An Anarchy of Families

An Anarchy of Families

State and Family in the Philippines

edited by

Alfred W. McCoy

published in cooperation with
The Center for Southeast Asian Studies
University of Wisconsin-Madison

Ateneo de Manila University Press

ATENEO DE MANILA UNIVERSITY PRESS
Bellarmine Hall, Katipunan Avenue
Loyola Heights, Quezon City
P.O. Box 154, 1099 Manila, Philippines
Tel.: (632) 426-59-84 / FAX (632) 426-59-09
E-mail: unipress@admu.edu.ph
Website: www.ateneopress.org

Philippine Copyright 1994 by Ateneo de Manila University
First printing 1994 / Second printing 1995
Third printing 1998 / Fourth printing 2002
Fifth printing 2007

Cover design by Fidel Rillo
Book design by Ingrid Slamer

Distributed in the Philippines exclusively by the Ateneo de Manila University
Press; in Asia by both the Ateneo and the Center for Southeast Asian Studies,
University of Wisconsin-Madison; and in the rest of the world by the Center for
Southeast Asian Studies, University of Wisconsin-Madison.

National Library Cataloging-in-Publication Data

Recommended entry:

Anarchy of families : state and
    family in the Philippines / edited
    by Alfred W. McCoy. – Quezon City :
    ADMU Press ; Wisconsin : University
    of Wisconsin Center for Southeast
    Asian Studies, c1993. – x, 542 p.
    : Ill., photos, maps

    1. Family – Philippine – Social
aspects. I. McCoy, Alfred W. 2. Title.

HQ680 306.85 1994 P944000182
ISBN 971-550-128-1

Cover: The governor of Antique Province, Enrique A. Zaldivar, photographed in
February 1986, while watching the funeral procession of murdered opposition leader
Evelio Javier. Many mourners believed that Javier had been killed on the orders of
a local pro-Marcos politician and joined the cortege as it wound its way through the
towns along Antique's coast. As the massive procession entered the provincial
capital, the governor assembled his entourage for a show of force. (*Credit:* Peter
Solness)

To

Harold C. Conklin

for service to his students
and contributions to the study
of the Philippines

Contents

Maps

Genealogies

About the Contributors

JEREMY BECKETT is associate professor of anthropology at Sydney University. He earned his Ph.D. in anthropology from the Australian National University with a dissertation on "Politics in the Torres Strait Islands" (1964). In addition to his work with the Maguindanao Muslims, he has continued his Australian research and has recently published *Torres Strait Islanders: Custom and Colonialism* (1987).

G. CARTER BENTLEY is an anthropologist and private consultant. He did his doctoral dissertation under Charles Keyes at University of Washington-Seattle on "Law, Disputing, and Ethnicity in Lanao" (1982). Drawing upon his fieldwork among the Maranao Muslims of the southern Philippines, he has published several articles on this subject.

MICHAEL CULLINANE is a historian of the Philippines and associate director of the Center for Southeast Asian Studies, University of Wisconsin-Madison. After six years of Philippine fieldwork in the mid 1970s, he completed his doctoral dissertation at the University of Michigan on "*Ilustrado* Politics: The Response of the Filipino Educated Elite to American Colonial Rule" (1989). He has continued to publish widely on the social history of Cebu and the political history of the Philippines.

BRIAN FEGAN is a senior lecturer in anthropology at Macquarie University. After fieldwork in Barrio Buga, San Miguel de Mayumo, in the early 1970s, he wrote his doctoral dissertation at Yale University with Harold C. Conklin under the title "Folk Capitalism: Economic Strategies in a Philippine Wet-Rice Village" (1979). Drawing upon his continuing fieldwork in San Miguel, he has published a series of academic articles on the politics and economics of Filipino peasant life.

ALFRED W. McCOY is professor of history at the University of Wisconsin-Madison. After field research in the region from 1973 to 1976, he wrote his dissertation at Yale University under Harold C. Conklin on the regional history of the Western Visayas, entitled "Ylo-ilo: Factional Conflict in a Colonial Economy" (1977). He has published academic essays on regional social history and Philippine national politics. In addition to his Philippine work, he has written on the political economy of the Southeast Asian opium trade and is author of *The Politics of Heroin* (1991).

x

RESIL B. MOJARES is professor of Cebuano Studies at the University of San Carlos in Cebu City. He did his Ph.D. at the University of the Philippines in 1979 and later published his dissertation under the title *Origins and Rise of the Filipino Novel* (1983). He is a leading authority on Philippine literature and social history. Among his publications are *Theater in Society, Society in Theater: Social History of a Cebuano Village* (1985), *The Man Who Would Be President: Serging Osmeña and Philippine Politics* (1986), and *Vicente Sotto: The Maverick Senator* (1992).

RUBY R. PAREDES is a historian of the Philippines and an academic planner at the University of Wisconsin-Madison. She wrote her doctoral dissertation at the University of Michigan on "The Partido Federal, 1900-1907: Political Collaboration in Colonial Manila" (1989). She has edited *Philippine Colonial Democracy* (1989) and continues to write on modern Philippine political history.

JOHN SIDEL is a graduate student in the Ph.D. program in Government at Cornell University. He has been conducting research in the Philippines since 1985 and is currently completing his doctoral dissertation on politics in Cavite and Cebu provinces under the supervision of Benedict Anderson.

"An Anarchy of Families":
The Historiography of State and
Family in the Philippines

Alfred W. McCoy

For historians of the First World, national history is often the sum of its institutional parts—corporations, parties, unions, legislature, and executive. Historians of Europe and America usually treat the family as an aspect of social history not as an institution that can direct a nation's destiny. In the Third World, by contrast, the elite family has long been a leading actor in the unfolding of the national pageant. More specifically, in the Philippines, elite families can be seen as both object and subject of history, shaping and being shaped by the processes of change.

Instead of treating the Philippine past solely as the interaction of state, private institutions, and popular movements, historians might well analyze its political history through the paradigm of elite families.[1] Indeed, these families have provided a strong element of continuity to the country's economic and political history over the century past. In her survey of Philippine politics, Jean Grossholtz described the family as "the strongest unit of society, demanding the deepest loyalties of the individual and coloring all social activity with its own set of demands." She then remarked, rather pointedly, that "the communal values of the family are often in conflict with the impersonal values of the institutions of the larger society."[2] Despite the apparent influence of family upon the wider society and its politics, most historians, both Filipino and foreign, have ignored this problem and still treat Philippine politics through its formal institutional structures.[3] Even social scientists, despite an obligatory bow in the direction of the family, have generally failed to incorporate substantive analysis of its dynamics into their rendering of the country's social and political processes.

As often happens in the study of the Philippines, social science thus diverges from social reality. Despite the oft-cited significance of elite families in Philippine politics, historical and contemporary analysis of their role remains superficial. Instead of studying family-based oligarchies, as their Latin American colleagues have done, Philippine historians have generally disregarded the leading Manila families on ideological grounds and largely ignored the provincial elites. Throughout much of this century, the small coterie of professional Filipino historians, many of them self-conscious nationalists, have dismissed the country's elites as politically treasonous or socially insignificant. For Teodoro Agoncillo, the doyen of postwar historians, the educated *ilustrados* of Manila's nineteenth-century elite had committed the original sin of betraying the Revolution of 1898 and collaborating thereafter with American colonialism. Concluding his study of the revolutionary Malolos Republic (1898–1901), Agoncillo describes Manila's elite, whom he calls "the haves," in language remarkable for its bitterness:[4]

> When one studies the Revolution in its first and second epochs one finds that . . . the middle class as a group betrayed the Revolution by a negative attitude: they refused to lift a finger to support the mass-movement because they did not believe it would succeed. . . . In the second epoch, the betrayal was consummated by positive action: they now entered the government by the front door and tried to sabotage it by the back door. . . .
>
> The betrayal in the first epoch may be forgiven, but that of the second can not. It is difficult, if not impossible, to rationalize the attitude of the "Haves," for when they accepted the high positions in the government they were, both from the legal and moral standpoints, expected to be loyal to that government. . . . [T]hey accepted the positions . . . but by insidious means undermined its foundations—through financial manipulations or through secret understandings with the Americans. Pardo de Tavera, Arellano, Paterno, Buencamino, Araneta, Legarda, and others . . . exemplified those who, while still in government, were already in sympathy with the American propaganda line of "benevolent assimilation." . . . [T]hese men, the first collaborators of the Americans, were also the first to receive the "blessings" of America and . . . to rise in the social and economic ladder of the country.

The nationalist historian Renato Constantino, Agoncillo's contemporary, has adopted a similarly dismissive attitude towards these same elite "collaborators" in his popular history of the Philippines. "Many of these individuals . . . prominent in the Aguinaldo government . . . had held other posts in the Spanish government," he noted:[5]

> Most . . . would again occupy good positions under the Americans. A few examples will . . . demonstrate the agility with which men of property and education switched their allegiance from one colonial power to another, with a short "revolutionary" career in between. T. H. Pardo de Tavera, Cayetano Arellano, Gregorio Araneta, and Benito Legarda went over to the Americans. . . .

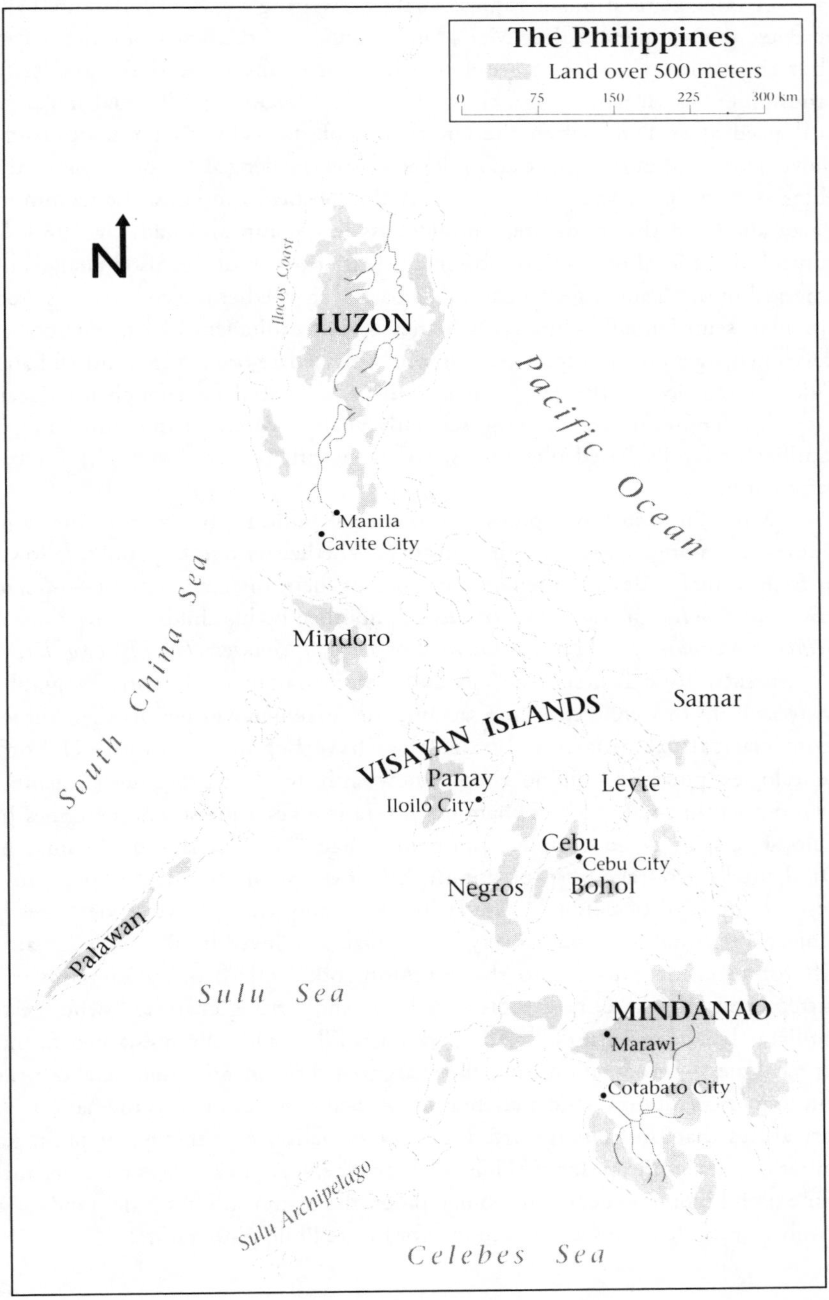

The Philippines
Land over 500 meters

0   75   150   225   300 km

N

Ilocos Coast

LUZON

Pacific Ocean

Manila
Cavite City

South China Sea

Mindoro

Samar

VISAYAN ISLANDS

Panay
Iloilo City

Leyte

Cebu
Cebu City

Negros   Bohol

Palawan

Sulu Sea

MINDANAO
Marawi
Cotabato City

Sulu Archipelago

Celebes Sea

A later generation of radical analysts, writing in the 1960s and 1970s, accepted the argument of Jose Maria Sison, founder of the new Communist Party, that the country's elites were a small, alien element—either rural feudal landholders or urban, *comprador* bourgeoisie.[6] Sison's intellectual hegemony collapsed after 1983 when the emergence of the yellow-ribbon opposition movement of Manila's upper and middle classes challenged his portrayal of these elites as an insignificant political force. Acting on his hypothesis, the Communist Party alienated the moderate, middle-class leadership and had, by 1986, lost control of the legal opposition movement. Left criticism of the Sison analysis later emerged in the "capitalism/feudalism" debate over whether the country was "semi-colonial, semi-feudal"— that is, whether or not capitalism had taken root and developed a genuine bourgeoisie.[7] Although the debate broke the informal ban on serious discussion of the *burgis*, it has not yet advanced far enough for research into elite family history. Lacking scholarly analysis of either individual Filipino families or family-based oligarchies, we must turn to elite biography for basic information.

Most Filipino biographies, the potential building blocks for elite-family studies, are more hagiography than history. Whether written by family, followers, or friends, their titles are often an apt index of their tone and content—*Master of His Soul: The Life of Norberto Ramualdez*, published by his children; *Jose Yulo: The Selfless Statesman* by Baldomero Olivera; or *Days of Courage: The Legacy of Dr. Jose P. Laurel* by Rose Laurel Avancena and Ileana Maramag.[8] Filipino biographers write as if death were a cleansing sacrament that somehow exempts their subjects from critical examination. Just as they have begun to compile elaborate genealogies, powerful Filipino families now enshrine their progenitors' memories in prose sentimental and sycophantic. Olivera invokes a priest who describes Jose Yulo as "a saint . . . a complete and perfect man."[9] Avancena and Maramag hail Dr. Laurel's "courage born of untarnished love for his country, a love proven beyond any cavil of doubt."[10] Maria Roces, in another such work, describes her subject, Fernando Lopez, as a "very likable man . . . 'loved by all'" with "a natural gift for reaching out . . . to the common folk." His brother Eugenio is an entrepreneur of "the utmost professionalism" and "strong character" who created "brilliant business ventures."[11] Such accounts fill a culturally prescribed formula for filial piety—exoneration from the charges of their enemies, silence about their cunning or corruptions, and a celebration of their contributions to the nation. The caricatures that thus emerge are devoid of sexuality, psychology, or fault, pale imitations of significant lives. While other Southeast Asian societies have produced some useful biographies and autobiographies, the region still has little nondynastic family history that can serve as a model for future Philippine research.[12]

Latin American Literature

In contrast to the paucity of Southeast Asian studies, Latin America offers a rich, theoretically informed literature on elite-family history that is applicable to other regions.[13] For several decades, Latin American historians have used detailed microstudies of elite families to discover new dimensions in their national histories. As Gilberto Freyre, a pioneer in this field, once argued, "anyone studying a people's past . . . will find that historical constants are more significant than ostensibly heroic episodes [and] . . . discover that what happened within the family . . . is far more important than . . . often-cited events . . . in presidential mansions, in parliaments and large factories." Applying this perspective to Brazil, Freyre found that its most distinctive elite families emerged in the sugar districts of the northeast during the sixteenth century— fusing land, sugar, and slaves to become patriarchs of "untrammeled power" and "total fiat." Arguing that the patriarchal family still exerts a subtle influence on the "the ethos of contemporary Brazilians," Freyre cites the case of President Epitacio Pessoa who in the early decades of this century was known as "Tio Pita" (Uncle Pita) in recognition of his penchant for appointing male relations to key government posts.[14]

By the late 1970s the field of family history was so well developed in Latin America that another Brazilian historian would describe the "family-based" approach to political history as a "commonplace in Brazilian history." Similarly, an essay on the role of kinship politics in Chile's independence movement began with the words "The importance of the family in Latin America goes unquestioned."[15] A decade later, Latin American historians were still unanimous in their belief that the elite family played a uniquely important political role in their region, one that required special consideration. Introducing eight essays for the *Journal of Family History*, Elizabeth Kuznesof and Robert Oppenheimer observed that "the family in Latin America is found to have been a more central and active force in shaping political, social, and economic institutions of the area than was true in Europe or the United States." Indeed, they found that "institutions in Latin American society make much more social sense, particularly in the nineteenth century, if viewed through the lens of family relationships."[16]

In her writing on the Pessoa family of Paraiba State in Brazil's northeast, historian Linda Lewin has produced some of the most refined historiographic reflections on the connections between familial and national history. Reacting to and reinforcing the weakness of the nation-state under the Old Republic (1889–1930), Brazilian families developed enormous political power. As Lewin explains in a seminal article, the "elite extended family has always loomed large in interpretations of Brazil's historical evolution, for the absence of a strong centralizing state as well as the lack of other competing institutions has meant its importance has long been recognized."[17]

Lewin suggests that, at least for the Pessoa family in Paraiba, there was a striking difference in the ethos of national and provincial politics. As one of the "tightly organized oligarchical elites who controlled state parties . . . by virtue of their delivery of [local] votes to the national presidential machine," the Pessoa family gained national influence, which further entrenched their local power in Paraiba.[18] Brazil's political leadership of this era was thus the product of family-based oligarchies—not parties, factions, or class-based social movements. "Without reference to the web of relationships woven by its members . . . it would be impossible to account for either Pessoa political control of their state or Epitacio's exceptional national career," writes Lewin about Brazil's President Epitacio Pessoa. "Consequently, in many respects this book attempts to interpret Epitacio as the creation of his political family."[19] Demonstrating a striking ideological flexibility, Epitacio Pessoa was "among . . . the world's most distinguished diplomats" at the Versailles peace conference of 1919 and a leading liberal on the national stage in Rio. Simultaneously, however, he operated as the pragmatic "state party boss" and "political patriarch" in provincial Paraiba.[20]

For Lewin, then, two key variables account for the extraordinary political power of Brazil's family-based oligarchies—kinship and the state. During the colonial era, when the state was not yet well established, elite families, reinforced by patriarchy and endogamy, captured control over land and labor in the country's productive hinterland. As the society changed during the late nineteenth century, patriarchy faded into conjugality and endogamy gave way to exogamy. But there was no "linear decline in the power of the elite family." Indeed, a small group of these families "continued to define a political elite" and "the *parentela* continued, in the absence of a strong state and class-defined society, to offer the greatest individual security." Despite modernization of the society, elite families in Brazil's northeast maintained "the same landed monopoly of commercial agriculture and coercive manipulation of the rural labor force."[21]

Surveying the scholarly literature on Brazilian state oligarchies under the Old Republic, Lewin found that the Pessoa family's power in Paraiba sprang from a political system with three overlapping types of authority, all of which depended upon "family-based groups and networks to some extent": (1) states such as Paraiba with a "primary dependence on the ties of family" and vertically integrated across socioeconomic lines; (2) other states such as Bahia or Pernambuco, which "can be characterized as personalistic oligarchies" that dovetailed personal ties with kinship; and (3) a unique pattern of purer party governance in Rio Grande do Sul with "an impressive degree of bureaucratization in its organizational structure."[22]

Other Latin American historians echo and elaborate upon these themes. On the final page of his richly detailed history of Mexico's powerful Sanchez family, Charles Harris offers an important insight into the political character of leading Latin American families that seems amply illustrated in his preceding three hundred pages: "If there is one element that runs through the Sanchez Navarros' political activities it is pragmatism, for they were prepared to work with anyone who would work with them."[23] In sum, Latin America's family-based oligarchies achieved their power because, in Eric Wolf's words, the state "yields its sovereignty to competitive groups that are allowed to function in its entrails."[24]

The Filipino Family

Even a cursory survey of the country's past indicates that in the Philippines, as in many Latin American settings, a weak state and powerful political oligarchies have combined to make a familial perspective on national history relevant. The Philippines has a long history of strong families assuring social survival when the nation-state is weak. In this century, the state has collapsed, partially or wholly, at least four times in the midst of war and revolution. After independence in 1946, moreover, the Philippine central government effectively lost control over the countryside to regional politicians, some so powerful that they became known as warlords. Reinforcing their economic power and political offices with private armies, these warlords terrorized the peasantry and extracted a de facto regional autonomy as the price for delivering their vote banks to Manila politicians.

After generations of experience Filipinos have learned to rely upon their families for the sorts of social services that the state provides in many developed nations. Indeed, the state itself has recognized the primacy of the family in Philippine society. In curiously loving language, Article 216 of the Philippine Civil Code states that "The family is a basic social institution which public policy cherishes and protects." In Article 219 the state admonishes its officials to respect the family's primary responsibility for social welfare: "Mutual aid, both moral and material, shall be rendered among members of the same family. Judicial and administrative officials shall foster this mutual assistance."[25] Similarly, in Article 2, section 12, the Philippine Constitution of 1986 makes the defense of the family a basic national principle: "The State recognizes the sanctity of family life and shall protect and strengthen the family as a basic autonomous social institution."[26]

Until recently the Roman Catholic Church, the nation's other leading source of power, either served the colonial state or its own institutional interests, remaining largely uninvolved in social welfare. Although the Church has developed strong social concerns since Vatican II, for most of its four centuries in the Philippines it remained an alien institution that extracted tribute and gave rituals in return.

What Church and state cannot provide the family must. In the century past, while three empires and five republics have come and gone, the Filipino family has survived. It provides employment and capital, educates and socializes the young, assures medical care, shelters its handicapped and aged, and strives, above all else, to transmit its name, honor, lands, capital, and values to the next generation. "The most important advantage of our family system," wrote educator Conrado Benitez in the 1932 edition of his classic high-school civics text, [27]

> is that it provides for the care of minors, the sick, the incompetent, and the dependent. In European and American countries, where the family is not so pronounced a civic unit, millions of pesos are spent by governments . . . taking care of the insane, the indigent sick. . . .

Thirty-five years later, a Philippine college sociology text explained the pragmatism underlying this practice: "The Filipino family . . . protects its members against all kinds of misfortunes since the good name of the family has to be protected."[28] Much of the passion, power, and loyalties diffused in First World societies are focused upon family within the Philippines. It commands an individual's highest loyalty, defines life chances, and can serve as an emotional touchstone.

Once we entertain the familial aspect, its centrality to many periods and problems in Philippine history becomes obvious. Reflecting upon social constraints to national development in the 1950s, anthropologist Robert Fox described the Philippines as "an anarchy of families."[29] Indeed, Philippine political parties usually have acted as coalitions of powerful families. Regimes can, as the Marcos era demonstrates, become tantamount to the private property of the ruling family. In the postwar period leading banks were often extensions of family capital (the Bank of Commerce was Cojuangco, while Manila Bank was Laurel). In his studies of Philippine banking, political scientist Paul Hutchcroft has found that: "There is little separation between the enterprise and the household, and it is often difficult to discern larger 'segments of capital' divided along coherent sectoral lines."[30] Similarly, the chief of the Securities and Exchange Commission, Rosario Lopez, noted in a July 1992 paper that only eighty corporations among the country's top one thousand were publicly listed because most Filipino companies "are actually glorified family corporations." Noting that Filipinos seem to prefer relatives as partners and shareholders, Lopez explained that: "There are sociocultural practices that endanger the situation, particularly the Filipino habit of having [an] extended family concept."[31] If banks and other major corporations are often synonymous with the history of a few elite families, so labor unions, Christian denominations, and even a communist party have been dominated by single families.

In Philippine politics a family name is a valuable asset. Along with their land and capital, elite families, as Jeremy Beckett argues in this volume, are often thought to transmit their character and characteristics to younger generations. Although new leaders often emerge through elections, parties and voters seem to feel that a candidate with a "good name" has an advantage. A Laurel in Batangas, an Osmeña in Cebu, a Cojuangco in Tarlac, or a Lopez in Iloilo stands a good chance of polling strongly. Believing that an established name carries cachet and qualification, parties often favor a promising scion of an old line when selecting candidates. Along with the division of lands and jewels, families often try to apportion candidacies for provincial or municipal offices among their heirs, sometimes producing intense conflicts over this intangible legacy. Just as the Cojuangco family's split in 1946–47 launched Jose Roy's long and distinguished career in Congress, so internal family battles can bear directly on the country's local and national politics. In the case of the Cojuangcos, this local battle over political legacy led Eduardo "Danding" Cojuangco into a lasting alliance with Ferdinand Marcos and life-long alienation from his cousin Corazon Cojuangco Aquino, an internal dispute compounded by her marriage into another powerful political family of the same province.

In applying the Latin American literature to the Philippines, it is useful to adapt the two key variables found in most Mexican or Brazilian family histories— strong elite families and a weak state. In particular, we must learn something of the character of Filipino kinship if we are to understand the influence of family upon Philippine politics. As anthropologist Roy Barton discovered in his prewar research among the highland Ifugao, the practice of bilateral descent is a central characteristic of Filipino kinship.[32] Summarizing what he calls an "anthropological truism," Jurg Helbling explains that bilateral kinship "produces overlapping, egocentric networks," fostering societies "characterized by vagueness and ambiguity, if not by disorder."[33] Unlike the patrilineal Chinese family, which could form unilineal kinship corporations to preserve property beyond three or four generations,[34] Filipinos define kinship bilaterally, thus widening their social networks and narrowing their generational consciousness. Instead of learning the principle of family loyalty by revering distant male ancestors, Filipinos act as principals in ever-extending bilateral networks of real and fictive kin.[35] "Filipino kinship system is cognatic or bilateral in form with an orientation towards ego," argues Yasushi Kikuchi. "The Filipino type of kinship group is, therefore, a generational corporate group devoid of lineal or vertical continuity but expanded horizontally within each generation with ego as the central figure."[36] Of course, not all egos are equal and there is often both hierarchy and leadership within this familial fluidity.

Supported by an informal ideology that legitimates the role of kinship in politics, elite Filipino families often perform a broad range of economic, social, and political functions. Not only does Filipino culture articulate strong beliefs about the family in the abstract but individuals, as both leaders and followers, are influenced by kinship concerns in making political decisions. In *Filipino Politics: Development and Decay*, David Wurfel explored the character of politics within a society based on bilateral kinship.[37]

> The family has long been the center of Filipino society. As in most parts of Southeast Asia kinship is essentially bilateral; that is, ancestry is traced through both the mother's and the father's line. Effective kinship ties are maintained with relatives of both parents. A bilateral system gives a potentially huge number of living kin, especially as five to ten children are not uncommon even today in each nuclear family of each generation.

Within these radiating bilateral networks of kin—four grandparents, several siblings, numerous aunts and uncles, dozens of godparents, scores of first-degree cousins, and hundreds of second- and third-degree cousins—an individual Filipino necessarily forges selective personal alliances to negotiate his or her way through the complexities of intrafamilial politics. Reinforcing this social fluidity, actual kinship relations often are superseded by the erratic influence of personal alliances and antipathies. Using fictive kinship, for example, an individual can elevate cousins to the status of siblings. Similarly, blood ties provide no guarantee that individuals will interact. In political terms, the word *family* does not simply mean *household*, as it is defined narrowly by demographers, nor does it mean *kinship*, as it is used more broadly by ethnographers. Seeking a term that describes the political role of *family*, we might use *kinship network*, that is, a working coalition drawn from a larger group related by blood, marriage, and ritual. As elite families bring such flexible kinship ties into the political arena, elections often assume a kaleidoscopic complexity of coalition and conflict, making Filipino politics appear volatile.

Once a stable "kinship network" is formed, such familial coalitions bring some real strengths to the competition for political office and profitable investments. A kinship network has a unique capacity to create an informal political team that assigns specialized roles to its members, thereby maximizing coordination and influence. Under the postwar Republic, for example, Eugenio Lopez became a leading businessman in Manila while his younger brother Fernando was an active politician at both the provincial and national levels. In particular, the pursuit of the state's economic largesse can depend upon the success of such teams, or kin-based coalitions, in delivering votes to a candidate for national office (senator or president). If elected, the politician will repay the investment many times over through low-cost government credit, selective enforcement of commercial regulations, or licenses for state-regulated enterprises such as logging and broadcasting.

The Weak State

Just as we must adapt the concept of the elite family to the Philippine context, so we must accommodate the particulars of the Philippine state. Since elite families and the state are engaged in a reciprocal relationship that constantly defines and redefines both, we need to place kinship networks within the larger locus of Philippine politics.

Reviewing the literature on the Philippine state selectively, two key elements seem to have contributed most directly to the formation of powerful political families—the rise of "rents" as a significant share of the nation's economy and a simultaneous attenuation of central government control over the provinces. Probing each of these aspects, rents and a de facto provincial autonomy, creates a broad political and historical context for the studies of the individual families found in this volume. In so doing, however, we must be careful not to separate phenomena that seem, in the Philippine context, synergistic. Simply put, privatization of public resources strengthens a few fortunate families while weakening the state's resources and its bureaucratic apparatus.

Within the literature on political economy, the theory of "rent seeking" best explains the economic relations between the Filipino elite and the Philippine state. As defined by economist James Buchanan, rents are created when a state gives an entrepreneur an artificial advantage by restricting "freedom of entry" into the market. When extreme restriction creates a monopoly, the consequences for the economy as a whole are decidedly negative: "No value is created in the process; indeed the monopolization involves a net destruction of value. The rents secured reflect a diversion of value from consumers generally to the favored rent seeker, with a net loss of value in the process." By restricting markets through regulation and awarding access to a favored few, states can spark an essentially political competition for such monopolies, a process called rent seeking.[38] Reviewing the past half century of Philippine history from this perspective, the theory of rent seeking seems appropriate to both elite politics as it functioned under the Republic and the "crony capitalism" that flourished under the regime of Ferdinand Marcos.

The emergence of the Republic as a weak postcolonial state augmented the power of rent-seeking political families—a development that further weakened the state's own resources. "The state, as it evolved out of the colonial context, remains a weak apparatus for economic development," explains political scientist Temario Rivera in his study of the postwar economy. "Enjoying little autonomy from dominant social classes and entrenched particularistic groups, the state is captured by . . . competing societal interests."[39]

This paradoxical relationship between a weak state and a strong society is not limited to the Philippines. Recent research on Third World politics has found that social units such as family, clan, or faction can block the state from translating its nominal authority into social action. "States are like big rocks thrown into small ponds," writes Joel Migdal; "they make waves from end to end, but they rarely catch any fish." He argues that Third World states suffer from an underlying duality—"their unmistakable strengths in penetrating societies and their surprising weakness in effecting goal-oriented social changes."[40] Seeking the source of the state's weakness, Migdal finds that social organizations such as "families, clans . . . tribes, patron-client dyads" continue to act as competing sources of authority. Thus, the "state leaders' drive for predominance—their quest for uncontested social control—has stalled in many countries because of tenacious and resilient organizations scattered throughout their societies."[41]

Summarizing the historical processes that produced such a state in the Philippines, it can be said that Spain and the United States tried to forge a strong bureaucratic apparatus based upon their own laws and social practice.[42] Since the modern Philippine state did not evolve organically from Filipino society, it could not induce compliance through shared myth or other forms of social sanction. Denied voluntary cooperation from their Filipino subjects, the Spanish and early American states derived much of their authority from the implied coercion of colonial rule. Compounding these contradictions, American colonials extended the powers of the central bureaucracy they had inherited from Spain while simultaneously experimenting with grassroots democracy in the form of local elections. In effect, the United States tried to moderate the imagined excesses of

Iberian centralization by introducing the Anglo-American tradition of local autonomy. Moving from local elections in 1901, to legislative elections in 1907, and presidential elections in 1935, the Americans built electoral politics from the municipality upward, thereby entrenching provincial families in both local and national offices. To restrain the abuses and autonomy of provincial elites, Manila Americans used their Philippine Constabulary as a political police force to check abuses of the peasantry by *caciques*—a term these colonials applied to Filipino local elites with an intentional Latin American connotation. During the early years of their rule, Americans used the term *cacique* to describe the provincial elites who combined local office with landed wealth to gain extraordinary control over the countryside. Similarly, the colonial executive tried to use insular auditors to restrain rent seeking by an emerging national elite. Although it was effectively penetrated and manipulated by these elites from the outset of American rule, the colonial bureaucracy managed to maintain its influence until the Commonwealth period of the 1930s.

After independence in 1946, the new Republic inherited the colonial task of restraining both rent seeking and provincial autonomy. Unlike the colonial governors appointed by Washington, however, Philippine presidents won office with the electoral support of provincial elites and Manila's oligarchs. As might be expected, much of the Republic's politics revolved about the contradiction between the president's dependence upon elite families to deliver votes and his duty to apply the laws against violence and corruption to these same supporters. These changes in the role of the executive compounded the pressures upon the bureaucracy, producing a rapid degeneration in the efficacy of this state apparatus. While the civil service had operated with integrity and efficiency under U.S. colonial rule, the postwar bureaucracy, in the words of O. D. Corpuz, was "characterized mainly by low prestige, incompetence, meager resources, and a large measure of cynical corruption." Compounding these corrosive influences, the intrusion of partisan politics into the realms of appointments and decision making soon compromised the autonomy of the civil service.[43] By the mid-1950s, the bureaucracy suffered from a "novel weakness" and was "highly vulnerable to attack by external parties (politicians)."[44]

Under the Republic (1946–72), Philippine presidents used the state's licensing powers as bargaining chips in their dealings with national and local elites, thereby creating benefices that favored the dominant political families. Viewed within the paradigm of rent-seeking politics, the Philippine political system was not based so much on the extraction of "surplus" from the production of new wealth but on a redistribution of existing resources and the artificial creation of rents—in effect, rewarding favored families by manipulating regulations to effect a reallocation of existing wealth.[45] The Republic regulated a wide range of enterprises—transport, media, mining, logging, banking, manufacturing, retail trade, construction, imports, and exports—to the extent that they required "protection from competition" to remain profitable.[46] Indeed, many entrepreneurs launched entire industries (textiles, for example) on the assumption that their investments would be protected.[47] While primary industries such as sugar and much of the manufacturing sector (textiles, autos, and steel) were creations of the state's licensing powers, provincial elites often relied upon other forms of state support. Instead of licenses per se, provincial elites required a free hand from Manila to exploit local populations, revenues, and resources, in effect, operating a benefice in the premodern sense of the term.

Starting from its role as the distributor of U.S. rehabilitation and Japanese reparation funds after World War II, the Philippine state played an increasingly important role in the economy through both its financial institutions and commercial regulations. By the late 1950s, the state role was so pronounced that an American financial consultant commented that "business is born, and flourishes or fails not so much in the marketplace as in the halls of the legislature."[48] Under the doctrines of economic nationalism and national development, the Republic eventually extended its nominal influence into almost every sector of the economy. Although the state had broad economic powers under the law, the Republic's record of implementing its development schemes was erratic. Elected with the support of rent-seeking political brokers, successive presidents were forced to pay off powerful politicians with local and national benefices, thereby compromising the state's integrity and diminishing its resources. The Republic thus developed as a state with both substantial economic resources and weak bureaucratic capacity.[49]

It is this paradoxical pairing of wealth and weakness that opened the state to predatory rent seeking by politicians. As resources drained from government coffers, the state apparatus weakened and political families gained strength. In his recent study of banking in the Philippines, Paul Hutchcroft explained the dynamics of a process that allowed the state to become "swamped by the particularistic demands of powerful oligarchic forces."[50]

> The Philippine bureaucracy . . . has long been penetrated by particularistic oligarchic interests, which have a firm independent economic base . . . yet rely heavily upon their access to the political machinery in order to promote private accumulation. . . . Because the state apparatus is unable to provide the calculability necessary for advanced capitalism, one finds instead a kind of rent capitalism based, ultimately, on the plunder of the state apparatus by powerful oligarchic interests.

The Republic's weakness also led to an attenuation of state control over the countryside and a loss of its near-monopoly on armed force. As the state reached into the provinces to promote democracy and development, it found itself competing with local elites for control over the instruments of coercion. The impact of this seemingly simple change upon Philippine politics was profound. In his analysis of Third World politics, for example, Migdal identifies effective coercion as a key attribute of a strong state: "First, leaders aim to hold a monopoly over the principal means of coercion in their societies by maintaining firm control over standing armies and police forces while eliminating nonstate controlled armies, militias, and gangs."[51]

In the Philippines, World War II and independence coincided to allow the rise of private armies that operated beyond Manila's control. Although the tendency towards political violence was already evident in prewar elections, politicians were not heavily armed and the state retained the power to intervene effectively in the provinces. During the war, however, the collapse of central authority and the distribution of infantry weapons to anti-Japanese guerrillas broke Manila's monopoly on firepower. Before 1935, the U.S. colonial state had used the Philippine Constabulary, the successor to the Spanish Guardia Civil, as its chief instrument of control, deploying its rifle companies to mediate between the demands of a modernizing center and the countervailing centripetal pull of provincial politics. When Manila's control over the countryside weakened after 1935, and attenuated with independence in 1946, provincial politicians demanded neutralization of the Constabulary as a condition for the delivery of their vote banks to presidential candidates, thereby fostering a de facto local autonomy and endemic political violence.

By the mid-1960s, official crime statistics indicated a level of violence that was extraordinarily high by international standards. In 1965, the year Ferdinand Marcos was first elected president, the Philippine homicide rate was about 35 per 100,000 persons—compared to just 25 for Colombia that same year during a time of upheaval known there as "La Violencia." The Philippine murder rate continued to climb, reaching a remarkable 42 per 100,000 persons in 1967. This violence was, however, neither random nor widespread. Statistical analysis indicates that it was integral to the electoral process. In Ilocos Sur, a province known for political violence, the murder rate ebbed to 1 or 2 in the months between elections and jumped to 30 during the November 1965 presidential campaign. Two years later, during the 1967 congressional elections, one municipality in Ilocos Sur achieved a remarkable annual homicide rate of 134 per 100,000.[52]

The proliferation of arms and a parallel erosion of central authority allowed the rise of provincial politicians known as the warlords. Under the postwar Republic, politicians who reinforced their influence with private armies included Floro Crisologo (in Ilocos Sur), Armando Gustilo (Negros Occidental), Ramon Durano, Sr. (Cebu), Mohamad Ali Dimaporo (Lanao del Sur), and Rafael Lacson (Negros Occidental). Although warlords were active throughout the Philippines, they were not found in every province. Powerful, semi-autonomous politicians controlled much of the Philippine countryside but only some reinforced their positions with paramilitary force in a way that made them warlords.

Looking back upon the Republic two decades later, several factors appear to have encouraged the emergence of warlordism. Private armies seem to have been more likely to appear in areas in which Manila's control was comparatively weak. Specifically, systemic political violence emerged in periods or provinces marked by some significant instability. After World War II, the combination of loose firearms and weak central control allowed warlords to emerge in many provinces. In later decades, warlordism often reemerged in regions where instability was fostered by the land frontier, protracted ethnic rivalry, or particular economic circumstance. On the frontiers, for example, local elites formed private armies to defend their extraction of natural resources through logging, mining, or fishing—the basis for wealth in many localities. Licenses for such extraction could be won formally through access to national politicians in Manila or informally by violent competition in the countryside. In these and other rural areas violence often occurred during elections when rivals competed to deliver blocs of votes for presidential candidates in the hope of winning rents as their reward.

Moreover, local politicians used private armies in provinces where a key element of production or processing was vulnerable to expropriation through armed force. To cite the most notorious example, human settlement in the province of Ilocos Sur is concentrated along a narrow coastal plain that seems almost pinched between the Cordillera and the South China Sea. Since most transport moves along a single national highway that enters from Ilocos Norte and exits south into La Union towards Manila, paramilitary groups could monitor most of the province's commerce from a few roadside checkpoints. Although peasants produced Virginia tobacco, the province's main export, on farms scattered along this coastal plain, the processing, or redrying, of the raw leaves created another choke point for a powerful family, the Crisologos, to extract a share of the surplus. During the 1960s, they maintained a private army of over a hundred men and engaged in political violence that gave the province a homicide rate far higher than the national average.[53] Anyone who tried to export tobacco from Ilocos Sur without drying it at the Crisologo factory and paying their extralegal export "tax" suffered confiscation at the family's checkpoint near the provincial boundary. By contrast, there were no comparable means by which a putative warlord could control the flow of rice produced in the vast Central Luzon Plain. The highway grid that crisscrosses the plain lacked comparable choke points, while both the production and processing of rice was widely dispersed.

Compounding this complexity, there are individual factors that lead certain provincial politicians to both adopt and abandon the use of private armies. A minor *datu* such as Ali Dimaporo or an ambitious peasant like Faustino Dy has very little choice but to use violence to establish his political and economic base. After securing wealth and power in a locality through armed force, provincial politicians can begin to barter votes to win both immunity from prosecution and benefices in the form of rents, cheap credit, or licenses. With his position thus legitimized, the family's founder, or his heirs, can enter a mature phase of old wealth and respectable politics. While the aging warlord usually retains an aura of ruthlessness akin to outlaw status, his children can study at Manila's elite schools, become lawyers or professionals, and marry into established families, thereby accelerating the process of legitimation that discourages the continuing use of political violence.

More than any other national leader of the Republican era, Ferdinand Marcos was a product of this provincial violence. Marcos learned politics in his father's prewar campaigns for the National Assembly, and he began his own political career as a defendant charged with murdering his father's rival in their home province of Ilocos Norte just after the 1935 legislative elections. Hardened by wartime experience in combat, black marketeering, and fraud, Marcos emerged as a politician who combined a statesman's vision with the violence of a provincial politician. During his second term (1969–73), he built an informal, clandestine, command structure within the armed forces to execute special operations and also cultivated close relations with provincial warlords. During the political crisis of 1971–72, he was the author of much of the terror bombing that traumatized national political life.

After his declaration of martial law in 1972, Marcos's authoritarian state exhibited both a punctilious public concern for legal proprieties and regular recourse to extralegal violence. In a practice that Filipinos came to call "salvaging," loyalist factions within the Marcos-controlled military detained and tortured opponents, discarding their brutalized remains in public places. Although Marcos rapidly amassed ample wealth for entry into the Manila elite, his use of their children as hostages, and later the public execution of a well-born rival, marked him as a man apart. In the end, it was his use of violence, along with economic mismanagement, that forced the national elite to turn against him.

In fashioning his mechanisms of authoritarian control, Marcos exploited the family paradigm in an attempt to remake the Philippines into his image of a "New Society." In the months following the declaration of martial law in 1972, veteran psychological warfare specialist Jose Ma. Crisol, working through the Philippine Army's Office of Civil Relations, convened an academic think tank to construct a master plan for social reform. Their report, *Towards the Restructuring of Filipino Values*, argued that Marcos should exploit the Filipino family paradigm to purge the country of negative values.[54]

> What is recommended therefore is an expansion of the family to a larger group—the country. We should treat the country as our very own family, where the President of the Republic is the father and all the citizens as our brothers. From this new value we develop a strong sense of oneness, loyalty to the country, and a feeling of nationalism. Because all Filipinos are brothers, we become just and sincere. There will develop in us a feeling of trust such that values, such as lamangan, pakitang-tao, bahala na, etc. will be eliminated from our system. . . .

> Because the New Society provides us with an opportunity to grow, it is the most appropriate time to develop our very selves. The Philippines needs to be economically stable and it is only when we develop a value of self-reliance,

self-discipline and a high sense of self-esteem that we could come up a progressive country. . . .

From the contemporary value system we hope to modify it—geared towards the aims of the New Society.

Apparently acting on this report, the Marcos regime organized a massive youth organization, the Kabataang Barangay, led by his eldest daughter Imee. Under Presidential Decree No. 684, of April 1975, all youths aged fifteen to eighteen were required to join one of these groups and many were sent to remote rural camps for training through "secret rituals" that tried to instill in them a primal loyalty to the first couple.[55] After days of intensive indoctrination, the youths would assemble in a candlelight ceremony to swear loyalty to the father and mother of the nation before larger-than-life portraits of Ferdinand and Imelda.

Although Marcos posed as a social reformer, his regime rested upon a coalition of rent-seeking families not unlike those that had dominated electoral politics before martial law. Backed by an expanding military and an influx of foreign loan capital that eventually totaled U.S. $26 billion, Marcos effectively centralized political power in the archipelago for the first time since the late 1930s, making once-autonomous provincial politicians supplicants and reducing the political process to palace intrigues. During the early years of the new regime, Marcos used his martial-law powers to punish enemies among the old oligarchy, stripping them of assets and denying them the political access needed to rebuild. Simultaneously, he provided his retinue of kin and cronies with extraordinary financial opportunities, creating unprecedented private wealth.

Instead of using his broad martial-law powers to promote development, Marcos expanded the role of rents within the economy, fostering a virtual florescence of the political corruption he had once promised to eradicate. In 1981, the business magazine *Fortune* sparked a storm of controversy with a report on this aspect of his constitutional regime, the New Republic: "Marcos' principal achievement in 15 years in power has been to help his friends and relatives build giant conglomerates."[56] Three years later, economists at the University of the Philippines produced a detailed study of rents as they had operated under Marcos, listing all of the 688 presidential decrees and 283 letters of instruction "which represent government intervention in the economy in one form or another." Seeking to explain how such "massive intervention" had led to the "domination of certain private interests over the government," the study concluded:[57]

The issue of exclusive rights to import, export, or exploit certain areas, the collection of large funds which are then privately controlled and expropriated, and the preferential treatment of certain firms in an industry for purposes of credit or credit restructuring are among the many instruments that have been utilized in the process.

Illuminating these broad trends with detailed case studies of corruption by individual cronies, Ricardo Manapat described the Marcos regime as a veritable apotheosis of rent seeking, which had divided "the whole economy . . . into different fiefs managed by relatives and cronies who regularly shared their earnings with the dictator."[58]

As a mix of regime paralysis, economic decline, and failing physical health eroded his authority after 1978, Marcos became increasingly reliant upon courtiers to deliver the blocs of provincial votes that he would need for a new mandate. Since the basis of crony wealth was accidental personal ties to the president rather than economic acumen, most, though not all, of these family-based conglomerates proved unstable. Plagued by mismanagement and corruption, these corporations collapsed with spectacular speed when the economy began to contract after 1981. As Marcos's provincial political machinery withered, he suffered sharp reverses in the 1984 and 1986 elections, producing a crisis of legitimacy for his regime.

President Corazon Aquino came to power in February 1986 with a revolutionary mandate for change and few debts to any of the prominent political families allied with Marcos's ruling KBL Party. Mindful of the abuses of the Marcos era, Aquino's appointive Constitutional Commission debated an antidynastic clause at length, seeking to prevent another president from making the Palace a familial preserve. In Article 7, section 13, the 1986 Constitution bars presidential relatives from office.[59]

> The spouse and relatives by consanguinity or affinity within the fourth civil degree of the President shall not during his tenure be appointed Members of the Constitutional Commissions, or the Office of Ombudsman, or as Secretaries, Undersecretaries, chairmen or heads of bureaus or offices, including government-owned or controlled corporations and their subsidiaries.

Over time, however, political pressures forced President Aquino to compromise the spirit of this extraordinarily strict constitutional principle when she revived the legislature. In the May 1987 elections, many of the president's relatives by blood or marriage won seats with the support of the ruling political party headed by her brother, Jose Cojuangco. Moreover, Aquino, occupying a narrowing political center between the communist left and the military right, gradually moved into an alliance with the provincial elites who had chafed under Marcos's centralized regime. Although initially hostile to her reforms, regional politicians allied themselves with her when she reopened Congress as an assembly of elites with the authority to frame land-reform legislation. After a careful survey of the election results, the Institute for Popular Democracy concluded that: "The May 1987 elections for the Legislature . . . saw political clans reasserting themselves as the real source of power in Philippine electoral politics." Indeed, 166 congressmen, or 83 percent of House membership, were from established "political clans," as were 56 percent of the local officials elected in 1988.[60] Paralleling this provincial restoration, Aquino returned expropriated corporations to Manila's old economic oligarchy. Stripped of their assets and driven into exile by Marcos, the Lopez family, to cite one example, returned to Manila in 1986 and began reclaiming both its corporations and its provincial power base.

In the first hours of Fidel Ramos's administration, the rhetoric of the new president provided an even sharper contrast between the principles and practice of family politics. In his inaugural address, delivered on 1 July 1992, Ramos launched a stinging attack on the country's pervasive system of rent-seeking familial politics and pledged himself to reform.[61]

> We must make hard decisions. We shall have to resort to remedies close to surgery—to swift and decisive reform. (1.) First, we must restore civic order. . . . (2.) Then, we must make politics serve—not the family, faction or the party—but the nation. (3.) And we must restructure the entire regime of regulation and control that rewards people who do not produce at the expense of those who do, a system that enables persons with political influence to extract wealth without effort from the economy.

Less than twenty-four hours later, however, Ramos proved the poignancy of his own social critique when he signed Executive Order No. 1 granting cement manufacturers the right to import cement duty-free for three years. While President Quezon had used the potent symbolism of his Commonwealth Act No. 1 to establish the country's Department of Defense in 1935, Ramos had expended the drama of his first presidential act upon a customs decree granting a coterie of established manufacturers a "stranglehold" over cement supplies. Observers noted that the order had been drafted by the incoming finance secretary, Ramon del Rosario, a Ramos confidante whose family corporation was a leading cement producer.[62]

Seeking to apply these general observations to particular case studies, this volume's familial approach to Philippine politics carries with it a series of linked hypotheses: (a) that family-based oligarchies are, to state the obvious, a significant factor in Philippine history; (b) that relations among these elite "families" have a discernible influence on the course of Philippine politics; (c) that elite families, organized on complex patterns of bilateral kinship, bring a contradictory mix of unified kinship networks and a fissiparous, even volatile, factionalism into the political arena; and (d) that the interaction between powerful rent-seeking families and a correspondingly weak Philippine state has been synergistic.

Case Studies of Filipino Families

As noted above, the Republic's emergence as a weak, postcolonial state was a necessary precondition for the rise of powerful political families. During the troubled transition to independence after World War II, the country's civil service, once an effective instrument of the colonial and Commonwealth states, became demoralized and politicized. Unrestrained by an efficient central bureaucracy, provincial politicians challenged Manila's control over the countryside while national entrepreneurs turned public weal into private wealth. As Manila lost its near-monopoly on armed force, some politicians mobilized private armies, producing an extreme form of local autonomy in a number of provinces.

Focusing on key factors within these larger processes, the essays in this volume revolve around the twin themes of corruption in the capital and violence in the provinces. Indeed, a quick survey of the families profiled here produces a spectrum of political leadership ranging from provincial warlords like Ramon Durano to rent-seeking entrepreneurs such as the Lopez brothers. As emphasized in several of these studies, the Republic's failure to regain control over the provinces after independence in 1946 allowed provincial elites across the archipelago to assume a de facto autonomy. Some of these politicians formed private paramilitary units, producing such warlords as Durano, Justiniano Montano, and Mohamad Ali Dimaporo. Similarly, the systematic corruption that accompanied the executive's episodic attempts at economic development encouraged rent seeking by entrepreneurial families such as the Lopezes and Osmeñas. Despite their pedigree and erudition, families with *ilustrado* antecedents such as the Pardo de Taveras, who lived largely off old capital and their good name, suffered a protracted political eclipse until marriage or personal ties hitched their fortunes to newer families that were prospering through provincial politics and rent seeking.

It would be a mistake, however, to impose a simple dichotomy upon the complex web of postwar Philippine politics. We could identify both national entrepreneurs without a provincial base and local warlords with only tenuous ties to the capital. Most political families, however, fused local power with national access. Indeed, many found that they could not compete effectively in Manila for rents unless they could deliver, by whatever means, a substantial bloc of votes to national politicians. Even the most violent of provincial warlords tried to win lucrative rents, either through allies in Manila or by exercise of their de facto local autonomy. Many of these families assigned members complementary roles as national or provincial leaders, demonstrating an efficiency that made family a formidable force in the political arena. To cite the most prominent case, Eugenio Lopez used his commercial and legal skills to become the Republic's leading rent-seeking entrepreneur. Simultaneously, his younger brother Fernando maintained the family's political base in the home province of Iloilo and used it to bolster his climb to national elective office.

Given a paradoxical pairing of the personal and the official within the term *political family*, it is not surprising that a remarkable variety of politicians should arise to defy any neat dichotomy or typology. Focusing on individuals instead of models or paradigms highlights the enormous variety in style and tactics found in the Philippine electoral arena. Rather than forcing this complexity into a procrustean bed of fixed categories, we have felt it best to allow our analytical framework to arise from the data. Let us illustrate this approach by taking out an imaginary piece of graph paper and plotting a horizontal axis of provincial autonomy and a vertical axis of national access. As we reduce individual careers to these two variables, and then to imaginary dots, each representing a single politician, the resulting graph would probably spread randomly across the page, revealing an enormous diversity of tactics. Complicating this two-dimensional representation of a three-dimensional reality, our dots would start to slip and slide across the page, reflecting changes in the character of individual families over time.

Focusing on major themes within this universe of possible tactics suggests that two elements—political violence and rent seeking—seem most significant in the history of many political families. Reflecting basic differences in landscape and livelihood, the strategy of each operates largely within a distinct domain. Under most circumstances, political violence is prevalent in the provinces and the competition for rents is concentrated in the capital. Unlike the Manila elites who operate within a culture of metropolitan civility, provincial families are forced to engage in systemic political violence either as agents or opponents. With its competition over public lands, precincts, and transportation routes, provincial politics involves a zero-sum struggle for hegemony over an electoral or commercial territory that encourages organized violence. By contrast, any aspirant for a major rent, whether financier or warlord, must compete within Manila's courtier society with its complex of palace intrigues, legislative coalitions, ideological debate, and bureaucratic regulations. While the provinces have often produced warlords, national politics in Manila has, at times, promoted leaders who combine the skills of both factional broker and national statesman.

Since independence in 1946, the territorial aspect of provincial politics has encouraged the extreme form of de facto local autonomy known as warlordism. As the state's control over the provinces receded after independence, warlords such as Durano, Dimaporo, and Montano used private armies to control localities and thereby gain a more secure tenure over elected offices. Elite families that did not mobilize their own militia still had to deal with the inherent violence of the provinces, either manipulating it, as the Lopezes have done, or confronting it like the Osmeñas. Returning to his home province in the late 1920s after years of legal studies at the University of the Philippines and Harvard, Eugenio Lopez allied himself with Iloilo City's criminals to seize control of the province's largest bus company. When Lopez later moved to Manila, he became a financier and philanthropist, assuming the aura of a cultured, cosmopolitan entrepreneur and avoiding direct involvement in political violence.

The Osmeñas of Cebu represent a contrasting case that nonetheless highlights the significance of provincial violence. As one of the first families to ascend from provincial to national prominence during the American period, the Osmeñas rarely employed violence. Soon after the U.S. Army landed in Cebu at century's turn, the family's founder, Sergio Osmeña, Sr., launched his political career by arranging the surrender of armed bands of former revolutionaries who were still marauding in the mountains of the interior. After his election as speaker of the Philippine Assembly in 1907, he acquired the patrician air of a national statesman. When his family's later generations came home to Cebu City from California or Manila to launch their political careers in the 1950s and 1980s, they were still forced to combat the organized violence of their rivals—the Duranos, Cuencos, and other local warlords. These latter-day generations of Osmeñas were able to evoke a familial aura of statesmanship and an ethos of managerial competence. Most recently, as Resil Mojares argues in his essay, the Osmeñas' collective persona as modern managers, the antithesis and alternative to the province's warlords, has become central to their political revival in contemporary Cebu. If only in their opposition to their rivals' use of private armies, violence has been a significant factor in the Osmeñas' careers as provincial politicians.

Although violence is their most visible aspect, all warlord families must seek rents or state revenues in some form to assure their political survival. Despite some striking differences, political families at both the provincial and national levels thus share a common involvement in rent-seeking politics, a process of turning political capital into commercial opportunity. There is an obvious economic dimension to provincial politics that encourages rent seeking. Aside from the periodic need for state funding to generate patronage and cash during elections, even the most violent warlord requires an autonomous source of revenue to sustain his retinue and private army. Ultimately these financial imperatives breach the barriers within any putative typology that might seek to separate provincial power from national access, making rent seeking a critical adjunct to the paramilitary power of even the most autonomous of warlords.

While a flair for violence and military organization are essential in a warlord's rise, it is financial acumen that assures his longevity. After using violence to establish political dominion over Danao City in the early 1950s, Ramon Durano, the subject of Michael Cullinane's essay, delivered votes to President Carlos Garcia in exchange for Japanese reparation funds used to construct the Danao industrial complex. With this independent financial base, Durano then possessed the manpower and matériel to survive in the unfavorable political climate that followed. Although his wealth allowed him to pose as a philanthropist and financier in his later years, Durano remained a warlord to the end, drawing upon private resources to mobilize goons for elections through the mid-1980s. Among its many enterprises, Danao City became the national center for the manufacture of firearms, called *paltik*. Durano's role as patron and protector of these local arms factories gave him access to an arsenal even after Marcos's martial-law regime confiscated nearly half a million firearms from private armies across the archipelago. Under martial law, Danao City's *paltik* industry became, through Durano's influence, a particular sort of protected industry. By banning imports of firearms after 1972 and failing to enforce the strict prohibition on their manufacture in Danao City, the Marcos regime inflated the black-market price for illegal firearms and created a rent of extraordinary value for Durano's clientele. Durano himself did not own the factories but still he benefited as the patron of a high-profit industry operating exclusively within his territory. The *paltik* is thus an apt metaphor for the Janus-faced character of the Philippine warlord—a weapon of primordial violence within Danao City and a precision manufacture that commands markets in the world beyond.

Illustrating the importance of rent seeking for a warlord's long-term survival, John Sidel recounts how Justiniano Montano's failures in Manila ultimately overwhelmed his success as a provincial warlord. For nearly thirty years, Montano was Cavite's preeminent leader, reinforcing his position as governor and senator with an armed retinue of extraordinary ruthlessness in a province notorious for its political violence. In the end, however, some signal failures at the national level insured Montano's eclipse as a provincial politician. In the late 1960s, the Montanos turned against President Marcos and found themselves purged from office after the declaration of martial law in 1972. Denied access to state patronage, Montano fell back on family resources that were insufficient to sustain his political influence. Inept in the process of using public office to create private wealth, Montano had failed to build an autonomous economic base that would allow him to survive a period of alienation from the regime in power. At the end of the Marcos era, Montano, despite his long dominion over a wealthy province, lacked the resources for a political revival, returning to Cavite from exile and living out his life in obscurity. Moreover, since Montano, unlike the Lopezes and Osmeñas, did not produce an effective political heir, he could not perpetuate his lineage—a key failing within the Filipino familial paradigm.

As a provincial politician in Muslim Mindanao, Mohamad Ali Dimaporo maintained a purer form of warlordism, described in G. Carter Bentley's essay, with fewer of the rent-seeking attributes of his counterparts elsewhere in the archipelago. Since he used violence to defend his constituency of Maranao Muslims against Christian settlers, Dimaporo's mobilization of a private army, known as the Barracudas, reinforced his political popularity among an embattled minority. Although he seemed interested in business, his political base among an impoverished minority living on a violent frontier denied him the sorts of economic opportunities available in Cavite or Cebu. Instead of manufacturing or real estate transactions, Ali engaged in a crude form of rent seeking, using the payroll and construction contracts at Mindanao State University as his prime source of operational funds. He also engaged in logging, a simple form of rent seeking, but he made no moves towards commercial or industrial enterprises. Despite his reliance on these limited and localized rents, Dimaporo's role as a paramilitary leader at the margin of the Philippine state allowed him to survive for nearly half a century. After the declaration of martial law, Marcos used the armed forces to reduce Dimaporo's private army. But a decade later, desperate to mobilize votes for his declining regime, Marcos rearmed the Barracudas with military weapons. In the aftermath of the "People Power" uprising of 1986, Dimaporo's reputation as a staunch Marcos ally and abusive warlord aroused the hostility of the Aquino administration. Still he retained sufficient firepower and following to weather a period of alienation from the center until he could reconcile himself with elements of the new regime. Ironically, it was his role as a leader of a cultural minority that allowed him to become the country's archetypal warlord, a form of leadership that remains more complex and multifaceted elsewhere in the archipelago. Like Montano, however, Dimaporo's relative financial failure will probably bar him from passing on substantial wealth, the basis of political power, to the next generation.

These chronicles of failure serve as an important corrective to the thrust of most of the essays in this volume. By selecting prominent politicians and recounting the stories of their inexorable rise, this collection could give the impression that all political families succeed. Over the long term, however, most seem to experience decline and defeat. Bilateral inheritance fragments property accumulated during the life of a powerful politician. Although strong leaders can leave name and money to their children, they cannot transmit the personal mix of charisma, courage, and cunning that guided their success.

At multiple levels within most of these essays, there is then an interweaving of individual biography and family history. To summarize very broadly, the underlying paradigm is familial but the narrative focus is often individual. That is, reflecting what the authors perceive to be the cultural ethos of the country, these essays describe individual actors operating within a familial context. In both politics and business, these actors seem to draw upon their kin networks to mobilize the support they need for success. Despite this familial basis for both perception and action, individual biography remains an important element of family history. Within the volatile, pressured markets of finance and politics, most competition is individual—one candidate for each political office and a single chief executive at the apex of a corporate hierarchy. Even among large families—such as the Lopezes, who count thousands of members spread over many generations—extraordinary individuals have played a seminal role in taking lineages to new plateaus of wealth and power.

Similarly, even the most dynamic individual competitor seeks to associate himself with an established family. Rising financiers and politicians reinforce their positions by identifying with prominent ancestors. Within a society based on bilateral kinship, individuals have some flexibility in the construction of their genealogy, selecting from maternal and paternal lines to create the most advantageous lineage for public advertisement. As Jeremy Beckett explains in his discussion of the Maguindanao elite, a family name is a negotiable political asset that commands attention among voters and allegiance among followers.

Many politicians try to transform their electoral offices into lasting family assets, building what Filipinos call a "political dynasty." Once entrenched, influential politicians often work to bequeath power and position to their children, in effect seeking to transform the public office that they have won into a private legacy for their family. For all politicians, provincial or national, office is inevitably ephemeral. But private wealth gained during their term in power, if substantial, can be passed on, giving succeeding generations the means to compete for office. Although the probability of a zero return on any investment in elections is at least 50 percent, the profits from a successful congressional campaign are so high that the risk is amply justified. Hence, the most successful politicians are those who can invest their heirs with the wealth and the good name needed to campaign effectively for office—a factor that blends the individual with the familial, the provincial with the national, and warlordism with rent seeking.

In seeking the variables that account for the ability of politicians to capitalize upon the opportunities of office, one factor seems to stand out—legal skills. Although he was by all accounts a skilled corporate executive, Eugenio Lopez was educated in the law not in business or finance. Similarly, though Ramon Durano, Sr., was a quintessential warlord whose taste for violence was legendary in Cebu, he also had a sound legal education that allowed him to translate his political influence into private wealth. To cite a contrasting case, Ali Dimaporo, who was poorly educated, has failed to move beyond localized benefices to exploit the obvious opportunities for rent seeking in Manila. In sum, he failed to use his bailiwick as a stepping stone into the national elite and thereby to gain access to economic rewards beyond the meager resources of his province. Although the Philippine state's enforcement apparatus remains weak, its legal codes governing elections, commerce, and corporations are complex and comprehensive, enveloping the whole universe of politics and business with nominally strict regulations. Through legal education, politicians learn to manipulate these regulations in their quest for rents. With this introduction to the country's legal culture, even the most virulent warlord has the tools to succeed as a rent-seeking entrepreneur. Marcos, for example, combined these disparate elements. After a youthful career in violent provincial politics, he became a consummate constitutional lawyer in one guise and an ambitious rent-seeking politician in another. Once elected president, he used a mix of state violence and legal manipulation to acquire a vast array of rent-seeking corporations for himself and his entourage.

In terms of historiography, the essays presented here share a common attempt to write Philippine national history from the vantage of the leaders of specific "families" that have played a dominant role in national or provincial politics. Instead of using familial anecdotes to illustrate a national history marked by wars and empires, these essays, in effect, subsume these larger events within the microhistorical perspective of individual families. Through their very structure, these essays mimic the familial world view of their subjects, reducing the panorama of a national election to one family's business opportunity or viewing a decade of dictatorship, with all of its agonies, as a personal misfortune. Although these essays move forward chronologically, and major events naturally intrude upon the lives of their subjects, the national is subordinated to the familial throughout. By following a political narrative marked by baptisms, marriages, murders, and board meetings—rather than war, revolution, or diplomacy—readers hopefully will gain an understanding of, even an empathy for, the perspective of a Filipino political family.

Although the essays in this volume share these larger concerns in one form or another, there are significant differences in emphasis. Instead of detailing the history of the Osmeña family, as he has done in his earlier biography of Serging,[63] Resil Mojares offers a theoretical reflection on the meaning of family identity within a system of electoral politics. Similarly, Jeremy Beckett probes the significance of a family name as a political asset in the Philippines and then illuminates this theme with a brief history of political competition among the Maguindanao. Moving from family history to political biography, several authors analyze the careers of the Republic's leading warlords. Whether peasant, lawyer, or Muslim aristocrat, provincial politicians with a flair for paramilitary mobilization used violence to gain office under the Republic, becoming, in Brian Fegan's words, entrepreneurs in violence. Although their private armies and defiance of the law made them seem autonomous, if not independent, these warlords proved, like Manila's rent seekers, remarkably vulnerable to state pressure when Marcos declared martial law.

Finally, other essays provide detailed, multigenerational studies of two of Manila's most prominent political families, the Pardo de Taveras and the Lopezes. Reflecting the distinctive character of each family, Ruby Paredes emphasizes the role of the Pardo de Tavera women and Alfred McCoy examines the career of a leading Lopez male. Starting with the career of Dr. Mita Pardo de Tavera, the secretary of social welfare in the Aquino administration, Paredes provides an interior view of an elite family's ideological and material life—its struggle to maintain a lineage in the *ilustrado* tradition and its bitter internal disputes over inheritance. Although Mita's grandfather, Dr. T. H. Pardo de Tavera, founded the Philippines' first political party and dominated the country's politics for nearly a decade at century's end, Paredes turns away from the male, public realm to focus on the domestic sphere controlled by the family's strong women. Through this emphasis on the household, Paredes illuminates key issues of marriage, inheritance, and succession implicit within the volume's other essays.

Indeed, the central event in this family history, the 1892 murder of Paz Pardo de Tavera by her husband Juan Luna, provides powerful testimony to the efficacy of this volume's familial approach to Philippine history. This murder has been excised from the nation's history and reduced to an exculpatory footnote in the biographies of Juan Luna, a brilliant painter and a Philippine national hero. Within the national story, the civic canonization of Juan Luna required the villification, even the extinction, of his wife and victim Paz.[64] In studying this era from the perspective of a single family, Paredes rediscovered the murder itself and uncovered original police reports that she has used to create a new understanding of the Filipino nationalist movement. Her essay restores the victim Paz to the national chronicle, unifies the political and the domestic, and articulates, for the first time, the way in which Filipino nationalists constructed gender under an oppressive colonialism. By retelling the old story with a new character and a new dialogue drawn from the domestic sphere, Paredes deepens and enriches our understanding of Philippine national history.

Adopting a more conventional approach, Alfred McCoy's study of the Lopez family chronicles the career of Eugenio Lopez as the most successful rent-seeking entrepreneur of the Republican era. His spectacular rise and sudden fall highlights the paramount role of public-sector manipulation in shaping the careers of even the most powerful of patriarchs.

Despite their differences of approach, the essays in this volume share a common concern with the role of family in Philippine politics and seek to open thereby a novel perspective on the study of Philippine history.

N OTES

During 1987–88, this essay began to take form amid a series of long conversations in Sydney with Dr. Brian Fegan of Macquarie University. Not only did he influence the initial theoretical perspective but in later correspondence he made extensive critical comments that have been incorporated into my final draft. During the paper's first presentation at the Association for Asian Studies meetings in San Francisco in 1988, the panel's discussant, Professor Benedict Anderson of Cornell University, offered some yeasty, even provocative, remarks that inspired further refinements in conceptualization. As these ideas later took shape in Madison, the University of Wisconsin's community of Philippine scholars—Ruby Paredes, Paul Hutchcroft, Michael Cullinane, and Daniel Doeppers—contributed careful readings that led to significant changes in the text. I am also grateful to Professor Florencia Mallon, a colleague in the History Department, for a thoughtful reading of the Latin American section. This essay, like all those in the volume, has benefited from the careful editing of Jan Opdyke. Finally, I would like to thank Sean Kirkpatrick, the Center's editorial coordinator, for his assiduous attention to the myriad details that make up this entire volume.

[1]There is, of course, a well-developed literature on the ways in which, in Jane Schneider's words, "corporate groups and formal institutions are often 'infiltrated' by powerful personal networks." For the role of such networks—"whether they are of kinship, friendship or patronage"—in serving as social alternatives to impersonal institutions in Sicily, see Jane Schneider, "Family Patrimonies and Economic Behavior in Western Sicily," *Anthropological Quarterly* 42, no. 3 (1969): 109–10; Peter Schneider, "Honor and Conflict in a Sicilian Town," *Anthropological Quarterly* 42, no. 3 (1969): 130–54; Anton Blok, "Peasants, Patrons and Brokers in Western Sicily," *Anthropological Quarterly* 42, no. 3 (1969): 155–70; and Anton Blok, *The Mafia of a Sicilian Village, 1860–1960: A Study of Violent Peasant Entrepreneurs* (New York: Harper and Row, 1975), 5–16.

At a broader comparative level, Eric Wolf surveys the influence of a range of personal associations, kinship included, upon social and political relations in "complex societies." He concludes that "anthropologists need to pay more attention to the rise and fall of families than they have done in the past." Starting from Lewis Henry Morgan's dichotomy between *societas* based on kinship and *civitas* where "relations of political economy . . . curtail the functions of kinship," Wolf then asks why families should be the main functional entity "within kin circles." Aside from performing key economic and social functions, the family remains the dominant form of kinship because it is "maximally adaptive to the conditions that define and circumscribe its existence." See Eric Wolf, "Kinship, Friendship, and Patron-Client Relations in Complex Societies," in Michael Banton, ed., *The Social Anthropology of Complex Societies* (London: Tavistock, 1966), 2, 6–9.

Although Philippine social research has been influenced by some of this literature, it has generally ignored Wolf's emphasis on the importance of the family and family history.

The more general literature on dyadic relations in the Philippines has shown how personal relations and political factions have shaped the character of the wider society. For those interested in family-based oligarchies, however, the Philippine literature on personal associations does have distinct limitations. Aside from explaining how such networks moderate and mediate the influence of institutions in this developing society, the literature is too broadly focused to probe the nature of family-based oligarchies. The Philippine literature on reciprocity and clientelism thus subsumes family within the larger category of personal networks in a way that conceals as much as it reveals about the infiltration of families into national institutions. Similarly, the focus on an amorphous and ill-defined "Filipino elite" has done little to illuminate the role of specific families or a system of family-based oligarchies. For a discussion of patron-client relations in Southeast Asia and the Philippines, see James C. Scott and Ben Kerkvliet, "The Politics of Survival: Peasant Response to 'Progress' in Southeast Asia," *Journal of Southeast Asian Studies* 4 (1973): 241–68; James C. Scott, "The Erosion of Patron-Client Bonds and Social Change in Southeast Asia," *Journal of Asian Studies* 32, no. 1 (1972): 5–37; and James C. Scott, "Patron-Client Politics and Political Change in Southeast Asia," *American Political Science Review* 66, no. 1 (1972): 91–113.

For the now classic studies of lowland Philippine reciprocity, see Charles Kaut, *"Utang Na Loob:* A System of Contractual Obligation Among Tagalogs," *Southwestern Journal of Anthropology* 17, no. 3 (1961): 256–72; Frank Lynch, *Social Class in a Bikol Town*, Research Series, no. 1 (Chicago: Philippine Studies Program, Department of Anthropology, University of Chicago, 1959), 126–40; Mary R. Hollnsteiner, "Reciprocity in the Lowland Philippines," in *Four Readings on Philippine Values*, edited by Frank Lynch and Alfonso de Guzman II (Quezon City: Ateneo de Manila University Press, 1973), 69–92; Mary R. Hollnsteiner, *The Dynamics of Power in a Philippine Municipality* (Quezon City: Community Development Research Council, University of the Philippines, 1964); Frank Lynch, "Social Acceptance Reconsidered," in Lynch and Guzman, *Four Readings*, 1–68; and Jaime C. Bulatao, "Hiya," *Philippine Studies* 12, no. 3 (1964): 424–38.

For work on the Philippine elite, critical and otherwise, see Mark McDonald Turner, "Interpretations of Class and Status in the Philippines: A Critical Evaluation," *Cultures et developpment* 10, no. 2 (1979): 265–96; Thomas C. Nowak, "The Philippines Before Martial Law: A Study in Politics and Administration," *American Political Science Review* 71 (1973): 522–39; and Justin J. Green, "Social Backgrounds, Attitudes and Political Behavior: A Study of a Philippine Elite," *Southeast Asia: An International Quarterly* 2, no. 3 (1973): 301–38.

[2]Jean Grossholtz, *Politics in the Philippines* (Boston: Little Brown, 1964), 86–87.

[3]There are some notable exceptions to this generalization that indicate the promise of the familial approach to Philippine history. In his general survey of Cebu City's social history written over a decade ago, Michael Cullinane pays particular attention to the significance of the household as a social unit and family life as a formative influence upon the city's society. In his biography of Sergio Osmeña, Jr., a leading Cebuano politician and one-time presidential candidate, Resil Mojares adopts a self-conscious familial approach. See Michael Cullinane, "The Changing Nature of the Cebu Urban Elite in the 19th Century," in *Philippine Social History: Global Trade and Local Transformations*, edited by Alfred W. McCoy and Ed. C. de Jesus (Quezon City: Ateneo de Manila University Press, 1982), 251–96; and Resil B. Mojares, *The Man Who Would Be President: Serging Osmeña and Philippine Politics* (Cebu City: Maria Cacao Publishers, 1986).

[4]Teodoro A. Agoncillo, *Malolos: The Crisis of the Republic* (Quezon City: University of the Philippines Press, 1960), 644–45.

[5]Renato Constantino, *The Philippines: A Past Revisited* (Quezon City: Tala Publishing Services, 1975), 232.

[6]Amado Guerrero, *Philippine Society and Revolution* (Hong Kong: Ta Kung Pao, 1970), 113–17, 234–49.

[7]Temario C. Rivera et al., *Feudalism and Capitalism in the Philippines* (Quezon City: Foundation for Nationalist Studies, 1982); Carol Victoria, "A Reply to the Resolution," *Pratika* 1, no. 2 (August 1986): 75.

[8]Norberto Ramualdez Centennial Committee, *Master of His Soul: The Life of Norberto Ramualdez (1875–1941)* (Manila: National Historical Institute, 1975); Baldomero T. Olivera, *Jose Yulo: The Selfless Statesman* (Mandaluyong: University of the Philippines, Jorge B. Vargas Research Center, 1981); Maria Natividad Roces, "Kinship Politics in the Post-War Philippines: The Lopez Family, 1945–1989" (Ph.D. diss., University of Michigan, 1990); Rose Laurel Avancena and Ileana Maramag, *Days of Courage: The Legacy of Dr. Jose P. Laurel* (Manila: Avancena and Maramag, 1980).

[9]Olivera, *Jose Yulo*, 3.

[10]Avancena and Maramag, *Days of Courage*, 361.

[11]Roces, "Kinship Politics," 96–101.

[12]Jennifer Cushman's study of a Sino-Thai provincial family, one of the first and most detailed of family histories in Southeast Asia, still lacks the theoretical sophistication and empirical depth of the major Latin American studies. See Jennifer Cushman, *Family and State: The Formation of a Sino-Thai Mining Dynasty, 1797–1932* (Singapore: Oxford University Press, 1991). Within the literature on the Philippines, Resil Mojares's study of Sergio Osmeña, Jr., *The Man Who Would Be President*, stands out as an exception to this rule.

[13]Reflecting their rich historical traditions, Europe and America have also produced impressive family histories. In the United States, for example, the Adams family of Massachusetts has been the subject of autobiographical and biographical research. See David F. Musto, "The Adams Family," *Proceedings of the Massachusetts Historical Society* 93 (1981): 40–58. In their studies of Sicily and other southern European societies, anthropologists have explored the role of informal networks based on kinship, friendship, and patronage. This work, and similar studies of Latin America, have inspired a lively literature on the role of factions and clientelism in Philippine politics. Whether in Europe, the Caribbean, or Southeast Asia, however, such network studies have not focused on the poles of the problem, family and state, in the same way that Latin American historians have explored the family-based oligarchy, arguably the most central of these networks. For a good example of the European literature, see Blok, *The Mafia of a Sicilian Village.* For work on informal networks in the Philippines, see Carl H. Lande, *Leaders, Factions, and Parties: The Structure of Philippine Politics*, Southeast Asia Monographs, no. 6 (New Haven: Southeast Asia Program, Yale University, 1965).

[14]Gilberto Freyre, "The Patriarchal Basis of Brazilian Society," in *Politics of Change in Latin America*, edited by Joseph Maier and Richard W. Weatherhead (New York: Praeger, 1964), 155, 161.

[15]Linda Lewin, "Some Historical Implications of Kinship Organization for Family-based Politics in the Brazilian Northeast," *Comparative Studies in Society and History* 21, no. 2 (1979): 263; Mary Lowenthal Felstiner, "Kinship Politics in the Chilean Independence Movement," *Hispanic American Historical Review* 56, no. 1 (1976): 58. For another study of the importance of family history in Chile, see Diana Balmori and Robert Oppenheimer, "Family Clusters: Generational Nucleation in Nineteenth-Century Argentina and Chile," *Comparative Studies in Society and History* 21, no. 2 (1979): 231–61.

[16]Elizabeth Kuznesof and Robert Oppenheimer, "The Family and Society in Nineteenth-Century Latin America: An Historiographic Introduction," *Journal of Family History* 10, no. 3 (1985): 215. In the same tone, Diana Balmori's three-generation study of an Argentine family argues for "a shift in the framework we ordinarily use to understand political actions" by deemphasizing "individual behavior and the activities of political parties in favor of political behavior action of families." See Diana Balmori, "Family and Politics: Three Generations (1790–1890)," *Journal of Family History* 10, no. 3 (1985): 247.

[17]Lewin, "Historical Implications," 263. For other studies of elite families in Brazil, see Billy Jaynes Chandler, *The Feitosas and the Sertao dos Inhamuns: The History of a Family and a Community in Northeast Brazil, 1700–1930* (Gainesville: University of Florida Press, 1972); John Norman Kennedy, "Bahian Elites, 1750–1822," *Hispanic American Historical Review* 53, no. 3 (1973): 415–39; Anthony Leeds, "Brazilian Careers and Social Structure: An Evolutionary Model and Case History," *American Anthropologist* 66 (1964): 1321–45;

Joseph L. Love and Bert J. Barickman, "Rulers and Owners: A Brazilian Case Study in Comparative Perspective," *Hispanic American Historical Review* 66, no. 4 (1986): 743–65; and Alida C. Metcalf, "Fathers and Sons: The Politics of Inheritance in a Colonial Brazilian Township," *Hispanic American Historical Review* 66, no. 3 (1986): 455–84.

[18]Linda Lewin, *Politics and Parentela in Paraiba: A Case Study of Family-Based Oligarchy in Brazil* (Princeton: Princeton University Press, 1987), 19, 24.

[19]Ibid., 7.

[20]Ibid., 5–6.

[21]Lewin, "Historical Implications," 291–92. Although Lewin questions the "conventional view" epitomized by Freyre's emphasis on patriarchy in colonial Brazil, she admits that there is insufficient evidence to challenge his views and concludes that this issue cannot be resolved "until more research on elite family structure is undertaken" (ibid., 286–88).

[22]Lewin, *Politics and Parentela*, 22–33.

[23]Charles H. Harris, *A Mexican Family Empire: The* Latifundio *of the Sanchez Navarros, 1765–1867* (Austin: University of Texas Press, 1975), 314. See also Charles H. Harris, "The 'Overmighty Family': The Case of the Sanchez Navarros," in *Contemporary Mexico: Papers of the IV International Congress of Mexican History*, edited by James W. Wilkie, Michael C. Meyer, and Edna Monzon de Wilkie (Berkeley: University of California Press, 1976), 47–61.

For other studies of Mexican family history, see John E. Kicza, "The Great Families of Mexico: Elite Maintenance and Business Practices in Late Colonial Mexico City," *Hispanic American Historical Review* 62, no. 3 (1982): 429–57; and Allen Wells, "Family Elites in a Boom-and-Bust Economy: The Molinas and Peons of Porfirian Yucatan," *Hispanic American Historical Review* 62, no. 2 (1982): 224–53. More recently, a household survey in Mexico City showed that the ideal of the "grand-family"—a three-generation, consanguine unit bound together by obligations of economic support, familial rituals, and social recognition—was shared by families of all classes. With greater resources, upper-class families were more capable of achieving an ideal to which families of the lower and middle classes aspired. See Larissa A. Lomnitz and Marisol Perez-Lizaur, "Dynastic Growth and Survival Strategies: The Solidarity of Mexican Grand-Families," in *Kinship Ideology and Practice in Latin America*, edited by Raymond T. Smith (Chapel Hill: University of North Carolina Press, 1984), 183–95.

[24]Wolf, "Kinship, Friendship," 1–2.

[25]Remegio E. Agpalo, *The Political Elite and the People: A Study of Politics in Occidental Mindoro* (Manila: College of Public Administration, University of the Philippines, 1972), 122–23.

[26]Republic of the Philippines, *The Constitution of the Republic of the Philippines* (Manila: National Bookstore, 1986), 3.

[27]Conrado Benitez, *Philippine Civics: How We Govern Ourselves* (Boston: Ginn, 1932), 22.

[28]Felicidad V. Cordero and Isabel S. Panopio, *General Sociology: Focus on the Philippines* (Manila: College Professors Publishing, 1967), 272.

[29]Robert B. Fox, "The Study of Filipino Society and its Significance to Programs of Economic and Social Development," *Philippine Sociological Review* 7, nos. 1–2 (1959): 6.

[30]Paul D. Hutchcroft, "The Political Foundations of Booty Capitalism in the Philippines" (paper delivered at the annual meetings of the American Political Science Association, Chicago, Illinois, September 1992), 6.

[31]*Manila Chronicle*, 23 July 1992.

[32]R. F. Barton, *Ifugao Law* (Berkeley: University of California Press, 1969), xii–xiii, 18, 19, 44.

[33]Jurg Helbling, "Kinship and Politics: The Reproduction of Political Units among the Alangan-Mangyan in Mindoro Oriental," in *Philippine Kinship and Society*, edited by Yasushi Kikuchi (Quezon City: New Day, 1989), 125.

[34]Fei Hsiao-Tung and Chang Chih-I, *Earthbound China: A Study of Rural Economy in Yunnan* (London: Routledge and Kegan Paul, 1948), 109–14; Wolf, "Kinship, Friendship," 3–4.

[35]Yasushi Kikuchi, *Uncrystallized Philippine Society: A Social Anthropological Analysis* (Quezon City: New Day, 1991), 38–45, 55–57.

[36]Ibid., 55.

[37]David Wurfel, *Filipino Politics: Development and Decay* (Quezon City: Ateneo de Manila University Press, 1988), 34.

[38]James M. Buchanan, "Rent Seeking and Profit Seeking," in *Toward a Theory of the Rent-Seeking Society*, edited by James M. Buchanan, Robert D. Tollison, and Gordon Tullock (College Station: Texas A&M Press, 1980), 7–8.

[39]For an analysis of the state sympathetic to this discussion, see Temario C. Rivera, "Class, the State and Foreign Capital: The Politics of Philippine Industrialization, 1950–1986" (Ph.D. diss., University of Wisconsin, Madison, 1991), 213; Wurfel, *Filipino Politics*, 56, 326–30, 340; and Gary Hawes, *The Philippine State and the Marcos Regime: The Politics of Export* (Ithaca: Cornell University Press, 1987), chaps. 1 and 5. For more general analysis of the state in the Philippines and the Third World, see Fermin D. Adriano, "A Critique of the 'Bureaucratic Authoritarian State' Thesis: The Case of the Philippines," *Journal of Contemporary Asia* 14, no. 4 (1984), 459-84; Robert Stauffer, "The Philippine Political Economy: (Dependent) State Capitalism in the Corporatist Mode," in *Southeast Asia: Essays in the Political Economy of Structural Change*, edited by R. Higgot and R. Robison (London: Routledge and Kegan Paul, 1985); and Hamza Alavi, "The State in Post Colonial Societies," *New Left Review*, no. 74 (July-August 1972): 59–81.

[40]Joel S. Migdal, *Strong Societies and Weak States: State-Society Relations and State Capabilities in the Third World* (Princeton: Princeton University Press, 1988), 9.

[41]Ibid., 31–32.

[42]See O. D. Corpuz, *Bureaucracy in the Philippines* (Manila: Institute of Public Administration, University of the Philippines, 1957), 128–213.

[43]Ibid., 222–23.

[44]Ibid., 246–47.

[45]The reader will have noted that this essay employs five overlapping concepts—rent seeking, licensing power, benefice, protected industry, and redistribution. They can be readily defined for the purposes of this paper. As explained by Karl Polanyi and interpreted by both Eric Wolf and James C. Scott, redistribution is a useful integrative concept that defines a broad area of economic-cum-political activity. "Contenders for power," writes Wolf, "must accumulate adequate 'funds of power' and redistribute them selectively to gain followers, rather than open resources to general redistribution. Polanyi, to whom anthropology owes the introduction of the concept of redistribution, allowed us to visualize mechanisms of exchange beyond those covered by 'reciprocity' or 'market' exchange." Instead of actually producing goods and services, Southeast Asian elites use their authority—traditional, colonial, and contemporary—to expropriate a part of peasant produce en route to external markets. Similarly, Filipino political families use their offices to extract a share of government services and projects destined for their territory, using the extralegal take to build patronage networks of political followers. In both instances, elites are engaging in the redistribution of resources produced by others (see James C. Scott, *The Moral Economy of the Peasant: Rebellion and Subsistence in Southeast Asia* [New Haven: Yale University Press, 1976], 5–6; and Eric R. Wolf, *Europe and the People without History* [Berkeley: University of California Press, 1982], 97–98).

Within this broad category of redistributive activity, benefices, rents, licenses, and protected industries represent specific types or forms. In premodern Europe, a benefice was a royal privilege that assured a courtier income from land rent, customs revenues, or protected commerce. In contemporary usage, a rent, as defined above, is any form of economic activity protected from free-market competition by state regulation. Rents can take a specific form such as state licenses to broadcast, import, export, transport, or extract. Similarly, the state can restrict free-market activity in a more generative manner by fostering growth of protected industries through tariffs, regulated domestic markets, or the selective award of incentives such as low-cost government credit.

[46]Manuel Montes, "The Business Sector and Development Policy," in *National Development Policies and the Business Sector in the Philippines*, edited by Aiichiro Ishii, Edilberto de Jesus, Kenji Koike, Leoncio D. Miralao, Jr., Manuel Montes, and Gerardo Sanvictores (Tokyo: Institute of Developing Economies, 1988), 65.

[47]For a carefully researched case study of the influence of protection upon the textile industry, see Laurence D. Stifel, *The Textile Industry: A Case Study of Industrial Development in the Philippines*, Data Papers, no. 49 (Ithaca: Center for Southeast Asian Studies, Cornell University, 1963).

[48]Thomas R. McHale, "An Econecological Approach to Economic Development" (Ph.D. diss., Harvard University, 1959), 217, quoted in Hutchcroft, "Political Foundations of Booty Capitalism," 3.

[49]For detailed studies of the decline of Philippine bureaucracy under the postwar Republic, see Corpuz, *Bureaucracy in the Philippines*, 195–248; and Visitacion R. de la Torre, *History of the Philippine Civil Service* (Quezon City: New Day, 1986), 92–96.

[50]Hutchcroft, "Political Foundations of Booty Capitalism," 1, 4.

[51]Migdal, *Strong Societies and Weak States*, 18.

[52]H. A. Averch, F. H. Denton, and J. E. Koehler, *A Crisis of Ambiguity: Political and Economic Development in the Philippines* (Santa Monica: Rand Corporation, R-473-AID, 1970), 183–98; Wurfel, *Filipino Politics*, 103.

[53]Averch et al., *Crisis of Ambiguity*, 189–91.

[54]Jose M. Crisol, *Towards the Restructuring of Filipino Values* (Manila: Office of Civil Relations, Philippine Army, n.d.), 47.

[55]Wurfel, *Filipino Politics*, 130.

[56]*Fortune*, 27 July 1981.

[57]Emmanuel S. De Dios, ed., *An Analysis of the Philippine Economic Crisis* (Quezon City: University of the Philippines Press, 1984), 40–41.

[58]This study was originally published in 1979 in samizdat format. See Ricardo Manapat, *Some Are Smarter Than Others: The History of Marcos' Capitalism* (New York: Aletheia Publications, 1991), 85 and preface.

[59]Republic of the Philippines, *Constitution*, 20.

[60]Eric U. Gutierrez, Ildefonso G. Torrente, and Noli G. Narca, *All in the Family: A Study of Elites and Power Relations in the Philippines* (Quezon City: Institute for Popular Democracy, 1992), 160, 162-63.

[61]*Philippine Daily Inquirer* (Manila), 1 July 1992.

[62]*Manila Chronicle*, 18 July 1992.

[63]Mojares, *The Man*.

[64]In an example of such excision, historian Vicente Rafael has studied a photograph taken in Paris in 1890 of three Filipinos, including Juan Luna, who are attired in fencing outfits while a woman, Paz, sits on the stairs in the rear. Rafael comments:

> Posing with their swords planted firmly between their legs, the *Indios Bravos* display a masculine alternative to what they perceived to be the menacingly androgynous . . .regime of the Spanish friars. That image of masculine solidarity is further suggested by the barely visible figure of a woman—Paz Pardo de Tavera, Luna's wife—situated in the background, at the margins of the frame, as if to signal the sexual hierarchy that patriotism reinstitutes. . .[T]his picture has the effect of remapping the body of the colonized subject in ways that peel away from the grid of colonial assumptions.

In his celebration of masculine liberation, Rafael does not mention that Luna would later use this martial training to beat Paz regularly and skillfully with his cane before shooting her fatally. See Vicente L. Rafael, "Nationalism, Imagery, and the Filipino Intelligentsia in the Nineteenth Century," *Critical Inquiry* 16:3 (1990):605–07.

Entrepreneurs in Votes and Violence: Three Generations of a Peasant Political Family

Brian Fegan

We all know what kind of events make it into the news, into chronicles, sagas, commissions of inquiry, court records, and the documents that are the materials of conventional history. It is stories about great men, ambition, vice, folly, perfidy, conflict, and natural disaster. The everyday lives of ordinary, decent, good, and well-adjusted citizens do not interest their neighbors as the stuff of gossip any more than they interest outsiders or posterity. It is only recently that social historians, particularly those inspired by the *Annales* school, have tried to reconstruct the everyday lives of uninteresting people in uninteresting times.

Ordinary peoples' lives are undocumented. They appear by name in church registries of births, deaths, and marriages. Otherwise they enter history's written sources only when times become "interesting," and even then as anonymous collectivities, like the mob, the crowd, or the rebels, or they are reduced to numbers in a disaster report or an election result. In a 1986 special issue of the *Journal of Peasant Studies* the hidden lives of peasants were explored, that is, their "everyday resistance"—the covert, individual sabotage, pilfering, footdragging, evasion of rents and taxes, smuggling, poaching, draft dodging, desertion, playing dumb, and other devices used by the weak to resist the power of dominant classes and the state.[1] But, though the contributors set out to discover where the peasants go between the "interesting times" when they resist overtly and collectively, the focus remained upon conflict. That discourse about the unrecorded was not about the unrecorded lives of ordinary people but about their unrecorded strife.

Personal Perspective

I have no training in history, much less in social history. But in the early 1970s, in the course of doing a village study, I found it necessary to investigate the past in order to understand the present. My central interests, as an economic anthropologist doing fieldwork, were in the social relations involved in rice agriculture in a village of Central Luzon, Philippines. But those social relations did not end with the village. Its rice farmers were tenants whose landlords lived in town or in Manila. Many peasants worked in the city. There was land reform afoot, and part of the reason for that was the history of landlord-tenant conflict in the area. It had generated tenant unions in the 1920s, the anti-Japanese Hukbalahap guerrillas during the Pacific War, and then a rebellion in the late 1940s that made the villages into battlefields. My village was peaceful in the 1970s but one had to ask what had caused the collapse of the armed revolt. I read everything I could about the region's past and its politics, and then set out to try to make sense of them by exploring the changes in the natural environment, the organization of farming, relations between landlord, overseer, and tenant, the rise and fall of the unions and the rebellion, local politics, and how people who participated in these changes thought about them at the time. Since regional history was becoming popular on its own terms, Al McCoy persuaded me to revise a chapter of my dissertation for *Philippine Social History*.[2]

I went back to the field in 1980 with the object of making a study of the town elites, particularly those connected to the village, to complement the village study. On the way, I became involved in writing a history of electoral politics in the town in order to trace the fortunes of its political elite. Between my work on more contemporary matters, historical questions led me increasingly into personal history and family history. Looking back on that work now, I realize that my inquiry into these broad questions of social change became focused on a single family—specifically, on tracing the political history of a village family, the de Guzmans, whose members at times used violence as a means to assist their rise from poverty.

I had to pursue this story. Since I first entered the village of Buga in mid-1971 I had been hearing stories about the de Guzmans. They remained the village's dominant political family even though the most prominent men of the older generation lived elsewhere. Andron, of the communist-led Huk Rebellion, was in 1971 an armed guard for LVN Pictures, Inc., in Manila, a movie studio founded by the wealthy landowner Doña Narcisa Buencamino-de Leon. From his headquarters in Cabanatuan City to the north, Andron's brother Grasing, overseer of some twenty-five hundred tenants of Doña Narcisa's heirs, ran the estates she had founded in five towns of the adjacent province. There Grasing was a millionaire and political king maker in his own right. Kardeng, (known as "the Limp") a man of legend like his brothers, had died two years before I arrived but when I rented his abandoned house from his son, the village headman, villagers asked darkly whether I had found many guns in its rotting walls and roof. Doña Narcisa was the richest person to spring from the town elite, and her husband's first cousin was the wife of

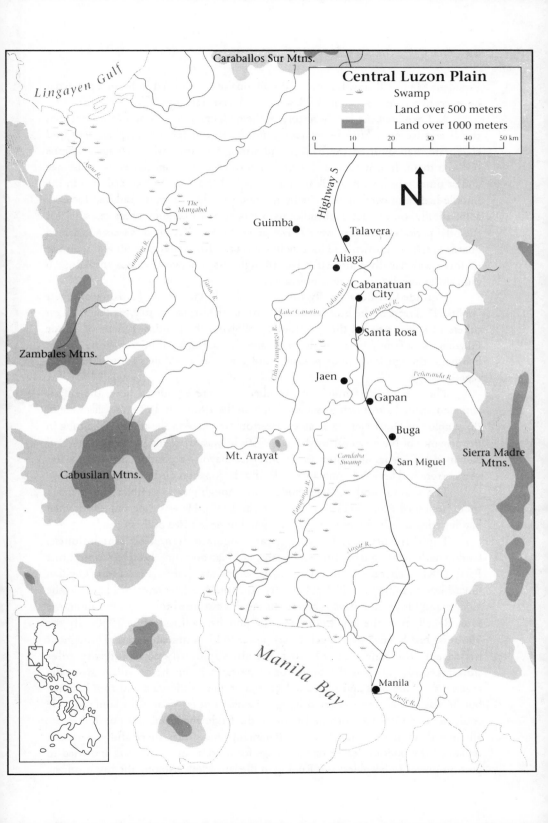

President Manuel Roxas. But her multimillionaire family lived in Manila protected by layers of servants, accountants, lawyers, and lesser relations.

As I explored the family history of the de Guzmans, it became apparent that the literature on relations between landowner and tenant, or politician and electorate, had omitted the bailiffs and strong-arm men who manage relations between them. In a system of absentee landowners, one characterized by resistance and at times rebellion, it struck me forcefully in 1980 that these crucial men in the middle had been overlooked. The literature on rural violence instead had focused, romantically, on the deeds of millenarian rebels, social bandits, unionists, and, for the brief periods when they were active, peasant rebels. Yet the overseers and armed guards of the landowners and local politicians had always been present and their use of force was usually more effective, though less newsworthy, less inspiring to radicals, or less disturbing to conservatives.

I decided to do a family history of the de Guzmans, focusing on their "political" careers in the broadest sense—that is, their capacity to exert their will on others in affairs beyond the household. Following the political careers of the de Guzmans as a family breaks with the village-centric model of microhistory, for the brothers, though born poor peasants and raised as a widow's sons, acted on a regional stage.

The first of the family's five brothers to achieve political note, the eldest, Amando, gained a reputation as a tough-guy in the 1920s. By 1925 his skills were in the employ of Doña Narcisa as an overseer on her estate in the town of Guimba in the province of Nueva Ecija. By the late 1930s he was managing her estate there and had used his talents in politics to become vice-mayor—a position that until a few years before had been held only by rich landlords. Amando died rich in the 1960s.

The second brother, Bienvenido, was a tough-guy, a gambler, and a crack shot. He joined Amando as an overseer in the 1930s. He was shot and killed when bandits tried to rob him of a big win in 1943 but he left two of them dead.

The third brother, Kardeng, is an enigmatic figure, peasant unionist, landowner's estate guard, pro-American guerrilla, one-time host to Communist Party (PKP) general secretary Jesus Lava, municipal politician, bandit, Civilian Guard leader, buffalo rustler, and political kingpin. Kardeng remained based in the village, and his greatest days occurred during the disturbed times of Liberation, the Huk Rebellion of the late 1940s, and the populist politics of the 1950s. By the 1960s he had handed over much of his power to his formidable sons. Throughout his career, Kardeng was able to maintain apparently contradictory roles simultaneously. He was the protector of peasants in his home village from the exactions of landlords and the unwelcome attention of the state and rival badmen but he was also an overseer controlling peasants in other villages for landlords. He could act as an overseer for one faction of the landowners and as a political leader allied with their rivals in elections. Balancing these roles successfully, Kardeng remained the political leader of the village for more than thirty years and tried to pass his power to his oldest son Rubing in the late 1960s. Among the five brothers, only Kardeng's children remained in the village to play an active role in its postwar politics.

The fourth brother, Andron, earned a reputation as an athlete and a man of great bravery and energy in the 1930s when he became a passionately committed member of the quasi-Marxist KPMP peasant confederation. During the Japanese occupation, he rose quickly to become an intelligence officer of the Hukbalahap guerrillas, acquiring a reputation for the ability to appear and disappear at will before the eyes of his enemies. By war's end, Andron was a Huk commander, and in the Huk Rebellion he attained the distinction of being the most wanted man in the municipality. In 1948 he arranged his own surrender to President Roxas, through his brothers and Doña Narcisa, having taken the decision that the rebellion was doomed. Doña Narcisa made him an armed guard in her LVN movie company. That took him to live in Manila, safely out of the region.

Grasing, the youngest brother, began his career as a harvest checker for Doña Narcisa in the late 1930s, rose to the position of overseer in her Cabanatuan City estate, and, during the Japanese occupation, to manager. By war's end, he was managing all her Nueva Ecija estates, with some twenty-five hundred tenants and nine thousand residents. He made alliances severally with the Huk, with bandits, Civilian Guards, municipal police, the Philippine Constabulary (PC), the army, and with the political private armies of those disturbed times. In the late 1940s he was a political figure of some note. Through his control of the vote on the estates and his complex alliances, Grasing was able to control mayorships in four towns and influence the outcome of elections for mayor of Cabanatuan City, the governor, and the local congressman. He was at times on the run from the authorities, from political enemies, and from others disturbed by a commoner with too much power. In the early 1950s, to give some flavor of the man, there were two attempts on his life. In one, three hundred troops surrounded his house in Laloma, a Manila suburb, and shot it up with automatic weapons for reasons arising out of a personal dispute between Grasing and a relative of his wife. Though one of his men was killed, Grasing was safely absent—thanks to a tip from a friend at Camp Crame, the PC headquarters—hiding out at the house of the mayor of Quezon City. He was absolved of charges of multiple homicide when the then PC Commander in Central Luzon, General Mariano Castañeda, gave Grasing papers making him retrospectively a special agent of the NBI and the dead men wanted killers. As Grasing explained it to me, he ran the numbers game, *monte* and *faro* card games, in Cabanatuan City "out of civic duty," to supplement the salaries of underpaid and overworked public officials who included the chief of police, the provincial commander of the PC, and the governor. He earned no personal profit from the gambling. They were all his "friends." Even in hiding he continued to manage estates and politics astutely, holding Doña Narcisa's power of attorney in all matters of the estates.

It would be a mistake to imagine that the personal armed encounters of the brothers, their youthful careers as gunmen, was what made them effective in promoting their own interests and those of Doña Narcisa. Though they began as gunmen, the key to their long-term success was their intelligence and political astuteness. As they matured, the de Guzmans showed the capacity to find and control younger men to do the dirty work while making alliances with other "real men" in the armed forces and the police, and among the rebels, bandits, and the politically ambitious. Among *magaling na lalaki* ('efficacious men') there are simultaneous rivalry and mutual recognition of spheres of influence, territories, and enterprises. They follow each others' careers as carefully as do prize fighters and actors. They meet to arrange settlements of homicide, to fix politics, and to settle other matters of import "out of court." Other men, respectable citizens, seek out their company in order to be seen with men of reputation. The poor and weak come to them for assistance in their troubles. Ordinary men are fascinated by their ability to breach the moral order with impunity. Kardeng and Andron were even credited with possessing magical amulets, conferring in one case invulnerability and in the other invisibility, to account for their charmed lives. Andron laughed at the notion—people were mistaking "tactics and propaganda" for magic.

Interviewing old politicians had prepared me for what otherwise would have surprised me: the de Guzman men were not at all inclined to conceal or whitewash their illegal deeds. They were eager to give me what amounted to depositions concerning their criminal and political misdeeds, however nefarious those might have been. Moreover, the details were usually confirmed by documentary sources and by testimony from their enemies or neutrals. Often these cast the de Guzmans, and both retired and active politicians, in a worse light, in legal terms, than did other sources. I found myself captured by the raciness of their accounts, by the intelligence of their observations and analyses of what they, their allies, and their competitors were doing and of the society that was their arena. These were men of considerable intelligence who in the course of practical politics habitually analyzed political opportunities, worked out scenarios, and made and tested theories of the behavior of men and trends in the systems of relations between them. Their special feature was their readiness to act to manipulate, to change, and to control outcomes to their advantage.

In short, between and within racy accounts of political skullduggery I was being presented with theories of politics, social relations, and social change. Those presenting them were intelligent men whose success (indeed, whose physical survival) had depended upon the accuracy of their theories as often as on their capacity for swift, ruthless action. This process puts the interviewer in a difficult position. One knows that the selection and relative salience of "facts" presented by the informant embodies his own theories as well as his desire to present himself in a certain light. Yet, bringing one's own theories to the session, one has to probe behind and around for other information that might constitute the "facts" that confirm or disconfirm one's theories. If this does not occur, the "data" that one later sits down to analyze can only bring one to the conclusions of the theorist who presented it; that is, one becomes an intellectual captive of one's informants. The interview becomes a battle of wits, a symposium. To keep ahead in it, the interviewer must be very thoroughly briefed by reading every available document, cross-checking interview data from other informants, and preparing questions to probe matters that expose informants' biases, accuracy of recall, and theories.

Why, I asked myself, are Filipino politicians so indiscreet? Why do they reveal—and insist the interviewer write down—matters that implicate them in grave crimes? The most economical explanation is that they wish to present themselves as *magaling na lalaki* ('real men'), men who get their way in contests for dominance with other men. Dominance over women is not a test or demonstration of being a "real man," though women might become the prizes or appurtenances of one who has earned the reputation in encounters with other males. The real man exerts his will over other men in contests of power. That he uses illegal means forbidden to ordinary men, and gets away with it, confirms that the *magaling na lalaki* is not an ordinary man. He is above such limits. Thus, unlike a public figure in America or Australia who would publicly and vehemently deny that he asked a judge a favor, Grasing de Guzman, known as the Godfather, described to me how by a combination of force, terror, and bribery of his opponents' lawyers, of witnesses, judges, police, and prosecutors, he routinely obtained favorable decisions for himself or for the hacienda he managed for Doña Narcisa. He was proud that he had won his cases, and reflected that with his skills he could have been a great lawyer. Then he laughed and said:

> No. I could never have survived as a lawyer. I am a man of honor. If I make a deal in a case I keep it. If someone made a deal with me and broke it I would kill him. As a lawyer I would have to bribe judges out of responsibility to my client. But judges are venal and may sell the case to the other side if it intervenes with a higher bid. Then I would have to kill the judge. Killing judges is perhaps a thing too difficult to make an *areglo* about. It is well that I used my talents otherwise.

Another explanation for what seems like indiscretion might be that these events are old, that the contest or crime occurred long ago, and there is no probability of its revival or prosecution. But active politicians have conducted the *areglo* ('amicable settlement') of homicide cases in my presence, arranging the disposition of money paid by defendants among victims' kin, witnesses, police, and others, with no sense that it would be politic to divert my attention. Similarly, they have conducted electoral skullduggery in front of me, or discussed arrangements for it in advance, and carried out corrupt negotiations about misuse of public property with no thought that this might be indiscreet. In some sense they were showing trust in my discretion. Equally, though, these are the everyday activities of politicians, and they had *invited* me to observe how they conduct politics. They also knew the rules, and, switching to English, could discuss politics in a civics-lecture format about as interesting and realistic as reading the Philippine Constitution or the country's Administrative Code.

In few cases was there an element of the confessional. One ex-mayor, who had got religion in his sixties, was regarded as both a religious crank and the most honest administrator the town had seen in the postwar years. When we were discussing his political career, I asked whether he had sold land to finance his first campaign. He began a long story of how he had made a fortune in the Liberation period by managing the financial affairs of prostitutes, setting up a number of them with considerable assets, including prime commercial sites that he bartered from starving landowners in Manila in exchange for rice purchased with the girls' dollar earnings from U.S. soldiers. Seven years later, when he asked one of these now-prosperous businesswomen whether he should run for mayor, she called together her ex-prostitute friends. They financed his victorious campaign. "You see," he said, "I bought the election with the proceeds of selling vulva to the foreigners."

For others, confession and guilt were not part of their ethos. The Godfather, Grasing de Guzman, nearly seventy in 1980, was running his own short-time "motel," piggeries, the numbers racket, gambling, a tractor pool, and a bakery. He continued to manage the lands of Doña Narcisa's heirs, including a cemetery and an urban subdivision, and to influence politicians. He considered himself to have reached an apex of power at which he seldom had to use crude force to gain his way but had turned to persuasion and peacemaking. But he had not dismissed his staff of bodyguards and special agents nor had he given up his less savory enterprises. Indeed, he conducted me around them, left me to discuss the economics and social relations of his motel/brothel with the staff, and conducted negotiations about a homicide settlement with a visitor at his office while I sat with them. He had seen the movie *The Godfather* and was proud to be known by that title in the local newspapers. As a former employee of Doña Narcisa's LVN movie company, and a connoisseur of the world of real men, he approved of *The Godfather, Part I*, but thought the sequel inferior. It had no moral lesson. The first film showed how a young man by energy and guts can rise despite adversity, defend himself against enemies by whatever means are expedient, grow wealthy and powerful, and help his friends. *That* was a story worth telling. He was prepared to tell me his whole story and particularly eager that it should be made into a movie. He laid it out in six acts, citing the dramatic high points of each. Though no other interviewee had such a keen cinematic eye, much in their accounts of themselves had the same flavor, a mix of Tagalog action films and Hollywood B-grade movies, in the bits they were most eager to tell and to have me record.

That brings me back to the starting point. Much in the lives of these men concerned their roles as worthy husbands and fathers, neighbors, friends, and entrepreneurs. But what they wanted to describe was not the part of their lives that confirms the moral and natural order but the extraordinary deeds that had breached it. They wanted to present themselves as the embodiment of those heroic figures who do not take the world and its rules for granted but try to rise above its limitations by breaking the rules, defying the constituted order by making it known that they are immune to and above them. Their lives were dramatic, the stuff of gossip, of news, and of history. Though their deeds made it into police blotters often, they were seldom brought to trial. If they were, they escaped punishment through daring or with the assistance of even more powerful allies. By doing so, in the different ways of Andron the rebel, of Kardeng the bandit and local politician, and of Grasing the Godfather, they gave others hope, heroes, and models.

But the curious and tragic thing about them is that all of the de Guzman brothers of that generation served the richest and most powerful family in their home town, a family that could permit them their depredations and arrange for the state to condone them, precisely because the de Guzmans were useful in maintaining the system of economic and political power that this great family and others like it control. The perplexing irony underlying the lives of these five brothers requires that we examine the nature of peasant politics and political families in the Philippines before we can make sense of the de Guzmans' history as political entrepreneurs in their home village over the span of three generations.

The Persistence of Political Families

Filipinos talk about political continuity in terms of the transfer of power within a territory between members of a family, and about political competition in terms of rivalry between families. Newspapers, political scientists, campaign organizers, and ordinary folk seldom discuss electoral politics in terms of parties, interest groups, or ideology. They usually talk about candidates as "standard bearers" of political families: the Laurels of Batangas, the Osmeñas of Cebu, the Romualdezes of Leyte, the Cojuangcos of Tarlac, the Singsons and the Crisologos of Ilocos Sur. Powerful political families are pejoratively called "oligarchs" and "political dynasties." Throughout this century, they have proven a persistent feature of Philippine politics. Under his martial-law regime, President Ferdinand Marcos promised to destroy the oligarchs. He did strip those who were his political rivals, like the Lopezes, of office and assets. He split some, like the Cojuangcos, allied himself with others, like his in-laws the Romualdezes, and created new ones. One plank of the 1987 Constitution granted the incoming Congress the power to make laws to prohibit political dynasties, roughly defined as close members of one family holding multiple positions in the state. But the winning candidates in the congressional elections of May 1987 included many members of old political families, some with close kin in the Palace or in high appointive office. Congress did *not* legislate to prevent its members' close relatives from running in the January 1988 local elections, and the constitutional clause lacked implementing legislation in the May 1992 national and local elections.

Part of the purpose of this paper is to ask why the family persists as the primary unit of political organization in the Philippines. Although focused on the history of one peasant family, this paper deals, in part, with the cooperation and conflict over several generations of two political families in a northern Bulacan rice-monocrop town. The landed de Leons have dominated municipal politics in San

Miguel since the Spanish regime. The peasant de Guzmans have dominated their village, over half of which is de Leon land, since the 1930s.

To probe this question, I will deal with an intermediate level between the individual and the state. At this middle level in the Philippines, family is the most significant political unit. One practical reason is that families are big and well organized there. Moreover, there is a strong ideology dictating that kinsmen should help each other in elections, share the honor of victory, and suffer the shame of defeat.

Since kinship ties are supported by this powerful ideology of solidarity, both landed and peasant families, with their numerous members, provide an unpaid and persisting political organization into which others collapse between evanescent election campaigns. Nonfamily coalitions have little to keep them together in the face of recriminations after a failure. They also tend to split after a success over the division of spoils and rivalry between the heads of component units for leadership in the next contest. By contrast, the family staff of unpaid campaign workers mobilize all their social assets in the hope of shared family honor and the fear of shame from a collective defeat. In this paper, I examine the way in which material capital in the form of land and other wealth; cultural capital in the form of education, political skills, and personal and family reputation; and social capital in the form of allies, clients, patrons, staff, enforcers, and protectors are all accumulated, conserved, dissipated, transmitted, and mobilized for electoral and class politics in the rural Philippines.

Peasants as Political Entrepreneurs

Reflecting my personal experiences and the personalities of the five de Guzman brothers, this paper describes how members of three generations of a peasant family have acted as political entrepreneurs, focusing on the family as a political unit. To begin with a general definition, a political entrepreneur uses his personal resources—plus the resources of those over whom he has authority, or whom can persuade, induce, or force—to compete for the power to make decisions affecting the inhabitants of an area.

The resources that a peasant can mobilize and promise to potential coalition allies consist of his several social capitals. These are difficult to measure and sum, except comparatively against rivals in a competition, and therefore are inherently unstable. Unlike an elite candidate, a peasant is seldom able to acquire the stable base of land or other capital that can provide an income or be mortgaged to provide funds for campaign spending and vote buying.

No peasant can afford to compete in campaign spending with rich candidates for the executive positions of mayor or governor, let alone those of congressman or senator. A peasant is limited to contesting local elections where his social capital (in the form of personal and family reputation, kindred, clients, allies, and networks), plus direct campaigning and lavish use of unpaid helpers, can substitute for funds.

Thus, peasant politicians are limited to campaigns for the positions of *barangay* captain, municipal councilor, and, rarely, provincial board member. At those levels the legal emoluments of office are not large enough to repay the cost of the last election, and the economic rents available to a winner are seldom big or lasting enough to allow him to establish a fortune.

Although a win brings an enhanced reputation, which is itself a resource for the future, it also brings ongoing costs. An incumbent faces an endless stream of visitors to his house at all hours. Supporters seek reciprocation of favors. Constituents seek interventions; sponsorship of community projects; sponsorship of baptisms, confirmations, and weddings; personal help in emergencies; recommendations; and assistance with papers and advice. Allies want to discuss tactics, and visiting officials, contractors, and businessmen seek to curry influence. The norms of rural hospitality and the politician's need to keep and increase support (by self-presentation as a personal friend, a generous man, and a man of the people) require an incumbent to offer at least snacks and coffee to all comers and meals to those who come from far away. The household of a candidate or incumbent becomes the court of a minipotentate but lacks the revenue to support it. He has travel expenses and the cost of entertainment and gifts when approaching officials and higher-level politicians in the township, provincial or regional capital, and Manila to seek interventions and the release of funds for pork-barrel projects. When one supporter is involved in a dispute with another he may contribute to the compensation to bring about an early *areglo*. Further, an incumbent is tempted to invest any increased income in seeking new supporters and alliances for the next contest at the same or a higher level of office.

Thus, for a peasant with limited funds, political entrepreneurship involves translating money capital (via generosity, vote buying, and campaign spending) into political capital, and translating all forms of social capital (in Pierre Bourdieu's sense) into political capital.[3] He stakes that political capital in a winner-take-all political competition with a number of other candidates. The risk is high since most candidates must lose. The prize is not wealth but prestige and limited power.

An election allows a candidate and his family the chance to demonstrate publicly that the sum of their social capital, translated into political support and measured in votes, is greater than that of their rivals, entitling them to higher prestige. This prestige is tested easily enough within a village by the support a person can assemble from kin, affines, *kumpadres, barkarda*, neighbors, clients, and friends. Village faction leaders calculate how to assemble a winning ticket by taking into account the number of kin and allies who would side with each potential candidate (that is, his conflict kindred).

It is more difficult to measure the support that a person from one village can demonstrate in votes in the municipality at large, pitted against candidates from other villages whose kinds of social capital differ. In this wider arena the direct votes of a large conflict kindred cannot suffice: its members are significant only if he can enlist their family and parochial pride to mobilize them as unpaid campaign workers and tap their personal networks that extend beyond the home village. A peasant who aspires to office beyond his village must have social capital in the form of a name and reputation that are known beyond his home base.

Prestige is the main prize of office. The victor in one election is looked to by politicians as a potentially valuable member of future tickets. He is a person who will be taken into account in future political calculations because of the support he has demonstrated. He has established his reputation as a *lider* who can muster votes and may deliver them to candidates for higher office in exchange for interventions on his behalf and on behalf of his clients, one who perhaps should be included in future rent-seeking deals.

But the greatest reward lies in the *galang* ('respect') that victory engenders at large. This reputation is particularly sweet when won at the expense of long-time rivals. In the rural Philippines any person who has once won office retains its respect title for life—alone as an address term such as *kapitan, konsehal,* or *alkalde,* or prefixed to his *palayaw* (his shortened personal name) as a reference term such as Kapitan Jose or Konsehal Rading.

The prizes for which peasant political entrepreneurs compete are largely nonmaterial: prestige and power, with a limited opportunity for additional income, that may be more than balanced by the cost of winning office and the upkeep of a political household. That is, the prizes for which candidates compete are unstable, difficult to translate back into money capital, and entail ongoing monetary costs.

Peasants as Entrepreneurs in Violence

For academics, Eric Hobsbawm's *Primitive Rebels* established the distinction, long cherished by peasants, between predatory and social bandits.[4] The social bandit robs the rich and gives to the poor, rights wrongs, and stands for justice for the poor and the oppressed. Like the primitive rebel and the millenarian leader, he is, in Hobsbawm's view, "pre-modern" for he fails to move beyond the redress of individual wrongs or attacks on particularly odious incumbents of a structurally unjust system.

In reality, a poor man who acquires a reputation for violence not only finds that he is constrained by the expectations of others but that his reputation is a resource that he can either put at the disposal of another party to conflict or use for himself as a political entrepreneur. At different times in his career, or at one time in relation to different others, an entrepreneur in violence may act as social bandit, predatory bandit, rebel, millenarian cultist, or revolutionary.

Further, the protector of some of the poor may act as a predatory bandit toward strangers (rich or poor) or as a protector of some of the rich. We often find social bandits and former rebels, along with discharged guerrillas and former soldiers, among landlords' rent and debt collectors, or working as guards of their crops, cattle, houses, businesses, and bodies; employed as strikebreakers and goons carrying out evictions of tenants and squatters; among the armed followings of members of the elite in their political contests; working as ward heelers and poll watchers, intimidating voters and guarding, seizing, or stuffing the ballot boxes; serving as agents charged with persuading, intimidating, eliminating, or spying on potential peasant leaders; or otherwise serving one or more members of the dominant classes as guardians of their persons, property, or incomes, controllers of the poor, or supporters in intra-elite contests.

Such men thrive where the state is weak and has not acquired the monopoly on violence that converts the followings of local power holders into its citizens. Conversely, such men are a resource for the dominant classes, helping them to control local agrarian conflicts and politics independent of the central state's forces, and thereby to maintain the inhabitants of their territory as dependents. Nevertheless, when private force fails, local power holders may, as a last resort, call upon state force to supplement their own forms of violence.[5]

In the politics of rural regions, men of intelligence and organizing capacity, who have acquired a reputation for personal violence or for commanding young men who can supply it, can mobilize local followings because they protect their clients and allies from like entrepreneurs and can extract benefits from power holders. Such men find it necessary to form alliances or coalitions with power holders to get a free hand for their local activities and to act as brokers for interventions delivered in return for control and support.

In the Philippines it is a rule of thumb of political calculation that "politics is addition," that is, it is strategically better to draw to one's own side, rather than to eliminate, the potentially most dangerous allies of one's competitor. To do so both reduces the number and power of an opponent's supporters and simultaneously increases one's own. As the careers of the de Guzman brothers show, one application of this adage is that members of the dominant class take note of young peasants who have acquired a reputation for effective violence and seek to add them to their staffs. Similarly, members of the landed elite often seek out local leaders of peasant unions, who have acquired a reputation for standing up to estate overseers and have shown a capacity for organization, and make them overseers in areas outside of their home villages. Though a tough peasant leader may be able to protect his own area from the attentions of "outside" overseers, the total effect of such a system is a general intimidation of the peasantry through the display of arms and of men ready to use them, producing a fine-tuned protection of the rich.

Since each must be allied more or less consistently with a faction of the rural elite, these entrepreneurs in violence often appear to be at odds with one another. They tend, therefore, to create factions among the lower class paralleling those existing among the elite, thereby subverting potential lower-class unity. The opportunity for a talented man of the rural poor to rise in this way helps to decapitate lower-class organizations such as peasant unions. Once present, and allied with upper-class protectors, such men can be enlisted to control and intimidate potential lower-class leaders.

Theories of Philippine Politics

The usual problematic for studies of politics in the Philippines has been to ask how candidates from wealthy landed families compete with each other to gain office, and how candidates drawn from these families mobilize support from the poor majority. That problematic fits with a two-class or elite-mass dichotomy in which the elite may be individuated into active, rational, individual actors but the non-elite is treated as a passive, undifferentiated mass. This two-group analysis is paralleled by the two-position, patron-client model, which, in turn, is often equated to the two-position, landlord-tenant relation. This latter dyad is analyzed in terms of an ahistoric golden age of "traditional," that is, morally praiseworthy, landlord-tenant relations that are assumed to have prevailed throughout the Philippines until that Eden's deflowering by capitalist penetration caused a moral fall. But the memory of those traditional relations (rather than the ahistoric model or ideal) is said to linger on.

Carl Lande went further, arguing that the logic of coalition formation dictates that the competition for power in each town or electoral district, on whatever scale, brings about two factions, each based on a core elite family.[6] Some writers frame the awful symmetry of this array of dichotomies as a picture that "explains" how contemporary candidates win office. They equate all the dyads. Thus:

ELITE	=	LANDLORD	=	PATRON	=	CANDIDATE
MASS	=	TENANT	=	CLIENT	=	VOTER

No one laughs, even though many candidates are not landlords, landlord-tenant relations are marked as often as not by anonymity or conflict, and it is a rare landlord family that ever had tenants enough to constitute a majority of voters in any electoral district. Something more must be going on.

To supplement this model some scholars have introduced extra actors: the *lider,* the "political machine," and the professional politician.[7] These ideas have allowed some writers to retain the dyadic models as the basic building blocks of the political system but to complicate their analysis by introducing the state and its resources and including consideration of various kinds and levels of professional brokerage between state, candidate, machine, and voter.

All these models work within a wider model in social-science theory that postulates that consensus and peaceful exchange under law characterize politics within the territory of a state, whereas political conflict and war characterize relations between states. But, because politics is about competition for power, a peaceful exchange model cannot be exhaustive. A model or theory that depends on exchange theory alone confuses what we would like politics to be with what politics is.

In the real historical world those who contest control of the state (or control of the resources of part of its territory) use whatever means seem most efficacious. Historically, in the Philippines, those means have included vote buying, the use of bullies and armed men to force the electorate to vote as directed or not vote at all, fraudulent manipulation of voting lists to exclude supporters of the opposition and include "flying voters" (who vote early and often), stuffing ballot boxes, seizing ballot boxes to alter the count, conducting false counts at the precinct level, falsifying reports of the count at higher levels, and a host of other stratagems. Those in control of many states use force to suppress internal opposition. Meantime, there are questions about how power is exercised to determine what kind of person can enter the political arena and what kinds of issues are included, tolerated, or excluded from the political agenda and policy debate.

Peaceful-exchange models distract social scientists from addressing styles of political competition that Filipino popular journalists have long labeled "guns, goons, and gold" or "force, fraud, and terror." The social-science models have allowed academic writers to introduce a moral preference into both description and analysis, and thus to dismiss the use of force as an aberration (typical only of the Marcos regime, for example, or of a local, temporary warlord), rather than acknowledging violence as an integral part of the political process in the Philippines.

Yet there is no inherent reason why an exchange model could not include negative exchange, as is done in games theory. Negative exchange involves the exchange of injuries to the person, resources, or supporters of a rival, which, when successful on both sides, results in revenge cycles. Since humans are capable of foresight, any analysis of this kind of politics must take into account the efforts of rivals to guard their persons, resources, and supporters from losses to neutrals or even more costly losses to rivals. Hence, political actors seek intelligence about the whole field of potential resources held by allies, neutrals, and rivals, as well as the intentions, political capacities, and vulnerabilities of all of them.

Marxists, who start from a conflict rather than a consensus theory, seem content to dismiss research and theory about electoral politics as a bourgeois, microtheory distraction from analysis of what really matters: the political economy of the Philippines in relation to the United States and international capitalism, semifeudal class relations, and how these might be overthrown by mobilizing a people's war. Unable to win elections, Marxist-Leninists denounce them as a bourgeois trick.

In its application to the Philippines, the literature of sociology and anthropology have been equally deficient. The sociological analysis of descent, kinship, and marriage alliance in small-scale societies with unilineal kinship was the obsession of British social anthropology up to the 1960s. It had just begun to take an interest in cognatic kinship systems and complex societies when the paradigm shifted. In the Philippines, American cultural anthropology took a different tack, concentrating on culture and personality issues until it was overtaken by a related paradigm shift in the 1960s. A major problem with the work of that period was that it began and ended with kinship as a normative system and as a closed and exhaustive system of explanation of relations within small-scale communities.

In the Philippines, sociology focused its attention on how kinship works in lowland societies, presenting it as a lamentable traditionalistic barrier to modernization. In modernization theory's continuum between the traditional and the modern, the Philippines and the United States were assigned positions exactly at the traditional and modern poles. The morally superior pole was inhabited by Americans with universalistic values, governed by laws not by men. The morally backward pole was inhabited by Filipinos with particularistic (or, worse, familistic) values that made their politics corrupt.[8]

About the only serious attempts to look at how bilateral kindreds might work were made by three Americans working in the British social-anthropology rather than the cultural-anthropology paradigms.[9] Charles Kaut argued that the bilateral kinship system of Tagalogs does not work as a rigid set of rules inflexible in time, place, and social position. Rather it is a flexible system in which behavior varies locally but is *justified* by rules as people adapt to necessity and opportunity. Francis Murray claimed that northern Tagalogs recognized two kinds of local kin groups, *tiyan* and *angkan,* which arose out of a rule or preference that kin should live beside each other. The only work I can locate that discusses action groups based on the personal kindred is Daniel Scheans who found work groups in Ilocos based thus.[10]

No attention was paid to a finding common in other societies with bilateral kinship, including Western European societies, that, although kindreds overlap, each person can stand as the reference point in disputes for what I call an agonistic, conflict, or led kindred. The conflict kindred has been the central unit in political and legal processes in the custom law of Philippine groups, as it was in Europe before the nation-state suppressed and supplanted its legal functions by the imposition of criminal law.

The conflict kindred consists of the set of close kinsmen who have a duty in customary law to support a person in disputes with nonkin, or with more distantly related kin, to demand *wergild* ('blood compensation') for death or injury to him, and, failing its payment, to exact.vengeance. In actual cases, the conflict kindred may be augmented by affines, close neighbors, allies, a more powerful backer, and clients and henchmen of the above. Whether it is augmented, and by how many people with what political resources, depends not on application of a kin rule but on the politics of the dispute and the presence of an able political leader.

Thus, it is useful to talk in terms of the conflict or led kindred, that is, all the persons who will support a leader on the basis of being related to him, even though some may be more closely related to the leader of an opposed kindred. This grouping, unlike the unqualified kindred, is a political unit that can have a continuing core membership formed around an effective leader to whom others look to undertake their disputes.

Whereas Murray defines *angkan* as a bilateral stock or localized kindred, northern Tagalogs in Buga would accept these definitions among the meanings for the term but also use it as the term for a conflict or led kindred. Thus, in calculating the electoral chances of two candidates for the post of village leader, or *barangay kapitan,* they could say:

> *Daig si Pilo. Matatalo siya sa bilangan. Malaki ang angkan ng kalaban na si Rodi. Kahit magpinsan buo sa ama sila magkalaban, papanig kay Rodi ang karamihan ng kamaganak.*

(Pilo is overwhelmed. He'll be beaten at the count. His opponent Rodi has a bigger *angkan.* Though the contestants are first cousins on their fathers' side, a majority of their relatives will side with Rodi.)

Divisions in elite political families like the Cojuangcos and the Osmeñas in the May 1992 elections confirm that the conflict or led kindred is a more useful tool for the analysis of political families than is the muddle caused by a notion that they are formed by genealogical links alone.

In my analysis, the Filipino political family corresponds to the led kindred. This political family is a persistent unit in societies that (1) have cognatic or bilateral kinship, and (2) a weak state that has not successfully suppressed self-help in disputes by replacing it with an enforced criminal law. Where category-based interest groups are not organized as political conflict groups, the led kindred or political family is the basic unit of political competition and conflict. It is not essential to the analysis (though it tends to confirm it) that this minimal political unit is covered by one of the meanings of the Tagalog term *angkan.*

In northern Tagalog rural society the term *matanda,* or *pinakamatanda,* is used to refer to the political head of a household or of a wider kin grouping. A *matanda* is an adult, married male who has grown children, is head of his own household, and can speak for it in public affairs because his father is dead or politically retired. He is the family's representative in serious disputes, in political faction-making and in matters relating to the wider state. The *pinakamatanda* is the political leader of a wider kindred than the household, the one who serves as its collective *matanda,* whether or not he is its oldest member. In theory the *pinakamatanda* of a large sibling group of senior adults is the one with the inclination and talent for conducting its affairs; in practice this is often the eldest brother, who, when the siblings were young, had over them the authority of their father's lieutenant. The *matanda,* as external representative of the family, guards his reputation to be able to deliver its undivided political support. It is his ability to speak for all the members and deliver all their votes that makes his voice heard by others. His ability to get favorable outcomes for family members in disputes with outsiders and obtain benefits distributed on the basis of voting power reinforces his authority to direct the conduct of members in public matters, including the vote.

Such leadership is a serious matter in a society with a weak state. The Philippine state has never been able to convince the population that its officials, acting without fear or favor in impartial pursuance of the law, can reliably protect the life, property, and honor of its citizens. Nor has it been able to convince them that those laws that grant benefits to citizens falling into certain legally defined categories will be automatically and speedily implemented in their favor.

Instead, Filipinos act as if the state is not an abstract set of anonymous functionaries but a loose alliance of individuals who have gained office by political favoritism and have their own individual interests, allies, and enemies. In that context, the populace looks to self-help and political negotiation as the only reliable sources of security and assistance.

Whether for the purposes of self-help or negotiation, it is essential to convince enemies that they cannot harm members of the family with impunity and to signal those who can give political support or supply armed force that the family can reciprocate. The kind of reciprocation most in demand is the political support of all members of the family, its dependents, clients, and allies. In this political context an isolated individual feels exposed and in danger. So he puts himself under the protection of a strong leader or family. Small families, poor families, and those with few men or no strong leader put themselves under the protection of a branch of the family of a husband or wife that has sufficient numbers to be taken into account. Thus, political families under their *matanda*—together with factions composed of alliances of such families under an effective leader—are the main political units in the countryside. The *matanda* of large families, not the individual voters, are courted by faction leaders and politicians. In effect, higher-level politicians deal with *matanda* as vote wholesalers. One index of the efficacy of this system is to look at the *kumpadres* acquired by a senior man at the marriages of his children. The *matanda* of a significant political family can get *kumpadres* from above his class—political office holders, candidates, and prominent persons with political ambitions. The head of an insignificant family that follows the leader of another family has few if any higher-class *kumpadres*.

It is this process that makes room for the career of a political entrepreneur as a faction leader. To keep control of the votes of the component families in his faction, a leader has to be able to deliver protection from their enemies and the unwelcome attentions of the state. Moreover, he has to be able to tap and distribute benefits from the wider political system. Delivering protection and controlling potential defectors demands that the leader have a credible ability to use armed force, whether on his own or by means of the younger men of his family, the allegiance of violent men, or an alliance with an armed leader.

Political Families and their Kindreds

Since the literature on Philippine politics has, for the reasons discussed above, generally avoided detailed discussion of the family as a political unit, we need to think about this issue. Why do rural Filipinos so often participate in politics as members of a family rather than as individual actors? A family is a more effective political unit than an individual because it has a permanent identity as a named unit, making its reputation, loyalties, and alliances transferable from members who die or retire to its new standard bearer. Being born into the household of a political family provides role models and an apprenticeship as well as an identity as a member of a prestigious family.

The Filipino family is the most enduring political unit and the one into which, failing some wider principle of organization, all other units dissolve. In a society that lacks interest groups organized as persistent voting blocks based on some category such as class, ethnicity, religion, or ideology, families are the units that compete for power within a local area and combine into ever-changing factions. If we make a reasonable assumption that each couple in the Philippines has an average of 6 children, then it follows that an average individual has some 5 siblings, 6 children, 30 nieces and nephews, 10 uncles and aunts, 60 first cousins, 120 first cousins of his parents, and 720 second cousins. If all of these are married, they link the individual into the similar families of each of their spouses. Each individual also has *kumpadres* acquired at baptisms, confirmations, and the weddings of his children and those made when he was invited to sponsor rituals for the children of his allies, plus classmates, village mates, business associates, and friends. In practice, overlaps between these categories reduce the extent of the circle. Not all the links can be activated, for some members of the circle will be linked by similar ties to a rival candidate and some kin may be lukewarm, neutral, or hostile to the candidate. But, when it comes to a contest with an outsider, even distant kin usually back their kinsman enthusiastically. In a congressional district or province comprised of several towns, the candidate or political leader able to mobilize his kinship links as the core of a political faction has a large organization but, because it is more or less localized to one town, he needs other bases of reputation and support—or money.

The family of a candidate constitutes an enduring political organization in which the closer kinsmen—particularly siblings, adult children, and some first cousins—provide a full-time, unpaid, and loyal staff. These assistants identify their personal interests with those of the candidate on whose success the political fate of the family hangs. The different genders, talents, training, contact networks, and other attributes of the members provide a potential specialization within that kin-based staff. In some political families one sibling may take responsibility for the family's use of violence, another for publicity, and still others for relations with particular localities, interest groups, and associations.

A family that has once contested an office, particularly if it has once won it, sets its eye on that office as its permanent right. The excitement of the campaign and the prestige won in it places a family above the ordinary in its own eyes and those of others. A political family has corporate pride in its status, is jealous of its reputation, and gains a sense of destiny. Such a family does not easily let go of office or cease contesting it even when to do so is quixotic. All the members of such a family share in the status of the incumbent. People call on them for tidbits of political gossip and to curry favor with the politician. The opinions of family members are given more weight by others. Ordinary people avoid giving them offense. When something of importance to another family or to the district at large is at stake, the political family is drawn into it. All these circumstances foster a collective pride from the inside, and a reputation from the outside, that this family is concerned with important matters. Not only do political families acquire a strong taste for office but their success gives them a clear advantage in elections against less prestigious rivals. Specifically, the mechanics of the Philippine write-in system of voting in multicandidate constituencies make name-recall strategic, reinforcing the electoral visibility of established political families.

The History of a Peasant Political Family

The following account traces the political biographies of three generations among the men of the de Guzman family, all of them born in Barrio Buga of San Miguel, the northernmost town of the province of Bulacan in Central Luzon, Philippines (see map on page 35). San Miguel is a rice-monocrop municipality located some eighty kilometers from Manila. Buga is a peasant village, in which almost all the farmers have been tenants since the turn of the century. The region saw extensive fighting in the period from 1896 to 1902, first in the 1896 Revolution against Spain, then in the war of resistance against the American invasion from 1898 to 1902. During the Pacific War, from 1942 to 1945, the town was racked again by fighting. In the Huk Rebellion that followed, from 1946 to 1952, the town experienced its most intense localized violence. Underlying conflict between landowner and tenant gave rise to peasant unions, beginning around 1918, which finally resulted in a land-reform program after 1972 that broke up the large absentee estates. Some aspects of the social history of the village and the politics of the town are recounted elsewhere.[11]

The de Guzman family were peasant rice cultivators in the late nineteenth century, owning 1.5 hectares of nonirrigated rice land, but were tenants on other land. During the turn-of-the-century wars, Jacinto de Guzman first fought the Spanish, then, under Colonel Pablo Tecson-Ocampo, fought as a guerrilla against the Americans. He was captured once by the Macabebe Scouts, Filipino auxiliaries of the Americans, and subjected to the water-cure torture. Old men say that Jacinto did not reveal his guerrilla connections under torture but found an opportunity to wound his guard and escape. Jacinto de Guzman may have begun the family's reputation for being *matapang* (brave or potent) or continued it. Rural Tagalogs, unlike the Irish, do not cherish stories from a past more distant than their own time or the time of people they have met.

When Colonel Tecson-Ocampo surrendered in 1901, Jacinto resumed life as a peasant. He married and began a family. But the land had been lost to debt and he became a tenant farmer. He stayed in contact with old comrades-in-arms and was involved in nationalist secret societies that drilled by night from 1906 to 1914 in the hope that Japan would land guns so that they might renew the national struggle. Jacinto was small in stature but his reputation for ferocity, his military experience, and his skill in arms were fortified by a reputed ability to call upon the assistance of fellow veterans. He was both feared and respected in the village.

Jacinto died prematurely in 1917, leaving seven children, the youngest an infant. The widow held a three-hectare tenant farm in Barrio Buga, plus three buffalo. At first none of her five sons was big enough to do the heavy work of plowing. The first year, she hired her late husband's brother Juan as a farmhand, contracting to pay him half of the tenant's 50 percent share of the crop. But Juan was a gambler and at harvest time used the whole of the tenant's share to pay off his debts, leaving the widow destitute. The family survived by gleaning, fishing, and hiring out to do any work available. The widow also found a trader to supply her with cooking pots on credit, and she sold them door to door. The second year, her oldest sons Amando and Bienvenido plowed while the rest contracted to transplant and weed on other farms in exchange for grown men doing the heavy work of harrowing on the de Guzman land. The brothers grew up as widow's sons, inured to hardship and ambitious to lift the family from its poverty. As each matured, he took over the farm until he could find a tenancy or opportunity elsewhere. The older children had little schooling beyond basic literacy but Eduardo (Andron), the fourth, completed six years of primary school, and the fifth son, Grasing, was put through high school in the town by his brothers, an unusual accomplishment for a peasant in 1935.

Life was grim and the times troubled. San Miguel's population of peasants and buffalo had recovered from the devastation of the turn of the century wars and epidemics,[12] its rice-monocrop economy was established, and the town was connected by rail to Manila eighty kilometers south. But the landowners, firmly in the saddle politically, were tightening the system of extraction from their tenants by shifting from low fixed rents to 50-percent-share rents and raising interest on consumption loans.

Although the landowners were firmly entrenched in municipal, provincial, and national politics under the Americans, the Jones Law of 1916 threatened this dominion. From the time the islands underwent "pacification" around 1902, only those literate in Spanish or English, those who paid substantial property taxes, and former town officials under the Spanish could vote and hold office. The Jones Law expanded the franchise to all adult males literate in the vernacular. As the U.S. colonial education system was spreading literacy fast, in a population in which adult literacy in the vernacular was already about 30 percent, the town-resident landowners had to devise new means to deliver the village vote, and find new men to do it, or they would lose control of politics. Since voting was by open rather than secret ballot, coercing tenant voters would become an important means of electoral competition. Though there probably always were tough village leaders, particularly in more distant *barrios*, there are neither written records nor surviving memories to demonstrate their presence in the past. Whether the elite's need for a new style of estate management, and for tough thresher operators, as well as a means to coerce the vote, created tough village leaders or merely gave them new functions, the period from around 1920 to 1960 is the time of the *barako, magaling na lalaki,* or *kinikilalang lalaki.* All these terms focus on masculinity, male potency, and the capacity to achieve ends through the use or threat of force. Jacinto de Guzman's sons displayed these traits abundantly and through them escaped the peasant's lot.

The Rise of the de Guzman Brothers

The careers of Jacinto de Guzman's five sons display the full range of positions in the delivery of violence, except for that of common soldiers in private employ, for they were men of intelligence and ambition. Their careers depended upon alliances with members of a rich and powerful landowner-politician family, whose attention the elder brothers earned by displaying their capacity for violence. By combining this capacity with political skill and ambition, each brother in turn drew upon the resources and alliances of the others to advance his career or protect him in crises. Significantly, the influence of the de Guzman brothers increased in periods when the state was weak and declined when it became strong.

In the 1920s, tensions were rising between landowners and the emerging tenant union and nationalist secret societies. The de Guzman brothers' cousin, Emiliano Macapagal, had been evicted from a tenancy in 1918 for leading a protest against conditions on the Hacienda Sevilla-de Leon. In Buga, the Kapatirang Magsasaka secret society cum peasant union increased in strength under Macapagal's leadership throughout the 1920s. The troubles of the 1920s and depression of the 1930s brought the brothers to the attention of landlord politicians who needed tough and ambitious men on their staffs.

The eldest brother, Amando de Guzman, was the first to establish a reputation for that combination of ferocity and astuteness that makes a man formidable. It brought him to the attention of Doña Narcisa Buencamino-de Leon ("Doña Sisang"), the most vigorous entrepreneur among the town elite, and it became his passport out of peasant hardship. Doña Sisang's brother, Don Gomercindo Buencamino owned tenanted land in Buga adjacent to the de Guzman farm, and Doña Sisang owned land scattered in nearby villages. However, it would be in her expanding tenanted haciendas in the adjacent province of Nueva Ecija that four of the five de Guzman brothers would find a mutually beneficial alliance with her. Doña Sisang made Amando an offer to work in her fast-expanding estates in Nueva Ecija. He began as a lowly harvest checker on her estate in Guimba in 1925 but rose quickly through his ambition and special talents. On the eve of the Pacific War, in 1941, he was managing the estate of 575 hectares and some 230 tenants, had been elected a town councilor with the highest vote, and was serving as acting municipal mayor.

Narcisa Buencamino was born into a Chinese-*mestizo* family of the landed and educated town elite but had been given little formal schooling. Her father,

Justo Buencamino, was killed in an ambush in 1901 by Filipino guerrillas under Colonel Pablo Tecson on his way to be installed by U.S. occupation troops as San Miguel's town mayor. When her mother married her late husband's brother, Narcisa managed the household. Around 1905, she married Don Jose de Leon ("Kapitan Pepe"), an educated but not very wealthy landowner, and turned her talents and energy to building a great fortune in rice haciendas and urban investments. In her rise as an entrepreneur Doña Sisang was assisted by the political influence of her Buencamino kin, including her uncle Don Felipe Buencamino, one of the founders of the Federalista Party and a prominent figure in colonial politics during the early years of the century. Her cousin, Felipe Buencamino, Jr., was a nationally powerful congressman for Nueva Ecija Province for many years. Among her husband's kin and in-laws were provincial governors, congressmen, Senator Ceferino de Leon, and his daughter Doña Trinidad de Leon, the wife of Manuel Roxas, Speaker of the House in the 1930s and president of the newly independent Philippines from 1946 to 1948. In 1938, Doña Sisang founded LVN Pictures, Inc., which under her management produced up to twenty-six Tagalog feature films per year from that time until the early 1960s. Through political connections she was able to borrow large sums on cheap government credit for her investments.[13] In return, she managed the strategy of the de Leon political faction in their home town of San Miguel. From there, and through her overseers on her Nueva Ecija farms, she delivered large parcels of votes to provincial and national politicians.

In the 1930s, the discontented peasants of Central Luzon turned to demonstrations, strikes, burning rice-sheaf stacks (mandala), and resistance to the landlords' overseers. After the collapse of the Tanggulan secret society in 1931 and the Sakdal rising in 1935, the scattered early unions of the secret-society type coalesced under the already strong National Confederation of Philippine Peasants (KPMP), founded in 1922, which was led by Manila Tagalog communists and allied with the AMT union of the Kapampangan Socialist Party. From about 1925, the landlords organized counterunions of strike breakers, led by their overseers and filled with landless peasants eager to show their loyalty in the hope of securing the farm of an evicted tenant.

The San Miguel elite was divided from 1901 to the 1950s into two rival factions, the de Leons and the Tecsons.[14] The existence of two elite factions contesting for local control is common in Philippine politics.[15] In San Miguel's case the distinction was not arbitrary due to the families' somewhat different resources and styles of getting out the vote.

By the 1910s, San Miguel's leading elite family, the de Leons, had become a closed aristocracy, delaying and controlling the marriages of its members so as to prevent the division of its estates among many heirs. The family arranged marriages between first cousins to reunite lands divided by inheritance, while they married outside only to the heirs of families of similar wealth and power. The wealthiest branches of the family mixed only with members of the national elite. Until the rise in popularity of Baguio after the Pacific War, Manila's wealthy came to Sibul

Springs in the Sierra Madre foothills of San Miguel in the hot season to take the waters and enjoy its forest setting. The de Leons entertained them in their grand houses in the town, reinforcing their elite connections.[16] The wealthiest branches of the de Leons had moved to Manila in the 1920s where they invested revenues from the estates that had been left in control of managers and poor relations. In Manila some pursued careers in the professions and politics, others enjoyed a leisurely lifestyle. The de Leon women attended Mass daily, were devoted to family life, and followed their strict convent upbringings by making daily devotions to the religious images of the family's patron saints. The men occupied themselves with business, politics, golf, gambling, and mistresses. They visited San Miguel only at fiesta, Easter, and during the resort season. But this strategy had political costs, for the family no longer had direct contact with its tenants and no vigorous members on the spot to organize local politics and manage the control of the peasants. Into the gap stepped Doña Sisang and the Sevilla brothers.

Catalino and Regino Sevilla were born into a family of rich peasants who owned five hectares in Barrio Pinambaran, adjacent to Barrio Buga. They had little education but a driving ambition. By about 1910, they were local overseers on de Leon land and frequented the big house in town on estate business. The brothers perceived the opportunity provided them by the de Leon strategy of delaying the marriages of its daughters. They laid siege to the affections of two rich spinsters, one a sister of Don Jose ("Kapitan Pepe") de Leon, and the other of his wife, Doña Sisang. With these strategic marriages the Sevilla brothers controlled the lands of their wives and were placed as managing overseers of other de Leon estates in San Miguel. Under Doña Sisang's strategic direction, they took up the standard of the de Leon faction in municipal politics. Between them, Catalino or Regino Sevilla held the mayorship during the terms of 1916–19, 1928–31, and 1937–40. They also expanded their personal fortunes in ways not based directly on owning land: cockpits and steam threshing machines. For much of this work—as estate overseers, election ward heelers, operators of the unpopular threshing machines, and controllers of gambling—the Sevillas needed tough men.

In the villages, the protection of water buffalo, a peasant's most important property, required and reinforced the special talents of the strong men. Anyone who wanted to keep his buffalo safe would place himself under the protection of the local strong man, who sometimes kept a corral where the village buffalo were guarded. Anyone who had fallen out with a strong man or refused to accept his protection was exposed to rustling. Should his buffalo disappear, a peasant had no recourse but to approach the strong man to undertake its recovery—even when he had excellent reason to believe that the strong man had arranged its disappearance to extort ransom or to make a political point. The police and the Constabulary were incapable of protecting or recovering buffalo, in part because mayors appointed and controlled the police and were indebted to some strong men as *liders* (vote brokers) who delivered the vote. In the 1930s, the third de Guzman brother, Ricardo ("Kardeng"), collected the buffalo of Barrio Buga at the end of the work season and drove them to pasture in the foothills near Sibul under the armed guard of his men. He also had the reputation of rustling buffalo for profit and politics.

The three youngest de Guzman brothers, Kardeng, Andron, and Grasing, made their name and that of Buga *sikat* ('shining') in the 1930s through their sporting prowess and as *magaling na lalaki*. In the late 1920s, the second brother, Bienvenido, had followed Amando to Guimba in neighboring Nueva Ecija Province to work as an overseer for Doña Sisang during the tense harvest season. But in the wet season he farmed in the adjacent *barrio*, Pinambaran, and had acquired a reputation beyond the immediate area because of his displays of ferocity at Don Catalino Sevilla's cockpit, where he was a big gambler.

Amando, the oldest, had risen in Doña Sisang's service to become manager of her Guimba estate by the mid-1930s. The three youngest brothers stayed in Buga, where they formed the core of a village softball team that regularly won the municipal league and represented the town in provincial meets. Tall Andron was famous as a softball pitcher, foot runner, and buffalo racer. He won foot races as far away as Manila, where he was pressed by an American professional trainer to go to the United States to race for money. He kept champion racing buffalo to work his three farms, ran them in dry-season saddle and cart races, and ran with them in the wet-season mud of harrowed fields. Kardeng was short but skilled in the martial art of *arnis,* or *escrima* (fencing with wooden swords), and carried a sword stick. Though Grasing was in high school until 1935 he already had acquired a reputation for ferocity when challenged and for the capacity to lead.

Kardeng took over the family farm in his turn and built his house there. When Andron married, Kardeng passed the farm to him since he had already found another. He protected his followers and allies but was ferocious toward enemies or defectors and treated strangers as either wolves or prey. After his cousin Emiliano Macapagal died of tuberculosis in 1928, Kardeng took over leadership of the Kapatirang Magsasaka (KM) peasant union in the village. With his organizational genius, and the popularity won by the family's sporting prowess and protection, he was able to reorganize the rice-farming tasks by using the KM's ideology of brotherhood to unify the village in a euphoric effervescence of mutual aid. Village men who were his contemporaries proudly display the triangular initiation brand of the KM, burned into their shoulders, and the scar on the wrist from which they drew blood to sign the KM oath. During the early 1930s, transplanting and harvest were reorganized in a village-wide labor pool. Village elders kept a register in which the labor days contributed by a household's members on other farms were recorded as credits and days received on its farm as debits. At the end of the season surplus-labor-receiving households reimbursed the pool in rice; households that had contributed a net labor surplus were paid from the pool. The work, with the group singing songs for unison, was merry. The KM used a military style: the *kabisilya* (labor-team organizer) blew calls on a bugle to signal reveille, the start of work, and snack breaks.

Kardeng's activities, even at this time, confound the sociological typology of rural leaders. On the one hand, he was the leader of KM, overtly a moderate tenure-reform union. But KM had a secret inner core of millenarian nationalists looking to promote an armed, anticolonial, antilandlord uprising. Kardeng protected his own villagers from the landlords' men over issues of agrarian conflict and voting, protected their buffalo from rustlers, and guarded their lives and property from rival strong men and bandits. But at the same time he used his reputation and following to deliver the vote from Buga-Pinambaran to landowner politicians, and acquired, as a ward heeler of the rich, the political protection that allowed him to operate as a union leader.

At that time Catalino Sevilla controlled, through overseers and by virtue of his marriage, about a quarter of Buga's land. Another branch of the de Leon family owned about half the village land. The remaining quarter was divided among several small- and medium-sized owners, among them Buencamino kin of Doña Sisang. In the surrounding area, landowners often evicted tenants who had voted against their directions or had joined a peasant union. Old peasants refer to the 1930s as *panahon ng buhat bahay*, "the time of carrying houses," for eviction from a farm meant that the tenant must call upon neighbors to carry his house to a new site. Catalino Sevilla evicted two Buga tenants in the 1930s for voting against his instructions, a fault easily detected by his overseers who need only consult the open voting list. Under Kardeng's leadership, the affected farms stood idle until selected unionist tenants received approval to reoccupy them. Kardeng himself took up tenancy on a de Leon farm from which a gunman-peasant, Jose Manalo, had been evicted for concealing the harvest.

When the KM's national leader, Attorney Vicente Almazar, died in 1933 after beatings and a jail term, Kardeng found himself with the undivided loyalty of local initiates of an organization that had disintegrated above the village level. He continued to protect his fellow villagers from abusive overseers on the Sevilla-de Leon and de Leon estates. Meantime, Kardeng's two older brothers, as overseers for a branch of the de Leon family in the adjacent province, were carrying out the same activities on behalf of Doña Sisang from which he protected his kin and neighbors in the home village. Kardeng was invited to join his brothers as an overseer, and also was urged by Andron's socialist and communist friends to join another socialist peasant confederation, the KPMP. Still, he took his own path, using his growing reputation and following as a political entrepreneur.

In 1933, Don Regino Sevilla observed Kardeng's ferocity in a fray in the town in which he left two men gravely wounded. Sevilla hired Kardeng to run the family threshing machines, presented him with his first firearms, and allowed him to select his own crews to guard and operate the machines. Meanwhile, Kardeng allied himself with the Tecsons, political enemies of the Sevillas, to whom he delivered the vote. In 1934, he fell out with the Sevillas but the Tecsons rewarded him with the management of their stable of threshing machines. In this capacity he was everywhere in threshing season, with a loyal crew of kinsmen and fellow villagers, the majority of them unionists.

According to old men, the Janus-faced stance of holding alliances with members of apparently opposed elite factions and serving conflicting class interests was common. Several overseers for large estates were *magaling na lalaki* employed to manage lands not in their home village because their reputations for violence cowed tenants into submission and discouraged them from concealing the harvest. But, at least in part, the same men had acquired their reputations for ferocity and leadership by intimidating the overseers of estates in their home villages and protecting the villagers there.

The fourth brother, Andron, with his reputation for sporting prowess, was a popular figure. He had also displayed, in more muted form, the family capacity for bravery and leadership. In the mid-1930s, he held the home farm and two tenancies downstream from Buga, towards the edge of Candaba Swamp, in an area of mixed Kapampangan- and Tagalog-speaking communities. That vast depression, bordering three provinces, is a lake in the wet season but in the dry months it is a dusty plain with dense thickets of tall tropical grasses. It has been a refuge for rebels and bandits since Spanish times. Andron did not join the KM as a youth because he "objected to people being branded like cattle" but in the mid-1930s the Candaba Swamp fringe was an area of maximum peasant unrest. Lope de la Rosa, a KPMP unionist led an armed band there from 1931, hunted by the Constabulary while performing Robin Hood deeds of resistance. De la Rosa's ideas were Marxist-Leninist, and he was a member of, but regarded as left-deviationist by, the Communist Party (PKP). Luis Taruc, a Kapampangan from across the swamp, worked as a tailor on the fringe of San Miguel town. Taruc spread the message of the Socialist Party and its Association of Poor Workers (AMT). Andron listened to both and became an active KPMP member. Unlike Kardeng—who was concerned to protect those under his personal sway and to extend that influence as far as opportunity allowed—Andron was concerned with notions of justice. His moral range included the abstract other, extending to strangers whom he thought should be treated like brothers. Where Kardeng dealt in the dyadic exchange of favors and injuries, Andron strove to see the other's point of view and to seek a just compromise by appealing to higher values.

With three farms to work and his racing buffalo to care for, Andron was both busy and prosperous. He married and built a house, large by village standards, on the highway. After Kardeng took over the Tecson threshing machines, Andron was approached to organize carts to haul the grain from the threshing sites to the landlords' warehouses in town. By 1936, he headed a harvest-season pool of thirty-five carts, many of them driven by his buffalo-racing friends. He was not allied with any elite politician; he was a farmer, sportsman, and carter by day, a unionist by night. But he was on good terms with some young members of the town-dwelling, landowner class and he was an acute observer of politics.

In 1936, the youngest brother Graciano ("Grasing") finished high school in town with the help of his brothers. He took a temporary job as a substitute teacher but was laid off, and then went to work on the roads in Guimba, Nueva Ecija, in a patronage job arranged by his oldest brother Amando. Amando was by then the manager of Doña Sisang's Guimba estate. Through the vote of its tenants and his notoriety as a tough guy he had won election as "topnotcher" town councilor. One day Doña Sisang noticed Grasing digging in the road near Amando's house. Was he not Amando's brother, the "teacher"? Why was he wasting himself on the roads? Go to Cabanatuan! Grasing began as a harvest checker in 1937 on Doña Sisang's estate on the fringe of Cabanatuan City but she soon switched him to other jobs in her network of enterprises. He was sent to cinemas all over the archipelago to see that managers and their staffs did not understate the box-office receipts in order to cheat her LVN Pictures of its 50 percent share.

Grasing rose quickly in Doña Sisang's service, developing a reputation as a man who could handle problems on the spot with discretion, using the threat of violence when expedient and the real thing when necessary. With three of the de Guzmans now in Doña Sisang's service (Amando, Bienvenido, and Grasing), the alliance between the peasant family and entrepreneurial landlord would become stronger in the disturbed times of the Japanese occupation and the Huk Rebellion. The remaining brothers would go their own ways—Kardeng as a political entrepreneur and Andron as a rebel. But during the rebellion each would come to owe his life to the capacity of his brothers to secure Doña Sisang's intervention with the national authorities.

The Pacific War: Guns and Guerrillas

The Pacific War opened new opportunities for political strong men drawn from classes below the old landed elite. In San Miguel, retreating U.S. forces blew the bridges and abandoned much matériel at an army camp near Sibul Springs. The townspeople evacuated to the hills in expectation of bombing and those near the highway in Barrio Buga moved away from the road and rail bridges.

Kardeng saw his opportunity and led a convoy of carts that hauled away everything movable from the abandoned army camp, acquiring hundreds of rifles and great stocks of ammunition. He armed his men and gave guns to allies, including Dioscoro de Leon of Gapan, and buried spare weapons in the yard. In Guimba, Amando was managing Doña Sisang's 230 tenants and serving as first councilor of the municipal government. When the Japanese landed at Lingayen for the drive south to Manila it was harvest time on the estate. The mayor was sick and the vice-mayor dead, so the Americans installed Amando as acting mayor. As the fighting approached he fled home to Buga. When the battle moved on, he returned to find that the Guimba tenants had hidden the harvest and were refusing to hand over the estate's share. He sent for his brothers, who came in an armed party, overseer and unionist alike with their men, and "persuaded" the tenants to relinquish Doña Sisang's share. Amando was able to stay "neutral" during the war because the Japanese installed his cousin Pablo, who had a Japanese son-in-law, as town mayor. According to his brothers, Amando enriched himself during and after the war in estate management and politics. Later he would fall out with Doña Sisang (in 1952) and the estate would pass to Grasing's management. Grasing says that Amando was no longer *matapang* ('brave') after the war "because he was afraid of losing his wealth." He died rich.

The second brother, Bienvenido, kept his own farm and worked as an overseer only during harvest. He was a notorious gunman and gambler who was "cowboy" brave and generous, and "go for broke," unafraid of the odds in gaming or a fight. After a big win in 1943, he was set upon by bandits. He killed two and wounded another but was shot dead in the gunfight. His daughter Nati later married a young man, Faustino Dy, in the *matapang* tradition, and followed him to the frontier province of Isabela, across the mountains in northern Luzon. There Faustino Dy would rise during the "Wild West" conflicts of land grabbing, logging, politics, and rebellion to become, by the late 1960s, governor, provincial warlord, and a logging millionaire.

With his guns Kardeng turned his followers into an armed force, which he affiliated loosely with the pro-U.S. guerrillas of the United States Armed Forces in the Far East (USAFFE). He acted as a minor warlord who found in the war an opportunity. There was an interregnum, with a hated foreign government ensconced in the capital, working through the prewar Philippine Constabulary. In the town the Japanese had the overt collaboration of the mayor and therefore of the municipal police. But the mayor, Kardeng's prewar patron Eugenio Tecson, was secretly in league with two groups of anti-Japanese guerrillas to whom he sent supplies and information. By mid-1943, the USAFFE guerrillas, commanded by American officers under Colonel Bernard Anderson, set up a base on Mt. Corona in the Sierra Madre east of town. The territory under their control was restricted to the mountain fringe and hilly *barrios* upstream of Highway 5. Downstream the Marxist-led Hukbalahap, based on the KPMP union, held sway. Kardeng stood on the fringes of these competing guerrilla movements, with his son Rubing acting as a USAFFE scout, his brother Andron as a Huk leader, and the mayor as an ally. Kardeng himself had guns, followers, a strategic position just a kilometer off the highway between the rail and road bridges, and the tactical talent to use them. Within a short time he was exploiting these advantages to become a powerful armed leader. The war justified robbing "collaborator" merchants moving valuable cargoes along the highway. Kardeng distributed part of the proceeds to the USAFFE and Huk guerrillas, in a style that was at once supportive of the patriots fighting a national enemy and payment of a kind of tribute by an independent political entrepreneur in recognition of superior force. Meanwhile, following the logic of guerrillas, social bandits, and long-sighted predatory bandits, he distributed part of the loot among his men and his neighbors, making them accomplices with nothing to gain, and much to lose, in betraying him.

In order to divert the collaborationist Constabulary and Japanese forces, robberies and ambushes by Kardeng's men were carried out well away from his home village. Since the Japanese conducted reprisals against villages that harbored guerrillas, the Huk and USAFFE commanders tried to carry out their actions near the villages of enemy leaders. When either guerrilla force intended to pass through

Buga and needed billets, food, medical care, or information, they contacted Kardeng first. The men were billeted according to his judgment of the capacity of households to bear the burden of extra mouths.

Kardeng's reputation for tactical and political ability was reinforced by a reputation for invulnerability, rationalized by his acquisition of an *anting-anting*, an amulet supposed to protect him from blade or bullet. But he had other problems, some with old personal enemies and some with Ganaps, mostly Sakdals, who out of racial, anticolonial sentiments supported the Japanese. Some were prepared to betray guerrillas. For most, Kardeng's reputation and his alliances with the USAFFE and Huk guerrillas were a sufficient deterrent. But his wife's sister's husband, a Constabulary trooper and ex-Sakdal turned Ganap, betrayed Kardeng to the Japanese secret police, the Kempeitai, in late 1943. Truckloads of Japanese soldiers and Constabulary troops raided Kardeng's house and dug up the cache of guns. Curiously, though the Kempeitai tortured him and threatened execution, Kardeng was allowed to live. He was taken to Manila and thrown into the dungeons of the old Spanish Fort Santiago from which few emerged alive.

Back in the village, his pro-USAFFE men came under the command of his son Rubing. Under Rubing and older men, the guerrillas became quiescent in the home area, though several men from the village joined the USAFFE camps in the mountains. In 1944, they took part in the epic trek through the forests of the Sierra Madre, under the leadership of Colonel Anderson, to meet a U.S. submarine on the east coast and return carrying new weapons, radios, and propaganda material.

Andron's wartime career took a different path. Instead of an independent entrepreneur in political violence he became a member of the Hukbalahap apparatus and rose in it. As early as March 1942, with the Japanese barely established, guerrilla units were forming along the edges of Candaba Swamp. At first these included both American survivors of Bataan and KPMP unionists. On 27 March, Andron attended a joint meeting at Arayat from which he emerged as a supply officer. Two days later the Marxist leaders founded the Hukbo ng Bayan Laban sa Hapon (People's Anti-Japanese Army), shortened to Hukbalahap, or Huk. Its military *supremo* was Luis Taruc, head of the Kapampangan AMT union and Socialist Party. Within a few weeks, Huk units were set up along the swamp fringe, and KPMP unionists were invited to join. The Huk set about collecting weapons. KPMP and AMT unionists in fishing villages of the Pampanga River delta brought boatloads of weapons from the Bataan battlefields. The Huk established an organization to govern the villages and organized armed squadrons, intelligence, and supplies. Andron went to Bataan with Felipa Culala, a woman commander known as Dayang-Dayang, to gather guns and ammunition. In 1943, when the Japanese were active in his area repairing the road and bridge, they noted the strategic position of Andron's large house, located on the highway opposite the Salacot school, and billeted their officers with him.

At first Andron was a contact and supply officer, collecting milled rice, money, weapons, clothing, and intelligence for the Huk units. Having the Japanese in his house afforded him excellent cover. For a while he continued to farm. But during the early wet season of 1943 he was arrested on suspicion of being a Huk. He was tortured but released.

Andron immediately went underground and sent his family to stay with kin. Ganap collaborators burned the house. Andron became a Huk officer under the alias Kumander Andy or Kumander Bangus, a nickname that referred to his fair skin and his habit of wearing white clothing. By that time, the early informal bands were giving way to organized squadrons, affiliated with either the Huk or USAFFE, with an emerging division of territories between them. The Huk were established first in Nueva Ecija, with squadrons 25, 55, and 28. Colonel Sta. Maria initially commanded two platoons in Barrio Batasan and Barrio Mandile of San Miguel. But, after they ambushed Japanese troops and were bombed, he went over to USAFFE. His successor, a local leader named Lipana, set up a squadron in Barrio Batasan of San Miguel but his men were co-opted by the Nueva Ecija group. He then set up his own Bulacan–San Miguel force, which he called Squadron 105.

Andron says that he refused offers from several Pampangan commanders from Nueva Ecija in order to accept the position of vice-commander of Squadron 105. The two commanders—Nicanor Lipana ("Rosales") and Anong Batas ("Tagumpay")—he dismisses as *duwag*, cowards, afraid to lead their men in encounters. His own reputation is of outstanding bravery, seeming invulnerability, and the power to appear and disappear at will. Old soldiers recount how in fire fights Andron would stand up to direct the fire of his concealed men. Squadron 105 at that time had some 135 to 145 men permanently under arms as full-time guerrillas, though the units that lived and operated together were platoons of around 30 men. The Huk had more volunteers from the immediate area than they could arm, and these were supplemented by some young fishermen from Hagonoy whom Lipana had brought back as carriers from an expedition to the delta to collect arms brought from Bataan.

The Huk were popular. Platoons moved by night, leaving the people of the place they had left no idea of their next destination. Upon arrival at a village they would contact the *teniente del barrio* (headman) who would distribute the men among the houses, two to four per dwelling, according to the capacity of households to feed them. They posted guards on village tracks and roads to prevent anyone from leaving and to warn of approaching strangers or enemies. While in a village the Huk called meetings, set up village governments, and organized "so that the local organization could support the armed organization." Individuals who opposed or resisted the Huk were taken along on their next move, lectured daily, and held until they changed their viewpoint.

According to Andron, the antilandlord struggle was dropped in favor of a united front for the duration of the occupation. He denies that there was a Huk policy of withholding rice from the landlords and claims that in fact the rich, especially the Tecsons, helped the guerrillas. Some Tecson landlords stayed on in Barrio Batasan as evacuees, although it was deep in Huk territory and had a Huk government. *Engkargados* (managing overseers) of the de Leon haciendas "voluntarily" gave the Huk one *cavan* (fifty kilos) of rice per farmer from the owner's share.

Grasing de Guzman began the war as one of eleven overseers on Doña Sisang's seven-hundred-hectare estate on the edge of Cabanatuan City, the rice-milling capital of Central Luzon. Bordering on the township, the estate included warehouses that received every year some one hundred thousand *cavans* (five thousand tons) of rice from de Leon lands. The fortunes of war made an opportunity when the *engkargado* was killed in a bombing raid. Grasing replaced him at the age of twenty-six. With communications to Manila cut, he was granted full power of attorney by Doña Sisang to act in her name. After the initial fighting receded, Japanese troops entered the town and installed their military administration, working partly through the Philippine Constabulary. Grasing continued to collect rents and debts from the tenants, despite the presence of the Huk, USAFFE, and *tulisanes* (bandits) in the villages, because he ingratiated himself with their leaders. By night, USAFFE and Huk guerrillas who came to the warehouse were given rice. By day, Grasing did business with the Japanese. He had USAFFE, Huk, and *tulisan* leaders stay at his house, opening alliances that served him well in wartime and would become important in postwar politics.

Liberation

In San Miguel during the first weeks of 1945, the war's final battles for the "Liberation" of the Philippines opened with the retreating Japanese setting fire to the warehouses while Mayor Tecson and the rich fled to the nearby hills. The Huk guerrillas entered the town, mopped up a Japanese rear-guard force, collected guns, and distributed Japanese goods to the populace. When the advance columns of the U.S. Army drove into San Miguel, Andron de Guzman's Huk were in control of the town. He gave the Americans three guides for their advance on Manila, while his unit continued searching for enemy stragglers. Several days later, a runner came to tell the three squadrons then in the township that the Huk battalion of Kumander Banal, which had guided U.S. forces to Manila and fought beside them, had been disarmed and massacred by USAFFE forces under Colonel Maclang at Malolos, Bulacan. The Huk guerrillas retired to the fields and the U.S. forces installed a series of USAFFE officers in the San Miguel mayorship.

Relations between the Huks and USAFFE guerrillas were strained after the massacre. No civilians were able to cross Highway 5, the boundary between their territories, and each side took hostages. Andron arranged peace talks with acting mayor Colonel Sta. Maria in April 1945. They released hostages on both sides, opened the "border" to citizens, and ceased contesting the other's territory. Meantime, the peasants had abandoned the wartime policy of postponing class conflict over the land in favor of a united, anti-Japanese front. Some tenants held guns as Huks or had picked them up on the battlefields. Few were ready to revert to

The de Guzmans: A Political Genealogy

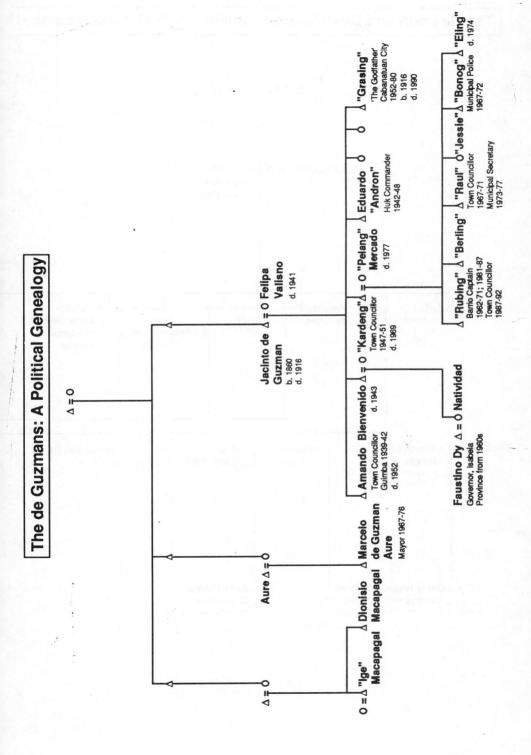

The de Leon and Buencamino Families: A Political Genealogy

de Leon Family

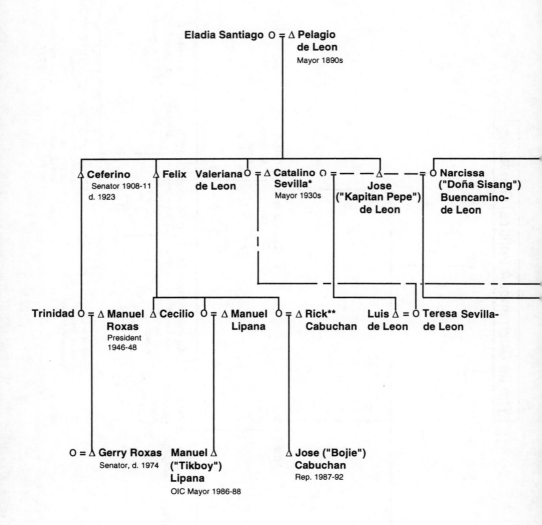

Eladia Santiago O = Δ Pelagio de Leon
Mayor 1890s

Δ **Ceferino**
Senator 1908-11
d. 1923

Δ **Felix**

Valeriana de Leon O = Δ **Catalino Sevilla***
Mayor 1930s

O = — — Δ — — = O **Narcissa ("Doña Sisang") Buencamino-de Leon**

Jose ("Kapitan Pepe") de Leon

Trinidad O = Δ **Manuel Roxas**
President 1946-48

Δ **Cecilio** O = Δ **Manuel Lipana**

O = Δ **Rick** Cabuchan**

Luis Δ = O **Teresa Sevilla-de Leon**

O = Δ **Gerry Roxas**
Senator, d. 1974

Manuel Δ ("Tikboy") Lipana
OIC Mayor 1986-88

Δ **Jose ("Bojie") Cabuchan**
Rep. 1987-92

Buencamino Family

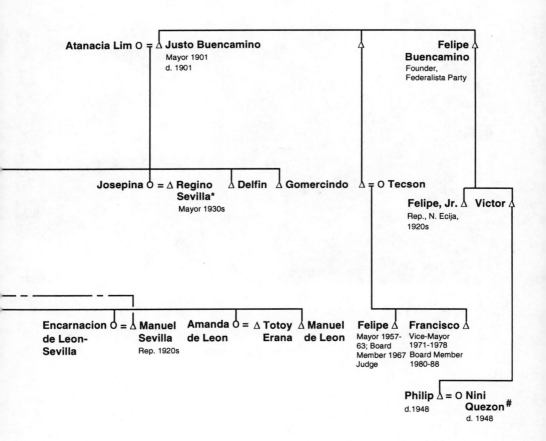

#daughter of Manuel Quezon, president, 1935-1945
*Catalino and Regino Sevilla are brothers
**Rick Cabuchan is brother of Gerry Cabuchan,
  elected Representative in 1987

At the July 1972 anniversary of the death of his father Kardeng, Berling de Guzman lets his infant son play with a Colt .45 automatic pistol in Barrio Buga, San Miguel. (*Credit:* Brian Fegan)

A 1972 reunion of the de Guzman family at Barrio Buga, San Miguel, on the anniversary of Kardeng's death brings together his kinsmen, political allies, *magaling na lalaki*, and henchmen. Seated (left to right around the table) are: unidentified; Asto Santiago, political middleman and construction contractor of Barrio Salacot; Resti Cruz, municipal secretary; Berling de Guzman, second child of Kardeng; Marcelo de Guzman Aure (in flowered shirt), mayor of San Miguel; Faustino Dy, husband of Naty de Guzman and warlord/governor of Isabela Province; Andron de Guzman (in glasses), Kardeng's brother and a former Huk commander; two unidentified men; Grasing de Guzman (wearing glasses and holding nose), Kardeng's brother and the political godfather of Cabanatuan City and southern Nueva Ecija Province; Kanor Castillo, a de Leon overseer; and unidentified. Standing behind Grasing are Henyo Lazaro (cap, dark glasses), an ex-Huk turned de Leon overseer; and (behind him to the right) Rubing de Guzman, Kardeng's son and political heir. (*Credit:* Brian Fegan)

A tense village meeting of Liberal Party leaders in Barrio Buga convened to choose a candidate for *barrio* captain in the January 1972 elections. Mayor Marcelo de Guzman Aure (right, with cigarette), unable to persuade two rival candidates to stand aside, chose Dionisio Macapagal as the party's candidate. While the meeting was in progress, the mayor's bodyguards, including the man in the far rear, provided protection with carbines and walkie-talkies.
(*Credit:* Brian Fegan)

In January 1972, at the end of what would
become the last free elections in the Philippines
for fourteen years, poll watchers scrutinize the
vote count for village officials at Barrio Buga.
Six months later, after flooding washed out
bridges and local toughs demanded a "toll" to
use a temporary crossing, bodyguards protect
their boss at a bridge in nearby Barrio Salacot.
(Credit: Brian Fegan)

During the dry season of 1973, the landlord's crew measures the harvest at the threshing machine on Hacienda Sevilla-de Leon in Barrio Buga. Used by landlords to maximize rent collection, the machine aroused the ire of peasants who resented the weeks of delay before they received their share of the harvest. The big threshing machine died with the advent of President Marcos's land reform in 1972.

the payment of high rents after three years of determining village affairs and ignoring the landlords' overseers. When the U.S. Army arrived in San Miguel in January, it was already late in the harvest period. The tenants of downstream *barrios* near the Candaba Swamp had paid little or nothing in rent. The landowners asked how they could get some rice for themselves and for the survivors of a burned-out Manila. They asked for a meeting with Huk leaders at Don Mariano Tecson's house. Kumanders Rosales and Andron agreed to persuade the farmers to relinquish more rice. They campaigned in the villages, asking those who had harvested one hundred *cavans* to pay twenty, which the Huk carted to town. Soon the prewar tenant organization was revived, though this time as a single union, the National Confederation of Peasants (PKM), led by men who had been wartime Huk commanders.

In Barrio Buga, Kardeng de Guzman returned pitifully emaciated from his incarceration at Manila's Fort Santiago dungeons and determined to make up for lost time. He regained control of his wartime men and guns, supported by his older sons, Rubing and Berling, who had become able guerrillas. In the chaos of Liberation there were convoys of U.S. trucks moving up towards the front in the mountains of Quiangan with men and supplies, others returning empty. Manila was burned and prostrate, desperate for lumber and food. Kardeng's men "found" broken-down American and Japanese trucks abandoned along the highways and repaired them for use as cargo haulers and buses. They "bought" the much-admired U.S. Army's 6 x 6 trucks from American drivers for a few bottles of rum, some fresh food, or a few minutes with a woman. With the addition of a winch, the 6 x 6 truck was able to haul heavy logs on steep and muddy mountain trails. Demand for lumber to rebuild Manila and the availability of the trucks combined to deforest the first slopes of the Sierra Madre. Kardeng's ex-USAFFE men knew the mountains and prospered as log haulers. His enemies allege that at Liberation he resumed as banditry the wartime habit of preying upon cargoes along the highway.

But Kardeng had split with his prewar ally and protector, Mayor Eugenio Tecson, whom he blamed for failing to intervene vigorously enough on his behalf with the Japanese. He allied himself with the USAFFE guerrilla leaders under the command of Colonel Alejo Santos, wartime commander of the Bulacan Military Area. Meantime, he was approached through his overseer brothers Amando and Grasing to take over administration of Doña Sisang's estates in San Miguel. Collection of rents had become difficult there in the context of the revived peasant union and wide distribution of firearms. Kardeng's personal reputation, his ability to back it with armed men, and the support of his brother, Huk commander Andron, made him a good choice.

Liberation politics provided a break with the past and opened the way for new men. The rich families had left for Manila. If they were to regain control of their estates and have any influence in electoral politics, then they must act through men who lived in the villages and could control them through personal followings backed by force. The old elite would no longer be in a position in which candidacy for the mayorship and provincial office was restricted to factional representatives of the town-dwelling landlord families. For families like the de Leons, however, national political office remained an enormously important prize. Manuel Roxas, whose wife was Doña Trinidad de Leon, first cousin of Doña Sisang's husband, broke away from the Nacionalista Party (NP) to run for president as leader of the new Liberal Party (LP). In his break with the NP, Roxas took with him a large part of the old elite and the party machine, including his in-laws the de Leons.

In July 1945, at the outset of the campaign for the April 1946 presidential elections, the wartime USAFFE and Huk guerrilla organizations temporarily buried their differences to form the Democratic Alliance Party (DA). The DA opposed Roxas on the collaboration issue and put up a joint slate for congressional seats in Central Luzon. The DA candidates in Bulacan were USAFFE colonel Alejo Santos and the Communist Party's secretary general Dr. Jesus Lava.

At war's end, Andron de Guzman had returned to farming. But the election campaign exacerbated the tensions between PKM/Huk and the landowners. During the war, the Philippine Constabulary had been employed by the Japanese as auxiliaries and had been at the forefront of the anti-Huk campaign. During the Liberation period, the Constabulary was renamed the Military Police (MP), rearmed, and reinforced with former USAFFE men. Some twenty-two thousand MPs were assigned to Central Luzon under officers loyal to Roxas. During the election period, they began a reign of terror. To bring about a Roxas victory they rounded up identifiable PKM/Huk, many of whom "disappeared." Andron's Huk were popular in the *barrios* downstream from Highway 5 where the Military Police concentrated their attentions. Meanwhile, the landowners' association began to form Civilian Guard units, concentrating their efforts in the same areas to bring in the late 1945 harvest.

In Cabanatuan City, Grasing de Guzman was in a very powerful position. He had contacts in all the forces (PKM/Huk, USAFFE, Military Police, Civilian Guards, and bandits) dating back to the war, plus his own men. Doña Sisang allowed him 5 percent of the hacienda receipts to support a Civilian Guard force. Grasing chose his own way. On each hacienda he managed he picked five or six men who were the local *matinik* ('spiky ones') and made them his men. These might be from any of the above organizations or simply *magaling na lalaki*. Grasing gave them guns, loaned them money, protected them from legal investigation, and used them as "confidential agents." The latter phrase covers a number of roles, including those of informer, provocateur, hit man, and special ally. In addition, from the Liberation period onward, Grasing controlled seven estates for Doña Sisang with full powers (see table 1).

TABLE 1 : **Buencamino-de Leon Estates Controlled by Grasing de Guzman**

Municipality	Estate Area (hectares)	Number. of Tenants	Votes (tenants x 5)	Year Grasing was Empowered
Cabanatuan	700	500	2500	1943
San Felipe	(?)	270	1350	1947
Sta. Rosa	105	52	260	1945
Jaen	110	51	250	1945
Guimba*	510	**300	1500	1952
Aliaga	575	**300	1500	1945–46
Talavera	** 200	**400	2000	1947
Total	** 2200	1873	9360	

*Under the control of Amando de Guzman until 1952
**Estimate

The nine-thousand-odd votes he could potentially mobilize for candidates competing for the second congressional seat of Nueva Ecija, the provincial governorship, and mayoralties in several municipalities made Grasing politically powerful. In return for his support, should any of his men be subjected to legal interference, Grasing could approach the mayor, the chief of police, the provincial commander of the Military Police, or the governor and say *Bata ko yaon, pawalan mo siya e* ("He is my lad, let him go"). Between 1957 and 1962, Grasing came to control gambling in Cabanatuan City, from the proceeds of which he regularly paid off the chief of police and the provincial commander, as well as the mayor and governor. In his own account, the *jueteng* (numbers game), *monte,* and other gambling rackets, which he ran as manager for a principal in Quezon City, gave him a cash flow sufficient to make such payoffs and to employ some of his toughs.

Towards the end of the 1946 election campaign, Doña Sisang asked Grasing to arrange a conference in Manila with wartime Huk commanders Juan Feleo, of Sta. Rosa, and "Dimasalang," of Aliaga—towns in which she had haciendas. These men were the top PKM union leaders of the province; indeed, Feleo was the national head of the PKM. But the meeting turned out to concern matters other than agrarian conditions on the estates. Meeting Doña Sisang in Manila, they were taken to see Manuel Roxas. Feleo and Dimasalang agreed to let the villagers vote for Roxas for president without pressure or intimidation if Roxas would relieve Civilian Guard and MP pressure on the populace to vote for Liberal candidates for Congress. In the event, southern Nueva Ecija returned substantial majorities for both the leftist DA's congressional candidates and the arch-conservative Roxas's presidential ticket. Through this deal, Feleo, Dimasalang, and the PKM leaders under them breached the DA's anti-Roxas policy, even though Feleo was a Politburo member of the Communist Party of the Philippines.

In San Miguel, the radical peasants were feeling confident after the DA swept the Central Luzon congressional seats. President Roxas appointed Eugenio Tecson as mayor, replacing a USAFFE guerrilla installed on the advice of Colonel Santos, now a DA congressman. Just after the April elections, PKM leaders met at the municipal cockpit to plan a 30 April start to a march to join a 1 May parade in Manila. Militia under "Banding," one of Mayor Tecson's Civilian Guard officers, picked up PKM leader Jose Ligon who was not seen alive again. About three weeks later, another PKM leader, Delfin Manuzon, suffered the same fate. The repercussions put Andron and Kardeng de Guzman under threat.

In late May, Andron visited a masseur in Salacot where he encountered Ligon's sons waiting in ambush for Banding. Andron persuaded the Ligons to remove the ambush but they blocked Banding's jeep a mile away, at Sacdalan. There was a gun battle. Andron ran out and captured Banding, who had run out of ammunition, and handed him over to the Ligons who were bent on revenge. Andron became a "wanted" man. He sent his wife and children away and went back underground to the Huk.

Kardeng de Guzman was then chief overseer in San Miguel for Doña Sisang. In June 1946, he took a party of tenants to the town hall to certify their applications for a crop loan. As he walked away from the meeting and passed the house of Mayor Tecson, Civilian Guard friends of Banding opened fire with a submachine gun, riddling Kardeng's thighs with bullets. Taking him to the nearby warehouse of the National Administration for Rice and Corn (NARIC), Civilian Guards prevented Kardeng from receiving medical treatment and stood about to watch him bleed to death.

Meanwhile, several of Kardeng's men ran to the *barrios* to spread the word. Andron assembled three or four hundred Huk of squadrons 24, 105, and 25, then in standing camps. They gathered just north of the township and commandeered trucks, loading some with petrol drums. Kardeng's former USAFFE unit assembled flatcars to pole down the railway line. Messages were sent north to Grasing and Amando. The combined Huk and USAFFE units sent messages informing the townspeople that if Kardeng died they would burn the town and wipe out the Civilian Guard units and municipal officials. Grasing drove posthaste to Manila down the Pampangan side of the plain to tell Doña Sisang that Civilian Guards had attacked his brother, her overseer. Doña Sisang rang President Roxas while Grasing collected a friend, MP Major Kakait, from a nightclub. With a military ambulance and escort they drove to San Miguel, faced down the Civilian Guards, and took Kardeng to a hospital.

Once Kardeng was given treatment, the Huk and USAFFE units dispersed. But Andron's status as a fugitive had increased. Kardeng's wounding did not destroy his reputation for invulnerability, for it soon became the stuff of legend that while he was held by the Japanese he had given the pants of his "coat of mail" talisman to a fellow prisoner. Thus the Civilian Guards had been unable to hit him above the thighs. He recovered but from then on had a limp, earning the name

Kardeng Pilay ("Kardeng the Limp"). Despite her intervention on his behalf, Kardeng did not resume his duties for Doña Sisang.

Peasant War in Central Luzon

Meantime, the Huk Rebellion broke out in full force in July 1946. Mayor Tecson, installed by Roxas, tried to temper the Civilian Guard units by choosing their leaders from the ranks of men who were both personally loyal to him and clearly identified with the locality. Among them, when he recovered, was Kardeng, who found himself with even more arms than previously. Andron's Huk adopted a double policy towards the Civilian Guard. Many were local peasants sympathetic to the PKM/Huk, whom they approached with the news that they had been offered Civilian Guard arms. Should they join? Andron's Huk said "Join, but do not abuse the people and hang back in action. We will not attack your village unit." The countryside soon became a checkerboard of *barrios* controlled by the Huk, by Civilian Guard units loyal to their landowner paymasters, by Civilian Guard units loyal to their own villages, and by bandit groups. Through this maze, the Military Police and army units conducted campaigns against the Huk, presenting the villagers with a bewildering array of forces.

But across the lines of class and ideological warfare friendships persisted between *magaling na lalaki*. Andron had several friends in the Military Police, the Civilian Guard, and even in the army. These contacts were used to convene frequent local truce conferences and meetings between the opposed armed forces in the rebellion, at which personal acquaintance, mutual admiration, and family links could be invoked as the basis of trust. In late 1946, the Huk in San Miguel posted notices and scattered leaflets to the Military Police. The sense of the message read:

> You are only the dogs of the proprietors. A man with a gun keeps a dog but when the dog catches a deer or pig it is not fed to the dog. He is given only the bones. Take notice of your true situation. Your father is a farmer and poor. Which of you PC is the son of a millionaire?

In the early months of this war, Captain Kakait, who was by then MP commander for San Miguel, sent word that he would like to meet Andron personally. Accompanied by Commander Rosales, Andron met him by arrangement at Salacot where they discussed the reasons why the Huk continued to fight. Kakait and Andron came to have *galang* respect for each other. The captain disciplined his troops to prevent abuses but could not restrain the Civilian Guard. He was rumored to have told *barrio* people: "Don't point out to us where the Huk are. If Andron and the Huk are downstream, we'll raid upstream if we have to raid somewhere to follow orders." Andron met Kakait at other times at the NARIC warehouse. In early 1947, however, Kakait was shot and killed by his own sergeant when he tried to prevent the abuse of some women during an MP drinking spree.

Major Chavez, provincial commander of the Military Police at Malolos, had been a prewar friend of Andron and at Liberation had presented him with a horse, a .45 automatic pistol, and a gun license. After Andron became "wanted," Chavez sent a message that he desired a personal meeting, to which both should come unarmed. Andron had his men check the meeting place for an ambush and sent sharpshooters into the fields and approach positions where they could stop any raid. Then he jumped off a passing truck at the meeting place, further enhancing his reputation for mysterious appearances and disappearances. Chavez flattered Andron, describing him as the *tala*, the *may manda*, the *lintik*, and the *matinik* (the bright star, the one in command, the lightning, the clever one) in that area. As an MP commander, Chavez had a problem with bandits who were plaguing the highway between San Miguel and Gapan. Could Andron help? Andron promised that, if Chavez would remove the MP checkpoints on the highway, he would deliver the robbers within a week, be they Huk, Civilian Guard, MP, or just *tulisan*. Within three days Andron delivered the three robbers to Chavez in Malolos, in a truck under the guard of Kumander Fandango, a Huk. They turned out to be soldiers of the Military Police.

In April 1947, at the fiesta of Andron's home *barrio* of Salacot, the Civilian Guard detachments of San Miguel and Gapan to the north had arranged a softball match attended by some four to five hundred men, most under arms. The MP under Major Chavez were conducting a large operation with another four to five hundred men in the Sierra Madre, hunting Andron and the Huk. Andron, dressed in his "trademark" white sombrero, shirt, and pants, and wearing a gun on each hip, slipped through the crowd at the match. He wore over his whites a colored overshirt and coolie hat. He liked softball and remembered the days before the war when he had been famous locally as a pitcher. His comrades warned that to be there was suicide.

Andron quietly approached the grandstand where Chavez, the San Miguel chief of police, and commanders of the two Civilian Guard companies sat in the seats of honor with the fiesta president. Andron dropped his overclothes and sat on the chief of police's right, "so that he couldn't draw." He greeted the commanders, whose mission it was to kill him, and proposed a truce until sundown. The fiesta president greeted him loudly, and the crowd took up the cry, closing in and calling his name. The officers "guaranteed" Andron's safety until sundown and the fiesta president called on him to referee the match.

Andron refereed the match amid hundreds of enemy soldiers. The game was tied and went into extra innings. Andron's comrades were terrified. Sundown was approaching. Major Chavez had radioed the extra four hundred or so troops to abandon the fruitless hunt in the mountains and to place a cordon round the fiesta. They warned him to leave lest he be *madukot* (picked up), as he had no more than thirty men with concealed arms in the crowd. Close to sundown, the San Miguel Civilian Guard team won the game and the crowd ran onto the field. Andron's trademark white clothing made him easy to spot but with the crowd about him it was impossible to shoot. Popular legend has it that Andron once again disappeared before the eyes of some nine hundred armed enemies. His account is more prosaic: he switched hats, then shirts, while others switched items of clothing to provide several decoys all in white. Andron slipped away, while the Civilian Guard and the MP were confused "like termites when their nest is kicked over and all search for the queen." He came across a lad taking his buffalo to water, commandeered the beast, and rode it to the creek in a sleepy, age-old, sundown scene, passing through the soldiers easily. Several hours later, after the troops had abandoned the search and retired to their own bases for the night, Andron returned to Salacot quietly, appearing in the midst of the crowd watching a *zarzuela* (popular opera). The incident added to his legend while making good propaganda for the Huk at the expense of their clumsy enemies.

In November 1947, elections were held for municipal, provincial, and Senate seats. The mayors installed by Roxas were in a strong position, having control of the Civilian Guard units, to deliver the vote. Military Police forces were partial to Liberal Party candidates; their support ranged from assistance, to guarding polling places in Huk areas, to terror.

In San Miguel, Kardeng de Guzman was influential as an ex-USAFFE guerrilla widely admired as a *magaling na lalaki*, prosperous from his logging deals, and strongly supported by Andron's Huk. He was well connected with Congressman Colonel Alejo Santos, then provincial leader of the Nacionalista Party and the most powerful man in the province. The LP had become the party of the proprietors, with both the Tecson and de Leon factions united under President Roxas's patronage. From 1946 to the 1960s, by contrast, the NP was the party of the *taga-bukid*, the villagers, and was becoming a well-organized machine dominated by the more prosperous peasants, overseers, and *magaling na lalaki*.

Kardeng ran for municipal councilor, gained the highest vote in the villages, was in the top three in the township, and was topnotcher for the municipality as a whole. This combination placed him in a powerful position: in the new politics, a topnotcher councilor would be scrutinized as a potential mayoral candidate, particularly if the incumbent was a mayor of the opposing party. Kardeng found himself first councilor to his prewar ally, Mayor Eugenio Tecson, whose Civilian Guard allies had augmented his vote. But they were of opposing parties, and Andron was a thorn in the side of the military. In late 1947, expelled congressman Dr. Jesus Lava, secretary general of the Communist Party and the most "wanted" fugitive in the land, was brought by Andron's men to Kardeng's house in Buga, suffering from tuberculosis. Kardeng's men guarded the house while Lava recuperated and "honeymooned" with his wife for two weeks.

By early 1948, however, Kardeng's situation had become impossible. As the hunt intensified for his brother, Kumander Andron the Huk, the Civilian Guards of San Miguel were once again bent on killing Kardeng. As ex-USAFFE guerrillas, his sons Rubing and Berling had recently joined the Civilian Guards. But Major Kotong, who had replaced Captain Kakait in command of the Military Police, claimed that they were "not capable of shooting their uncle Andron" and accused them of being spies. Kardeng, Rubing, and Berling went on the run with some of their men, hunted by the San Miguel Civilian Guards. They took refuge with Mayor Dioscoro de Leon, *kumpare* of Grasing de Guzman, who was the commander of the Civilian Guards in the next town, Gapan.

In Cabanatuan City, Grasing had his own troubles in the 1947 election. The mayor, Totoy Ocampo, and Civilian Guard chief Rafael Valisno were disturbed at Grasing's growing power and the number of toughs allied to him. His estimate of their motive was that they decided: *Barilin natin yaon at darating ang araw na siyang hari dito!* ("Let's kill that one, lest the day come when he is the king hereabouts!"). Valisno opened fire on Grasing's house one night with a .30 caliber machine gun mounted on a jeep. One of Grasing's cart drivers was killed and his own gunmen returned fire. Next day, he took his family to San Miguel but returned after three days with eleven men under Dioscoro de Leon and an ally, Velayo of Gapan, in an armored command car and two jeeps with mounted machine guns. They called for Mayor Ocampo and Valisno at the town hall, ordering them to throw out their weapons and come out one by one, or be burned out. De Leon demanded that Ocampo and Valisno apologize and "guarantee" that they would not again attack Grasing. Satisfied, he delivered a last warning: "My Kumpare Grasing wants to forgive you your debts. OK. But if you move, *never* go through Gapan!"

In April 1948, President Roxas died suddenly at the U.S. air base in Clark Field, Pampanga. His vice-president, Elpidio Quirino, resumed negotiations with the Huk under a truce that extended from late June to the end of August. By the time the "amnesty" period ended on 1 September, negotiations had broken down. Meantime, the army had been reorganized, expanded, and beefed up with U.S. arms and advisors. All over Central Luzon the end of the truce marked the beginning of a struggle more violent than anything experienced in three years under the Japanese and two under Roxas.

In San Miguel, Kardeng de Guzman and his sons were away logging in the mountains, bringing their logs down to Gapan where Dioscoro de Leon sheltered them. The Huk command had sent Andron south to Laguna Province on an expansion mission. He received orders to return urgently, as the new war was the worst yet and his men lacked active leaders. Andron walked home through the Sierra Madre forests, descending into a deserted countryside. In September 1948 the combined forces of the army, Military Police, and Civil Guard, acting under martial law, had forcibly evacuated the inhabitants of the *barrios* to the town. There the peasants lived in the streets, rejected by the townspeople and denied food, water, and shelter. The army's policy was to cut off the Huk from food, recruits, and information. Anyone found outside the township without military escort could be shot on sight. Meanwhile, armed forces pillaged the peasants' houses and slaughtered their forcibly abandoned livestock. In the town, men were killed out of hand as suspected Huk, and their corpses dumped in the river, simply because they had a Japanese watch or had defended a woman from rape. Babies and young children died from epidemics in the unsanitary conditions. Old people say that so many bodies floated in the rivers that people who had drawn water there all their lives dug wells or carried water from rare and distant tubewells.

Andron sought out his Huk associates, basing himself first in abandoned Buga with some twenty-five men. Gradually he sent them home—there was no food and some were sick. He slept on a bench hidden in the middle of the standing rice. The forced evacuation was very effective. Determined to see how matters stood, he crawled in the mud behind a dike to question some harvesters sent out under guard to reap. "Life in town is tight indeed," he was told. "The PC are killing people without reason and stealing. If a man protests, he is 'suspect' and floats in the river a few days later." Andron slipped into town to see for himself, question contacts, and get food. Conditions were very bad and the people were suffering. Meanwhile, in his estimation the Huk were not strong enough on a national scale to earn any kind of victory from this hardship. The expanded and resupplied army was too big to fight. Its new weapons—jeeps, artillery, tanks, and airplanes, all used ruthlessly with forcible concentration—were unanswerable. He sent the father of his bodyguard to Don Sindoy Buencamino, brother of Doña Sisang, to say that he was ready to *mamahinga*, rest from the struggle. Could Don Sindoy help?

Sindoy went to General Castañeda, commander in chief of the Military Police, to ask that national soldiers pick up Andron, as Civilian Guards might kill him on surrender. A convoy of jeeps—the first with MPs, the other carrying Major Alec Pala, Major Milosantos, and Andron's brothers Kardeng and Grasing—went to Salacot. Andron had been warned by Kardeng's son Raul that they were coming, and lay in the rice by the road, jumping up as the convoy came abreast, so it would not know from whence he had come. He was allowed to change clothes, to keep his guns, and was taken to town where MPs and Civilian Guards were sent away. Members of the town elite shook hands with him. That night there were fireworks and celebrations in San Miguel and the provincial capital, Malolos, as Andron's surrender would signal peace for all of Bulacan. He was taken to Manila where Grasing fed and entertained the escort generously overnight. Andron spent the evening talking with his brothers at Grasing's Manila house. Next day, he was taken to Camp Crame, the MP headquarters, for interrogation. His account of the questioning is not that of a defiant rebel or a social bandit forced to the wall. At least in retrospect, his answers seem modeled on the Christ of the Tagalog *Pasyon* verse epic:

MP: Why did you surrender?

Andron: When I came from another town I saw my town mates and barrio mates had been forced to suffer because of me. It is better that one man be punished than that thousands suffer. If I will be shot or jailed for life, I accept that rather than that the many suffer.

In Andron's account he was not tortured or pressured to give information about his Huk superiors, disposition of forces, or other intelligence. Later he was taken to President Quirino, who asked similar questions, including why Doña Sisang had made representations on his behalf. Andron answered that he did not know. Today, he offers the shrewd guess that it was because she found his brothers useful and his surrender an opportunity to demoralize Huk remnants in San Miguel. After further interrogations, he was held for less than a month, then released under a "guarantee" from Doña Sisang. There were two conditions only. Andron must not return to San Miguel and he must not rejoin the Huk.

Postwar Politics

Within a month of his surrender, Andron was back under arms, this time as a guard at Doña Sisang's LVN Pictures. All five of the de Guzman brothers had come to serve this influential woman. The Huk movement continued, winding down as the people became demoralized. In San Miguel, Andron's replacement was Silvestre Tecson, "Kumander Ester," who surrendered around 1958–59 when Secretary General Lava decided that all Huk should return to peaceful life. Andron got him a job with LVN.

Andron's surrender in 1948, and the guarantees arranged by Doña Sisang, reduced the dangerous attention paid to Kardeng and his sons by the Civilian Guard and Military Police. They returned to their home village where the sons farmed and continued with their logging. Backed by his formidable older sons, who were by then notorious in their own right, Kardeng resumed political control of the village and its surrounding area. His USAFFE connections enabled him to compile back-pay lists for guerrillas and their widows. Votes from his own area, from the remnants of Andron's Huk following in the swamp-fringe area, and support from admirers and allies made him a powerful broker in politics. Enemies of the family allege that they and their ex-guerrilla supporters continued to dabble in truck hijacking, buffalo rustling, and illegal gambling. But criminal charges laid against Kardeng and his first and second sons repeatedly failed for lack of evidence. On one occasion the second son, Berling, had charges of triple homicide dismissed against him in Manila when a paper was produced from General Castañeda, head of the MP, stating that Berling was a special agent of the National Bureau of Investigation and the dead men wanted criminals. The reputations of the village branch of the family in the 1950s correspond to those of *mafiosi*, in the Sicilian sense of men of honor who use private violence to settle matters without reference to the law.

After Ramon Magsaysay's successful 1953 presidential campaign, rural politics changed in style and personnel. Backed by U.S. funds and psychological warfare advisers sent to help in the anti-Huk war, Magsaysay built an electoral machine for the Nacionalista Party based on village-level brokers who exchanged pork-barrel benefits and interventions for votes. Within a few years, the flood of central-government money washed away those *magaling na lalaki* who failed to adapt. Kardeng was one who managed to add the new methods to the old, remaining an important political figure until his death in 1969.

In Cabanatuan, Grasing continued to manage Doña Sisang's estates, and, through his astute political dealings, to influence mayoral elections in the five estate municipalities and Cabanatuan City, as well as the governorship and the congressional seat. He was at times wanted for homicide but managed to have all charges dismissed, once through an intervention by General Castañeda on lines similar to the ploy that had saved his nephew. An assassination attempt failed, in the early 1950s, because Grasing was lying low at the home of a prominent politician. Even when underground, evading personal enemies or the law, he continued to hold Doña Sisang's power of attorney, acting for her in all matters affecting the estates, and was able to keep his apparatus of toughs, overseers, and agents running.

After his criminal notoriety of the 1950s faded, Grasing's career and reputation matured into those of a political king maker, businessman, and philanthropist. His influence in regional politics and with national government officials made him an effective go-between and peacemaker in provincial rivalries. His intervention on behalf of an accused man could get charges dropped by the police and the PC, or cause witnesses to forget their evidence. On behalf of Doña Sisang and her heirs, he manipulated tenants on the estates in such a way that the land reforms of presidents Magsaysay in 1954 and Macapagal in 1963 had little effect on estate income. In a very direct way, his behind-the-scenes maneuvers enabled these vast estates, which ought to have been a prime target, to escape redistribution. The connections of Doña Sisang and her family worked in the same way at the national level, protecting both the estate and Kardeng.

As Cabanatuan City expanded, the seven-hundred-hectare estate on its outskirts became valuable urban land. Grasing manipulated its tenants into surrendering their cultivation rights, allowing the Buencamino-de Leon estate to convert rice land into the Kapitan Pepe Memorial Park cemetery and urban subdivision, both of which he managed. Growing rich from this managerial and political base, Grasing invested in land in Nueva Ecija and Bulacan provinces, in piggeries, a tractor pool, a short-time motel, and urban real estate. He became a patron of fiestas, sporting competitions, and athletic teams, and a "friend of the poor" on whose largesse and interventions a constant stream of supplicants waited.

Grasing presents himself in his mellow years as a man of the people, a poor man who rose by guts and energy to become a self-made millionaire and an example for others. He regards himself as a man on the side of the common people against their oppressors. He keeps in his pocket a list from the *Readers Digest* of the twenty greatest men in the world, each of whom rose from the lowest order of his society to its peaks of wealth and power. He affects white suits, keeps a white Mercedes and a white Ford, both, like his office, upholstered in white. Despite his conversion to a man of peace in his late sixties, he retains the ethics of a bravo, epitomized in his presentation of the *magaling na lalaki* facing his Maker as a kind of cowboy showdown: *Alisin mo ang yabang, tatapat ka sa magaling sa iyo!* ("Give up your boastfulness for you will face one who is more *magaling* than you!").

After President Marcos imposed martial law in 1972, Grasing's talents and the political influence of the Buencamino-de Leons were insufficient to protect the estates outside Cabanatuan City from land reform. Marcos owed no political debts to the de Leons, whose political flag bearer was Senator Gerry de Leon-Roxas, son of the late President Roxas and of Doña Sisang's cousin, Doña Trinidad de Leon. Since Gerry Roxas was president of the rival Liberal Party, Marcos simply jailed him.

From 1972 to 1979, Marcos was bent on a strong centralizing program, in which he closed the Congress and severely reduced the powers of mayors and governors. Without electoral politics, or connections to the Palace, Grasing's major assets were lost. The 1972 land reform dictated the transfer of land to the tenants of large estates. Tenants were to buy their farms in fixed annual amortization over fifteen years. Although Grasing was able to delay the shift from share tenancy to land transfer, and to force up the transfer price per hectare, he could not prevent the bureaucracy from carrying out the will of the newly strengthened central state.

The de Guzmans as Local Politicians

In the smaller world of Barrio Buga, Kardeng de Guzman's decline and demise in the late 1960s coincided with the emergence of his sons as a new generation of village political leaders. During the two decades between Liberation and his death in 1969, Kardeng resided in San Miguel and resumed his role as a political broker, combining his negotiating skills and reputation for violence to become an influential local leader in the new populist politics that developed after 1953. In rebuilding his political influence, and thereby maintaining his family's mystique, Kardeng prepared the ground for the next generation to succeed him as the leaders of Barrio Buga.

Informants remark that the watershed in San Miguel's municipal politics was Ramon Magsaysay's campaign for president in 1953. Until then, town politics had been dominated by the de Leon-Tecson struggle within the elite, though both factions had supported Roxas's Liberal Party in postwar years. However, the Tecsons were in disarray after the death of their senior generation who had spent the family fortune in repeated contests for municipal office and failed to recoup their expenses while in office. These earlier municipal governments had few resources, aside from *areglo*, to profit an incumbent mayor. Meantime, the top elite had left town and the Sevilla brothers, who had run for office under the de Leon banner, were weakened likewise. They had not been able to link themselves with the *barako*, who competed with them for management of the estates of their de Leon in-laws. The old multifunctional town elite of landed wealth, education, professions, and politics had fled to Manila leaving behind remnants that were badly demoralized.

During his campaign for the presidency in 1953, Magsaysay had the backing of a number of moderate intellectuals. More importantly, he had enormous financial, logistical, and propaganda backing from the U.S. government. He used this support to build a personal machine capable of carrying his campaign to every *barrio*, and backed his rhetoric with use of the reformed, disciplined, armed forces to carry out local pork-barrel projects in the form of roads, bridges, schools, and water pumps. This flood of resources directed downward from the central government was a new phenomenon. Power over allocation of contracts for public works, licenses, and jobs became an important resource for ambitious men in the countryside. After he became president, Magsaysay's national machine used these resources to attract a new kind of local vote broker and build them into a permanent machine for the Nacionalista Party.

The Nacionalistas changed local politics from a system in which candidates were selected by family factions of the town elite to one in which a party convention selected and financed the candidates. They set up a party committee in every *barrio*, with a broader-based leadership than the old *barako*, although many *barako* made a successful transition to the new politics. Representatives from the *barrios* met as a board of directors and chose candidates whose campaign expenses were supplemented by funds from the national party. Once in office, there was new wealth to be made from the allocation of the "roads and bridges" construction and other central-government supplements of the municipal land taxes. In Magsaysay's time, the NP municipal machine was virtually a party of small farmers, many of them attracted by his promises of land reform and government cleanup.

The new politics of the party machine helped Felipe Buencamino of the Nacionalista Party to win office as mayor, in 1956, with almost a clean sweep of San Miguel's municipal council positions. Buencamino was of a middle-class branch of the family, one not connected closely with the de Leons. He had a wife who was actually a Tecson. Meanwhile, the mass voter-registration campaign launched after the dirty 1949 national elections, and a change in the way polling was conducted, made the ballot secret. This reform weakened the hold of the hard men. The *barako* would not disappear for another couple of decades but with few exceptions they lost their capacity to deliver zero opposition votes from their bailiwicks, where machine brokers now organized votes. Several old *barako* found new political careers as local bosses, combining the old *barako* methods with the new politics of pork-barrel, influence peddling, and vote trading. In the course of so doing, they abandoned the loyalty of the *barako* to a single leader. Some became adept at shifting sides to deliver the bloc of votes they controlled to the highest bidder.

The town councils were no longer places where well-educated, landed proprietors and professionals presided over the spending of a small budget raised from taxes on their own land. From the mid-1950s onward, the councilors were often men of limited education who pursued politics as a livelihood. They presided over the spending of relatively large sums of money allocated by national-level politicians with pork-barrel objectives. This change opened the way for better-educated mayors to put council resolutions in legal language, the implications of which were neither understood nor debated by the council, reducing it at times to a rubber-stamp body. While prewar mayors sometimes lost their fortunes in politics, from the 1950s onward it was possible for mayors to leave office richer than when they had entered it because of the flow of wealth passing through their hands unchecked by the compliant town councils.

The resurgence of the Nacionalista Party and its new machine structure had two curious effects. First, it forced the remnants of the old Tecson and de Leon factions into an uneasy alliance. The de Leons had a special interest in keeping a Liberal Party machine going because of the unique position of Trinidad de Leon-Roxas in the LP national office. Her son Gerry became a senator and in the early 1970s the leader of the Liberal Party. Having scattered their wealth among numerous heirs, and much reduced in fortune, the Tecsons engaged in some desperate spending during the mid-1950s in an attempt to recover office for the family. The failure of this unlikely alliance to win office for the Liberal Party opened the way for new men to carry the LP banner and then to reform the party along machine lines.

Felipe Buencamino served two terms as mayor but stepped aside to run successfully for the Bulacan provincial board in 1963. His successor as the NP candidate, Bernardo Sempio, a de Leon through his mother, was unable to match the massive spending of the new-rich logger Felix Tayag who was helped to victory in the mayoral race by his party mate President Macapagal. On the other hand, Tayag could not carry Dr. Pedro Tecson with him as vice-mayor. That position and a majority of council seats went to the NP candidates—reflecting the continued superiority of the NP machine whenever extraordinary personal spending was not a factor.

By 1967, however, a new man, former assistant *fiscal* Marcelo de Guzman-Aure, took over from Mayor Tayag who had stepped aside to run for the provincial board. Aure pushed aside the old town elite, who had controlled the LP, and created a village-based party machine, recruiting the same kind of village faction leaders, vote brokers, and *barako* as those who dominated the NP apparatus, which Buencamino continued to control. Aure was assisted in this effort by the old *barako* Kardeng de Guzman and his maternal de Guzman kin in the villages. In the 1967 and 1971 elections for mayor of San Miguel, Aure's wins under the LP banner took place against the backdrop of an NP president, NP congressman, and NP governor. Fortunately for Aure, his campaign on both occasions was assisted by a local split in the NP between two rival candidates for mayor. His wins reflect the skills of a professional politician adept at creating and enthusing a political machine despite a restricted flow of pork-barrel funds. This scarcity of national patronage forced Aure to exploit every municipal resource open to a mayor in order to reward his supporters. Moreover, he managed to use links with LP senators and the national machine to attract sufficient funds to make his municipal machine function effectively, quietly assisted by NP congressman Rogaciano Mercado.

Mayor Aure's administration facilitated the emergence of a third generation of his de Guzman kin as the new political leaders in Barrio Buga. Not only did Aure's style of machine politics advance the interests of village-level brokers throughout the municipality, but his blood ties and political debts to the aging Kardeng, still influential in his locality, made the mayor sympathetic to the needs of the old man's sons, now making their political debut.

In 1965, two years before Aure's election, Kardeng had launched a successful campaign by his eldest son Rubing for the office of *barrio* captain, recently established as an elective position. In the November 1967 elections, Aure ran with Kardeng's support and the old man's third son Raul as one of his candidates for San Miguel's municipal council. While Aure scored an impressive margin of 4,587 votes to 3,901 against his Nacionalista rival, Raul gained a lesser 3,776 votes to capture seventh place among the eight successful council candidates.

In the 1971 elections, Raul slipped to sixteenth place, with only 2,705 votes, losing his seat on the council. But his ally Aure was reelected mayor with a comfortable margin and, still indebted to the de Guzmans, appointed Raul as his municipal secretary—an office that allowed the family some significant extralegal rewards. By the time Kardeng died in 1969, his family was at the peak of its political powers, with his relations serving simultaneously as town mayor, town councilor, and as Buga's *barrio* captain.

Martial Law and its Aftermath

On the eve of martial law in 1972, the old landed elite was absent from the town, though its foremost members still owned lands there and had some influence through electoral donations to town politicians. The absent elite no longer provided the local political or professional elite. New men, of families without *principalia*, *ilustrado*, or *hacienda* lineage but with professional training in medicine, the law, and accountancy contested the mayorship. Their electoral success rested not on membership in old, landed, family factions but on the support of village-based party machines that were branches of the national parties. The political party, not the elite family, had become the major source of funds, supplemented by donations from a few prominent well-wishers and the energetic support of party-faction leaders in the village, the more powerful of whom were now professional political brokers.

At the municipal level, the mayoral and many council candidates were themselves full-time or part-time political entrepreneurs who derived a large part of their incomes from political fixing. The mayorship was now a valuable prize. Its salary and the perquisites of office—allocation of the roads and bridges fund, the *areglo* of crimes, *tong* from illegal logging, a cut from the *jueteng* numbers game, and the allocation of market licenses—could provide great returns to an incumbent. Moreover, the mayorship could be the stepping stone to greater power within both the party machine and electoral politics. To cite the best-known example, San

Miguel mayors Buencamino and Tayag had moved up to the provincial board. High political connections served to protect the incumbent from scrutiny about his use of the spoils of office, providing him with privileged information about government plans that afforded him lucrative investments. Under Marcos's martial-law regime, however, much of this system changed, forcing the third generation of de Guzman politicians to adapt again.

After Marcos declared martial law in 1972, the influence of all the de Guzman politicians was seriously weakened locally, just as the Buencamino-de Leon family's was weakened nationally, by a strong president ruling through decree. The essence of the change was that personal networks among powerful figures with independent political resources in a relatively autonomous province were no longer decisive. The central state had disarmed and disrupted the private forces of such figures; closed down the national legislature and suspended the elections that allowed both symbolic and real contests to demonstrate autonomous power; purged local government offices, leaving only supporters of the president; centralized finances and pork barrel to prevent the creation of new machines; and jailed many of the old politicians. Marcos installed new central-government officials in the towns—some representing pork-barrel ministries operated to attach support to the president and his wife, others looking over the shoulders of the purged governors and mayors.

Moreover, Marcos reduced the significance of private force by means of an arms roundup in 1972, a later transfer of municipal police command from local mayors to the central Philippine Constabulary, and the rapid reassignment of any PC officers who established cozy arrangements with local politicians and/or *mafiosi*. In late 1972, there were widespread arrests and assassinations of *magaling na lalaki* who were staff or allies of provincial politicians or connected with the Huk remnants or the New People's Army (NPA), the armed wing of the Maoist Communist Party (CPP), founded in 1968.

Under martial law, the de Guzman family, like other local strong men, suffered a protracted eclipse. As a centralized authoritarian state, the Marcos regime tried to rule through its military and reduce its reliance upon local mediators like the de Guzmans. In the periodic purges that followed martial law, Mayor Aure and his municipal secretary Raul de Guzman eventually lost office. In what turned out to be a major political misstep, Rubing had resigned his post as *barrio* captain of Buga before the 1972 elections to seek work with his uncle Grasing in neighboring Nueva Ecija Province. Since Marcos decided to leave incumbents in *barrio* offices until the 1980 local elections, Rubing's political retirement effectively denied his family access to local power for nearly a decade.

But beneath the newly strengthened state apparatus, the old centrifugal political forces survived and eventually reemerged. Over the long term, Marcos had little success in his attempt to create a national ideology through state propaganda, the education system, and a single national party. The regime turned into a monarchy or "conjugal dictatorship" presided over by technocrats but lampooned as a "marital law" characterized by "crony capitalism" and centralized corruption.

As the dictator's health declined, external pressures mounted from the United States, the International Monetary Fund, and business leaders to install a system of succession that would prevent Imelda Marcos from coming to power, create stable business conditions, and gain a new aura of legitimacy in foreign and local eyes.

Once Marcos began the program of "normalization" by restoring elections in 1978, he was forced to progressively dismantle the centralized apparatus because it was incompatible with the kind of local strong men and strong-arm methods necessary to get out the vote in remote areas. After 1979, Marcos returned a measure of autonomous power to the mayors, governors, and the new national assemblymen, although it was plain to all that the conditions under which elections were held made it virtually impossible for any but a candidate of the ruling party, the Kilusang Bagong Lipunan (KBL), to win.

As the Marcos regime began to weaken from within and its reach into the countryside attenuated, the de Guzmans, like other local influentials across Central Luzon, began to reclaim both their formal and informal authority. In the 1980 local elections that accompanied Marcos's establishment of a cosmetic New Republic, Raul de Guzman ran unsuccessfully for municipal vice-mayor on the opposition ticket—scoring a respectable 5,845 votes against 16,490 for the candidate of the KBL. Two years later, in the 1982 village elections, Rubing ran as a non-KBL candidate and regained his post as Buga's *barrio* captain, restoring the family to a position of power in its bailiwick. After the election he switched to the KBL in order to be able to secure pork-barrel benefits for his village. He was received as a prodigal and showered with public-works projects.

By the mid-1980s, the decentralization process had gone far enough to seriously weaken the central state, allowing the *magaling na lalaki* and local power holders to revive. After February 1986, the new regime of President Corazon Aquino faced not only rebellions by Muslim and communist guerrillas, a politicized officer corps, a demoralized central bureaucracy, and a bankrupt treasury but also a revival of autonomous armed forces controlled by local power holders in the provinces, towns, and villages.

Among those who seized this opportunity was the recently reelected Rubing de Guzman. During Marcos's last years, he used his skill, reputation, and contacts to deliver a disproportionate share of the regime's quota of patronage for the entire municipality of San Miguel to his home village of Buga. During the dictator's last year, he played the role of an enthusiastic loyalist and his clientele prospered accordingly. After Marcos's fall, he led his family through a successful transition from the dictatorship to a restored democracy under Corazon Aquino—a time of change that challenged the abilities of politicians at all levels. In particular, the 1986 presidential elections required a delicate balancing act for the local KBL machine and supporters like Rubing de Guzman.

The 1986 Elections in Barrio Buga

In Barrio Buga, Captain Rubing de Guzman campaigned for Marcos by mobilizing his political faction—a group based on the de Guzman-Macapagal families of the old Liberal Party, supplemented by some former Nacionalista families that had switched sides. Among these new allies was Jose Lazaro, Buga's NP/KBL *barrio* captain from 1972 to 1982. Lazaro had gone over to the de Guzmans as part of a 1980 reconciliation after twenty-six years of estrangement from his *kumpadre* Dionisio Macapagal, the man he defeated in his campaign for *barrio* captain in 1972. Another of Rubing's factional allies, Melencio Macapagal—who had two daughters married to members of Colonel Irwin Ver's Presidential Guard and a son who had been made a policeman under Defense Minister Juan Ponce Enrile—campaigned vigorously for Marcos. The local devotees of the Iglesia ni Cristo (Church of Christ) had supported Rubing with their forty-four disciplined votes in 1982 and now were committed by orders from their national head to vote for Marcos.

This dominant KBL coalition campaigned for village unity behind Marcos with the apolitical slogan *Marcos alang alang sa mehora* ("Marcos, out of regard for the pork-barrel projects"). Rubing used his consummate knowledge of the ins and outs of village politics to add to the ranks waverers who owed personal debts of gratitude to him or the KBL incumbent in San Miguel's *municipio*, Mayor Juan de la Cruz. Although many who would vote KBL were unhappy with Marcos, in Barrio Buga—where about half the land is still owned by the Hacienda de Leon and another quarter by the Hacienda Sevilla-de Leon—there was, not surprisingly, a strong sentiment from many land-reform beneficiaries that Marcos had a right to their support. Like most land-reform tenants across the Central Luzon Plain, those in Barrio Buga still held a mere Certificate of Land Transfer (CLT), a temporary document that denied them the security of tenure embodied in the final Torrens titles that Marcos had promised. Since those leading the Aquino campaign in San Miguel were de Leon landowners and their kin, the land-reform issue seemed etched with particular clarity in Barrio Buga.

The campaign for Aquino in Buga was led by the anti-de Guzman faction whose core was a set of families that had been Nacionalista in the 1971 local elections, had won the 1972 village election with the NP captain Jose Lazaro, and had ruled through him from then until 1982 by dispensing with the solidly Liberal village council. In the 1982 village elections, this NP faction had run under the KBL banner but had been totally shut out of office by de Guzman and his NUL council slate, who subsequently were received into the KBL as prodigals. That left the old NP/KBL with no connection to the Marcos administration. Many of the anti–de Guzman NP political orphans linked up behind a younger generation of prosperous villagers whose political ambitions had been frustrated by two generations of de Guzmans. These leaders subsequently linked themselves with the anti-Marcos opposition.

In another sense, however, the core of the Aquino campaign was the loyal tenants and clients of the de Leons—notably, individuals who were overseers or had off-farm jobs deriving from the de Leons. These loyalists were joined by the large Toledo family, which counted two members who had been represented in legal cases by Attorney Jose ("Bojie") de Leon-Cabuchan, heir to the de Leon land in Buga. Elected first village councilor on the de Guzman NUL slate in 1982, the bus driver Bidi Toledo and his wife, and the former LP village councilor Adoreng Toledo, brought their fourteen children, most of them married, into the ranks of Aquino's local campaign. This family's defection caused much bitterness with Rubing de Guzman, whose wife was a Toledo.

Hitherto, campaigning in the village had as its first strategy winning over the *matanda*—the male political head of a family who committed all its votes. In return, large families were given considerable leverage in faction making and in broker benefits. However, poll watching *liders* say that in this election the young and women ignored elders. Families were divided and male elders could not be sure that members would follow their direction. There is a possibility that some elders, obligated by their promises to campaign organizers, were attributing to unruly youth their own unwillingness to vote according to party, faction, and immediate personal benefit. Some of the young were influenced by new currents in the Church, others by ideas from college campuses, NPA contacts (the NPA was already organizing in adjacent Barrio Sapang), the anti-Marcos media, and their own evaluation and discussion of what was good for the country. Many young people rejected as *pulitika* or *maruming pulitika* (dirty politics) the pragmatic deals that male elders were making to exchange their votes for favors from the regime. They suspected that the KBL would once again manipulate the vote somewhere above the precinct level. As a researcher working two years after these events, I found it difficult to evaluate the degree to which people of all ages may have been caught up in an emotional, almost millenarian, sense of the stormy end of one era and the dawn of another. Tagalogs tend to present themselves as rational and prescient after the event.

In the confused evaluation of which candidate to vote for, one factor strongly favoring Aquino was the perception that, whatever her faults, her victory would provide the last chance to restore democracy or at least stable government. If Marcos won by his usual foul means, the insurgency would worsen. Many young people could see no alternative but civil war to unseat him. If he succumbed to ill health, his probable successors, Imelda Marcos and General Ver, no doubt would be even more incompetent, corrupt, and brutal. Therefore, a Marcos victory would mean facing the bleak prospect of no long-term option other than the dictatorship of the right or the NPA left. An Aquino victory would put an end to the Marcos dictatorship, bring down from the hills those who had fled his abuses, disprove the communist slogan that there was no alternative to dictatorship but armed revolution, and give democracy a chance.

Starting with his inauguration in January 1966, Marcos's rule had lasted twenty years. In a population in which a majority of the voters were under thirty, many had known no other president. The first couple's portraits were in every schoolroom, every government office, and on calendars in a majority of homes. Since 1972, youth had been subjected at all levels of education to a revised New Society curriculum designed to instill the ideals of the ruling KBL Party and loyalty to the president. Much of the print media, most of the radio stations, and all of the TV channels were controlled by the regime. Moreover, the Kabataang Barangay (KB), the regime's youth association, had some real meaning to young people in San Miguel. The topnotch town councilor in the 1980 elections was Vivian Miranda, a twenty-five-year-old woman and KB president. In the 1988 local elections—without bloc voting—another young KB woman president, Nenet Talusan, only eighteen years old, would win as topnotch municipal councilor. It therefore says much for the capacity of young Filipinos to resist state indoctrination that a large portion of the young claim what political leaders confirm—that they voted overwhelmingly for Aquino, even against the direction of their parents. Marcos had failed to capture the idealism of the youth, and the murder of Benigno Aquino, Jr., had convinced them that the regime was immoral. For youth, it was time for a change.

On election day in February 1986, Marcos won in Barrio Buga with a ratio of 2.13 to 1. But in adjacent Barangay Pinambaran his margin was an impressive 5.03 to 1, and in the Huk/HMB base in Barangay Mandile, on the edge of Candaba Swamp and in the Kapampangan speech area, he scored the highest with 5.8 to 1. Dionisio Macapagal, a life-long oppositionist and LP stalwart, wrote to me a few days after the EDSA "revolution," which he had followed on radio and television. First, he boasted that the former LP opposition faction (the one that had followed Captain Rubing de Guzman, after his 1982 defeat of the NP/KBL, into alliance with the town KBL mayor) had achieved unprecedented unity in the village, campaigning on that slogan of *alang alang sa mehora*, "in consideration of the pork-barrel projects," including the irrigation extension and the road and bridge renovations, flood-control works, and multipurpose rice-drying platforms already gained from the administration, and the new school buildings "approved" but promised for delivery *after* the elections. But when Macapagal, his family, and their political followers, clustered around the television, heard that Marcos and General Ver had flown to Hawaii, they cheered with tears in their eyes, "even though it was we who had voted for him." The *dambuhala*, the legendary monster, had been defeated.

All over the Philippines the transition period from February 1986 to the local elections of January 1988 was full of frantic and bitter contests for the appointed posts of OIC (Officer in Charge) governor and mayor. Important to the institutionalization of the Marcos-Aquino transition—involving the conduct of the February 1987 constitutional referendum, the May 1987 congressional elections, and the January 1988 local elections—was the political maneuvering by these OIC officials in dismissing and appointing municipal councilors and *barrio* captains. Politically what was at stake was the creation of political machines to replace or recycle the Marcos machine down to the grassroots level.

To understand the importance of this transitional phase it is necessary to keep in mind that the Philippine state has never had a centralized, disciplined civil service reaching down to the village level. The Spanish colonial legacy of a highly centralized state is in large part an illusion. The state's civil apparatus penetrates little beyond Manila, and where it does it is a poor instrument since its directives are subverted by its officials' alliances with local power holders who work for their own particular interests. Until martial law, there were remarkably few central-government officials in the rural townships apart from the schoolteachers. Instead of a centripetal, salaried, national bureaucracy, the provinces, towns, and villages were administered by centrifugal elected officials whose tenure of office, income, policies, and discipline were autonomous. Moreover, when elements of the transplanted U.S. model of local government were adapted to Philippine political culture, local elites were able to manipulate them to continue and reinforce the long history of "everyday resistance" by local elites against an alien state power and its colonial law. They used autonomy of municipal government, municipal police, and the courts to maintain local customary law and their prerogatives as a rural oligarchy. Elite aims could best be achieved by keeping the central-state officials out, weak, or controlled, thereby preventing the state from converting their clients and dependents into its citizens. Thus, under the postwar Republic, local officials maintaining private armies had considerable control over police and the power to intervene in criminal cases to bring about *areglo*, thus setting aside the state's criminal law.

In short, the central state lacked the ability to enforce its laws and policies throughout its territory. It also lacked a monopoly on armed force, even in "normal" situations, a failing the centrifugal tendencies of which were manifested by the existence of private armies of local power holders at all levels from the village to the province. In addition, by the late 1980s, ethnic and ideological rebels, lost commands, or mutinous army factions were in the field, some cooperating with local officials. In effect, the central state could not give orders to local officials as a right but had to cajole, bargain, and treat with them. This paralysis produced little administration and much politics, for officials at each level of the system were forced to make "arrangements" with all the autonomous elected officials below them in order to get their will done.

Between 1972 and 1978, Marcos had attempted to disarm or co-opt private forces and to centralize the administrative system by subordinating relatively autonomous, elected, local politicians to both central government salaried officials and the KBL's cadre. From 1979, when Marcos sought foreign legitimacy through manipulated elections, he restored several powers to local officials. But he also tried to remove their political autonomy by making access to office dependent upon the approval of the centralized KBL machine rather than on autonomous local support. The aim was to use the KBL party machine, paralleled by the relevant civil bureaucracies (the Ministry of Human Settlements [MHS] and the Ministry of Local Government and Community Development [MLGCD]), to give Marcos's central government control down to the *barrio* level.

The downfall of Marcos in the extraordinary events of February 1986 changed the character of the Philippine presidency, the apex of the central administration. The new coalition under Corazon Aquino swiftly set about allotting the spoils— cabinet positions and directorships of government departments—to its victors. But for any real transition from Marcos to Aquino to occur outside Manila it would be necessary to break up the apparatus of the KBL machine and the KBL-aligned MLGCD and MHS officials. The cadre of KBL local officials needed only a credible leader to support a Marcos restoration, via a Napoleonic sequel to February, under Defense Secretary Juan Ponce Enrile, or a KBL resurgence in later elections, which might be accomplished under Bulacan's Blas Ople. (In early 1980, Ople had proposed to head a loyal opposition if the National Assembly were reopened.) Within the fragile military-civilian coalition of 1986, these possibilities were not lost on Enrile, nor were they ignored by those close to Aquino who feared his ambitions. It was Aquilino Pimentel's task as secretary of local government to dismiss Marcos's governors and mayors, in order to destroy one apparatus, while appointing officers in charge to establish another. Given Aquino's desire to restore electoral democracy as soon as possible, it was plain that those granted OIC positions would share in Aquino's legitimacy and popularity, winning the chance to make their names known and to build a local machine.

In May 1986, one of President Aquino's aspiring political leaders in Bulacan, Attorney Jose ("Bojie") de Leon-Cabuchan, was given a free hand to seat his first cousin, landowner and Manila businessman Manuel ("Tikboy") de Leon-Lipana as the OIC mayor of San Miguel. The incumbent KBL mayor, Juan de la Cruz, yielded office gracefully, retiring to his farm, piggery, and trucking business in Barrio Sta. Ines, about nine kilometers from the town. Although he continued to receive old friends, de la Cruz made no move to keep the KBL alive as an organization and effectively withdrew from local politics.

Once sworn in, Mayor Lipana called for the "courtesy resignations" of all municipal employees of the town hall, market, slaughterhouse, ambulance and fire brigades, and road construction teams. Of the 105 town employees he replaced 21, principally the temporaries and those lacking civil-service qualifications. He used the vacated jobs to reward campaign helpers. Among these, he appointed Adoreng Toledo of Barrio Buga as the market master, and Doray Mendiola as a market revenue collector.

Moreover, Mayor Lipana dropped the elected KBL vice-mayor and councilors. Then, working through his hand-picked nominating committee, he sent a short list of the "best qualified" aspirants for these vacated council positions to the Department of Local Government. The new OIC vice-mayor and eight OIC councilors had all worked for the Aquino campaign. The dismissed KBL councilors made a legal appeal and later were granted reinstatement and allowed to serve until the end of their elected terms.

Lipana also dismissed twenty-one of the forty-five *barrio* captains, on the grounds that he had no use for old KBL politicians, even though some held awards from Marcos's MLGCD citing them as outstanding captains. In their place he appointed people who had campaigned for Aquino without regard to the formal succession rules, which proceed down the line of *barangay* councilors in the order of their vote counts in the last election.

Significantly, Lipana chose new local officials on the recommendation of his family and a few friends, notably his municipal secretary, Councilor Artemio Garcia, and several tenants of the de Leons—people who were his dependents and in no position to offer advice he did not want to hear. He did not seek the advice of old politicians, and refused to accept it when it came his way. Since he had grown up in Manila and had lived in New York for several years during the 1970s, Lipana lacked sufficient immersion in small-town politics, and familiarity with the personal reputations of those who attached themselves to his star, to avoid some bad choices in his appointments. His cousin, Attorney Jose de Leon-Cabuchan was in a similar position, and not able to meet the deficit in local intelligence, since his strengths were self-confidence, energetic organization, and the orator's capacity to stimulate a crowd rather than a politician's ability to build a coalition.

As a result of this conflict between their ambitions and those of local aspirants, Lipana and Cabuchan made enemies of a number of older municipal politicians of the elite and drove them into the camps of the opposition. They alienated the dismissed town councilors and *barrio* captains who had considerable followings, political talent, great energy, and the chameleon's ability to change their political coats. In the place of these proven performers, Lipana and Cabuchan built a machine that was inexperienced and overconfident at the top and rather shaky at its grassroots base. Nor were they motivated by ideological consistency, for they did not entirely reject those tainted with Marcos's brush, and had, in fact, picked up their share of turncoats along the way.

The elected captains made a more effective response to dismissal than did the town councilors. Thrown together in adversity, they fought back politically rather than legally, making an alliance with Bulacan's OIC governor Roberto Pagdanganan, who welcomed them on the principle that the enemy of an enemy is a friend and that he could only gain by the gift of a cadre of experienced grassroots politicians in the home town of his rival Cabuchan. Pagdanganan already had begun to deny discretionary funds to the mayors who opposed him in a bid to make them look incompetent as patrons in the delivery of "infrastructure" maintenance or improvements. But this tactic could backfire with voters unless he found another channel through which to deliver funds.

Approached by the recently dismissed *barrio* captain Rubing de Guzman of Buga, Governor Pagdanganan agreed to attend a meeting there of the dismissed captains and councilors to hear their complaints. Good politics was bad manners. The governor had twice failed to attend meetings with the Mayor Lipana, a wealthy landowner. Now he accepted the invitation of a peasant, again bypassing the mayor. Thereafter, Governor Pagdanganan channeled provincial discretionary funds through the dismissed captains, insisting that the mayor had no right to dismiss them without cause and due process before their terms expired in June 1988. Justifying this strategy legalistically, the governor accepted only the signatures of the elected captains on *barangay* requests or receipts, or those of officials appointed as OICs by virtue of succession when a captain had died, resigned, or been dismissed with cause.

Local Struggles and National Issues: The February 1987 Plebiscite

By February 1987, it was plain that President Aquino was in office to stay. The mood of national hope for a non-Marcos, noncommunist future had captured everyone. But peasants were critical of the land-reform plank in the new draft Constitution on the ground that it granted too much power to what they feared would be a landlord-controlled Congress. Moreover, they were angry over the January 1987 massacre of some twenty peasant marchers at Plaza Mendiola before the gates of Malacañang Palace. Landowners were angry that land reform was even mentioned in the Constitution. But such criticism was pushed into the background because most people felt that, the Constitution aside, they were being asked to decide only one question: whether President Aquino and Vice-President Laurel should stay in office for the term of the new Congress. This focus turned the plebiscite, as former Defense Secretary Enrile complained, into a presidential election without an opponent. The campaign focused on the approval or disapproval of the "housewife in the palace" rather than on the details of the draft Constitution, which was certainly the world's longest and perhaps its most complex.

Although both the left (the National Democratic Front, Partido ng Bayan, and the Kilusang Mayo Uno) and the right (the KBL and NP) opposed the Constitution's ratification, the final percentages voting "yes" and "no" should not be read as indicating the actual depth of support for either vote. In San Miguel, for example, local political maneuvers accounted for a relatively poor showing by the "yes" vote.

On the surface of politics, all the pro-Aquino coalition parties and figures in Bulacan Province seemed to campaign openly for "yes." OIC Governor Pagdanganan let it be known that OIC mayors were expected to get out a substantial affirmative vote or they would face replacement. Pagdanganan welcomed President Aquino at a huge rally that he organized in the provincial capital of Malolos in early January, where they appeared together as the main speakers. Indeed, the governor and his allies campaigned vigorously for a "yes" vote throughout most of the province. But the rift between Pagdanganan and San Miguel's aspirant governor Cabuchan made it politic to weaken the latter's reputation with both the administration and the voters by encouraging a low percentage of affirmative votes in his home town of San Miguel. Accordingly,

Pagdanganan stayed out of San Miguel to humiliate his enemy. Indicative of the Manila press corps' grasp of these complexities, a news item in the "Hometown News Section" of the *Manila Times*, dated 11 January 1987, reported that some of Bulacan's key politicians were campaigning against ratification of the Constitution. Specifically mentioned were former minister Rogaciano Mercado, board member Pete Gonzales, *and* Roberto Pagdanganan.

Governor Pagdanganan's maneuvers at the provincial level fitted the interests of Cabuchan's rivals in the Third Congressional District of Bulacan, Lipana's rivals for the San Miguel mayorship, and the local politicians that these two cousins had dismissed. Accordingly, while overtly in favor of the Constitution, members of the old municipal elite and younger aspirants did not exert themselves, and some secretly encouraged a "no" vote by their followers. *Barrio* captains claim that Pagdanganan let them know that he would regard it as a signal of their support if they campaigned quietly against "yes" in their villages. Although the Constitution was approved in San Miguel, the town had a low voter turnout. Moreover, only 74 percent of those who turned up at the polls voted "yes," one of the lowest percentages in the province.

In Barrio Buga, Rubing de Guzman is said by his enemies to have campaigned secretly for a "no" vote to avenge himself on the landlord cousins, Lipana and Cabuchan. The village's "yes" campaign was led by the anti–de Guzman faction centered around OIC councilor Alex Cacatian, OIC captain Alejo Mendiola, and Mayor Lipana's market appointees Adoreng Toledo and Doray Mendiola. Pilo Castillo, three times elected Buga's first councilor, switched to the "Cabuchan for Congress" camp after working for Marcos in the snap election. Given the strength of the de Guzmans, it is not surprising that the "yes" percentage in Barrio Buga was even lower than that recorded in the municipality as a whole.

With the Constitution ratified, the Aquino administration moved quickly to restore political stability by holding congressional elections in May 1987 and local elections seven months later. Within the municipality of San Miguel, these two elections effectively blunted the de Guzmans' aspirations for national office while affirming their influence at the *barangay* and municipal levels. In the May elections, San Miguel's pre–martial law mayor, Marcel de Guzman-Aure, sought to revive his eclipsed political career by running for the House of Representatives from Bulacan's Third District. In the final balloting, he placed only seventh, with 2,069 votes against the winning candidate's 27,626. This dismal performance eliminated Aure as a significant political figure in San Miguel, depriving the de Guzmans of their most successful politician.

In the January 1988 local elections, however, Rubing de Guzman placed second in the balloting for the town council—a significant victory that both affirmed and extended his influence. In these same elections, the incumbent mayor Manuel de Leon-Lipana, a descendant of the de Leons who shared his family's aloofness from the villages, lost to the town's former police chief, Fernando B. Mendez. Although a product of Marcos's centralized national police, and thereby a nominal agent of repression, Mendez had proven himself an effective populist politician. During his years as a Marcos police officer, he had used his office to build both a positive reputation and a political following in the villages. After switching his allegiance to the pro-Aquino party after the EDSA uprising of 1986, Mendez scored an impressive victory in the January 1988 elections, winning with 12,895 votes compared to Lipana's 8,191. Since Lipana had been supported by his congressman cousin Jose de Leon-Cabuchan, and he was also the standard bearer of the landed de Leon family, the outcome was significant.

The land-reform issue played a central role in Lipana's defeat. As the leaders among San Miguel's peasant voters knew well, Mayor Lipana's father, Manuel Lipana, Sr., had married one de Leon heiress and worked as a manager of lands for Doña Trinidad de Leon, the widow of President Manuel Roxas. Moreover, the elder Manuel's brother-in-law was Attorney Don Cecilio de Leon, the managing heir for all the lands of Don Felix de Leon, including his substantial holdings in Barrio Buga. These elder de Leons, Manuel Lipana, Sr., and Cecilio, were die-hard opponents of land reform and led an opposition movement of major landlords during the 1970s. Indeed, these two were known among San Miguel's peasants, from the early 1970s to the mid-1980s, as the brains behind the landlords' resistance to Marcos's land reforms. The de Leons set up a landowners' association that commissioned the renowned corporate lawyer Juan T. David to marshall legal cases against tenants who tried to get what was supposed to be mandatory under the Marcos decree. Working through David, who filed plea after plea in the Court of Appeals and the Supreme Court, the de Leons tried to invalidate seemingly insignificant planks in the land-reform legislation, clause by clause. In the short run, these tactics served to intimidate tenants. Over the longer run, the legal strategy was designed to set precedents that would accumulate in such a way as to make land reform unworkable. Ultimately, it was hoped, the Supreme Court would have to heed its own minor decisions and rule the entire legislation unconstitutional. These endless legal proceedings against tenants—first to block leasehold and then to stop land transfer—damaged the reputation of the de Leon clan among the peasantry. Organized peasants opposed the family. Once they sobered from the euphoria of the EDSA Revolution, and were whipped up by peasant leaders allied to Mendez and other local leaders, they took their revenge on Mayor de Leon-Lipana.

Showing the acumen to ally himself with Mendez, a candidate who at first glance seemed an improbable winner, Rubing de Guzman made the transition to the new politics of the post-Marcos era. After his dismissal as *barrio* captain in 1986, he left the KBL Party and ran for the municipal council two years later on Mendez's pro-Aquino ticket. Despite an unprecedented swarm of competitors for all offices, Rubing placed second among the thirty candidates for San Miguel's council. Since the number-one councilor was a young woman who had gained prominence through Marcos's Kabataan Barangay youth movement, and was soon to go abroad, Rubing was in a strong position to exercise leadership at the municipal level and extend his family's influence into the 1990s.

Although Rubing does not have the commanding aura or the legendary status of his father Kardeng, he nonetheless won his seat on the council by opposing Lipana, the annointed leader of the de Leons. Though less powerful than his father, Rubing seems to have more real independence of action as a political leader. He was the first de Guzman in this century to break definitively with the de Leons. Its wisdom confirmed by subsequent events, this breach between the aristocratic de Leons and the de Guzmans, who a generation before had been their retainers, confirms the end of the hacienda system of large estates run for absentee landlords by strong-man overseers drawn from the peasantry.

The de Guzmans Today

The de Guzman family has dominated the politics of their *barangay* for two generations, from the 1930s to the 1990s. Rubing was twice *barangay* captain (1965–72, 1981–87) and later town councilor (1988–92). His father Kardeng was topnotcher town councilor during Liberation and a kingmaker in municipal politics until about 1967. Rubing's third brother, Raul, was town councilor from 1967 to 1971 and then municipal secretary until 1978.

As of 1990, only one branch of the family is currently residing in the village: now part of the family's senior generation, Rubing is still a municipal politician living with some of his children and grandchildren in Barrio Buga. His second brother, Virgilio ("Berling"), has a small business in Manila, as does their sister Jessie. The third brother, Raul, who lives in San Miguel's *poblacion* with his wife, a high school teacher, is currently a political middleman. The fourth brother, Onorato ("Bonog"), has a farm in the village but lives outside it on the highway where he has a second holding. His wife is a rice trader and also employs women to make baby dresses on a piecework basis. The youngest male, Eliseo ("Eling"), was drafted after completing his university education and became an officer in the Armed Forces. Later he died in combat against Muslim rebels in Mindanao.

There is no other de Guzman household in the village. However, the largest family residing there are the Macapagals, who count a de Guzman ancestress. They have "always" aligned themselves with the de Guzmans. On their mother's side the de Guzmans have relatively few kin, as their mother and two sisters married into the village from outside. Rubing married within the village, but into the Toledo family, the largest branch of which aligns itself against the de Guzmans. Despite its diminished numbers, this comparatively small family enjoys considerable local prestige and remains the leading political family of Barrio Buga.

The de Guzmans' economic base in the village cannot account for their political prominence. Their land consists of one tenant farm of 3.5 hectares, held since the 1930s, plus a second of 4.5 hectares held from the 1950s, now worked by the youngest and eldest brothers, respectively. Both farms were held under share tenancy until the mid-1970s when they received a Certificate of Land Transfer under the Marcos land reform. This land base amounts to about 8 hectares of a total of 200 hectares in the village, or about 4 percent of village agricultural land. Although several other sibling sets hold more land, the family was already politically dominant in the 1930s when it held only the smaller farm.

Nor does the political power of the de Guzmans in their home village rest on having the most common surname or the greatest number of bilateral kin. Seven surnames have more members, and many *matanda* (political elders of families) have much larger kindreds in the sense of numbers of adult bilateral kin. The de Guzmans' dominant position rests on their success as political entrepreneurs, leaders who have drawn into their political clientele other, more numerous families. It is in this sense that the de Guzmans are said to have a big *angkan*. It is a led kindred, most branches of which have only a distant relationship but side with the de Guzman faction against groupings led by men with whom they have closer genealogical relationships. Kinship is thus an idiom in which support is contested and expressed, a kind of discourse, rather than a set of rules that unequivocally directs support according to the closeness of genealogical linkage.

The de Guzmans' ability to protect their supporters from danger and obtain satisfactory outcomes for them in disputes with enemies, from the courts, and from state officials is an essential part of the services they provide. The majority of the members of the de Guzman faction within the village are drawn from more numerous but less politically able families, who render *galang* respect to them as champions protecting them from various perceived threats. It is not lost on their followers or their enemies that the de Guzmans have at times used violence to repay insult, and that in the past several de Guzman men have killed enemies, but that in no case did they go to jail or pay *areglo* blood money as settlement. They have powerful allies among other political entrepreneurs, strong men, and politicians with whom they exchange votes and favors. Rubing, the current leader of the family, has been since the 1960s on first-name terms with a number of past and present congressmen, governors, and mayors. His son is a municipal policeman, who has legitimate cause to keep high-powered firearms in the family's house and to carry them.

In addition to providing protection for the family's supporters, Rubing de Guzman has exerted himself to obtain collective benefits for his village in the form of *mehora* (improvements) funded by the national government. It is universally understood that Manila receives more demands than it can fund, and that the same applies to its provincial and municipal units. Thus, funds spent in one village are not spent elsewhere. Since each level of government approves more projects than it can pay for, the art of pork barrel is to "follow up papers" (that is, move them through the bureaucratic labyrinth) and cultivate contacts who can arrange that scarce funds will be allocated to a project in one's own constituency. By making and maintaining strategic relationships with up-and-coming politicians, even when these crossed apparent party affiliations, the de Guzman chief won a windfall of projects for his village during the Marcos years, with funding well beyond any *barrio*'s reasonable share. This success was well known and served as a source of jealous admiration throughout the municipality. When Rubing campaigned successfully for town councilor in the 1988 local elections, he turned this success to advantage, presenting himself as an ordinary peasant, a man without oratorical skills or flowery speech, who wanted to be judged by what he had proven he could do for the ordinary people not by empty promises.

Although they are peasant farmers, petty entrepreneurs, and local politicians who have never risen higher than the post of municipal councilor, the de Guzmans of Buga are just as much a "political family" as are the families of great wealth. My criterion for defining a political family is simple: that both outsiders and its own members view it as a political unit whose power—either to get its will done or block its opponents—is, first, transferable from one member to another over time, and, second, extends beyond its blood members to allow it a leading role in the politics of its particular area.

The de Guzmans, their fellow villagers, and professional politicians say that since the early 1930s *ang de Guzman ang namumuno duon* ("they are the ones who are important or who lead there"). This perception is not based on numbers, for those bearing the surname in the home village have never numbered more than six adult men or 3 resident households within a village whose population has ranged between 150 and 300 households.

The de Guzmans, their fellow villagers, and outside observers expect the family to contest office; to take a leading role whenever municipal, provincial, or national politicians and official or nongovernment organizations are making decisions that directly affect the village and its environs; and to prevent, openly or covertly, implementation of decisions about which they were not consulted or that they do not like. Criminals, police, armed strong men, rebels, lawyers, and judges expect the de Guzmans to intervene in cases involving their supporters or fellow villagers.

Although they have not been involved in killings in several decades, two members of the current, dominant, sibling set retain reputations as dangerous men. These reputations were acquired during the Japanese occupation when they were USAFFE guerrillas, in the disturbed times of Liberation, and in the violence of the Huk Rebellion, when, as young men, their father commanded a Civilian Guard unit while they were involved in logging, reputed banditry, and rustling. That their grandfather was a *kinikilalang lalaki* or *magaling na lalaki,* a notorious tough guy, and their father Kardeng and all his brothers had similar reputations, has always been part of the aura surrounding this sibling group.

At the heart of their continuous political prominence lies an esprit de corps and sense of corporate honor that binds the family and impels it to throw itself into public affairs as a unit rather than withdraw to the concerns of the member households. The de Guzmans persist in engagement even when such action has been a source of physical danger and financial burden. This involvement extends to the de Guzmans living outside the village. During an election campaign, they come home to Barrio Buga and throw their resources behind the family's standard bearer.

Despite decades of living in Manila, Rubing's siblings have managed to remain listed as voters in the village. They participate in, organize and donate to, and attend the annual gatherings at Buga's *bisita* chapel for Easter and Pasalamat, the harvest Thanksgiving.

The de Guzmans are fiercely proud of the fact that the family has always included *kinikilalang lalaki*; that neither friend nor foe can overlook them *hindi kami mga hindi pinapansin* ("we are not people who are ignored"); and that both ordinary and powerful people treat them with *galang* respect. Although reputations made in the disturbed era of the 1930s through the 1950s are fading, the de Guzmans cherish the tales of those relations who were peasant rebels, guerrillas, and bandits. The aura of their father and grandfather's glory still hovers about the current generation.

The other element in their political success is a sense of destiny: the de Guzmans think of themselves as having a right, even a kind of duty, to participate in public affairs, to stand out above ordinary folk, and to recover the birthright position that their kinsmen once achieved. That his late father had been elected topnotcher town councilor in the early postwar period was one spur to Raul in contesting the post of councilor in 1967 and 1971. Similarly, in 1988, this sense of family inspired Rubing, after many years as *barangay* captain, to run for municipal councilor on behalf of the family.

Significantly, Rubing's role as village leader, town councilor, and municipal influential parallels, rather precisely, the roles that his father Kardeng first played in the 1930s. Over the space of a half century marked by war, revolution, dictatorship, and rebellion, two de Guzmans, father and son, have remained influential political leaders within Barrio Buga and its surrounding municipality of San Miguel. This continuity is more than coincidental. Their remarkable political tenacity indicates that the de Guzman family has, in its own way, won a position of political influence in San Miguel as entrenched and established as that enjoyed by the Osmeñas in Cebu City or the Cojuangcos in Tarlac Province.

A PPENDIX : Political Biodata of the de Guzmans

Jacinto de Guzman (b. ca. 1860, d. 1916)

A member of the KKK revolution against Spain in 1896–98, Jacinto de Guzman fought against the Americans from 1898 until his unit, under Colonel Pablo Tecson-Ocampo, surrendered in 1900. Reputed to be *matapang* ('brave, ferocious'), and an expert swordsman, he drove out an American rinderpest inoculation team around 1908. He belonged to the Veteranos de la Revolucion and was a member of various millenarian nationalist movements between 1900 and 1916.

Felipa Valisno-de Guzman (d. 1941)

The wife of Jacinto de Guzman, Felipa Valisno-de Guzman was widowed 1916. She raised seven children in poverty until the older sons were able to find work as farm laborers. Her five sons became *matapang* and *kinikilalang lalaki* ('notorious men').

Amando V. de Guzman (d. 1971)

The eldest son of Jacinto and Felipa, Amando de Guzman was *matapang*. He began his career as a harvest checker and later worked as an overseer for Narcisa ("Doña Sisang") Buencamino-de Leon's estate in Guimba, Nueva Ecija. He was elected topnotch town councilor of Guimba in 1935, appointed acting mayor in 1942, serving until he was deposed by the Japanese. In later life he abandoned the roles of *matapang* and politico for private life. He died rich in 1971.

Bienvenido V. de Guzman (d. 1943)

The second son, Bienvenido was *matapang*, a crack shot, and a gambler. He worked as an overseer on Doña Sisang's Guimba estate under his brother Amando, and was killed by bandits in 1943. His daughter Natividad ("Naty") married Guimba *matapang* Faustino Dy, a logger, political entrepreneur, and governor of Isabela from the 1960s.

Ricardo V. ("Kardeng") de Guzman (d. 1969)

Also *matapang*, the third brother, Kardeng, was a Kapatirang Magsasaka peasant-union leader in the 1930s while employed as a threshing manager, first for the de Leons and later for their political rivals the Tecsons. Distributing arms looted from an abandoned U.S. camp, Kardeng became a USAFFE guerrilla chief during the Pacific War. Arrested by the Kempeitai 1943, he was held for a time at Fort Santiago. He was reputed to possess a "coat of mail" talisman, which rendered him invulnerable above the thighs. He was elected topnotcher municipal-council member in 1946, and was also employed as an overseer for Doña Sisang in San Miguel. He was machine-gunned in the thighs by Civilian Guards in 1947 because of his brother Kumander Andron, the Huk. Kardeng maintained political control of his home area around Buga and was influential in municipal politics, despite accusations of rustling and banditry, from 1946 to 1969.

Eduardo V. ("Kumander Andron") de Guzman (d. 1992)

The fourth brother, Andron, was renowned in the 1930s as an athlete and KPMP unionist, while earning his livelihood as a tenant farmer. He was a Huk supply officer and intelligence officer from 1942 to 1945, and a Huk-HMB commander from 1944 to 1948. He surrendered, via Doña Sisang and her cousin Doña Trinidad de Leon-Roxas, to President Roxas in September 1948, and was later employed as an armed guard with Doña Sisang's LVN Pictures, Inc., from 1949 until the 1970s.

Graciano V. ("Grasing") de Guzman (b. 1916, d. 1990)

The fifth brother, Grasing, was a high school graduate who began his career as a primary school teacher in 1935. Considered *matapang*, he was employed as a checker for Doña Sisang's LVN Pictures in 1936, as a hacienda overseer in 1937, and as an *engkargado* (managing overseer) in Nueva Ecija from 1942 to 1981, during which time he controlled estates in seven municipalities. He was a political leader in Nueva Ecija from 1946 to 1952, and is known to have paid off the mayor, the governor, the police, and the provincial PC commander to protect his control of gambling rackets in Cabanatuan City between 1945 and 1960. He was accused of homicide five times and survived three assassination attempts. In his later years he was employed as a manager for the heirs of Doña Sisang in their Kapitan Pepe Memorial Park and Subdivision in Cabanatuan City.

Petong de Guzman (d. 1990)

A second cousin of the de Guzman brothers, Petong was also *matapang*. He moved to Manila in the 1930s where he acquired a tough-guy reputation and a following in the Pasay City bars. Called upon by female textile strikers to protect them from company goons, he became a union boss with sideline interests in "rent-a-demo" rowdies, toughs who could be hired to man or break up picket lines or political rallies. When martial law was declared in 1972, a prohibition on strikes ruined Petong's business.

Bernabe M. ("Rubing") de Guzman (b. 1924)

The eldest son of Kardeng, Rubing de Guzman finished high school in 1942. He was *matapang*, a USAFFE scout from 1942 to 1945, a logger in the Sierra Madre and a Civilian Guard from 1946 to 1948, and on the run with Kardeng in Gapan in 1947. He served as Kardeng's chief assistant in village and municipal politics between 1946 and 1969. Continuing as a tenant farmer, Rubing was accused of rustling and banditry in the 1950s. He served as Liberal Party *barrio* captain from 1962 to 1972. He remained anti-Marcos with the LP then the National Union for Liberation, and in 1981 defeated the KBL captain, but was inducted into the KBL soon after his election. He helped organize opposition to the Cabuchan-Lipanan resurgence of the de Leons in 1986-87, was elected a Lakas ng Bansa municipal councilor in 1988, but lost a reelection bid in 1992.

Virgilio M. ("Berling") de Guzman (b. 1926)
Berling, the second son of Kardeng de Guzman, was a *matapang* in the 1950s and 1960s. He took up logging in the 1940s and went to Manila in the 1950s. There he committed a multiple homicide but was exonerated upon the production of backdated papers from General Castañeda, an ally of his uncle Grasing, showing him to be an NBI agent. Berling is an aficionado of "police characters" in Manila and has contacts among politicians and "notorious men" due to his business interests at ten-pin bowling alleys. He contributes cloth, silkscreen printing, money, basketballs, and time to his brother Rubing's election campaigns.

Rogelio M. ("Raul") de Guzman (b. 1933)
The third son of Kardeng de Guzman, Raul studied law and became a political entrepreneur. He served as Liberal Party municipal councilor from 1967 to 1971, and as municipal secretary from 1971 to 1979. He lost a bid for the vice-mayorship in 1980 running for the NUL. He has acted as a strategist for his "uncle" Marcelo G. Aure and his brother Rubing in their election campaigns.

Jessica M. ("Jessie") de Guzman-Maño (b. 1934)
Jessica de Guzman is a Manila businesswoman, the daughter of Kardeng. She is a fiercely partisan campaigner and a contributor to her brother's election campaigns.

Honorato ("Bonog") de Guzman (b. 1937)
Bonog is the fourth son of Kardeng de Guzman. He served as an appointed municipal policeman during the administration of his "uncle," Mayor Marcelo G. Aure, from 1967 to 1978. Bonog is a tenant farmer with two farms; his wife is a rice trader. He contributes money, vehicles, contacts, and time to his brother's election campaigns.

Marcelo G. Aure (b. 1922?)
Marcelo Aure, who had a de Guzman mother and a father from Cavite, is a lawyer and political entrepreneur. Aure served as assistant provincial *fiscal* in the 1960s. He was elected Liberal Party mayor in 1967 and 1971, and served until 1978 when he was deposed on charges of *estafa* (fraud). Since then he has suffered several defeats under the Liberal and NUL banners, and remains the head of the remnant LP. Aure is respected by his de Guzman "nephews," including his protégé Raul who served as his municipal secretary.

Dionisio Macapagal (b. 1904)
A tenant farmer in the 1930s, Macapagal was a member of the Tanggulan, Sakdal, Kapatiran Magsasaka, and the KPMP. He was a Ganap during the war and once was saved from execution as a collaborator by his cousin Andron de Guzman. With the proceeds from logging in the Sierra Madre in the 1940s he was able to buy his two small farms. Macapagal served as *barrio teniente* and *kapitan* from the 1930s to

1962 when he passed the office to his "nephew," Rubing de Guzman. He is the political *matanda* of the large Macapagal *angkan*, whose votes he delivers to his Aure and de Guzman kinsmen. He is known as a supporter of land reform. For more on Dionisio Macapagal, see Fegan, "Social History."

Melencio Macapagal (b. 1930)

Melencio Macapagal is a former seaman, professional photographer, and a village councilor. A de Guzman ally, he leads the larger branch of the Macapagal *angkan*. Two of his daughters married Presidential Guards in the Marcos period, reinforcing the family's influence.

N OTES

[1]This special issue of the *Journal of Peasant Studies* (13, no. 2 [January 1986]) was later published in monograph form as James C. Scott and Benedict Kerkvliet, eds., *Everyday Forms of Peasant Resistance in Southeast Asia* (London: Frank Cass, 1986). The volume was inspired by James C. Scott's *Everyday Forms of Peasant Resistance* (New Haven: Yale University Press, 1987).

[2]Alfred W. McCoy and Ed. C. de Jesus, eds., *Philippine Social History: Global Trade and Local Transformations* (Manila: Ateneo de Manila University Press, 1982).

[3]Pierre Bourdieu, *The Logic of Practice* (Cambridge: Cambridge University Press, 1990).

[4]Eric Hobsbawm, *Primitive Rebels: Studies in Archaic Forms of Social Movements in the 19th and 20th Centuries* (New York: Norton, 1959).

[5]Anton Blok, *The Mafia of a Sicilian Village, 1860–1960: A Study of Violent Peasant Entrepreneurs* (New York: Harper and Row, 1974).

[6]Carl Lande, *Leaders, Factions, and Parties: The Structure of Philippine Politics*, Southeast Asia Monographs, no. 6 (New Haven: Southeast Asian Studies, Yale University, 1965).

[7]On *liders*, see Mary R. Hollnsteiner, *The Dynamics of Power in a Philippine Municipality* (Quezon City: Community Development Research Council, University of the Philippines, 1963). For theories concerning the "political machine," see Kit Machado, "From Traditional Faction to Machine: Changing Patterns of Leadership and Organization in the Rural Philippines," *Journal of Asian Studies* 33 (1974): 523–47; and Thomas C. Nowak and Kay A. Snyder, "Economic Concentration and Political Change in the Philippines," in *Political Change in the Philippines: Studies of Local Politics Preceding Martial Law*, edited by Benedict J. Kerkvliet, Asian Studies Program Papers, no. 14 (Honolulu: University of Hawaii Press, 1974), 153–241. On the "professional politician," see Machado, "From Traditional Faction to Machine."

[8]Frank Lynch, "Social Acceptance Reconsidered," in *Four Readings on Philippine Values*, edited by Frank Lynch and Alfonso de Guzman II (Quezon City: Ateneo de Manila University Press, 1973), 1–68; Jaime C. Bulatao, "Hiya," *Philippine Studies* 12, no. 3 (1964): 424–38.

[9]Charles Kaut,"The Principle of Contingency in Tagalog Society," *Asian Studies* 3, no. 1 (April 1965): 1–18; Charles Kaut, "Process and Social Structure in a Philippine Lowland Settlement," in *Studies on Asia, 1960*, edited by Robert K. Sakai (Lincoln: University of Nebraska Press, 1960), 35–50; Francis J. Murray, "Lowland Social Organisation I: Local Kin Groups in a Central Luzon Barrio," *Philippine Sociological Review* 21, no. 1 (1973): 29–36; Francis J. Murray, "Lowland Social Organisation II: Ambilineal

Kin Groups in a Central Luzon Barrio," *Philippine Sociological Review* 21, no. 2 (1973): 159–68.

[10]Daniel Scheans, "Kith-Centred Action Groups in an Ilocano Barrio," *Ethnology* 3, no. 4 (1964): 364–68.

[11]Brian Fegan, "The Social History of a Central Luzon Barrio," in McCoy and de Jesus, *Philippine Social History*, 91–129; Brian Fegan, "Politics in a Central Luzon Town (1880–1980)," *Lipunan* 2, no. 3 (1981): 73–97.

[12]Marshall S. McLennan, *The Central Luzon Plain: Land and Society on the Inland Frontier* (Quezon City: Alemar-Phoenix, 1980); Fegan, "Social History."

[13]Monina A. Mercado, *Doña Sisang and Filipino Movies* (Manila: Vera-Reyes, 1977).

[14]Fegan, "Politics in a Central Luzon Town"; "History and Cultural Life of San Miguel, Bulacan," Historical Data Papers, Philippine National Library (typescript, ca. 1950–51). The data were supplemented and elucidated by extensive interviews with members of those families.

[15]Hollnsteiner, *Dynamics of Power*; Lande, *Leaders*.

[16]"History and Cultural Life of San Miguel, Bulacan."

Walking in the Shadow of the Big Man: Justiniano Montano and Failed Dynasty Building in Cavite 1935–1972

John Sidel

Throughout precolonial Southeast Asia, the "big man" ruled supreme, his power essentially personal, based neither on lineage nor on office.[1] In Weberian terms, authority was essentially "charismatic" rather than "traditional." The self-made "big man" was compelled to reaffirm his leadership on a continual basis, most importantly through violence. He had to demonstrate again and again that he possessed those qualities—whether magical powers, oratorical skills, spiritual refinement, or bravery in war—that commanded the respect and loyalty of his followers. Given conditions of land abundance, dispersed settlement, and shifting cultivation, precolonial Philippine polities cohered only insofar as "big men" were able to project or impose their "prowess" upon subject populations, and economic power derived from control over men and violence rather than ownership of land or other fixed assets. Thus, in Philippine societies at the time of Spanish contact, the size of followings defined the powers of the *datus* (big men), and "slaves comprise[d] the greatest wealth and capital of the natives of these islands."[2]

With kinship reckoned cognatically (bilaterally), and lineage ineffective in regulating succession to political leadership, the possibilities for "dynasty" building in precolonial Southeast Asia were severely circumscribed. Even in the more extensively elaborated and institutionalized hierarchies of political authority found in mainland Southeast Asia, Sumatra, and Java, "kingship" was essentially a personal achievement, and lineage failed to compensate for an absence of those personal qualities necessary for leadership. Thus, as O. W. Wolters wryly notes, "Moral stigma was not attached to what the Chinese regarded as 'usurpation', for an overlord's power was not protected by the concept of a 'dynasty' in a society with a plethora of half-brothers."[3]

In Burma, for example, at least eight of the nine kings of the Pagan "dynasty" (11th–13th centuries) about whom we have inscriptional information of any worth were not in the immediate or direct line of succession. Of the later Konbaung "dynasty," only three of eleven kings were blood heirs.[4] In the Philippines, where political authority remained largely uninstitutionalized and confined to the nucleated settlement (that is, the *barangay*), the obstacles to the retention of power by a given family across generations were all the more apparent. Even in Islamicized Sulu, succession to the sultanate depended ultimately on "prowess" rather than on claims based on genealogical descent.[5]

Overall, "family" served not as an "unassailable organizing principle of authority"[6] but rather as a means of identifying and creating networks of personal loyalty. Marriages, for example, served as mechanisms for the forging of alliances through the creation of new affinal bonds. The "achievement of founding a line of descent [was] emphasized rather than that of perpetuating an old one,"[7] and hence the prodigious generation of offspring was valorized as a sign of a "big man's" personal power.

External influences worked to expand the possibilities for "dynasty" building in Philippine society. Where Islam penetrated, it favored the closer association of political leadership with certain lineages and the stabilization of succession through the establishment of genealogies and rules for leadership transition.[8] The Spanish colonial regime, moreover, established a system of colonial administration that formally empowered the native *datus* as village headmen (*cabezas de barangay*) and petty governors (*gobernadorcillos*), and allowed hereditary succession to govern ascension to these posts until late in the eighteenth century.[9] Finally, the incorporation of the Philippines into the world economy and the ensuing commercialization of agriculture in the nineteenth century allowed Chinese *mestizos* with roots in the burgeoning cash economy to accumulate land and other fixed economic assets that could be passed from generation to generation.[10]

As elsewhere in the modern world, capitalism spawned Filipino family fortunes of "dynastic" proportions. Thus, like nineteenth-century, small-town America, the archipelago has yielded an abundance of local landed families. Just as northeast Brazil is famous for its *parentela*, the Philippines, too, offers numerous cases of long-standing, *hacienda*-based clans: the Cojuangcos of Tarlac, the Fortiches of Bukidnon, and the various sugar baronetcies of Negros Occidental. While not quite matching Europe's great family shipping empires, Cebu boasts of the Aboitizes, Escaños and Chiongbians. And, as in New York, with its banking houses and real-estate dynasties,[11] Manila plays host to the Ayalas, Aranetas, Ortigases, and Tuasons.

In fact, the family's role as "the primary unit of capital accumulation and corporate control"[12] and the successful concentration and retention of proprietary wealth in family hands help to explain the longevity of the most prominent "dynasties" in contemporary Philippine society.[13] In some cases (in the Lopez family, for example), the conversion of landed properties into corporate vehicles has

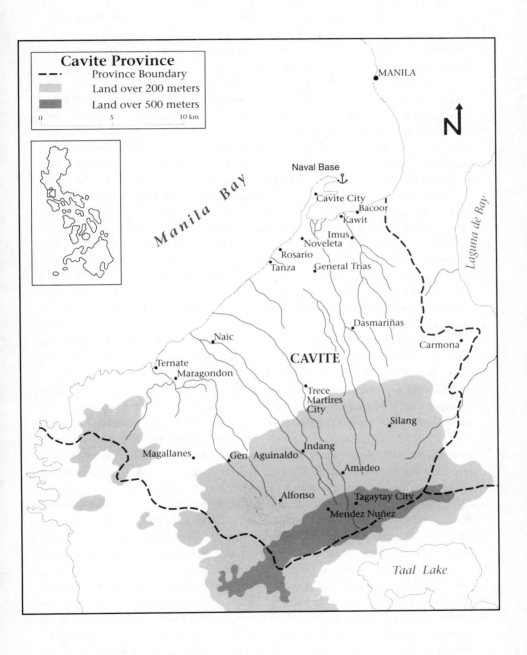

Cavite Province

- – - – Province Boundary
- Land over 200 meters
- Land over 500 meters

0   5   10 km

N

Manila Bay

MANILA

Naval Base

Cavite City

Bacoor

Kawit

Imus

Noveleta

Rosario

Tanza

General Trias

Dasmariñas

Carmona

Naic

CAVITE

Ternate

Maragondon

Trece
Martires
City

Silang

Magallanes

Gen. Aguinaldo

Indang

Amadeo

Alfonso

Tagaytay City

Mendez Nuñez

Laguna de Bay

Taal Lake

facilitated continued familial solidity over the generations. In other families, such as the Tuasons, the diffusion and dilution of family wealth through inheritance, intermarriage, and investment diversification has speeded the dissolution of the "dynasty." In any case, the alternative trajectories are clear: either an increase in familial power or dynastic self-liquidation.

To be sure, political context has in large part determined the longevity of Philippine "dynasties." The availability of electoral positions has allowed *hacenderos* throughout the archipelago to set up their scions as town mayors, congressmen, and provincial governors, to such an extent that political office remains seemingly inherited or passed along within the family. Moreover, the patrimonial nature of the state apparatus has encouraged such "political clans" to accumulate, expand, and upgrade their proprietary wealth through privileged access to contracts, concessions, licenses, and behest loans—the rentier mechanisms noted by Alfred McCoy in his essays in this volume. Economic might and political power have often proved to be mutually reinforcing, spinning an upward spiral of dynastic success. Yet those familial continuities frequently observable within the state apparatus—whether in the military or in the school system—exemplify nepotism more than so-called dynasticism. "Dynasties" survive as such over the generations by establishing a solid base in proprietary wealth that lies outside of the state apparatus and does not depend solely upon the ebb and flow of the family's political fortunes.

Where elective offices are linked not to proprietary wealth but to political machinery, illegal economic rackets, and violence, the limitations of dynasticism are clear. As in the criminal underworld, dynastic succession to political leadership in such settings is problematic and familial solidity unlikely. When political longevity is impressive, it bears witness not to the strength of a family dynasty but to the survival of a single big man recast as today's provincial "warlord" or urban "boss."

In this vein, the story of Cavite's Justiniano S. Montano, Sr., is exemplary, a clear case of both failed dynasty building and successful big man rule. For Montano remained the dominant figure in Cavite politics from 1935 until 1972 and served an almost uninterrupted tenure in the legislature from the birth of the Commonwealth until the onset of martial law. By the 1960s he had even installed three of his sons in positions of political and economic prominence. Yet in the end Montano was unable to establish the permanent base that would have left his family's preeminence intact. His story is thus revealing of both the obstacles to dynasty and the opportunities for big men evident in postwar Philippine politics.

Like the precolonial big man, Montano projected his own distinctive form of "prowess." He was a fearsome pugilist and an aggressive interloper who depended for his success not only on bluster, bravado, and bullying but on the persistent threat and use of violence. In the course of his career, Montano made headlines by brawling with rivals on the stairs of Cavite's Capitol Building and whipping out his .45 caliber revolver before fellow congressmen on the floor of the House of Representatives.[14] Though now retired and well into his eighties, the barrel-chested

Caviteño can still send a hapless interviewer reeling with one of his unintentionally powerful jabs or slaps on the back. Chuckling, he muses over the numerous fist fights and shouting matches that peppered his years in politics, admitting, with characteristic understatement, "I have no tact!"

As with the classic big man, violence was a crucial element in Montano's political success. In 1938 he personally administered a bloody beating to Cavite's acting provincial *fiscal*, Vicente Llanes, who had voiced opposition to the proclamation by the provincial board of canvassers of Montano's reelection in November of that year. Storming unannounced into Llanes's office, the newly reelected assemblyman destroyed the furniture, broke a chair over Llanes, and left, shouting, according to witnesses, "I'll kill you, damn you."[15] Montano also survived several assassination attempts, the first of which occurred only two days prior to his initial proclamation as assemblyman in 1935, and he was implicated in a series of political killings that spanned his entire career. While serving as a senator, for example, in 1952, he was imprisoned briefly following charges that he had masterminded the killing of the mayor of Maragondon, Severino Rillo, and several of his policemen. He was later linked to the 1965 slaying of Manuel Verzosa, a ranking clerk of the House Electoral Tribunal, who was reviewing an electoral protest against him. Over the course of his long tenure as Cavite's political kingpin, Montano faced repeated accusations of sponsoring election-related terrorism and of maintaining a so-called private army in the province.

In addition to political murders and instances of "warlordism," Montano was long associated with various criminal activities. In the late 1940s and 1950s, his Cavite entourage included notorious bandits, rustlers, highwaymen, and hired killers. Indeed, Cavite's most famous criminal—Leonardo Manecio, alias Nardong Putik—first emerged in the limelight as one of the assassins allegedly enlisted by Montano in 1952 for the so called Maragondon Massacre referred to above. In the 1960s, Montano was consistently linked to a major smuggling syndicate, while his sons were variously implicated in extortion, questionable real-estate deals, and rigged horse races and boxing matches.

"Big man" Montano projected "prowess" not only through violence but through skillful exploitation and manipulation of the law and of his position within a faction-ridden and eminently privatizable state apparatus. His considerable—and widely acclaimed—legal skills served him well in numerous court cases and in the halls of the legislature, while his well-placed connections allowed him to install countless protégés in customs, the courts, and other strategic branches of the bureaucracy. Moreover, like preceding and succeeding Cavite kingpins, Montano came to occupy the role of an intermediary, or broker, shuttling between national-level politicos in Manila, covetous of his province's votes, and the thuggish town mayors, gambling den operators, bandits, carnappers, and smugglers who dominated the political and economic landscape of Cavite. Montano's impressive longevity in Cavite politics thus depended on his ability to serve up the electorate to Manila politicos and to deliver patronage and protection to Cavite criminals using violence and state power as the essential resources for accomplishing both tasks. To this extent, at least, Montano's story parallels that of so-called provincial warlords in other parts of the country where the "commanding heights" of the local economy—illegal activities or transportation choke points rather than established concentrations of land and capital—may be monopolized through coercion and control over agencies of the state.

Yet Montano's career is instructive in its limitations as well as its longevity, for the finality of his political demise in 1972 is as revealing as his dramatic emergence as a provincial power broker in 1935. When compared to such seemingly permanent fixtures in Philippine politics as the Lopez and Osmeña clans, his failure to survive the Marcos era or to pass the Montano mantle to his progeny in dynasty form appears as noteworthy as his earlier success. In fact, his inability to propel himself beyond Cavite or to establish a more enduring foothold outside of the state machinery reflects the distinctive structure of Cavite's local political economy, revealing the importance of state power at the provincial level in the control of this suburban province's most precious prizes: its valuable lands and its extensive illegal economies. To understand the limitations of dynasty and the opportunities for modern-day big men in Cavite—and Philippine—politics, it is necessary to examine Montano and the evolving national and provincial context in which he emerged, flourished, and eventually fell.

Aguinaldo's Cavite: Inquilinos, Tulisanes, Caudillos (1895—1935)

The peculiar history of Cavite under Spanish rule and its central role in the Philippine Revolution decisively shaped the contours of the province's political landscape in the American and postwar periods. The early presence of Spanish ecclesiastical and military power established the close linkage in Cavite between access to the state bureaucracy and the accumulation of land and capital. In Cavite El Puerto (known today as Cavite City), which had long served as a major port of embarkation for merchant vessels, a Spanish naval station, arsenal, and shipyard encouraged the evolution of a wealthy and well-educated urban, proprietary, *ilustrado* class dominated by Chinese *mestizos*. By the late nineteenth century, the port had developed close communications and transportation links with nearby Manila, and its streets featured several churches, theaters, casinos, and government offices, as well as a large tobacco factory.[16] Urban proprietors drew considerable incomes from various commercial establishments in the port, served as contractors to the Spanish naval authorities, and acquired from the colonial state monopoly rights to the rich salt beds in the swampy areas along Cavite's extensive coastline.[17]

In inland Cavite, the predominant pattern of land ownership linked capital accumulation to the Spanish frailocracy. Divided among the Dominicans' *haciendas* in Naic and Santa Cruz de Malabon, the Augustinians' tracts in San Francisco de

Malabon and Rosario, and the Recollects' estate in Imus, property belonging to the monastic orders totalled well over thirty-five thousand hectares of prime land, which encompassed virtually all of settled Cavite by the end of the Spanish colonial era.[18] As scholars have noted, the size, extent, and economic significance of these friar estates effectively precluded the emergence of the dominant class of Chinese *mestizo* landowners found elsewhere in the archipelago during the nineteenth century.[19] Rather, the ascendant nineteenth-century elites in the towns of coastal and inland Cavite consisted of *inquilino* tenants, who subleased the friar lands to subtenant-cultivators, thereby garnering rentier profits sufficient to acquire such amenities as horse-drawn carriages and impressive stone houses for themselves, and expensive Manila educations for their offspring.

Significantly, the relative position of these *inquilino* elites depended on the degree of favor they enjoyed with the friars who administered the estates. According to the most comprehensive scholarly work published to date on Spanish Cavite,

> . . . the [friar] hacenderos controlling the estates gave favors to their Filipino paramours and relatives who became rich owing to the many lands and kataasan or loma (high level land suited for agriculture) available to them from the special relations, while those whom they hated were dispossessed of lands through mere whispers of servants, paramours and relatives.[20]

As generation succeeded generation, continued currying of the friars' affections served to secure the renewal of loyal families' *inquilino* contracts and to facilitate the expansion of these contracts to include larger tracts of rice and sugar land. For example, Mariano Paredes, son of a leading *inquilino* on the Recollects' Hacienda de Imus, is said to have "profited very much to be sure from the relationship that his father had with the parish priest of Imus, which friendship he continued to cultivate. In time he obtained more leaseholds on ricelands which were increasing in acreage."[21] Scions of leading *inquilino* families married among themselves, and, under the friars' careful scrutiny, competed in highly restricted elections for the local offices of *gobernadorcillo* (town mayor) and *cabeza de barangay* (*barangay* captain).[22] Paredes, for example, married his daughter Jacoba to a certain Guillermo Tirona, whose father —like Paredes himself— had served as *gobernadorcillo* of Imus and had acquired leaseholds on prime tracts of the town's rice fields.[23] Thus, by the end of the nineteenth century petty *inquilino* "dynasties" had emerged, the members of which occupied local political offices and held the lucrative contracts to Cavite's vast friar lands. These small-town clans were to dominate the political and economic lives of Cavite towns for years to come: the Aguinaldos of Cavite Viejo (Kawit); the Tironas and Topacios of Imus; the Cuencas of Bacoor; the Camposes of Dasmariñas; the Alvarezes of Noveleta; the Triases, Viniegras, and Ferrers of San Francisco de Malabon (today's General Trias); the Nazarenos of Naic; the Mojicas of Alfonso, Indang, and Mendez; and the Kiamsons of Silang.

Paralleling this process of class formation, Spanish rule over Cavite also spawned a tradition of predatory and "criminal" activities, such that by the end of the nineteenth century the province was known as *La madre de los ladrones,* the "mother of thieves." As the monastic orders—spurred by the opening of Philippine ports to international trade in the early 1800s—expanded their landholdings, intensified sugar cultivation, and supervised the erection of new towns in Cavite, the growth of Spanish "rule by law" expanded the province's "outlaw" sphere.[24] Preying on the wealthy *inquilino* families in the lowland towns, rustling cattle in upland pastures, and kidnapping sugar merchants en route to Manila, Cavite's bandits fled via various river networks to the coast or hid in the dense forests covering the Tagaytay Ridge that rose two thousand feet above sea level along the southern border of the province.[25]

Significantly, many of these outlaw elements operated in connivance with the local law-enforcement agencies of the colonial state, establishing the close connection between crime and politics that would endure in Cavite for years to come. Cattle-rustling gangs typically consisted of disgruntled former *cuadrilleros* (town policemen) or *cabezas de barangay* in cahoots with local officials, who facilitated the approval or forgery of documents required for the sale of livestock.[26] Regular elections for the positions of *cabeza de barangay* and *gobernadorcillo* created a "revolving door" of sorts, as the newly chosen town executives filled the ranks of the *cuadrilleros* with their clients. Those discharged often switched from duties as *pulisya* to escapades as *tulisanes* (bandits). In exceptional cases, banditry even proved an effective means of upward mobility within the ranks of the establishment: the famous *tulisan* Luis Parang was named *capitan de cuadrilleros* of Imus soon after his 1828 surrender and won election as the town's *gobernadorcillo* in 1834.[27] Similarly, the legendary Casimiro Camerino, whose gang of more than fifty men long operated out of the forests of Dasmariñas, was granted amnesty in 1869 and integrated into the provincial militia as a colonel and head of the Compania de Guias de la Provincia de Cavite.[28]

Against this backdrop of *inquilino* and *tulisan* ascendance, the mobilization by Emilio Aguinaldo of his "revolutionary" following in 1896 represented the first bid by a Caviteño for province-wide power. Aguinaldo's family had long held leaseholds on Recollect land in Cavite Viejo (Kawit) and his father and older brother had both served as *gobernadorcillo* of the town. Emilio himself won election in 1895 as *capitan municipal* (the new Spanish title for the *gobernadorcillo*) after serving for eight years as the *cabeza de barangay*.[29] It was from this vantage point of small-town economic and political prominence that he emerged at the helm of the Katipunan's recruitment drive in Kawit at the outbreak of the Philippine Revolution.

While the Spaniards shot thirteen of the wealthiest *ilustrados* of Cavite El Puerto in September 1896 in retaliation for their Masonic and Katipunan affiliations,[30] Aguinaldo was forming his "Revolutionary Government" in Imus from the ranks of Cavite's petty elite clans, drawing *inquilinos* and *tulisanes* alike into his following. In Kawit, he patched up family feuds between rival *inquilino* clans, rallied the forty *cuadrilleros* under his command, and invited the *tulisanes* who had long plagued the town to join his cause.[31] Expanding his political base through a network of friends and relatives, Aguinaldo filled his Cabinet with members of the prominent families of the northern towns that comprised the Recollects' Hacienda de Imus: Candido Tria Tirona of Kawit, Cayetano and Glicerio Topacio of Imus, and Felix Cuenca of Bacoor.[32] The young Aguinaldo also brought into the ranks of his army such scions of local dynasties based in other parts of the province as Placido Campos of Dasmariñas, Marcelino Aure of Mendez, Ambrosio Mojica of Indang, Gregorio Jocson of Naic, and Vito Belarmino of Silang. Occupying municipal offices and enjoying long-standing leaseholds on the friar lands, these Aguinaldo subordinates provided an ample base for further recruitment from among their client *cuadrilleros,* affiliated *tulisanes,* and subtenant farmers of more modest means and status.[33]

From its beginnings, the Revolution set the enduring pattern for the armed factional conflict and competition that would shape Cavite politics for decades to come, based as it was on rivalry between Aguinaldo and Tirona's Sangguniang Magdalo (Magdalo Council), located in Imus and Kawit, and the Alvarez family's Sangguniang Magdiwang (Magdiwang Council), centered in the neighboring town of Noveleta. Mariano Alvarez, *capitan municipal* of Noveleta and a relative by marriage of Katipunan supremo Andres Bonifacio, had drawn upon his own network of friends and relatives among Cavite's town elites, filling the Sangguniang Magdiwang with the likes of his sons Pascual and Santiago of Noveleta, Mariano Trias of Cavite El Puerto, Emiliano Riego de Dios of Maragondon, and Diego Mojica of Indang.[34] Thus, at the outbreak of the first phase of the Revolution, the Sangguniang Magdiwang claimed jurisdiction over the towns belonging to the Dominican and Augustinian estates stretching along the coast below Kawit and inland to the upland towns in the southern reaches of the province.[35] Aguinaldo's Sangguniang Magdalo, on the other hand, had a solid base on the Recollects' vast *haciendas,* which encompassed populous Kawit and Imus in the north as well as a broad swath of territory that extended east to Carmona and south towards Tagaytay Ridge to include Dasmariñas, Silang, and Mendez.[36] In the course of the Revolution the Magdalo faction subordinated its Magdiwang rivals, as Aguinaldo managed to eliminate Bonifacio and to establish himself, however briefly, as supreme *caudillo* throughout much of Luzon.

Following their much vaunted escapades as Aguinaldo's "revolutionary" lieutenants during this brief *caudillist* interlude, the scions of these petty Cavite "dynasties" whose forefathers had flourished as *inquilinos* and *gobernadorcillos* in the nineteenth century retreated to the familiar arena of small-town politics, triumphing handily in the highly restricted municipal elections held by the American colonial regime in 1901.[37] Moreover, those families that had held *inquilino* leaseholds on monastic lands in the province managed to acquire ownership rights to the same tracts they had previously subleased following the

American government's purchase of the friar estates and their subsequent sale to "previous tenants" by the corrupt Bureau of Lands.[38] Many such sales involved concessional, long-term, payment schedules and were financed by government loans, which more often than not remained unpaid for years.[39] Counting on the leniency of their friends in the Bureau of Lands or the intercession of legislators, many Cavite town notables retained ownership of lands they never paid for. As late as 1934 the accounts for some 1,350 lots covering nearly twelve thousand hectares remained in arrears.[40]

Control over municipal office facilitated not only acquisition of landholdings but also involvement in local criminal activity. By law, municipal *presidentes* (mayors) enjoyed complete discretion over the appointment and removal of municipal policemen, who thus, in the words of the director of the Philippine Constabulary in 1909, became mere "messengers, muchachos, and servants" of the towns' chief executives.[41] Pitted against these "agents of the law" were rogue elements of Aguinaldo's forces, who remained armed and at large after the General's capitulation in 1901, extorting cash and crops from the local population.[42] This state of "lawlessness" led to a harsh crackdown by the newly established colonial regime in Manila. In 1903 alone, some 173 Caviteños were convicted for banditry. A year later, the provincial jail was overflowing, draining provincial funds and forcing the transfer of prisoners to corrective facilities in Manila, the imposition of martial law on Cavite, and the postponement of elections until 1907.[43] Despite the American provincial authorities' vigorous campaign, the bandits enjoyed not just the connivance but the active sponsorship of leading local families. Cavite's provincial *fiscal* (state prosecutor) complained in 1909 of persistent intimidation of complainants and witnesses in cattle rustling cases by unnamed "influential persons in the province." As late as 1940 the situation remained essentially unchanged, with frequent reports of cattle thieves enjoying protection from municipal officials.[44]

Mayoral control over the police also tended to link municipal politics in Cavite with contests for control over the lucrative *jueteng* gambling racket, since the selective enforcement of statutes against these illegal and frequently rigged lotteries generated substantial sums of protection money. Philippine Constabulary sources throughout the American colonial period noted the involvement of municipal police in the protection of *jueteng* throughout the province, claiming in 1926 that weekly "hush money" payments were averaging one hundred pesos for a municipal *presidente*, fifty pesos for a chief of police, and five pesos each for policemen, stipends that dwarfed official government salaries.[45] Meanwhile, replacement of the Spanish arsenal with an American naval station transformed the former Cavite El Puerto into a renamed Cavite City, renowned for its brothels, cabarets, and gambling dens, a milieu that helped facilitate the smuggling of American-made firearms into the province.[46]

While small-town politics followed the patterns of the Spanish era, the transfer of provincial-level power into local hands under the Americans linked the fortunes of Aguinaldo's nascent political machine to the forces of the national government radiating out of Manila. In 1901 General Mariano Trias, a close associate of Aguinaldo, was appointed to the provincial governorship—and with American support elected to that post by Cavite's municipal executives a year later.[47] The declaration of martial law in Cavite in January 1904 led to the replacement of Trias with an American governor and the postponement of subsequent gubernatorial elections until 1907, while leaving provincial treasurer Daniel Tirona, the second Magdalo minister of war and younger brother of Aguinaldo's "cherished *compadre*" (*minamahal na kumpare*), Candido Tirona, rather fortuitously in place as the highest-ranking Filipino official in the province.[48]

As was the case in most of the Philippines, the elections of 1907 for governorships and seats in the Philippine Assembly marked the historic linkage of Cavite's municipal and provincial politics with Manila-centered, national-government patronage, wedding the revolutionary veteran-politicos of the province to the dominant Partido Nacionalista machine.[49] In February, former provincial secretary Leonardo Osorio, scion of what may have been the wealthiest family of Cavite El Puerto, won the governorship as the candidate of Manila-based Nacionalista Party leader Dominador Gomez, who reportedly selected Osorio and personally managed his campaign.[50] Opponents charged that Osorio's narrow victory—66 of a total of 117 votes—had been obtained at the price of thirty-five pesos per vote, and hinted that Gomez had sold his endorsement and campaign efforts to Osorio for a handsome sum.[51]

Prominent Manila journalist and attorney, Rafael Palma, who ran and won as the Nacionalista candidate for Cavite's seat in the Assembly in July 1907, had little need to resort to such tactics as the wide margin of his victory amply attested.[52] Renting a house in the province for a year to meet residency requirements, Palma found himself besieged with endorsements from all camps—from Ateneo classmate Governor Osorio, from former governor Mariano Trias, and from General Aguinaldo himself.[53] "My election was assured at the very start," Palma later remarked in his memoirs, noting that one of his opponents, Emiliano Tria Tirona of Kawit, a former student of his at the Escuela de Derecho, had even asked Palma's permission to run as a candidate, so that he might make a name for himself in politics.[54]

The outcome of the 1907 electoral contests in Cavite, brokered as they were between the kingpins of the province and Manila-based *ilustrado* politicians, constituted triumphs not just for the Nacionalista Party but for the Aguinaldo machine as well. Tirona was not only Palma's protégé but also the brother-in-law of Aguinaldo, having married Maria del Rosario, the younger sister of the General's wife.[55] In 1908, when Assemblyman Palma, one of the leaders of the Partido Nacionalista and a close associate of newly elected Assembly Speaker Sergio Osmeña, was named the first Nacionalista member of the Philippine Commission, he resigned from the legislature and endorsed Tirona, then president of the Nacionalista Committee of Kawit, in the ensuing special election.[56] The 1909 election to the provincial governorship of Nacionalista Tomas Mascardo, a Kawit-born revolutionary general commissioned by Aguinaldo, and also a close friend of Nacionalista leader Manuel Quezon, aptly complemented Tirona's reelection to the Assembly the same year.[57]

Subsequent years saw a break in this pattern of Nacionalista dominance as Tirona emerged as the acknowledged master of Cavite politics and a leading oppositionist to the Nacionalista regime. Twice reelected as the lone Cavite representative to the national legislature, and later serving two terms as senator from the Fourth Senatorial District, by the 1920s he was a leading light of the Democrata Party. Although the Democratas remained a small minority opposing the Nacionalista regime, at times they controlled crucial "swing" votes when the faction-ridden majority party was split.[58] Despite the Nacionalista Party's virtual monopoly on patronage, splits within the ruling bloc allowed Tirona and his Democrata machine to survive in Cavite. Thus the Democratas won both the Cavite governorship and the province's lone seat in the lower house of the legislature in 1922, 1931, and 1934, when the Nacionalista Party was most divided. Tirona's most successful protégé, Pedro Espiritu, twice won election to the legislature and twice more to the provincial governorship. Espiritu, whose Imus-based family subsequently won the franchise to supply electricity to Cavite's northern towns, happened to be the personal secretary of Tirona's brother-in-law and close associate, General Emilio Aguinaldo. Indeed, Tirona's status as Cavite's first "provincial kingpin" remained linked to Aguinaldo's Magdalo machine throughout the pre-Commonwealth period.

Tirona's political fortunes were closely entwined with—and in considerable measure dependent upon—the privileged position of Aguinaldo in the national political arena. As the preeminent *caudillo* of the Revolution and a hero of the struggle against the American invaders, Aguinaldo commanded considerable public attention. Through his leadership of the Association of the Veterans of the Philippine Revolution he maintained a following among some fifty thousand war veterans, whose ranks included prominent political figures scattered throughout Central and Southern Luzon.[59] In the 1920s, moreover, Aguinaldo's close relationship with American Governor General Leonard Wood afforded him considerable influence over executive appointments. Thus, Jose P. Melencio, the General's son-in-law, was appointed as representative for Cotabato in the legislature, and his law partner, A. G. Escamilla, was named delegate for Nueva Vizcaya. As one commentator noted:

> From the mere clerk job to the exalted office of appointive representative, the veterans' president had always utilized his influence to [*sic*] the Governor General. He was virtually responsible for the appointments of Christian Filipino representatives for non-Christian provinces. These were his own men. In the municipal board of the city of Manila, Aguinaldo has always a

look. In fact he has succeeded more than once in having some of his aides and trusted subordinates filled [*sic*] unoccupied seats in the council.[60]

Aguinaldo's relationship with Senate president and Nacionalista Party leader Manuel Quezon also worked to their mutual personal advantage. In 1920, for example, Quezon arranged for the passage of a bill providing the retired General with a generous pension of one thousand pesos per month.[61] More importantly, with Quezon's connivance, Aguinaldo had since 1908 occupied a broad swath of former friar land in the town of Dasmariñas without a contract, finally purchasing the tract in a public auction in 1927. Amounting to 1,185 hectares of prime sugar land, the estate was divided into sixty-nine lots to circumvent the limitation on individual purchases of public land to 144 hectares, through the use of various Aguinaldo children and grandchildren as "dummies" in the sale.[62] Moreover, the purchase was made on an installment basis, and over the years the General consistently welshed on his payments to the government. By 1934 he had paid less than 10 percent of the purchase price and an even smaller portion of the accumulating interest.[63] Bureau of Lands officials calculated in 1929 that the aging *caudillo* had managed to avoid paying well over half a million pesos by squatting on the land since 1908, and that he still owed more than half that amount in debts to government lending agencies.[64] While Quezon facilitated both legislative approval of the original transaction and executive laxity in the collection of Aguinaldo's interest payments, the General expressed his gratitude at crucial junctures, supporting Quezon in his formation of the Partido Nacionalista Colectivista in 1922 and in his opposition to the Hare-Hawes-Cutting Act in 1933.[65]

Yet Quezon was not content to rely solely on the General as his "man in Cavite" and also worked to promote the career of his close friend and fellow Nacionalista, Antero Soriano, who thus emerged as a latter-day Magdiwang counterforce to Aguinaldo's Magdalo machine. Soriano, a big-time gambler and Quezon crony who hailed from the southern coastal town of Tanza, won a seat on the board of directors of the Manila Railroad Company and through rigged auctions and two dummy corporations acquired extensive landholdings in his home town and in neighboring Naic.[66] In 1912, he won the Cavite governorship, to which he was reelected in 1916. In 1919 he defeated Tirona for the Fifth District senatorial seat, and in 1925 he won the special election for Cavite's seat in the House of Representatives after the death by natural causes of his protégé, Augusto Reyes. By 1926, Manila journalists were writing of a "Soriano Bloc" in the lower chamber of the legislature, a force that remained powerful until Soriano's death after a prolonged illness in 1929.[67] While protégés then serving as Cavite's governor and congressman were voted out in 1931, Soriano's recommendee for Cavite City mayor, Ramon Samonte, remained in this appointed post for several years after his mentor's death.

Overall, the electoral system installed by the American colonial regime preserved and enhanced the political power that Aguinaldo had amassed in the course of the Revolution. His followers, drawn primarily from among the Spanish-era, small-town elite clans, were quick to reassert control over the provincial apparatus, easily winning the highly restricted mayoral elections in the early years of American rule. As they had done under the Spaniards, they used their political influence to secure rights to land, and through mayoral control over the municipal police they continued to involve themselves in such criminal activities as cattle rustling, kidnapping, and banditry. Moreover, with the watchful friars gone, the mayors and their minions were free to participate as financiers, operators, or protectors of *jueteng* operations in their towns, especially if they enjoyed friendly relations with the provincial authorities.

With the removal of the friars and the linkage of municipal, provincial, and national politics in 1907, a new, previously unattainable niche of provincial-level power was created, one that promised considerable control over the "commanding heights" of Cavite's economy. With his Magdalo machine in place, Aguinaldo and his ally Tirona were perfectly positioned to occupy this niche and make it their own. For nearly three decades they did so, using their influence over the expanding Cavite electorate to establish ties with such national-level, Manila politicians as Rafael Palma, Leonard Wood, and Manuel Quezon, ties which themselves worked to enhance their hold over the province. Aguinaldo secured for himself a large monthly pension, the largest and richest tract of land in Cavite, and extensive privileges and patronage in Manila. His protégés, the congressmen and governors, enjoyed control over Cavite-bound pork barrel and handsome shares of the daily *jueteng* take while they cultivated their clients among the town mayors with whispered asides to the provincial *fiscal* and carefully penned notes to the director of the Bureau of Lands.

Yet, as Quezon's occasional rifts with Aguinaldo and his promotion of Soriano as a "spoiler" forewarned, this happy state of affairs depended heavily upon the maintenance of reciprocal—if not genuinely friendly—ties with powerful patrons in Manila. If Cavite's provincial kingpins challenged or otherwise antagonized the national-level powers, funds for road construction would dry up, lands would be confiscated, unsympathetic Constabulary officers and *fiscals* would be rotated to Cavite, and the loyalty of town mayors would fall into doubt. Such was the dynamic that would unravel Aguinaldo and Tirona's machine in 1935, paving the way for Montano's succession to the provincial throne.

Montano as Cavite Kingpin: The Early Years [1935–1945]

As the grandson of a revolutionary captain with Magdiwang and pro-Bonifacio sympathies, and as a Tanza-born townmate of the late Quezon man, Soriano, the young attorney Justiniano S. Montano was an appropriate challenger to Aguinaldo and Tirona's Magdalo hold on Cavite. Fresh out of the University of the

Philippines' College of Law, he placed second in the bar examinations of 1929 and was immediately rewarded by Cavite Governor Fabian Pugeda (a Nacionalista and Soriano protégé) with appointment as assistant provincial *fiscal* in his home province, an office created by Pugeda after Montano rejected his offer of service as justice of the peace in the southern town of Silang.[68] This position gave Montano a taste of provincial-level power, exposed him to the shady back-room deals that cemented "crime" and "politics," and allowed him to establish throughout Cavite a lasting reputation for his considerable legal skills. In 1932, however, he was forced to resign when Pugeda was succeeded as governor by Democrata Pedro Espiritu, the protégé of Aguinaldo and Tirona.

Despite this apparent setback, local political developments worked in Montano's favor. Since his election in 1931, Governor Espiritu had engaged in a highly publicized, though selective, campaign against provincial *jueteng* operations, perhaps prompted by fears that revelations about the involvement in *jueteng* of the governor of neighboring Laguna Province might lead to a similar scandal in Cavite.[69] Taking full advantage of his gubernatorial powers, Espiritu added a large number of "special agents" to the provincial payroll, suspended several hostile town mayors, and closed down small *jueteng* dens so that his wealthy ally, the notorious Cavite City "Jueteng King," Honorio Rojas, could expand his operations.[70] Montano, meanwhile, began a private law practice, defending the suspended mayors against Espiritu's accusations and taking on the election protest cases of Nacionalista candidates who had lost in the 1931 municipal contests.[71] Though Montano's 1934 bid for the governorship failed to unseat Espiritu, the latter's death in May 1935 left the office in the hands of Nacionalista provincial board member Ramon Samonte, a Montano supporter.[72] Thus Montano came to enjoy the support of several incumbent or former town mayors and an ally in the provincial capital, as well as a modest base in Tanza, where his family owned substantial landholdings, and in Naic, where his wife's clan, the Nazarenos, had long held sway.

A widening split between Aguinaldo and Quezon also guaranteed strong Nacionalista backing for Montano. In November 1934, Director of Lands Simeon Ramos, with the approval of Secretary of Commerce and Agriculture Eulogio Rodriguez, had issued an executive order revoking the sale of the sixty-nine lots to Aguinaldo and confiscating the estate in its entirety.[73] Subsequently, Aguinaldo and Tirona let it be known that previous understandings between the Democratas and the Nacionalistas that divided the spoils of office would no longer be honored.[74] In the spring of 1935, Aguinaldo announced his intention to run against Quezon in September for the presidency of the new Commonwealth. Having abandoned his strategy of appeasement, Quezon was no doubt eager to create real trouble for the General in his own bailiwick. Relying on the advice of his trusted aide and Cavite troubleshooter, former congressman Emilio P. Virata, Quezon eventually settled upon Montano as the Nacionalista Party's candidate for Cavite's Assembly seat in the September race against Democrata stalwart Emiliano Tria Tirona, counting on the young lawyer to draw some of the province's votes from the opposition camp.

He was not disappointed. After a tumultuous race during which Montano was frequently urged to withdraw, he beat Tirona by a respectable margin and held Aguinaldo's home-town lead over Quezon in Cavite to only 5,000-odd votes, thus helping the "gentleman from Tayabas" to his landslide victory over the aging General.[75] Montano, later hailed as the victorious Quezon's "savior" in Cavite, had clearly employed a fair share of "dirty tricks" to pull off such a coup on Aguinaldo's home turf.[76] For example, by the opposition's account, he had arranged the illegal registration of hundreds of voters in several Cavite towns.[77] More importantly, he overcame Tirona's threats of retribution against his supporters and did not fall victim to his opponent's notoriously unscrupulous tactics.[78] With Samonte standing guard over the canvassing of the votes in the provincial capital and a Constabulary that was clearly sympathetic to the Nacionalista ticket, Democrata attempts in at least seven towns to intimidate voters and election inspectors in favor of Aguinaldo and Tirona failed.[79] After the election, some seven hundred Aguinaldo-Tirona supporters massed in Kawit where they beat two Constabulary officers and threatened more violence.[80] Yet Montano survived a postelection ambush and assumed his seat in the Assembly.[81]

Anxious to defend his newly won position, Montano was quick to cement ties with Manila patrons who could help rig future contests in his favor. With Quezon's blessings, he successfully engineered the passage in the Assembly of a bill that provided for the subdivision and sale of all portions of the former friar estates "remaining undisposed of" and disqualified as purchasers all those—like Aguinaldo—who had previously been delinquent in payments for this land. Montano's bill, which Quezon approved in 1936, further facilitated the transfer of Cavite land from Aguinaldista to Montanista hands by retaining the original prices fixed when the plots were first offered for sale, by providing highly concessional installment schedules, and by offering preference to "bona fide occupants" at the discretion of Secretary of Agriculture and Commerce Benigno S. Aquino, Sr., who had taken Montano under his wing.[82] Montano also helped his ally Ramon Samonte to victory in the gubernatorial elections of 1937 and won official Nacionalista endorsement as the party's candidate in the 1938 elections for the Assembly. Here he enjoyed the backing of his mentor, Aquino, who as Nacionalista campaign manager had a virtually free hand in the choice of the party's candidates for the legislature.[83] Montano's Aguinaldista opponents regrouped, however, joining forces with Aquino's rivals in the Nacionalista Party to support Manuel Rojas, son of the famous "Jueteng King" and owner of substantial properties in Cavite City, coconut lands in Silang, and salt beds and fishponds along the provincial coast.[84] Yet what Rojas had in "gold" Montano matched in "goons," and the latter's election-day ballot-snatching activities won him the Assembly seat by a slim margin.[85]

Aquino's enemies in Manila continued to work against Montano, however, forcing him to resign his seat just a year after the election. By this time Quezon's declining health was keeping rival camps in the Nacionalista leadership jockeying for position in anticipation of the 1941 presidential elections. Thus, cabinet secretaries Manuel Roxas (Finance), Rafael Alunan (Interior), and Aquino (Agriculture and Commerce) were angling against Assembly Speaker Jose Yulo and his partner Majority Floor Leader Quintin Paredes. In a ploy to undermine Aquino, Yulo and Paredes schemed to oust his protégé Montano in favor of Rojas, allegedly encouraged by a bribe of several thousand pesos paid by the "Jueteng King" to the financially strapped Paredes.[86] Acting on an election protest filed by Rojas and on assault charges mounted against Montano by Acting Provincial Fiscal Llanes, Yulo directed the Assembly's Committee on Interior Government to conduct an investigation of the 1938 election. In October 1939 the Electoral Commission ruled in Rojas's favor, awarding him Cavite's lone Assembly seat while finding Montano "guilty of disorderly conduct, of dereliction [*sic*] of a public trust, an act that incapacitates him and makes him unworthy to continue in his position as Member of the National Assembly."[87] Though Montano resigned before the committee recommended his expulsion, the Assembly passed—at Yulo's request—a motion condemning the young legislator's behavior.[88]

Simultaneously, Yulo moved to undermine Montano's fragile grip on Cavite's electoral machinery, asserting his right under the Election Code as president of the Nacionalista party and chairman of its governing body to recommend the appointment of new election inspectors representing his party in that province.[89] Secretary of the Interior Rafael Alunan—an Aquino ally—argued against this, asserting his department's supervisory role over the boards of election inspectors.[90] Ignoring this gesture, Yulo named newly proclaimed Assemblyman Manuel Rojas the Nacionalista Party's representative in Cavite, with full authorization to propose election inspectors, thus encouraging him to replace the protégés of Montano and of Governor Samonte with his own henchmen.[91] When Rojas, acting on Yulo's instructions, allowed three sympathetic mayors to install their own flunkies as inspectors, Samonte responded by suspending the three mayors and replacing them with Montano loyalists—a move affirmed by Secretary Alunan who ruled that the original, pro-Montano inspectors would remain.[92]

After a period of heated public debate, President Quezon intervened, suspending Samonte briefly (on the pretext that he had acted on his own and without Alunan's approval), along with the three mayors, but allowing Montano's men to stay on as Nacionalista election inspectors.[93] This stand-off in Cavite persisted up to the beginning of World War II. Samonte lost to Luis Ferrer (backed by Rojas and the Yulo-Paredes faction) in the gubernatorial race of 1940 but Montano recaptured his Assembly seat (although Tirona won election to the Senate) the following year. Both the Montano-Samonte combine and the rival machine of Rojas, Ferrer, and eventually Tirona, operated within the confines of the Nacionalista Party, with Quezon professing neutrality even as various cliques and cabals around him intervened on one or the other Cavite faction's behalf.[94] In this early period of Montano's career, his political survival remained conspicuously dependent upon the ebb and flow of national-level, factional politics and the sponsorship of Manila leaders like Alunan and Aquino.

Ties to patrons in the national government also kept Montano "afloat" politically during the Japanese occupation of the Philippines from 1942 to 1945. While Aguinaldo and Tirona served as ranking members of the puppet regime in Manila, and their protégé Ferrer remained in place as governor of Cavite, Montano won an early appointment as mayor of Cavite City. This he achieved through the good graces of his mentor Aquino (who had been appointed commissioner of the interior by the Japanese in January 1942) and as a result of the impressions he made upon Japanese officers in Cavite.[95] Given Cavite's proximity to military headquarters in Manila and its strategic importance for naval operations, the province was closely supervised by the Japanese Military Police, making collaboration a far more attractive option than resistance, especially in Cavite City where the Japanese Naval Yard and the provincial headquarters of the Military Police were located.[96] As one historian of the Japanese occupation of Cavite has noted, "only limited guerrilla activities were conducted during the period 1942–1944. These activities included sabotage and harassment of Japanese posts and sentries and the infiltration of town government positions."[97] Montano skillfully balanced his position as Cavite City mayor with friendly ties to the "guerrillas" operating in the vicinity, offering them food, supplies, and other forms of assistance.[98] By late 1944, sensing the impending American invasion, he had distanced himself from the Japanese, establishing close contact with various "guerrilla" groups and relinquishing his municipal position.

The absence of a unified resistance movement in Cavite prevented Montano's postwar displacement by guerrilla leaders emerging during the war. By the end of 1942, more than a dozen self-proclaimed guerrilla groups had emerged in Cavite but most were engaged in purely predatory activities, warring among themselves in bandit fashion for control over roads and turf that could be "taxed" for cash, produce, and labor.[99] By the time of the province's liberation, in February 1945, three groups held most of Cavite under their control: the Fil-American Cavite Guerrilla Forces under Mariano Castañeda (who served as provincial governor from May to December of 1944), Patricio Erni's Guerrillas (named after its leader, a notorious bandit), and the Mag-irog Unit led by Magno Iruguin, a former policeman in the town of General Trias.[100] Each group, consisting of two to four hundred armed men, had several towns firmly in its clutches while it squabbled with the rival bands for other municipalities.[101]

At first glance, it appears that Montano found his political position preserved, if not enhanced, at the time of Cavite's liberation in February 1945. Aguinaldo and Tirona's high-profile participation in Laurel's puppet government did little to enhance their postwar political credentials in Manila, and Tirona's flight to northern Luzon in early 1945, and subsequent imprisonment at the hands of American counterintelligence, exacted its cost on his health, although he remained in the Senate until his death in 1952. Montano had maintained friendly relations with the Mag-Irog Unit and with notorious guerrilla bandit Patricio Erni and his band in Tanza and Amadeo, which, upon liberating Cavite City, installed

Montano's trusted ally Ramon Samonte as mayor.[102] With his contacts in Manila—including his close friend Defense Secretary Tomas Cabili—and his legendary legal skills, Montano proved a useful patron to Cavite "guerrilla" leaders seeking recognition and USAFFE back pay or fighting charges of wartime killings and other misdeeds. Montano also had an ally in Mariano Castañeda, who temporarily reassumed the governorship of Cavite during Osmeña's brief presidency and later served as Military Police provost marshal general under Roxas.[103] Yet in the early postwar years Montano found his aspirations to dominance over Cavite thwarted by a ruthless rival, the heir apparent to Aguinaldo's Kawit-Imus-based machine, Dominador Camerino.

Montano and the Camerino Challenge: Roxas to Garcia (1946–1961)

A descendant of legendary nineteenth-century bandit Casimiro Camerino and revolutionary colonel Lucas Camerino, Imus-born Dominador Camerino was a home-grown heir to Cavite's *tulisan* tradition and to Aguinaldo's Magdalo machine. An up-and-coming flunky in the prewar Aguinaldo-Tirona entourage, with only a fourth-grade education, Camerino had served first as a *barrio* captain (1928–31), then as mayor of Imus from 1931 until 1941, when he won a seat on the provincial board. Opponents during the late prewar years linked Camerino to the lucrative *jueteng* racket and to a number of kidnapping cases.[104] Under the Japanese occupation, he remained a provincial board member until December 1944 when he assumed the governorship following Mariano Castañeda's supposed flight to the hills to lead the resistance. Though displaced by the return of Castañeda as Cavite governor in early 1945, under Osmeña, Camerino returned to power as the new governor appointed by the Roxas administration in 1946. He immediately replaced with his own protégés all Cavite town mayors earlier appointed by Osmeña on Montano's recommendation, in the process handing perennial Montano foe Manuel Rojas the powerful Cavite City mayorship.

As in the years after the Revolution, there was an upsurge in violence and criminality in the aftermath of the Second World War.[105] The Japanese occupation and guerrilla resistance had left an estimated three to five thousand firearms still in the province.[106] Resistance groups of dubious reputation "liberated" the towns and for months thereafter fought among themselves over turf.[107] Bandits, rustlers, and highway robbers were said to hold "undisputed sway" in many areas, while kidnappers held even the provincial *fiscal* for ransom.[108] Manila dailies featured stories detailing a seemingly endless stream of murders and robberies in Cavite towns.[109]

As Casimiro Camerino had done eighty years earlier, the new Governor Camerino mixed crime and politics to his personal advantage, relying on strong-arm tactics to guarantee his hold on provincial power. After the 1946 elections, he released highway robbers and other outlaws jailed during the early "liberation" period and employed them as policemen and "special agents."[110] Bandits held in the provincial jail in Cavite City escaped under suspicious circumstances in late October 1947, making themselves available to assist in Camerino's successful campaign for the governorship that November.[111] On the campaign trail, Camerino supplemented a legendary "common touch" with a brash display of muscle. As a military intelligence agent noted in October, "In every political meeting that Camerino holds in the different towns of Cavite province, he has with him from two to three truckloads of men armed with rifles of different kinds, pistols, and revolvers."[112] Moreover, Camerino used his protégé mayors' powers of appointment to build a standing private army. One commentator remarked that "Governor Camerino kept his municipal police forces well armed besides an army of special agents who are all loyal to him."[113] Thus armed, Camerino easily won election to the governorship in 1947 and reelection in 1951, while his protégés captured fourteen of the province's nineteen elective mayorships in 1947 and sixteen in 1951.

Knowing well how to play the game, Camerino deployed his coercive resources not only to ensure his own election, and that of "his" mayors, but to deliver votes to his Liberal Party patrons in Malacañang. In the 1946 presidential race, he helped to secure Roxas a margin of twenty-seven thousand votes over Osmeña in Cavite, and in 1949 he instigated a virtual "reign of terror," which guaranteed a thirty-nine-thousand-vote lead for Quirino over Laurel. Numerous reports detailing the intimidation of Cavite voters, Nacionalista election inspectors, and Nacionalista candidates appeared in the Manila papers, and an investigation soon proved that on average twenty thousand fraudulent votes had been manufactured in the province for each of the Liberal Party's senatorial candidates.[114] According to the Nacionalista Party's subsequent petition for annulment of the 1949 Cavite election results, Camerino and his armed special agents had threatened violence to local Nacionalista leaders, assaulted those who continued to campaign, and on election day drove Nacionalista voters from the polls at gunpoint, ordering election inspectors to enter returns favorable to Quirino's Liberal Party.[115] November 1953 found Camerino again doing battle on Quirino's behalf. His "armed goons and special agents roamed around the barrios," a later court decision noted, and "in some instances went from house to house, [and] threatened the leaders and adherents of the opposition against voting on election day," warning them "to stay home if they wish[ed] to remain alive."[116]

Roxas and Quirino amply rewarded Camerino's services on their behalf with patronage and special favors. They acceded to Camerino's recommendations for successive provincial military commanders, *fiscals*, and treasurers as well as for the relevant district engineers and division superintendents of schools.[117] Moreover, under both Roxas and Quirino, the appointed position of Cavite City mayor was awarded to various members of the Rojas family, thus placing anti-Montano forces at the helm of Cavite's most populous and prosperous municipality. Control over Cavite City, home to the U.S. Naval Station at Sangley Point, oiled Camerino's emerging machine with regular collections extorted from the town's brothels, cabarets, and gambling dens. Pork barrel supplemented protection money to guarantee a considerable "war chest": Camerino's 1947–51 term as governor saw the construction of some three million pesos worth of public works projects, while the release of P150,000 ("for the construction of barrio schools") in late October 1951 and of P500,000 (from the road and bridge improvements fund) in mid-1953 funded vote-buying blitzes in the November elections of those two years.[118]

Against Camerino's well entrenched machine, Montano countered with his own display of local "muscle," relying on a rough band of ex-mayors, guerrilla leaders, and former policemen. Typical of these protégés were Artemio Quion, a town police chief dismissed in 1946 who took up cattle rustling and banditry, and Martin Torres, a former town mayor whose band of one-time guerrillas regularly attacked Batangas-bound buses passing through Cavite in the early postwar years.[119] Political competition grew exceedingly violent. In the last two months of 1946, alone, the Camerino-Montano feud left seven dead.[120] The following year, while campaigning with bodyguards and supporters in the town of Maragondon, Montano and his candidate for governor clashed with town police led by Mayor Patrocinio Gulapa, a Camerino man, leaving four dead and others wounded.[121] In February of 1949, Gulapa was fatally shot in a cockpit in the town of Noveleta, followed several months later by Bailen mayor Hugo Beratio, another Camerino Liberal, who fell to hostile gunfire in the town plaza.[122] In September 1952, Gulapa's successor in Maragondon, Severino Rillo, was kidnapped and stabbed to death along with the Maragondon chief of police and several of his officers, all Camerino men.[123] Dubbed the Maragondon Massacre, this incident led to a protracted court case in which Senator Montano—along with several of his protégés and alleged hired gun Leonardo Manecio (alias Nardong Putik)—was accused of the killing. During the November 1953 election campaign, Bacoor vice-mayor Eduardo Ocampo, Jr., and four of his henchmen, also Camerino Liberals, suffered a similar fate to that of their counterparts in Maragondon.[124] All told, five Cavite town mayors and eight municipal police chiefs lost their lives to assassins' bullets in the tumultuous decade following World War II.

Having recaptured the province's lone seat in the House of Representatives in 1946, Montano supplemented this frontal assault in Cavite with back-room maneuvers in Manila. Though officially a Liberal, he pitted Nacionalista Lamberto Javalera, whose brief postwar stint as Manila chief of police had ended amid considerable scandal,[125] against Camerino in the 1947 gubernatorial race, no doubt hoping that Javalera's close relationship with General Mariano Castañeda, the Roxas-appointed Military Police Command provost marshal, would vitiate the advantages enjoyed by Camerino as the appointed incumbent.[126] While Javalera lost to Camerino by over nineteen thousand votes, Montano's dalliance with the opposition soon paid off. Two years later, when Quirino and Camerino nominated long-time Montano rival Manuel Rojas as the administration's candidate for Montano's House seat, Montano landed himself a spot on the Liberal Party's 1949 senatorial slate by promising to keep Cavite solidly pro-Quirino, despite its vulnerability to penetration by Nacionalista presidential candidate Jose Laurel, a native son of the neighboring province of Batangas.

Yet this pre-election deal, brokered in mid-1949 by Quirino Liberal Party president and general manager Eugenio Perez,[127] failed to keep the irrepressible Montano from his old tricks: though a Liberal senatorial candidate, he crossed party lines to back his law partner and protégé, Nacionalista candidate Jose T. Cajulis, a former Cavite provincial *fiscal*, against Rojas for the House seat. Camerino engineered a wide margin for Quirino over Laurel in Cavite, and Rojas easily defeated Cajulis, but Montano, having won a Senate seat, quickly turned the tables. Soon after his election, he began to attack the Quirino administration, joining his close friend Senator Tomas Cabili and several other Liberal senators to form a bloc known as the "Little Senate." The Senate Blue Ribbon Committee, which Montano established, began to investigate growing allegations of graft and corruption in the new Liberal government, and its exposures caused the president and his entourage considerable embarrassment.[128] Exasperated, Quirino offered Montano a cabinet position as secretary of labor but the wily Caviteño refused, keeping his distance from the increasingly unpopular administration.[129] Thus, while Camerino solidified his base in Cavite—winning reelection in 1951 by a twenty-five-thousand-vote margin and securing sixteen of the province's nineteen mayorships for his men—Montano positioned himself well in Manila, poised to follow Defense Secretary Ramon Magsaysay into the Nacionalista camp.

When Quirino went down in defeat in 1953, so did Camerino. His well-publicized promises and threats had failed to win his Malacañang patron a victory over Magsaysay in Cavite, nor did his efforts on Quirino's behalf stand him in good stead with the new Nacionalista administration. Though Liberal candidate Manuel Rojas was proclaimed in November as the winner of the provincial congressional race, the slim margin of victory allowed Montano protégé Jose Cajulis—after an election protest convened before the now Nacionalista-controlled House Electoral Tribunal—to capture the seat in the end. Similarly, by early 1954 Montano had been cleared of the charge of having masterminded the Maragondon Massacre, which had led to his arrest in late September of 1952.[130] Camerino soon found himself on trial for a series of crimes, most notably the 10 November 1953 killing of Jacinto Morales, son of a Nacionalista leader in Bacoor.[131]

Magsaysay moved quickly to reward Montano for his support in the 1953 elections. Camerino was suspended in 1954 and replaced with a Montano protégé who proceeded to fire the governor's three hundred provincial guards and "special agents" and to harass recalcitrant pro-Camerino mayors with suspensions and court cases.[132] Montano's protégés won appointment to the Tagaytay City mayorship and to the positions of mayor, chief of police, and city *fiscal* in Cavite City. Well-publicized closings of brothels, raids on illegal gambling dens, round-ups of unregistered jeepneys, and "mass screenings" of resident Chinese followed in Cavite City, thinly veiled mechanisms for extorting higher rates of protection money for

In June 1949, Cavite congressman Justiniano Montano addresses the Liberal Party (Quirino Wing) convention at the Sta. Ana Cabaret in Manila.

In the years following World War II, many Cavite villages had impressive arsenals of U.S. infantry weapons. Photographed in August 1959, Unit No. 3 of the "Society for Peace and Progress" of Barrio Bayan Luma, Imus, was organized by the Constabulary's provincial commander. This proliferation of arms contributed to endemic electoral violence in Cavite that required a military presence to maintain order. In November 1961, for example, troops of the 20th Battalion Combat Team were on duty at Imus while Congressman Justiniano Montano was running for reelection.

Senator Justiniano Montano (in cowboy hat, with cigar), photographed on the steps of the Cavite provincial capitol.

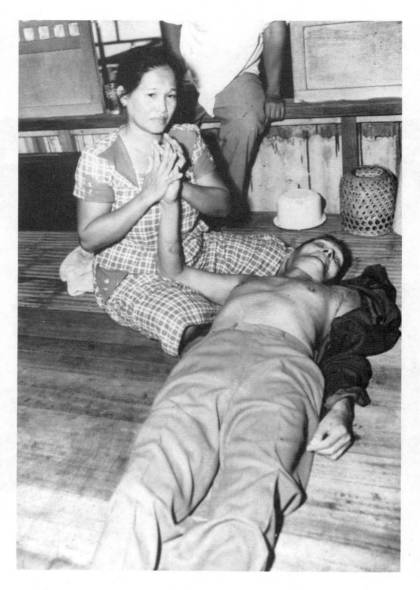

Corpse of a campaign worker murdered during the November 1953
elections in Cavite Province.

Famous Cavite bandit Leonardo Manecio ("Nardong Putik") photographed shortly after his capture in 1958–59. His shirt is open to show tattoos that, in combination with a magical medallion, reputedly rendered him invulnerable to bullets. The amulets proved ineffective, for in October 1971 he was shot by agents of the National Bureau of Investigation. After escaping from Muntinglupa Prison in October 1969, in order to avoid an assassin reportedly hired by Senator Justiniano Montano, Manecio had operated in Cavite for two years, regaining much of the local influence that he had enjoyed before his incarceration.

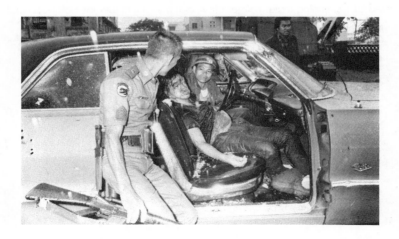

At the Cavite Province convention of the Nacionalista Party in August 1971, legendary smuggler Lino Bocalan (second from left) is proclaimed the candidate for provincial governor and former governor Dominador Camerino (third from left) is confirmed as his running mate. Former provincial board member Jose Nolasco and Manuel Paredes (far left and far right) hold up the candidates' hands.

Montano's "boys."[133] The Rojas family was forced to cough up eighty-eight thousand pesos in "amusement taxes" on its two cinema houses after passage of a city ordinance imposed a tax on such establishments.[134]

Magsaysay "gifts" combined with these key appointments to prepare Montano's emerging machine for the November 1955 local elections. Malacañang released two million pesos in pork barrel funds for improvements to government highways and waterworks in Cavite in the summer of 1955, thus providing substantial liquid funds for vote buying and other campaign expenses.[135] Magsaysay also signed into law a bill sponsored by Montano that transferred the provincial capital from Cavite City to "Trece Martires City," formerly a sleepy inland *barrio* in Tanza largely owned by the Montano family. The relocation of the Capitol Building and other provincial offices to this unlikely site raised the value of the Montanos' land from twenty-five to fifty centavos per square meter according to well-informed sources.[136] Moreover, according to the bill's provisions the provincial governor would serve as ex-officio mayor of Trece Martires, thus enjoying discretion over the appointment of the municipal police force and considerable insulation from public scrutiny in his administration of the province's affairs.

Thus fortified by Magsaysay, Montano's emerging machine went on to defeat Camerino in the mayoral and gubernatorial elections in November 1955. The Commission on Elections (Comelec) placed the municipal police forces of sixteen of Cavite's nineteen towns under the control of the Philippine Constabulary (PC), conveniently leaving only Montano's strongholds free from supervision.[137] Thwarted by this neutralization of his armed following, Camerino was unable to recoup through strong-arm tactics in Cavite the considerable losses he had suffered in Manila under Magsaysay. With the provincial returns tallied in the secluded new Capitol Building under the watchful gaze of Montano protégés, Camerino was powerless to intervene. He lost the governorship to Montano's son, Delfin, while his loyal Liberal mayoral candidates went down in defeat in all but seven municipalities. A year later Camerino was back in Bilibid prison serving the first months of a long sentence for his role in 1953 election "terrorism." In Cavite his once monolithic machine lay idle, deprived of Manila support.

Yet the death of Magsaysay in 1957 and the ascension to the presidency of Vice-President Carlos Garcia revived the perennial challenger to Montano's hold over Cavite. By the end of January 1957, Camerino was a free man, pardoned by Garcia at the urging of the new president's son-in-law, Caviteño Fernando C. Campos, whose Dasmariñas-based clan had long supported Aguinaldo's, then Camerino's, Imus-Kawit machine.[138] Moreover, Nacionalista Party leaders decided against renaming Montano to their 1957 senatorial slate, and, when Montano nudged Cajulis to step aside and let him retake Cavite's seat in the House, his former protégé proved recalcitrant and joined forces with Camerino and Campos. Yet, with most of the mayors in his camp and the provincial Constabulary command on his side, Montano defeated Cajulis handily.[139] Two years later his son Delfin won reelection to the Cavite governorship, defeating Camerino by a slim margin, while pro-Montano mayors were elected in twelve of the nineteen municipalities.

With Garcia's support and encouragement, Camerino and Campos strove to unseat Montano in the November elections of 1961. Campos, who announced his own candidacy for Montano's House seat in the summer of that year, arranged for Malacañang to freeze funds for Cavite projects and managed to obtain Nacionalista designation of the province as a "free zone."[140] This arrangement allowed him to name half of the Nacionalista election inspectors while his ally Camerino appointed those representing the Liberal Party, leaving Montano with sympathetic poll-watchers in only half of Cavite's precincts.[141] Moreover, Campos intrigued to insure that the Philippine Constabulary's provincial command in Cavite would be sympathetic to his bid for Montano's seat.[142] The Montanos later charged that Constabulary forces in Cavite failed to provide security in "critical areas," ignored violence and intimidation exercised by armed men in Campos's employ, and even participated in election-day terrorism and fraud.[143] More specifically, the pro-Montano mayor of Tagaytay City asserted that PC Rangers assigned to insure peaceful elections in his municipality had actually kept some two thousand voters from casting their ballots.[144]

Against this Garcia-supported cabal Montano deployed the resources of the provincial government, reaping the benefits of having installed his son Delfin as governor. On election day Governor Montano unleashed more than four hundred armed "special agents" (ignoring the PC chief's order that they surrender their firearms), while the provincial board of canvassers reviewed returns in the Capitol Building under his watchful eye.[145] In many precincts Montano's protégé mayors and their armed henchmen allegedly "accompanied, followed, watched, assisted and/or prepared the ballots of the registered voters inside the voting booths during the voting," such that a handwriting expert later testified that over 8,800 ballots had been "prepared in groups, each group by one hand, or ballots each written by two or more persons."[146] By such means the elder Montano managed to retain his House seat while delivering Cavite to the victorious Liberal Party presidential candidate, Diosdado Macapagal, by a whopping 33,000-vote margin.[147] Having survived four years of an unfriendly administration, Montano once again could count on the advantages accompanying the installment in Malacañang of a president sympathetic and politically indebted to him.

Montano Entrenched, Montano Dislodged: The "Octopus" (1962-1972)

Justiniano Montano—or "Tatang," as he had come to be known—reaped the spoils of victory with gusto. Soon after Macapagal assumed the presidency in January 1962, Montano won election as House majority floor leader (as a resurrected Liberal), thus increasing his share of pork barrel allotments, his quota of appointees, and his cut of grease money from lobbyists interested in the success or demise of bills under consideration by the legislature. The new president also appointed Montano's youngest son, Justiniano, Jr.—a boxing enthusiast and horse breeder—as chairman of the powerful Games and Amusements Board (GAB), the government agency charged with the supervision of horse racing, jai alai, and boxing. As GAB chairman, the younger Montano was later implicated in match rigging, race fixing, toleration of illegal betting, and the management of boxers through "dummies" for his personal profit.[148] More importantly, Delfin Montano won reelection to the governorship in 1963, this time by a margin of more than thirty-six thousand votes, while Liberal candidates beholden to the Montanos swept into sixteen of the nineteen traditional mayoralties and captured two newly established offices in Cavite City and Tagaytay City. Camerino, sensing the futility of another gubernatorial bid, retreated to the safety of his bailiwick, settling for the mayorship of Imus. Even in this stronghold he found himself embattled, with policemen loyal to the former mayor refusing to heed his orders.[149]

Meanwhile, Montano's entrenched position in Cavite and enhanced stature in the national arena offered him unprecedented opportunities for personal economic advancement in the early 1960s, as nearby Manila's industrial and demographic growth increased the value of Cavite property. The Montanos' discretionary powers over the disposition of public land in Cavite provided the family substantial opportunities for profit, as the controversy surrounding the Manila Bay Reclamation Project suggested. Congressman Montano, in fact, sponsored the 1958 bill to extend Manila's Dewey Boulevard (now Roxas Boulevard) to Cavite City, allowing private contractors to reclaim some twenty-five hundred hectares of foreshore land along Manila Bay and then sell the property at a considerable profit. Yet by 1959 he had grown antagonistic towards the efforts of the Republic Real Estate Corporation (representing powerful Manila politicians and American businessman Harry Stonehill) to sign contracts with various municipalities in the Manila-Cavite City belt, perhaps disappointed with his share of the lucre. Delfin Montano demonstrated considerable creativity in thwarting the RREC deal, first engineering a publicity stunt that exposed Stonehill's efforts to bribe him in exchange for approval of the reclamation project and later invoking various legal technicalities and threatening a lawsuit.[150] These antics served as a clear warning to prospective real-estate moguls—those interested in "developing" Cavite's suburban properties must keep the Montanos' interests in mind.

With the provincial government under Delfin's thumb and Cavite's congressional pork barrel allocations in his own hands, Montano literally paved the way for his son Ciriaco's successful management of the family's expanding real-estate investments. Receiving generous support from the national government's Home Financing Corporation and other government agencies and financial institutions, the family investments in Cavite certainly prospered. With Ciriaco at the helm, Montano-controlled companies developed real estate for subdivisions in northern suburbs of the expanding Manila metropolis, while hundreds of hectares of tracts in the south of the province were bought and converted to agro-business, including a piggery and two thousand hectares of sugar land.[151] In the name of "progress" and "the development of Cavite," Congressman Montano and his son the governor pushed the selective expansion of roads and public works, insuring rapid appreciation of the value of these properties.

While his control over state discretionary powers facilitated this real-estate bonanza in inland Cavite, Montano's grip on state coercive resources secured him considerable benefits from the booming illegal economy centered on the extensive northwestern coastline of the province along Manila Bay. By the late 1950s, Tanza, Montano's home town and stronghold, had emerged as the key port for the smuggling of foreign "blue-seal" cigarettes and other goods from Borneo, thanks to the town's location and its superior "natural anchorage facilities."[152] According to government documents that surfaced in 1964, an average of twenty-four hundred cases of blue-seal cigarettes—yielding six hundred thousand pesos in profits—arrived monthly on Tanza's shores, along with substantial quantities of firearms, ammunition, gunpowder, and perfume.[153] Tanza thus benefited handsomely from the Philippine government's efforts, since the 1950s, to promote the local tobacco industry through subsidies and restrictions on the importation of foreign cigarettes. Capipisa, one of the town's coastal *barrios*, became famous for its plush residences and paved streets, sponsored largely by *barrio* resident Lino Bocalan. This "modest fisherman" turned millionaire also came to own homes in Makati's exclusive Urdaneta Village and in San Francisco, California, and he enjoyed a police escort when he drove through Cavite in his Mercedes Benz.[154]

Though based in Tanza, these smuggling operations evolved into an economy of considerable scale—a veritable "octopus"—entailing transport to and from Cavite as well as distribution and marketing in Manila, and involving officials at all levels of government. While a syndicate of smugglers in Cavite, Sulu, and Zamboanga financed and provided transport for the shipment of the contraband goods, and local procurers handled distribution in Manila, "protection" rested essentially in Montano hands. The Montanos, who had allegedly forced themselves on the smugglers, used their political power to guarantee "selective" antismuggling efforts on Cavite's shores and roads and to secure the release of confiscated goods and apprehended syndicate members.[155] Position within the state apparatus determined the division of labor between father and son. The efforts of Governor Montano insured local police cooperation. His father, as House majority floor leader, Macapagal ally, and long-time chum of Defense Secretary Macario Peralta, Jr., enjoyed ample access to the military establishment and considerable influence over the assignment of military officers to his home province. Hush money supplemented career concerns to guarantee military cooperation: the smuggling syndicate's payroll included substantial monthly "salaries" for such Constabulary officials as the Second Zone chief, the provincial commander in Cavite, and ranking officers of the Criminal Investigative Service.[156] In exchange for such compensation, various military units not only turned a blind eye to the syndicate's smuggling operations but in fact made available the coercive resources of the state for use in the policing and enforcement of the syndicate's monopoly against potential competitors.

While profits from this smuggling racket—useful for meeting vote-buying and other election-related expenses, or recyclable through real-estate investments—strengthened Montano's political and economic position in Cavite, they also pitted him against powerful forces in the national arena. By 1964, the volume of blue-seal cigarettes smuggled into the country was estimated by government sources to be averaging seventy thousand cases a month. With fifty cartons in a case, and each carton worth at least ten pesos, by conservative estimates this racket comprised an economy of well over four hundred million pesos a year, an empire that no one provincial politico could hope to claim for himself.[157] Moreover, a combination of the continued availability of foreign cigarettes and the low quality of locally grown leaf spelled the death of the heavily subsidized, Ilocos-based, infant tobacco industry. By 1964, the Philippine Virginia Tobacco Administration (PVTA)—the government's corrupt tobacco monopoly/monopsony agency—was effectively bankrupt, having incurred well over three hundred million pesos in debts to the Central Bank, and millions of pesos worth of unmarketable, low-quality tobacco were rotting away in PVTA *bodegas*.[158] Parties with a vested interest in the tobacco industry's survival began to fight for the destruction of the Cavite-centered smuggling empire.

Thus the Montanos inevitably found themselves at odds with powerful Ilocano politicians whose economic and political fortunes were closely linked to the tobacco industry. One such politician was Senate president Ferdinand E. Marcos. In March 1964, Marcos launched his pre-election attack on the Macapagal administration by generating a highly publicized exposé of the smuggling operation, detailing the involvement of the Montanos and their accomplices in high government circles, including top military officials, cabinet members, and the president's brother, Angel Macapagal.[159] The Montanos countered with a campaign against the tobacco subsidy, drawing public attention to the diversion of government funds from national projects to prop up the Ilocos region's flagging economy.[160] More importantly, Montano worked hard to thwart Marcos's presidential ambitions. When Marcos defected from the Liberal Party and ran for president as a Nacionalista in 1965, Montano stood by the incumbent Liberal administration, delivering the Cavite vote to Macapagal by a margin of nearly twenty-eight thousand votes. When Marcos emerged victorious in November, Cavite became "opposition country" with Montano at loggerheads with Malacañang.

Marcos-inspired schemes to undermine Montano's position in Cavite were soon under way, beginning with an effort to eliminate the veteran legislator's role as "protector" of Lino Bocalan's Tanza-based smuggling operations. In September 1966, Congressman Floro Crisologo of Ilocos Sur, a Nacionalista and member of the tobacco bloc, suddenly came forth on behalf of five enlisted men from the Philippine Constabulary's Civil Affairs Office (CAO) who had been caught escorting Bocalan's sister through an antismuggling checkpoint in Cavite.

Crisologo claimed that the CAO men were in fact military intelligence agents assisting him in his capacity as a member of the House Committee on National Defense.[161] Later he unveiled documents purportedly compiled by these CAO "agents," including an alleged "blue book," which listed the names of civilian and military officials involved in the smuggling operations. Congressman Montano and his son the governor appeared at the top of the list. Also named were congressmen and provincial governors of neighboring Laguna and Batangas, as well as military officers up and down the Armed Forces of the Philippines hierarchy, from the 137th PC Company in Cavite to the office of the secretary of national defense.[162] The Montanos' countercharges that Crisologo and the CAO agents claiming to represent President Marcos were blackmailing Bocalan remain unverifiable but it is clear that the exposé was intended to demonstrate Montano's inability to provide adequate protection and to encourage Bocalan to bypass the provincial kingpin and deal directly with Malacañang.[163]

Marcos's carrot-and-stick courtship of Bocalan proceeded, with Malacañang first threatening then rewarding the notorious smuggling lord. A government suit against Bocalan for undeclared 1964 and 1965 income taxes dragged on in the courts with no apparent resolution.[164] Then, in July of 1968, customs agents at Manila International Airport prevented Bocalan's lawyer from leaving Manila for Hong Kong when they discovered that he was carrying $100,000 in cash. After the attorney produced a special communication from the Central Bank stating that no restrictions on such carry-on currency schemes applied, Customs Commissioner Juan Ponce Enrile allowed him to leave.[165] Thus Marcos made clear to Bocalan that "business as usual" depended on direct relations with Malacañang, rendering Montano's services as broker redundant.

Marcos also battled Montano on the electoral front, encouraging long-time rival Dominador Camerino to run for the governorship in 1967 and then deploying national resources to favor him. The Commission on Elections assumed control over all towns and cities of the province, deputizing the Constabulary to oversee the municipal and city police, provincial guards, and "special agents" of the governor.[166] Selectively implementing a Malacañang-imposed firearms ban, the Constabulary disarmed pro-Montano mayors and policemen while allegedly allowing Camerino henchmen to hold onto their guns.[167] Moreover, just two weeks before the November 1967 election, Marcos removed the pro-Montano provincial *fiscal,* appointing in his stead Bienvenido Reyes, an assistant provincial *fiscal* who had won his job on Camerino's recommendation.[168] As acting provincial *fiscal,* Reyes chaired the provincial board of canvassers and thus guaranteed some restraints on Governor Montano's ability to "manufacture" the desired election results in the provincial capital. Although these interventions worked in Camerino's favor, they did not suffice to dislodge the Montanos: Delfin captured the governorship by a margin of more than four thousand votes while pro-Montano mayors won election in twelve municipalities and in Cavite and Tagaytay cities.

Two years later, Marcos and Montano went to battle again. The latter, who had earned a reputation as one of the president's "bitterest critics," filed a resolution in May 1969 calling for Marcos's impeachment, raising corruption charges in connection with public-works allocations for Cavite, and questioning the president's nominees for two vacant seats on the Supreme Court.[169] After this measure failed to garner congressional support, Marcos, eager for revenge, worked to obstruct Montano's 1969 bid for reelection to Cavite's seat in the House while he sought another term in Malacañang for himself. Unwilling to choose between two of his Upsilonian fraternity brothers, Marcos first sponsored long-time Montano foe Fernando Campos, who had served as Marcos's undersecretary of commerce since 1966, as the official Nacionalista candidate. In the role of a third-man "spoiler," Marcos added Juanito Remulla, a provincial board member and former Montano supporter who had won more votes than Delfin Montano in 1967. Once again, the Commission on Elections placed all of Cavite's towns and cities under its control, subordinating municipal and city police, provincial guards, and "special agents" to the control of the Comelec-deputized PC.[170] Moreover, just a few weeks before the election, the legendary Cavite bandit Leonardo Manecio "mysteriously escaped" from the Bilibid prison in Muntinlupa and returned to Cavite to assist anti-Montano forces in the election campaign.[171] Manecio, who had served time for his role in the 1952 Maragondon Massacre while Montano went free, was no doubt eager for revenge: the prison authorities who helped him "escape" claim to have saved him from certain death at the hands of a "hit man" contracted by an unnamed politician.[172] Yet these subterfuges failed to dislodge Montano, for "dark horse" Remulla outpolled Campos and split the anti-Montano vote. Marcos's two fraternity brothers, however, succeeded in serving up Cavite to their "brod" in Malacañang, giving him a sixteen-thousand-vote margin in the province over Liberal presidential candidate Serging Osmeña. Thus, for the first time since the defeat by Roxas of Osmeña's father in 1946, Montano had failed to secure in Cavite a winning margin for the presidential candidate he supported.

The election's outcome, and Marcos's subsequent success in engineering the ouster of Montano from the position of House minority floor leader,[173] no doubt encouraged the long-awaited defection of Lino Bocalan to the Marcos camp. Once Bocalan had allied himself with Marcos, Montano was deprived of a secure home base in Tanza and denied a share of the fruits of its illegal economy. Bocalan's newly established intimacy with the incumbent administration became apparent with the appointment of Brigadier General Zosimo Paredes, Bocalan's *compadre,* as chief of the Second PC Zone, which covered the provinces of Southern Luzon.[174] At Marcos's urging, Bocalan announced that he would run for governor as a Nacionalista against Delfin Montano in the 1971 election with long-time Montano rival Dominador Camerino as his running mate. Predictably, Bocalan and Camerino reaped the benefits of administration support: the Commission on Elections placed eight towns with pro-Montano mayors under PC control, allowing Paredes considerable scope for intervention on his *compadre's* behalf.[175] Moreover, citing the thirteen lives that had been lost during the campaign and "the tense situation which prevailed in the province even after the election," Comelec held the final canvassing of Cavite election returns in the commission's central offices in Manila.[176] With the electoral machinery thus "sanitized" in his favor, Bocalan defeated Delfin Montano for the Cavite governorship. Sweeping in on his coattails, Camerino was elected as vice-governor, perennial Montano foe Manuel Rojas as Cavite City mayor, and eleven other Nacionalistas as municipal mayors.

Though injured by his defeat in this rigged match, Montano went down fighting. When Bocalan assumed the governorship in January 1972, he found the pro-Montano police in the provincial capital armed, hostile, and unwilling to step down.[177] Moreover, several newly elected mayors in Bocalan's camp failed to serve more than a few months of their terms. By the end of February, the mayors of Cavite City, General Aguinaldo, and Magallanes, as well as the chief of police of Naic, had fallen to assassins' bullets.[178] These incidents, however, merely played into the hands of Bocalan. Reacting to the violence, Marcos in March of 1972 ordered Philippine Constabulary forces under the command of Second PC Zone chief Paredes to assume control and supervision of the police forces in all of Cavite's towns and cities, thus securing the province for Bocalan's political and economic benefit.[179]

With both national and provincial government forces arrayed against him and his home base in Tanza stolen by Bocalan, Montano could neither profit from Cavite's illegal economy nor summon the muscle and machinery needed for electoral success. Hamstrung by this new political alliance, his chances of recapturing the Cavite House seat were slim. His best chance for a rebound now lay with the Aquino-for-President campaign that could sweep him back into power on the coattails of a new administration in 1973 much as the Nacionalistas' Magsaysay ticket had done twenty years earlier. Benigno Aquino, Jr., was indebted to Montano for the provision of crucial "manpower" in a previous election, and the Cavite legislator could bank on repayment if the Liberal senator from Tarlac managed to capture the presidency. Recalling the elder Aquino's role in his 1938 reelection, Montano no doubt hoped for a replay, this time with his late patron's son guaranteeing retention of the Cavite House seat.

Developments in the national political arena—culminating in Marcos's declaration of martial law in September 1972, the closing of Congress, and detention of leading opposition figures, including Aquino—dashed whatever hopes Montano had entertained for a comeback. Having left for a visit to the United States in early September, he was, by coincidence or design, absent when martial law was proclaimed, and he remained abroad for the duration of Marcos's reign. As if surgically removed, the supposed "lord and master of Cavite politics" literally vanished from the provincial arena.

Conclusion

When, after Marcos' downfall in 1986, Montano eventually returned to the Philippines, he found himself politically irrelevant. Though readmitted into Liberal Party circles in Manila, he was largely ignored. Bocalan, whom Marcos had ousted soon after he declared martial law, sought him out and begged forgiveness, yet without political capital he had only tears of remorse to offer his townmate and former associate. Camerino, who had assumed the governorship following Bocalan's removal, had died in 1979 but his successor, Juanito "Johnny" Remulla, had emerged in the final years of Marcos's rule as the undisputed kingpin of Cavite. Having amassed both a considerable fortune and a substantial political following during his seven uninterrupted years as provincial governor under Marcos (1979-86), Remulla switched to the Aquino camp after EDSA. From there he helped his protégés to capture Cavite's three House seats in May 1987 and won reelection to the governorship in January 1988. Later he regained control over properties and companies temporarily sequestered by the Aquino government, established close links with a number of important domestic and foreign firms investing heavily in Cavite, and expanded his already extensive landholdings in the province. In May 1992, he easily won reelection, while a close ally, Caviteño film star Ramon Revilla, captured a Senate seat. Numerous Remulla protégés also returned to office in various towns.

Meanwhile, Justiniano Montano, now well into his eighties, has been left to spend his days at home with his grandchildren, puffing on his pipe and reading French magazines. After all his years as Cavite's "lord and master," he is now worthy only of an occasional, nostalgic note in newspaper columns, and merely capable of harassing Remulla through various court cases. His remarkable disappearance, even more than his emergence, on the political stage highlights the elusiveness of his power: what was it that "made" Montano in the first place, allowed him to endure for so long, and failed him in the end?

Montano's long tenure as provincial "kingpin" must first be understood in the context of the economic and political evolution of Cavite in the twentieth century. Over the years the evolution of metropolitan Manila spurred changes in land use in the suburban province, so that agro-business, residential subdivisions, and eventually industrial estates came to overshadow rice fields, pastures, fishponds, coconut groves, and coffee and sugarcane plantations as mainstays of the Cavite economy. Population growth and the extension of suffrage expanded the Cavite electorate from some 7,000 voters in 1912 to more than 27,000 in 1934, 82,000 in 1957, and 133,000 in 1969, according to the records of the Commission on Elections. Despite these developments, certain political patterns persisted. In Cavite's municipalities, successive generations of small-town, political "dynasties" of *inquilino* lineage prospered, intermarried, and competed for local political office, gradually shifting profits from their farmlands and rice mills into ice plants and electric companies, cockpits and movie theaters, golf courses and beach resorts.

At the provincial level, successive "kingpins" rose and fell according to a different rhythm, one closely attuned to the ebb and flow of national politics. Lacking *haciendas* on the scale of those found in Negros or Tarlac, Cavite's provincial landscape did not lend itself to dynastic domination by sugar barons the likes of the Montelibanos or the Cojuangcos. With its population and economic resources dispersed among what today constitute twenty municipalities and three cities, the province also eluded control by a single big-town boss in the tradition of Caloocan's Asistio, Pasay's Cuneta, or even Danao's Durano, whose Chicago-style domination of large population centers with thriving illegal economies has facilitated domination of entire congressional districts. Nonetheless, as Montano's lengthy career attests, "kingpin" status was in fact attainable in Cavite.

As in the case of the Aguinaldo-Tirona machine, Montano's status was in large part derivative, dependent on the flow of national power emanating from Manila. For just as the success of Aguinaldo and Tirona resulted in considerable measure from their influence in Manila and the favors of such patrons as Leonard Wood and Manuel Quezon, so Montano consistently allied himself with Malacañang, placing his bet on the winning presidential ticket in every election from 1949 to 1965 and running his son as a candidate of incumbent administrations in the gubernatorial races of 1955, 1959, and 1963. Like Aguinaldo and Tirona in periods of Nacionalista Party reconsolidation, Montano found his position least secure when local rivals obtained the support of powerful national politicians, as occurred during Fernando Campos's Garcia-backed 1961 campaign for Cavite's congressional seat. Just as Aguinaldo's showdown with Quezon precipitated the General's "loss" of Cavite in 1935, so Montano's prolonged confrontation with Marcos led to his political demise in 1972. Significantly, his heavy reliance on violence and state resources rendered him particularly vulnerable to a hostile chief executive, as the use of coercion in obtaining electoral victories and protecting illegal economic activities required the collusion of various agencies of the national government.

From the onset, Montano's strong-man rule rested on public office and state resources rather than on land or popular support. Just as Aguinaldo's election as *capitan municipal* of Kawit in 1895 prefigured his leadership role in the Revolution, so Montano's appointment as assistant provincial *fiscal* in 1929 allowed him to assemble the clientele that he mobilized in the 1935 election. Once in Congress, Montano used the Cavite seat to secure and advance his position in a number of ways, much as Tirona and his minions in the legislature did in the heyday of the Aguinaldo machine. First, his power over the allocation of Cavite-bound pork barrel accorded him great leverage over the province's nineteen municipalities and three chartered cities, providing patronage resources useful for sustaining a following among the mayors. Second, Montano's seat in Congress guaranteed him a measure of discretion over the assignment of various government officials to Cavite—the provincial Constabulary commander, the judge of the Court of First Instance, the provincial *fiscal*, the provincial treasurer—which further buttressed his command over the mayors and other local power brokers. He also enjoyed enough influence in the national arena to install numerous protégés in strategic positions within the national bureaucracy. Finally, over the years Montano's seat in the legislature offered him increasing opportunities for personal advancement through real-estate speculation, "horse trading," lobbying, and other "rentier" activities, as the controversy surrounding the Manila Bay Reclamation Project suggests.

By the late 1950s, Montano's control over public office had facilitated the appropriation and conversion of the bulk of Cavite's state coercive resources into a "private army" that buttressed his hold over the province. With the election of his son Delfin to the governorship in 1955, provincial guards, "special agents," and prisoners under the jurisdiction of the provincial warden fell under Montano's command, along with the municipal police forces directed by pro-Montano mayors. With the provincial Constabulary commander and other officers in his pocket, Montano by the early 1960s was in a position to control the lucrative Cavite smuggling racket and to guarantee favorable election results for himself and his patrons in Malacañang. Thus his privatization of state resources helped to perpetuate his rule, with national politicians' acknowledgment of his kingpin status reinforcing the tendency towards entrenchment and monopoly. As in the case of Aguinaldo's clash with Quezon in 1935, only conflict with a hostile administration in Malacañang could produce a dynamic capable of disrupting this upward spiral of success, and in this case it plummeted Montano to the depths of political insignificance after 1972.

In large part, then, Montano's reputation as "provincial warlord," "kingpin," and "lord and master of Cavite" was a fiction, a myth of sorts, as the completeness of his downfall amply attests. Cut off from national patronage, his putative political machine quickly crumbled—mayors defected or failed to win reelection, provincial offices fell to rivals, and the number of loyal municipal policemen, provincial guards, and "special agents" shrunk accordingly. Denied the sympathies of Comelec and the Constabulary, Montano's supposed "private army" could neither deliver the votes nor protect the Tanza-based smugglers. Refused recognition, he ultimately proved a paper tiger, his carefully constructed empire in Cavite a collapsible Potemkin village.

Ultimately, then, Montano's long-standing preeminence in Cavite politics rested on his projection of personal prowess reaffirmed time and again through the selective use of violence. Violence was instrumental in purely practical terms—in the elimination of enemies, the manipulation of elections, and enforcement of the smuggling racket's monopoly on the traffic in contraband. Banditry and illegal economic activities had flourished in Cavite even before the Revolution, and violence had long constituted an essential resource for political and economic competition. In this context, acts of violence themselves conveyed and asserted the reaches of power, dramatizing the power holder's presence and strength for Manila newspaper readers and Cavite gossip-mongers alike. Thus Montano's tough guy theatrics and the spate of killings that marked his ascension in the 1950s and his downfall in the 1970s aimed to impress upon all that he was a force to be reckoned with, a contender not to be ignored. Like the "big man" of bygone days, Montano was to the end a champion performer with Cavite as his stage.

A PPENDIX : Patrons and Clients in Cavite Politics, 1946–1972

The Liberals in Power (1946–1953): Roxas, Quirino, and Camerino

1946	National	Roxas (Liberal) defeats Osmeña (Nacionalista).
	Cavite	Camerino helps Roxas to 27,000-vote margin in the province. Montano backs Osmeña, wins House seat as Nacionalista. Roxas names Camerino governor and names twenty Camerino protégés as mayors.
1947	Cavite	Camerino wins governorship by 19,000 votes. Fourteen (pro-Camerino) Liberal mayors elected. Liberal appointed mayor of Cavite City.
1949	National	Quirino (Liberal) defeats Laurel (Nacionalista).
	Cavite	Camerino helps Quirino to 38,000-vote margin in the provinc Manuel Rojas (Liberal) wins House seat. Montano (Liberal) wins Senate seat.
1951	Cavite	Camerino (Liberal) reelected by 25,000-vote margin. Sixteen (pro-Camerino) Liberal mayors elected.

Montano Entrenched: Magsaysay, Garcia, and Macapagal (1953–1965)

1953	National	Magsaysay (Nacionalista) defeats Quirino.
	Cavite	Montano helps Magsaysay to 10,000-vote margin.
		Montano protégé José Cajulis wins House seat as Nacionalista (after protest).
		Montano protégé appointed mayor of Cavite City.
1955	Cavite	Delfin Montano (Nacionalista) defeats Camerino (Liberal) for governorship.
		Sixteen (pro-Montano) Nacionalista mayors elected.
1957	National	Garcia (Nacionalista) wins presidency.
	Cavite	Camerino and Montano help Garcia to 14,000-vote margin in Cavite.
		Montano (Nacionalista) wins House seat.
1959	Cavite	Governor Montano (Nacionalista) reelected.
		Thirteen (pro-Montano) Nacionalista mayors elected.
1961	National	Macapagal (Liberal) wins presidency.
	Cavite	Montano helps Macapagal to 33,000-vote margin.
		Montano reelected to House, becomes Liberal.
1963	Cavite	Governor Montano reelected.
		Eighteen (pro-Montano) Liberal mayors elected.

Montano Dislodged: The Marcos Years (1965–1972)

1965	National	Marcos (Nacionalista) wins presidency.
	Cavite	Montano opposes Marcos, delivers 27,000-vote margin to Macapagal (Liberal).
		Montano (Liberal) reelected to House.
1967	Cavite	Governor Montano (Liberal) reelected.
		Fourteen (pro-Montano) Liberal mayors elected.
1969	National	Marcos (Nacionalista) reelected.
	Cavite	Montano supports Osmeña (Liberal), but Marcos garners 16,000-vote margin.
		Montano (Liberal) reelected to House.
1971	Cavite	Lino Bocalan (Nacionalista) defeats Delfin Montano (Liberal) for the governorship.
		Eleven Nacionalista mayors elected.

Elections and Cavite Politics, 1946–1972

Year	Presidency	House Seat/Governorship	Mayors
1946	Roxas (Liberal) wins in Cavite	House: Montano (Nacionalista) Governor: Camerino (Liberal)	
1947		Camerino (Liberal) elected governor	14 Liberals 5 Nacionalistas
1949	Quirino (Liberal) wins in Cavite	House: Rojas (Liberal) Senate: Montano (Liberal)	
1951		Camerino (Liberal) reelected governor	16 Liberals 3 Nacionalistas
1953	Magsaysay (Nacionalista) wins in Cavite	House: Cajulis (Nacionalista)	
1955		D. Montano (Nacionalista) elected governor	14 Nacionalistas 7 Liberals
1957	Garcia (Nacionalista) wins in Cavite	House: Montano (Nacionalista)	
1959		D. Montano (Nacionalista) reelected governor	13 Nacionalistas 8 Liberals
1961	Macapagal (Liberal) wins in Cavite	House: Montano (Liberal)	

continued

1963		D. Montano (Liberal) reelected governor	18 Liberals 3 Nacionalistas
1965	Marcos (Nacionalista) loses in Cavite	House: Montano (Liberal)	
1967		D. Montano (Liberal) reelected governor	14 Liberals 7 Nacionalistas
1969	Marcos (Nacionalista) wins in Cavite	House: Montano (Liberal)	
1971		Bocalan (Nacionalista) elected governor	11 Nacionalistas 10 Liberals

Montano's Mayors

Year	Party in Power	Montano's Party	Cavite Mayors
1947	Liberal	Nacionalista	14 Liberals 5 Nacionalistas
1951	Liberal	Nacionalista*	16 Liberals 3 Nacionalistas
1955	Nacionalista	Nacionalista	14 Nacionalistas 7 Liberals
1959	Nacionalista**	Nacionalista	13 Nacionalistas 8 Liberals
1963	Liberal	Liberal	18 Liberals 3 Nacionalistas
1967	Nacionalista	Liberal	14 Liberals 7 Nacionalistas
1971	Nacionalista	Liberal	10 Liberals 11 Nacionalistas

*In 1951, though a Liberal, Montano sponsored a Nacionalista slate in Cavite.
**In 1959, the Nacionalista Garcia administration supported Camerino, a Liberal, and his slate in Cavite.

Long-Time "Montanista" Mayors in Cavite

Amadeo:	Santos Ambagan (1951–1967)
Bacoor:	Pablo Sarino (1959–1967, 1971–1986)
Carmona:	Cesar Casal (1955–1979)
Cavite City:	Fidel Dones (1955–1979)
Bailen/Gen. Aguinaldo:	Rafael Dalusag (1955–1959, 1963–1980)
Gen. Trias:	Ernesto Genuino (1959–1971)
Indang:	Fulgencio Guevarra (1963–1980)
Magallanes:	Anatolio Reyes (1963–1980)
Maragondon:	Telesforo Unas (1955–1986)
Naic:	Macario Peña (1955–1976)
Rosario:	Calixto Enriquez (1963–1986)
Tagaytay City:	Isaac Tolentino (1955–1980)

N OTES

Research for this essay was carried out under fellowships from the National Science Foundation and the Olin Foundation. The author would like to express his gratitude to these sponsors and to Jojo Abinales, Ben Anderson, Mary Callahan, Lotta Hedman, Paul Hutchcroft, Al McCoy, Jim Ockey, and Jim Rush for their comments, criticisms, and suggestions. Many thanks also to Neil Oshima for help with the photographs. Needless to say, neither the sponsors nor the friendly readers mentioned above bear any responsibility for the shortcomings of this essay.

[1]See Marshall D. Sahlins, "Poor Man, Rich Man, Big-Man, Chief: Political Types in Melanesia and Polynesia," *Comparative Studies in Society and History* 10, no. 3 (April 1963): 285–303.

[2]Dr. Antonio de Morga, "Events in the Filipinas Islands," in Emma Helen Blair and James Alexander Robertson, eds., *The Philippine Islands, 1493–1803* (Cleveland: A. H. Clark, 1903–19), 26:127.

[3]O. W. Wolters, "Khmer 'Hinduism' in the Seventh Century," in R. B. Smith and W. Watson, eds., *Early South East Asia: Essays in Archaeology, History and Historical Geography* (New York: Oxford University Press, 1979), 429.

[4]Michael Aung-Thwin, "Divinity, Spirit, and Human: Conceptions of Classical Burmese Kingship," in Lorraine Gesick, ed., *Centers, Symbols, and Hierarchies: Essays on the Classical States of Southeast Asia*, Southeast Asia Monographs, no. 26 (New Haven: Yale University, Southeast Asia Program, 1983), 81–84.

[5]Cesar A. Majul, "Succession in the Old Sulu Sultanate," *Philippine Historical Review* 1, no. 1 (1964): 252–71.

[6]Vicente L. Rafael, *Contracting Colonialism: Translation and Christian Conversion in Tagalog Society under Early Spanish Rule* (Quezon City: Ateneo de Manila University Press, 1988), 14.

[7]O. W. Wolters, *History, Culture, and Region in Southeast Asian Perspective* (Singapore: Institute of Southeast Asian Studies, 1982), 4–5, cited in Rafael, *Contracting Colonialism*, 13.

[8]On the spread of Islam throughout the Malay world and Islamic influences on Malay conceptions of kingship, see Barbara Watson Andaya, "The Nature of the State in Eighteenth Century Perak," and L. F. Brakel, "State and Statecraft in 17th Century Aceh," in Anthony Reid and Lance Castles, eds., *Pre-Colonial State Systems in Southeast Asia: The Malay Peninsula, Sumatra, Bali-Lombok, South Celebes* (Kuala Lumpur: Malaysian Branch of the Royal Asiatic Society, 1975); and G. W. J. Drewes, "New Light on the Coming of Islam to Indonesia?," *Bijdragen tot de Taal-, Land-, en Volkenkunde* 124, no. 4 (1968): 433–59.

[9]O. D. Corpuz, *The Roots of the Filipino Nation* (Quezon City: Aklahi Foundation, 1989), 1:179–82; and John Leddy Phelan, *The Hispanization of the Philippines: Spanish Aims and Filipino Responses, 1565–1700* (Madison: University of Wisconsin Press, 1959), 123.

[10]See Michael Cullinane, "The Changing Nature of the Cebu Urban Elite in the 19th Century," in Alfred W. McCoy and Ed. C. de Jesus, eds., *Philippine Social History: Global Trade and Local Transformations* (Quezon City: Ateneo de Manila University Press, 1982); John A. Larkin, *The Pampangans: Colonial Society in a Philippine Province* (Berkeley: University of California Press, 1972), especially chapter 4 ("Cash-Crop Society"); Benito Fernandez Legarda, Jr., "Foreign Trade, Economic Change and Entrepreneurship in the Nineteenth-Century Philippines" (Ph.D. diss., Harvard University, 1955); and Edgar Wickberg, *The Chinese in Philippine Life, 1851–1898* (New Haven: Yale University Press, 1965), especially chapters 2 and 3.

[11]See, for example, Ron Chernow, *The House of Morgan: An American Banking Dynasty and the Rise of Modern Finance* (New York: Simon and Schuster, 1990); and Tom Schactman, *Skyscraper Dreams: The Great Real Estate Dynasties of New York* (Boston: Little, Brown, 1991).

[12]Thomas C. Nowak and Kay Snyder, "Economic Concentration and Political Change in the Philippines," in Benedict J. Kerkvliet, ed., *Political Change in the Philippines: Studies of Local Politics Preceding Martial Law* (Honolulu: University Press of Hawaii, 1974), 161.

[13]For the most comprehensive studies of the national oligarchy and its economic bases, see Temario Campos Rivera, "Class, the State and Foreign Capital: The Politics of Philippine Industrialization, 1950–1986" (Ph.D. diss., University of Wisconsin, Madison, 1991); and Dante Simbulan, "A Study of the Socio-economic Elite in Philippine Politics and Government" (Ph.D. diss., Australian National University, 1964).

[14]For examples of such theatrical episodes, see Reynaldo Naval, "Montano, Nueno Stage Fist Fight," *Manila Times,* 9 August 1957, 1; and "Montano, Nueno Fight," *Daily Mirror,* 8 August 1957, 1.

[15]"News of the Week," *Philippines Free Press,* 3 December 1938, 27. See also "Montano's Trial Opens," *The Tribune,* 17 October 1939, 14; and "Courts: Montano to Jail?" *Philippines Free Press,* 12 December 1939, 30.

[16]Soledad Borromeo, "El Cadiz Filipino: Colonial Cavite, 1571–1896" (Ph.D. diss., University of California, Berkeley, 1973), 142, 151.

[17]Soledad Borromeo-Buehler, "The *Inquilinos* of Cavite: A Social Class in Nineteenth-Century Philippines," *Journal of Southeast Asian Studies* 26, no. 1 (March 1985): 81.

[18]D. C. Shanks, "Report of the Governor of Cavite," in Bureau of Insular Affairs, War Department, *Fifth Annual Report of the Philippine Commission, 1904, Part 1* (Washington, D.C.: Government Printing Office, 1905), 450.

[19]See Borromeo, "El Cadiz Filipino," 68; and Borromeo-Buehler, "The *Inquilinos* of Cavite," 75. For classic descriptions of the emergence of the largely Chinese-*mestizo* landowning elite in the provinces during the course of the nineteenth century, see Larkin, *The Pampangans*; and Wickberg, *The Chinese in Philippine Life.*

[20]Isagani R. Medina, "Cavite Before the Revolution, 1571–1896" (Ph.D. diss., University of the Philippines, 1985), 216.

[21]E. Arsenio Manuel, "Biography of Tomas Tirona," *The Diliman Review* 14, no. 4 (1966): 290.

[22]See Medina, "Cavite Before the Revolution"; as well as Glenn A. May, "Civic Ritual and Political Reality: Municipal Elections in the Late Nineteenth Century," in Ruby R. Paredes, ed., *Philippine Colonial Democracy* (Quezon City: Ateneo de Manila University Press, 1989).

[23]Medina, "Cavite Before the Revolution," 222; Manuel, "Biography of Tomas Tirona," 303.

[24]This process is the theme of the chapter on *"tulisanismo"* in Medina, "Cavite Before the Revolution," 120–210.

[25]Ibid., 174.

[26]Ibid., 155–63.

[27]Ibid., 132–40.

[28]Ibid., 149–51. See also Manuel Artigas y Cuerva, *Los Sucesos de 1872: Resena Historica Bio-bibliographica* [The events of 1872: An historical and bio-bibliographical review] (Manila: La Vanguardia, 1911), 94–95.

[29]Emilio Aguinaldo, *Mga Gunita ng Himagsikan* (Manila: Cristina Aguinaldo Suntay, 1964), 5–6, 25.

[30]Ibid., 101–2.

[31]Ibid., 45–68.

[32]Ibid., 103, 143. I have crosschecked the names of these revolutionary figures against the lists of Chinese-*mestizo principales* in Cavite towns provided in Borromeo, "The *Inquilinos* of Cavite," 75; and Borromeo-Buehler, "El Cadiz Filipino," 111–14. This pattern of revolutionary recruitment is similar to that portrayed by Glenn A. May in his article

"Filipino Revolutionaries in the Making: The Old School Tie in Late Nineteenth-Century Batangas," *Bulletin of the American Historical Collection* 9 (July–September 1981): 53–64; and more recently in his book *Battle for Batangas: A Philippine Province at War* (New Haven: Yale University Press, 1991).

[33]Aguinaldo, *Mga Gunita ng Himagsikan,* 49. May's article and book elaborate upon this argument with reference to the pattern of mobilization in Batangas (see note 32).

[34]Aguinaldo, *Mga Gunita ng Himagsikan,* 139, 142.

[35]Ibid., 142.

[36]Ibid., 143.

[37]Shanks, "Report of the Governor of Cavite," 454–58.

[38]See, for example, "Documentos Tomados . . . Expediente Incoado por el Comite de Defensa de los Derechos de los Proprietarios de Terrenos en Imus, Cavite . . . I.F., Despues de su Organizacion, Marzo 1911" [Captured documents: Preliminary despatch by the Committee for the Defense of the Rights of the Owners of Land in Imus, Cavite. . . .], in the 1908–1911 folder, Box 248, Series 7, of the Manuel L. Quezon Papers, Filipiniana Division, National Library, Manila.

[39]See, for example, the letter of 1 March 1926 from Tomas Mascardo to Quezon in the "Imus, Cavite—1926" folder, Box 42, Series 7, Quezon Papers. Mascardo wrote: "Hindi ako lamang ang nagkakautang sa ating Pamahalaan, tungkol sa paghohornal sa lupa; kami'y napakarami at ang mga iba sa amin, ay patuloy sa kanilang pananangkilik at pakikinabang sa lupa, kahima't hindi nakasusulong ng hornal. . . ." [I am not the only one who owes money to our Government, in terms of installment payments on land; we are quite numerous and some among us have continued to invest in and profit from the land, although without advancing installment payments. . . .]. Similar correspondence may be found in the "Naic—1928" folder, Box 44; and the "April 1–June 30, 1934" folder, Box 250, Series 7, Quezon Papers.

[40]See "How They Evade Property Taxes in Cavite," *Philippine Free Press,* 3 February 1934, 8, 37.

[41]"Report of Acting Director of Constabulary, Department of Commerce and Police, Bureau of Constabulary, Manila, P.I., August 8, 1908," in Bureau of Insular Affairs, War Department, *Report of the Philippine Commission to the Secretary of War, 1908, Part 2* (Washington, D.C.: Government Printing Office, 1909), 372.

[42]Shanks, "Report of the Governor of Cavite," 452.

[43]Ibid., 448, 454. See also Luke E. Wright, (acting civil governor), "Executive Order No. 8, The Government of the Philippine Islands, Executive Bureau, Manila, January 27, 1904," in Bureau of Insular Affairs, War Department, *Fifth Annual Report of the Philippine Commission, 1904, Part 1,* 692–93; as well as D.C. Shanks, "Report of the Governor of the Province of Cavite," in Bureau of Insular Affairs, War Department, *Sixth Annual Report of the Philippine Commission, 1905, Part 1* (Washington, D.C.: Government Printing Office, 1906), 212.

[44]The 1909 report of Francisco Santamaria, Cavite provincial *fiscal,* is found in Ignacio Villamor, *Criminality in the Philippine Islands, 1903–1908* (Manila: Bureau of Printing, 1909), 59–60. On the connivance of local officials and police with cattle rustlers in Cavite in later years, see "What's Wrong With Cavite?" *Philippine Free Press,* 13 January 1940, 20–21.

[45]For evidence of widespread *jueteng* operations in Cavite, see these sources: letter of 27 October 1922 from Claro Cuevas of Bacoor to the Honorable Secretary of the Interior through Hon. Manuel L. Quezon, Senator, Fifth Senatorial District, in the "Bacoor, Cavite: 1921–1923" folder, Box 41, Series 7, Quezon Papers; the 1909 report of the Philippine Constabulary inspector, in W. Cameron Forbes, *The Philippine Islands* (Boston: Houghton Mifflin, 1928), 1:167; "'Jueteng King' is Unmolested," *The Tribune,* 13 May 1931, 3; "The Jueteng Business," *Philippines Free Press,* 4 November 1933, 2–3, 40–41; and Emmanuel A. Baja, *Philippine Police System and its Problems* (Manila: Pobre's Press, 1933), 356.

[46]"Governor Planning Clean-up of Cavite Where Vice of All Varieties Reported Rampant," *Manila Daily Bulletin*, 15 April 1922, 1; "Cavite Cabarets," *The Tribune*, 19 December 1928, 4.

[47]See "The Cavite Election," *Manila Times*, 5 February 1902, 1; and "Big Contest is on in Cavite," *Manila Times*, 5 February 1907, 1.

[48]Wright, "Executive Order No. 8," 1:692–93.

[49]See Michael Cullinane, "*Ilustrado* Politics: The Response of the Filipino Educated Elite to American Colonial Rule, 1898–1907" (Ph.D. diss., University of Michigan, 1989), 437–516.

[50]"Osorio Wins Out in Cavite," *Manila Times*, 7 February 1907, 1.

[51]"Votes and Guns: To the Caviteños," *Manila Times*, 11 February 1907, 1; "Must Toe the Mark," *Manila Times*, 23 April 1907, 1, 6.

[52]Palma received 1,894 votes as opposed to 446 for Eugenio Inocencio, 285 for Emilio Tria Tirona, and 77 for Jose M. del Rosario ("The Election in Cavite Province," *Manila Times*, 2 August 1907, 3).

[53]Rafael Palma, *My Autobiography* (Manila: Capitol Publishing House, 1953), 60–61.

[54]Ibid.

[55]Aguinaldo, *Mga Gunita ng Himagsikan*, 37.

[56]For more details concerning Palma's political career, see Cullinane, "*Ilustrado* Politics," 491–92, 505.

[57]General Mascardo served in the Revolution as commander of the Filipino sector in Central Luzon where he was Manuel Quezon's commanding officer. The two men remained friends during the American period, with Quezon supporting the studies of the general's son and naming him aide-de-camp to his wife, Doña Aurora Quezon. See Leon S. del Rosario, "General Tomas Mascardo," *Philippines Free Press*, 29 August 1953, 16, 45.

[58]Carlos Quirino, *Quezon: Paladin of Philippine Freedom* (Manila: Filipiniana Book Guild, 1971), 149.

[59]Successful *revolucionario*-politicos included long-time Laguna governor Juan Cailles and Bulacan kingpin Teodoro Sandiko.

[60]Jose V. Clarino, *General Aguinaldo and Philippine Politics* (Manila: Fajardo Press, 1928), 37.

[61]See "Aguinaldo Mere 'Tool,'" *The Tribune*, 13 August 1935, 10; and Teodoro M. Locsin, "Aguinaldo at Eighty," *Philippines Free Press*, 11 June 1949, 70.

[62]See Jorge B. Vargas, "General Aguinaldo and the Bureau of Lands" (dated 30 September 1927) in the "January 20–December 31, 1927" folder, Box 250, Series 7, Quezon Papers.

[63]Ibid.

[64]See the 27 July 1929 letter of Serafin P. Hilado (director of lands) to Quezon in the "1922–1927" folder, Emilio Aguinaldo file, in the Major Correspondents' Series, Quezon Papers. See, in particular, the attached "Statement of the Accounts of General Emilio Aguinaldo with the Bureau of Lands (Friar Lands Division)."

[65]Isabelo P. Caballero and M. De Gracia Concepcion, *Quezon: The Story of a Nation and its Foremost Statesman* (Manila: United Publishers, 1935), 213, 315.

[66]See the letter of 14 September 1918 from Antero Ganuja et al., of Naic, Cavite, in "Bureau of Lands—1918" folder, Box 248, Series 7, Quezon Papers.

[67]"Soriano Bloc Launches Its First Attack," *The Tribune*, 22 July 1929, 1.

[68]Justiniano S. Montano, Sr., interviews with the author, San Juan, Metro Manila, 18 October 1990 and 15 August 1991.

[69]"The Jueteng Business," 2–3, 40–41.

[70]"Espiritu Wars Against Jueteng," *Philippines Free Press*, 9 September 1933, 56–57.

[71]Montano interviews, 18 October 1990 and 15 August 1991.

[72]Ibid.

[73]See "Rodriguez Orders Lands Confiscated," *The Tribune*, 29 November 1934, 3; "Aguinaldo Land Case Within Law," ibid., 29 November 1934, 10; and Quirino, *Amang*, 49–50.

74"Paredes to Patch Up Mess in Cavite," *The Tribune*, 28 November 1934, 1.

75"Coalition Ticket Wins by Landslide," *Philippines Free Press*, 21 September 1935, 30.

76"Montano Savior," *The Tribune*, 19 September 1935, 2.

77"Poll Officials to Observe Law," ibid., 17 September 1935, 2.

78Caballero and Concepcion, *Story of a Nation*, 440.

79"*Confidencial*" letter of 11 September 1935 from Juan Nolasco (president, Comite Nacional de Campana) to General Basilio Valdes (brigadier general, Philippine Constabulary, Manila): "Tenemos informes confidenciales que los Aguinaldistas forzaran a los electores en dichos municipios a votar por el General Aguinaldo, y que durante el escrutinio los mismos Aguinaldistas obligaran a los inspectores de eleccion para que leyeran las balotas a favor del General Aguinaldo comoquiera que nuestra gente no loerara semejante acto de violencia. . . . [We have received confidential reports that the Aguinaldistas will force voters in the said towns to vote for General Aguinaldo, and that during the counting the same Aguinaldistas will compel election inspectors to read ballots in favor of General Aguinaldo (whereas) our people will not (engage in) such acts of violence. . . .].

80"Three P.C. Men Beaten in Kawit," *The Tribune*, 3 October 1935, 1.

81Justiniano S. Montano, Sr., interview with the author, San Juan, Metro Manila, 14 September 1990.

82First National Assembly, First Session, Bill No. 1101, Commonwealth Act No. 32, "An Act Providing for the Subdivision and Sale of All the Portion of the Friar Lands Estates Remaining Undisposed of," Approved, 15 September 1936.

83See "Cabinet Men to Call on Aquino," *Manila Daily Bulletin*, 29 June 1938, 2; Joseph Ralston Hayden, *The Philippines: A Study in National Development* (New York: Macmillan, 1942), 440; and "Political Notes," *Philippines Free Press*, 29 October 1938, 31.

84"Newcomer," ibid., 11 November 1939, 24C–24D.

85"Political Notes: Draw," ibid., 21 October 1939, 43. See also "Election Records Seized in Cavite: Tally Sheets, Minutes in 9 Towns Taken," *The Tribune*, 11 November 1938, 1, 2.

86See the undated, unsigned note in the "Cavite, June-July 1947" folder, Box 6, Series 2, Manuel A. Roxas Papers, Filipiniana Division, National Library, Manila. Excerpts from this note include the following: "When Paredes went to America by Clipper, he stopped in the house of Don Honorio Rojas, Jueteng King, and father of Manuel S. Rojas, where they had a long conference. . . . Paredes was given a "Pabagsak" of P4,000.00 and in turn he promised the Rojas family that Manuel will surely win the protest. . . . We know that Paredes is financially broke, and perhaps you Manila people know it too. But when Floor Leader Paredes intervened in the Rojas-Montano protest case, Paredes was able to settle some of his pending bills."

87"Noticias de la Semana," *Philippines Free Press*, 21 October 1939, 68; Baldomero T. ("Toto") Olivera, *Jose Yulo: The Selfless Statesman* (Manila: University of the Philippines, Jorge B. Vargas Filipiniana Research Center, 1981), 82–83.

88Ibid., 83.

89"Yulo, Alunan in Poll Dispute," *The Tribune*, 8 October 1939, 1, 2, 26.

90Ibid.

91Ibid.

92Ibid.

93"Political Notes: Draw," 43.

94"Quezon Denies That He Was Backing Cavite Candidate," *The Tribune*, 27 November 1940, 3.

95Montano interview, 18 October 1990.

96Melinda C. Tria, "The Resistance Movement In Cavite, 1942–1945" (M.A. thesis, University of the Philippines, 1966), 31.

97Ibid., 47.

[98]Montano interview, 18 October 1990; and Tria, "The Resistance Movement," 78.
[99]Tria, "The Resistance Movement," 31–32.
[100]Ibid., 23–27.
[101]Ibid., 130–37.
[102]Ibid., 119–20.
[103]Ibid., 78.
[104]Montano interview, 18 October 1990.
[105]See Carolyn Sobritchea, "Banditry in Cavite during the Post World War II Period," *Asian Studies* 22–24 (1984–86): 10–27.
[106]See "Bandits Harass Cavite People," *Sunday Times*, 13 January 1946, 1, 8; and Uldarico S. Baclagon, *Lessons from the Huk Campaign in the Philippines* (Manila: M. Colcol, 1960), 206. Baclagon served in 1945–46 as the chief intelligence and investigating officer of the Military Police in Cavite.
[107]Tria, "The Resistance Movement," 119–20.
[108]See "Bandits Harass Cavite People," 1, 8; and "Cavite Fiscal, Another Held for Ransom," *Manila Times*, 21 February 1946, 1, 4.
[109]See, for early 1946, for example, "Imus Folk Killed by Armed Robbers," *Manila Times*, 4 February 1946, 7; "Cavite Bandits Held, Charged," ibid., 9 March 1946, 1; and "Cavite Man Found Slain," ibid., 27 March 1946, 3.
[110]"Speech of Mr. Cajulis," in *Congressional Record, Republic of the Philippines, House of Representatives*, 3d Cong., 1st sess., 27 April 1954, 1, no. 61, 2006–14.
[111]Baclagon, *Lessons from the Huk Campaign*, 207.
[112]Letter of 28 October 1947 from Agent 844 to the commanding general, MPC, in the "Cavite: September-October 1947" folder, Box 6, Series 2, Roxas Papers.
[113]"The Cavite Incident," *Manila Chronicle*, 5 November 1947, 4.
[114]See "Poll Commish Acts Swiftly on Complaints," *Manila Times*, 9 November 1949, 2; "The Local Scene," *Philippines Free Press*, 12 November 1949; and "Voice from Cavite," ibid., 26 November 1949, 54. See also the 13 April 1952 "Decision" of the Senate Electoral Tribunal in the case of Claro M. Recto, Alejo Mabanag, Trinidad Legarda, Jose O. Vera, Jose Ma. Veloso, Marcelo Addua, Pedro Hernaez, and Domucao Alonto, Protestants, versus Quintin Paredes, Esteban R. Abada, Lorenzo Sumulong, Enrique B. Magalona, Tomas L. Cabili, Macario Peralta, Jr., Justiniano Montano, and Teodoro De Vera, copy filed in the Elpidio Quirino Papers, Ayala Museum, Manila.
[115]"NP Protests Cavite Vote," *Manila Times*, 11 November 1949, 1, 16.
[116]See the 18 May 1957 "Resolution" of the Electoral Tribunal of the House of Representatives, Electoral Case no. 102, Manuel S. Rojas, Protestant, versus Jose T. Cajulis, Protestee, 452.
[117]See, for example, "The Cavite Incident," 4.
[118]See the following sources on Camerino's pork-barrel allotments from Quirino: 23 October 1951 letter from House Speaker Eugenio Perez to President Quirino, in the "Cavite" folder, Box 45, Elpidio Quirino Papers, Ayala Museum, Manila; "Dominador M. Camerino, Candidate for Governor of Cavite (Liberal)," *Philippine News Service*, sheet no. 18, 4 November 1951; and "P.5 Million Cavite Road Fund Shortage Bared," *Daily Mirror*, 11 January 1954.
[119]On Quion, see "Undisclosed Terms Given Quirino Nod," ibid., 21 April 1951; on the Torres brothers, see Andres Callanta and Jose L. Llanes, "4 Slain, 5 Wounded as Cavite Feud Flares," *Manila Times*, 30 November 1946, 1, 20.
[120]See "Says Politics Behind Clash," *Manila Daily Bulletin*, 3 December 1946, 2; and "The Local Scene," *Philippines Free Press*, 7 December 1946, 33.
[121]See the series of articles on this incident featured in the *Manila Chronicle*, 4–8 November 1947.
[122]"Maragondon Mayor Found Slain," ibid., 26 February 1949, 1, 4; L. O. Ty, "Cavite's Political Vendetta," *Philippines Free Press*, 8 May 1954, 14.

[123]"Cavite Killings Traced To Camerino-Montano Feud," *Manila Chronicle*, 4 September 1952, 1, 9; "Cavite Situation Tense; Raiders Kill Four Men," *Manila Times*, 4 September 1952, 2; "Politics and Murder," *Philippines Free Press*, 30 September 1952, 2–3.

[124]"PC Brings Full Order To Cavite," *Manila Chronicle*, 11 November 1953, 1, 3.

[125]See "Report of the Special Committee to Investigate the Alleged Anomalies and Irregularities in the Police Department of the City of Manila," House of Representatives, Republic of the Philippines, 1st Cong., 2d sess., 22 April 1947.

[126]"MP Chief's Alleged Meddling in Politics May Precipitate Crisis," *Manila Chronicle*, 5 November 1947, 16, 12.

[127]Montano interview, 14 September 1990.

[128]Ibid.; and L. O. Ty, "The Man Who Came Back," *Philippines Free Press*, 24 June 1950, 9, 54–55.

[129]Ibid.; and Montano interview, 14 September 1990.

[130]See "Sen. Montano Accused: Maragondon Raid Blamed on 25 Men," *Manila Chronicle*, 30 September 1952, 1, 8; and "Senator Arrested, Fights Back," *Daily Mirror*, 30 September 1952, 1.

[131]See "Cavite Killer Claims Probers Forced Him to Drag in Camerino," *Manila Daily Bulletin*, 11 March 1954, 1; "Camerino Counsel Ask [*sic*] for New Trial," *Manila Times*, 10 June 1954, 1; and "Discard Plan to Contest Decision," *Manila Daily Bulletin*, 10 June 1954, 8.

[132]"Camerino Agents Fired by Rodriguez; Montano in Cavite," *Manila Times*, 7 January 1954; "Mayor Faces Sedition Rap," *Sunday Chronicle*, 10 January 1954; "Cavite Slay [*sic*] Witness Hostile, Fiscal Claims," *Daily Mirror*, 25 January 1954; "Violence Seen in Cavite," *Manila Times*, 16 September 1954; "Rosario Mayor Defies Mangubat," *Daily Mirror*, 16 September 1954.

[133]"Cavite City Mayor Padlocks Night Spots," *Manila Times*, 26 July 1954; "Screening of Aliens Ordered in Cavite," ibid., 7 August 1954; "200 'Colorum' Operators Fall," *Daily Mirror*, 9 August 1954; "City Police Chief Accused," ibid., 18 February 1955.

[134]"P88,000 Cavite City Suit Dropped," *Manila Times*, 12 February 1956.

[135]"P2(M) for Cavite," ibid., 4 May 1955.

[136]See Rogelio L. Ordonez, "Ang Kabite at Ang Mga Montano" [Cavite and the Montanos], *Asia-Philippines Leader* 1, no. 4 (30 April 1971): 47; as well as the article by Ernesto O. Granada published in the 26 January 1955 issue of the *Philippines Herald*.

[137]Republic of the Philippines, Commission on Elections, *Report of the Commission on Elections to the President and the Congress on the Manner the Elections Were Held on November 8, 1955* (Manila: Bureau of Printing, 1956), 19, 139, 141–42.

[138]"Cavite NPs Hit CG Son-in-law's 'Deals' with LP," *Manila Times*, 21 June 1957, 1.

[139]The notorious bandit Leonardo Manecio, better known as Nardong Putik (whose July 1955 escape from the Imus PC stockade Camerino had engineered for campaign purposes) gunned down Cavite's provincial PC commander, Lieutenant Colonel Laureano Maraña, and eight of his men in Imus on election day. See Romeo R. Lachica, "Shot Down by Pursuing PC Police," *Manila Times*, 24 November 1957.

[140]"Garcia In-law, Montano Clash," ibid., 8 August 1961, 1.

[141]"Montano Charges Poll Fraud Plot," ibid., 30 October 1961, 2.

[142]See "Poll Body Gets Montano Plea," ibid., 5 September 1961, 1; and "Montano Invites Press Observers to Cavite," ibid., 12 October 1961, 2.

[143]"Montano Raps PC Chief, Aids [*sic*]," ibid., 30 December 1961, 13.

[144]"Gov. Montano, CG's Kin Grapple," ibid., 20 August 1963, 1.

[145]See "Monta, Campos Trade Charges," ibid., 2 September 1961, 1; "Campo Says His Aim is Poll Safety," ibid., 21 September 1961, 1; "Montano to Take Agents' Disarming Case to Court," ibid., 23 September 1961, 1; and Filemon V. Tutay, "Clean and Free Elections?" *Philippines Free Press*, 4 November 1961, 7.

[146]Estelito P. Mendoza, "Memorandum for the Protestant," in Electoral Tribunal of the House of Representatives, Electoral Case no. 137, Fernando C. Campos, Protestant, versus Justiniano S. Montano, Protestee, 18 August 1963, 3–4, 10.

[147]"Montano Accused of Buying Votes," *Manila Times*, 7 November 1961, 22.

[148]See "Montano Claims Charges Not True," ibid., 19 July 1969, 2; "Montano Denies Charges Against GAB Officials," ibid., 21 April 1970, 1; and "Sarreal Jr., Elorde Criticize Montano," ibid., 14 May 1972, 30.

[149]See "Tension Grips Cavite Town," ibid., 13 January 1964, 1.

[150]See Napoleon G. Rama, "The People and the Manila Bay Reclamation Deal," *Philippines Free Press*, 3 September 1960, 36–37, 39; Napoleon G. Rama, "More on the Manila Bay Reclamation Project," ibid., 15 October 1960, 39; and "Court Halts Reclamation Project," ibid., 5 May 1962, 8.

[151]Articles in the *Manila Times*, 1963–70, as well as Securities and Exchange Commission documents, offer considerable insight into the machinations of such Montano companies as Cirmont Industries, Monta-Monte Realty, C. N. Montano and Associates, Trece Martires Development Corp., Cavite Farms Corp., Naic Farms Corp., and Tanza Farms Corp.

[152]See Ireneo Torres, "Fact and Myth about Tiny Cavite Barrio Described," *Manila Chronicle*, 24 March 1964, 10. By 1958, Sandakan, British North Borneo, had become the world's largest importer of American cigarettes, the overwhelming majority of which were bound for Philippine shores ("Import Control, High Taxes, and Smuggling," *American Chamber of Commerce Journal* 24, no. 5 [May 1959]: 197). By contrast, Imus, Camerino's home town, had become the site of extensive marijuana cultivation and a base for auto-theft operations in nearby Manila. See Jose de Vera, "Anatomy of 'Carnaping': Thugs, Cops, Politicos Linked," *Manila Daily Bulletin*, 22 March 1962, 1, 15; and "Politician Denounced," *Manila Times*, 27 May 1963, 2.

[153]These estimates appeared in documents submitted by Acting Executive Secretary Calixto O. Zaldivar to Secretary of Justice Salvador Marino in March 1964, later published in the Manila press. See "Documents Expose Extent of Smuggling Operations," *Manila Chronicle*, 19 March 1964, 1, 2.

[154]See "Lino Bocalan: Susunod na Gobernador ng Kabite?" [Lino Bocalan: The next governor of Cavite?], *Asia-Philippines Leader* 1, no. 11 (18 June 1971): 44–45.

[155]See "Documents Bare Extent of Smuggle [sic] Operations," *Manila Chronicle*, 20 March 1964, 1, 5; as well as Jose de Vera, "Blue-Seal Cigarette Hoard Seized; PC Hold Ex-Fiscal," *Manila Daily Bulletin*, 25 January 1962, 14; and "P.C. Troops Raid Smugglers' Lair," ibid., 15 March 1962, 2.

[156]Documents detailing the syndicate's operations cited the following monthly payoffs: chief of major AFP command, P20,000; chief of CIS, P10,000; area chief of CIS, P5,000; major, unit commander, P10,000; major, assistant unit commander, P8,000; captain, unit commander, P5,000 ("Documents Bare Extent of Smuggle [sic] Operations," 1, 5). In 1966, subsequent revelations identified the following members of the military establishment under the Macapagal administration as recipients of "hush money" from the syndicate: Secretary of Defense Macario Peralta, PC chief Brig. Gen. Nicanor Garcia, Second PC Zone chief Brig. Gen. Segundo Gazmin, Second PC Zone chief of staff Col. Miguel Sison, Second PC Zone assistant chief of staff Lt. Col. Teodoro Mascardo, Cavite PC commander Lt. Col. Isidro Villa, and 137th PC Company commander Capt. Pedrito Arroyo. See Primitivo Mijares, "3 Solons, 27 AFP Men in Smugglers' Book: 'Double Agents' Defended," *Saturday Chronicle*, 3 September 1966, 1, 2; and Filemon V. Tutay, "Three's a Crowd: Crisologo vs. Montano vs. (?) Bocalan," *Philippines Free Press*, 10 September 1966, 71–74.

[157]These figures represent the estimates made by Customs Commissioner Jose Lingad, as cited in Napoleon G. Rama, "The Octopus," ibid., 21 March 1964, 3, 81.

[158]See Patricia Torres Mejia, *Philippine Virginia Tobacco: 30 Years of Increasing Dependency*, The Philippines in the Third World Papers, no. 9 (Quezon City: Third World Studies Center, University of the Philippines, 1982).

159See Francisco De Leon, "Marcos Gives Dossier to DM," *Manila Chronicle*, 18 March 1964, 1, 2; and "Manahan Identifies Fisherman from Cavite as Top Smuggler," ibid., 17 March 1964, 1, 2.

160Edward R. Kiunsala, "Tobacco Law Under Fire," *Philippines Free Press*, June 1964, 10, 75.

161See Mijares, "Solons, AFP Men," 1, 2; Iluminado Varela, Jr., "Smuggling Row: It All Started at a Checkpoint," *Manila Chronicle*, 5 September 1966, 1, 20; and Primitivo Mijares, "CAO Agents Cleared at Smuggling Quiz," ibid., 9 September 1966, 1, 20.

162See Mijares, "Solons, AFP Men," 1, 2.

163See "Montano Counter [*sic*] Expose," *Manila Chronicle*, 4 September 1966, 1, 2; and Tutay, "Three's a Crowd," 71–74.

164See Manuel Silva, "Lawyer with $100,000 Held at MIA," *Daily Mirror*, 9 July 1968, 1; and "Bocalan Man with $100,000; OK, Says Enrile," *Manila Times*, 10 July 1968, 1.

165Juan V. Borra (chairman of the Commission on Elections), Resolution no. RR-552, promulgated on November 2, 1967, No. 77, Appendix GG, in Republic of the Philippines, Commission on Elections, *Report of the Commission on Elections to the President and the Congress of the Philippines on the Manner the Elections Were Held on November 14, 1967* (Manila: Bureau of Printing, 1969), 140–42.

166"Cavite Governor Hits Political Color in Palace Firearms Ban," *Daily Mirror*, 11 February 1967, 2; "Comelec Relieves Three PC Officers," *Manila Chronicle*, 1 November 1967, 11.

167Jovito R. Salonga, Abraham F. Sarmiento, and Antonio Jose F. Cortes, "Motion for Reconsideration and Rehearsing," filed 1 January 1968, in Fernando C. Campos et al., Petitioners, versus Commission on Elections et al. (Respondent G.R. No. L-28439, Supreme Court, Republic of the Philippines, Manila).

168See "Another Anti-FM Bombshell Coming," *Daily Mirror*, 20 May 1969, 1.

169Montano had charged that Marcos had conspired with Senator Helena Benitez to arrange for the construction of a public road cutting across the Benitez estate in Dasmariñas, Cavite. Moreover, he had raised embarrassing questions about Marcos's nominees for vacant positions on the Supreme Court, Claudio Teehankee and Antonio Barredo. See "Palace Poises Ax on Montano," *Daily Mirror*, 22 May 1969, 1.

170"List of Police Forces Placed by the Commission on Elections under Commission Control in the 1967 Elections," Appendix Z, in Republic of the Philippines, Commission On Elections, *Report on Elections Held November 14, 1967*, 118–19.

171Max Buan, Jr., "Manecio Will Yield If. . . ." *Daily Mirror*, 8 June 1971, 1.

172Unnamed former Bibilid prison official, interview with the author, Pasay City, 20 January 1992.

173F. H. Magno, "House LPs Decide to Change Leader," *Daily Mirror*, 19 March 1971, 1; Isagani Yambot, "Montano Ousted; Mitra Takes Over," *Manila Times*, 23 March 1971, 1; Primitivo Mijares, *The Conjugal Dictatorship of Ferdinand and Imelda Marcos I* (San Francisco: Union Square Publications, 1976), 159.

174"President Orders Probe of Montano-Paredes Row," *Manila Times*, 3 June 1971, 24; "DND Quizzes Second PC Zone Chief," *Daily Mirror*, 2 June 1971, 2.

175Michael Duenas, "Montano vs. Bocalan," *Philippines Free Press*, 30 October 1971, 8, 53–54.

176Filemon V. Tutay, "Bloodiest Election Yet," ibid., 20 November 1971, 4–5, 40.

177"Polcom Team to Cavite," *Daily Mirror*, 3 January 1972, 1; "New Clash in Trece Martires," *Manila Times*, 3 January 1972, 1.

178"Cavite Mayor's Ambushers Identified," *Daily Mirror*, 16 February 1972, 1; "2 Charged in Cavite Ambush," *Manila Times*, 21 February 1972, 26; Ireneo Torres, Jr., "Cavite City Loses Mayor in Ambush," *Manila Daily Bulletin*, 26 February 1972, 1, 2; Filemon V. Tutay, "No Mayors Land," *Philippines Free Press*, 11 March 1972, 6–7.

179"PC Takes Over 19 Towns, Three Cities of Cavite," *Manila Daily Bulletin*, 8 March 1972, 24.

Patron as Client: Warlord Politics and the Duranos of Danao

Michael Cullinane

For nearly forty years following World War II, Ramon Durano, Sr., was the dominant political power holder in the northeastern towns of Cebu Province. Today his heirs continue to hold sway over this area. Between 1949 and 1972, he was the congressman from Cebu's First District (see map) and his youngest son Nito has held the same seat since 1987. Since 1955, except for a brief period after February 1986, the mayorship of Danao, the district's wealthiest and most populous municipality, has remained in the family's hands—at first under Ramon's wife Beatriz (1955–71), then under their eldest son Boy (1971–86), and most recently under another son, Don (since 1988). As one reporter concluded, Danao City, Ramon's home town and the family's political and economic base, is owned by the Duranos "lock, stock, and votes."

From Danao, the Duranos have exerted wide influence over provincial politics, forming the nucleus of political coalitions that have contended for control of the province since the early 1950s. As patriarch, Don Ramon used his family to consolidate his realm, while simultaneously expanding his external relationships to protect its political and economic assets. During the 1984 election campaign for the National Assembly, Ramon Durano, the aging Cebuano warlord, was questioned by a foreign journalist about the many family members holding government positions in Danao City. Durano informed the reporter that "politics is not something you can entrust to non-relatives."[1]

Always a controversial figure, Ramon Durano projected two contradictory images: the loving Christian father and the ruthless political warlord. As father and patron, he was a rather simple man whose lifestyle and political sensibilities were rooted in the local politics of Cebu. Depicting himself as the folksy *provinciano* who often spoke in parables drawn from local lore or Christian scripture, he frequently told interviewers that "I'm just a town boy." In his later years, Manong Amon, as he was fondly called, found solace in the role of the jovial grandpa, sitting modestly with a contented grin, surrounded by his descendants, as his many well-wishers sang "I'll be loving you, always." Beyond the family circle he was the benevolent patron of his people, one who cared for his followers "from the cradle to the grave." And always he was a devout Catholic, fond of showing visitors the deep holes worn by his knees in the carpet beside the conjugal bed where he regularly prayed. His biographers provide an exhaustive list of his donations in support of church edifices and religious celebrations and causes, depicting Don Ramon as the Philippines' leading philanthropist.[2]

As a warlord, Ramon Durano was a powerful local potentate once photographed standing in front of the Danao City Hall brandishing a sword and challenging enemies to smite him. His opponents often accused him of maintaining control through intimidation, assassination, and corruption. During the early part of his political career, he was known for his propensity to eliminate political rivals while serving as a guerrilla officer during the Japanese occupation and establishing his dominance over Danao after the war. In the 1960s, Durano's heavily armed hired enforcers were the archetypal goons, the *mga bungutun* ('bearded ones') of Cebu politics, who were caricatured in the election parades of his opponents as creatures so monstrous that they frightened children in the crowds. By his own admission, Durano governed his political life with the slogan "When somebody tries to outsmart you, do not get mad, get even." "Politics in Cebu," he wrote in his autobiography, "is a battle of survival in a very physical sense. . . . You simply cannot allow yourself to be shot by gangsters."[3]

Throughout his long and turbulent career, Ramon Durano used both family and patrons to control the lives of thousands of people in his district. Though in many ways he was a warlord and undisputed master of his local domain, within the context of the Philippine political system he was required to participate in elections, both to affirm his political authority and to attract the patrons needed to protect his local prerogatives. To a great extent, his success as a warlord can be attributed to his ability to manage his family's control of "Durano country" and to find powerful patrons, both provincial and national, willing to barter his votes for their privileged access to national power. Herein lies the central irony: Ramon Durano, the "Caesar of Cebu," seemingly the personification of provincial warlordism, was both created and sustained by the nation-state. Though he appeared to be the most autonomous warlord beyond the reach of Manila, his very survival depended upon the state.

Thus, this study of Ramon Durano and his family will concentrate on the dynamics of local politics, on the one hand, and the interaction between the warlord and his provincial and national patrons on the other. After tracing the rise of Ramon Durano and the political history of the family, the essay will analyze the mechanisms it uses to maintain political and economic control.

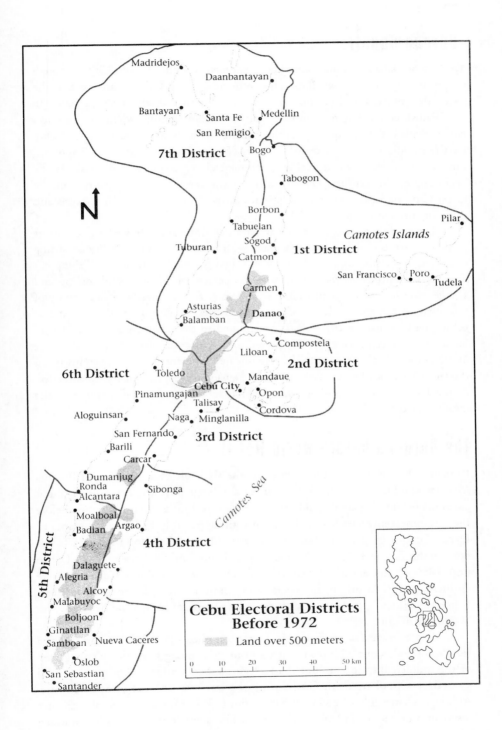

Madridejos

Daanbantayan

Bantayan

Santa Fe

Medellin

San Remigio

7th District

Bogo

Tabogon

N

Borbon

Tabuelan

Pilar

Sogod

Camotes Islands

Tuburan

Catmon

1st District

San Francisco

Poro

Tudela

Carmen

Asturias

Danao

Balamban

Compostela

Liloan

2nd District

6th District

Toledo

Mandaue

Pinamungajan

Cebu City

Opon

Talisay

Cordova

Aloguinsan

Naga

Minglanilla

San Fernando

3rd District

Barili

Carcar

Dumanjug

Ronda

Sibonga

Camotes Sea

Alcantara

Moalboal

Badian

Argao

4th District

Dalaguete

5th District

Alegria

Alcoy

Malabuyoc

Boljoon

Ginatilan

Samboan

Nueva Caceres

Oslob

San Sebastian

Santander

Cebu Electoral Districts Before 1972

Land over 500 meters

0   10   20   30   40   50 km

"Durano Country"

The city of Danao is located some thirty kilometers north of Cebu City. Although it appears to have been an important settlement along Cebu's east coast in the sixteenth century, it did not become a major political and religious jurisdiction in the Spanish colonial system until the late eighteenth century when the Recollect fathers made it the headquarters of their missionary activities in northeastern Cebu. By the middle of the nineteenth century, Danao had become more populous, functioning as the ecclesiastical and commercial center of the northeast. At the beginning of this century, Danao was the most developed municipality north of Cebu City, had the largest population, and was a major center for interisland shipping throughout the Visayas.[4]

Danao does not possess a rich agricultural hinterland. Only 30 percent of its total land area is classified as arable plain, with most of the municipality consisting of rolling or steeply sloped hills not well suited for staple agriculture. Fishing has long been the primary livelihood of some 45 percent of the town's inhabitants and a large majority of the population lives in coastal *barrios*, mostly in the vicinity of the town center, the *poblacion*. Cottage industries, ranging from the weaving of fishing nets to making cheese, also contributed to the commercial life of Danao. Since the nineteenth century, the presence of substantial deposits of coal in the mountainous interior has led to the sporadic development of a mining industry. In the late 1950s, nearby coal deposits made Danao an ideal site for the construction of the Durano-owned cement plant, which soon consumed 80 percent of the locally mined coal.[5]

The Duranos Before World War II

Born in 1905, Ramon Durano, Sr., was the sixth of seven children of Bibiana Mercado and Demetrio Tan Durano. In his autobiography he relates nothing about ancestors before his parents, and other sources reveal little about the family before the late nineteenth century, although his kin apparently had been residents of Danao for two generations. Ramon's mother Bibiana Mercado (1867–1957) was born in the Zapatera district of Cebu City and apparently did not move to Danao until 1886 when she married Demetrio. Although the Mercados of Cebu City were Chinese-*mestizo* in origin, her social and ethnic background remains unclear. Demetrio Durano (1863–1948) was reputedly a native of Danao and he clearly was of Chinese origin.[6]

Before his marriage, Demetrio Durano studied Spanish in Danao under a local tutor and, along with his brother Fausto, was among some thirty young men of the municipality to enroll at the Colegio de San Carlos, the only recognized secondary school in Cebu City during the last two decades of Spanish rule. Although Demetrio's schooling at San Carlos (1881–83) was limited and did not result in a degree, it undoubtedly accorded him some local status as an educated man, or *ilustrado*. In the late 1890s, he converted this status into a bureaucratic post when he was appointed *juez de paz* (justice of the peace) of Danao. There is also some evidence that Demetrio held the post of *teniente*, a local office equivalent to that of municipal councilor. By the end of Spanish rule, he was part of Danao's *principalia*, the upper stratum of local office holders and notable citizens. In this capacity his name appeared on a list of members of the municipality's *junta popular* who protested the imposition of American rule over Danao in 1900.[7]

Demetrio and Bibiana were neither wealthy nor landed. But neither were they poor. During Ramon's lifetime, his father appears to have been an itinerant merchant—trading local products and operating a fleet of small sailing vessels that plied the inland seas between the north coast of Cebu and the west coast of Leyte.[8] Reflecting its station, the family lived in the large coastal *barrio* of Suba, contiguous to the *poblacion*, and apparently it did not own any agricultural land. Thus, its livelihood was closely associated with the commercial life of the municipality and its market place, dependent upon the varied entrepreneurial activities made possible by Danao's location as a regional center of interisland trade.

Although Demetrio was among Danao's *principales* at the century's turn, the Duranos were not one of the municipality's leading families. Throughout the prewar years, Danao's political and economic life was dominated by several prominent, wealthier families. Nevertheless, Demetrio, his brother Fausto, and his eldest son Mariano engaged in municipal politics with some success. Mariano was elected to the Danao municipal council and appears to have been active in political affairs.[9] Socially and politically, the Duranos were linked to several of Danao's more prominent families. Ramon's baptismal godfather, Salvador Gonzales, was a wealthy landowner from a leading family.[10] More importantly, Demetrio's eldest daughter, Elisea, was married to the town's most powerful prewar political leader, Paulo Almendras, a wealthy landowner who cultivated the young Ramon. Welcomed into the Almendras household, Ramon formed close ties to his nephews Priscillano, Jovenal, Josefino, and Alejandro, all of whom later became influential political leaders in the provinces of Cebu and Davao. Clearly, Durano's associations with the Almendras family provided him with political experience and influence within Danao.[11]

Ramon's marriage to Beatriz Duterte provided another important link. The Dutertes had long been a significant political family in Danao, one with strong roots in Cebu City. The father of Beatriz, Severo Duterte, was politically active and competed for the mayorship before the war. Ramon's marriage to Don Severo's daughter was a politically significant match. Their marriage produced seven children: Beatriz, who married Emerito S. ("Tito") Calderon of a politically powerful family from the southern Cebu town of Samboan; Lydia; Ramon, Jr. ("Boy"); Jesus ("Don"); Rosemarie ("Judy"), who married Celestino ("Dodong") Sybico, a politically influential resident of Balamban on Cebu's west coast; Thaddeus ("Deo"); and Ramon III ("Nito").[12]

Much of Ramon Durano's early life was spent in school, since his parents insisted that their children obtain as much education as possible. Unlike his father and uncle, Ramon was educated in the English-language public schools set up under the Americans. At age seven, in 1912, he began his studies at the public elementary school in Danao, graduating in 1919. The following year he entered the Cebu Provincial High School in Cebu City, receiving his diploma in 1926. He then enrolled at the Cebu Junior College, an institution administered by the University of the Philippines, also in Cebu City. Two years later, with an associate of arts degree, he left for Manila to pursue a bachelor's degree in education at the University of the Philippines. In 1930, he returned to Danao with a B.S.E. degree, having graduated, he proudly noted, in the same class as Josefa Edralin, the mother of Ferdinand Marcos.[13] In April 1931, he married Beatriz Duterte, then an elementary-school teacher and a student at the Cebu Normal School.[14]

Although the young Durano taught for a short time at the Cebu Provincial High School, he soon discovered that teaching was a poorly paid profession, ill suited for a man with his ambitions. After a brief stint as a clerk in the treasurer's office of nearby Mandaue, he obtained an appointment through the Almendras family as a toll-bridge superintendent in Davao. There he resided for nearly two years in the early 1930s. The salary and extralegal collections deriving from this position, as well as a furniture-making business, permitted Durano to accumulate substantial savings.[15]

When he returned to Danao sometime around 1933, he initiated the dual career—politics and business—that would dominate the rest of his life. Allied with his prominent brother-in-law and mayor of Danao, Paulo Almendras, he won his first political office and served as municipal councilor from 1934 to 1938. At the same time he invested his newly acquired capital in four sailing vessels and established himself, like his father, as an itinerant trader. His ships operated throughout the Visayan Sea and reached as far as Palawan, usually carrying corn and *tungug,* a mangrove bark used for tanning and for coloring the popular coconut drink, *tuba.*[16]

His business ventures proved successful and in 1935, as his life became more settled, he decided to achieve what he professed to be one of his earlier goals: to become a lawyer. While still a merchant and municipal councilor of Danao, he entered the law school of the Southern Institute, a small private college in Cebu City, where he obtained his degree in only one year. He then attended a law review course at the University of Santo Tomas in Manila, passed the bar examination, and returned to Cebu as an attorney.[17] After a brief stint in a law office in Cebu City, he returned home to expand his entrepreneurial and political activities. Although Durano seems to have had no real affection for the law, his legal credentials would be critical to his growing political ambitions. "I considered the bar examination," he later explained, "as my passport to the future." Without legal qualifications, "my political enemies will have cause to say that I have no business asserting my leadership in Danao politics."[18]

Although he says little in his autobiography about his political activities during the late 1930s, Durano surfaced at the end of the decade as a rising leader within the expanding network of Mariano Jesus Cuenco, the most powerful anti-Osmeña politician of Cebu City and a member of President Manuel Quezon's Commonwealth cabinet. The Cuenco-Durano alliance was not strictly political, for it appears to have developed out of their mutual interest in exploiting the coal resources of Danao. The partnership produced a relatively lucrative business that mined the coal and sold it to the Cebu Portland Cement Company (CEPOC), a government-operated enterprise in Naga, a municipality south of Cebu City. Cuenco's influential position in President Quezon's cabinet, and his appointment as general manager of CEPOC in 1940, ensured the regular sale of the partnership's coal to the government cement works and greatly facilitated their drive to control the majority of the mines in the Danao area.[19]

With its coal deposits and its large population, Danao was also an attractive venue for the political ambitions of Cuenco, who was, in alliance with Quezon, seeking to undercut the political dominance of Sergio Osmeña in Cebu Province. By the late 1930s, Durano's political alliance with Cuenco led to a break with his relatives and long-time political allies, the Almendras family, who were widely acknowledged as the leading Osmeñistas of Danao. Although the reason for the split is not entirely clear, it produced an Almendras-Durano feud that persists to the present day.

In the years preceding World War II, Durano emerged as a major leader of the Cuenco faction. Under its political umbrella, he entered provincial politics in 1941 as an opposition candidate in the Frente Popular for Cebu's First District congressional seat. He was soundly defeated by the pro-Osmeña Nacionalista, Celestino Rodriguez, a political luminary and wealthy sugar landowner of northern Cebu.[20] The Japanese occupation, however, disrupted the rhythms of Philippine politics, providing Durano with his introduction to extralegal violence.

Wartime Politics

Durano chose the guerrilla resistance as his wartime political arena. Some months after the Japanese occupied Cebu, he was commissioned as a captain in the Cebu Area Command, a guerrilla force under the command of two Americans—Harry Fenton, in charge of administration, and James Cushing, the head of military operations. After his induction into the guerrillas by Fenton, Durano spent much of the early part of the war serving as his supply and intelligence officer, providing this controversial American with everything from prewar pesos, to scarce commodities, to young women. Under Fenton's authority, Durano is said to have used his position in the guerrillas to arrest, try, and summarily execute prewar political figures in the First District suspected of collaborating with the Japanese. After the war, it was alleged that many of these executions were part of a systematic elimination of the political allies of Celestino Rodriguez. The execution of Harry Fenton lends credibility to the allegations. In September 1943, Fenton was arrested and executed by his fellow guerrillas for a series of crimes that included hoarding of supplies and sexual abuses. Indeed, Fenton's own diary for a six-month period from July to December 1942 records more than sixty executions, a number of which targeted politically prominent Cebuanos. Those who have written of Fenton's excesses generally have blamed his peculiar psychology, never asking how an isolated foreigner largely ignorant of Cebu politics could have gained the information and inclination to execute so many local influentials. Circumstances indicate that Fenton's Filipino aides played key roles in this process.[21]

Since he was, as he put it, "identified with the Fenton group," Durano reportedly was arrested by guerrillas in late 1943 but was spared execution by the intercession of Cushing and influential relatives.[22] Though many of the details remain unclear, Durano appears to have sat out much of the remainder of the Japanese occupation in a guerrilla stockade. Near the end of the war he claims that he managed, together with his family, to make his way to Leyte. There he took advantage of the burgeoning underground economy of the immediate Liberation period to act as the supplier of a range of commodities during this time of extreme hardship. Targeting American GI dollars, Durano also marketed local handicrafts as wartime souvenirs. This lucrative trade kept him in Leyte for some time after peace was restored but in mid-1946 he returned to Cebu with his newly acquired wealth.[23]

By the end of 1946, two political factors had become apparent: Durano's position vis-à-vis his political enemies in Danao and elsewhere in the First District had improved substantially, and as a result his usefulness to his political patron, Mariano Cuenco, had greatly increased. Durano's wartime exploits had brought him wide notoriety but no threatening recriminations. Instead he had earned a reputation as a man willing to go to great extremes to improve his lot and protect his family's interests. The war years had provided him with valuable experience and abundant resources, creating a new environment for the achievement of his ambitions.

Postwar Political Maneuvers

The retirement of Sergio Osmeña, Sr., from politics after his defeat in the 1946 presidential election left Cebu in the hands of the Cuencos. They quickly tightened their control over the provincial government by forming a close alliance with the newly elected president, Manuel Roxas, the founder of the new Liberal Party. As a local leader in the rapidly expanding "Bando Cuenco," Ramon Durano received valuable patronage from the most powerful political network in postwar Cebu.[24] Since he was not yet in a position to run for Congress during the first postwar elections held in 1946, Roxas appointed him head of the Cebu branch of the government-operated National Coconut Corporation (NACOCO) sometime later that year. According to contemporary observers, this allowed him to line his pockets with funds siphoned from the regional copra trade. Operating out of Cebu City, Durano also established a small printing company, the University Press, where for a brief period he published a vernacular magazine, *Ang Balita*.[25]

By 1949, Durano was ready to enter politics. He was nominated as the Cuenquista congressional candidate for the First District on the Liberal Party ticket under President Elpidio Quirino. The incumbent, Durano's nephew Jovenal Almendras, a pro-Osmeña Nacionalista, decided not to run, leaving the field open. In an election dominated by the Bando Cuenco, Durano easily defeated his Nacionalista opponent, Florencio Urot, who had received limited support within the district since the collapse of the Osmeña family.[26] In 1950, Ramon Durano began his career in the House of Representatives as a freshman congressman from Cebu.

The Takeover of Danao

Although he was victorious in the congressional elections of 1949, Durano was not yet the dominant political figure in Danao or the surrounding district. Contemporary accounts of Danao usually describe it as a rustic municipality inhabited by farmers and fishermen with no powerful landlords. Politics at the time revolved around strongly contested electoral struggles between factions of locally prominent families with no single family or faction monopolizing office. As one schoolteacher wrote in the early 1950s, politics in Danao is "very hot" and "doesn't recognize any blood relation."[27]

By the late 1940s, Danao politics was centered around two competing blocs: the Almendras family, long influential in political affairs and closely allied with the Osmeñas; and a newer faction headed by Ramon Durano, the close ally of the Cuencos.[28] In the 1949 and 1951 municipal elections, pro-Durano candidate Pedro Sepulveda won the mayorship but this victory by no means sealed Durano's grip on town politics.[29] His takeover of Danao would require a violent struggle.

The ensuing conflict was not strictly a local one but was part of a larger, increasingly intense contest for control of Cebu provincial politics between the Cuencos and the Osmeña family, recently revived under Sergio ("Serging") Osmeña, Jr. After the war, as one contemporary politician noted, the Cuencos "practically had complete control of Cebu," for with only one exception "all the other 51 municipalities were manned by Cuenquistas, both elective and appointive." "All the judges and *fiscals*," he insisted, "paid homage to the Cuencos because Don Mariano was 'padrino' [sponsor] of their appointments."[30]

The situation changed in 1951. In the gubernatorial election of that year, Serging Osmeña entered politics and formed a major political alliance, the Bando Osmeña, which challenged the Cuencos both in Cebu and on the national level. With the support of President Quirino, Serging Osmeña defeated Manuel Cuenco, the incumbent governor, in 1951, sending shock waves through Cebu politics and reestablishing the central presence of the Osmeñas in provincial affairs. In early 1952, the new governor embarked on a campaign to remove a number of Cuenquista mayors around the province, alleging that they were corrupt. Among those targeted was Mayor Sepulveda of Danao, an ally of both Cuenco and the First District congressman, Ramon Durano.[31]

Governor Osmeña's suspension of Mayor Sepulveda in April 1952 led to serious political conflict in Danao. Pending the disposition of administrative charges against Sepulveda, Osmeña appointed an ally, Pedro Tecala, as acting mayor. As Tecala was a close associate and kinsman of the Almendras family, his appointment was considered a direct challenge to Durano's influence in Danao. The conflict exploded into violence on 25 May when Tecala was shot and killed at a Parent-Teachers Association meeting at the Danao Provincial High School by Manuel Yray, the vice-mayor and a Durano relative. Witnesses alleged that Durano, also armed with a revolver, ordered Yray to shoot Tecala, who had been insisting over Durano's objections that as mayor he should preside over the meeting. Before he died Tecala declared that Durano was responsible for his assassination. The Philippine Constabulary (PC) occupied Danao, later arresting both Durano and Yray on charges of murder.[32]

After a sensational trial, which dragged on until February 1954, Durano was acquitted and Yray was sentenced to seventeen years' imprisonment. In the meantime, Danao politics was in chaos. After Tecala's murder, Governor Osmeña appointed Josefino Almendras to the mayorship in an effort to place Danao directly under his allies. When the Cuenco-Durano forces protested, the Supreme Court eventually appointed Jose Pantoja, the municipal councilor who had received the highest vote count in the 1951 election. In 1954, when the administrative charges against former mayor Sepulveda collapsed, he was reinstated. He remained in office until the next election in 1955.[33] Meanwhile, Durano's acquittal paved the way for his takeover of Danao politics by demonstrating to local residents that he could withstand the efforts of Governor Osmeña and the Almendras family to undercut his local influence. He emerged from his trial with the aura of a local hero who had resisted the efforts of the Cebu City politicians to interfere in Danao's affairs.

To bring the town under its direct control, the Durano family backed Ramon's wife, Beatriz Duterte Durano, for the Danao mayorship in the elections of 1955. Beatriz won easily and held the mayorship for the next sixteen years, stepping down in 1971 to run unsuccessfully for governor. Boy Durano succeeded his mother to the mayorship in 1971 and held the post until 1986. After 1955, electoral contests in Danao became monotonous events, with Beatriz Durano or her son running unopposed or against candidates who appear to have been set up by the Duranos to create the illusion of a partisan struggle. Soon other positions in the municipal government were filled by family members or close associates. After Danao became a city in 1961, these trends accelerated until Danao became tightly controlled by the Durano family.[34]

Combines and Patrons in the 1960s

While the home front was secured by the late 1950s, new problems were arising in the Duranos' external relations. By that time Don Ramon's traditional patron, Mariano J. Cuenco, was no longer a dominant local and national figure, and the

Bando Cuenco was disintegrating. After its defeat by Serging Osmeña in 1951, the Cuenco faction had begun to weaken, losing both its national clout and its local following in Cebu's increasingly volatile politics. The alliance gradually eroded until the Cuencos, in 1959, joined their long-time enemies in a political coalition known as the "Cuenco-Osmeña Fusion." During the 1960s, though rife with tension and frequent internal conflicts, the Fusion emerged as the dominant political coalition in Cebu provincial politics.[35] As the Cuencos faltered and drew closer to the Osmeñas, Durano and his associates were abandoned.[36]

In response to his patron's decline, Ramon Durano organized new local alliances aimed at replacing the Bando Cuenco. Over the next two decades, Durano headed several political coalitions, known locally as "Combines," that played important roles in Cebu politics. The first emerged out of existing alliances within the Bando Cuenco and centered around politicians who were Durano's relatives and allies. The earliest combine allied Durano with Manuel Zosa, a cousin from the southwestern municipality of Barili. Zosa, like Durano, had been a strong Cuenquista leader and had dominated Cebu's Sixth District since 1947. In the 1953 and 1957 elections, Durano and Zosa ran under the aegis of the Bando Cuenco (as Democratas and as Nacionalistas, respectively) but did so in full awareness that their days as Cuenquistas were numbered. Even before the Cuencos joined Osmeña in 1959, the Durano-Zosa combine had emerged as a separate political bloc allied with President Carlos Garcia, a Cebuano from the neighboring island of Bohol.[37]

In 1961, the Durano-Zosa combine expanded to include Tereso Dumon, a political ally from the northwestern municipality of Daanbantayan. A businessman and labor leader, Dumon emerged as a prominent figure in local and national affairs in the 1950s and held the Seventh District congressional seat for most of the 1960s. During the early years of that decade, Durano, Zosa, and Dumon formed the "DZD Combine."[38] In the late 1960s, this combine underwent changes as Durano elevated his two sons-in-law—Tito Calderon (of Samboan in the Fifth District) and Dodong Sybico (of Balamban in the Seventh District)—forming the Durano-Calderon-Sybico (or DCS) Combine.

The 1960s witnessed the height of Durano influence in Cebu electoral politics. Between 1957 and 1972, the leaders of the Durano-led Combines were victorious in most elections within four of Cebu's seven congressional districts—Durano in the First, Zosa in the Sixth, Calderon in the Fifth, and Dumon and Sybico in the Seventh. The DCS Combine remained intact until 1986 when it collapsed in the post-Marcos period under the strains of provincial politics and internal family feuds.

Durano and his allies used these provincial Combines as vote-gathering machines to forge alliances with national figures who needed provincial support. The Durano-controlled Combines were linked at one time or another to all three presidents of this period. Though most were affiliated with the Nacionalista Party, the Durano-Zosa Combine briefly joined the Liberal Party in an effort to court President Macapagal in 1962. A closer look at these provincial Combines provides insight into the relationship between local politics and national affairs.

In the early 1950s, Durano and Zosa were successful pro-Cuenco politicians, in Congress as members of the Liberal Party and in Cebu elections as members of the Bando Cuenco. They operated as leaders *under* Mariano J. Cuenco, who called the shots and provided access to the national leadership through alliances with presidents Roxas and Quirino. When the Cuenco-Quirino bond collapsed in the aftermath of the 1951 elections, the Cuencos switched their loyalty to Ramon Magsaysay—joining the Magsaysay for President Movement, becoming members of the Nacionalista Party, and bringing both Durano and Zosa with them. With firm support in their districts, Durano and Zosa easily won reelection in 1953 as Cuenquistas and Nacionalistas allied with Magsaysay. Significantly, Durano won reelection to Congress in 1953 even before his acquittal in the Tecala murder trial.

While the Cuencos were losing both national influence and local power in the late 1950s, Durano for the first time was building his own personal relationship with a national ally, Vice-President Carlos Garcia, who would become president in May 1957 when Magsaysay died. In the November 1957 presidential elections, Durano and Zosa formed their provincial combine and, as Nacionalistas, actively supported Garcia for election as president in his own right. At odds with Serging Osmeña for some time, Garcia welcomed the delivery of Cebuano votes independent of both the Osmeñas and the Cuencos.

For his part, Durano's 1957 electoral battle against an influential Osmeña-backed candidate was one of the closest in his political career. He defeated his opponent by fewer than four thousand votes, despite what the Cuenco-owned newspaper reported as the "terrorist" activities of Durano goons.[39] Nevertheless, Garcia's victory and the reelection of Durano and Zosa gave life to their combine, which entered the political arena as a faction with proven provincial constituencies and a friend in Malacañang Palace. By the time the Cuenco-Osmeña Fusion was formally launched, in June 1959, with a distinctly anti-Garcia orientation, the Durano-Zosa Combine was the only viable political organization in the province with strong ties to the new president.

In 1959, his deepening alliance with President Garcia led Durano into one of only two electoral contests he waged outside his political domain. As part of Garcia's efforts to undermine the political influence of Osmeña and Cuenco in Cebu, Durano, with little to lose and everything to gain, was persuaded to run for the governorship against the Fusion candidate, Jose Briones. Durano lost the election by fewer than five thousand votes, a very creditable showing. In so doing he solidified his relationship with Garcia, who by now realized that Durano and the DZD Combine could deliver and would be his only hope for Cebuano votes in his quest for reelection in 1961.[40] The Garcia-Durano alliance was strengthened in 1959 when Rosita Dimataga-Almendras (the younger sister of Garcia's wife who was married to Durano's nephew, Josefino) became the running mate of Beatriz Durano in the mayoral elections in Danao. The two women won easily and held these posts for the next eleven years.[41]

As the leader of the largest pro-Garcia voting bloc in the Central Visayas during the late 1950s, Ramon Durano found himself in an enviable position to receive presidential pork barrel. By fortuitous circumstance, Garcia was disposed to reward his Cebuano ally, and did so out of the Japanese reparations then being distributed by the Philippine executive. Between 1957 and 1960, Durano received money and machinery amounting to more than six million pesos for the establishment of the Universal Cement Company (UNICEMCO), which provided the basis for what would later become the Danao Industrial Complex. In September 1958, the first lady, Leonila Dimataga Garcia, herself a Cebuana, presided over the laying of the cornerstone for UNICEMCO.[42] As an additional favor, Garcia appointed Ramon's "favorite brother," Antonio Durano, to the post of assistant director of the Bureau of Agriculture in August 1958.[43]

The presence of a major cement works in Danao, and its promise of increased revenues, permitted Durano to lobby for Danao's elevation to city status. There were numerous advantages in this change, not the least of which was that city status would bring with it nearly complete independence from provincial supervision. Using his influence with Garcia and his contacts in the legislature, Durano successfully negotiated the passage of Republic Act 3028 in June 1961, reclassifying Danao from municipality to city. Under this law, Danao acquired a status equivalent to that of Cebu City, and its elected officials would no longer fall under the jurisdiction of the governor. The city now would function more directly under the office of the Philippine president. In effect, this change cleared the way for the Duranos to tighten their control over nearly every aspect of life in Danao. In an effort to maximize his gains, Durano immediately introduced a bill in Congress that would have partitioned Cebu into two provinces, north and south. The northern portion was to consist of the First and Seventh districts, making the city of Danao its capital and the Duranos its undisputed masters. Strongly opposed by the Osmeñas and Cuencos, the bill failed to pass. Nonetheless, on 17 September 1961, Danao City was inaugurated, making it the premier municipality of northern Cebu. Today it remains the only city in the old First and Seventh congressional districts.[44]

In return for these favors, Durano and the DZD Combine delivered a substantial portion of the 1961 Cebuano vote to Garcia. In his losing campaign for reelection against Diosdado Macapagal, Garcia received more votes in Cebu than in any other province. This time Durano himself was easily reelected to Congress, defeating his pro-Osmeña opponent by more than twenty thousand votes. The other two leading figures of the DZD Combine, Zosa and Dumon, also won by large margins in the Sixth and Seventh districts.[45] By the time Garcia left office at the end of 1961, Durano had retained his congressional seat, strengthened his provincial combine, transformed Danao into a city with a growing "industrial complex," and greatly consolidated his family's hold over "Durano country."

Despite these successes, Durano and the DZD Combine, as pro-Garcia Nacionalistas, had little to look forward to as Macapagal entered the presidential palace in early 1962. Before long Durano and Zosa broke with the Nacionalistas and rejoined the Liberal Party in an effort to establish a less adversarial relationship with Macapagal. Realizing that there was little reason for Macapagal to favor his combine over Osmeña's Fusion, Durano decided to challenge the Fusion directly in the 1963 local elections. In his boldest attempt to confront Serging Osmeña, Durano announced his candidacy for the mayorship of Cebu City, while his son-in-law, Tito Calderon, entered the race for the vice-governorship. Building his campaign around charges of corruption aimed at the incumbent mayor, Osmeña, Durano succeeded in attracting support from a number of disaffected Fusion leaders. Although he collected more than twenty-two thousand votes in the heart of Osmeña's stronghold, Durano lost the election by sixteen thousand votes. Calderon lost by an even greater margin to the Osmeña candidate.[46] Only in Danao were the Duranos successful. Running as Liberals, Beatriz Durano and Rosita D. Almendras were reelected mayor and vice-mayor by large margins, and Jesus ("Don") Durano, Beatriz and Ramon's son, received the highest number of votes for the city council. Indeed, in 1963 no Nacionalista won office in Danao.[47]

Nonetheless, the DZD Combine's defeat in the race for key provincial offices against Osmeña made it difficult for Durano and Zosa to attract Macapagal's support. By 1964, Macapagal was courting Osmeña in preparation for the 1965 presidential election. Miffed at Osmeña's appointment as head of the Liberal Party in Cebu, and realizing they had little to gain from Macapagal, Durano and Zosa returned to the Nacionalistas. There they soon found common cause with presidential hopeful Ferdinand E. Marcos, himself a recent convert to the Nacionalistas. By the mid-1960s, despite his inability to capture electoral posts beyond his home territory, Durano's combine had clearly established itself as a viable opposition to the Osmeña-dominated Fusion. Marcos's search for Visayan friends and Cebuano votes led to a long relationship with Durano. Though Macapagal chose wisely in Cebu in 1965, where Osmeña delivered the majority of the provincial votes, he lost the election to Marcos, who was inaugurated as president in January 1966. Realizing the danger Osmeña posed as a rival for national leadership, Marcos worked to build a solid Cebuano alliance in support of his reelection. Ramon Durano emerged as a key player in Marcos's electoral strategy.[48]

As a major Marcos ally during the late 1960s, Durano's influence in provincial politics increased. In the 1965 election he was easily reelected to his congressional seat, as was his ally Dumon in the Seventh District. The other two DZD leaders lost their elections, however, with Zosa suffering his first defeat since 1949 in the Sixth District and Tito Calderon beaten in his first attempt to capture the Fifth. This election was the last for the DZD, which was soon reorganized into the DCS Combine, in which Calderon and Dodong Sybico surfaced as central figures under the direction of their father-in-law, Don Ramon. For the next four years Durano and Serging Osmeña engaged in an increasingly intense and violent struggle for control of Cebu politics, with Marcos intervening whenever possible in support of the anti-Osmeña forces. As the two political blocs squared off in preparation for the 1969 presidential elections, political assassinations increased and slanderous allegations escalated.[49]

The local elections of 1967 were a testing ground for the building confrontation, and the results were mixed. In an alliance with Rene Espina, the Marcos candidate for governor, the DCS Combine played an important role in handing Osmeña a major defeat. Espina was reelected as governor over Osmeña's choice, Priscillano Almendras, a Durano nephew and political enemy. Osmeña's candidates also lost all but four of the province's fifty-six mayorships. Osmeña maintained his political base only by winning reelection as mayor of Cebu City along with his bloc of councilors.[50] But, despite this poor showing, he continued his efforts to capture the presidential nomination of the Liberal Party in 1969. Meanwhile, the Duranos, in league with Marcos, maneuvered to deny Osmeña the support he needed to deliver his own province in the presidential campaign.

Although membership in the larger alliance against Serging Osmeña varied considerably during this period, its core in Cebu was the DCS Combine, focused on four congressional districts under the control of four influential leaders—Durano, Calderon, Zosa, and Sybico—all relatives as well as allies. In 1967, the Durano family reconfirmed its dominance over Danao City. Running as mayor, vice-mayor, and councilor, respectively, Beatriz Durano, Rosita D. Almendras, and Don Durano, now Nacionalistas all, won their seats in Danao City unopposed, sweeping in the other Duranista candidates on their coattails. Outside of Danao and the First District, the most thorough effort to replicate the Durano pattern was being initiated in southern Cebu, where the Calderons succeeded in dominating a major municipality, Samboan. This town became the base for their efforts to gain control of the Fifth District, which had remained a Cuenco-dominated area since the earliest postwar elections. In the 1967 election, Beatriz Durano Calderon, Tito's wife and Ramon's eldest daughter, captured the mayorship of Samboan with 95 percent of the vote.[51] By 1969, with Samboan firmly in the family's hands, Tito Calderon moved to capture the district. At the same time, Ramon Durano was working to expand his direct control over the Seventh District. In early 1969, the Durano propaganda machine began publicizing a movement initiated by the district's mayors to petition Durano to run for Congress in that jurisdiction. Durano, in turn, was promoting his son-in-law, Dodong Sybico, working to install him in Congress as the Seventh District successor to Tereso Dumon.[52]

The pinnacle of Durano's political influence in Cebu politics was reached in 1969. Not only did he and his associates succeed in delivering the majority of Cebuano votes to Marcos but they won overwhelmingly nearly every provincial office they contested. As in 1967, Serging Osmeña was able to carry a majority only in Cebu City and the surrounding Second District, while the rest of the province fell to Durano and other Marcos allies. With the exception of Josefino D. Almendras, the Duranista candidate in the Second District who lost to John Osmeña (Serging's nephew), all the combine's leaders won their congressional seats.

In the First District the presidential election results were unprecedented, with Marcos defeating Osmeña by a margin of more than four to one, while the Nacionalista congressional candidates "made a clean sweep" in the district. In Danao City the final count was almost embarrassing: Marcos emerged with 15,422 votes to Osmeña's 877. Referring to this election, Durano later boasted that "without my blessings no candidate could win in the province of Cebu."[53]

When the dust settled, Durano not only emerged as Cebu's dominant provincial politician but he found himself with an even stronger ally in the presidential palace. While Osmeña endeavored to overturn the election results through litigation, claiming massive fraud by Marcos and his allies, Durano basked in his victories, almost oblivious to the dramatic changes that were beginning to take place throughout the Philippines.[54] Political turmoil followed the unprecedented reelection of Marcos, as political elites everywhere scrambled to protect their interests and new political organizations surfaced to demand radical changes in the decaying economic and political milieu. A vigorous youth movement emerged under the influence of the resurgent left while a growing nationalist movement sought to restructure society and end the "neocolonial" dominance by the United States. The bombing of a Liberal Party rally at Manila's Plaza Miranda in August 1971, widely believed to have been instigated by Marcos, led to increased opposition. In Cebu, sympathy for Serging Osmeña and his nephew John, both wounded in the bombing, had a considerable impact on provincial politics, particularly when Serging returned to campaign for the November local elections.

Building upon their 1969 success, the Duranos, with strong Marcos support, set their sights on the long-coveted Cebu governorship in the 1971 elections. Although defeated in their earlier attempt to win the governorship in 1959, the Duranos were now in a much stronger position. One sign of the combine's growing power had come in November 1970 when Durano's daughter, Lydia Durano Rodriguez, was elected as a delegate to the Constitutional Convention from Cebu's First District. Confident of victory in the 1971 race, the Duranos and the Nacionalistas chose Beatriz Durano as their gubernatorial candidate. In the bloodiest election in Cebu history, she lost to the Osmeña candidate, Osmundo Rama, a stunning defeat that formed part of a complete reversal of political fortunes in Cebu. The Osmeñas won every city and provincial office. Serging Osmeña was reelected as mayor of Cebu City, scoring the largest majority he ever achieved in his five races for this office. Moreover, the eight Liberal senatorial candidates, all Osmeña endorsed, swept the province.[55] Despite their expanded power, the Duranos again were unable to capture key offices beyond their domain. On the eve of Marcos's declaration of martial law, the influence of the Duranos and their combine allies had been reduced to their core territory once more.

Warlord Politics in the "New Society"

The period of authoritarian rule under Marcos, which lasted until 1986, created a series of new challenges for the warlord and his family. In order to preserve their territory and retain the fiscal and economic resources they had accumulated over the years, the Duranos were forced to adjust to the new form of national politics. When Congress was dissolved at the onset of martial law in 1972, Don Ramon suddenly found himself without the key national office he had held for twenty-two years. This change was paralleled by the emergence of a new generation of political leaders within the family. Until his death in 1988, Don Ramon remained the central figure in his family's political maneuverings but under Marcos's dictatorship his children began to play a more prominent role in the political life of "Durano country."

During the first six years of dictatorial rule, the Duranos enjoyed a period of dominance made uneasy by the lack of elections with which to legitimate their local hegemony. Their national patron, Marcos, had no compelling reason to reward them since he ruled without the need for congressional approval or electoral mandate. Although the Durano-Marcos alliance remained intact, it adjusted to the imperatives of authoritarian rule.[56] Initially the Duranos maintained their control over Danao City. Boy Durano was serving as mayor, having been elected to the post in 1971 when his mother, the long-time incumbent, stepped down to run for the governorship. The Calderons retained their hold on Samboan where Beatriz Durano Calderon was mayor. Outside of these municipal enclaves, however, the Duranos and their close associates held no government offices. Compounding these problems, Governor Osmundo Rama, the Osmeñista who had defeated Beatriz Durano in 1971, would remain in office until 1976.

Until 1978, electoral politics ceased to exist. Instead of elections there were six carefully orchestrated plebiscites seeking popular approval for specific Marcos initiatives. These referendums required only yes or no votes, and the results were largely fabricated to demonstrate growing popular support for the dictatorship.[57] The vote counts, that is, those submitted by the various constituencies, seemed to serve only one purpose—verification of loyalty from local leaders and their ability to deliver. In these not-so-subtle tests the Duranos went to absurd lengths to demonstrate their loyalty to the president. In the 1973 referendum, which posed the question of whether Marcos should continue in office, the Danao tally was 28,902 yes and 7 no. In the 1976 referendum, on the continuation of martial law and related constitutional amendments, Danao voted 34,439 yes and 14 no.[58] There was no reason for Marcos to question the loyalty of the Duranos but there was a growing need to impose some restraint on the overzealous warlord.

In 1976, after careful consideration, Marcos and his advisers decided to reorganize the Cebu provincial government. They did this by replacing Governor Rama with an appointee, Eduardo ("Eddie") Gullas. An attorney and owner of the largest private university in the Visayas, Gullas had been allied with the anti-

Osmeña political forces in Cebu City for some time. In 1969, he had won the Third District congressional seat as a pro-Marcos Nacionalista and had reaffirmed his loyalty to the president after the declaration of martial law. In early 1973, Marcos had appointed Gullas as his commissioner of professional regulations, a post he retained after assuming the governor's office.[59] From Marcos's viewpoint, Gullas had three important qualities in his favor: he was a popular political leader from Cebu City, an Osmeña stronghold; he was personally loyal to the dictator; and he was not linked to the Duranos.

The appointment of Gullas rather than a loyal Duranista was a clear sign that Marcos had no intention to deliver Cebu to his loyal ally Don Ramon. Gullas had been selected as a foil and his appointment set into motion a series of careful machinations by Marcos aimed at retaining the loyalty of the Duranos while restraining them from running Cebu—a situation the regime believed would cause local discontent.[60] Able to do little to contest the Gullas appointment, the Duranos were forced to operate in an uneasy alliance with the new governor. Not until 1978, when the first offices were opened up for election, did the Durano-Gullas conflict become public. Between 1978 and 1986, the rivalry continued during the six elections of the Marcos dictatorship: in 1978 for the members of the Interim National Assembly (Batasang Pambansa); in 1980 for municipal and provincial offices; in 1981 for president; in 1982 for *barangay* officials; in 1984 for members of the National Assembly; and in 1986 for president.

In 1978, the announcement of elections for the Interim National Assembly revived political activity. For six years there had been only one active political organization throughout the Philippines, Marcos's own party, the Kilusang Bagong Lipunan (KBL). In Cebu the KBL became increasingly divided, with one faction led by the Duranos and the other by Gullas. In 1978, the factions were more focused on the nominations of KBL candidates than on the election itself. As Gullas later put it, Marcos's policy of "deep selection" would decide the results in advance.[61] In close consultation with Marcos and his minister of local governments, Jose Roño, the party was careful in its selection of the thirteen KBL candidates for Region VII, which included Cebu. To satisfy the leading political figures in Cebu, the KBL candidates were drawn from both factions: Eddie Gullas, Rene Espina, Nito Durano, and Tito Calderon from the old Nacionalista group; and Lito Osmeña (Serging's nephew) and Tony Cuenco (the son of Manuel) representing the old Fusion.[62]

Outside Manila there was little organized resistance to KBL candidates. In Region VII, however, particularly in Cebu, an aggressive new opposition party, the Pusyon Bisaya, nominated a full slate of candidates to challenge the KBL. During the campaign, the Pusyon generated widespread, enthusiastic support. In response, Marcos seems to have sanctioned the likelihood of victory by Pusyon candidates everywhere in the region except in the core area of Cebu where he intended to retain KBL control.[63] When the votes came in, it became obvious that the KBL in Cebu had failed to manipulate the results effectively enough to secure even the four core seats. Flagrant KBL violations were obvious to the public and its overwhelming support for the opposition threatened violence. Only in Danao and the municipalities under Durano's sway did the KBL candidates win decisively. In the end even this was not enough. The region's Board of Canvassers, with Marcos's apparent approval, conceded all thirteen seats to the Pusyon Bisaya over the strong protests of the Duranos.[64] When the results were announced, neither the Duranos, Gullas, nor any of their associates had won seats in the Interim National Assembly. Clearly the only winner in the election was Marcos. He permitted the opposition to surface, to let off steam and win empty offices, while leaving the political balance of power in Cebu intact. His hand-picked governor, Eddie Gullas, retained his post, and the Duranos, who had once again demonstrated their loyalty, were still confined to Danao.[65]

The next encounter came in 1980, when Marcos announced the first local elections since 1971. Three opposition parties quickly emerged in Cebu, each with its own candidate for the governorship. Within the KBL a struggle ensued between Gullas and the Duranos over the KBL nominee. In December 1979, after long consultations in Manila with Marcos and his advisors, Gullas emerged as the KBL candidate and Nito Durano as his running mate. The two Cebu factions of the KBL were, it seems, left to their own devices in selecting candidates for municipal mayoralties throughout the province. Unlike the situation in 1978, the pro-Marcos forces were fully prepared for the 1980 election. When the results were announced, Gullas and Durano had won easily, carrying with them a full array of KBL mayors, most allied with the Duranos.[66] Once again, however, Marcos was the real winner, for the opposition had been crushed, KBL officials dominated the province, his choice for governor had been elected, and the Duranos, as loyal as ever, were still contained.

The 1980 elections permitted the Duranos to reaffirm and expand their family's control over the municipalities of the old First District. Boy Durano was reelected mayor of Danao, while his son, Ramon ("Boboy") Durano IV, was elected city councilor. Boy's brother, Deo Durano, won the office of mayor of Sogod, a municipality north of Danao, and pro-Durano mayors captured the district's other towns. In the southern municipality of Samboan, the Calderons continued their dominance over the mayorship and influenced the election of mayors elsewhere in the old Fifth District. Moreover, Tito's son, Raymond D. Calderon, was elected to the Cebu provincial board, presided over by Gullas and Nito Durano. Although the Duranos had failed again to capture the prized post of governor, they had strengthened their local bases. Of equal importance, the next generation of Duranos was following in its parents' footsteps.

In another move intended to legitimize his authoritarian regime, Marcos lifted martial law in January 1981 and promised that presidential elections would be held in June. Since no creditable candidates came forward to run against the president, the election was a farce. Nevertheless, this "demonstration election" won the approval of the Reagan administration in Washington and provided another venue in which Filipino politicians could register support for the dictator. Taking full advantage of the moment, the Duranos went all out. Less than two months before the election, Ferdinand and Imelda Marcos were the major sponsors at a large celebration in Cebu commemorating the fiftieth wedding anniversary of Don Ramon and Beatriz. During the election itself, in a superfluous show of loyalty, Danao City delivered 51,408 votes to Marcos and only 148 to his rivals.[67]

After this crushing victory, Marcos began to loosen the political reins. Shortly after the KBL demonstrated its strength in the elections for *barangay* officials in March 1982, he announced that elections for the National Assembly would be held in May 1984. With ample lead time, political organizations proliferated. In Cebu a number of local opposition groups surfaced, some new and others forming around remnants of the Pusyon Bisaya. The bloc with the greatest potential for success was the Coalition Panaghiusa, which soon came under the leadership of the Osmeñas and Cuencos. The local KBL remained firmly in the grasp of Marcos and its two local leaders, Durano and Gullas.

As the 1984 elections approached, the internal struggle between Gullas and Durano intensified. Despite Durano's opposition, Gullas was still serving as Cebu's governor and in 1983 had been named the only provincial representative to Marcos's Executive Committee, a body of advisors that functioned as the regime's collective vice-presidency. When the KBL candidates for Cebu's eight seats in the National Assembly were selected at a private caucus in Manila, Gullas and Durano were given three candidates each for the province's six legislative seats while Marcos himself selected the candidates for two new Cebu City seats.[68]

In an awesome demonstration of their ability to control electoral results, the Duranos delivered an overwhelming majority from "Durano country" and the old First and Seventh districts, placing their three candidates at the top of the winners' list. Gullas delivered the Third and Sixth districts but his KBL candidate in the Fourth District lost to Nenita Daluz, a popular Panaghiusa radio commentator from Cebu City. As expected, the two city seats were won by the opposition's Panaghiusa candidates. In late May, allegations of electoral fraud, leveled particularly against the Duranos, led to a violent protest in Cebu City against the KBL and continued Marcos rule.[69] By the end of 1984, the province was divided into three political factions: the Duranos, the Gullas bloc, and the opposition, led now by the Panaghiusa, which was allying itself with UNIDO, an anti-Marcos coalition in Manila.

At the time of their patriarch's eightieth birthday in 1985, the Duranos were well situated within Cebu officialdom, holding even more key political offices than they did at the height of their electoral power in the late 1960s. Ramon Durano's youngest son, Ramon III ("Nito"), and his son-in-law Tito Calderon were representing Cebu in the National Assembly; his daughter Beatriz Durano Calderon was vice-governor; his grandson Raymond D. Calderon was a provincial board member; his eldest son Boy was mayor of Danao; his son Deo was mayor of Sogod; his grandson Boboy was a Danao city councilor; and Don Ramon himself was a *barangay* captain. Moreover, the newly appointed mayor of Cebu City, Ronald Duterte, was Beatriz Durano's nephew.[70]

Despite the many Duranos in Cebu government, the family still did not dominate provincial politics. Marcos curtailed Durano's attempts to monopolize the arena by supporting Gullas, who retained the governorship to the end. Gullas was even floated as a possible vice-presidential running mate when Marcos announced that he would hold a presidential election in February 1986. Although always willing to acknowledge Durano's loyalty, Marcos was clearly reluctant to indulge the warlord's hegemonic ambitions. Thus, as Marcos courted Gullas in December 1985, the KBL selected Beatriz Durano to serve on the prestigious, though powerless, committee that would notify Marcos of the party's endorsement of his candidacy.[71] Marcos used every possible manipulation to maintain a balance of power in Cebu that, above all, favored the dictator's control over local politics.

In early December, two months before the February 1986 elections, Durano boldly declared that Marcos would win and that he would "slug it out" with the opposition to guarantee his patron's victory. With his loyalty to Marcos thus demonstrated, however, the aging warlord devoted most of his time to fighting Gullas, as the two vied for control of the pro-Marcos campaign. In a local meeting of the KBL held in mid-December, the provincial leaders attempted unsuccessfully to coordinate their campaign efforts and map out a strategy that would deliver votes to Marcos while alleviating tensions between the feuding factions. After sending in an arbitrator and summoning Durano to Manila for consultation, Marcos and his advisors, in apparent frustration, attempted to forge a truce by persuading the two politicians to agree at least on separate campaign jurisdictions.

Despite these efforts at unity, the Durano-Gullas split persisted.[72] On the occasion of his birthday, on 24 December, Ramon Durano invited the forty-eight mayors of Cebu to a celebration in Danao where he presented his plan for the KBL division of the province. The Duranos would control the old First and Seventh districts in the north, Gullas would control the Second and Third districts that flanked Cebu City, Tito Calderon would manage the Fifth District of the south, and the Fourth and Sixth districts would be divided among three loyal KBL leaders from those areas. Although this scheme was not particularly favorable to Gullas, the governor remained publicly silent for the remainder of the campaign, possibly to prevent further escalation of the conflict.[73]

A month before the elections Durano engaged in a series of publicity stunts. He challenged Corazon Aquino and Salvador Laurel, Marcos's opponents, to campaign in Danao. When they took him up on the offer and showed up in town, they encountered a large billboard in front of the main church reading "Welcome to Ferdinand E. Marcos Country." He also offered to bet anyone in the opposition a million pesos that Marcos would not only win the election but would receive more votes than Cory in both Cebu and in Benigno Aquino's home province of Tarlac.[74]

As reports circulated of pending electoral violations and unusually large increases in voter registration in Danao, both the National Citizens Movement for

Free Elections (NAMFREL) and a number of international observers targeted Danao as a "hot spot" that would require close inspection. NAMFREL, in particular, made "Duranoland" one of the focal points of its national campaign to guarantee an honest election. When the voting ended it was apparent that the efforts of hundreds of volunteers had failed. Most reports concluded that there had been no election at all in Danao, the results having been fabricated in advance. At the start of the campaign, Danao mayor Boy Durano had announced that Marcos would win all of the city's 58,000 votes. Indeed, when the results came in they were among the most lopsided in the province—57,225 for Marcos and 342 for Aquino.[75]

Although the political developments of February 1986 made the final count irrelevant, the election results in Cebu appear to have been genuinely mixed. Although Marcos is reported to have lost in Cebu Province, it is believed that he won by a slight majority in the areas outside Cebu City. Gullas was unable to reverse the tidal wave of opposition support in Cebu City, where Aquino won a large majority of the votes. The Duranos, as noted, delivered Danao and the old First District. But, unlike the situation in 1984, even the Duranos were unable to secure victories for Marcos in three municipalities. Clearly, "cracks" had begun to appear in Durano's solid north. In the south the situation was even worse, since Marcos reportedly lost in the Calderon stronghold of Samboan.[76] The Osmeñas and Cuencos, as leaders of the opposition, had successfully reasserted themselves in Cebu politics.

Surviving Marcos

The unexpected departure of Ferdinand Marcos, their patron of twenty years, forced the Duranos to adjust yet again to changing political circumstances. Within days of Marcos's flight to Hawaii, Ramon Durano held a press conference at which he urged Filipinos to support Aquino. Unconvinced by these eleventh-hour gestures, the Aquino government was clearly hostile to the Duranos, who had given far more than perfunctory support to the Marcos regime. In the reorganization of local governments and the appointment of transitional officials, "officers in charge" (OIC), in early 1986, the Aquino regime removed Boy Durano from the mayorship of Danao and replaced him with long-time political adversary Jovenal Almendras. For the first time in more than thirty years the mayor of Danao was not a member of Ramon Durano's immediate family. The post of OIC vice-mayor was given to Rosalinda T. Tomboc, the daughter of Pedro Tecala, the Danao mayor murdered by Durano's henchman in 1953. To add insult to injury, Leonardo Capitan, the lone NAMFREL volunteer in Danao and an outspoken critic of Durano-engineered fraud in the February 1986 election, was named to the Danao City Council.[77] By mid-1986 it seemed that the complete dismantling of the Durano empire would soon follow.

Under the Aquino administration's policy of reconciliation, the political and military components of the Marcos era were left in place, while the pre–martial law electoral process was reestablished. The Aquino government did not attempt through extralegal means to end the economic and political controls that the Duranos exercised. With open elections as the primary weapon in the Aquino arsenal, the new government seemed to believe that it could vote the Duranos out of power. This naive policy grossly underestimated the Duranos' strength and demonstrated the new administration's poor grasp of the Philippine political process at the local level. Despite the presence of unfriendly "officers in charge" in Danao City, Aquino's policies allowed the Duranos to retain the coercive mechanisms they had built up over nearly forty years of political dominance.

When the new government reestablished electoral districts for the congressional elections of May 1987, Nito Durano was well placed to dominate the new Fifth District, which corresponded to the old First. President Aquino made Durano's defeat a high priority, giving her personal support to Nita Daluz, his Panaghiusa opponent. Three days before the election, Aquino herself campaigned for Daluz in Cebu, visiting Danao twice to urge voters to end the Durano dynasty. Speaking before several thousand people in the plaza, Daluz proclaimed that she would convert the Durano-owned industries into "semi-government entities to benefit the workers." Standing by her side, Aquino linked Daluz's victory to the restoration of democracy in Cebu.

The struggle in the Fifth District was billed as a battle between popularity (Daluz) and machinery (Durano). As the focal point of the elections in Cebu, the Fifth District produced an array of unusual alignments, including Nito Durano's endorsement by Minnie Osmeña, daughter of Serging. When the results were in, it was announced that Nito Durano had defeated Daluz by twenty thousand votes, taking almost 80 percent of Danao's tally. While opposition protests and allegations of fraud flooded in, Durano thanked the people of his district for conducting themselves in a peaceful and orderly manner and praised his opponent for the valiant effort that had helped make democracy "a reality" in Cebu.[78] In an election post mortem, a long-time political analyst of Cebu's politics concluded that "once again, the Durano machine proved unbeatable in the district."[79] For the Aquino government it was a painful lesson in local politics, a clear demonstration that "People Power" was ineffective against an entrenched and distant warlord.

Although the Duranos demonstrated their ability to deliver votes in their territory, elsewhere in the province the 1987 elections proved less favorable for the family's old DCS Combine. As they had done under Marcos, the Duranos, now led by son Nito, allied themselves with Tito Calderon and Dodong Sybico, Don Ramon's sons-in-law. All were affiliated with the revived Nacionalista Party–Grand Alliance for Democracy (NP-GAD) under Juan Ponce Enrile, Marcos's former defense minister and the leader of the military faction whose failed coup had brought Aquino to power. Under this banner, Calderon ran in the Second District and Sybico in the Third. In addition, Don Ramon's nephew, Ronald Duterte, the

Marcos-era mayor of Cebu City, ran as an NP-GAD candidate for the congressional seat of the city's southern district. All three of these allies lost, leaving Nito as the only Durano with a national political office under the new regime.[80] Although the Duranos were able to secure their home front, the rise of competing political forces in Cebu City and elsewhere in the province had overwhelmed their political influence beyond "Durano country." Even more alarming was the family's lack of a national patron. Although Enrile had the potential to achieve national leadership in 1987, the Aquino government's hostility prevented him from solving any of the Duranos' pressing economic problems.

Internal family disputes posed a more serious threat to the Duranos than Aquino's efforts to break their political power. Operating from a diminished power base, and without a viable national patron, long-standing tensions surfaced among Don Ramon's sons over the division of their father's dwindling economic and political spoils. In mid-1987, a family crisis erupted soon after the Aquino government announced that elections would be held for local offices in January 1988. The aging warlord soon found himself in the midst of a bitter clash among his sons over the mayorship of Danao. Boy Durano supported the candidacy of his son Boboy (Ramon IV). Boy's younger brother, Deo, the former mayor of Sogod, had early declared his intention to run. Both Don Ramon and Beatriz Durano eventually favored Don, brother of Boy and Deo. As the controversy grew, Beatriz Durano filed her own candidacy, apparently in order to discourage Deo from running. In complete disregard for his parents' efforts to reach a compromise, Deo pursued his campaign, establishing alliances with local and national politicians in an attempt to legitimize his candidacy. A short time before the election, Don Ramon himself publicly announced that he would run. He condemned his son for acting in violation of the Fourth Commandment, "Thou shalt honor thy father and thy mother." Deo persisted, accusing his family of abusing its power in Danao.

The situation was complicated further by the fourth brother, Nito, who initially seemed to be supporting Deo against their father. In mid-December, however, Nito announced: "My dad is my candidate for Danao City." With this endorsement, Nito then negotiated his father's affiliation with the newly organized Cebu Coalition under Congressman Filemon Fernandez, which shifted the family away from Enrile's NP-GAD Party and toward two national coalitions, the PDP-Laban and Lakas ng Bansa, the latter a group associated with Senator Ernesto Herrera.

These political maneuvers led to a major break in the DCS Combine, as relations with the Calderons of Samboan and Sybicos of Balamban deteriorated. Without the support of Nito Durano or his father, Tito Calderon and Dodong Sybico's son were running for provincial governor and provincial board member as Enrile Nacionalistas. On the eve of the election, Nito Durano disclaimed any affiliation with Calderon, who continued his quest for the governorship without Durano support. Calderon suffered a humiliating defeat in the gubernatorial race, finishing fourth. Simultaneously, the young Sybico failed to make the top fifteen in the race for the provincial board.[81]

In a turbulent, though ultimately manipulated, election in Danao, Don Ramon was elected mayor and his son Don vice-mayor. But Ramon's decisive victory did not bring an end to the family conflict that had been building throughout the campaign. Only days after the election, Don and a group of his goons intercepted Deo Durano in a Cebu City suburb, ran his car off the road, and left him with three bullet wounds. By the end of the month, the two brothers had filed charges against each other in the local courts. The family's internal conflicts and the breakup of its provincial combine led one political observer to proclaim, perhaps too quickly, that "we are probably witnessing the crumbling of the once respected and feared Durano political 'empire' in Cebu."[82] By early 1988, the ailing, eighty-three-year-old patriarch and his youngest son Nito were left with the tasks of bringing peace to the fractured family and rebuilding their decaying dynasty.[83]

Recognizing the fragility of their political base and the need to restore family unity, Nito and his father resumed the tedious effort to renegotiate the Duranos' relationships beyond Danao. Although the family still held the local congressional seat and the mayorship of Danao, its provincial power had been seriously eroded by the collapse of its political network and the loss of a national protector, a weakness amplified by a remarkable revival among the Osmeñas. The Duranos' reliance on goons and vote buying in the 1987 and 1988 elections accentuated their weakness. Moreover, the forced resignation of the family's military protector, General Edgardo Abenina, after his involvement in the August 1987 coup attempt, left them in an even more precarious position. Remarkably, however, only a short time before his death in October 1988, Don Ramon was talking enthusiastically about an impending alliance between the Duranos and the Aquino-Cojuangco bloc.[84] Today the political future of the Duranos remains unclear. The death of their patriarch has brought about a family reconciliation, mediated by Nito Durano, the apparent heir to his father's leadership of the family.

Winning Elections

Over the years Durano family life has been punctuated by elections, consumed by the intrigues of electioneering, and sustained by postelection patronage. Their success as the dominant family of Danao City and its surrounding congressional district depended upon winning elections. "Durano country" itself was an electoral zone where the Duranos controlled the votes and offered them to the highest bidder. By 1988, Ramon Durano, his wife Beatriz, and their children had participated in nineteen elections and six referendums and had campaigned for over thirty offices (see appendix). All the assets of the family's domain—revenues, land, agricultural commodities, industries, power, and influence—were derived from success at the polls. Similarly, much of the profits from their enterprises were invested in elections to guarantee the family's continued dominance. What Don Ramon and his family did best was to deliver the votes of "Durano country."

This achievement was also the cornerstone of the family's relationships with national patrons, all of whom, with the exception of wartime guerrilla leader Harry Fenton, allied themselves with the Duranos to gain the votes that the family could deliver. It is not surprising, therefore, to discover that during the first six years of martial law the Durano empire was in its most precarious state since 1955. When, after the longest period in this century without significant elections, Marcos finally reinstituted them in 1978, the Duranos participated vigorously, ready to demonstrate that they could still deliver the votes that would make them worthy of the president's patronage.

Since few election results are ever reversed through litigation or formal protests, any tactic resulting in electoral victory is, in the final analysis, legitimate. In electoral jurisdictions like Danao and the First District, entrenched warlords such as the Duranos have used various methods to control results. In most elections for which information exists, Danao and the First District were designated "hot spots," areas in which the Commission on Elections (Comelec) or NAMFREL requested the assignment of extra Constabulary detachments or additional election inspectors to provide security for voters and to guard against fraud at the polling places.[85] Such safeguards rarely have made much difference anywhere in the Philippines. In Danao they generally proved to be futile indeed. In the larger context, the Duranos' electoral success can be attributed to the fact that many of the city's voters are economically dependent on the family, making it easier to dictate voting behavior. Nevertheless, the family has used numerous techniques to manipulate election results—sometimes using force and vote buying, and other times relying on more subtle forms of manipulation made possible by greater control over the process itself: falsifying registrations, switching ballot boxes, and fabricating results.[86]

Guns, Goons, and Gold

In his campaign against his father for the Danao City mayorship in 1988, Deo Durano lashed out against the rest of his family, accusing them of dominating elections through the use of the three "Gs" of Philippine politics—guns, goons, and gold. This phrase has been popular for some time as a characterization of Philippine electoral politics. *Guns* and *goons* imply the use or threat of force in influencing electors, and *gold* implies the use of money or materials for vote buying. The Duranos were notorious for both.

Violence, real or potential, has played an important part in postwar electoral politics. The sight of armed men in the vicinity of polling places is not uncommon and campaigns often have been marked by political assassinations and gun battles between rival factions. The Duranos are no strangers to political violence. More like a marauder than a freedom fighter, Ramon Durano moved through the hills and towns of northern Cebu during the Japanese occupation with a group of armed guerrillas in search of political enemies and plunder. Many "executions," personal and political, have been attributed to these men. In the postwar period, violence remained an integral part of Durano's political life. He and his political associates carried guns themselves and, as the Tecala and other murders indicate, used them to strengthen their political positions.[87] Whenever it was necessary, the Duranos relied on force to win elections and to maintain control.

The Duranos never lacked for guns. Danao has long been a major center for the illicit manufacture of firearms. There is some evidence that guns were produced in Danao as early as the Philippine-American War, when gunsmiths in the hills behind Danao are said to have supplied the Cebuano rebels with locally made weapons. During the Japanese occupation, Danao again became a center for local gun manufacture, specializing in handguns known locally as *paltik* and supplying guerrillas in the uplands of Cebu. It was during the postwar years, however, that the manufacture of Danao-made guns came into its own. It is no coincidence that the expansion of production and sales of *paltik* corresponded with Durano's takeover of town politics in the early 1950s. Although the Duranos did not monopolize the arms business, they had their own factories, regulated production, and taxed sales. Moreover, they have protected and promoted the industry by means of local controls and external political arrangements, particularly alliances with regional military commanders.

Under Durano's leadership in the 1960s, the illicit trade in locally made guns, as well as other weapons, grew considerably. After 1961, when Danao became a city with the family more directly in control of its customs agency and local enforcement personnel, use of the port for the distribution of guns was considerably simplified. By the late 1960s, the manufacture of illicit handguns emerged in an economic survey as one of Danao City's major "cottage industries."[88] When martial law was declared in September 1972, there were reports that the Duranos were burying thousands of guns on land controlled by the family on the Camotes Islands between Cebu and Leyte.[89]

Although privately owned guns disappeared for some time during the early years of martial law, Danao's weapons industry had revived by the early 1980s. A key factor in this revival has been the family's collusion with the military, the primary enforcers of gun-control laws. Not only did military officers close their eyes to the presence of the factories, conducting periodic raids mainly for show, but it is also alleged that a number of senior officers have became major investors in the manufacture of guns and informal partners in their distribution. The skilled gunsmiths of Danao were soon producing arms that ranged from the traditional *paltik* to sophisticated reproductions of American-made rifles and semiautomatic weapons. By 1985, the industry had grown to the extent that the communist-led New Peoples Army in Cebu reportedly was planning to kidnap Danao gunsmiths to supply its soldiers with weapons. In December of that year, in an apparent gesture to his ally in Cebu, Marcos issued an executive order legalizing the manufacture of guns by certain registered companies. By the end of the year, the gun-making industry of Danao was booming. Indeed, one account noted that "almost every other house in Danao City is a gun factory." This report estimated that more than five thousand Danao residents were engaged in making guns and that some four thousand guns were produced in the city each month.[90]

As the industry expanded, it attracted foreign buyers, both individuals looking for cheap weapons and criminal syndicates from Japan and Taiwan. The Japanese *yakuza* is alleged to be a major client. Legal gun making was short lived, however, since the Aquino government revoked Marcos's order in early 1986 and reinstated restrictions on the manufacture of weapons. But, despite occasional raids conducted during the Aquino administration, Danao's industry continued to flourish. Since the reopening of the legislature under Aquino in 1987, Nito Durano has been promoting a bill that would legalize gun making by licensed companies, arguing that since considerable expertise exists in this industry the export of guns would contribute to the country's foreign exchange.[91] The legalization of gun manufacturing would benefit the Duranos' declining "industrial complex" by providing them with a profitable, legitimate business they could easily monopolize, both by selling guns legally and by smuggling them through well-established networks.

The gun industry contributes to the Duranos' revenues through the proceeds of sales from family-controlled factories as well as informal "taxes" collected from the other manufacturers operating in "Durano country." Moreover, the industry keeps the family well stocked with the weapons necessary for local political control. The Durano sons, in particular Boy and Deo, have their own factories and maintain large arsenals of weapons to supply to political goons during elections.[92] With ample guns at their disposal, the Duranos have been able to mobilize massive displays of armed force during elections.

"Goons," or political enforcers, have long played an integral part in the political life of the Durano family. They are drawn from a variety of sources: the urban gangs and ruffians of Cebu City, the personal bodyguards of family members, the Danao City police force, the Insular Security and Investment Agency, paramilitary units established after martial law, and the vigilante groups that have proliferated since 1986. As the Duranos have become more experienced in the ways of dominion, their methods of applying force and using armed men have diversified.

In the local idiom, there are two categories of goons: "casuals" and "regulars." The former term refers to temporary goons hired for short periods of time, while the latter refers to more permanent personnel. The family is always surrounded by a sizable body of loyal men drawn from the ranks of relatives and followers. The core of the regulars includes both personal bodyguards and Danao City police. Comprised of some fifty men loyal to the family, the Danao police force is an important component in the maintenance of Durano control. Indicative of their integration into the Durano security apparatus, its officers often supervise the casuals hired by the family. Likewise, employees of Danao City and local Durano-owned businesses supply the regular enforcers who can be armed and deployed during elections.[93]

During elections, when more enforcers are needed, the regulars are supplemented by casuals. Large numbers of men from Cebu City's slums have always been available for service as goons either during elections or for specific assignments at other times. These men are brought to Danao for instructions, issued weapons from the family's well-stocked arsenals, and assigned specific duties in and around "Durano country." When the elections are over, after returning their weapons and receiving their wages, they are mustered out of the service and sent home. Since they work for money, and not out of loyalty, they are supervised by family members, loyal political henchmen, or regulars. Usually assigned in more remote *barrios* of the city or district, their varied tasks include intimidating voters, distributing money to buy votes, detaining anti-Durano leaders, battling with opposing goons, and carrying out other activities dictated by the family. Although during the elections of the late 1960s and early 1970s most of the casuals were recruited from Cebu City, the Duranos also hired goons from other provinces, particularly from the Manila suburb of Tondo and the Ilocos provinces.

During the 1960s, the Duranos' use of goons and guns became institutionalized. Although they continued the old technique of recruiting casuals from outside, they also established the Insular Security and Investment Agency (ISIA) in Cebu City. Incorporated as the Insular Police Academy in 1966, the ISIA has been administered by Durano's daughter, Judy, in cooperation with other members of the family. ISIA's professed business is the training and placement of security guards, all of whom are registered with the Philippine Constabulary and licensed to carry weapons. Until their services are needed during elections, these men are employed in and around Cebu City or elsewhere. In addition, the company conducts brokerage, loading, and warehousing activities on the Cebu wharf, keeping it in contact with the city's dock workers. In this way the family has been able to maintain a permanent armed force, "a private army" estimated at a thousand men, which can be mobilized quickly for nearly any purpose. With corporate headquarters in the cities of Danao and Cebu, ISIA declared 116,510 pesos worth of firearms among its assets in 1984.[94]

During post-Marcos elections, the Durano strategy has been to place at least ten armed goons in each of the city's forty-two *barangays*, or *barrios*—a strategy requiring more than four hundred men in Danao and far greater numbers for coverage in the congressional districts. Starting work two days before the voting, goons are generally hired for three days at a rate of one hundred pesos a day plus expenses. It is felt that the presence of goons is made more effective if there is at least one political assassination on the election eve. During the 1987 elections, the acting OIC mayor of Danao alleged that there were five such assassinations. Most goons do not have to engage in violence since their presence alone serves as a warning to voters. The objective was clearly stated by the official slogan of the ISIA: "Be Sure and Get Results."[95]

In addition to hired goons, the politics of the 1970s and 1980s made possible the use of paramilitary units for political purposes. Mobilized by Marcos in 1976 to combat the New People's Army, the Civilian Home Defense Forces (CHDF) were locally recruited, self-defense units under nominal Constabulary jurisdiction. In reality they operated under the direction of the mayors. In Danao, the Duranos controlled the CHDF and, when necessary, used it for enforcement during elections. After the Aquino government abolished the CHDF in 1986, anticommunist, self-defense forces known as "vigilantes" emerged in many areas, again in close association with the local military and politicians. At first Danao did not need vigilantes, as the Duranos were able to control their territory without supplementing their regular forces. But by 1987 vigilante groups under Durano control emerged in several municipalities.

Deployment of CHDF, vigilantes, and private goons generally requires the cooperation of regional military authorities. The Duranos have always been careful to maintain good relations with the Constabulary officers in their area. During martial law, when the military gained greater power in the provinces, the Duranos made it a point to co-opt the commanding officers, a task that was simplified by their reputation as the leading Marcos loyalists in Cebu. It is widely believed that the Duranos bribed military officers—entertaining them lavishly, giving them gifts, and occasionally making them partners in their *paltik* business. Such closeness to the local Constabulary commanders made it easier for the Duranos to deploy armed goons, the CHDF, and vigilantes throughout their district during elections.[96]

The importance of military support became clear in late 1987 when the regional Constabulary commander, General Edgardo Abenina, a long-time Durano ally, was dismissed after his participation in the August 1987 coup attempt against Aquino. Though by no means hostile to the Duranos, his successor, Colonel Mariano Baccay, entered his post under a new administration and had to make symbolic efforts to distance himself from the warlords of the north. Under Baccay, the number of successful raids against the gun merchants of Danao increased and the perception of Durano control over the provincial military consequently changed, creating a more fluid interaction between Constabulary officers and anti-Durano provincial officials.[97] The post-Marcos era, while complicating the political situation, has not brought an end to the use of guns and goons by the Durano family.

Since they have been able to control election results by other means, the Duranos have not had to rely on "gold" to buy votes in elections. As a general rule, however, voters in Danao have been paid a nominal five pesos for their support, a sort of electoral bonus that sometimes comes with a sack of rice or corn. Such payments, delivered by Durano agents called *cabos*, or by the goons, also serves as a reminder that the family is watching. In the elections of May 1987 and January 1988, when Durano control was more seriously challenged, the family invested more heavily in vote buying. In 1987 there were reports that the Duranos were paying fifty pesos or more to individual voters, an allegation confirmed a year later when Deo Durano admitted that he had spent 200,000 pesos to defeat his father. For his part, Don Ramon reportedly paid 7 million pesos to buy "practically everyone in Danao City."[98]

Durano "gold" was more frequently used to pay for goons and to buy the loyalty of the public-school teachers who traditionally supervised the polling places, exercising direct control over the ballot boxes. Rather than buying individual votes, the Duranos carefully selected the teachers who would make the tallies and report the results to election officials. Three teachers were assigned in each of the forty-two *barangay* precincts where they played critical roles as guardians of the ballot box. Before each election, the selected teachers were invited to the Durano home for entertainment and instructions on election procedures. At the same time, they were reminded of the benefits of loyalty, warned of the price of betrayal, and paid between five hundred and a thousand pesos each.[99] A former teacher herself, Beatriz Durano maintained an easy rapport with the teachers, most of whom were women, and devoted much time to working with them and their supervisors, all of them well aware of her role in hiring and promotions.

Even the Popes Vote in Danao

In addition to coercive methods, the Duranos have other means of delivering election results—everything from padding the electorate to fabricating returns. A persistent charge against the family has been the gross inflation of the number of registered voters in Danao City. As table 1 demonstrates, the registered and actual numbers of voters reported in Danao began to increase rapidly after 1955, at a rate higher than that of population growth, peaking in the 1969 presidential election when almost four times as many voters were registered as had been the case in 1951. In Marcos's manipulated elections of the early 1980s, Danao's electorate expanded to the point of absurdity, approaching the total population of the city. After the Aquino government took power and the Danao registration process was subjected to more careful public scrutiny, the city's electorate was cut almost in half—from 58,645 voters in 1984 to 29,505 in 1987.[100] Inflated registration, when combined with high voter turnout and fabricated returns, facilitated the family's ability to dominate municipal offices, control the First District, influence provincial politics, and court national patrons searching for Cebuano votes.

The Duranos were rarely shy about altering election results and frequently did so with a boldness unmatched in Cebu. In seriousness it was said that "in Danao even the dead vote." It is believed that the unusually high number of electors in Danao resulted in part from the fact that registered voters who died were left on the books to cast their ballots for Durano-sponsored candidates. During the 1986 presidential campaign, Don Ramon boasted that all the concrete busts of the Catholic popes that lined a city park would vote for Marcos. Though offered as a jest to foreign journalists, the boast was taken seriously by many in Cebu since it was believed that Durano could deliver the votes of anyone he pleased.[101]

The referendums of the 1970s provide the best examples of the family's ability to produce votes. Desperate to reconfirm their loyalty to Marcos, the

Duranos delivered overwhelmingly large "yes" votes in support of the dictator's initiatives.[102] This power was also demonstrated in the 1988 election for Danao City mayor when Don Ramon defeated his son Deo. Ramon denied his son even a single vote in the precinct considered to be Deo's personal bailiwick. Although Deo accused his father of "dirty tactics," he did not file a protest, aware that such an action would be futile.[103] With the 1988 election in mind, one local observer commented: "I am beginning to think that clean and honest elections can never be expected for as long as Mr. Durano lives."[104]

TABLE 1 : **Population and Voters in Danao, 1949–1987**

Year of Election	Registered Voters	Actual Voters	Population
1949	—	4,405	26,461 (1948)
1951	—	4,522	—
1959	—	7,847	—
1961	12,082	8,616	32,826 (1960)
1963	12,567	8,561	—
1965	14,426	—	—
1967	14,444	10,522	—
1969	18,210	16,299	—
1970	18,039	—	47,662 (1970)
1971	—	13,433	—
1976	—	36,149	50,260 (1975)
1981	53,466	51,556	56,967 (1980)
1984	58,645	—	
1986	—	57,567	—
1987	—	29,505	73,000 (1990 est.)

Sources: See note 100.

The Duranos and the Church

To dominate Danao and its district, Ramon Durano expended vast resources, personal and financial, to court the Catholic Church. Paralleling the family's ties to key military leaders, he contributed to the Church's various charities and cultivate close relations with prominent clergymen. In a 1986 address to the Cebu Traders Association, Don Ramon proudly disclosed that he had donated a remarkable 22 million pesos to the Church. Only a short time before this announcement, he had appeared on television with Cebu's Cardinal Ricardo Vidal at the consecration of a new parish church built with a 5 million peso contribution from Don Ramon. His biographers present an exhaustive list of Church donations, including substantial contributions to international causes and foundations.[105] Through these donations, the family has co-opted influential figures in the Catholic hierarchy and received support from grateful clergy.

Until his retirement in 1982, Cardinal Julio Rosales, archbishop of Cebu since 1950, maintained close and cordial relations with the Duranos. Rosales also was known to be a good friend of the Marcos family, especially of Imelda Romualdez Marcos, a fellow Leyte-Samaran. These connections created a particularly favorable climate for Durano's influence with the Church during the martial-law years. Durano received public support from Cardinal Rosales and his leading administrator, Monsignor Manuel Salvador, who played a central role in the assignment of priests and articulation of the Church's political positions during the Rosales incumbency. Under his successor, Cardinal Vidal (whose appointment was resisted by Imelda Marcos), the relationship between the Durano family and the Church became less mutually supportive. Adopting a policy of "critical collaboration" with the Marcos regime after 1983, Cardinal Vidal operated more like Cardinal Jaime Sin of Manila and far less like his predecessor Rosales.[106]

In mid-1987 the Christians for National Liberation (CNL), an organization affiliated with the National Democratic Front, accused Cebu's Catholic hierarchy of favoring the family in assigning parish priests to "Durano country." The CNL charged that a recent reorganization of the Cebu diocese had assigned priests either related to or allied with the Duranos to the parishes of their district. Seven of the eleven parishes, including Danao itself, were staffed by Durano relatives, while all the other priests in the district had long-standing alliances with the family.

Although the Church hierarchy in Cebu denied these allegations, sources inside the diocese admitted that Don Ramon had long exercised influence over parish assignments, not so much because the church favored him but because unsympathetic priests feared assignment in "Durano country."[107] Whatever the reason, it is clear that the Duranos influenced the placement of priests in their territory.

Like the other residents of Danao and the First (later the Fifth) District, parish priests assigned to the area have had to come to terms with the repressive environment. Between 1958 and 1987, only two priests presided over the parish of

The Durano Family: A Selected Genealogy

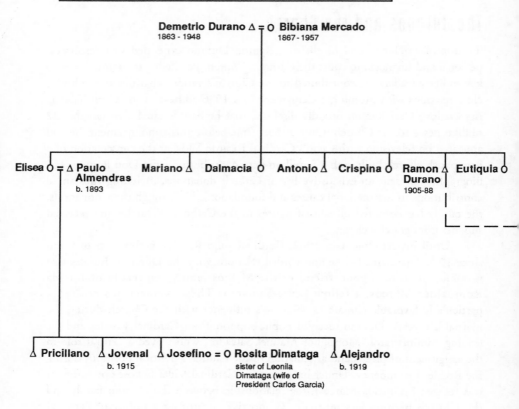

Demetrio Durano △ = ○ **Bibiana Mercado**
1863 - 1948   1867 - 1957

Elisea ○ = △ **Paulo**   **Mariano** △   **Dalmacia** ○   **Antonio** △   **Crispina** ○   **Ramon** △   **Eutiquia** ○
         Almendras   **Durano**
         b. 1893   1905-88

△ **Pricillano**   △ **Jovenal**   △ **Josefino** = ○ **Rosita Dimataga**   △ **Alejandro**
                     b. 1915   sister of Leonila   b. 1919
                                                    Dimataga (wife of
                                                    President Carlos Garcia)

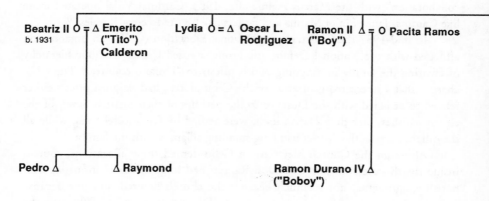

Beatriz II ○ = △ **Emerito**   **Lydia** ○ = △ **Oscar L.**   **Ramon II** △ = ○ **Pacita Ramos**
b. 1931   **("Tito")**   **Rodriguez**   **("Boy")**
                 Calderon

Pedro △   △ **Raymond**   **Ramon Durano IV** △
                                                                        ("Boboy")

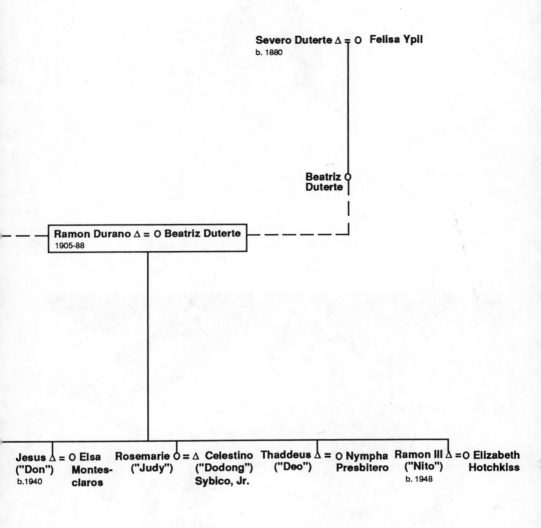

Severo Duterte △ = O Felisa Ypil
b. 1880

Beatriz O
Duterte

Ramon Durano △ = O Beatriz Duterte
1905-88

Jesus △ = O Elsa   Rosemarie O = △ Celestino   Thaddeus △ = O Nympha   Ramon III △ =O Elizabeth
("Don")   Montes-   ("Judy")   ("Dodong")   ("Deo")   Presbitero   ("Nito")   Hotchkiss
b.1940   claros   Sybico, Jr.   b. 1948

Ramon Durano, Sr., the warlord of Danao City, Cebu, photographed in 1985. (*Credit:* Resil Mojares)

During the 1986 election campaign, Ramon Durano, Sr., poses with members of his private army in Danao City.

Ramon ("Nito") Durano III, the youngest son and most likely successor of Ramon Durano, Sr., photographed in 1990. (*Credit:* Resil Mojares)

Thaddeus ("Deo") Durano, son of Ramon Durano, Sr., and a serious contender in the intrafamilial struggle to succeed him as the dominant politician in Danao City. (*Credit:* Resil Mojares)

A pro-Osmeña float in a 1967 election parade in Cebu City depicts Ramon Durano, Sr. (figure in the rear), as a killer with a skull and crossbones tattooed on his chest while victims, each named with a placard, lie at his feet. Like a puppet master, Durano holds three chains that lead to collars around the necks of the Durano-Marcos (Nacionalista Party) candidates at the front of the float: (left to right) Francisco Remotigue (NP candidate for vice-governor of Cebu), Rene Espina (NP candidate for governor), and Luis Diores (NP candidate for mayor of Cebu City). As shown on the facing page, the same parade featured horrific figures of goons in the employ of warlord Ramon Durano, Sr. (*Credit:* Michael Cullinane)

Danao: Fr. Cesar J. Alcoseba (1958–76) and Fr. Santos M. de la Serna (1976–87), neither of them a native of Danao or a relative of the Duranos. Both priests maintained a close public relationship with the Duranos, giving the impression of Church support for the family. Behind this facade, however, the coercive element of the Duranos' relationship with the Church occasionally emerged. Privately both priests described an atmosphere of fear that pervaded their lives and work in Danao. In the 1960s, Father Alcoseba, who at the time was sympathetic to the efforts of NAMFREL to encourage honest elections, refused to allow the organization to use his rectory as a headquarters, explaining later that he had been threatened by the Duranos.

In 1986, the uneasy relationship existing between the Duranos and Father De la Serna surfaced when the family tried to use the priest to discredit NAMFREL. When NAMFREL representatives announced that major election violations had occurred in Danao during the presidential elections, a press release signed by De la Serna appeared in the leading Cebu newspaper refuting the allegations and contending that the election had been "orderly and peaceful." Headlined "For the Public to Know," the priest's full-page statement, which was presented as a notarized affidavit, included attacks on both NAMFREL and the opposition party. The following day a nervous and distracted Father De la Serna, surrounded by diocesan leaders at a press conference, publicly denied that he had questioned NAMFREL's integrity. He claimed that he had no knowledge of how the election had been conducted in Danao and that his signed statement pertained only to what he had witnessed himself, ostensibly from the rectory. Moreover, he disclosed that the Duranos had paid for the "editorial," actually an advertisement, and claimed that he had refused to sign a more strident attack on NAMFREL prepared by Durano followers. He apologized for any damage he might have caused NAMFREL, which he praised for performing "a great service to our people against all odds."[108]

Although Father De la Serna insisted that he did not fear the Duranos' retribution for this act of independence, his confidence may have been misplaced. When the diocese was reorganized some months later, De la Serna was transferred from Danao to the remote parish of Guadalupe in the outer suburbs of Cebu City. The Danao parish was assigned to his assistant, Father Pascual Ypil, a native of Danao and a first cousin of Beatriz Durano.

Although priests in "Durano country" have been known to campaign for the family and its candidates, the primary role of the Church has been less direct, serving to legitimate the family's dominion and affirming Don Ramon's leadership. At the dedication of new Church buildings and renovations of old, clerical leaders are prominently displayed, giving blessings and expressing their appreciation for Don Ramon's Christian charity. As one observer noted, Durano has been successful in bribing God Himself.[109]

The City as Hacienda

"From a sleepy second class town to an industrial complex," reads the program commemorating the sixth anniversary of the City of Danao in 1967. Although Danao had long been a populous market town, until the 1960s it differed little from the other municipalities along Cebu's north coast. Two developments transformed Danao: the Duranos' "industrial complex" inaugurated in 1958 with the Universal Cement Company, and the enactment of a city charter in 1961. Both sprang from the political patronage of Ramon Durano's close ally, President Carlos Garcia, who used his authority to grant Durano Japanese reparations for his cement mill and to negotiate the legislation that made Danao a city. These changes made possible the city's evolution into a benefice of the Durano family.

The success of the Duranos in winning elections was based on the family's control over Danao's voters. Unlike most provincial elites, whose power is based on landed estates and whose control over voters depends on alliances with local power holders, Durano's grip on Danao was direct. Although he had not inherited much land and had based his early political career on diverse economic activities conducted within a community lacking large landowners, by the mid-1960s he was Danao's wealthiest citizen and one of the largest landlords in the province. By monopolizing city government, developing the "industrial complex," and acquiring an increasing amount of urban property, the Duranos made Danao City something of a family hacienda.

As Danao moved from public to private domain, the Duranos extracted wealth directly from the city's revenues and indirectly from public-service contracts—a process facilitated by the family's close relationship with regimes in Manila. Danao also served as the base for Durano's political power, as demonstrated by the family's control over both the city's captive voters and its public posts, from mayor to school janitors. With the public and private sectors under its control, and a large portion of the population in its employ, it was an ideal situation for the Durano family. Like a private hacienda, the family managed every aspect of the life of Danao City, treating the residents as tenants or dependents and subjecting them to their patronlike power.

The Industrial Complex

The family's wealth was derived from the industrial complex but from the outset the Durano business empire was rooted in politics and the political relationships of the patriarch. Shortly after his return to Cebu in 1946, Ramon Durano expanded his prewar commercial and coal-mining activities with the "sacks of money" he supposedly accumulated in Leyte during Liberation.[110] By the late 1940s, he had taken control of most of the workable mines in the Danao area, in collaboration with Mariano J. Cuenco, and was selling the bulk of the production to the Cebu Portland Cement Company in Naga.[111] In 1955, he consolidated his entrepreneurial activities and assets into a single enterprise, Durano and Company, Inc. Although he dates the beginning of Danao City's industrialization from the founding of this company, developments prior to 1958 were insignificant. The critical element in the family's initial success was not its entrepreneurial skill but simple political opportunity, the geology that gave Danao the two raw materials (coal and limestone) necessary for cement production, and the geography that located both close to the sea.

After a period of negotiation, which appears to have begun under President Magsaysay and concluded under Garcia, the latter granted his political ally a 6 million peso cement plant.[112] Construction began in early 1959 and UNICEMCO produced its first sack of cement on 13 May 1960.[113] It was just the beginning for the Duranos and for Danao. After 1960, the Durano business ventures expanded rapidly. By the beginning of martial law in late 1972, they numbered a dozen major enterprises. "You name it," Durano later boasted, "and I have it . . . even a bakery" (see table 2).[114] Most of the Durano business operations are located together along a three-kilometer portion of the main highway five kilometers north of the *poblacion* in the *barrio* of Dungo-an, an eighty-hectare site known as the Durano Industrial Estate. Once a sparsely inhabited marsh, Dungo-an had been reclaimed by the Duranos and converted to private ownership during the late 1950s and early 1960s.

Although the Duranos owned or controlled an impressive array of companies, most of them served Danao's two major industries—cement and sugar milling. The success or failure of most of the Durano companies was closely tied to these milling operations. Utility Enterprises manufactures sacks for cement and sugar; the drydock and lighterage facilities maintain the fleet of tugboats and barges used for cement and sugar transport; and Cebu Industries and Associated Foundry contribute a range of services to the plants. With few exceptions, the family-owned companies did no business outside the Durano industrial complex. While Dancar Industries was later incorporated into Danao City to serve it and neighboring municipalities, it was originally established to provide power and telephone service only to the industrial estate. In all, the industrial complex was a self-contained entity, dependent on cement, sugar, and the city of Danao.

All of Danao City's major enterprises were owned, controlled, and managed by members of the Durano family. Ramon Durano acted as overseer and minister of political affairs for the entire operation. Beatriz Durano, in addition to serving as Danao City mayor, was president and chair of UNICEMCO and the Danao City Development Bank, president of Durano and Company ("the holding company of the Durano empire"), and managing director of the Interisland Lighterage Company.[115]

By 1967, nearly every family member was involved in the business: daughter Beatriz Durano Calderon was vice-president of Durano and Co., Tito Calderon (her husband) was president of UNICEMCO, Lydia Durano Rodriguez was secretary-treasurer of Durano and Co. and Utility Enterprises, Oscar Rodriguez (Lydia's husband) was president of Durano and Co. and treasurer of UNICEMCO and Utility Insurance, Boy Durano was active in managing all the businesses, Pacita Ramos Durano (Boy's wife) was executive secretary of the Ramon Durano Foundation and treasurer of Dancar Industries, Don Durano was president of Utility Enterprises, Elsa Montesclaros Durano (Don's wife) was cashier for the Danao City Development Bank, Judy Durano Sybico was secretary of Dancar Industries, Dodong Sybico (Judy's husband) was chairman of the Danao City Development Bank, Deo Durano was general manager of Cebu Industries and Dancar Industries, Nympha Presbitero Durano (Deo's wife) was assistant manager of the Foundation Publishing House and corporate secretary of the Danao City Development Bank, and Nito Durano was assistant manager of UNICEMCO.[116] Thus, Danao City and its industrial complex functioned as a Durano enterprise with all the profit flowing to the family.

The number of Durano employees remains unclear. Don Ramon once claimed that his industrial complex employed "no less than 10,000 people" (nearly one of every five residents of Danao) and that his companies paid out some 2 million pesos a month in salaries.[117] Upon close inspection these figures seem greatly exaggerated, and in fact they are contradicted by records made available to researchers in the mid-1970s. At that time it was estimated that the number of employees of Durano's largest companies amounted to fewer than 1500 persons.[118] Although these figures may err on the low side, they seem closer to reality than Durano's, particularly since Don Ramon was politically motivated to inflate the number of employees as a justification for the burgeoning rate of voter registration in Danao.[119]

The core company, the one that sustained the others, was UNICEMCO. As politicians, the Duranos found in cement an ideal business. The family controlled the coal and limestone required to fuel the plant, owned milling facilities financed by the national government, and sold their product either to government contractors or at above-market prices set by political allies.[120] During the 1960s, as new processing kilns were added, the Durano cement plant had developed in three stages. The first unit was operational by 1960 and had a daily capacity of five thousand sacks of cement. The second unit, with a daily capacity of fifteen thousand sacks, began producing in 1965. In 1968, a much larger unit was installed, capable of producing fifty thousand sacks a day, greatly expanding the plant's capacity.[121] By 1970, UNICEMCO had joined the ranks of the leading cement producers in the country.

The Philippine cement industry has long been an essentially political enterprise, since the government, as one of the primary consumers of the commodity, is often engaged in both production and sales. When the demand for cement as a building material increased in the 1960s, cement was required for schools, government buildings, roads, and bridges. It is no coincidence that much of UNICEMCO's profits were made by selling cement to government contractors engaged in public works. The initial success of the company derived from sales in the Visayas, Mindanao, and the Bicol region where the demand was such that UNICEMCO could command high prices.[122]

TABLE 2: **Durano Family Businesses, ca. 1970**

Associated Foundry and Machine Shop Co. (Dungo-an, Danao, 1967; metal works)

Cebu Fishing and Manufacturing Co.
(Gato Island, off northern Cebu, ca. 1965; fishing and sea-snake hides)

Cebu Industries, Inc. (1966)
Duraweld (Dungo-an, Danao; welding construction rods, etc.)
Electric Wire and Cable Factory (Dungo-an, Danao)
Factory for Pedicab Side Carriages (Dungo-an, Danao)
Batching Plant (Dungo-an, Danao; mixing road cement)

Dancar Industries, Inc. (1960)
Dancar Electric Plant (Dungo-an, Danao, 1960)
Dancar Ice Plant (Dungo-an, Danao, 1960)
Dancar Acetylene and Oxygen Plant (Dungo-an, Danao, 1967)
Dancar Telephone System (Dungo-an, Danao, 1968)

Danao City Development Bank (Danao, 1967; rural banking)

Durano and Company, Inc. (1955)
Durano Coal Mines (interior of Danao, ca. 1930)
Dolomite Mines (interior of Danao; product sold for glass manufacturing in the
        late 1960s to San Miguel Corporation and Republic Glass)
San Jose Subdivision (Alabang, Rizal, acquired in 1958)
Durano Sugar Mill (Dungo-an, Danao; centrifugal milling plant in operation by
        the 1970s)

Foundation Publishing House, Inc. (Dungo-an, Danao, 1963)

Insular Security and Investment Agency (Cebu City and Danao City, 1966)

Interisland Lighterage Company, Inc. (Dungo-an, Danao, ca. 1965; operates
tugboats, barges, and trucks to transport cement and sugar and to handle incoming
raw materials; includes warehouse facilities)

Kraft Paper Plant (Dungo-an, Danao)

Republic Drydock Corp. (Dungo-an, Danao, 1965; some manufacturing but mostly
repair of tugboats and barges, mainly those of Interisland Lighterage; has slipway
facilities)

Royal Construction Co. (Dungo-an, Danao)

Universal Cement Co. (Dungo-an, Danao, 1958, operational in 1960)

Utility Enterprises Corp. (Dungo-an, Danao, 1960; manufacturing bags for
cement, sugar, and other commodities)

Utility Insurance and Surety Co. (Manila-based, 1958)

Sources: See note 114.

By the early 1970s, Danao City had become a community of concrete. Roads, bridges, and other public works were built with the local product. The Duranos frequently made much of their "cementation" of Danao, boasting that 85 percent of the city's roads were concrete, a sign of the family's love for the local residents.[123] With the Durano-dominated city acquiring concrete from the Durano-owned batching plant, these roads were also a source of family wealth.[124]

Though clearly a profitable endeavor, the cement business required repeated investments of political capital to sustain it. UNICEMCO, the sixth cement-manufacturing plant constructed in the Philippines, was initiated as a part of the import-substitution industrialization policies of the 1950s. Initially government planners attempted to replace foreign cement with domestic production, and by 1970 there were thirteen cement plants in operation. The problem now became overproduction, with rapidly growing surpluses outstripping demand and few potential foreign markets.[125] Five years later there were seventeen cement companies competing primarily for the domestic market.[126] Faced with such competition, UNICEMCO might stay afloat but it could not prosper.

By 1985, UNICEMCO was in serious decline, due in part to "technical problems" with its high-capacity processing units. By this time the original unit was no longer producing cement, having been converted to process lime for the Durano Sugar Mill. Neither of the two larger units were operating at full capacity, and both were in need of repair. By the end of the year, renovations on the second unit were underway and Durano had successfully negotiated a "credit," through the Marcos government, of 50 million dollars from the Japan Export-Import Bank to rehabilitate the entire plant. Although this loan appears to have accomplished little in terms of rebuilding the cement plant, one observer on the eve of the 1986 elections noted that 50 million dollars would certainly inspire Durano "to do battle for the President and the Kilusang Bagong Lipunan." With his protector gone by the end of 1986, the Durano cement company slid rapidly into bankruptcy. By the end of the next year, the Development Bank of the Philippines (DBP) had foreclosed on UNICEMCO, placing it in receivership.[127]

The Duranos' other industrial ventures were financed by cement profits, government loans, and the family's exactions from Danao City. The Durano companies have had uneven histories, contending not only with the vagaries of fluctuating markets and conflicting economic policies but also with the cycles of politics. Since little is known about the history of these companies, however, it is difficult to assess the overall impact of the changing political scene on the Durano business empire.

The story of the family's second-largest enterprise, the Durano Sugar Mill, differs from that of UNICEMCO but it also is replete with political influence. Construction of the "2,000-ton daily capacity sugar mill" began in 1967, with government financing totaling some 86 million pesos from the DBP.[128] Swept along by Marcos's unrealistic expansion of sugar production in the mid-1960s, Durano entered the business at a difficult time. By the time the mill was operational in 1970, sales of Philippine sugar to the United States, the industry's main market, were beginning to decline. Unprepared to compete on the world market, particularly during the depressed conditions following 1975, Durano and the other new sugar millers found an unfavorable environment for profit. These problems were exacerbated for the planters and millers when, between 1974 and 1977, the Marcos government imposed monopoly control on the sugar industry, eventually placing it under a Philippine Sugar Commission headed by the dictator's political ally, Roberto S. Benedicto.[129] While these changes led to financial disaster and heavy indebtedness to the Philippine National Bank for most planters, Durano appears to have been partially shielded by his political relationship with Marcos, who protected the Danao mill during the industry's periodic crises.

For the Duranos, locating raw cane for milling was often difficult. Since the war, the only significant sugar-growing area of Cebu has been in the northwestern portion of the island, mainly in the municipalities of Tuburan, Bogo, and Medellin. Since the inception of the modern sugar industry there in 1929, most cane had been milled at the Bogo-Medellin Central. The Duranos invested considerable effort, primarily through political allies and family connections, in attempting to divert this cane to their mill. At the same time they maneuvered to increase sugar cultivation in Danao. By the mid-1970s, most of the family-controlled land in Danao City "was devoted to sugar cane."[130] Despite these efforts, the Durano Sugar Mill was never able to operate at full capacity and by the mid-1980s had become a losing concern.[131]

Beyond cement and sugar, most of the Durano enterprises were either dependent, illicit, or insolvent. An interesting example of the latter was the Foundation Publishing House, the failure of which reveals the close relationship between the warlord's business operations and his political patrons. Listed as a major printing establishment in 1964, it had disappeared from industry directories by 1980.[132] During Foundation's heyday, from 1963 to 1972, the press was kept active with government contracts to print documents, in particular the records of congressional sessions. The press also published a Cebuano vernacular magazine, *Bag-ong Suga*, and a popular Cebuano comic series, *Kulba Hinam*. The former served as a propaganda magazine, highlighting Danao City events and Durano family activities, as well as engaging in polemics against the family's political enemies in Cebu City. Both *Bag-ong Suga* and *Kulba Hinam* had ceased publication by 1971. After the declaration of martial law and the demise of the Congress, the Durano publishing house had difficulty generating business. Without substantial government contracts it eventually was reduced to printing souvenir and fiesta programs for Danao and its neighboring communities.[133]

In retrospect, the tremendous growth in the illicit gun trade in Danao during the early 1980s must be viewed in the context of a decline in the family's major business concerns. It is certainly no coincidence that Nito Durano's efforts to legitimize gun manufacturing are part of the family's revitalization plan for the industrial complex.

As the Philippines under Marcos departed from a policy of protecting domestic industries and moved toward an export-oriented economy financed by foreign investment and loans, the Duranos found an increasingly less favorable environment for the expansion of their industrial endeavors. Ramon Durano's dependence on his political alliance with Marcos made that relationship all the more central to the survival of his businesses. Under martial law, Durano's firms were in their most precarious state and any break with Marcos would have meant disaster. Unable to attract an alternative patron during the authoritarian era that extended from 1972 to 1986, the Duranos were compelled to remain loyal.

By the early 1980s, the Duranos had managed to sustain operations but profits and total assets were declining rapidly. Although ranked nationally the 405th company in sales, and 8th among cement companies, in 1980 UNICEMCO slipped to 577th, a ranking of 10th among cement companies, in only a year. By 1984, none of the Durano enterprises was listed among the top two thousand corporations in the country.[134] While Durano remained loyal to his patron, Marcos, the economic changes set in motion by the dictator led to the gradual decline of the warlord's business interests. Unable to attract much business from elsewhere in the province, especially from the steadily developing Cebu-Mandaue-Lapu-Lapu urban zone only thirty kilometers to the south, the Durano industrial complex remained an isolated family estate rather than an industrialized city. Even before Marcos was forced into exile, several of the large industrial buildings of Danao City had become empty hulks. The potential of the late 1960s and early 1970s was never realized. But, although the Duranos had failed to bring sustainable prosperity to Danao, their industrialization schemes had succeeded in making them one of the country's richest families.

The City of Danao

The economic grip of the Duranos on Danao goes far beyond their "private-sector" interests. From the mid-1950s onward, the family's control of local politics led to de facto privatization of the municipality, reducing it to just another resource serving the family's interest. Danao's evolution from municipality to "chartered city" greatly facilitated this process. Like many chartered cities in the postwar Philippines, Danao's elevation to this status in 1961 was primarily for political rather than administrative reasons. Under administrative guidelines, municipalities were eligible to become cities when their populations exceeded fifty thousand and their annual incomes were greater than one million pesos. Significantly, more than six years after it became a city, Danao, like many others, still had not met either criteria.[135]

By 1970, Danao was one of the fifty-eight cities in the Philippines, most of them established through congressional legislation in the postwar period. Undoubtedly, the primary reason the Duranos sought city status for Danao was independence from supervision by Cebu's provincial government. As a city, Danao's

Durano-controlled government could avoid the scrutiny of their political enemies, the Osmeñas and the Cuencos, who dominated provincial government. In the 1950s, during Ramon Durano's early bid for dominion over Danao, Serging Osmeña had challenged his efforts by removing his hand-picked mayor, sparking conflicts that culminated in Durano's trial for the murder of the acting mayor. As a city, supervision of Danao's administration shifted to the central government and its executive branch.[136] For Durano this was a favorable arrangement. After an uneasy four years with Macapagal (1962–65), the Duranos enjoyed a close working relationship with the Philippines' longest-serving chief executive, Ferdinand Marcos (1966–86).

To the extent that Danao has become a Durano family institution, the interests of the city and the family are coterminous.[137] Between 1961 and 1986, the Durano family controlled all the key offices, elected and appointive. The posts of mayor and vice-mayor were held by members of the immediate family and the town councilors were always relatives or loyal followers. Subject to confirmation by Congress's Commission on Appointments, offices such as city treasurer, engineer, *fiscal*, health officer, superintendent of schools, and judge are nominated by a city's mayor and appointed by the president of the Philippines. During the Marcos years this procedure meant that for all intents and purposes the Durano family simply selected nominees who were automatically appointed by Manila. Moreover, the mayor was authorized to appoint other key personnel directly, among them the city assessor and the chiefs of police and the fire department. The appointment of large numbers of department heads, deputy officials, and clerical personnel also fell under the mayor's authority. As a result, the Duranos exercised control over the selection of all civil-service employees working within the city, including public-school teachers.[138] Every position within the city's jurisdiction was subject to Durano family control, and all officials and employees were aware that they owed their jobs to the Duranos.

The family's monopoly of key positions in city government did not go unnoticed. As early as 1963, Priscillano D. Almendras, Ramon's nephew and political opponent, attacked the Duranos on the radio, accusing them of running Danao as a family business. He named ten city offices held by Ramon Durano's relatives and charged that other kin were on the public payroll. His list included the mayor (Beatriz Durano), the vice-mayor (Rosita Dimataga-Almendras), the president of the City Council (Boy Durano), the chief of police (the husband of Beatriz's niece), the city assessor (the son of Ramon's cousin), the Bureau of Internal Revenue collecting agent (Ramon's nephew), the city health officer (Ramon's nephew), the city medical officer (the son of Ramon's cousin), the supervising nurse (Beatriz's niece), and the school division's head nurse (Ramon's sister).[139]

The uncontested control that the Duranos maintained over Danao City permitted the family to treat it as a private reserve. All functions—revenue collection, tax assessment, public utilities, port facilities, education, health services, rural development, and courts—were under their control. Allegations were rampant that they appropriated city property and services for their own use. For example, Dancar Electric and the Dancar Telephone Company, subsidiaries of the Durano-owned Dancar Industries, still provide most of the electric and telephone service for the city. Another family concern, the city's Dancar Ice Plant, supplies Danao's refrigeration needs.[140]

The two most frequent allegations made against the Duranos were the illicit use of the port facilities to smuggle commodities into and out of the province and widespread "landgrabbing." The private wharf of the Duranos was believed to be the entry point for everything from cigarettes to large equipment, much of which entered without customs inspection or payment of duties, and the exit point for illicit guns and other merchandise.[141] Although this essay does not do justice to the complex question of the family's acquisition of city land, the dramatic expansion of the Durano landholdings during the past twenty-five years has led to frequent accusations of abuse. Although the details of these transactions remain obscure, there is sufficient information to indicate that the Duranos' acquisition of city property was facilitated by their control of local government and their ties to the Marcos regime.[142]

Despite allegations, very few formal charges of misappropriation or abuse of the public domain have been made, and virtually none have reached the courts.[143] The Duranos' long history of arrogant corruption aroused excitement and anticipation among Cebuanos in 1986 when, after more than thirty years, a political opponent of the family became mayor of Danao. When the Aquino government came to power, it appointed Jovenal Almendras as OIC mayor of Danao with instructions to restore "democracy" to the beleaguered city. When Almendras finally took office at the end of May, it became clear that the Duranos had engaged in some hasty housecleaning. Nevertheless, in early 1987 Almendras was able to pull together a case against the family. Though its evidence was thin, it revealed a number of interesting aspects of Durano rule in Danao.

In Mayor Almendras's suit, the city accused the Duranos of evading their property taxes for 1986 and Manila's Department of Finance was authorized to bill the family for 2,782,423 pesos in back taxes. Durano and his family countersued, charging the mayor and the entire Danao City Council of libel, and requesting "moral damages." Far more interesting, the family alleged that Danao actually owed them 83,681,300 pesos for services supplied in the 1960s by UNICEMCO and Durano and Company. Quoting a September 1960 municipal resolution, the Durano lawyer claimed that Danao City had authorized the Durano-owned businesses to undertake, among other things, the "concreting" of city streets and the reclamation of swampy areas for the construction of public buildings. In return, the Durano companies had been exempted from tax obligations in perpetuity. Now that the city was charging them property taxes, the Duranos were billing the city for the cost of these services.[144] By the time these charges and countercharges were aired before the court in 1988, the Duranos had returned to City Hall along with a new coterie of elected councilors and city officials.

Except for its costly paved streets, the city of Danao does not seem to have prospered under the warlord. Despite the presence of the Durano industrial complex, Danao remained a fourth-class city throughout the 1960s, even after 1974 when Marcos enacted a reclassification scheme based on total city revenues. By the beginning of the 1980s, Danao was ranked lowest among Cebu Province's five cities in terms of revenue. Cebu and Toledo held the highest ranking (1st-A), Mandaue and Lapu-Lapu were listed as second-class cities, and Danao was designated fourth class.[145]

From Cradle to Grave

When questioned about his long reign over Danao, Ramon Durano frequently attributed his success to the fact that he takes care of his people. As he put it in his autobiography, "I feel it is not our fault that the people of Danao City love us. We serve them, as I always say, from the cradle to the grave."[146]

After more than a generation of Durano dominance over nearly every aspect of local life, it not surprising to find a culture of dependency in Danao. The nearly invisible line between the public and private domains in the city has placed its inhabitants in a predicament beyond their control. Many residents obtain their livelihoods from the Durano-owned industrial complex or the family-controlled city government. Employment under the Duranos undoubtedly has benefitted some families. For most, however, there are few other options. Those who work outside the Durano net survive as best they can in the more traditional occupations, farming or fishing, which predate Durano hegemony and have benefitted little from it. There is no evidence that the inhabitants of Danao are better off than those of any other Cebu municipality. They are no better educated nor are they less susceptible to the health problems facing other lower-income Filipinos.[147]

Despite all evidence to the contrary, Ramon Durano's rhetoric depicts an idyllic community in which an industrious, God-fearing family has devoted itself to uplifting its people in a manner not unlike that of a traditional *hacendero*. As he bestows personal favors upon those in need, many humble themselves before him and kiss his hand. Speaking like an old landlord, Don Ramon explains that "My workers are bonded to me." The older employees have stayed on and "today their children, nieces, nephews, and grandchildren are also working with me in the complex." In the manner of a benevolent patron, he continues:

> But if my workers have stayed on, it is also because we have become friends. All these years, I have been Manong (elder brother) to them. They come to me with their problems and I go to them with mine. It is a give-and-take relationship. I have shown them credibility and reliability and they have repaid me in kind.[148]

Indeed they have, for, as Durano aptly put it, "In this industrial complex lies the source of my political power."[149] Between the cradle and the grave, the citizens of Danao serve the Duranos in two critical ways: as manpower for the family's businesses and as voters for its political rule.[150] Little else really matters in Durano's Danao.

Conclusion: Patronizing the Warlord

Ramon Durano and his familial "kingdom" in northeastern Cebu were a unique product of the local politics. Under the postwar Republic, the family patriarch became the consummate warlord, ruling his public and private domains as both benevolent patron and armed enforcer. At no time did he entertain political ambitions beyond Cebu. Throughout his career his goal was always to be the political ruler of his province. Although he never achieved his ambition, he kept a firm hold on Danao City and its district for nearly forty years. Operating within a system of electoral politics, Durano's success as a warlord was based ultimately on his ability to deliver votes for himself, for family members and local supporters, and especially for national patrons. By so doing, the family was able to convert electoral victories into concessions from grateful patrons who in turn provided them with the means necessary to consolidate their wealth and local power.

Durano's patrons sustained him and made possible his long tenure as "the political kingpin of the north." He achieved his earliest political successes in Danao as a follower of his brother-in-law, the local leader Paulo Almendras. He emerged on the larger political scene as a vote-getter for the provincial leader Mariano Cuenco in the late 1930s. Even during the war, he worked as an agent for the notorious Harry Fenton from whom he learned the political utility of violence. As a local and congressional *lider* for the Bando Cuenco in the 1940s and 1950s, he matured as a politician, becoming savvy to the mechanics of the national political economy. But it was two Philippine presidents who contributed the most to the Durano family's political empire—Carlos Garcia and Ferdinand Marcos.

As the Cuencos gravitated toward their eventual alliance with the Osmeñas in the late 1950s, Durano found himself isolated and threatened with the demise of his regime in Danao. Instead, this crisis increased his wealth and power beyond his wildest dreams. Through family contacts he negotiated an alliance with Carlos Garcia, then desperate for support from Cebu, for his presidential campaigns of 1957 and 1961. Durano's ties with Garcia were instrumental in facilitating the financing for his industrial complex and in the establishment of Danao as a city— both central to the consolidation of the family's rule over "Durano country."

Durano's relationship with Marcos was more complicated and contradictory but it was no less important in preserving the hold of the Duranos over Danao. Marcos was careful to leash his Cebuano ally, always concerned to maintain his own control over Cebu politics. As Durano frequently pointed out, he never became a Marcos "crony."[151] It can be argued that this was not because Durano declined to become one. Rather, Marcos did not need him since the conditions of his authoritarian regime denied the warlord an alternative patron. In this precarious situation the Duranos remained loyal Marcos clients to the end. With most of his local controls well entrenched, Durano did not require Marcos's active support, simply the benign neglect that allowed him a free hand in his own territory. Unwilling to allow Durano control over the whole province, however, Marcos and his advisors promoted Eddie Gullas as a foil for Durano in Cebu. For the family it was an acceptable, though undoubtedly frustrating, arrangement. But with the state casting a blind eye upon their local operations, the Duranos were able to maintain their monopoly of power in Danao City, play a major role in provincial politics, and preserve much of their wealth.

Reaching Out to the Final Patron

Ramon Durano built a career by courting powerful patrons. He mastered the methods of exchanging loyalty for favors, votes for concessions. It is fitting, therefore, that late in life the aging warlord established his final relationship with the ultimate patron, God the Father. He was, wrote a long-time admirer, "in constant touch with God."[152] While he remained the feisty local politician, in his later years Durano devoted emotional energy, fulsome rhetoric, and hard cash to barter for his last concession—entry into heaven. It is within this context that we can comprehend Durano's posture as the penitent—his many charitable acts, his biblical musings, and his awkward identification with Christ. All of these gestures and rhetorical constructions seem odd—the actions and utterances of senility—unless we see them as things "not of this world," intended instead to win the patronage of the final arbiter.

To the dismay of journalists seeking a spectacle of warlordism, Durano preferred to talk about religion in all his later interviews. Throughout the 1980s, as he fought the final political battles for his earthly patron, Ferdinand Marcos, Durano developed a degree of popularity among Filipino and foreign correspondents, many of whom visited Danao to engage him in conversation and wander about the city at his side. Instead of a venomous warlord with the tough talk of a mafia don, they found a man babbling incomprehensible parables about the meaning of life, the afterlife, and the Gospels.

One of Durano's favorite topics concerned the parallels between his life and that of Jesus Christ. His parables usually emerged when he was asked about his "political dynasty" in Danao. Rather than condemning dynasties, he would transform the issue through the idiom of the Christian family, arguing that Christ clearly used his family to build the "dynasty" that gave birth to Christianity. In these explanations he often provided genealogical details to bolster his interpretations of the Gospels. He reminded his listeners that all but two of Jesus's twelve apostles were his relatives, implying that nepotism was nothing new and that he, Durano, was in good company. Continuing in this vein, he would explain that the two nonfamily members within Jesus's entourage were Judas, who betrayed him, and Thomas, who doubted him, eventually becoming, as Durano put it, a "subversive." With unassailable logic, he would explain that he, like Christ, trusted only family members.[153]

When it came time to negotiate his passage to paradise, the warlord publicly excluded his children from participation in his official charity, the Ramon Durano Foundation. Although it was established in 1961, the foundation did not emerge as a viable institution until the late 1970s when Durano began using it as a conduit for many of his donations. The foundation was intended to maintain orphanages and old-folks homes, and to support church construction.[154] The argument that it was established to obtain tax deductions does not explain Durano's late obsession with giving, a characteristic that must have concerned his children.

Throughout his autobiography, Durano frames his life in the image of the Good Samaritan, a man whose sole purpose is to serve the humble of the world. The first and last three chapters of this chatty discourse deal with pious acts: "Finding a Purpose in Life," "My Philanthropic Works: You Serve the Lord by Serving the Less Fortunate," "Ramon Durano Foundation, Inc.: The Open Arms of Generosity to Serve the People," and "Epilogue: Nearer My God Today." Declaring his life's purpose to be service to God through service to others, he concludes: "If I've stayed in politics for 60 years, it is because of this commitment to the people."[155]

It was not until he reached seventy, however, that Ramon Durano began to record his philanthropy, particularly his donations to causes of the Catholic Church. Ten years later, in 1986, these donations by his own count amounted to more than 37 million pesos.[156] With Heaven in mind, he concluded:

> The Holy Scripture says that we ourselves determine our own reward by our own good deeds. God . . . will reward you more for your generosity. For he who sows sparingly will reap sparingly. But he who sows in abundance will reap abundantly.[157]

As the "foremost Filipino philanthropist," Don Ramon Durano sowed what he had reaped on earth to reap even more abundantly beyond.[158]

A PPENDIX : **Durano Family Political History**

Election Year/ Candidate/ Office-Location	Local Alliance	National Party Affiliation	Presidential Ally
1890–1896			
DTD/JP-Danao*	unknown	na	na
1897–1899			
DTD/MC-Danao*	unknown	na	na
1901			
DTD/MC-Danao*	unknown	na	na
1903			
DTD/MC-Danao*	unknown	na	na
1905			
DTD/MC-Danao*	unknown	na	na
1907			
DTD/MC-Danao*	unknown	na	na
1909			
SD/MC-Danao*	unknown	na	na
1909			
SD/MC-Danao*	unknown	na	na
1911			
SD/MC-Danao*	unknown	na	na
1913			
SD/MC-Danao*	unknown	na	na
1916			
SD/MVP-Danao*	unknown	na	na
PGA/MC-Danao*	unknown	na	na
1919			
PGA/MVP-Danao*	Osmeña	Nacionalista	na
SD/MC-Danao*	unknown	unknown	na
1922			
PGA/MP-Danao*	Osmeña	Nacionalista	na
SD/MC-Danao*	unknown	unknown	na
1925			
SD/MC-Danao*	unknown	unknown	na
1928-1940			
PGA/MP-Danao*	Osmeña	Nacionalista	na
SD/MC-Danao*	unknown	unknown	na

Election Year/ Candidate/ Office-Location	Local Alliance	National Party Affiliation	Presidential Ally
1931			
PGA/MP-Danao*	Osmeña	Nacionalista	na
SD/MC-Danao*	unknown	unknown	na
1934			
PGA/MP-Danao*	Osmeña/Almendras	Nacionalista	na
SD/MC-Danao*	unknown	unknown	na
RMD/MC-Danao*	Osmeña/Almendras	Nacionalista	na
1937			
PGA/MP-Danao*	Osmeña/Almendras	Nacionalista	na
SD/MC-Danao*	unknown	unknown	na
1940			
RMD/HR-1st#	Cuenco/Sotto	Frente Popular	na
1946			
JDA1/HR-1st*	Osmeña	Nacionalista	Osmeña
MAZ/HR-6th*	Cuenco	Liberal	Roxas
1949			
RMD/HR-1st*	Bando Cuenco	Liberal	Quirino
MAZ/HR-6th*	Bando Cuenco	Liberal	Quirino
(1952: Tecala murder and trial)			
1953			
RMD/HR-1st*	Bando Cuenco	Democratic	Magsaysay
MAZ/HR-6th*	Bando Cuenco	Democratic	Magsaysay
1955			
BDD/M-Danao*	Bando Cuenco	Nacionalista	Magsaysay
1957			
RMD/HR-1st*	Bando Cuenco	Nacionalista	Garcia
MAZ/HR-6th*	Bando Cuenco	Nacionalista	Garcia
(1957-58: Reparations payments begin)			
(1959: Cuenco-Osmeña Fusion)			
1959			
RMD/PG-Cebu#	Durano-Zosa	Nacionalista	Garcia
BDD/M-Danao*	Durano-Zosa	Nacionalista	Garcia
RDA/VM-Danao*	Durano-Zosa	Nacionalista	Garcia
(1961: Danao becomes a city)			
1961			
RMD/HR-1st*	DZD Combine	Nacionalista	Garcia
MAZ/HR-6th*	DZD Combine	Nacionalista	Garcia

Election Year/ Candidate/ Office-Location	Local Alliance	National Party Affiliation	Presidential Ally
1963			
RMD/M-Cebu#	DZD Combine	Liberal	Macapagal
BDD/M-Danao*	DZD Combine	Liberal	na
RDA/VM-Danao*	DZD Combine	Liberal	na
JDD/CC-Danao*	DZD Combine	Liberal	na
ESC/PVG-Cebu*	DZD Combine	Liberal	na
1965			
RMD/HR-1st*	DZD Combine	Nacionalista	Marcos
ESC/HR-5th#	DZD Combine	Nacionalista	Marcos
MAZ/HR-6th#	DZD Combine	Nacionalista	Marcos
1967			
BDD/M-Danao*	DCS Combine	Nacionalista	Marcos
RDA/VM-Danao*	DCS Combine	Nacionalista	Marcos
JDD/CC-Danao*	DCS Combine	Nacionalista	Marcos
BDC/M-Samboan*	DCS Combine	Nacionalista	Marcos
1969			
RMD/HR-1st*	DCS Combine	Nacionalista	Marcos
JDA2/HR-2d#	DCS Combine	Nacionalista	Marcos
ESC/HR-5th*	DCS Combine	Nacionalista	Marcos
MAZ/HR-6th*	DCS Combine	Nacionalista	Marcos
CNS/HR-7th*	DCS Combine	Nacionalista	Marcos
1971			
BDD/PG-Cebu#	DCS Combine	Nacionalista	Marcos
RDDII/M-Danao*	DCS Combine	Nacionalista	Marcos
BDC/M-Samboan*	DCS Combine	Nacionalista	Marcos
LDR/CCD-1st*	DCS Combine	na	na
PDC/CCD-5th*	DCS Combine	na	na
FZ/CCD-6th*	DCS Combine	na	na
(1972: Martial Law declared)			
1978			
RDDIII/IBP#	DCS Combine	KBL	Marcos
ESC/IBP#	DCS Combine	KBL	Marcos
1980			
RDDIII-PVG-Cebu*	DCS Combine	KBL	Marcos
RDC/PBM-Cebu*	DCS Combine	KBL	Marcos
RDDII/M-Danao*	DCS Combine	KBL	Marcos
RDDIV/CC-Danao*	DCS Combine	KBL	Marcos
TDD/M-Sogod*	DCS Combine	KBL	Marcos
BDC/M-Samboan*	DCS Combine	KBL	Marcos

Election Year/ Candidate/ Office-Location	Local Alliance	National Party Affiliation	Presidential Ally
1984			
RDDIII/BP*	DCS Combine	KBL	Marcos
ESC/BP*	DCS Combine	KBL	Marcos
(1984: BDC appointed PVG-Cebu to replace RDDIII)			
1986			
JDA1/OIC-Danao	na	na	Aquino
(appointed by Corazon Aquino)			
1987			
RDDIII/BP-5th*	Durano	NP-GAD	Enrile
CNS/BP-2d#	Durano	NP-GAD	Enrile
ESC/BP-3rd#	Durano	NP-GAD	Enrile
RD/BP-Cebu City#	unknown	NP-GAD	Enrile
1988			
ESC/PG-Cebu#	unknown	NP	na
RMD/M-Danao*	Durano/Fernandez	LABAN-Cebu Coal.	na
TDD/M-Danao#	independent	PDP-Laban	na
JDD/VM-Danao*	Durano/Fernandez	LABAN-Cebu Coal.	na
1992			
JDD/M-Danao*	Durano	NPC	Cojuangco
BDD/M-Danao#	Durano	LDP	Mitra
RDDIV/VM-Danao*	Durano	NPC	Cojuangco
RD/M-Cebu City#	John Osmeña	NPC	Cojuangco
BDC/PBM-Cebu#	unknown	Lakas-NUCD	Ramos
RDDIII/BP-5th*	Durano	LDP	Mitra

* = electoral victory
\# = electoral defeat
na = not applicable

Abbreviations: Durano Family Candidates

BDC: Beatriz Durano Calderon (daughter of RMD-BDD, wife of ESC)
BDD: Beatriz Duterte Durano (wife of RMD)
CNS: Celestino N. ("Dodong") Sybico, Jr. (husband of Judy Durano)
DTD: Demetrio Tan Durano (father of RMD)
ESC: Emerito S. ("Tito") Calderon (husband of BDC)
FZ: Francis Zosa (son of MAZ?)
JDA1:   Jovenal Durano Almendras (nephew of RMD; son of PGA)
JDA2:   Josefino Durano Almendras (nephew of RMD; son of PGA)
JDD: Jesus Duterte ("Don") Durano (son of RMD-BDD)
LDR: Lydia Durano Rodriguez (daughter of RMD-BDD)

MAZ: Manuel A. Zosa (cousin of RMD)
PDC: Pedro Durano Calderon (son of BDC-ESC)
PGA: Paulo Gonzalez Almendras (brother-in-law of RMD)
RD: Ronald Duterte (cousin of BDD)
RDA: Rosita Dimataga Almendras (wife of JDA2)
RDC: Raymond Durano Calderon (son of BDC-ESC)
RDDII: Ramon Duterte ("Boy") Durano, Jr. (son of RMD-BDD)
RDDIII: Ramon Duterte ("Nito") Durano III (son of RMD-BDD)
RDDIV: Ramon D. Durano IV (son of RDDII)
RMD: Ramon Mercado Durano, Sr.
SD: Severo Duterte (father-in-law of RMD; father of BDD)
TDD: Thaddeus Duterte ("Deo") Durano (son of RMD-BDD)

Abbreviations: Party Affiliations and Political Offices
BP: Batasang Pambansa (National Assembly)
BP-5th: Batasang Pambansa-Fifth District, Cebu
CC: City Councilor
CCD: Constitutional Convention Delegate
DCS: Durano-Calderon-Sybico (Combine)
DZD: Durano-Zosa-Dumon (Combine)
GAD: Grand Alliance for Democracy
HR-1st: House of Representatives-First District, Cebu
IBP: Interim Batasang Pambansa (National Assembly)
JP: Juez de Paz (Justice of the Peace)
KBL: Kilusang Bagong Lipunan
LABAN: Lakas ng Bayan (also LnB, Lakas, Laban)
LDP: Laban ng Demokratikong Pilipino
M: Mayor
MC: Municipal Councilor
MP: Municipal President (Prewar Mayor)
MVP: Municipal Vice-President (Prewar Vice-Mayor)
NP: Nacionalista Party
NPC: Nationalist People's Coalition
NUCD: National Union of Christian Democrats
OIC: Officer-in-Charge
PBM: Provincial Board Member
PDP: Partido ng Demokratikong Pilipinas
PG: Provincial Governor
PVG: Provincial Vice-Governor
VM: Vice-Mayor

N OTES

I would like to acknowledge the assistance of, and express my thanks to, several people who helped in the preparation of this essay. Valuable source materials were provided by Rene Alburo, Alfred W. McCoy, Resil B. Mojares, Felicitas Padilla, John Sidel, and Margaret Sullivan. Editorial work by Alfred McCoy and Jan Opdyke contributed considerably to revisions of earlier drafts. Although reference is made throughout the essay to events after 1988, the primary focus is on the family's history up to the death of Ramon Durano, Sr., in October 1988.

[1]The first quote is by Nick Williams of the *Los Angeles Times*, as reproduced in Ramon M. Durano, *Ramon M. Durano: An Autobiography* (Danao: Ramon Durano Foundation, 1987), 152. The second is from *Asiaweek*, 18 May 1984.

[2]Jesus Vestil, interview with the author, Cebu City, 4 August 1987; Ramon M. Durano, interview with Manuel Satorre, Danao City, ca. 1982, available on tape at the Cebuano Studies Center, University of San Carlos, Cebu City. There are two lengthy biographical works on Ramon Durano: Durano, *Autobiography*; and Carlos Quirino and Laverne Y. Peralta, *Ramon Durano: The Story of the Foremost Filipino Philanthropist* (Danao: Ramon Durano Foundation, 1986). The Quirino and Peralta biography draws heavily upon the manuscript for Durano's autobiography, quoting from it extensively, but attempts to place Durano's life in the larger perspective of Philippine history. Durano's autobiography is used more often in this essay. During the 1980s, many journalists flocked to Danao to interview the colorful warlord and several of these have left memorable images of his last years. One of the most interesting is Kaa Byington, *Bantay ng Bayan: Stories from the NAMFREL Crusade (1984–1986)* (Manila: Bookmark, 1988), which devotes a chapter to NAMFREL's struggles in "Duranoland."

[3]Durano, *Autobiography*, 96.

[4]The population of Danao between 1903 and 1990 has changed as follows: 16,173 in 1903, 22,581 in 1918, 28,387 in 1939, 26,461 in 1948, 32,826 in 1960, 47,662 in 1970, 50,260 in 1975, 56,967 in 1980, and an estimated 73,000 in 1990. See U.S. Bureau of the Census, *Census of the Philippine Islands . . . 1903* (Washington, D.C.: Government Printing Office, 1905), 2:157; Philippine Islands, Census Office, *Census of the Philippine Islands . . . 1918* (Manila: Bureau of Printing, 1921), 2:156; Philippines (Republic), Bureau of the Census and Statistics, *Census of the Philippines, 1960: Population and Housing—Cebu* (Manila: N.p., 1962), 1:18/2; Philippines (Republic), Bureau of the Census and Statistics, *1970 Census of Population and Housing—Cebu* (Manila: N.p., 1972), 1:1; Philippines (Republic), National Census and Statistics Office, *1980 Census of Population and Housing—Cebu* (Manila: N.p., 1983), 1:1; and Philippines (Republic), National Statistical Coordination Board, *1991 Philippine Statistical Yearbook* (Manila: N.p., 1991), 1–10.

[5]*A Study of People Participation in the Conduct of Local Government, Administration and Politics of Danao* (Cebu: Department of Political Science, University of San Carlos, 1978), 4–18, 52–53 (hereafter cited as *San Carlos Study of Danao*); Cres. Batiquin, "The Net That Covers the Visayas and Mindanao," *Philippines Free Press*, 26 September 1959, 50–51; Cres. Batiquin, "The Cheese That Made Danao Famous," *Philippines Free Press*, 5 September 1959, 18. The presence and mining of coal in Danao and elsewhere in Cebu is discussed in some detail in Charles H. Burritt, comp., *The Coal Measures of the Philippines* (Washington, D.C.: Government Printing Office, 1901), 9, 21–22, 53–69, 104–7, 146–63; and Frank D. Spencer and Jose F. Vergara, *Coal Resources of the Philippines*, Special Reports, no. 20: *Coal* (Manila: Bureau of Mines, 1957), 27–32, 36–40. At the turn of the century Danao was described as a "commercial coaling station" with active mines in its interior, several of which were linked to the coast by "tram way" (what Durano called a *bagoneta*). See U.S. Bureau of Insular Affairs, *A Pronouncing Gazetteer and Geographical Dictionary of the Philippine Islands* (Washington, D.C.: Government Printing Office, 1902), 458, 487.

[6]The absence of prewar parish registers in Danao prevents researchers from obtaining the valuable information contained in the birth and marriage entries of the late Spanish period. Most of the information on Ramon Durano's parents derives from his own accounts, in particular from Durano, *Autobiography*, 23–30. *City of Danao, 6th Charter Anniversary, September 17, 1967* (Danao: N.p., 1967) also contains much information on the Durano family and their businesses. It is interesting to note that, according to Quirino and Peralta, *Durano*, "the Duranos believe that their mother, Dna. Bibiana, was a descendant of Juan Mercado of Biñan, Laguna, grandfather of Dr. Jose Rizal, the national hero" (p. 8). They claim that one of Juan's sons, the father of Bibiana, migrated to Cebu. This theory is based on the notion that "the family name of Mercado is a rarity in Cebu." Actually this is not the case nor is it likely that Durano's mother was related to Rizal. A large and influential Mercado family can be traced to Cebu City's Chinese-*mestizo* district, or *parian* (of which Zapatera was a part), in the early nineteenth century. Records on the Mercado family are available in the collection of *protocolos* for Cebu in the Philippine National Archives, and were part of the materials used in Michael Cullinane, "The Changing Nature of the Cebu Urban Elite in the 19th Century," in *Philippine Social History: Global Trade and Local Transformations*, edited by Alfred W. McCoy and Ed. C. de Jesus (Quezon City: Ateneo de Manila University Press, 1982), 251–96.

[7]Durano, *Autobiography*, 23–30; Colegio de San Carlos, Libros de Matrícula, 1880–1898 (a collection of matriculation records of the late nineteenth century available at the Minor Seminary in Mabolo, Cebu); *Guia oficial de las islas Filipinas 1898* (Manila: N.p., 1898), 978; *Danao, 6th Anniversary*. Whereas Demetrio is said to have been *juez de paz* from 1890 to 1896, and municipal councilor from 1897 to 1909, neither Demetrio nor Fausto Durano are mentioned in the election records for town officials between 1890 and 1893. See Philippine National Archives, Elecciones de Gobernadorcillos: Danao, 1890–93; and *Facts About the Filipinos: Taking the Southern Islands* (Boston: Philippine Information Society, 1901), 13–14.

[8]Durano, *Autobiography*, 23, 57; *Danao, 6th Anniversary*. Although Durano frequently claimed that his parents were poor, and that he rose "from rags to riches," his sister, Eutiquia, who entered a nunnery under the name Sor Maria Pudenciana, stated in an interview that the Duranos were never poor. See Sor Prudencia [*sic*], interview with Manuel Satorre, ca. 1982, available in the Cebuano Studies Center, University of San Carlos, Cebu City. Quirino and Peralta, in *Durano* (p. 8), describe Demetrio and Bibiana as part of the "lower middle class of Cebu society," and state that Demetrio invested income he derived from itinerant trading in small general stores (*sari-sari*) and farm land. In his autobiography (pp. 124–27), Durano describes some boyhood involvement in several of the economic activities of his mother and his father's sister. These women devoted much of their day to selling products such as tobacco at the municipal market.

[9]*Facts About the Filipinos*, 14; National Library of the Philippines, Historical Data Papers, Cebu Province: Danao (a collection of local histories gathered in the early 1950s by public-school teachers. For lists of the members of census advisory boards and enumerators, see U.S. Bureau of the Census, *Census of 1903*, 1:757; and Philippine Islands, Census Office, *Census of 1918*, vol. 1, appendix.

[10]Durano, *Autobiography*, 32. For information on the activities of Gonzales and Salvador as councilors, see Historical Data Papers: Danao.

[11]Eleuterio L. Ragas, *Handumanan: Mga Punoang Lungsodnon . . . sa 1934–1937 sa Kabisayan ug Mindanaw* (Cebu: Ragas Brothers, 1935), 98; Wilfredo P. Valenzuela, ed., *Know Them: A Book of Biographies* (Manila: Dotela, 1966), 2:35–37; *50 Years of Philippine Autonomy: The Golden Jubilee of the First Philippine Legislature, 1916–1966* (Manila: Philippine Historical Association, 1966), 49; *Official Directory of the House of Representatives, 1946–1949* (Manila: Bureau of Printing, 1949), 33; Andres R. Camasura, comp., *Cebu-Visayas Directory* (Manila: N.p., 1932), 423; Jovenal Almendras, interviews with the author, 7 August 1987, Danao City, and 9 August 1987, Cebu City; Historical Data Papers: Danao.

For glimpses of prewar Danao politics and the role of the Almendras family, see *Bag-ong Kusog*, 17 October 1924; and *Progress*, issues of 27 and 31 January 1931, and 12 February 1931.

[12]*Danao, 6th Anniversary*; Durano, *Autobiography*, 70–72; Quirino and Peralta, *Durano*, 43. In the latter, Durano is quoted as saying that "the famous Duterte clan" was "mostly composed of politicians and businessmen." On Severo Duterte, see Ragas, *Handumanan*, 98.

[13]It should be noted that the chronology of Ramon Durano's education and commercial activities before the war varies in different accounts. The summary here derives mostly from Durano, *Autobiography*, but is supplemented by other sources: *Danao, 6th Anniversary* (which states that his B.S.E. degree was obtained in 1932); *Official Directory of the House of Representatives, 1950–1953* (Manila, Bureau of Printing, 1950), 65–66; *Official Directory of the House of Representatives, 1958–1961* (Manila: Bureau of Printing, 1958), 109–10; and Magbanua, Mijares and Associates, *The Philippine Officials Review '67* (Pasay City: M & M Publications, 1967), 127.

[14]There is some confusion regarding the date of Ramon's marriage to Beatriz Duterte. In his autobiography he claims that they were married in 1928 (p. 62). This year is also given in Quirino and Peralta, *Durano* (p. 41). Nevertheless, on 4 April 1981 the couple celebrated their fiftieth wedding anniversary in Danao with Ferdinand and Imelda Marcos as their sponsors (*Morning Times*, 4 April 1981; *Republic News*, 15 April 1981). It is interesting to note that in his autobiography the caption under a photograph of the anniversary celebration states that it occurred in 1978. In an interview, Ramon's sister Eutiquia described Ramon's marriage to Beatriz as a secret affair opposed by their father. She also indicated that Beatriz was pregnant at the time of the marriage. See Sor Prudencia, interview with Manuel Satorre. The latter statement was confirmed by Jovenal Almendras (interviews, August 1987). Almendras also claimed that Beatriz was still enrolled in the Cebu Provincial High School at the time their relationship began. I have used the 1931 date for their marriage, assuming that the relationship (and the family) may have begun earlier but that the marriage occurred in that year, just prior to the birth of their first child, Beatriz Duterte Durano, born in Cebu City on 11 July 1931. See Commission on Elections, Certificate of Candidacy of Beatriz Durano Calderon, 21 March 1992, on record at the Office of the Provincial Supervisor, Cebu City (information provided by Resil Mojares).

[15]Durano, *Autobiography* (pp. 56–57), states that he took the job in Davao in 1933. See also *Danao, 6th Anniversary*, in which his employment in Davao is said to have begun in 1935. We can be fairly certain that Durano was back in Danao at least by 1934 since he was elected at that time to a three-year term on the Danao Municipal Council. Almendras (interviews) alleges that Durano's business ventures of the late 1930s were capitalized by money obtained in Davao through illicit bridge and road tolls and a furniture-making business.

[16]*Danao, 6th Anniversary*; *Directory of the House of Representatives, 1950–1953*, 65; Durano, *Autobiography*, 56–57, 77–78; *San Carlos Study of Danao*, 32–33. In an interesting personal account of Danao and its prewar life in the context of Ramon Durano's career, Francisco Morales, a prominent Cebu-based writer and columnist, noted that in the late 1920s the Duranos were allied closely with the Almendras family in municipal politics against the Sepulveda and Enriquez families (*Republic News*, 15 April 1981).

[17]The timing here is unclear. For various accounts, see Durano, *Autobiography*, 58–60; *Danao, 6th Anniversary*; and Jovenal Almendras, interviews. In *Directory of the House of Representatives, 1950–1953*, 65–66; and *Directory of the House of Representatives, 1958–1961*, 109–10, Durano is described as a teacher and lawyer by profession, as well as a businessman engaged in coal mining and real estate.

[18]Durano, *Autobiography*, 60.

[19]*Danao, 6th Anniversary*, claims that Durano's coal-mining activities in Danao began in 1927. Most accounts, however, state that his interest in coal mining began in the late

1930s. By 1950 he was said to own and operate "the biggest coal mines of the province" (Angel D. Quiambao, "Know Your Congressman," *Daily Mirror,* 27 February 1950, and 8 February 1958. Durano, *Autobiography* (pp. 65–68) discusses his early efforts to establish mining operations in the interior of Danao but provides no dates. The urgency to consolidate and expand his coal-mining activities in the late 1930s is undoubtedly related to the change in policy of the owners of CEPOC. After years of being criticized for purchasing coal outside the country at a high price, the plant authorities began in the late 1930s and early 1940s to acquire coal from mines in Cebu, establishing a nearby market in Naga that was linked to Danao by railway. See *Progress,* 14 September 1930, 8 February 1931, 10 April 1932, 14 August 1932; and *Bag-ong Kusog,* 9 September 1932, 5 February 1937, 10 February 1939. On Cuenco's involvement in CEPOC, see *The Nacionalista Party Before the Electorate* (Manila: Nacionalista Party, 1941), 40; *Official Directory [of the Senate of the Philippines], 1960–1961* (Manila: Bureau of Printing, 1960), 34. The close commercial link between Cuenco and Durano, in terms of their mining concerns and their sales contract with CEPOC, is demonstrated explicitly by Tereso M. Dosdos, a prominent Nacionalista politician, former congressman from the First District, and former registrar of deeds of Cebu, in a cable to Manuel Quezon sent on 13 October 1941. See Manuel L. Quezon Papers, Series VII, Box 156, File: Elections 1941, National Library of the Philippines. For information on the history of CEPOC, see Jose S. Zafra, "The Growing Cement Industry of the Philippines," in *1961 Fookien Times Yearbook* (Manila: Fookien Times, 1961), 98–100.

[20] At the time Durano ran for Congress in 1941 he was a Cuenquista but not in Cuenco's party since Cuenco was still allied formally with the Nacionalista leaders Quezon and Osmeña. Durano ran for office under the aegis of the Frente Popular, which in Cebu was organized by Vicente Sotto, a long-time political adversary of Osmeña. In Durano, *Autobiography* (pp. 86–91), Durano describes his first congressional election but fails to mention the support he received from Cuenco, indicating that since Cuenco was in the Nacionalista Party he was supporting Durano's opponent. His early links with the Cuencos, however, were widely acknowledged. See *Bag-ong Kusog,* 7 November 1941; *Danao, 6th Anniversary;* Celestino Rodriguez, *Episodios Nacionales: Horas Tragicas de Mi Pueblo* (Cebu: N.p., n.d.), 65–66; and Resil B. Mojares, *The Man Who Would Be President: Serging Osmeña and Philippine Politics* (Cebu: Maria Cacao, 1986), 49–50. Durano's 1941 campaign generated controversy among the Cebu Nacionalistas, many of whom complained to Quezon and alerted Osmeña that Durano was working with Cuenco to disrupt the party's provincial ticket. In what may have been his earliest effort to attract a national patron, Durano cabled Quezon himself in November, proclaiming his loyalty to the Commonwealth president, suggesting that he was not really a Frente Popular supporter, and hinting that he would attempt to switch to the Nacionalista Party before the election. These events are illuminated in an interesting series of cables filed in the Manuel L. Quezon Papers, Series VII, Box 156, File: Elections 1941, National Library of the Philippines (copies provided by Alfred McCoy). See especially Celestino Rodriguez to Quezon, 8 October 1941; [Tereso M.] Dosdos to Quezon, 13 October 1941; Ramon Durano to Quezon, 1 November 1941; M[ariano] Jesus Cuenco to Quezon, 9 November 1941; and Edring to Sergio Osmeña, 10 November 1941. Durano's alliance with Cuenco in 1941 was the earliest indication that he had split with the Almendras family since Paulo Almendras and his sons remained Osmeñistas.

[21] Rumors of Durano's wartime atrocities were widespread during the author's residence in Cebu in the late 1960s. These are most directly reported in Rodriguez, *Episodes Nacionales,* 39–48, 56–67, 126–28, 216–23, 231–36, 271–93; and in the Jovenal Almendras interviews. More general accounts that discuss Fenton's misdeeds do not directly implicate Durano. See Manuel F. Segura, *Tabunan: The Untold Exploits of the Famed Cebu Guerrillas in World War II* (Cebu: M. F. Segura, 1975), 128, 181, 185–204; and Cayetano M. Villamor, *My Guerrilla Years* (Cebu: Villamor Publishing House, 1955), 31–32. Villamor refers to Durano as a "faithful follower" of Fenton. In his fairly conservative account of guerrilla activities, Segura (p. 189) has this to say about Fenton: "[His] murderous tendency,

his preferred isolation, unfriendliness and disrespect for others (particularly women), alienated him from fighting man and civilian alike, who soon learned not only to dread him but hate him profoundly." Quirino and Peralta, *Durano* (pp. 83–84), describes Fenton as going "to extremes in the wanton killings of civilians," which "earned him the hatred of the relatives of his many victims." Fenton's isolation dictated heavy reliance upon his men to capture and accuse suspected collaborators. See "Diary of Harry Fenton, 1942," Charles T. R. Bohannan Collection, U.S. Military History Institute, Carlisle Barracks, Pennsylvania (notes provided by Alfred McCoy). Rodriguez, *Episodes Nacionales* (pp. 66–67, 126, 236), specifically accuses Durano of conspiring to "eliminate some 43 leaders of the Partido Nacionalista," his prewar political enemies. He lists twelve of these "victims of his vindictive fury" by name, among them the mayors of the First District towns of Danao, Carmen, Sogod, and Tabogon, one of whom was Demetrio Durano, Ramon's first cousin. Elsewhere Rodriguez claims that Durano and other officers under Fenton were responsible for the deaths of forty-six people. For his part (*Autobiography*, 73–83) Durano acknowledged his close association with Fenton, attributing his "unfortunate" demise to "intrigues and in-fighting," condemning "roving groups of armed men" who plundered and committed atrocities during the war, and distancing himself from involvement in the execution of collaborators. There is no mention of the accusations that he took part in the plundering and killing. In the eleven-page account of his wartime experiences, Durano devotes only three paragraphs to his time in the hills. The remainder of the chapter deals with more general issues, including the evils of the Japanese, the provision of sailboats and trucks to the Americans for their evacuation and war efforts, and his activities in Leyte during the final months of the war.

[22]Jovenal Almendras, interviews. Villamor, *Guerrilla Years*, (p. 32), states that Durano was arrested along with Fenton. Rodriguez, *Episodes Nacionales*, (pp. 288–93), though condemning Durano as one of Fenton's henchmen, states that Durano was freed since there was no proof against him at the time.

[23]Jovenal Almendras, interviews. In his autobiography (p. 80) Durano claims that he left Cebu when the executions of Filipino collaborators began, transferring his family by sailboat to Biliran Island, off the northern coast of Leyte. He gives no date for this move. In most accounts of his wartime activities, Durano is simply said to have attained the rank of captain while serving as an intelligence or supply officer with the Cebu guerrillas. See *Danao, 6th Anniversary; Directory of the House of Representatives, 1950–1953*, 65–66; and *Directory of the House of Representatives, 1958–1961*, 109–10. Durano, *Autobiography* (pp. 80–83), claims that he was on Biliran Island with his family during the months preceding the American landing in Leyte. He states that after they arrived he set up a transit business between Tacloban and Baybay and opened a "souvenir" shop where he sold handicrafts and local products to American soldiers. He says that he remained in Baybay, Leyte, for some time after the war, later returning to Danao with "several sacks of money" amounting to six hundred thousand pesos.

[24]*The Tribune* (Commonwealth Anniversary Supplement), 15 November 1941, 15; Angel D. Quiambao, "Know Your Congressmen," *Daily Mirror*, 27 February 1950, 8 February 1958.

[25]NACOCO suffered from a number of national and local scandals during the late 1940s. For accounts of those in Cebu, see *Morning Times*, 10 May 1947, and 16 July 1947 (references supplied by John Sidel). The newspaper's general allegations are confirmed in the Jovenal Almendras interviews and in Felicitas Padilla, interview with the author, 3 August 1987, Cebu City. Almendras claims that Durano was assisted in his efforts to defraud NACOCO by "the Duterte brothers," his relatives by marriage. Fraud of this sort was believed to have been rampant during the height of Cuenco control in late 1940s, at which time Mariano Cuenco was a senator, Miguel Cuenco a congressman, and Manuel Cuenco governor of Cebu. See Mojares, *The Man*, 49–50. In his autobiography Durano does not mention his employment with NACOCO. For information on his press and magazine, see *Bag-ong Suga*, 10–16 July 1966, 15, 88; and *Danao, 6th Anniversary*.

[26]See *Republic News*, 15 April 1981, wherein Francisco Morales describes Durano as the "protégé" of Cuenco and states that "through the backing" of Cuenco he was elected to office. See also *San Carlos Study of Danao*, 34–35. In his autobiography (p. 93), Durano refers to the incumbent Almendras as Sergio Osmeña's "hand picked" candidate. Almendras may have been forced to withdraw under pressure from Cuenco, and it also appears that the Almendras-Durano feud was exacerbated at this time. See *Pioneer Press*, issues of 23 April, 23 July, and 10 November 1949, which describe a Liberal Party "convention" held in the First District town of Catmon at which Mariano and Manuel Cuenco were both in attendance and Durano won the nomination easily. In the 1949 election, Durano defeated the Nacionalista Urot by a count of 2,796 to 1,609. For a general analysis of the election and the impressive Liberal Party victory, see Ma. Aurora Carbonell-Catilo, Josie H. de Leon, and Eleanor E. Nicolas, *Manipulated Elections* (N.p.: the authors, ca. 1985), 8–24.

[27]Historical Data Papers: Danao. See also *San Carlos Study of Danao*, 32–34. The latter states that before the Duranos took over Danao politics "there was the alternating pattern of political figures to the mayorship at various election periods." Francisco Morales, in *Republic News*, 15 April 1981, recalled that during his days as principal of the Danao Elementary School in the late 1920s the two political factions vying for control of Danao were the Almendras-Durano and Sepulveda-Enriquez alliances.

[28]*Manila Times*, 16 September 1952; Mojares, *The Man*, 54.

[29]In his autobiography Durano does not mention these political struggles. There is some evidence that Sepulveda defeated Jovenal Almendras in the mayoral race in 1947, while the latter was the incumbent congressman of the district, which would suggest that the Almendras-Durano feud was in full swing at that time. See *Pioneer Press*, 13 November 1947. The Almendras feud with Durano was due in part to his position as Cuenco's man in Danao (Jovenal has stressed in his interviews that Durano was "made by Cuenco"). The weakening of the Almendras family's political influence in Danao also may be due to the movement of Alejandro D. Almendras (Jovenal's brother) to Davao where he played a major role in postwar economic and political developments. See Valenzuela, *Know Them*, 2:35–37; and *50 Years of Autonomy*, 49.

[30]Vicente S. del Rosario, *Fighting is My Love: A Memoir* (Cebu: V. S. del Rosario, ca. 1986), 101. See also Mojares, *The Man*, 27–46.

[31]The best account of these developments is ibid., 35–58; see also del Rosario, *Fighting is My Love*, 106–9. For the election results, see *The Republic*, issues of 15, 17, 20, and 22 November 1951. In Danao, Manuel Cuenco defeated Osmeña by only 174 votes, indicating that the Almendras family—the local Osmeñista leaders—retained considerable influence. See *Daily Mirror*, 18 April 1952.

[32]Mojares, *The Man*, 54–55; *Republic Daily* (Cebu), issues of 27, 28, 29, and 30 May 1952; *Daily Mirror* (Manila), issues of 18 April, and 26, 27, 29, 30 May 1952; *Manila Times*, issues of 26, 27, 28, and 30 May 1952. In his autobiography (p. 139), Durano briefly discusses the Tecala murder but only in the context of the opportunity it provided for him to develop a relationship with Ferdinand Marcos who served as one of his attorneys in the case.

[33]Historical Data Papers: Danao; *San Carlos Study of Danao*, 32–34. The latter source suggests that Sepulveda was reelected in 1954 (presumably in a special election). See also *Daily News* (Cebu), issues of 7, 11 January 1953, 1, 6 November 1953, and 28 February 1954; *Daily Mirror*, 2, 6 June 1952, 1, 26 July 1952, 4, 5 August 1952, 27 January 1953, and 27 February 1954; and *Manila Times*, 4 June 1952, 5, 8, 9 August 1952, 16, 19 September 1952, 18 October 1952, and 7, 11, 27 January 1953. It is important to note that during the course of the trial the press reported two incidents in which Durano henchmen attempted to eliminate witnesses against him. It is also worth noting that Manuel Yray died in prison. His body was returned to Danao by Durano, who sponsored a large funeral procession and burial for his loyal follower (Jovenal Almendras, interviews; Quirino and Peralta, *Durano*, 116).

[34]These issues are discussed more fully below.

[35]The best account of Cebu politics during this period is Mojares, *The Man* (see particularly pages 89–93). See also del Rosario, *Fighting is My Love*. For accounts of the Cuenco demise and the developing Cuenco-Osmeña reconciliation, see *Manila Times*, 15, 16 February 1953, 17, 22 April 1954, 1 January 1956, 24 August 1957, and 3 September 1957; *Daily Mirror*, 23 February 1953, and 19 August 1954; *Bag-ong Adlaw*, 14 June 1954; and *Republic Daily*, 8, 11 November 1955, and 14 November 1957. During much of 1954 and 1955, both the Cuenco and Osmeña factions were affiliated with the Nacionalistas and vying for the support of President Magsaysay. Allying themselves with the Osmeñas must have been mortifying for the Cuencos, so much so that Miguel Cuenco, Mariano's younger brother, refused for some time to join the Fusion.

[36]It is not entirely clear why the Duranos never allied themselves with the Osmeñas but local lore suggests that there was a strong mutual animosity between Serging and Don Ramon, related in part to the murder of Pedro Tecala and the bitter struggles between the two during the 1950s and 1960s. A Durano-Osmeña Fusion would have been nearly inconceivable in the context of postwar Cebu politics. See Durano, *Autobiography*, 95–96; and del Rosario, *Fighting is My Love*, 131. Durano (p. 95) clearly describes his affection for Sergio, Sr., and his dislike for Serging, concluding with the statement "Osmeña and I bitterly fought for political ascendancy and supremacy in Cebu."

[37]Mojares, *The Man*, 116. On Zosa, see Durano, *Autobiography*, 103; *Directory of the House of Representatives, 1946–1949*, 114–15; *Directory of the House of Representatives, 1958–1961*, 125–26; and *Daily Republic*, 12, 14, 15 November 1957.

[38]On Dumon, see *50 Years of Autonomy*, 93; Valenzuela, *Know Them*, 3:50–52; and Magbanua, Mijares, *Philippine Officials*, 133.

[39]On Osmeña and Garcia, see Mojares, *The Man*, 83–87; and del Rosario, *Fighting is My Love*, 131. Durano, *Autobiography* (pp. 140–41), briefly mentions his having run in 1953 as a member of the Democratic Party, which suggests that at this time he may not have fully allied himself with Magsaysay. For some accounts of the shifting alliances in Cebu, see *Manila Times*, 17, 22 April 1954, 24 August 1957, and 3 September 1957. For local Cebu election results, see *Report of the Commission on Elections . . . 1957* (Manila: Bureau of Printing, 1958), 234–35, 246; and *Republic Daily*, 12, 14, 15, 17 November 1957.

[40]In the 1959 election for the governorship, Durano actually defeated Briones in the province but heavy losses in Cebu City led to his overall defeat. See *Morning Times*, 19 May 1963. Durano remained undefeated throughout this period in the First District, while Zosa won the Sixth District seat in all but one election (1965), holding it from 1946 to 1965 and again from 1969 to 1972. Calderon lost the Fifth District seat in 1965 but won it in the next election, holding it from 1969 to 1972. Dumon held the Seventh District seat from 1961 to 1969, with Sybico succeeding him from 1969 to 1972. See *Roster of Philippine Legislators, 1907 to 1987* (Manila: House of Representatives, Congressional Library, 1989), 168–71. As early as 1954, Durano was being considered as a Cuenquista candidate for governor against the Osmeñistas (*Daily Mirror*, 19 August 1954). For 1959 provincial election coverage, see Mojares, *The Man*, 116; Durano, *Autobiography*, 99–100 (wherein Durano seems to confuse this election with his campaign against Osmeña for mayor of Cebu City in 1963); *Daily News*, 23 July, and 8, 18 October 1959; *Republic Daily*, 3, 7, 10, 13, 14, 21 November, and 20 December 1959; *Manila Times*, 12 October 1959; *Philippines Free Press*, 8 August, 5, 12 September, 3 October, and 14, 28 November 1959. Durano protested his electoral loss to Jose Briones but nothing came of the suit. See *Report of the Commission on Elections . . . 1959* (Manila: Bureau of Printing, 1960), 475.

[41]Jose Martinez, "Cebuanas Triumphant," *Philippines Free Press*, 5 December 1959, 54; Mojares, *The Man*, 116. In his interviews, Jovenal Almendras suggested that the Durano-Garcia alliance resulted from Durano's links with Josefino Almendras (the son of Paulo and brother of Jovenal) and his wife Rosita Dimataga, concluding that through them Durano was able to establish a close and profitable connection with Garcia. Josefino Almendras was, it seems, the only member of his family to ally himself with the Duranos during this period.

[42] *Report of the Reparations Commission . . . to December 31, 1958* (Manila: [Bureau of Printing], n.d.), 16, 24, 36, 85; *Cebu Trade Directory, 1962* (Cebu: A. A. Altonaga, 1962), 229. Although no major study of the distribution of reparations has been made, it is clear that the allocation of these goods, services, and loans was strongly influenced by political considerations. The newspapers and magazines of the late 1950s and early 1960s provide a broad outline of how reparations were used by politicians. In his seminal study, *The Philippines: Public Policy and National Economic Development* (Ithaca: Cornell University Press, 1961), Frank H. Golay anticipates this problem, concluding that "the reparations program may be succumbing to the seamier side of Philippine political activity" (p. 311).

[43] Durano, *Autobiography*, 32; *Republic Daily*, 10 August 1958. Durano's relationship with Carlos Garcia is barely touched upon in his autobiography. Garcia is not even mentioned in connection with Durano's political life. He is mentioned in passing in a discussion of Durano's business concerns (p. 123), where it is simply said that he was president at the time Durano acquired his Kraft Paper Plant. He is also mentioned briefly in Durano's general assessment of the seven presidents he knew. There Garcia is praised as having been a "very good chief executive" but one who was indecisive and "rather slow in his judgment" (p. 131).

[44] On Danao's becoming a city, see Gervasio Lavilles, *Cebu: History of Its Four Cities and Forty-Nine Municipalities* (Cebu: Mely Press, 1965), 23, 25; and *Danao, 6th Anniversary*. On Durano's efforts to establish a second province in northern Cebu, see *Manila Times*, 22 April 1961, and 12 May 1961.

[45] For 1961 election coverage and results, see *Report of the Commission on Elections . . . 1961* (Manila: Bureau of Printing, 1962), 251–52, 273; *San Carlos Study of Danao*, 38–39; *Republic News*, 16, 17, 19 November 1961; and Martin Meadows, "Philippine Political Parties and the 1961 Election," *Pacific Affairs* 35, no. 3 (Fall 1962): 261–74. In Danao the Duranos delivered 92 percent of the vote to Garcia (8,058 to 697).

[46] Mojares, *The Man*, 116; del Rosario, *Fighting is My Love*, 153; Durano, *Autobiography*, 99–100. For some examples of the election coverage, see *Morning Times*, 19 May, 30 June, 19 September 1963; *Republic News*, 12, 27 September, 24 October, 12, 17 November 1963; and *Manila Times*, 20 February 1962.

[47] *Report of the Commission on Elections . . . 1963* (Manila: Bureau of Printing, 1964), 364; *San Carlos Study of Danao*, 40–41.

[48] Mojares, *The Man*, 112–14; Durano, *Autobiography*, 101, 137–45. In his autobiography, Durano describes his long association with Marcos, dating from their days as colleagues in Congress in 1949. On Durano and Zosa's bolting the Liberal Party, see *Manila Times*, 13, 14 July 1965.

[49] For examples of the accusations made by the two politicians against one another at the time, see *Bag-ong Suga*, 29 July 1966, 4–5, 79–81; *Manila Times*, 15 June 1966; *Philippines Free Press*, 16 July 1966; and Mojares, *The Man*, 115–19. On the results of the 1969 election, see *Report of the Commission on Elections . . . 1965* (Manila: Bureau of Printing, 1967), 298–99. It is interesting to note that the eventual reorganization of the DZD Combine into the DSC Combine was due in part to the 1965 election, in which Zosa lost the Sixth District by a wide margin to Dumon, who ran on the Liberal Party ticket, not as a Nacionalista. This suggests that Dumon had remained loyal to Macapagal, and possibly to Osmeña, in the complex political realignments of 1964–65.

[50] Mojares, *The Man*, 118; del Rosario, *Fighting is My Love*, 153–54. The 1967 election results for Danao are given in *San Carlos Study of Danao*, 44; see also *Report of the Commission on Elections . . . 1967* (Manila: Bureau of Printing, 1968), 253, 326.

[51] *San Carlos Study of Danao*, 42–45; *Morning Times*, 17 November 1967.

[52] *Bag-ong Suga*, 4 April 1969, 10.

[53] Durano, *Autobiography*, 71. See also Mojares, *The Man*, 142–43; del Rosario, *Fighting is My Love*, 154–55; and Gary Bacolod, "The Local Contest: 'Anatomy of Feudal Politics,'" *Partisan*, October 1971, 7–9. For election coverage, see *Morning Times*, 29

November 1969; and *San Carlos Study of Danao*, 45–46. The margin of Marcos's victory over Osmeña was bettered only by Durano's victory over his First District opponent, Mario Suson, who received only 396 votes in Danao compared to Durano's 15,602. Durano clearly saw his 1969 election success as one of his greatest political achievements, claiming that, although Osmeña and Macapagal "conducted a military operation against me in Cebu," he "was able to fight them toe-to-toe" (Quirino and Peralta, *Durano*, 125–26). It was at this time, he said, that he earned the title "king-maker" (Durano, *Autobiography*, 103).

[54]For an overall assessment of the 1969 election, see Carbonell-Catilo et al., *Manipulated Elections*, 38–53. On the changing political conditions of the late 1960s and early 1970s, see Mojares, *The Man*, 146–56; and Amando Doronila, "The Transformation of Patron-Client Relations and its Political Consequences in the Philippines," *Journal of Southeast Asian Studies* 16, no. 1 (March 1985): 99–116. For a contemporary glimpse of the new ideas germinating in Cebu and an analysis of local affairs on the eve of the 1971 election, see *Partisan*, October 1971.

[55]Mojares, *The Man*, 151–52; del Rosario, *Fighting is My Love*, 155–56. On the election results for delegates to the Constitutional Convention in 1970, see *Report of the Commission on Elections . . . 1970* (Manila: Bureau of Printing, 1971), 384–86. In addition to Lydia D. Rodriguez, the Durano alliance also succeeded in electing Francis M. Zosa (Sixth District) and Pedro B. Uy Calderon (Fifth District) to the Constitutional Convention. For additional 1971 election local coverage, see *The Freeman*, 8, 10, 14 November 1971.

[56]In early reports on the martial-law regime, there was some speculation that Marcos was cracking down on Durano, who was out of the country at the time. Clearly the Duranos were hurt financially by Marcos's initial takeover of all cement-milling facilities (including Durano's UNICEMCO) and the military's vigorous efforts to collect weapons and shut down illicit gun manufacturers (see, for example, *New York Times*, 2 October 1972). Rumors in Cebu at the time suggested that the Duranos turned in some of their guns but had the bulk of them removed to the Camotes Islands where they were buried until the manufacture and use of firearms received the tacit approval of the Marcos regime. Concerning his relationship with Marcos, Durano wrote "Marcos and I were very close prior to the election of 1965, but our bond of friendship became even stronger afterwards. In many of his political battles, I gave him substantial help and assistance for I believe in the greatness of the man" (*Autobiography*, 102–3).

[57]Carbonell-Catilo et al., *Manipulated Elections*, 58–60; Primitivo Mijares, *The Conjugal Dictatorship of Ferdinand and Imelda Marcos I* (San Francisco: Union Square, 1986), 450–52.

[58]*San Carlos Study of Danao*, 47–51.

[59]Eduardo ("Eddie") Gullas, interview with the author, 10 August 1987, Cebu City. Durano, *Autobiography* (p. 103), describes Gullas as the "protégé of Mrs. Durano" and someone he "could not trust," in part because he came from Cebu City. Nevertheless, he alleges, because of his wife's insistence "I took him under my wings" in 1969.

[60]In his interview, Eddie Gullas explained that Marcos viewed Cebu as "hostile territory" and chose him as governor to avoid polarizing the political forces there. Gullas also believed that Marcos wanted a "communicator type" like himself, someone with a "fresh face" and a "clean record." Clearly, considerable thought went into the appointment. At the height of the Gullas-Durano controversy in the mid-1980s, one of the stories circulating in Cebu was that Gullas originally had been offered the Cebu City mayorship but that on the advice of Marcos's local government minister, Jose Roño, he turned it down. Later, so the story goes, Gullas was offered the governorship over Tito Calderon, the Durano choice (see *Sun Star Daily*, 12 May 1985).

[61]Eduardo Gullas, interview.

[62]Eduardo Gullas, interview; see also del Rosario, *Fighting is My Love*, 173.

[63]In his interview, Gullas alleged that according to the plan the four KBL candidates earmarked for victory in Region VII were himself, Nito Durano, Lito Osmeña, and Tony

Cuenco. The other nine seats of Region VII were to be surrendered to the Pusyon Bisaya. On the Pusyon Bisaya, see ibid., 171–73, 181–89; and Jeruel N. Roa, "Casimiro M. Madarang, Jr.," *Vistas,* 4 April 1982, 8–9, 17, 22, 26.

[64]In his interview, Gullas admitted that in the unaltered vote count the Pusyon Bisaya nearly swept the election, winning twelve seats, while the thirteenth was actually won by him. Gullas chose not to file a protest because he preferred to keep the governorship of Cebu, resuming his post after the election. He also claimed that the original agreement among KBL leaders to retain four seats and allow the rest to the Pusyon was disrupted by someone (possibly with military links) who rearranged the results so that the KBL winners would be Gullas, Durano, Calderon, and Tomas Toledo (from Bohol). It was the attempt to obtain these latter results that was so badly bungled, forcing the Board of Canvassers, with Marcos's approval, to declare a complete victory for the Pusyon Bisaya candidates. Given the attempted reorganization of the results to include Calderon while eliminating Osmeña and Cuenco, and the implication that "military personnel" were involved, Gullas undoubtedly was placing the blame for the bungling on the Duranos, though he did not say so directly. See also Carbonell-Catilo et al., *Manipulated Elections,* 66–68; and del Rosario, *Fighting is My Love,* 183–84. For the published election results, see *Morning Times,* 15 April, 14 May 1978.

[65]Based on the Gullas interview and on stories circulating around Cebu at the time, it is interesting to speculate that the Pusyon Bisaya may have been a Marcos creation, a political trial balloon launched to test the turbulent waters of Cebu and identify areas of resistance. As a ploy, it undoubtedly served to humiliate the Osmeñas and Cuencos, by seducing them into the KBL and then letting them lose, thus demonstrating Marcos's control over the situation and his enemies' lack of popularity. For most of the members of the Pusyon in Cebu, however, the party's brief but dramatic success remained an important symbol of Cebuano resistance to Marcos. See, for example, del Rosario, *Fighting is My Love,* 171–92.

[66]In his interview, Gullas indicated that the competition between himself and the Duranos was intense, with Marcos clearly working to maintain a balance between them. Although Gullas had been willing to run against a Durano candidate, Marcos would not permit it. Gullas admits that in 1980 Durano controlled most of the mayors of Cebu but claims that he was rapidly becoming more influential in the province. Filemon Fernandez (personal communication, 1982) claims that at a December 1979 meeting at Malacañang he was asked to run for governor as a compromise candidate (between Gullas and Durano) but he declined. See also Jeruel N. Roa, "Assemblyman Filemon L. Fernandez," *Vistas,* 4 April 1982, 8. For general overviews of the 1980 election, see Carbonell-Catilo et al., *Manipulated Elections,* 69–75; and del Rosario, *Fighting is My Love,* 191–202. Del Rosario alleges that bribery of election inspectors was widespread and that massive fraud is the only explanation for the KBL victories.

[67]*Morning Times,* 4 April 1981; *Report of the Commission on Elections . . . 1981* (Manila: Bureau of Printing, 1982), 174. For a general account of this election, see Carbonell-Catilo et al., *Manipulated Elections,* 75–78.

[68]Del Rosario, *Fighting is My Love,* 208–9; Joseph Y. Punay, "Discordant Notes in KBL Harmony," *Mr. & Ms.,* 17 February 1984, 17–20; Joseph Y. Punay, "Pusyon Bisaya Takes Center Stage in Central Visayas," *Mr. & Ms.,* 16 March 1984, 20–21; Joseph Y. Punay, "Rumors of a P3-M Bribe Blast Credibility of Cebu Opposition," *Mr. & Ms.,* 23 March 1984, 20–22; "Complete List of Candidates for May 14th Batasan Election," *Mr. & Ms.,* 30 March 1984, 13; Godofredo M. Roperos, "Central Visayas Situationer," *Mr. & Ms.,* 4 May 1984; Joseph Y. Punay, "In Visayas-Mindanao: Towards the Campaign Homestretch," *Mr. & Ms.,* 11 May 1984, 22–24; "Philippines, Elections: And Now the Test," *Asiaweek,* 18 May 1984, 30–47. In his interview, Gullas explained that he got along quite well with Nito Durano but was generally at odds with his father. He disclosed that at the KBL organization meeting Durano wanted Marcos to approve the candidacy of his daughter, Judy Durano Sybico, but that Marcos and his associates refused. Marcos also may

have prevented the Duranos from running as KBL candidates in Cebu City. Though Ramon, his wife, and their daughter Lydia had declared their residency in the city before the deadline, they did not file for candidacy there. See Punay, "Discordant Notes."

[69]Del Rosario, *Fighting is My Love*, 209–10. For election coverage, see *Sun Star Daily*, 2, 14, 15, 16, 17, 18 May 1984; "Philippines, Elections," 30–47; Joseph Y. Punay, "Black Saturday in Cebu Politics," *Mr. & Ms.*, 25 May 1984, 16–18; Joseph Y. Punay, "Inday Nita Cortes-Daluz: Joan of Arc of Cebu Politics," *Mr. & Ms.*, 15 June 1984, 25–27; *Foreign Broadcast Information Service Report, Philippines*, 21 May 1984, pp.1–3, 24 May 1984, p. 4, 12 June 1984, p. 6 (hereafter cited as *FBIS Report*). For a general discussion of the 1984 election, see Carbonell-Catilo et al., *Manipulated Elections*, 78–90. Del Rosario (pp. 209–10) claims that the Duranos boasted that they permitted the victory of Nita Daluz since she would be "useless in the Batasan." If the Duranos did "let her win," it more likely would have been to discredit Gullas, whose candidate, Antonio Almirante (of the Fourth District), was defeated by Daluz. The results clearly favored the Duranos, and shortly after the election Almirante split with Gullas and joined the Durano bloc (see *Sun Star Daily*, 12 May 1985). The final vote count for the provincial seats, as announced on 9 June 1984, was as follows:

Ramon Durano III (KBL-Durano)	414,687
Emerito Calderon (KBL-Durano)	375,892
Adelino Sitoy (KBL-Durano)	349,318
Nenita Daluz (Panaghiusa)	335,698
Luisito Patalinghug (KBL-Gullas)	329,497
Regalado Maambong (KBL-Gullas)	326,525

[70]See the Durano tribute in *Cebu Executive Magazine*, December 1985, wherein Don Ramon is pictured and described as "the durable political kingpin." On the appointment of Beatriz D. Calderon as vice-governor, see Durano, *Autobiography*, 106–7. This appointment was a critical issue in the growing conflict between Gullas and Durano, with Gullas apparently working against the appointment of Durano's daughter. See Joseph Y. Punay, "How and Why the Durano-Gullas Rift Widened" (*Mr. & Ms.*, 19–25 July 1985, 13–14). Ramon Durano, Sr., was apparently elected *barangay* captain in Poro, a municipality on the Camotes Islands, in the 1980 elections. The Duranos had long been dominant in the politics of the three towns of the Camotes, which were a part of the old First District.

[71]Eduardo Gullas, interview; *Cebu Executive Magazine*, December 1985, 11. In the latter, the Cebu delegation to the KBL convention in Manila was described as "divided" between the Gullas and Durano factions. For details on the growing rift between Gullas and Durano, see *Bulletin Today*, 11 July 1985; Joseph Y. Punay, "Fusion and Confusion in Central Visayas Politics," *Mr. & Ms.*, 12–18 July 1985, 21–22; and Punay, "Durano-Gullas Rift," 13–14.

[72]*Sun Star Daily*, 9, 15, 18, 20, 22, 23, 29, 30 December 1985, 3 January 1986; *The Freeman*, 20, 24 December 1985; *Visayan Herald*, 23 December 1985.

[73]The conflict had repercussions in Manila where choosing between Gullas and Durano for leadership of the KBL in Cebu was a major dilemma for the regime. In Durano's view, Gullas had the support of Imelda Marcos and Minister Jose Roño, while he was confident that the president preferred his leadership (Durano, *Autobiography*, 148–49). An interesting manifestation of the Gullas-Durano feud was played out in the election of the head of Cebu's branch of the Kabataang Barangay, the national youth organization headed by Marcos's daughter Imee. The Cebu contest pitted the sons and daughters of local politicians against one another in a competition that clearly had wider implications and both Gullas and Durano worked for their favorites (see *Sun Star Daily*, 3, 4, 17, 18 January, and 17 February 1986. The feud continued unabated after the presidential election. Durano and Gullas even led separate delegations under the KBL banner to Manila to celebrate the Marcos victory (ibid., 24 February 1986).

[74]Ibid., 8, 9, 10, 11, 13 January 1986; *Philippine Daily Inquirer*, 9 January 1986; *FBIS Report*, 13 January 1986 (p. 4), 14 January 1986 (p. 11), 15 January 1986 (pp. 9–10).

[75]*Visayan Herald*, 7, 21 January 1986; *Sun Star Daily*, 20 December, 7, 8, 17, 24 January, 4, 7, 8, 11, 15, 16, 17, 28 February 1986; *The Freeman*, 21, 23, 26, 27, 30 January, 7, 8, 10, 13, 16, 20, 21 February 1986; J. R. Alibutud, "Danao City: Where the Election was Over Before the Voting," *Mr. & Ms.*, 14–20 February 1986, 20–21. For a more detailed account of NAMFREL's critique of the Duranos' rule, and its unsuccessful efforts to bring about a fair election in Danao and the old First District, see Byington, *Bantay ng Bayan*, 161–86. NAMFREL's general assessment of the 1986 election is presented in *The NAMFREL Report on the February 7, 1986 Philippine Presidential Elections* (N.p.: National Citizens Movement for Free Elections, [1986]). Durano, *Autobiography* (p. 150), boasts that in Danao Marcos won 99.6 percent of the vote, leaving Aquino with "only .4%." By NAMFREL's count, the Danao tally gave 99.2 percent to Marcos, and .8 percent to Aquino (Byington, *Bantay ng Bayan*, 176).

[76]*Sun Star Daily*, 18 February 1986; Eduardo Gullas, interview. Problems in several of the First District municipalities were evident before the election, especially in Bogo where the Martinezes, leading landowners in this sugar area, were openly opposing the Duranos (ibid., 7, 8 May 1985).

[77]After fleeing Danao along with other NAMFREL volunteers on election day, Leonardo Capitan gave a long interview on Radio Veritas in Manila in which he exposed many of the Durano-inspired election violations (see Byington, *Bantay ng Bayan*, 174–76). Although Jovenal Almendras was a Durano relative (Ramon's nephew), his appointment was considered hostile since he was identified with the Almendras brothers who had long opposed the Duranos' takeover of their town. The Duranos did not surrender City Hall without a fight. Although he was appointed in early March of 1986, Almendras was unable to take office until the end of May because the Duranos engaged in a series of legal ploys that allowed them time to make an orderly departure (Jovenal Almendras, interviews). In March 1986, Eddie Gullas was also removed from office and replaced by Osmundo Rama, the governor he had replaced in 1976. In April, when the KBL in Cebu formally disbanded, to no one's surprise it split into two competing factions, one under Durano and the other under Gullas (*FBIS Report*, 18 April 1986, 4–5). Although for some time Gullas was involved in organizing a new party, he withdrew from politics before the 1987 election and has not been actively engaged since that time. In Durano's message of support for the Aquino government he claimed to have decided to support Aquino because she was "recognized by the U.S. government" (*Sun Star Daily*, 28 February 1986).

[78]Manila Times, 6 December 1986; *Sun Star Daily*, 2, 3, 4, 6, 8, 9, 11, 13, 14, 15, 17, 18, 21 May, 5, 18 June 1987; *Mr. & Ms.*, 8–14 May 1987; *Veritas*, 14–20 May 1987; *FBIS Report*, 8 May 1987, 1. Minnie Osmeña's earlier flirtations with the Duranos are suggested in *FBIS Report*, 30 January 1986, 17.

[79]Quoting Godofredo Roperos in *Sun Star Daily*, 18 June 1987.

[80]Ibid., 17, 27 May, 5 June 1987.

[81]Ibid., 25, 28, 30 July 1987, 3, 4, 5, 15, 19 December 1987, 8, 10, 11, 12, 13, 14, 19, 21 January 1988; *The Freeman*, 8, 16, 19, 21 January 1988; *Manila Chronicle*, 15 January 1988. In an interview with Resil B. Mojares conducted on 5 March 1988 in Cebu City, Godofredo M. Roperos, a prominent journalist based in Cebu, noted that Calderon originally had been encouraged to run for governor by Ramon Durano, Sr., who offered Calderon one million pesos for his campaign in the hope of using him to gain leverage with the Enrile wing of the Nacionalistas. Durano eventually switched his support to Filemon Fernandez in an effort to achieve a national alliance with Senator Ernesto Herrera. As the story goes, Herrera had promised to help the Duranos recover UNICEMCO, which at the time had been placed in receivership by the Development Bank of the Philippines (interview transcript provided by Resil Mojares). The break between Dodong Sybico and the Durano

family was exacerbated by his separation from Judy Durano. Their marriage was later annulled despite the fact that they have seven children.

[82] *The Freeman*, 22, 23, 25, 26, 28, 29 January 1988; *Sun Star Daily*, 23, 25, 26 January 1988.

[83] Ibid., 24, 25, 31 January, 1 February 1988.

[84] Ramon Durano, Sr., interview with Margaret Sullivan, 15 January 1988 (transcript provided by Margaret Sullivan).

[85] *Report of the Commission on Elections . . . 1957*, 246; *Report of the Commission on Elections . . . 1967*, 118; *Report of the Commission of Elections . . . 1970*, 29, 273–74. See also *The Freeman*, 21, 30 January 1986, 7, 8, 24 February 1986, 6, 7, 17, 19, January 1988; *Sun Star Daily*, 24, 26, 27, 30 January 1986, 7, 8, 17 February 1986; 11, 19 January 1988.

[86] By controlling the political and administrative apparatus of Danao City and maintaining close relations with allies in Manila, Ramon Durano was in a favorable position to influence the appointment of key electoral officers in his jurisdictions. It has been alleged, for example, that Durano regularly controlled the appointments and assignments of Comelec personnel in his district, especially in the late 1970s and 1980s, guaranteeing his influence over these officers (Jovenal Almendras, interviews).

[87] In the late 1960s and early 1970s, Durano was known to carry a .38 caliber revolver in a bag along with his crucifix, rosary, missal, and photographs of his parents and grandparents (Jesus Vestil, interview).

[88] On the turn-of-the-century origins of gun making in Danao, see *New York Times*, 7 May 1987. In 1988, an American National Public Radio report on Danao gun manufacturers stated that the "industry" was begun by Mario Durano in 1928 (Allen Burlow, NPR Report, 18 August 1988). In his autobiography, Durano (p. 79) mentions, out of context, that while he was in the mountains of Cebu during the Japanese occupation he met a town mate who was a "manufacturer of Danao-made guns." For various reports on gun making and the hoarding of weapons for political purposes in Danao, see *Daily Mirror*, 3 May 1952; *Manila Times*, 9 April 1962; and *San Carlos Study of Danao*, 12, 17. For reports on gun running out of Cebu's northeastern coast, see *Manila Times*, 23 February, 12, 15 May, and 28 August 1952.

[89] *New York Times*, 6 October 1972.

[90] On 7 May 1987, the *New York Times* reported that in Danao there were three thousand gun manufacturers "who provide a livelihood, directly or indirectly, for 60 percent of the residents." Ramon Durano himself used the prevalence of home-made handguns in Danao to explain why communist "terrorism" could not succeed there. The terrorists would be outgunned, he reported, and simply shot (*Sun Star Daily*, 4 February 1986). For a range of reports on the manufacture and sale of Danao guns, see ibid., 19 December 1985, 18 January 1986, 24 May 1987, 12 June 1987, 4 September 1987, 8 January 1988; *Visayan Herald*, 3 January 1986; *The Freeman*, 1 February 1986, 7 August 1987; *Manila Chronicle*, 14 June 1990; *Philippine Daily Inquirer*, 7 August 1987 (describing a raid that seized some 140 *paltik* worth 210,000 pesos); and *FBIS Report*, 7 November 1985, 19 (reporting on the seizure in Cebu City of a carload of 93 *paltik* worth about 100,000 pesos). The latter report claims that at the time a *paltik* sold for about 1,000 pesos in Cebu but that smugglers could sell them in Taiwan for 15,000 pesos each.

[91] Information on the Japanese *yakusa* connection comes from newspaper accounts, from conversations with people in Cebu during the summers of 1986 and 1987, and, in particular, from interviews conducted in Danao with a family of gun merchants by Robert Uy in June 1990. The interviews reveal that guns are sold to the *yakusa* by means of off-shore trading between local sellers and Japanese fishing boats. For a major report on the Danao gun trade with Taiwan, also accomplished through smuggling on fishing boats, see *FBIS Report*, 26 June 1989, 53–54. The reputation of Danao's gun industry has attracted a number of foreign journalists. In early 1986, a Japanese film crew went to Danao to collect

footage on the city's gun manufacturers for a documentary describing "interesting spots in Cebu" for Japanese tourists to visit (*Sun Star Daily*, 18 January 1986).

[92]Jovenal Almendras, interviews; Eduardo Gullas, interview. Gullas described a visit to Boy Durano's armory in Danao City where he saw an impressive array of weaponry from *paltik* to "stateside" attack rifles and other military armaments. In an extremely rare raid on the Durano home, conducted shortly after the military came under the control of Corazon Aquino, soldiers found six pistols, a shotgun, and an eighteen-inch *bolo* (sword). The family claimed that the shotgun and two of the pistols (a .357 magnum and a .38 revolver) did not belong to them but that the *bolo* was the one regularly carried by Don Ramon. As far as can be determined, no one in the family was arrested or cited for an illegal act (*FBIS Report*, 19 June 1986, 15).

[93]One visitor to Danao during the campaign for the February 1986 election noted that Ramon Durano "always has four or five bodyguards lounging nearby, more if he is in his home compound, where they multiply geometrically" (Byington, *Bantay ng Bayan*, 162–63). For a description of Cuenco goons in the late 1940s, see del Rosario, *Fighting is My Love*, 98–100.

[94]Eduardo Gullas, interview; AR (a former goon employed on several occasions by the Durano family), interview with Rene Alburo, Cebu City, 15 February 1988. For an example of criminal elements among the Durano goons, see *Sun Star Daily*, 7 May 1985. For accounts of raids by Durano goons on towns in the Camotes, see *The Freeman*, 10 February 1986; and *Visayan Herald*, 4 February 1986, wherein it is alleged that Danao (though unnamed) was the center of a province-wide network of goons linked by walkie-talkies and engaged in an effort to "terrorize" people into voting for Marcos. An eyewitness account of the actions of Durano goons in the Camotes Islands during the February 1986 elections alleged that the towns there were "full of Durano's long guns" and that the channel between Cebu and the Camotes was patrolled by "an armed tugboat" that regulated traffic from Cebu City and Danao in order to prevent NAMFREL volunteers from travelling to the islands (Byington, *Bantay ng Bayan*, 169). On ISIA, see General Information Sheets for 1977, 1979, 1986, and 1987, Securities and Exchange Commission, Region VII Office, Cebu City: entries for "Insular Police Agency, Inc." and "Insular Security and Investment Agency" (information supplied by Resil B. Mojares); *Cebu Telephone Directory*, 1985–86; *Cebu City Telephone Directory*, 1986–87; *Cebu Executive Magazine*, December 1985, 25; Jovenal Almendras, interviews.

[95]Jovenal Almendras, interviews; AR, interview with Rene Alburo; Eduardo Gullas, interview; *Cebu City Telephone Directory*, 1986–87. For reports of Durano goons being used during elections in Danao and the First District, see *Republic Daily*, 12, 14, 15 November 1957; *Manila Times*, 12 October 1959; *Daily Mirror*, 28 September 1961; *Visayan Herald*, 8 February 1986; *Sun Star Daily*, 15 May 1984, 20 February 1986, 12, 17, 29 May 1987; and *The Freeman*, 17, 19 January 1988.

[96]See the allegations of Deo Durano in *Sun Star Daily*, 8, 20 January 1988; *The Freeman*, 8, 13, 14 January 1988; and those of Celestino Martinez, of Bogo, in *Sun Star Daily*, 7 May 1985; *The Freeman*, 8 May 1985. Deo Durano also alleged that his father's associates and their military supporters were issuing military uniforms to goons and CHDF men to provide an official cover for their harassment of voters. See also Eduardo Gullas, interview, and Jovenal Almendras, interviews, wherein both men stress that Durano's close association with the provincial military authorities was always an important factor in the family's political success. In his interviews, Almendras also explains how the Duranos began to recruit vigilantes (many of whom were former members of the CHDF) in the late 1980s, in part simply to maintain control over these men. Representatives of the National Democratic Front operating in Cebu in late 1987 also confirm that the Duranos and Sybicos (of Balamban) were actively recruiting and forming vigilante groups for political purposes (Ka Dodong, Ka Albert, and Ka Trining, interview with the author, 10 August 1987, Cebu City).

[97] Close relations between the Duranos and Abenina were widely acknowledged, and the strong criticism lodged against Abenina by the opposition party, the Panaghiusa, was in part intended to disrupt the strong ties between the military and the Duranos' political forces in Cebu (*Sun Star Daily*, 26 May 1987; *Philippine News and Features*, 13, 20 July 1987). On the coup attempt and its aftermath, see *The Freeman*, 29 August 1987; and *Los Angeles Times*, 29 August 1987.

[98] Jovenal Almendras, interviews; *Philippine Daily Inquirer*, 3 February 1988; *The Freeman*, 18 January 1988; *Sun Star Daily*, 12 May 1987, 13 January 1988. For interesting allegations of systematic vote buying by the Duranos in the 1986 election, see *Veritas*, 2 February 1986; *Sun Star Daily*, 31 January 1986; and *FBIS Report*, 30 January 1986, 16–17. For reports on vote buying by the Duranos, see *Republic Daily*, 7 November 1959; *Sun Star Daily*, 31 January 1986, 12, 17 May 1987, 19 January 1988; *The Freeman*, 17, 19 January 1988; and "The Cebuanos Couldn't Be Bought," *Philippines Free Press*, 28 November 1959. According to the latter source, millions of pesos, mostly from government agencies, were released by President Garcia to assist Durano in his struggle against the Osmeñas' candidate for governor, Jose Briones. The routine payment by the Duranos of 5 pesos for votes is also reported in *The Freeman*, 3, 4 November 1971. In his autobiography (pp. 114–15), Durano condemns vote buying as a tool of "crooked politicians," distancing himself from such corrupt acts and stressing that he did not need to buy votes since he earned political support by providing voters with employment in his industrial complex. In a later effort to demonstrate his honesty, he states (pp. 151–52) that the Marcos administration sent him a check for 5 million pesos to be used for vote buying in the February 1986 presidential election. Durano claims to have returned the check uncashed after the election, eliciting the Marcos response: "See, it's only Monching who is returning the money!" A copy of the returned check is reproduced in Quirino and Peralta, *Durano*, 139.

[99] Jovenal Almendras, interviews.

[100] The data for table 1 derive from a variety of sources. Population data come from the censuses cited in note 4. Election data come from *Pioneer Press*, 10 November 1949; *Times 400*, 10 November 1951; *Republic Daily*, 10 November 1959; *Morning Times*, 29 November 1969; *The Freeman*, 14 November 1971, 23 January 1986, 11 February 1986; *Visayan Herald*, 7, 23 January 1986; *Sun Star Daily*, 6 February 1986, 5 June 1988; *San Carlos Study of Danao*, 38, 40, 44, 51; and various issues of the *Report of the Commission on Elections* (1961, pp. 243, 246; 1963, p. 332; 1965, p. 252; 1967, p. 214; 1970, p. 427; and 1981, p. 174). For complaints and commentary on fraudulent registration in Danao, see *Asiaweek*, 18 May 1984; *Washington Post*, 13 August 1984; *Visayan Herald*, 7, 21 January 1986; *Sun Star Daily*, 2 May 1984, 7, 8 January 1985; 20 February 1986; *The Freeman*, 23 January 1986, 10, 20, 21 February 1986. In 1959, Comelec officials disclosed that the Danao registry lists were "full of Caviteños," illicit voters from the province of Cavite (*Republic Daily*, 3 November 1959). Another report on the discrepancies between the Danao electorate before and after 1986 disclosed that in the February 1986 presidential election "nearly all 64,000 residents were classified as voters" but that when registration was carried out in April 1987 there were only 35,000 qualified voters (*FBIS Report*, 8 May 1987, 1). In his autobiography, Durano (p. 118) responded to charges of illicit registration by claiming that the population of extra voters in Danao must be attributed to the large number of "migrant workers" employed by his family's industrial concerns who prefer to register and vote in Danao rather than return to their homes. This contradicts his earlier claim (p. 117) that the strength of his businesses is that from the beginning they employed local residents who "stayed on" into the third generation. The number of employees in the Durano industrial complex never accounted for a significant portion of the number of registered voters even during the 1960s and 1970s when these businesses were at their height. In 1975–76, when the population of Danao was officially 50,260 and the number of actual voters was 36,149 (for the 1976 referendum), the total number of employees in the four largest Durano-owned companies was 1,299 (3.5 percent of the electorate). The largest

occupational group in Danao at the time was fishermen, who are estimated to have made up 45 percent of the population (*San Carlos Study of Danao*, 15–16). It is interesting to note that at the time in Danao there were more schoolteachers (368) and people engaged in dressmaking and embroidery (200) than there were employees of the Durano Sugar Mill (205). The number of voters in the 1976 referendum represented nearly 72 percent of the population, which demographically is highly suspect. Even if the number of Durano employees is doubled to account for resident "migrant workers" hired for seasonal labor, the entire body of employees would have comprised only 7 percent of the electorate.

[101] *Visayan Herald*, 28 January 1986; *The Freeman*, 1 February 1986.

[102] *San Carlos Study of Danao*, 37–51. Similar vote counts in Danao precincts were not uncommon; see, for example, *Republic News*, 19 November 1961. Former Durano follower and Marcos-appointed Comelec commissioner, Casimiro Madarang, filed a formal petition with Comelec protesting a series of Durano electoral frauds in the May 1984 election (*Mr. & Ms.*, 15 June 1984). It was even alleged that the Duranos could control the electoral process from start to finish (see *The Freeman*, 13 February 1986).

[103] *Sun Star Daily*, 2 January 1988. The Danao election results in 1986 were considered by many observers to have been completely fabricated. One article exposing some of the frauds was entitled "Danao City: Where the Election Was Over Before the Voting" (*Mr. & Ms.*, 14–20 February 1986).

[104] *Sun Star Daily*, 12 January 1986.

[105] Ibid., 23 December 1985, 4 January 1986; *The Parish and Church of Santo Tomas de Villanueva: A Historical Record . . . Danao City . . . December 1985* (souvenir program). See also an editorial in the *Visayan Herald* (10 January 1986), which accuses Durano of manipulating the Church and the cardinal for political purposes. For the long list of Durano's donations, see Quirino and Peralta, *Durano*, 181–97. For an early account of politically motivated gifts to the parish priests of Cebu Province during Durano's campaign for the governorship, see *Daily News*, 18 October 1959.

[106] See Robert L. Youngblood, *Marcos Against the Church: Economic Development and Political Repression in the Philippines* (Ithaca: Cornell University Press, 1990), 72, 126, 175–76, 193–94, 200; and Catholic Bishops' Conference of the Philippines, *1983 Catholic Directory of the Philippines* (Manila: CBCP, n.d), 136, 155. Rosales retired in 1982 and died in 1983. In the early 1980s, the Catholic Church hierarchy began more openly to distance itself from the Marcos regime. Though Cardinal Sin engaged in this activity with considerable caution, he became the symbol of the Church's effort to take a more critical stance toward the dictator and his wife while at the same time not directly resisting the regime.

[107] *Sun Star Daily*, 5 May 1987; Resil B. Mojares, personal communication, 20 October 1987.

[108] Jovenal Almendras, interviews; *Sun Star Daily*, 15, 16 February 1986; *The Freeman*, 16 February 1986. Father De la Serna's testimony was considered so important in confirming the validity of the 1986 election results in Danao that Durano referred to it in his autobiography (p. 150) and reproduced the entire affidavit as an appendix (pp. 210–11). It declared, claimed Durano, "that the situation in Danao City before, during and after the election was peaceful and orderly."

[109] That Durano was successful in "bribing God" is a commonly heard expression in Cebu and it is not always mentioned as a negative trait.

[110] In his autobiography (pp. 82, 115), Durano alleges that the profits from his business ventures in Leyte amounted to six hundred thousand pesos. Though not mentioned, it is clear that his business activities during this period also were capitalized by money obtained from his brief but profitable employment with NACOCO (see also note 22, above).

[111] Durano's prewar mining activities were concentrated in the two remote *barrios* of Dunga and Kahumayhumayan. By the late 1940s his coal-mining ventures had expanded

considerably (see, for example, *Daily Mirror*, 18 March, 22 September 1952; and *Manila Times*, 19 March 1952, 11 May 1954). In the *Manila Times*, Durano was accused of major fraud between 1946 and 1950 for not declaring for tax purposes, among other things, the profits he made on coal sales to CEPOC. The total amount of alleged tax fraud was more than 150,000 pesos, with less than 6,000 attributed to coal profits, indicating that his political enemies (principally Osmeña) were aware of his "other" income, undoubtedly that deriving from NACOCO. By the mid-1950s, as his schemes to establish a cement plant developed, he began to expand his coal-mining interests even more. With reparations payments, he acquired or leased more than two thousand hectares of coal land in Danao's interior and by the 1970s he had control of all the major mines around Danao. Citing Board of Energy statistics, he stated that his mining enterprises were the second largest in the country (Durano, *Autobiography*, 115, 120; *Cebu Trade Directory, 1962*, 229). On CEPOC, which later became the Apo Cement Company, see Zafra, "Cement Industry," 98–99. For information concerning coal mined for the Cebu Portland Cement Company and the increasing profits generated by these sales, see Cebu Portland Cement Company, *Annual Report of the General Manager for the Fiscal Year Ending June 30, 1950* (Cebu City: Cebu Portland Cement Co., 1950); and Lolita Gil Gozum, "A Historical Survey of the Postwar Operation of the Cebu Portland Cement Company, with Particular Attention to the Province of Cebu" (M.A. thesis, University of San Carlos, 1955). The latter two documents were supplied by John Sidel. See also Spencer and Vergara, *Coal Resources*, 27–32, 36–40.

[112]All the raw materials necessary for cement production could be found within nine kilometers of the plant (*Cebu Trade Directory, 1962*, 229; *San Carlos Study of Danao*, 15). It is interesting to note that the *Cebu Trade Directory, 1962* describes UNICEMCO as a concern owned by "a group of Filipino businessmen" with no mention of Durano. The only person mentioned in the full-page description of the new plant is Leonila D. Garcia, President Garcia's wife, who "laid the cornerstone" of the plant on 9 September 1958. It is likely that the idea for the plant emerged in the early 1950s and on Durano's initiative the plans were set in motion. In his autobiography (p. 116), Durano attributes the success of his industrial complex to a group of "boy-wizards of President Magsaysay," who, as mechanical and mining engineers, assisted him in setting up the business. Moreover, Quirino and Peralta (*Durano*, 142) state that in 1954 he hired Cloatilde ("Diding") Quirolgico (an Ilocana with an M.A. from Philippine Women's University) who had been for some years the secretary-treasurer of the Cebu Portland Cement Company, and that she became his "business consultant," organized UNICEMCO, and "later managed the acquisition" of the Durano Sugar Mill. Although Durano does not mention her in his autobiography, Quirino and Peralta claim that without Quirolgico the industrial complex "would not have become a reality" (p. 142). They quote Durano as saying that "In one way or another, she was responsible for its foundation" (ibid.). In the larger political context, it is important to note that within Congress Durano held committee posts that allowed him to monitor and influence economic and business policies. During his critical third term (1957–60), when his personal business empire was launched, he was chair of the Committee on Commerce and Industry. He is said to have devoted his energies as chairman to the promotion of "local industries" (*Daily Mirror*, 8 February 1958). An interesting example of Ramon Durano's propensity to use his official position as a congressman to promote the family's business endeavors was exposed in early 1962. At that time an official probe into his actions in Congress was initiated, and charges of corruption were leveled against him, when it was disclosed that he had endorsed a bill to franchise the operation of a Manila taxi company by Cebu Heavy Industries, a corporation owned by his brother Antonio, his son Don, and son-in-law Oscar Rodriguez. Durano himself was one of the major investors in the company. See *Daily Mirror*, 23 April 1962; and *Manila Times*, 24 April, 5 May 1962.

[113]*Cebu Trade Directory, 1962*, 229.

[114]Durano, *Autobiography*, 120. In table 2, names of the key companies are italicized. The names and activities of the companies derive from *Danao, 6th Anniversary, San Carlos*

Study of Danao, 14–17; Durano, *Autobiography,* 120–23; and Quirino and Peralta, *Durano,* 141. The latter describes Dancar Industries as "an assembly plant for Japanese Datsun cars." Little is known about the San Jose Subdivision in Alabang but by the 1970s this would have been a lucrative piece of property. Having come into Durano's hands in 1958, it is tempting to speculate that it somehow was acquired with reparations funds. An obvious omission from table 2 is illegal gun manufacturing, which by the 1980s was an important source of family income. Over the years some other companies were added to the Durano holdings but until a comprehensive history becomes available, this list will suffice.

[115]By 1958, all the shares of UNICEMCO were "fully subscribed" (*Cebu Trade Directory, 1962,* 229). On Beatriz Durano's directorships, see Quirino and Peralta, *Durano,* 41.

[116]*Danao, 6th Anniversary.*

[117]Durano, *Autobiography,* 120.

[118]*San Carlos Study of Danao,* 13–17.

[119]See, for example, Durano, *Autobiography,* 117–18; and note 100, above. In this context it is interesting to note that the UNICEMCO plant was constructed with machinery intended to require less labor than most; the original plant needed "only a 170-man labor force" (*Cebu Trade Directory, 1962,* 229). The figure of 10,000 employees becomes more believeable if we include among his employees all those holding positions in the Danao City government, including teachers.

[120]In his study of Philippine industrialization, Yoshihara Kunio stressed that Durano was among a small number of politicians who took advantage of the government's industrial-promotion schemes to build his business empire—first with cement, utilities, and insurance, and later with sugar. See Yoshihara Kunio, *Philippine Industrialization: Foreign and Domestic Capital* (Quezon City: Ateneo de Manila University Press, 1985), 134. A recent and useful study of the postwar interaction between politics and economic development is Amando Doronila, *The State, Economic Transformation, and Political Change in the Philippines, 1946–1972* (Singapore: Oxford University Press, 1992).

[121]*Sun Star Daily,* 9 December 1985.

[122]*Cebu Trade Directory, 1962,* 229.

[123]*Danao, 6th Anniversary.*

[124]Allegations regarding the profits that accrued to the Duranos from their "cementation" projects were rampant. See, for example, *Republic News,* 27 September 1963, wherein Priscillano Almendras speculates that if Durano could win the Cebu City mayorship that year he would construct sidewalks throughout the city with cement from his plant and charge property owners for the service. In the same vein, it is easy to see how some of Ramon Durano's donations of Church buildings could serve two ends: improving his public image and unloading surplus cement.

[125]Zafra, "Cement Industry," 98–100; Yoshihara, *Philippine Industrialization,* 37, 134; *Philippine Industry* (Manila: Department of Commerce and Industry, n.d.), 135–36; Geronimo Z. Velasco, "Growth of Manufacturing Industries" in *The Philippine Economy in the 1970's* (Quezon City: University of the Philippines, Institute of Economic Development and Research and the Private Development Corporation of the Philippines, 1972), 85–87; Gerardo P. Sicat, *Economic Policy and Philippine Development* (Quezon City: University of the Philippines Press, 1972), 3–4, 241–42. Sicat uses the cement industry as an example of how "oligopolistic" power restricts national production in order to serve domestic companies and prevent the development of surpluses for export.

[126]Only about 18 percent of the Philippine cement produced in 1975 was exported. See *Book of the Philippines, 1976* (Manila: Research and Analysis Center for Communications and Aardvark Associates, 1976), 222.

[127]*Sun Star Daily,* 9 December 1985; *Visayan Herald,* 14 December 1985; Godofredo M. Roperos, interview of Resil B. Mojares.

[128]In his autobiography (pp. 120–21, 123), Ramon Durano describes two DBP loans obtained for establishing and maintaining his industrial operations, one for 23 million pesos

and the other for 63 million. Both were presumably for the sugar mill. Durano claims that these loans were repaid by 1983, a year before they were due. Approval and financing of the Durano Sugar Mill, as with all the new sugar *centrals* of this period, proceeded under the close scrutiny of the Marcos regime. This strongly suggests that the Danao mill was approved only because of Durano's importance to Marcos's political ambitions in the late 1960s. See Gary Hawes, *The Philippine State and the Marcos Regime: The Politics of Export* (Ithaca: Cornell University Press, 1987), 91–94, 172–73.

[129]Ibid., 93–96.

[130] *San Carlos Study of Danao*, 5. Although the soil and slope of the land in Danao are not particularly suitable for sugar cultivation, cane was planted everywhere it would grow. During the early 1980s, the Duranos were also actively seeking cane in Negros Occidental and transporting it to Danao by barge for milling.

[131]The Durano Sugar Mill was owned by the family holding company, Durano and Co. In 1980, Durano and Co. was ranked 885th among Philippine corporations in sales (the figures in pesos being 32,433,000 in sales, 954,000 in net income, and 57,368,000 in total assets). In subsequent years neither Durano and Co. nor the Durano Sugar Mill made the top 1,000; they were not among the top 5,000 by 1989.

[132]Felipe L. Gonzaga, comp., *Directory of Philippine Printers and Publishers* (Manila: Bureau of Public Libraries, 1964), 7; *Directory of Philippine Printers and Buyer's Guide, 1980* (Manila: Printing Industries Association of the Philippines, n.d.).

[133] *Danao, 6th Anniversary*, Resil B. Mojares, *Cebuano Literature: A Survey and Bio-Bibliography with Finding List* (Cebu: San Carlos Publications, 1975), 83. According to the latter source, *Bag-ong Suga* was published between 1963 and 1971. See also *Kulba Hinam Komiks* 1, no. 5 (31 August 1967). On visits to the Foundation Publishing House in 1974 and 1987, I found that business had all but come to a standstill. The large printing presses and other machinery sat idle inside the huge building, gathering dust.

[134]"Top 1000 Corporations in the Philippines," in *1981–82 Fookien Times Philippines Yearbook*, 126–40; "Top 1000 Corporations in the Philippines," *1982–83 Fookien Times Philippines Yearbook* (Manila: Fookien Times, 1983), 150–62. The figures in pesos for 1980 were 74,041,000 in sales, a deficit of 10,504,000 in net income, and 110,322,000 in total assets. For 1981 they were 64,481,000 in sales, a deficit of 14,970,000 in net income, and 103,002,000 in total assets. In 1984, when no Durano enterprises were listed among the country's top two thousand corporations, fourteen cement manufacturers and twenty-two sugar-milling companies (including Bogo-Medellin) were listed. See *Business Day 1000 Top Corporations in the Philippines* (Quezon City: Businessday, 1985), 30–69, 106, 142–81. No Durano enterprises were ranked among the top five thousand corporations for 1989, at which time twelve cement manufacturers and twenty-one sugar millers were listed. See *Philippine-Business Profiles, 1990–91: 5,000 Top Corporations* (Manila: Philippine Business Profiles and Perspectives, Inc. and Center for Research and Communications, 1990), 412–68.

[135]Daisy G. Bernabe, *Philippine City Charters: A Formal Comparison* (Manila: University of the Philippines, College of Public Administration, 1969), 4, appendices 2 and 3.

[136]On the jurisdictions of cities and their relationships with the national government, see ibid.; and Jose Veloso Abueva and Raul P. de Guzman, eds., *Handbook of Philippine Public Administration* (Manila: University of the Philippines, College of Public Administration, 1967), 354. The latter states that "the creation of the city makes it an independent political entity separate from and independent of the province within which it is located, unless otherwise provided by law." See also John H. Romani and M. Ladd Thomas, *A Survey of Local Government in the Philippines* (Manila: University of the Philippines, Institute of Public Administration, 1954), 86–87, wherein the authors discuss the implications of changing the legal status of cities and the "political considerations" that "play an important, and in some cases determining, role in deciding whether or not a municipality will be converted into a city." For a detailed study of two cities in terms of the

influence of politics on government, see Howard M. Leichter, *Political Regime and Public Policy in the Philippines: A Comparison of Bacolod and Iloilo Cities,* Special Reports, no. 11 (DeKalb: Northern Illinois University, Center for Southeast Asian Studies, 1975).

[137]See *San Carlos Study of Danao.,* 57–62, which concludes by stressing the all-encompassing impact of the Durano family on the social, political, and economic affairs of the city.

[138]For the legal guidelines relating to these matters, see Bernabe, *City Charters,* 56–57.

[139] *Republic News,* 27 September 1963.

[140] *San Carlos Study of Danao,* 15–16.

[141]See, for example, *Republic News,* 1 July 1983, in which it is alleged that a multimillion-peso shipment of trucks and vans was smuggled into Danao at the Durano wharf.

[142]For one example, see *Daily Mirror,* 27, 28 January 1972; and *Manila Times,* 17, 18 February 1972.

[143]A good example of the kind of broad charges leveled against the Duranos is the statement made in 1963 by Priscillano Almendras, a close observer of Danao affairs (*Republic News,* 27 September 1963).

[144] *Sun Star Daily,* 29 March, 25 July 1987. The reclaimed land is undoubtedly the site on which the Durano industrial estate was built. The only other major semiofficial accusations lodged against the Duranos during the period of transition (March 1986 to February 1988) came from an Aquino-appointed city councilor, Leonardo Capitan. In an interview focusing on the "rape of democracy" in Danao, conducted by the Manila-based newspaper *Malaya,* Capitan claimed that under the administration of Mayor Beatriz Durano (1955–71), the family had engaged in massive landgrabbing. A few days later Beatriz Durano filed a two-million-peso libel suit against the newspaper and Capitan (*The Freeman,* 16 December 1987). Apparently Capitan never formalized his accusations and the Durano lawsuit was still in the courts when the family reasserted itself in Danao politics in 1988.

[145]Bernabe, *City Charters,* 16–17; Antonio Orendain, *Local Governments in A New Setting: An Annotated Compilation of Presidential Decrees Affecting Local Governments* (Manila: Alpha Omega, 1977), 1:51–52, 372–77; *Philippine Yearbook, 1979* (Manila: National Economic and Development Authority, 1979), 988–89. In the context of these revenue-based classifications (with most of the revenue deriving from the taxation of local businesses), it is interesting to compare Toledo and Danao. The government and politics of Toledo have never been dominated by a single family or political group, nor has there been a direct connection between elected political officials and the owners of the city's "industrial complex," the Altas Consolidated Mining and Development Corp. (The presence of Atlas in Toledo is what justifies its city status.) The biggest difference, however, is in city revenues. Toledo, which collects more than 7 million pesos in taxes annually, is classified as a 1st-A city; Danao collects less than a million and remains a fourth-class city.

[146]Durano, *Autobiography,* 71.

[147]This was the conclusion of the *San Carlos Study of Danao* in the late 1970s.

[148]Durano, *Autobiography,* 117–18. Descriptions of people kissing Durano's hand, and his contention that this act demonstrates the respect "his people" show him, are provided in Byington, *Bantay ng Bayan,* 163–64. The latter concludes that "Durano's people are very, very poor and his favors very humble." When asked if he was a warlord, Ramon Durano frequently, and quite fittingly, responded: "I like the lord, but not the war."

[149]Durano, *Autobiography,* 117. Durano was fully aware of the association between politics and business. Chapter 9 of his autobiography (pp. 113–27), which deals with his business activities, was subtitled "You Say Business and Politics Cannot Go Together. If They Cannot, There is Something Wrong with Your Politics." He stresses that he learned about "the workings of business" while studying the "intricacies of politics" during his "long sojourn in the legislative body."

[150]To put a humorous twist on Don Ramon's favorite saying, it could be said that many citizens of Danao cast their votes from the cradle and the grave.

[151]Ibid., 123–24; Byington, *Bantay ng Bayan,* 163. See also Quirino and Peralta, *Durano,* 159. The latter provides the locations and account numbers of "all" Durano's dollar accounts in the United States, totalling $91,665. For a revealing study of Marcos's cronies and their rapacious activities, see Belinda A. Aquino, *Politics of Plunder: The Philippines under Marcos* (Quezon City: Great Books Trading and the University of the Philippines' College of Public Administration, 1987).

[152]Quirino and Peralta, *Durano,* 159, quoting Jose Guevara, former congressman and Manila columnist, who wrote the foreword for Durano's autobiography.

[153]These sentiments are clearly expressed in Ramon Durano, interview with Margaret Sullivan; and in *Asiaweek,* 18 May 1984.

[154]Durano, *Autobiography,* 192–94.

[155]Ibid., 22.

[156]Ibid., 159–60. A complete list is reproduced in Quirino and Peralta, *Durano,* 181–97.

[157]Durano, *Autobiography,* 158–59.

[158]In reference to Ramon Durano, a local observer noted in a letter in the Cebu press that it is not uncommon for older people "who feel their end is near and that they will soon face their God and make an accounting of their deeds, to spend the remaining few years of their lives in constant prayer and communion with God and doing charitable works to make amends for whatever evil deeds in the past and to appease the wrath of God" (*Sun Star Daily,* 4 January 1986).

Mohamad Ali Dimaporo:
A Modern Maranao Datu

G. Carter Bentley

Mohamad Ali Dimaporo rose from obscurity in the wilds of Lanao to become a provincial governor, congressman, university president, advisor to President Marcos, and operator of the most powerful political machine in Mindanao. While others among Marcos's coterie of close associates have fallen from power, Dimaporo defied the Aquino government and the Philippine Army and has continued to prosper. He is reputed to be the luckiest man in Mindanao. The three G's of Philippine politics, guns, goons, and gold, swirl around him with manic abandon. Even while he professes no ambition other than to serve his country, he has been called the "Marcos of Mindanao," the "Chief of Staff for Mindanao," even the "Mad Dog of Mindanao."[1] For much of the Philippine reading public, Mohamad Ali Dimaporo is the archetypal Moro warlord. His flamboyant political style makes such good copy that, even during the big *palabas* of the Marcos-Aquino transition, Dimaporo's struggle to hold power in central Mindanao drew attention in the national dailies. In the Aquino era he remains high profile: "Whatever he says and does is always front-page material."[2]

In many ways Ali Dimaporo is an anomaly. He is a Muslim who reached the highest levels of power within the Philippine government while the Muslim minority and that government were at war. He is a man of relatively modest origins who attained an extremely high position among the Maranao hereditary nobility. Many find him outrageous, even laughable, but he commands respect because, in the desperately competitive world of Maranao (and of Philippine) politics, he wins. His is a political dynasty only one generation deep, but he is already laying the groundwork to extend it into the future.

Mohamad Ali Dimaporo was born on 15 June 1918 in the small municipality of Binidayan, south of Lake Lanao.[3] He is the eldest of the five sons and three daughters of Datu Dimaporo Marahom and Potri-Maamor Borngao Marahom, though one of his sisters had a different mother.[4] His father was the sultan of Binidayan, though the title passed to one of Ali's cousins. His father also served as *presidente* of the *municipio* for a time. Ali knew nothing of these details during his early years. He says: "I did not know I was the child of my mother and my father. I thought all the while my grandparents were my parents." He was named by his grandparents and lived with them until he left to attend elementary school in the provincial capital. He describes his grandfather as "also a well respected fellow, a very good speaker, and expert in genealogy. He taught me how to read Quran." Ali recalls with affection the loving care given him by his grandfather.[5] There is little indication that he ever knew his own father.

After entering elementary school in Binidayan in 1928, Ali was sent to Camp Keithley Elementary School in Dansalan, the colonial administrative center in Lanao. Classmates there recall him as an industrious but not overly intelligent student. He finished his elementary years in Ganassi, having completed the seven-year course in five years, "because I was accelerated twice. At that time, brilliant students were accelerated."[6] Much of Ali's energy during this time was devoted to earning money. He spent weekends and holidays selling fruit, betel leaves, salt, and sugar. At one point he fell from a *madang* tree while picking fruit and was nearly killed.

Ali attended the Lanao High School in Dansalan, one of the outstanding public high schools in the Philippines at that time. He graduated in 1938, proceeding on to the University of the Philippines where he completed a prelaw bachelor's course and began studies in law. During his second year there two notable events occurred. First, a star student in the law school, Ferdinand Marcos, was arrested for murder while preparing for his bar exam. Marcos's impassioned and ultimately successful pleading before the Philippine Supreme Court captured the imagination of the nation and of his fellow law students, including Ali Dimaporo. Second, Ali was drafted on 29 October 1941.

On 30 October, Ali was commissioned a third lieutenant in the Tenth Battalion of the 101st Infantry Division of the Philippine Army, the unit responsible for the defense of Mindanao and Sulu. Lieutenant Dimaporo's unit was assigned a defensive position in Davao. After Davao fell to the Japanese, Ali's unit withdrew to Bukidnon. He was then ordered by the United States Armed Forces Far East (USAFFE) high command to report to General Guy O. Fort, a long-time Philippine Constabulary commander who had arrived in early 1942 to organize the defense of northern Mindanao. Dimaporo says he first became General Fort's aide de camp and then was given responsibility for organizing the "Bolo Battalion," an irregular force of Maranao warriors armed initially only with bolos and homemade shotguns.[7] American commanders hoped this force would harass Japanese troops as effectively as had Maguindanao units after the invasion of Davao.[8] However, when a Japanese invasion force landed on the Cotabato coast, on 27 April 1942, and pushed through Parang and Malabang toward Lake Lanao, the "Bolo Battalion"

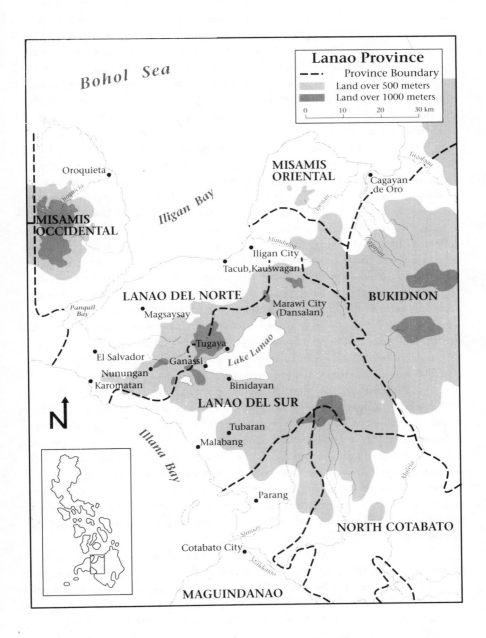

Bohol Sea

Lanao Province
- - - Province Boundary
Land over 500 meters
Land over 1000 meters

0   10   20   30 km

Oroquieta

**MISAMIS
ORIENTAL**

Cagayan
de Oro

Tagadan

Oroquieta

**MISAMIS
OCCIDENTAL**

Iligan Bay

Mandulog

Agusan

Cagayan

Iligan City

Tacub, Kauswagan

LANAO DEL NORTE

BUKIDNON

*Panguil
Bay*

Magsaysay

Marawi City
(Dansalan)

Tugaya

El Salvador

Ganassi

Lake Lanao

Nunungan
Karomatan

Binidayan

LANAO DEL SUR

N

Tubaran

Malabang

Illana Bay

Muleta

Parang

NORTH COTABATO

Simuay

Cotabato City

Mindanao

MAGUINDANAO

could provide little resistance.[9] By May, "Japanese Imperial Forces rumbled along the Malabang-Ganassi-Dansalan road as conquerors."[10] Dimaporo was forced to retreat with his fellow "Bolomen" to Karomatan where he was promoted to first lieutenant for saving the life of an American officer.[11] Facing an overwhelming Japanese military force, Fort (along with General Vachon in Cotabato) ordered a general surrender on 27 May. Lieutenant Dimaporo, a "loyal and obedient soldier," complied with the order, though he recalls it as a "bitter pill."[12] Following his surrender, Dimaporo was held in Camp Keithley. He was released in early July after promising his Japanese captors that he would help them pacify the Maranao populace. For this purpose, the Japanese Army gave him thirty rifles and two launches for use on Lake Lanao. He also pledged to bring about the surrender of Captain Mamarinta Lao and Major Manalao Mindalano, the highest ranking Muslim officer in USAFFE.[13] To fulfill his promise, Ali delivered speeches praising the Japanese fighting spirit and their plans for the Greater East Asia Co-Prosperity Sphere, and urged his audience to plant their crops and live in peace. He also collected firearms for surrender to the occupation force.[14] In return for these services, he was given the use of two trucks, with which he developed a profitable trade in rice, coffee, and tobacco between Lanao and Misamis Oriental. He also began providing protection for traders coming from Jolo to trade at Malabang, eventually establishing a monopoly on the Sulu trade in the district.

But, even while he served as a leader in the Japanese pacification effort, Ali maintained contact with the increasingly active guerrilla movement in Lanao.[15] He lent his launches to Major Mindalano and frequently, he later claimed, supplied the guerrillas with food, money, shelter, and ammunition.

Japanese officers regarded Dimaporo as a firm ally. They brought him to Manila on a propaganda junket, along with Domocao Alonto, Bato Ali, and other Muslim notables of Lanao. The visitors were "quartered at the Manila hotel, entertained lavishly at banquets and parties [and] met Laurel, Aquino, Vargas and other prominent figures in Manila."[16] In January 1944, Dimaporo, along with Malabang mayor Gandamasir Diambangan, undertook for a good price to provide laborers and armed guards for construction of a landing field in Malabang. When Major Mindalano announced that he would attack the landing field and would kill any laborers found working there, Dimaporo countered that he would defend the laborers and the landing field from attack.[17]

By June 1944, the Japanese commander at Malabang, Captain Ishima, was becoming increasingly suspicious of his erstwhile ally. On 13 June, Dimaporo was detained on charges that he was pro-American, had provided food to Americans, and regularly consorted with guerrillas. After a harrowing interview, he managed to persuade Ishima that the charges were false. Ishima released him only after compelling him to shake hands with his accuser, an act greatly offensive to his *maratabat* (honor). Dimaporo immediately began plotting revenge on Ishima and the Japanese.[18]

On 24 June, he found his opportunity when, with several relatives and twenty-six of their men, he undertook to provide security for laborers working on the Malabang-Parang road. Also present were Captain Ishima, twelve Japanese soldiers, Mayor Diambangan, and ten of his armed guards. During the lunch break, Dimaporo and his men shot and killed Ishima and the Japanese soldiers. With Diambangan's men, they proceeded to Malabang where they killed most of the Japanese garrison. After the attack, a blocking force led by Dimaporo's brother-in-law, Macapangcat Tomara, held off Japanese reinforcements at the Matling bridge. Dimaporo sent runners to secure reinforcements, hoping to hold Malabang permanently. When these failed to materialize and Japanese units began arriving from Cotabato, he retreated to his home town of Binidayan. In all, forty-three Japanese soldiers were killed in the attack.[19] In response, Japanese warships bombarded coastal areas where the guerrillas might be hiding. While they held Mayor Diambangan and other civilians responsible for the action, Dimaporo took full credit, announcing to all that he alone was responsible. He used a variety of ruses to delay the expected Japanese attack, offering to surrender and then dickering over conditions. He invited the Japanese to meet him for a peace conference in Binidayan or Wato; they offered him safe conduct to a meeting in Malabang or Dansalan. Neither was so foolish as to fall into the other's trap. During this same period, Dimaporo was instructed to prepare for a general uprising planned to coincide with the anticipated American landing. He took part in operations so successful that when American forces landed on 17 April 1945 Malabang and its airport were entirely in guerrilla hands. Patrols sent along the highway toward Lake Lanao encountered no Japanese resistance at all.[20]

Ali Dimaporo's wartime exploits established his reputation as a fighter and a man to be feared. He survived charges of collaboration with the Japanese and earned plaudits from American and Filipino officials alike. He was lauded as "the outstanding hero of the people of Malabang . . . idolized and respected by all."[21] He was praised for phrasing his propaganda speeches to subtly ridicule and undermine the Japanese, even while praising them, and for taking their pay while plotting their demise.[22] At the same time an agent in Binidayan, observing that many confiscated weapons had found their way into Dimaporo's local armory, warned, "Watch him, for he is a dangerous man."[23]

Dimaporo claims to be "the man who liberated Lanao." He also disclaims any motive other than patriotism. Unlike former President Marcos, who "dreamed to be a big man even then," Dimaporo says, "I had no ambition except to fight and defend our country. That is why I did not even make reports. I was not after any credit whatsoever." He remembers that he received many medals but does not recall them all. Some were lost, he says, but "I did not really care. I was not after glory."[24]

After Lanao was liberated in October 1944, Dimaporo was assigned to the Military Police Command in Malabang.[25] During this period the MPs were responsible for collecting arms from civilians, weapons that the Maranao were loathe to give up. Dimaporo reports collecting arms "by the truckload" in the town and surrounding areas and encountering little difficulty because he was by then "reputed to be a very brave man."[26] He also claims to have released all persons kidnapped and enslaved during the war. He was effective enough in this work to be promoted to captain and was assigned the reestablishment of governmental authority in Tugaya, a particularly intractable municipality on the west shore of Lake Lanao. According to a profile published by Mindanao State University:

> If his over-all strategy was simple, the young captain's tactics were even simpler. For example, Ali knew well enough that local headmen hoarded weapons and ammunition, and kept in slavery numerous kidnapped persons. To convince them of his "sincerity and determination to enforce the law," he held a conference with all of them. But he made sure that the talk was conducted within the deadly range of a 50-caliber machine-gun he had previously emplaced atop a hill. The headmen, therefore, not totally ignorant of the damage to one's health the monster weapon could inflict, left the session never doubting a word of the captain's. Soon they were back to surrender truckloads of their own loose weaponry and their slaves.[27]

This show of force added to Dimaporo's already formidable reputation.

Wartime service in the resistance helped further many political careers in the postwar period. Salvador Lluch and Tomas Cabili, both established leaders of the Christian community in Lanao, used their service records to reinforce their political leadership.[28] Following Philippine independence in 1946, however, Muslims were being brought into the electoral process for the first time and national party leaders began seeking prospective Muslim candidates.[29] Dimaporo was one, recruited by Liberal Party leaders as a candidate for the Philippine Congress.[30] He has described his candidacy as the product of a populist bandwagon, reporting that, "One day, a Friday, when I was busy in my camp, a delegation of *datus* came to me. When we went to the mosque for the Friday prayer, they put their hands on top of the other and swore by the Koran that they will make me their candidate. I won as Congressman by a landslide."[31] Indeed, among five candidates, including two of his high-school classmates, Dimaporo won a congressional seat handily. He was thirty-one.

His campaign for reelection in 1953, however, had a different outcome. The Liberal Party was then in decline, the popularity of its leader, Elpidio Quirino, having fallen dramatically. Dimaporo's opponent in the election was Ahmad Domocao Alonto, the son of Alauya Alonto, Sultan sa Ramain, signatory of the Commonwealth Constitution, former senator, and the most prominent Maranao collaborator during Japanese rule.[32] Like Dimaporo, Alonto had attended the University of the Philippines Law School. Unlike him, Alonto had graduated. Alonto also had advantages of lineage and wealth that Dimaporo lacked. In a bitterly contested campaign, Dimaporo lost his seat. He claims that this was due largely to military interference in the elections, further asserting that:

[T]he army and constabulary—still loyal to the erstwhile secretary of national defense, Ramon Magsaysay, who was the Nacionalista candidate for President—interfered in the elections. For one thing, General Manuel Cabal, the commanding general in the province, was the brother-in-law of Magsaysay's. Dimaporo had to protest the results of the election before the House Electoral Tribunal. He was proclaimed winner ultimately when only six months were left of his legitimate term.[33]

Despite this vindication, Dimaporo was not seated in Congress. He ran once more in 1957 but lost again, this time by three thousand votes, as he, Valerio Rovira, and Camilo Cabili split the Liberal Party vote. Nacionalista Alonto was reelected. Disavowing any further interest in politics, Dimaporo retired to attend to his farms in Karomatan, intending to make his fortune growing cassava.

The political landscape changed dramatically in 1959 when the province of Lanao was divided into Lanao del Norte and Lanao del Sur. Partition gave contending Christian and Muslim dynasties in Lanao separate domains. It also responded to rising demands from Maranao for a proportional share of government jobs. Prior to this time, the government bureaucracy had been dominated by Christian Visayans, many of whom commuted daily from their homes in coastal Christian communities to offices in the provincial capital in Dansalan. Of the two new provinces, the population of Lanao del Sur was more than 90 percent Muslim, and of Lanao del Norte 70 percent Christian.

Partition gave Dimaporo a chance to revive his political career. While "the Alonto-Lucman clan achieved complete political hegemony in Lanao del Sur," the Lluch family was facing increasing opposition from other important families (such as the Cabilis and Quibranzas) in Lanao del Norte.[34] In the 1959 elections Dimaporo ran as a Liberal Party candidate for governor, though he was not expected to win. His profiler writes that "The LP was desperate. No less than LP stalwarts like Vice-president Diosdado Macapagal, Senator Ferdinand E. Marcos and House Speaker Cornelio Villareal descended upon Cassava Planter Dimaporo, practically telling him to commit political suicide by locking horns with Lluch."[35] Dimaporo says that he chose to run in the north because "If I run in Lanao del Sur, I would have been the most unpopular man there because nobody was paying taxes and I was going to impose taxes."[36]

In this election, Dimaporo faced numerous obstacles. He was a Muslim in a predominantly Christian province who had announced his candidacy only two months before the election.[37] Only two of the nineteen municipal mayors endorsed him. He lacked the degree of descent rank that would have solidified a Maranao following, and he was not particularly wealthy. In his favor, the Lluch family had made many important enemies. Because the Lluchs failed to take Dimaporo's candidacy seriously, they failed to mount a concerted campaign against him. He drew support from strong Christian factions opposed to Lluch, including the prestigious Cabili and Quibranza families.[38] In the end, Dimaporo handed Lluch a stinging defeat, taking the governorship of Lanao del Norte by a mere 275 votes. In this and subsequent elections, Dimaporo displayed his acumen as a political organizer, his almost uncanny ability to turn an apparently weak position into a winning one.[39]

Subsequent election victories came easier. Dimaporo ran for reelection in 1963 and won by eight thousand votes. His profiler comments:

> As governor of Lanao del Norte, Dimaporo fostered the good relations between Muslims and Christians, improved appreciably the peace-and-order situation, introduced numerous public works projects, increased tax collections and raised the province's classification from fifth to third class.[40]

Dimaporo ran for Congress in 1965 and was elected with a majority of twenty thousand votes. Still a member of the Liberal Party, he supported incumbent President Diosdado Macapagal, though he says that in his heart he hoped Ferdinand Marcos would win. He claims that he would have supported Marcos (at the time still a Liberal Party member) if Marcos had not assured him that he would not run.[41] He recalls inviting Marcos to Iligan and introducing him as the next president of the Republic. Marcos demurred, asserting that his candidate was Macapagal. During this visit, Dimaporo's wife went into labor. Marcos accompanied him to the hospital, and Dimaporo named his son Ferdinand Marcos Dimaporo. When Marcos decided to run for the presidency as a Nacionalista, he reportedly sent Dimaporo a telegram and several checks to help in the campaign but Dimaporo returned them on the grounds that he was committed already to the support of Macapagal's candidacy.

As evidence of his honesty, Dimaporo reports that:

> During the counting of the votes, [he] stood off emissaries from his own Liberal Party, who petitioned him to "alter the election results overwhelmingly in favor of President Macapagal." He gave them a flat, "no, over my dead body." As a result, Macapagal won by only a "sizeable margin" in Lanao Norte.[42]

Dimaporo's rectitude in this instance presumably earned him favor with President Marcos. In any case, he joined Marcos under the Nacionalista banner in 1966 and supported him unswervingly thereafter, especially during a number of difficult episodes in the latter's career. For instance, Dimaporo helped shepherd through Congress a controversial bill sending Philippine troops to Vietnam, a move favored by Marcos but opposed by Filipino nationalists, including many in his own party. Even more tellingly, Dimaporo supported Marcos after the Jabidah massacre in which several dozen Muslim recruits to a secret Philippine Army unit were killed by their Christian officers as they prepared to leave their training base on Corregidor Island.[43] This incident galvanized Muslim opposition to the government.

As no other single incident had done since independence, Jabidah made all sections of Muslims—secular and religious, modern and backward alike—concerned about their future. Muslims organized demonstrations all over Manila, especially in front of Congress and the Malacanang Palace. Demonstrators called the Jabidah shooting the "worst crime of the century."[44]

Almost alone among Muslim leaders, Ali Dimaporo defended the president against strident demands that he be held accountable. Instead of joining in calls to impeach him, Dimaporo produced witnesses who claimed that no massacre had ever taken place. While these "witnesses" were later discredited, Dimaporo's obfuscation contributed to the acquittal at court martial of all the officers accused of murder.[45] In this crisis, Dimaporo's willingness to subordinate his Muslim identity to personal and party loyalty earned him Marcos's gratitude.

As President Marcos consolidated his hold on power, Dimaporo's star continued to rise. In 1969, when Marcos won an unprecedented second term, Dimaporo was reelected to the House by twenty-five thousand votes over Pacificador Lluch, scion of the still-powerful Lluch family. He also became chairman of the Public Works Committee in the House of Representatives, one of the most sought after positions in Philippine politics. By this time Dimaporo had built a formidable political machine in north-central Mindanao and had begun to emerge as a leader of national consequence.

Despite his apparently solid hold on the electorate, the 1969 elections betrayed ominous signs of sectarian violence. Manila election officials complained that politicians in the two Lanao provinces defied orders from both Malacañang and the Commission on Elections (Comelec) by maintaining private armies. Indeed, the regional Philippine Constabulary (PC) commander was relieved of duty for his failure to carry out orders that such armies be disbanded.[46] Four people were reported killed in violence related to the race between Lluch and Dimaporo. This was not a particularly large number compared to the severe violence witnessed in Ilocos Sur but in view of the long-standing polarization of Muslims and Christians in Mindanao, any violence along religious lines was viewed with alarm.

During the next round of elections, in November 1971, the cross-religious political front created to oppose the Lluch dynasty was shattered. When former ally, Governor Carmelo Quibranza, ran for reelection, Congressman Dimaporo supported Vice-Governor Mamalig Umpa, a Muslim, against him. According to one observer:

> Friends who fall out are fierce enemies. As the Quibranza and Dimaporo camps faced each other, terror came into its own in Lanao del Norte. . . . Private armies had a field day. Killings and burnings became routine. Once-bustling communities became ghost towns as people abandoned their ripening crops and escaped in the nick of time. Christians and Muslims fled, each in a different direction. Communities who were supposed to be fighting

each other were running away from each other. But the fighting went on, for the gangs and their political masters did not flee.[47]

The conflict began in mid-July and intensified as the elections approached, creating over one hundred thousand refugees by election day. Governor Quibranza, Iligan mayor Camilo Cabili, and other Christian officials charged that Ali Dimaporo and his brother Naga were masters of the "Barracudas," the name given to a loosely articulated gang of some three hundred men (primarily policemen, Muslim PC, and bodyguards) who terrorized Christian settlers in the hills and valleys between Karomatan (where Naga Dimaporo was mayor) and Iligan City. Dimaporo denied funding or tolerating the Barracudas, suggesting that they were a figment of overheated imaginations.[48] During a speech in Congress, he also charged that Governor Quibranza had organized three liquidation squads to ensure his reelection.[49] Dimaporo challenged reporters to come to Karomatan, where he maintained that peace and order reigned. He offered food and transportation, and "said he will even place his wife and children in Iligan City as guarantee for the safety of observers. The lawmaker asserted that Karomatan is a 'most peaceful town' and said he is for clean elections but that it is hard to convince people who have not gone to the town."[50] Reporters who accepted the invitation reported that armed gangs were running Karomatan and other towns in Lanao del Norte and that both Muslim and Christian members of the Philippine Constabulary regularly fraternized with Barracuda and Ilaga members in their areas.[51]

Eventually the violence became so severe in Lanao del Norte that President Marcos was forced to intervene personally. Under an arrangement made under his auspices, both Governor Quibranza and Vice-Governor Umpa agreed to withdraw from the race in favor of recently appointed Brigadier General Wilfrado Encarnacion (a long-time resident of Marawi City)[52] who would retire from active duty to run for governor. Although both candidates signed an agreement to this effect, after Comelec chairman Jaime Ferrer opined that Encarnacion could not be placed on the ballot because he had missed the statutory registration deadline, both Umpa and Quibranza reactivated their campaigns, with the latter now running as a Liberal Party "guest candidate." Although both Comelec and the Supreme Court eventually allowed Encarnacion's candidacy, the fragile peace disintegrated and "the tumult resumed with intensified viciousness."[53] A Barracuda attack on a Constabulary outpost in Magsaysay, Lanao del Norte, killed seventeen Philippine Army soldiers. In response, the army flew in more than a thousand troops, mounting a battalion-scale assault, which left sixty-six Muslims dead.[54] Despite the professed determination of Philippine Army commanders to liquidate the outlaw gangs, the Barracudas continued to operate because, some refugees suggested, "the Muslim official concerned openly boasts of his 'good connections' with a high-ranking national official who values his friendship—and who needs his captive Lanao votes."[55] The unnamed parties are clearly Congressman Dimaporo and President Marcos. Recently, Dimaporo recalled that prior to martial law he had about eight hundred firearms and two armored cars under his control. He reports, "I told the President that there is something wrong. I said Mr. President, we are the party in power but the opposition has an armored car and a private army. The President told me to go ahead. So I bought two armored cars."[56] Among the pre–martial law private armies, Dimaporo's was probably the largest in Mindanao.

Unlike previous elections in Lanao del Norte, the 1971 round pitted Muslims against Christians, and in this contest the numerically superior Christians won. All the Christian candidates for mayor were elected, and even the lone Muslim on Quibranza's adopted Liberal Party slate lost badly.[57] Moreover, the tensions generated by this election hardly had begun to cool before special elections scheduled for 22 November in Sapad, Magsaysay, Salvador, and Nunungan (in Lanao del Norte) and Malabang (in Lanao del Sur) fanned them again into full blaze.[58] The special election had national significance because Alejandro Almendras and Manuel Elizalde, both Christian Nacionalistas, stood only a few thousand votes apart in the race for the last available Senate seat. The outcome of their race hinged on the twenty-two thousand votes to be cast in these remote Lanao municipalities. Voting in the Lanao del Norte towns thus focused national attention on the Dimaporo-Quibranza confrontation since Dimaporo supported Elizalde and Quibranza supported Almendras. But this was not the only office at issue. Princess Tarhata Alonto Lucman, sister of Dimaporo's old nemesis, Domocao Alonto, and wife of former congressman Harun al-Rascid Lucman, ran as the Liberal Party candidate for the governorship of Lanao del Sur against incumbent Linang Mandangan, a Nacionalista and a close relative of Dimaporo's. Princess Tarhata's chances for election hinged on a strong showing in Malabang, the Lanao del Sur municipality directly adjacent to Dimaporo's Karomatan stronghold.[59] Terror played an increasingly prominent role as the election drew near and Dimaporo proved unable to control the outcome. Princess Tarhata was elected governor of Lanao del Sur, while Ali's candidate, Manuel Elizalde, lost his Senate race. However, the fortunes of individual dynasty builders were overshadowed on election day by the outbreak of mass violence, including the massacre of more than thirty unarmed Muslim voters returning from polling places in Magsaysay where they had been turned away by the Ilagas who controlled the town. The slayers were identified as Philippine Army troops stationed in Tacub, Kauswagan.[60] The Tacub Massacre set off an intensifying spiral of violence as Muslim irregulars and government troops each sought revenge for wrongs suffered at the hands of the other. The massacre had outraged Muslims throughout the Philippines, and had drawn international attention, eliciting charges of genocide from a number of quarters. In this expanded conflict, all Muslim belligerents in Lanao came to be called Barracudas, so that the name lost its earlier association with Dimaporo.[61]

In the aftermath of the election campaign, Muslim-Christian polarization continued to intensify. More and more persons on both sides became refugees as they abandoned their homes and fled to more secure locales. Muslims poured into Marawi City, Christians into Iligan. Residents of Iligan began an economic boycott of Marawi City, and with the help of police set up checkpoints along the highway linking the two provincial capitals. Thereafter, "When drivers and passengers from one city ran into those from the other, they fell upon each other."[62]

In this increasingly volatile situation, Ali Dimaporo continued to hold his anomalous position as a Muslim Congressman from a province increasingly dominated by Christians both numerically and politically. But his power base contracted to Karomatan and the few other Maranao-dominated towns in Lanao del Norte, while in Lanao del Sur his influence was circumscribed by Tarhata Lucman's accession to the governorship. His star appeared to be in decline. He was saved from complete eclipse when President Marcos declared martial law on 21 September 1972 and dissolved the Congress. At the time Dimaporo was in Tripoli, Libya. He recalls wiring Marcos and placing himself at the president's disposal, since he felt he displayed "sincere unfailing wisdom and compassion" in making the difficult decision to suspend normal political processes.[63] Since martial law had aborted his congressional career, Ali retired to tend the extensive fishponds he had acquired during his legislative tenure.

Although formally out of politics, Dimaporo continued to advise President Marcos on Muslim affairs. "I became what you would say a troubleshooter," he recalls.[64] In many ways it was a natural alliance, since Dimaporo's regional interests coincided with the national interests of Marcos. After October 1972 the national government faced an armed Muslim secession movement led by the Moro National Liberation Front (MNLF), which in Lanao had strong links to Dimaporo's opponents the Alontos and Lucmans. Formation of the MNLF was initiated by Rascid Lucman, former congressman and husband of Governor Tarhata Lucman. One of the MNLF's founding co-chairs was Abul Khayr Alonto, scion of the Alonto-Lucman clan and the vice-mayor of Marawi City. The MNLF attacked Dimaporo as a member of the Muslim political elite, which it held responsible for the decline of Muslim autonomy due to its avid pursuit of personal wealth and power. Hence Dimaporo's interests were as threatened by Muslim secessionists as were those of the national elite in Manila. Unlike most other Maranao politicians, Dimaporo spoke openly and often against Muslim secession. He also cooperated with the Philippine Army in its drives against Muslim secessionists. According to him, "No leader in Mindanao attacked the MNLF except me."[65]

Dimaporo's loyalty was rewarded on 31 March 1976 when Marcos appointed him to replace Brigadier General Mamarinta Lao as acting governor of Lanao del Sur.[66] Thus he gained through presidential appointment what he could not achieve through election—control over the provincial government of Lanao del Sur. Moreover, in the reshuffling of local governments under martial law, he was able to place his people in control of many municipal governments. Those opponents he could not supplant, he co-opted or neutralized. Throughout his tenure he was backed by President Marcos and Philippine Army and Constabulary forces in the province. The military gave him a free hand to use force for his own purposes. In return, he cleared the armed forces to fight Maranao rebels in virtually any manner they wished. He supported the declaration of free-fire zones, mass evacuations and arrests, house-to-house searches, and search-and-destroy missions throughout the province. He even offered to bivouac Philippine Marines on portions of the Mindanao State University campus.[67]

Only a few months after he became governor of Lanao del Sur, the administration of the Mindanao State University was placed under Dimaporo's charge. Since its founding in the mid-1960s, MSU had struggled to remedy the historical failings of public education in Mindanao but it had become entangled in local and regional political conflicts. By 1976, radical proposals for reform were emanating from all quarters, with the Board of Regents threatening a vote of no confidence in MSU President Mauyag Tamano (brother of former senator Mamintal Tamano). Tamano, for his part, asked that his office and the finance office be moved from the Marawi campus to Cagayan de Oro to escape the crossfire.[68] Half-finished buildings littered the campus, construction and instruction budgets evaporated as funds were siphoned off in all directions, and the university's educational mission receded ever further into the background. Although responsibility for the deterioration was laid at President Tamano's door, few believed that he had profited unduly from his position. He failed, however, to keep this unwieldy institution under control. So President Marcos appointed his troubleshooter, Governor Dimaporo, to tame MSU.

The Mindanao State University was extremely important to the government, and to Governor Dimaporo, for a number of reasons. By 1976 it had become by far the largest employer in Muslim Mindanao, and its expenditures per student far exceeded those of any other Philippine state university. Politicians in the region were acutely aware of the concentration of wealth at MSU and of its value as a source of patronage. The government and the military knew that the university had become a prime recruiting ground for the MNLF. By 1976, MSU was dominated by the conflicting political forces surrounding it. Governor Dimaporo used it to support his political machine, even while bringing a modicum of order to the campus. He expanded the university's security force to 450 men and reactivated the Lanao del Sur Provincial Guard (LSPG) Striking Force. He began recruiting supporters to Civilian Home Defense Force (CHDF) units. Using the MSU budget, he also employed a variety of "special agents," including notorious killers, whose duties included anticipating, intercepting, and liquidating threats to his administration. Under this regime, Dimaporo's opponents found they had to act more circumspectly, for those who failed to do so were subjected to the governor's wrath. A few faculty members with suspect political associations were killed on the campus during Governor Dimaporo's tenure as president.

More frequent methods used by Governor Dimaporo for dealing with campus dissent are illustrated by the case of the musical group *Mga Anak ng BQ,* a quintet of junior faculty members who sang two satirical songs during a Founders Day talent contest in August 1978.[69] The songs pointedly criticized conditions on campus, addressing the lack of classroom materials, late pay, deficient health services, book shortages, bloated budgets, misappropriation of university resources, and the governor's obsession with keeping the campus golf course trimmed. The songs struck a responsive chord in the audience and the performance was received with uproarious laughter and applause. To conclude their performance they sang "If I Loved You," from the musical *Carousel*, dedicating it to the university and pledging themselves to work for its future improvement. Throughout the performance Governor Dimaporo sat in the front row accompanied by several guests.

After leaving the performance hall, the members of *Mga Anak ng BQ* were told that Governor Dimaporo was livid, fuming that they had insulted both him and the university. Warned that they might be in physical danger, the instructors retreated to their living quarters where they remained for several days. Their attempts to apologize to Dimaporo were rebuffed, they were placed on preventive suspension, and administrative proceedings were instituted against them for sedition within the university. Since the criticisms in their songs were generally regarded as valid, there was widespread sentiment supporting *Mga Anak ng BQ* among MSU faculty and students. Moreover, the suspension placed the graduation of 650 members of the senior class in jeopardy since they would be unable to complete required courses taught by the five instructors. For these reasons a majority of the faculty hoped that the suspension would be lifted, although the mere threat of Dimaporo's displeasure was sufficient to prevent them from adopting any public position. At a meeting convened to consider the issue, faculty council members nearly passed a resolution asking that the five teachers be provisionally reinstated but, upon being warned by one of Ali Dimaporo's assistants that this might attract the governor's displeasure, they recanted. The nature of the threat was not explicit but its ramifications were abundantly clear to the audience. A few days earlier, one of the suspended teachers (a member of the Alonto family) had been beaten in his room by several men later identified as members of the LSPG Striking Force. They were led by one of Governor Dimaporo's sons. The position of the members of *Mga Anak ng BQ* was so precarious that they could not find an attorney willing to undertake their defense even though the Lanao del Sur chapter of the Integrated Bar of the Philippines listed well over one hundred members. In the end the five submitted a plea for understanding and leniency in lieu of a formal defense. In due course they were found guilty of the charges and their fates were handed over to Dimaporo. He issued a "severe reprimand" but reinstated them to their former positions. Privately all five were advised to find positions elsewhere as their safety could no longer be guaranteed at MSU. They did so.

In addition to the *Mga Anak ng BQ* case, administrative proceedings were begun against three faculty members who refused the governor's "request" that they take on the suspended teachers' classes as overloads without pay. These three were also suspended, and at the end of the proceedings they were dismissed from the university with prejudice (a condition precluding any future government employment). Campus ópinion held that Dimaporo had adeptly exploited the situation to rid himself of three professors he deemed undesirable. The most prominent of them, a Catholic activist who had been a gadfly to previous administrations, fought the decision and remained on the campus, though she no longer held any official position in the university. With Dimaporo's removal from the university presidency in March 1986, her case was reopened in Manila, though this time its disposition became entangled in a new round of campus politics.

Dimaporo's extreme response to what elsewhere would have been regarded as harmless campus protest attracted disparaging coverage in the Manila papers, as did the conditions *Mga Anak ng BQ* had highlighted in their songs. Still, the university's educational functions languished and funds continued to be diverted to Dimaporo's private interests.[70] In fact, the governor's standing steadily increased in the eyes of his patron, President Marcos. Eventually Dimaporo was appointed to Marcos's exclusive Executive Committee, the most prestigious and powerful position attained by any Muslim under the Marcos regime.

This is not to say that Dimaporo's dominance went unchallenged. The May 1978 Interim Batasang Pambansa (IBP) elections provoked outraged cries from opposition candidates. They claimed that elections had never been held in many parts of Lanao del Sur and that returns reported for the areas that had held elections were entirely manufactured. The accusations were sufficiently serious that the Philippine Supreme Court nullified the initial canvass of election returns and ordered the Commission on Elections to convene a special canvassing board. Not surprisingly, the special board confirmed an overwhelming sweep by the Kilusang Bagong Lipunan (KBL) ruling party. Even so, the Comelec board found results from Karomatan, Dimaporo's home base in Lanao del Norte, so suspect that it delayed their confirmation for several weeks. In the end KBL lawyers squelched opposition by threatening action for criminal libel against those who had charged electoral fraud.[71] Finding their position hopeless, Dimaporo's opponents let the issue lapse. In fact, the 1978 IBP elections had involved fraud flagrant even by the relaxed standards of Lanao del Sur, where a popular saying has it that "even the birds and the flowers can vote." In several locales "official" results were announced the day before elections were held, rendering actual voting problematic at best. After the elections, several ballot boxes were found floating in Lake Lanao. Revelation of these blatant irregularities, however, did Dimaporo no harm. Rather, it confirmed his ability to manipulate the electoral and legal processes to any end he desired.

The same was true of the level of fraud attained during his governance. Funds disappeared as rapidly from the provincial coffers as they had from the MSU budget. In early 1979, provincial transportation authorities issued a report, complete with photographs, celebrating completion of a long-planned highway around Lake Lanao. In fact, the pavement ended only a few kilometers east of Marawi City. Marawi wags quipped that the highway could have been paved three times, in gold, for all the money that had been spent on it. Still, Dimaporo's ability to draw funding from Manila remained unimpaired.

In fact, many projects were completed during the years of his rule. Numerous structures were added to the MSU campus, including a physical-education complex and buildings for the schools of education, business, engineering, law, and fisheries. Benefits of this boom spread beyond the campus through construction employment and pilfering of building materials. Some of the structures remained closed, since money for furnishings and teaching materials was harder to acquire, but the campus expansion certainly looked good.

The same was true of successes Dimaporo reported against the Moro National Liberation Front. Throughout November and December of 1977, Philippine Army units conducted large-scale operations against suspected rebel bases, declaring free-fire zones, conducting mass arrests and house-to-house searches, and generally making life difficult for nearly everyone. These operations had little actual effect on rebel forces but extravagant results were claimed. In December 1977, a top MNLF field commander, Abul Khayr Alonto, "returned to the fold of the law." Governor Dimaporo suffered some embarrassment when this highly publicized surrender was delayed for three days while a sufficient number of plausible "rebel returnees" were recruited from surrounding communities. In June 1978, Rear Admiral Romulo Espaldon reported the collapse of the Northern Mindanao Revolutionary Command with the surrender of 1,215 rebels who were expected to return to their peacetime occupations as farmers and fishermen.[72] Dimaporo happily claimed credit for this coup, which added to his prestige in Manila. By late 1978, Admiral Espaldon reported that a total of 35,411 Muslim rebels had surrendered.[73] In fact, a substantial fraction of them had done so in Lanao del Sur, many several times, so that they could receive surrender bonuses over and over again. It served the interests of Governor Dimaporo, Admiral Espaldon, and President Marcos to confirm these exalted estimates of their joint success.

In the areas Marcos apparently considered most important, Dimaporo was eminently successful. He kept his part of Mindanao under control. However deep and broad were popular grievances against his rule, few dared utter words against him in public. In effect, under the patronage of Marcos, Dimaporo constructed an exemplary Maranao datuship in north-central Mindanao. This success was symbolized by his accession, in December 1982, to the title of Sultan sa Masiu over the objections of several other Maranao sultans. Dimaporo's successful claim to a position at the highest level of Maranao nobility gave vivid illustration to his remarkable accumulation of power.

By the time of the 1984 elections to the Batasang Pambansa (National Assembly), Dimaporo had achieved a stranglehold on the political machinery of central Mindanao. An assessment of electoral conditions in Mindanao noted that: "It was only in Region XII that the mighty KBL machine worked with express precision . . . Region XII has nine assemblymen. The one who would call the shots for the whole region is Ali Dimaporo."[74] The same article predicted confidently that Region XII would witness the election of Abdullah Dimaporo (Ali's son), of his brother Macacuna, and his brother-in-law, Marawi City mayor Omar Dianalan.[75] The other assemblymen would be selected at Ali's discretion. In the fractured world of Mindanao politics, with divisions by religion (Muslim and Christian), ethnicity (Maranao, Maguindanao, Ilongo, Ilocano, and Cebuano), region, and class, Dimaporo's domination of the whole political process was remarkable.

Still, his control did not remain uncontested. In early 1985, Dimaporo and his brother-in-law, Dianalan, clashed over an appointment to the post of speaker pro tempore of the Batasang Pambansa. Dimaporo wanted the position for his son, Abdullah, while Dianalan claimed to have been promised it no less than three times. President Marcos reportedly considered Abdullah, at thirty-five, too young for the post, so Dimaporo suggested that it go to the oldest Mindanao legislator, his brother Macacuna, aged fifty-five. Marcos announced the appointment on 19 February, setting off a flurry of accusations and challenges between Dimaporo and Dianalan partisans. According to reports at the time, "The dispute teetered dangerously near violence on two successive nights at the Batasan, with the protagonists hurling invectives, if not fists, at each other, with their followers in the galleries shouting threats and dares to 'settle it in Lanao.'"[76] Marcos referred the issue to the KBL Assembly caucus, which, not surprisingly, confirmed his decision by the overwhelming vote of 81 to 9.[77] Batasan observers speculated at the time that Dimaporo had broken his promise to Dianalan as part of a larger plan to eliminate him as a potential opponent, the first step having been to ensure his assembly election so as to remove him from his local power-base in Marawi City.[78] During a Malacañang meeting among the contending forces, Marcos reportedly asked the assembled politicians "Who is the real leader in Lanao?" Governor Dimaporo is supposed to have replied "Mr. President, I can make you win if you will not stop me from changing the election returns!"[79] The president's involvement in this episode echoes that of 1971, when an electoral conflict between Dimaporo and a Lanao opponent was settled by Marcos in Dimaporo's favor.

In consolidating his empire Dimaporo showed a remarkable ability to anticipate, preempt, and defeat challenges to his power. However, just as the Marcos regime began to erode following the assassination of Benigno Aquino, similar difficulties began to arise in Lanao. A young lawyer, Saidamen Pangarungan, opened a Lakas ng Bayan (LABAN) opposition party office in Marawi City. More significant was the lingering rancor between Dimaporo and Omar Dianalan. With the announcement of the "snap presidential election" in December 1985, and the rise of the Aquino-Laurel ticket as a plausible challenge to Marcos, Dianalan found a vehicle for pursuing his grudge. He left the KBL at this time, telling the Catholic newspaper *Veritas* that:

> [H]e could no longer stand being treated shabbily by Dimaporo and the ruling party. "Since [I contested the post of Batasan speaker pro tempore] all my men, including those whose appointments I had a hand in, have been

fired. Not even those with qualifications and civil-service eligibilities were spared. What they merely lacked was Ali-gibilities and Ali-fications," Dianalan charged.[80]

Together with his younger brother, Jiamil, and his father-in-law, former governor Dimakuta, Dianalan joined forces with the Alonto-Lucman faction. Of this new arrangement, Dianalan remarked: "Politics make strange bedfellows. This is our first time to work together with the Alontos."[81] In the days preceding the snap election Dianalan took the offensive, charging that Dimaporo was "forcing government employees to swear before the Koran that they'll vote for the ruling party." He further noted that:

> "The Mindanao State University, of which Ali is the president, has a 450-man security guard, which Ali has converted into his own private army. Can you imagine, a campus which used to have only a handful of security guards, now guarded by 450?" Dianalan said. . . . He added that Ali also has 300 special action men, 200 provincial guards, 250 security guards in his different business interests, and 1,500 CHDF's distributed in 37 towns. "All these men are armed with high-powered guns," he said, in stressing why it is very urgent that Comelec place the province under its control.[82]

To further bolster Dimaporo's power in the weeks before the election, Lanao military commanders received orders from Manila to give the governor a large number of mostly semiautomatic and automatic weapons (1,792 according to Philippine Army records), which he then distributed to relatives, employees, and other supporters.[83]

At the same time, opposition figures such as Dianalan were issuing grave warnings about the likely conduct of the election. Dianalan urged Comelec to purge voter lists of an estimated forty thousand "ghost voters" in Lanao del Sur and thirty thousand in Lanao del Norte. By election time, in mid-February, many eligible voters found that a purge had taken place but that their names had been stricken from the registration lists. Voters and vote tabulators were subjected to intense pressure to produce the outcome desired by the party in power, though in some cases they were reported to have resisted.[84] As usually happens after Lanao elections, the reported results were challenged, but the Batasan canvass gave Marcos 191,755 votes to Aquino's 28,070 for Lanao del Sur as a whole. The totals in Marawi City were somewhat closer, 16,203 for Marcos and 10,829 for Aquino. Results in the vice-presidential race between Tolentino and Laurel were similar, though not quite so lopsided. These results confirmed, again, Governor Dimaporo's control over the Lanao political scene.

This election signaled the beginning rather than the end of the open struggle for power. Dimaporo stood with President Marcos. In a television interview granted only a few days after the election, he warned of "bitter and bloody strifes should the combined efforts of the opposition, Namfrel, and the church leaders succeed in dividing the Filipino people." He went on to argue that:

> [T]he overall margin of about 600,000 votes [held by] President Marcos over Corazon Aquino in the two autonomous regions (Regions 9 and 12) were votes cast by greatful [*sic*] Muslims and Christians in recognition of the many developments that the President has given to the two regions. . . . He denied charges of alleged terrorism and rampant poll irregularities committed by the KBL. The charges were attributed to Member of Parliament Omar Dimaporo [*sic*]. . . . He said there were instances in which MP Dianalan and his followers provoked KBL men during the election but they always avoided him [Dianalan] because a confrontation could trigger a bloody clash among his followers and Dianalan's armed men.[85]

Despite the thinly veiled threat, the political tide in Mindanao began to turn against Dimaporo. Many of those who earlier had kept silent out of fear began to speak openly against him. A variety of prominent Muslims attended a Manila meeting held on 18 February, which denounced the conduct of the elections in Regions IX and XII. Among those who joined in this denunciation were former senator Mamintal Tamano, Omar Dianalan, Jiamil Dianalan, Saidamen Pangarungan (chair of the Lanao del Sur LABAN and president of the Muslim Association of the Philippines), and numerous representatives of Lanao del Sur voluntary associations.[86] At the same time, students and faculty at MSU began to agitate openly for campus reform. In response to prayer meetings and protest rallies, Governor Dimaporo brought units of his Special Action Force onto the campus. Fearing bloodshed, most Christian students and many Muslims left the area.

As events moved toward a climax in Manila, conflict intensified in Marawi as well. On 24 February, the day of the People Power coup in Manila, troops loyal to Dimaporo ringed an Islamic school in Marawi where a prayer rally had been scheduled. To avoid violence, the rally was cancelled. Shortly after Marcos's midnight flight from Manila, Dimaporo retreated to the MSU campus with his armed supporters, reportedly vowing, "I will fight and protect the 'MSU-ans' to the last drop of my blood. We are going to protect this republic. We are going to protect this university from any forces that will attack."[87] Within days, on the advice of Minister of Local Government Aquilino Pimentel, Corazon Aquino appointed her provincial party chairman Saidamen Pangarungan as OIC governor of Lanao del Sur.

Despite his defiant declaration a few days earlier, Dimaporo and his armed supporters retired from the campus on 1 March under pressure from Philippine Army units. In order to forestall military action against him, Dimaporo called on Defense Minister Juan Ponce Enrile on 3 March. During this meeting he told Enrile that, while he was still a Marcos loyalist, "I am neutral to Cory Aquino and I pledge my support to you."[88] In an agreement with Regional Unified Command (RUC) XII chief General Rodrigo Gutang, Dimaporo promised to surrender the

Mohamad Ali Dimaporo, former governor of Lanao del Sur Province, photographed in January 1987.

In the January 1986 presidential campaign, Governor Mohamad Ali Dimaporo
appears with President Ferdinand E. Marcos at a rally for the ruling KBL
at Iligan City.

After his surrender to President Aquino in 1986, Marcos loyalist Mohamad Ali Dimaporo appears with the press to surrender what he claims to be the entire cache of firearms of his notorious private army, the "Barracudas."

On 16 June 1986 (see photo, upper right), in an effort to defuse tensions in Lanao, warlord Mohamad Ali Dimaporo (pointing) meets with leaders of the Philippine Armed Forces at Camp Aguinaldo, Manila: (left to right) Defense Secretary Juan Ponce Enrile, Armed Forces Chief of Staff Fidel V. Ramos, and General Renato de Villa. Mohamad Ali Dimaporo (see photo lower right) concludes this conference by shaking hands with his local antagonist, Brigadier General Rod B. Gutang, then commander of Region XII.

Mohamad Ali Dimaporo posing for the press in 1986 at his home in Corinthian Gardens, an exclusive Manila subdivision favored by members of the Philippine military who had become wealthy during the administration of Ferdinand Marcos.

arms that had been given to him in the weeks before the election, though over the next several months he managed to avoid doing so.

Despite this concession, Dimaporo clung to his position as governor of Lanao del Sur. Hopes for an orderly succession were complicated by the age differential between the two contenders (Pangarungan was thirty-five and Dimaporo sixty-eight).[89] Pangarungan had in hand the order from Pimentel appointing him OIC governor, and the Philippine Supreme Court had ruled that Pimentel had the authority to order such replacements. Still, Dimaporo refused to give up his position until Pangarungan approached him personally, presented his credentials, and allowed him to exit gracefully with the ceremonial honors he felt were his due.[90] This Pangarungan refused to do. Instead he sent copies of the relevant documents by messenger, reportedly fearing that Dimaporo might destroy the originals.[91] This preremptory treatment violated Maranao etiquette and further exacerbated already strained feelings. Dimaporo's position hardened. He demanded that Pangarungan's appointment be tested in court and proceeded to fortify the provincial capitol building with more than sixty of his men, some of them provincial guards, some reportedly Barracudas.[92] As Pangarungan lacked the power to remove Dimaporo by force, in the resulting stalemate the provincial government froze into immobility.

The situation finally was resolved on 25–26 April while Dimaporo was in Manila. On Friday morning, 25 April, a composite army and Constabulary force led by Pangarungan's uncle, PC Colonel Omar Manabilang (who had been appointed provincial commander only nine days earlier), moved to take over the capitol. Six of Dimaporo's guards were surprised by the force (others were performing ablutions in the nearby Agus River preparatory for Friday prayers), several automatic weapons and an M-79 grenade launcher were confiscated, and Pangarungan's people began moving in.[93] Although Dimaporo had lost the capitol, he was far from finished. His brother, Monib, began assembling armed supporters from such strongholds as Binidayan, Tubaran, Marugam, and Karomatan. These began moving into Marawi City around midnight. By the early morning hours of 26 April, some three hundred armed Dimaporo supporters began a series of "harassments." Some were minor, such as incidents that occurred near the capital and near the Mantapuli Philippine Army detachment headquarters on the outskirts of Marawi, which mainly involved firing guns into the air. Others were more serious. Pangarungan family residences and businesses were attacked with grenades, injuring Pangarungan's father and three other family members.[94] According to reports at the time,

> By 9 a.m., Dimaporo's force, in effect, hostaged the city when they blocked the two Sadok bridges leading to the highways [linking Marawi City and the coast]. A massive evacuation had already started, to as far as Iligan City (37 kms. away) as Dimaporo's fatigue or black-clad army reinforced the barricades already littered with rocks, logs, and tires. No vehicles could pass through.[95]

While police and army units remained on alert, a variety of prominent Marawi residents, including Maranao religious leaders and General Mamarinta Lao (retired), who was related to both Pangarungan and Dimaporo, undertook to mediate the conflict. They told both sides that "it would be un-Islamic to fight and not to go down to the negotiating table."[96] Dimaporo initially demanded that government troops be removed from the capitol, but relented when he was assured that their presence was intended only to secure a provincial property audit. Faced with a threat from RUC XII chief Gutang that the military would act if he did not remove his forces, subjected to moral suasion from Islamic religious personnel, and recognizing that his position was no longer tenable, Dimaporo issued a statement on the provincial radio station, asking his supporters to return home and promising that nothing would happen to them. Early in the evening of 26 April, Dimaporo and his supporters (including ten municipal mayors who had helped plot strategy during the crisis) left the capital in trucks and motor launches. He explained that it pained him to clash with allies with whom he had fought the NPA and MNLF and that he would not fight the army because of his friendship with Defense Minister Enrile and Chief of Staff Fidel Ramos, saying, "If only for them I would not fight the military."[97]

In the following weeks Dimaporo was pressed by the government to surrender the firearms he had been issued by former president Marcos. By mid-May of 1986 fewer than two hundred had been surrendered, most of them old and unserviceable.[98] Armed forces personnel reported that none of these arms carried serial numbers matching those of the modern weapons given him earlier.[99] Dimaporo responded that he needed the guns to protect his fishponds and that, in any case, he no longer knew where many of them were. He offered to have his men identify persons possessing loose firearms if the Philippine Constabulary would pursue them in earnest. But he pleaded that his own men be allowed to keep their arms because "they have killed many NPAs and MNLFs and they themselves will be easy targets if they'll [sic] lose their firearms, 'just like the late Gov. Federico Peralta of Tarlac after the military confiscated his guns.'"[100] He refused to disclose his future plans but continued to claim that he was the legitimate governor of Lanao del Sur. He sought to protect his supporters among the municipal mayors, arguing that special elections should be held to settle leadership issues once and for all. He also warned, ominously, that many of the thirty-seven KBL mayors in Lanao del Sur had made a pact never to relinquish their positions.[101] In fact, many OIC mayors designated by the Aquino government were prevented from assuming their posts by armed resistance initiated by incumbent mayors. A year later most municipalities were still controlled by the KBL mayors selected by Dimaporo under martial law.

Still fearing attack from army and Constabulary units now controlled by his enemies, Dimaporo and his supporters entrenched themselves in and around his Binidayan home. They dug foxholes and blockaded roads leading to Binidayan. Dimaporo explained, "I had no choice. Before they could finish us off, we could finish them off."[102] While he claimed that he had told his supporters to go home following the April settlement negotiated by General Lao, observers on 23 June remarked that, "Dimaporo's house and mosque looked like a fortress, with heavily armed men roaming all over."[103]

Despite the loss of his offices, Dimaporo remained a force to reckon with. In addition to his armed supporters:

> He is considered one of the richest men in Mindanao. He has at least five cars (including a Mercedes Benz and a limousine). He has three motorboats. He has a "3000 hectare fishpond, a 30 or 40 thousand hectare logging concession, two or three plantations, and a house in Los Angeles." None of these has been questioned by the present administration. He says he got his fishpond from Vice-president Fernando Lopez who was then Secretary of Agriculture; his logging concession ("which is almost exhausted now") from Speaker Eulogio Rodriguez who was "President of NP when I was LP," and his plantations and house in the States and at the Corinthian Gardens "out of the profits I have generated from operating my logging concessions and fishpond."[104]

Despite his notoriety as one of Marcos's closest cronies, his widely rumored misappropriation of government funds, and his continuing resistance to the new regime, the Aquino government never attacked Dimaporo's financial assets. Although he was the quintessential Marcos-era warlord, he, almost alone among Marcos's inner circle, escaped the scrutiny of the Presidential Commission on Good Government (PCGG).[105]

Dimaporo also maintained a relatively high political profile. He supported a call by defeated presidential candidate and former Cagayan de Oro city mayor Ruben Canoy for Mindanao to declare its independence from the Philippine Republic, an ironic position in view of his long-term fight against Bangsamoro secessionism.[106] He explained his position on Mindanao autonomy to an interviewer: "I told this to [MNLF chairman Nur] Misuari, if he wants independence not only for the Muslim [sic] but for all the people of Mindanao, then maybe many people will join you."[107] His confidence remained high. He told interviewers that he had advised President Marcos in the weeks before the election to retire General Ver in order to placate the Americans who were in a position to "destroy us politically and financially." He claimed that he might have been vice-president had not Imelda Marcos interposed her own ambitious designs, and that: "If Marcos chose me to be his Vice-President, I think we will still be in Malacañang now."[108] He gave no indication that he might retire from politics, declaring instead that, come election time, he would defeat OIC governor Pangarungan, even in his home town.[109]

After Dimaporo was finally dislodged from his dominant position in Lanao del Sur politics, the tenuously unified Lanao opposition fragmented as his many opponents fought over the spoils of victory. Dimaporo and other Marcos loyalists sought to heighten the disorder and thereby to demonstrate the new regime's inability to govern. A spate of well-publicized kidnapings highlighted provincial problems. Fr. Michel de Gigord, Catholic chaplain at the Mindanao State University, was kidnaped from his home on the campus on 4 June, ten nuns were abducted from Marawi on 11 July, and Brian Lawrence, a Protestant missionary stationed at MSU, was kidnaped on 12 July. One long-time observer of Lanao politics concluded that:

> Certainly Dimaporo's relatives and followers were responsible for the kidnaping of Father Michel de Gigord on June 4 from the campus of Mindanao State University, and probably also for that of Brian Lawrence on July 12. Probably they were not involved in the kidnaping of ten nuns in Marawi on July 11, though the actors seemed to have identical motives: revenge against the government, which had taken away power and positions, and extortion. In Father Michel's case there was an additional, personal motivation: he had been outspoken in his criticism of the Dimaporo era at MSU.[110]

The kidnapings demonstrated in dramatic fashion that Dimaporo's successors lacked the power to maintain public order.[111]

The details of Fr. Gigord's kidnaping and release are particularly revealing of Maranao politics, and of Ali Dimaporo's mastery of them.[112] The choice of the victim and the place and time of the kidnaping were calculated for maximum political effect. Gigord had been vocal in his criticism of Dimaporo's actions at MSU. Moreover, Catholic student organizations associated with Gigord had pressed strongly for campus reform and provided a focus for anti-Marcos activities on the campus. Gigord was therefore implicated among the forces that had led to Dimaporo's removal, doubly so since he was a French citizen and France had been the first nation to recognize the Aquino government (on 25 February 1986). Because Fr. Gigord was the first priest kidnaped under the Aquino administration, the event drew maximum publicity. And because the kidnaping occurred at the Mindanao State University, with its concentration of financial resources and patronage, it dramatized the vulnerability of this key institution to attack. Significantly, Gigord was kidnaped on the day President Aquino appointed Dr. Ahmad Alonto, Jr., as president of the university. It also occurred as RUC XII chief Gutang, under orders from President Aquino to disband private armies, once again threatened Dimaporo with military action unless he surrendered his firearms.[113] It was widely believed that Dimaporo used Gigord as a shield to prevent Gutang from acting against him. Moreover, Dimaporo's forces were so strong in the region in which Gigord was believed to be held (Binidayan and the Balt Islands in nearby Lake Lanao) that the provincial PC commander, Saidamen Pangarungan's uncle Colonel Manabilang, dared neither to send forces nor emissaries into the area. Thus, the kidnaping served to impress upon Dimaporo's enemies just how little the current government could do to protect them.

While Dimaporo formally denied any involvement in the kidnaping, he also let it be known that he would have to be included in any negotiations for Gigord's release. While there seems to have been little doubt that he would eventually be freed, local military authorities and political leaders agreed that the negotiation process was complicated by Maranao factional politics. While Governor Pangarungan remained in Manila, where he and Princess Tarhata Lucman had been fighting over the provincial governorship, the princess flew to Marawi to seek Fr. Gigord's release. As she explained to reporters, "I owe gratitude to the French government for being the first to recognize Cory's government; for the French ambassador who attended Cory's February 25 proclamation and because of the French government's neutral stand when Reagan ordered the bombing of Libya."[114] She also identified Dimaporo as the key figure in the drama, saying, "One thing is very sure. If something happens to the priest, I will hold Dimaporo responsible."[115] She asserted that Gigord was being held near Binidayan, Dimaporo's home town, and stated openly that "The priest is in the hands of the Dimaporos."[116] After Princess Tarhata arrived in Lanao, Dimaporo made her wait several days before he flew in from Manila and serious negotiations could begin.

> During the interim, Princess Tarhata and partisans of Governor Pangarungan sparred with each other. According to a reporter on the scene, Col. Omar Manabilang, Lanao Sur Provincial Commander said the efforts of the negotiators are noteworthy but lack of coordination has somehow confused the abductors. Retired Gen. Mamarinta Lao was the first to volunteer his services as negotiator, Manabilang said . . . Manabilang believes that Gen. Lao could have easily negotiated for the release of Fr. Michel. Though not directly harping on Princess Tarhata's efforts, Manabilang said politics has delayed the release of the priest. Princess Tarhata, however, minced no words when she told *Veritas* Manabilang "is not doing anything." . . . Princess Tarhata has demanded for [sic] the relief of Manabilang. Manabilang on the other hand insists he was installed Provincial Commander on the basis of his performance. . . . Lt. Col. Magasuga Dandanum, who reports to Princess Tarhata, told *Veritas* that there are those who say that if ever the priest is released to Princess Tarhata, she will become the Governor. . . . Bishop [Bienvenido] Tudtud [of the Prelature of Marawi] told *Veritas* "dili man simbagan ang tumong nila" (it is not the Church they are after).[117]

As Princess Tarhata and Governor Pangarungan vied over credit for freeing Fr. Gigord, Ali Dimaporo loomed in the background, a political presence no one could ignore.

In the end, Dimaporo managed to control the circumstances of Gigord's release, to claim the credit for it, and to secure the plaudits that followed. He had earlier promised the French ambassador that Gigord would be released on 21 June. Given this assurance, Princess Tarhata prepared welcoming ceremonies for the returned priest among his parishioners at MSU. At the last minute Dimaporo announced that negotiations had stalled and that the release would be delayed, thereby disrupting Princess Tarhata's public-relations plans. At his Binidayan residence on Monday, 24 June, Dimaporo told assembled reporters that Gigord would be:

> released 80 per cent tonight or tomorrow morning. . . . He will be in my hands if not by tonight or [*sic*] tomorrow to be ready on Wednesday when the Generals (Southcom Chief Maj. Gen. Jose Magno and RUC X Chief Gen. Adalem) will be here. I understand there are some foreign press coming. That's why I have got to work very hard to see to it that these people will not be disappointed.[118]

When the invited press arrived by helicopter on Tuesday morning he told them to come back the next day at 10 o'clock instead. According to *Veritas*, "Originally, the plan was for the priest to proceed to MSU. Dimaporo, however, outsmarted Princess Tarhata. Dimaporo had scheduled 'turnover' rites at ten o'clock the following day."[119] In fact, Fr. Gigord arrived at Dimaporo's residence on Tuesday evening but his ceremonial release was delayed until the reporters had reassembled. As one journalist described the scene, "The Barracudas and the people of Binidayan were all at the Multi-purpose Hall. The media men from Manila, friends of Dimaporo, arrived with the Colonel [Raul] Aquino. The video tape rolled. The cameras clicked. And Dimaporo was proclaimed hero."[120] Fr. Gigord wanted to return to MSU, which would have suited Princess Tarhata's purposes, but instead, "In a hasty bid to present the priest to authorities in Manila, Fr. Michel was allowed only a few minutes at the Chaplaincy at MSU and then immediately whisked off to the Cagayan de Oro Airport for the 3:35 flight to Manila. The following day, Dimaporo would be seen flashing that now all-too-familiar grin on the front pages of the national dailies."[121]

While Dimaporo proudly claimed credit for Fr. Gigord's release, he was less decisive in denying responsibility for the kidnaping in the first place. When asked by reporters about his role, he responded:

> In the beginning, they were making allusions that I have something to do with it. I asked the military to investigate, to pinpoint responsibility. Now that the military believes I have nothing to do with it, it could be some of my men, it could be the rebels, it could be anybody. But I cannot deny that it could be some of my men for reasons I do not know. But as [*sic*] all other kidnapped persons including American priests, Chinese, Koreans, Japanese and some businessmen that were kidnapped specially [*sic*] during the height of the trouble, I was mainly responsible to have them released.[122]

Indeed, some former members of Dimaporo's MSU security force were implicated in the kidnaping itself and a number of his relatives were identified among those who held Gigord captive. Even while denying direct responsibility for the kidnapings, Dimaporo conveyed through his statement the message that he alone held the reins of chaos and terror. Security and violence were his to dispense at will. Despite this ominous note, the national publicity he received as a result of the Gigord kidnaping was, on the whole, positive. Even at the lowest ebb of his fortunes, Ali Dimaporo remained a force to be reckoned with in Mindanao politics.

In the months following the Gigord kidnaping, Pangarungan, Lucman, Dianalan, and others continued to struggle for control of the provincial government.[123] External events, including abortive negotiations between the Aquino government and various Bangsamoro nationalist factions, further complicated the political scene.[124] Finally, in September 1986, President Aquino appointed Princess Tarhata Lucman to replace Pangarungan as OIC governor of Lanao del Sur. Peace and order continued to be a problem.[125] As Princess Tarhata worked to consolidate her rule and Pangarungan sought to regain his position, all the political contenders began preparing for the congressional elections scheduled for 11 May 1987, the first electoral contest to be held under the Aquino regime. Ali Dimaporo also began preparing his political comeback. In April, reportedly responding to a deathbed request by Omar Dianalan's father, leaders of the Dianalan and Dimaporo families met to resolve their differences. Their successful rapprochement resulted in some curious alliances in the May elections. Dimaporo, a declared Marcos loyalist, ran as the KBL candidate for Congress in Lanao del Sur District 2, while Omar Dianalan stood as Cory Aquino's PDP-LABAN candidate in Lanao del Sur District 1. Ironically, the two cooperated against UNIDO (Liberal) Party governor Lucman and her nephew Ahmad (Jun) Alonto at MSU.[126] In the initial canvass, both Dimaporo and Dianalan were declared winners in their respective districts. In addition, Dimaporo's son Abdullah won a clear victory in Lanao del Norte's District 2. The results in both Lanao del Sur districts were relatively close. Dimaporo was credited with 37 percent of the vote, with his nearest competitor, Jamail Lucman, receiving 32 percent. Dianalan won 30 percent of the vote in District 1, compared to some 22 percent received by Mamintal Adiong, the candidate backed by the Alontos.[127] These results were challenged by nearly all candidates and the resulting flurry of legal submissions, affidavits, and other documents postponed the final declaration of the winners for several months. By late August, although the Congress had been in session for more than two months, no representative from Lanao del Sur had yet been seated. Nevertheless, Ali Dimaporo spoke and acted in both Mindanao and Manila as if his election had been formally proclaimed. In an August 1987 interview, he gave his view of the election challenges.

> You know, according to the provincial canvass, I won [by] 3,474 votes and they claim there was terrorism committed by my men. In their own (i.e. COMELEC's) cross examination it had been proven that it's absolutely false

> because in the first place, General Hermosa reported that I won in a clean, honest and orderly election. In the hearings my witnesses were the Brigade Commander, the Station Commander and the COMELEC registrar. . . . I am staking my political career for anybody—the NBI [National Bureau of Investigation] or any of the people of Lucman to investigate and if they can pinpoint any single man who went around Binidayan . . . and if I cannot have him delivered to them I give up my election.[128]

Eventually Dimaporo's election was confirmed and he regained a congressional seat, though not the one he had held prior to martial law.

In the aftermath of the election, the number of kidnapings and other acts of violence again increased in Lanao del Sur.[129] In early June 1987 several blocks in the Iligan City business district burned to the ground. The Maranao men apprehended and accused of the crime were later released to the custody of Congressman-elect Dimaporo. On 8 July two social-service workers were kidnaped in Lanao del Sur, and released unharmed five days later. On 9 July a female student was shot to death in a restroom at MSU, apparently by a recently fired, Dimaporo-loyalist, security guard. On 22 July two teachers at the MSU High School were kidnaped by armed men during a flag-raising ceremony at the center of the campus.[130] On 16 July Dimaporo complained in a radio interview that no one was in control in Lanao del Sur and predicted that more trouble could be expected.

On 7 August sixteen people from MSU, including thirteen students, two faculty members, and one staff member, were kidnaped from a vehicle shortly after it left the campus on its way to Iligan. After several days the victims and their abductors were located on Balt Island, the same island identified during the Gigord kidnaping as a Barracuda stronghold. The kidnapers initially demanded a ransom of half a million pesos, but later raised their demand to 62.5 million, one-fourth the annual MSU budget.[131] They also demanded the removal of MSU president Alonto, one vice-president, and the chief of security. When Dimaporo was approached about obtaining the victims' release, he declined to become involved unless Governor Lucman personally appealed to him for help. This she refused to do. After ten days of negotiations conducted by her son, and the rumored payment of a substantial ransom by the governor's family, the captives were released.[132] On the day the MSU victims were released, the wife of the National Power Corporation's Mindanao manager was kidnaped from her home. Of all these incidents, only the last was not credited to Dimaporo, his relatives, or his supporters.

Only a few weeks later, rumors linked Dimaporo (along with former defense secretary Juan Ponce Enrile and a few others) to the August 1987 coup attempt against the Aquino government led by Colonel Gregorio Honasan. Widely circulated reports suggested that the coup was plotted during meetings held at Dimaporo's Corinthian Gardens residence outside Manila. Eventually Dimaporo issued a public denial of involvement, though as usual his statement was less than definitive.

Dimaporo's "warlord" image, the perception that he is a supremely dangerous person, appears to have done him little harm either in Manila or in Lanao. He retained his standing in the Congress. He continued to sidestep government demands that he relinquish his weapons and disband his private army. His wealth continued to grow as he converted his immense fishpond holdings to prawn culture.[133] His star continued to rise in Lanao del Sur as his opponents, the Alontos and Lucmans, struggled to contain the forces of chaos and to meet challenges from the Pangarungans and other rising political families. Dimaporo placed his favorite son, Abdullah, in a relatively safe seat in Congress (Lanao del Norte) from which he could build the next generation of the Dimaporo dynasty. He still had the support of a majority of local officials in Lanao del Sur, where he could mobilize more men with more guns than anyone else in Lanao. He had repeatedly turned back political and military challenges from the national government. Even the Philippine Army dared not challenge him in his home territory. In sum he seemed to have come through the trauma of Marcos's fall remarkably unscathed.

On the surface there is little to mark Ali Dimaporo for such an exceptional political career. He is not a particularly good public speaker. He has little of the winning bonhomie of a Ninoy Aquino. He is physically unprepossessing. According to Maranao standards, his behavior tends to be coarse, more typical of a commoner than of the aristocrat he claims to be. But he has repeatedly shown a subtlety in political maneuvering unmatched in the fiercely competitive arena of Maranao politics. He took advantage of the dissolution of civil government during World War II to build a band of armed followers. From his attacks on the Japanese in Malabang he gained a reputation for audacity, organizational ability, and military command. His Military Police service consolidated his reputation for winning through intimidation. When he entered politics he used the same abilities to organize, manipulate, and intimidate.

While Ali Dimaporo does not embody Maranao images of nobility, his career exemplifies certain aspects of datuship in the Muslim Philippines. As elsewhere in Southeast Asia, political structure in the Islamic Philippines traditionally has been defined by centers, accumulations of power by, and in, particular individuals.[134] As Jeremy Beckett notes of Maguindanao political structure, "The datu represented the centralizing principle in a volatile society in which centrifugal forces were strong."[135] In the absence of status ascribed according to lineal kinship, leadership depends substantially on an individual's ability to attract and maintain a following.[136] Constructing a supporting faction depends upon creating relations of reciprocity with supporters either through gift-giving or imposition of indebtedness.[137] In principle, it makes little difference whether debt is created by a gift voluntarily received or an injury involuntarily sustained. As Beckett points out with reference to Maguindanao datus:

In his struggle to maintain his following, against disintegration on the one hand, and against predatory datus on the other, his personal attributes were recognized to be critical, above all his ability to command fear and respect. Thus elevated, personal power could never be contained by notions of order or legitimacy; to a degree power became its own legitimation. If a datu were strong enough to enforce folk-Islamic or adat law, he was also strong enough to transgress it. If he could command the goods of his followers, he could refuse to distribute them, as a kind datu was supposed to do. The followers might be entitled to leave him, but the likelihood of their doing so was in inverse proportion to the fear in which they held him. Thus, finally, a datu was what a datu did.[138]

Failure to understand this process has left observers of Philippine datus unable to account for their ability to attract and hold followers. As datus display apparently contradictory character traits, it would seem logical that persons attracted to a datu by one set of qualities would be repelled by a display of the opposite. Yet often this does not happen. Reynaldo Ileto, for instance, describes the confused impressions of Datu Uto of Buayan recorded by Spanish commentators during the late nineteenth century. While some attributed his leadership to physical prowess and personal valor, others emphasized his timidity and fearfulness, others his "intelligence and audacity," still others his prudence, wisdom, cunning, bad morality, flexibility, apparent selflessness and paternal care in his relations with his supporters, and so on.[139] What comes through in the Spanish accounts is Datu Uto's success in cultivating clients and enemies at the same time that he intimidated them. The Spaniards noticed Uto's "ingenuity in manipulating friendships and debt relationships to suit his ends" but they found it hard to accept the fact that he would greet his enemies with open arms and profuse declarations of friendship even while he was sending his slave armies to destroy them.[140] How, outsiders wondered, could a datu engender trust and loyalty under these circumstances? They failed to realize that this was the wrong question, that support was not elicited from autonomous individuals exercising voluntary will, but that leadership succeeded to the extent that it commanded respect, that it made domination (being ruled) seem inevitable. In this arena, to be predictable (and therefore worthy of loyalty and trust by external standards) was to be outmaneuvered. Thus, security for followers lay in proximity to power, not in any ethical criteria governing its sources or exercise.

Ali Dimaporo displays "contradictions" of character and an apparent lack of scruples similar to those attributed to Datu Uto. To the outside world he often presents an innocuous face. He speaks frequently of his devotion to the concepts of brotherhood and love, telling one interviewer:

I believe that good Christians and good Muslims should do our best to guide our misguided brothers and sisters, for the interest and good of the great majority. I believe that it [is] in unity that we can promote peace, and it is in peace that could be the key to progress, happiness and prosperity in the future of our people. . . . I am going to do everything possible within my power to promote this brotherly relationship between Christians and Muslims. In fact, I have gone one step ahead. My son, Abdullah, the best of my children is married to a Christian. Now I have five grandchildren who are Christians.[141]

Yet, if Dimaporo's rhetoric is often paternalistic, displaying a deep concern for those under his tutelage, he inspires awe and fear in them as well. This is the man feared by Christian residents of Lanao as the godfather of the Barracudas, who sent Christian students at MSU scurrying for cover during the Marcos-Aquino transition. Yet these Christians repeatedly elected him to high political office. This is also the man who contracted a marriage for his son that was despised by most Maranao. Yet they elected him once again to Congress. He rails almost maniacally against those who might attack him, swearing before God that he will destroy them. He dares the Commission on Audit to prove that he stole money from MSU and defies his enemies to establish his connection to the Barracudas. He challenges reporters to prove that he is responsible for the kidnaping of Fr. Gigord or that he was involved in planning the August 1987 coup attempt. Far from trying to avoid connection with the often outrageous accusations against him, he seems to revel in them.[142] His denials, when he offers them at all, are always equivocal, allowing that he might be involved but implying that no one has power enough to hold him accountable. His defiance of the Aquino government during the period after Marcos's fall only enhanced his reputation. When even the army and the national government were unable or unwilling to engage this giant of Lanao, what chance has any lowly individual against him? He breaks all the rules, yet he prospers.[143] It is precisely this ability to transcend the limits of normal human action that makes Dimaporo a datu.[144]

As a datu, Dimaporo's disruptive aspect complements the tutelary relations he cultivates just as assiduously. Just as he provides security and efficacy for those who follow him, he brings chaos and violence to those who oppose him. His attractiveness lies precisely in his power, the proven efficacy of his actions, his ability to outmaneuver, neutralize, and destroy those who seek to bring him low. By his power he brings order into the world; by the same power he can destroy that order. In the old days, cattle rustling was a preoccupation among Maranao. More recently, kidnaping has served the same purpose, to test the resources, power, and personal prowess of contenders for political power. Implication in kidnapings, coups, fraud, venality, and murder do a Maranao datu's reputation no harm, so long as he gets away with it, and in this Dimaporo has excelled.[145]

Dimaporo's extraordinary achievements are symbolized by his successful assumption of the title Sultan sa Masiu. In terms of actual political power, titles at this level of the Maranao titular hierarchy have traditionally been purely honorific, since no Maranao prior to Dimaporo was able to accumulate sufficient power to dominate such a large segment of the populace.[146] So long as he can maintain that dominance, by whatever means, he will stand as a pillar in a fluid and dangerous social world. All this suggests that in many ways Dimaporo's career is exemplary of Maranao datuship, a successful adaptation of traditional ideas and symbols to a radically changed political setting.

This conclusion is supported by an experience I had in July 1987 while visiting the mosque of Sheik Mukhdum on Simunul Island near Tawi-Tawi. This is reputedly the oldest mosque in the Philippines, by common reckoning having been established in 1380 A.D. During the visit, I was invited to pray to the sheik for whatever I might desire since his spiritual power (*barakat*) was so intense that God would surely answer any prayer made in the precincts of his tomb. Indeed, I was told, when Ferdinand Marcos was president of the Senate he had come and prayed that he would become president of the nation. Obviously his prayer had been answered, and if Marcos was president no longer it was as a result of his own failures and not the sheik's. I mentioned to my companions that Ali Dimaporo had survived Marcos's fall and appeared to be prospering in defiance of the Aquino government. They responded that Dimaporo is smarter, more cunning, and luckier, than Marcos. One of the tomb's caretakers added that Dimaporo's *barakat* must be very great indeed. Indeed!

Notes

[1] *Mindanaw Week*, 16–20 August 1987, 9–10.
[2] Carolyn O. Arguillas, "The Warlord as Marcos Loyalist," *Veritas*, 7–9 July 1986, 15.
[3] This account of Dimaporo's early career is drawn primarily from biographical documents prepared under his direction by public relations personnel at the Mindanao State University. They were distributed on ceremonial occasions such as his investiture in 1982 as Sultan sa Masiu. Since they were intended to legitimate Dimaporo's positions within the government and the Maranao titular hierarchy, a good deal of self-fashioning and myth making can be assumed to have taken place. Where possible I have tried to verify the "facts" in Ali's official biography.
[4] Military records list his father as Dimaporo Mamalapat, Sultan sa Binidayan, and his mother as Borugas Marahom (Counter Intelligence Corp Case Report, Dimaporo, Mohamad-Ali, Binidayan, Lanao, Mindanao; 210th CIC Det., APO 310; File: 210/30.CC–3–7, 14 August 1945; People's Court, Box 96, Folder 9, University of the Philippines Archives).
[5] Ben Trio Rufin, "Dimaporo: A Profile," *Yesterday/Today* (official organ of the Office of Alumni Relations, Mindanao State University), 2 April 1981, 1.
[6] Arguillas, "The Warlord," 15.
[7] Cooperating with Dimaporo was Captain Mamarinta Lao, later to achieve distinction as the first Muslim to attain the rank of general in the Philippine Army.
[8] John Hugh McGee, *Rice and Salt: A History of the Defense and Occupation of Mindanao During World War II* (San Antonio: Naylor, 1961), 43–44.
[9] Ralph Benjamin Thomas, "Muslim but Filipino: The Integration of Philippine Muslims, 1917–1946" (Ph.D. diss., University of Pennsylvania, 1971), 290.
[10] Rufin, "Dimaporo," 2.

[11]Ibid.

[12]Ibid.

[13]While Captain Lao surrendered in December 1942, Mindalano never did.

[14]Anticipating a similar episode some forty-five years later, Dimaporo only turned in old, unusable weapons (CIC Case Report, Exhibit I, 2).

[15]Given the limited forces with which they attempted to control the extensive territories and populations in Mindanao, the Japanese were able to garrison only a few Lanao towns, including Malabang, Ganassi, Dansalan, and Iligan. With elimination of the prewar civil administration and the Japanese failure to establish an effective replacement, law and order disintegrated in Lanao. Armed gangs preyed upon the Japanese but also on their enemies among the Muslim and Christian populations. Some semblance of order was restored under a "Free Lanao" government established under a unified guerrilla command in 1943. See Thomas, "Muslim but Filipino," 294.

[16]CIC Case Report, Exhibit I, 2.

[17]In later testimony, both Dimaporo and Mindalano claimed that this confrontation was staged, that Ali had already conveyed his intention to attack the airfield using his own men, and that Mindalano approved of his determination to protect the field and its men (CIC Case Report, 10).

[18]Ali described this episode in characteristically dramatic terms (quoted in Arguillas, "The Warlord," 16):

> The Japanese found out that I gave the cigarettes and sugar rationed to me to the guerrillas. But you see, it was part of my campaign. They eventually arrested me. It was only the will of Allah that I wasn't killed. I told the Japanese I was only trying to help them. I even spat on the face of the Japanese commander and told him if they want, they could kill me. They released me on condition that if I am reported helping the guerrillas, they would chop my neck. I was arrested and detained for one day. The next day, I looked for places I could ambush them. And I found the opportunity.

[19]A report prepared by Mamarinta Lao lists twenty-two soldiers killed: ten at the Cotabato-Lanao boundary, four at the Malabang garrison, three at the landing field, and five at the "Cota" (CIC Case Report, "Lao to Provincial Governor," 1).

[20]See United States Eighth Army, "Report of the Commanding General Eighth Army on the Mindanao Operation, Victor V," n.d., declassified 29 April 1946.

[21]CIC Case Report, 10. The investigating CIC officer noted that "the Christian residents of Malabang appear extremely grateful to him and he seems more friendly to them than even to the local Moro leaders. The Christian residents of Malabang are most appreciative of his intervention in their behalf with the Japanese garrison" (ibid., 13).

[22]Ibid., 9, 13.

[23]Ibid., 29 July 1945. An attachment entitled "Information" (dated 29 July 1945) is referenced here.

[24]In fact, Dimaporo submitted several reports to military and civilian authorities, detailing the plans and actions surrounding the "Malabang incident" (ibid., Exhibit I and Attachments dated 26 June, 27 June, and 8 July 1944).

[25]Dimaporo was given a letter of commendation for his part in the October 1944 United States Forces in the Philippines (USFIP) attack on Malabang (ibid., Exhibit IX).

[26]Arguillas, "The Warlord," 15.

[27]Ibid.

[28]Lluch and Cabili both figured in Dimaporo's subsequent political career, both as allies and as opponents. Like Dimaporo, Cabili served as a guerrilla leader during the war. Lluch served as civil administrator in the Free Lanao government.

[29]Other Muslim politicians who got their start in the guerrilla movement include Salipada Pendatun in Cotabato and Rascid Lucman, later elected to Congress from Lanao.

[30]Rufin, "Dimaporo," 4.

[31]Arguillas, "The Warlord," 16.

[32]Recall that Alonto and Dimaporo had both traveled to Manila as guests of the Japanese in 1943. Dimaporo reports that during this trip "I was offered the position of Congressman. Domocao Alonto and Governor Kogoh, Japanese civilian administrator of Lanao, assured me that my election would be certain. I refused" (CIC Case Report, Exhibit I, 2).

[33]Rufin, "Dimaporo," 4.

[34]T. J. S. George, *Revolt in Mindanao: The Rise of Islam in Philippine Politics* (Singapore: Oxford University Press, 1980), 171.

[35]Rufin, "Dimaporo," 5.

[36]Arguillas, "The Warlord," 16.

[37]Recall that Dimaporo had made himself a hero in the eyes of Christian families by defending them against depredations by Japanese occupation forces (see note 21).

[38]So strong was the antagonism between Lluch and Cabili that the latter "worked for the guerrilla movement in Bukidnon and Occidental Misamis, staying out of Lanao to avoid any conflict among his own and Lluch's followers that might harm the guerrilla movement" (Thomas, "Muslim but Filipino," 297).

[39]See George, *Revolt in Mindanao*, 171n.

[40]Rufin, "Dimaporo," 5.

[41]Arguillas, "The Warlord," 16.

[42]Rufin, "Dimaporo," 5. This story plays on several themes simultaneously. In relating it, Dimaporo tells us that he could have altered the election outcome had he chosen to do so but that he refrained out of personal honesty, loyalty to the democratic process, and personal feelings for Ferdinand Marcos.

[43]For details, see George, *Revolt in Mindanao*, 122–28; and Cesar A. Majul, *The Contemporary Muslim Movement in the Philippines* (Berkeley: Mizzan Press, 1985), 40–45.

[44]George, *Revolt in Mindanao*, 125–26, 127.

[45]Arguillas, "The Warlord," 17.

[46]*Manila Times*, 5 October 1969, 1.

[47]George, *Revolt in Mindanao*, 172.

[48]*Manila Times*, 2 September 1971, 1; 24 October 1971, 1.

[49]George, *Revolt in Mindanao*, 172.

[50]*Manila Times*, 1 September 1971, 1.

[51]Ibid., 3 September 1971, 1.

[52]Marawi City is the provincial capital of Lanao del Sur, formerly Dansalan.

[53]George, *Revolt in Mindanao*, 173.

[54]Ibid., 174.

[55]*Manila Times*, 28 October 1971, 23; 29 October 1971, 1, 12.

[56]Arguillas, "The Warlord," 18.

[57]George, *Revolt in Mindanao*, 174.

[58]Voting had been postponed in the first three of these municipalities by a resolution of the Commission on Elections (Comelec) endorsed by the Supreme Court. In the last two (along with Luuk, Jolo) Comelec had declared a failure of election after finding that no voting had taken place (*Manila Times*, 8 November 1971, 1; 13 November 1971, 1).

[59]Ibid., 17 November 1971.

[60]See George, *Revolt in Mindanao*, 174–76; and Majul, *Contemporary Muslim Movement*, 56–57.

[61]Dimaporo's role in the violence surrounding the 1971 election has never been made clear. He, of course, challenges his accusers to prove his involvement. Interestingly, reports emanating from Binidayan in 1986 described arrangements strikingly similar to those rumored fifteen years earlier. In both instances, Naga Dimaporo, Ali's younger brother, is identified as the Barracudas' commander. See "Dimaporo's Barracudas," *Veritas*, 7–9 July 1986, 17.

[62]George, *Revolt in Mindanao,* 179.

[63]Rufin, "Dimaporo," 6.

[64]Arguillas, "The Warlord," 17.

[65]Ibid.

[66]*Bulletin Today,* 1 April 1976, 1.

[67]Abuses against students eventually caused these units to be removed to a safe distance from the campus.

[68]The MSU Board of Regents was constituted in a manner assured to highlight Muslim-Christian conflict. Five of the members were Maranao from Lanao del Sur; the other five were Christians connected with interests in Iligan City (ibid., 25 June 1976).

[69]I attended all hearings and examined all documents connected with this case. In addition, I interviewed all the principal parties, witnesses, and the hearing officer. For details, see G. Carter Bentley, "Administrative Law at the Margins: Disciplinary Cases at the Mindanao State University" (paper presented at the First International Philippine Studies Conference, Kalamazoo, Michigan, 1980).

[70]For instance, the costs of his son Abdullah's lavish Makati wedding reception were paid out of an MSU "discretionary fund" under Ali's control, as were the costs of campaign literature during Abdullah's 1978 run for a seat in the Interim Batasang Pambansa (National Assembly).

[71]*Daily Express,* 13 June 1978, 2.

[72]Ibid., 8 June 1978, 1, 2.

[73]Ibid., 11 December 1978, 6.

[74]Horacio V. Paredes, "Mindanao's Goliaths Play Power Politics," *Mr. and Ms.,* 10 February 1984, 8, 11.

[75]Ibid., 11.

[76]Lita Torralba Logarta, "After Dimaporo and Dianalan, Who's Next to Threaten KBL Unity," *Mr. and Ms.,* 15–21 March 1985, 13.

[77]Ibid.

[78]Ibid., 14.

[79]Ibid.

[80]*Veritas,* 29 January 1986, quoted in Lela Garner Noble, "Muslim Grievances and the Muslim Rebellion," in *Rebuilding a Nation: Philippine Challenges and American Policy,* edited by Carl Lande (Washington, D.C.: Washington Institute Press, 1987), 426.

[81]Ibid.

[82]Ibid., 426–27. Shortly before the election, a Manila columnist described Dimaporo's forces as follows (Ramon Tulfo, "Private Army," *Bulletin Today,* 4 February 1986, 12):

Dimaporo calls his private army the "special action force." They wear a funny blend of fatigue and jungle suit uniforms complete with patches of scout rangers, special forces, and jungle fighters (although most of them haven't had formal military training). Most of them are comfortable going around without shoes.

To top their comic sight, these uniformed pseudo-military men sport ranks of real military personnel. We are told that one of the men sports a captain's rank on his shoulder and a sergeant's chevron on his arm.

What is not funny about them, however, is their array of weapons: M-16 and M-14 Armalite rifles, the old reliable Garand and Browning Automatic Rifle (BAR) and the M-79 grenade launcher.

We are told that the local PC Commander looks the other way on the existence of Dimaporo's private army, what with his strong connections.

Even local media men cringe in fear at the thought of exposing the private army. The death of *Bulletin Today*'s Demosthenes "Demy" Dingcong in Iligan City in 1980 is still fresh in their memory.

[83]Arguillas, "The Warlord," 18.
[84]Noble, "Muslim Grievances," 427.
[85]*Bulletin Today*, 15 February 1986.
[86]Ibid., 19 February 1986, 1, 5.
[87]Noble, "Muslim Grievances," 427.
[88]*Bulletin Today*, 4 March 1986, 1, 8.
[89]Dimaporo was not alone in making Pangarungan's youth an issue. During a Malacanang meeting Princess Tarhata Lucman, Maranao matriarch, former Lanao del Sur governor, and UNIDO partisan, reportedly told Pangarungan that "he was still young and could still get hold of many positions in the future" (*Mr. and Ms.*, 16–22 May 1986, 19).
[90]Ibid., 19–20.
[91]Ibid., 20.
[92]Ibid.
[93]Ibid.
[94]Ibid.
[95]Ibid.
[96]Ibid.
[97]Ibid., 21. The leadership transfer at MSU took place more smoothly. Colonel Mamiguin Magomnang, designated regent-in-charge, quietly approached Dimaporo and presented his appointment papers. There followed a "low key but well attended ceremony on the campus" (ibid.).
[98]Ibid.; see also Arguillas, "The Warlord," 18.
[99]*Mr. and Ms.*, 16–22 May 1986, 21.
[100]*Veritas*, 27 April 1986, 2.
[101]*Mr. and Ms.*, 16–22 May 1986, 21.
[102]Arguillas, "The Warlord," 18.
[103]Ibid., 17.
[104]Ibid.
[105]The Presidential Commission on Good Government was established early in the Aquino regime to seek out and recover assets misappropriated by government officials under the previous regime. It served as one of the Aquino government's principal means of harassing its predecessors.
[106]*Asiaweek*, 11 May 1986.
[107]*Mindanaw Week*, 10–16 August 1987, 9.
[108]Arguillas, "The Warlord," 17; see also *Mindanaw Week*, 10–16 August 1987, 8.
[109]Arguillas, "The Warlord," 18.
[110]Noble, "Muslim Grievances," 432.
[111]The kidnapings benefited others besides Dimaporo. As part of her drive to regain her former position as provincial governor, Princess Tarhata Alonto Lucman began a publicity campaign aimed at demonstrating Governor Pangarungan's ineffectiveness. Pangarungan's alleged failure to prevent and then to resolve the kidnapings played a central role in this campaign.
[112]The details of the kidnaping are drawn from reports in *Veritas*, 26–29 June 1986, 10–11; and 30 June–2 July 1986, 9–13.
[113]Gutang's drive was expected to begin on 10 June at the end of the Ramadhan fast period. *Veritas*, 26–29 June 1986, 10–11.
[114]Ibid., 10.
[115]Ibid.
[116]Ibid.

[117]Ibid., 11.

[118]*Veritas*, 30 June–2 July 1986, 10.

[119]Ibid., 11.

[120]In fact, the promised "generals" did not attend the release ceremony.

[121]*Veritas*, 30 June–2 July 1986, 10–11.

[122]Ibid., 11.

[123]See G. Carter Bentley, "People Power and After in the Islamic City of Marawi," in *From Marcos to Aquino: Local Perspectives on Political Transition in the Philippines*, edited by Benedict A. Kerkvliet and Resil B. Mojares (Honolulu and Quezon City: University of Hawaii Press and Ateneo de Manila University Press, 1991), 46–47.

[124]Ibid., 47–48.

[125]While kidnap attempts continued, fewer succeeded. A second attempt to kidnap the Carmelite nuns foundered when, facing death, they refused to leave their convent. Two Protestant missionaries narrowly escaped a kidnap attempt in early 1987 when a young woman accompanying them recognized one of the abductors as her cousin.

[126]Dimaporo's personal candidate in the District 1 race was reportedly attorney Mangontawar Guro, a fellow KBL member. However, Dimaporo failed to campaign actively on his behalf, leaving the race open to Dianalan.

[127]Adiong might have won had not Normallah Pacasum, Governor Lucman's daughter, entered the race and thereby split the votes of the Alonto-Lucman supporters. Pacasum won 10 percent of the vote.

[128]*Mindanaw Week*, 10–16 August 1987, 8.

[129]Bentley, "People Power and After," 50–51.

[130]*Malaya*, 24 July 1987, 6.

[131]*Philippine Daily Inquirer*, 12 August 1987, 1, 9.

[132]See Bentley, "People Power and After," 51.

[133]*Mindanaw Week*, 10–16 August 1987, 9.

[134]On patterns of political leadership in Southeast Asia as a whole, see, for example, O.W. Wolters, *History, Culture, and Region in Southeast Asian Perspective* (Singapore: Institute of Southeast Asian Studies, 1982); and G. Carter Bentley, "Indigenous States of Southeast Asia," *Annual Review of Anthropology* 15 (1986): 275–305. Wolters, in particular, explores the selective appropriation of symbols and rituals from world religions to support leadership cults in the region. For more specific examinations of the dynamics of power and its representation, see Benedict R. O'G. Anderson, "The Idea of Power in Javanese Culture," in *Culture and Politics in Indonesia*, edited by Claire Holt (Ithaca: Cornell University Press, 1972), 1–70; Stanley J. Tambiah, *World Conqueror and World Renouncer* (Cambridge: Cambridge University Press, 1976); Clifford Geertz, *Negara: The Theater State in Nineteenth Century Bali* (Princeton: Princeton University Press, 1980); Lorraine Gesick, ed., *Centers, Symbols, and Hierarchies: Essays on the Classical States of Southeast Asia* (New Haven: Yale University, Southeast Asian Program, 1983); and A. C. Milner, *Kerajaan* (Tucson: University of Arizona Press, 1983).

[135]Jeremy Beckett, "The Defiant and the Compliant: The Datus of Magindanao under Colonial Rule," in *Philippine Social History: Global Trade and Local Transformations*, edited by Alfred W. McCoy and Ed. C. de Jesus (Honolulu: University of Hawaii Press, 1982), 396.

[136]The implications for political structure of predominantly cognatic kin-reckoning in Southeast Asia have been explored by a number of authors. See, for example, George Peter Murdock, ed., *Social Structure in Southeast Asia* (New York: Wenner-Gren, 1960); Robert L. Winzeler, "Ecology, Culture, Social Organization, and State Formation in Southeast Asia," *Current Anthropology* 17 (1976): 623–32; Wolters, *History, Culture, and Region*; and Bentley, "Indigenous States," 290–92. On the Maranao, see Melvin Mednick, *Encampment of the Lake: The Social Organization of a Moslem-Philippine (Moro) People*, Research Series, no. 5 (Chicago: Philippine Studies Program, Department of Anthropology, University of Chicago,

1965); and David Baradas, "Ambiguities in Maranao Rank Differentiation," *Philippine Sociological Review* 21 (1973): 273–78.

[137]For useful theoretical perspectives on reciprocity and the formation of political hierarchies, see Pierre Bourdieu, *Outline of a Theory of Practice* (Cambridge: Cambridge University Press, 1977), 159–97; and Annette B. Weiner, *Women of Value, Men of Renown: New Perspectives on Trobriand Exchange* (Austin: University of Texas Press, 1976). For a discussion of these issues in Tagalog society, see Vicente Rafael, *Contracting Colonialism: Translation and Conversion in Tagalog Society Under Early Spanish Rule* (Quezon City: Ateneo de Manila University Press, 1988), 137–46.

[138]Beckett, "The Defiant and the Compliant," 396. This conclusion echoes Anderson's points about Javanese ideas of power, especially that, in contrast to western conceptions, the exercise of power does not raise the issue of legitimacy. Anderson writes, "To the Javanese way of thinking it would be meaningless to claim the right to rule on the basis of differential sources of power—for example, to say that power based on wealth is legitimate, whereas power based on guns is illegitimate. Power is neither legitimate nor illegitimate. Power is" (Anderson, "The Idea of Power," 8).

[139]See Reynaldo Clemena Ileto, *Magindanao, 1860–1888: The Career of Datu Uto of Buayan,* Data Papers, no. 82 (Ithaca: Southeast Asia Program, Department of Asian Studies, Cornell University, 1971), 38–40.

[140]Ibid., 39.

[141]*Mindanaw Week,* 10–16 August 1987, 9.

[142]During my various stays in Lanao del Sur, I heard a variety of rumors concerning Dimaporo's personal life. The more lurid maintained that he kept some two dozen concubines in addition to three (or, un-Islamically, five) wives, and that he had personally killed a wife and one of his kinsmen who had been carrying on an affair. These stories, true or not, added unnatural sexual prowess to his mystique and further confirmed his well-known ruthlessness.

[143]In a similar vein, Ileto asks, with regard to Datu Uto, Spain's greatest nineteenth-century nemesis in Mindanao, "How does one, for example, account for his wish to have his son Magindara go and study in Spain?" See Ileto, *Magindanao,* 39. A variety of similarly puzzling episodes are described in Cesar A. Majul, *Muslims in the Philippines* (Quezon City: Philippine Center for Advanced Studies, University of the Philippines System, 1973).

[144]The theme of transcendence or the containment of opposites in the person of the king recurs in the literature on Southeast Asian political leadership. See Bentley, "Indigenous States," 294–97.

[145]For examples of how status in Maranao society has been enhanced by actions contrary to law, see Mamitua Saber, Mauyag Tamano, and Charles K. Warriner, "The Maratabat of the Maranao," *Philippine Sociological Review* 8 (1960): 10–5; Mednick, *Encampment of the Lake*; Carleton L. Reimer, "Maranao Maratabat and the Concepts of Pride, Honor and Self Esteem," Dansalan Research Center Occasional Papers, no. 4 (Marawi City: Dansalan Research Center, 1976); and G. Carter Bentley, "Law, Disputing, and Ethnicity in Lanao, Philippines" (Ph.D. diss., University of Washington, 1982), 150–207.

[146]By comparison, in the mid-1970s President Marcos managed to coax Rascid Lucman, former congressman and founding sponsor of the Moro National Liberation Front, back from his Middle East exile. In celebration, Marcos proclaimed Lucman "Sultan sa Mindanao," a presumption almost universally regarded as ludicrous, first because such titles were not in Marcos's power to dispense, and, second, because Lucman, while no political lightweight, possessed insufficient power to command respect from the whole population of Mindanao.

Political Families and Family Politics among the Muslim Maguindanaon of Cotabato

Jeremy Beckett

In the Philippines the idea of family structures public perceptions of the relations among and within the various elites. Although political parties have existed since early in the century, talk is more likely to turn on the careers of certain families who are powers to be reckoned with whenever offices and resources are to be distributed. Among these are virtual dynasties so long established that they carry a born-to-rule mystique. The realities are less certain. A family is identified by a patronymic but the acting aggregate may not include all those entitled to carry the name, and may include individuals connected through female links and even affines. Moreover, the extent to which such aggregations are unified varies from case to case and over time; political families are by no means proof against internal rivalry and schism. Filipinos nevertheless perceive them as elements of relative stability amid the flux of political life, and as such they inform political strategy.

Such formations, indeed familism generally, are at variance with the conventional view of modernization, according to which "primordial" loyalties give way to rules and rationality. But over the last decade studies have confirmed the continuing importance of family, most notably among Latin American elites. One of these goes so far as to assert that "corporate descent groups may be a systematic feature of the top strata of even the most technologically advanced countries, even including the United States."[1] In some parts of the Philippines, elite families have moved from the countryside to the city and from politics to business, giving way, according to Kit Machado, to the professional politician.[2] Ferdinand Marcos, following his seizure of power in 1972, promised an end to what he called "the oligarchy" and succeeded at least temporarily in reducing the wealth and power of some well-known groups. But, as the Marcos regime itself showed, the fall of particular families does not spell the end of familism itself, and we do not know whether Machado's professional politicians have tried to pass their offices on to kin rather than to other professionals.

During the run up to the 1984 elections, there was again talk of preventing the formation of "dynasties" but with equivocal results. Following the deposition of Marcos by "People Power," it seemed that a new Philippine politics might crystallize around differences over doctrine and platform but, although the political culture is now more complex and heterogeneous than it was before 1972, family is still a factor, even at the highest level. Meanwhile, in the Muslim south, a number of Maguindanaon political families have managed to survive during three colonial regimes, a democratic republic, the Marcos regime, and the return to parliamentary government of the late 1980s.

The Maguindanaon ethno-linguistic group numbers approximately four hundred thousand persons, living mainly in the Cotabato region of southwestern Mindanao.[3] They are Muslims who kept themselves outside the pale of the Spanish Philippines until the last years of the nineteenth century, and who remained somewhat alienated from the predominantly Christian society even before the secessionist struggle of the past twenty years. Nevertheless, they have participated in national political institutions in much the same way as other Filipinos and the political family has taken the same general form. One may see this as a perpetuation of primordial social forms common to the entire archipelago and predating both Islam and Christianity. But this is not a sufficient explanation, even if it can be shown to be true. Deeper understanding must be sought through an examination of political system and social structure.

Structure and Process in Philippine Politics

The classic work on Philippine politics is Carl Lande's *Leaders, Factions, and Parties*.[4] Although written twenty-five years ago and primarily addressing the electoral democracy of the time, it remains the only systematic attempt to link politics and everyday life by laying bare the structural principles underlying both. As such it is relevant to any discussion of subsequent developments.

Under Spain, politics was confined to the municipal level and engaged only a handful of landowners. Under the United States, provincial and national offices became subject to election, while the franchise was gradually expanded until, with the proclamation of the Republic in 1946, it included all adults. Quite early in this history a two-party structure emerged, not just on the national level but at the grassroots. Indeed, Lande derived it from the characteristic bifactionalism of the municipality, where electoral politics began and where a significant degree of power still resided.[5] In keeping with this, the parties were not distinguished according to ideology, and differed not at all as to the politics or social and regional origins of their leaders. They were loose, unstable coalitions of regional power holders, each

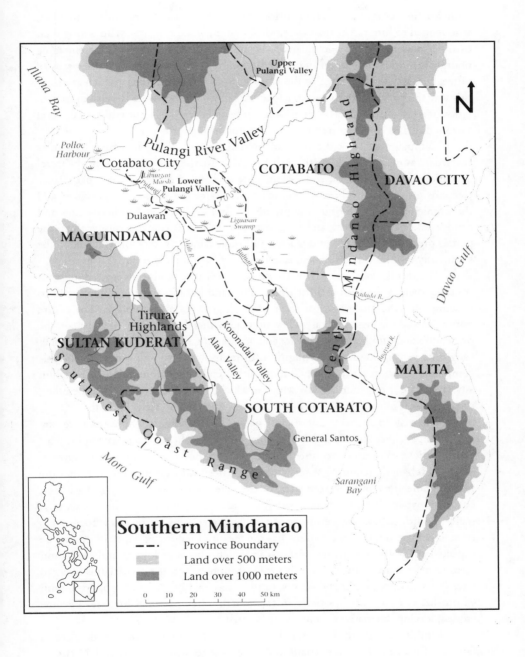

Illana Bay

Polloc
Harbour

Upper
Pulangi Valley

Pulangi River Valley

Cotabato City

Libungan
Marsh

Lower
Pulangi Valley

COTABATO

Central Mindanao Highland

DAVAO CITY

Pulangi R.

Dulawan

Liguasan
Swamp

Davao Gulf

MAGUINDANAO

Mali R.

Pulangi R.

Padada R.

Tiruray
Highlands

Koronadal Valley

Alah Valley

Buayan R.

MALITA

SULTAN KUDERAT

Southwest Coast Range

SOUTH COTABATO

General Santos

Moro Gulf

Sarangani
Bay

Southern Mindanao

- - - Province Boundary

Land over 500 meters

Land over 1000 meters

0   10   20   30   40   50 km

with his (or occasionally her) own following of *caciques, liders,* and landowners, who looked to him rather than to national figures, while similarly maintaining their own personal followings and alliances. While the big landowners and the emerging bourgeoisie, who were often one and the same, gained most from the rewards of office, enough trickled down to the "common *tao*" to secure their participation. In this way the parties, like the personal factions of which they were largely composed, crosscut and obscured class divisions. Only in a few areas, notably in Central Luzon, did class consciousness threaten the bonds of clientelism.

Campaigning took the form of myriad separate deals, in which particular rewards, ranging from a small cash payment to the promise of a pork-barrel allocation or a government concession, were exchanged for votes. Moreover, since elections for different offices were synchronized—for the Senate, the province, and the municipality at one time, the presidency and Congress at another—votes and funds could be traded back and forth between the levels. Under scrutiny, then, the parties proved to be chains and clusters of dyadic contracts, each of which could be summarily terminated and reestablished with a different partner virtually at will.

The dyadic contract, a term Lande borrowed from anthropology,[6] along with concepts such as the patron-client relationship, and kinship and friendship, tends to obscure—for the analyst as for the actors—highly variable combinations of the normative and the instrumental.[7] They afflict us with a double vision of actors, on the one hand selling to the highest bidder and abandoning sinking ships but on the other caught in webs of loyalty and obligation. In reality, political followings are unstable compounds of short-term deals and more or less enduring commitments. Though in any given case it may not be clear which is which, and one may turn into the other, the distinction must be maintained because the system has a "need" for both.

It is easy to see why this should be so. The candidate whose resources are limited must collect on old debts and draw on credit where he can, saving his hard cash for those who can be recruited by no other means. Thus politics is a matter of delayed exchanges, requiring voters and candidates to trust one another. Either the reward comes first and the vote later, or the vote comes first and the reward later, occurring when the candidate takes office—always assuming that he has won. A major reward, such as a government job, a logging concession, or a new road, takes time to deliver. So, unless a creditor has the means of enforcing payment, he can be expected to prefer preexisting relations in which norms of loyalty and obligation seem to offer some security. For this very reason, however, the politician is likely to stretch his credit with kin and clients, until he has paid his debts to supporters with whom his relationship is strictly instrumental. Thus personal loyalties become eroded, leaving the material component exposed.

Kinship belongs to the normative end of the continuum, and Lande places a family—for example, a dominant sibling group to which other individuals or sibling groups are allied by marriage—at the core of a local faction. However, kinship is continuous with the network of dyadic ties and, despite its normative strength, is liable to fragmentation.

Lande locates the origins of this structure in a traditional kinship system that, being cognatic, lacks the power to generate bounded groups.[8] But this explanation depends upon the assumption of cultural continuity without considering contemporary conditions. In any case, the question is not whether bounded groups exist but how sharply they are defined and what areas of life they structure. In almost any situation the advantages of individual maneuverability are to some degree offset by countervailing advantages of coalescence, closure, and solidarity. Conceptually as well as practically, a plethora of dyadic ties cries out for some kind of aggregation, even though this may stop short of incorporation. Noncorporate coalitions, from which the parties may withdraw with their resources intact, emerge to resolve the contradictions: hence the faction and the political family.[9]

The idea of family has the capacity to construct aggregates because it is predicated upon continuity—a dimension that Lande tended to ignore in his search for structure. Integral to the concept of filiation is the belief that, along with physical characteristics, personal qualities such as courage, assertiveness, and shrewdness are transmitted from generation to generation rather than dying with the individuals who manifest them at a particular time. The very familiarity of this notion can seduce us into accepting the transformation that it effects: the transcoding of structures of domination into terms that are part of everyone's experience.

If in no other way, a family is a corporation to the extent that it has a reputation as a power to be reckoned with. It is this reputation that draws followers and attracts the attention of politicians farther up the system hierarchy. It also motivates some members to maintain the family reputation and others to support them. However, what Durkheim called the mechanical solidarity that reputation engenders exists in tension with the reality that the rewards of political action are always limited, and that, particularly in the case of public office, which is indivisible, they are liable to be unequally distributed. The younger members may be prepared to wait their turn. Others may be content to remain dependents, benefiting from and mediating access to the powerful, and basking in reflected glory. For the ambitious, a cognatic system offers the possibility of defecting to another family in which prospects are brighter. As families expand with the generations there is some tendency for one branch to monopolize reputation and reward, leaving the rest to dwindle into poor relations or to align themselves elsewhere.

But, while a family may be divided or fragmented momentarily, the norms and sentiments that define it transcend particularities, and so secrete the power to generate a reaggregation. Thus anger is forgotten, siblings reconciled, and families reunited.

At the time Lande wrote about Philippine politics, power was widely diffused, with the central government precariously balanced on the apex of a pyramid of regional and local alliances. Martial law centralized power and gave the country respite from electioneering. Family remained important, however, as a means of distributing the rewards required to maintain a measure of contentment and legitimacy—considerations that became increasingly important as the New

People's Army (NPA) and Muslim insurgency intensified. Under the controlled form of electoral process introduced under international pressure in 1978, securing nomination in the official party (the Kilusang Bagong Lipunan, or KBL) was more important than winning the favor of the voter. Nevertheless, preserving the semblance of electoral process while securing the desired result could only be achieved with the kind of collusion that influential families could provide. The post-Marcos era is by no means a replica of what existed before 1972 but the revival of relatively free elections has seen the return of many old families both in Cotabato and elsewhere in the Philippines.

The Datus of the Pulangi Valley

The heartland of the Maguindanaon people is the valley of the great Pulangi River, known to the Spaniards as the Rio Grande de Cotabato (see map). This area was the domain of a number of title holders, the best known to history being the sultans of Maguindanao who rose to commercial and military power at the end of the sixteenth century and survived into the nineteenth.[10]

Like the other polities of the Malay world, those of the Pulangi were segmentary, the basic building blocks of which were local datudoms.[11] These enjoyed a considerable degree of autonomy, but were oriented towards a courtly center for trade and civility, and periodically articulated into wider alliances for attack and defense.

The primary meaning of *datu* is 'ruler', but its secondary meaning is 'one entitled to rule by virtue of descent from datus', which is signified by reference to a hereditary title, a place, and traditional associations with servile and supporting groups. The sons of such a ruler could all be called datu, but only one could succeed to the title. Unless disputes over the succession resulted in the division of the domain, the datus without title could either dwindle into dependents or seek their fortunes elsewhere. Over the generations the dependents became numerous, and, while some maintained a measure of dignity as cadet lines, others declined to a point at which they were omitted from the genealogical record. At this point continuing use of the title might bring ridicule rather than respect. Although titles and servile attachments declined during the American period, the underlying structures persist in the form of the contemporary political family.

The descent principle received further elaboration in the constitution of nobility. All the title holders in the valley were, at least in theory, descended from the sharif (who, according to local history, brought Islam to Mindanao) and so ultimately from the Prophet Mohammed.[12] Although the political order that this belief once supported has crumbled, the sense of nobility is very much alive among those who can locate ancestors on the ancient genealogies.[13]

The Spaniards did not gain a foothold in the Pulangi Valley until the second half of the nineteenth century, and, despite a series of military victories, they were able to control the hinterland only through the agency of friendly datus.[14] The

Americans, who succeeded the Spaniards in 1898, established a permanent presence in the interior but were indebted to local leaders for the peace that prevailed after 1904. They were also indebted to the datus for their cooperation in the drive to exploit the region's vast natural resources, and to leaven the "backward" native population with go-ahead immigrants from the overcrowded islands to the north.[15]

The upheavals of the late Spanish and early American periods had reduced the old political order to a shambles. But, while some of the high nobility had lost their followers and been reduced to penury, new datus had emerged who gained in power and wealth by making themselves useful to the colonial authorities. The two dominant figures of the colonial period were Datu Piang of the Upper Valley and Datu Sinsuat (see table 1) of the Lower Valley.[16] Both were appointed at different times to represent the province in Manila, and so were able to acquire the experience and connections that would stand them (or their sons) in good stead when elections began in the Commonwealth period. In 1936, Sinsuat defeated a son of Piang for a seat in the National Assembly, and then lost the seat to another Piang son in 1940.[17]

Like the Americans before them, the Japanese occupation authorities came looking for important families through whom they could control a people they did not understand.[18] They duly appointed Sinsuat's son, Duma, and a son of Piang to the Assembly. At the same time, both families had members in the resistance. While the Japanese controlled the delta and a few interior centers, the hinterland reverted to a situation similar to that obtaining around the turn of the century in which local leaders controlled their domains with armed retainers. Some of these supported the Japanese; others, including some Christian immigrants, were guerrillas, nominally under U.S. Army command but in practice independent for much of the time.

The representation of important families in both camps should not be interpreted as division. Some families claim to have arranged matters this way in order to hedge their bets, and it is clear that there was contact across the lines. In the process a few lost their lives at the hands of the Japanese but no one suffered unduly for collaboration after the return of American forces.

Electoral Politics Under the Republic

With the inauguration of the Republic of the Philippines in 1946, political office assumed greater importance than it had under colonial rule. The rewards and powers of a congressional seat were considerable, and increased as national politics took shape, but even the mayor of a small, rural municipality had government funds to spend, jobs to allocate, police to command, and the courtship of big politicians at election time. Incumbents tended to be powers in their own right and to turn their offices into personal fiefs, so that, for example, the municipal police came to resemble a personal retinue, even a bodyguard. It was common also for mayors to act as informal arbitrators, even in matters such as murder, providing a

TABLE 1 : **Winners and Principal Contestants in Elections for Congressman and Governor of Cotabato and North Cotabato, 1946-71**

Date	Contest	Winner	Other Candidates
1946	Congress	Gumbay Piang	Duma Sinsuat, *J. Kimpo*
1949	Congress	Blah Sinsuat	Ugtog Matalam, Gumbay Piang
1953	Congress	Luminog Mangilen	Mando Sinsuat, Blah Sinsuat
1955	Governor	Ugtog Matalam	Duma Sinsuat, *P. Guagas*
1957	Congress	Salipada Pendatun	*Gil Gadi,* Duma Sinsuat
1959	Governor	Ugtog Matalam	*P. Rosete,* B. Lidasan
1961	Congress	Salipada Pendatun	*H. Pedro,* Blah Sinsuat
1963	Governor	Ugtog Matalam	*Gil Gadi*
1965	Congress	Salipada Pendatun	*M. Sucadito*
1967*	Governor	Salipada Pendatun	A. Sangki (Ampatuan)
1969*	Congress	Salipada Pendatun	Blah Sinsuat
1971*	Governor	*Carlos Cajelo*	Simeon Datumanong

Note: Names in italics are Christian; names in roman are Muslim.
* Indicates elections for North Cotabato, after the subdivision of the old province.

cheaper, and quicker, alternative to the courts. If the offending party was unable to pay the compensation, he might enter the mayor's service, much as debt slaves had done in earlier times.

In the frontier province of Cotabato (which at that time included the present provinces of North and South Cotabato, Maguindanao, and Sultan Kudarat) political office acquired added importance in a context of rapid, if unorganized and sometimes disorderly, development. Lightly populated, with wide arable and grazing lands, and valuable stands of timber in the uplands, it attracted an ever-increasing flow of Christian settlers, particularly from the overpopulated Visayas, until by 1970 all the accessible land had been taken up. The production of rice, corn, coconuts, cattle, and lumber rose steadily, with a corresponding increase in the service sector and the emergence of Cotabato City as a major center. Since much of the land had been classified as virgin, its allocation was a government responsibility but the process proved more political than bureaucratic. The same was true for timber concessions. Legal occupation of land was often effected at the expense of traditional occupants and squatters whose violent resistance provided loggers and *hacenderos* with a reason to maintain armed guards. The increasing traffic of people and produce through the interior gave rise to banditry. However, although the bandits were often displaced peasants, they were sometimes protected by politicians, and in some places bandits, police, and armed retainers were hard to distinguish. Under such conditions, politics became so intertwined with economics and security that no one could afford to stay out of it. Soon everyone was taking a hand, if not as a candidate then as the controller of a block of votes, or as a simple follower.

In the emerging multiethnic society, the Chinese maintained control over the rice and corn trade and over much of the general retailing in Cotabato City.[19] But, being barred from politics, their participation in that realm was confined to backing candidates. Christians predominated in banks, national and international companies, and the professions, while gaining an ever-increasing representation in primary production. Maguindanaon, while slowly gaining a foothold in the legal professions, were concentrated in the rural sector. Most remained small holders or tenants, often producing little beyond what they needed to subsist.[20] But there were numbers of progressive, middle-sized farmers, and some big owners who, as they prospered, diversified their interests in rice and corn, cattle, coconuts, logging, and transportation. The big Christian owners followed a similar strategy with the result that, although there was pervasive conflict over land and concessions, there were no lobbies around particular industries.

Until the upheavals of 1971, Cotabato saw little in the way of agrarian conflict. Although Maguindanaon peasants were steadily displaced by Christian settlers, they tended to move to the frontier, and seemed to believe that new land was still available for some time after this ceased to be the case. Local conflicts erupted from time to time but the datus usually defused them, and so maintained good relations with Christian allies. According to some accounts, they tended to favor the Christians, regarding the incoming settlers as better and more progressive farmers than the Maguindanaon peasantry.

In politics, however, the Christians remained the junior partners until the elections of 1971. Though some ran for high office, Maguindanaon not only retained the congressional seat but provided all the main challengers. In the governorship, similarly, the principal candidates were always Maguindanaon, running with Christian vice-gubernatorial candidates. Evidently Maguindanaon politicians had certain advantages over the Christians, for they maintained control over the principal offices for some time even after they were outnumbered in the electorate.[21] Among their own people they could activate widely ramifying kinship and friendship networks as well as traditional loyalties among the lower orders. Their approach to the Christians was more likely to be instrumental. By contrast, the settlers' kinship networks were truncated due to emigration, and, while the Maguindanaon politicians usually spoke English and one or more Filipino languages, few of the Christians could speak Maguindanaon, and their attitude to the "Moros" was characterized more by fear than by understanding. Thus, when Muslims voted for Christian candidates, it was at the behest of their own leaders rather than as a result of direct contact. As they were manifestly less effective in the field, Christian politicians also were less attractive to the national parties.

The Maguindanaon politicians could not maintain their ascendancy indefinitely, however. In 1965 the province and congressional district of North Cotabato, where most Maguindanaon lived, was separated from South Cotabato, which had a preponderance of Christians. The latter elected Christians in the next election, while the former returned the Muslim incumbents. By 1970, the Maguindanaon were outnumbered even in their own heartland, and it seems likely that the fighting between Muslims and Christians that erupted in 1971 was as much the result of political as of agrarian rivalries.[22]

National office effectively removed a politician from his constituency, particularly when the constituency was as remote from Manila as was Cotabato. Thus Salipada Pendatun, who served a term in the postwar Senate and sat in Congress from 1957 to 1972, spent most of his time in the capital and eventually married into a Manila family.[23] Although he retained a house in Cotabato City and land in the interior, he had to rely on local leaders for the organization of support. His sister's husband, who was governor for much of the period, was a critical ally. These leaders might keep a house in the city, but their bailiwicks were in the countryside. Here they occupied large concrete houses, surrounded by high walls, topped with barbed wire, and guarded by armed men. Round about lived their kinsmen, tenants, laborers, and henchmen.

Cotabato turned violent during the 1950s and politicians began to go about with armed bodyguards. The more prominent also retained a hundred or more men, equipped with modern firearms and transported by jeeps. These private armies were never deployed in serious engagements but were brought out for purposes of intimidation and for displays of prepotency. On one occasion, the house of the incumbent congressman in Cotabato City was blockaded by the men of his rival, though no shot was fired. On another occasion, the appearance of two armed bands around the provincial court brought about the indefinite adjournment of a legal dispute between two powerful leaders. In elections armed men might be used to protect friendly precincts, to intimidate voters elsewhere, or to capture a precinct loyal to a rival with a view to scattering voters and forging the ballots. Some politicians acquired, perhaps even cultivated, a murderous reputation but in fact the few assassinations that occurred during this period were ambushes with the assailants unidentified.

A few municipalities were so well controlled that elections went uncontested but most contained a number of factions and coalitions of varying importance, which either challenged the incumbent mayor or waited to be wooed. Certainly no person or family could control a whole province or congressional constituency unaided. Candidates had to gather their support piecemeal, among great electors, local *caciques*, vote jobbers, village leaders, and family heads. This they accomplished by mobilizing kinship ties, promising to use influence in government, and offering direct financial inducements.

The bargaining and double dealing that accompanied such transactions, combined with the relative scarcity of money, was conducive to the use of violence, on the one hand, and to the exploitation of personal ties on the other. The means of coercion must, in the nature of things, be concentrated but personal connections were more useful when dispersed. At home a kinsman was likely to be either a dependent with no followers or a competitor for economic and political rewards. Established elsewhere, in his own bailiwick, perhaps running a plantation, a logging concession, or a smuggling operation, with votes under his control, the same relative could be a valuable ally. In the frontier conditions that characterized Cotabato during these years, the more enterprising members of a family usually took up new lands on their own account rather than relying on patrimony. The political family, then, typically consisted of a number of independently based kinsmen, and perhaps affines, who combined their resources to secure an office for one of their number.

It is not my intention to write a comprehensive electoral history of Cotabato: the region is too vast and heterogeneous. Though the electorate was a mere 34,478 in 1946, it approached a quarter of a million by the mid-1960s. Instead I shall outline the careers of the Maguindanaon candidates and their families who contested gubernatorial and congressional office during the period 1946–71 (see Table 1). I shall then focus on a municipality, the politics of which were largely monopolized by a single family.

Piangs, Sinsuats, and the M-P-M Alliance

The first postwar congressional election in Cotabato saw the revival of prewar rivalries, with a son of the now deceased Datu Piang defeating Duma, the son of Datu Sinsuat. Duma, however, was a supporter of the incoming President Roxas, who appointed him to the governorship, which he already had held under the Japanese.[24] In the 1949 gubernatorial election, Duma's half-brother, Blah Sinsuat, defeated the Piang incumbent, who died soon after. With this death, which had been preceded by the deaths of the other three politically active brothers, the Piangs fell into disarray and never again bid for office outside their home municipality.

In the 1953 congressional contest, Blah Sinsuat lost office to Luminog Mangilen, heading an alliance based in the Upper Valley and known as M-P-M, after its principal members, Matalam, Pendatun and Mangilen himself. Pendatun, whose career was to continue into the 1980s, could claim noble descent but he had been born in poor circumstances and owed his education to an American schoolteacher. With Duma Sinsuat and one of the Piangs, he was among the first Maguindanaon attorneys. Before the outbreak of war he had secured election to the Provincial Board but it was as a guerrilla leader during the Japanese occupation that he acquired the national reputation that got him into the postwar Senate.[25] During the same period he made wide-ranging connections, which served him well in his political career. Pendatun was supported by a brother who was mayor of the home municipality, in which he had acquired a great deal of land, and by his sister's husband, Ugtog Matalam. The latter was also the son of a titled family but economically and politically speaking he was a self-made man who had achieved sufficient prominence as a guerrilla to be appointed governor in the period between the end of the war and the proclamation of the Republic. He had failed in a bid for the congressional seat in 1949 but regained the governorship in the elections of 1955. In the meantime, however, it was Luminog Mangilen who ran for and won the congressional seat. Another guerrilla leader, he had placed both Christians and Muslims in his debt by supplying them with rice captured from the Japanese. In the postwar period he had prospered and become well known, transporting immigrants into and produce out of the interior. His brother, Samat, looked after his bailiwick by occupying the position of mayor.

M-P-M scored another victory in 1955, when Ugtog Matalam defeated Duma Sinsuat in the first election for governor, winning three more contests against various opponents (see Table 1). With the death of Mangilen, Pendatun, now out of the Senate, secured the congressional seat against Duma Sinsuat in 1957, and against Blah Sinsuat in 1961. He defeated Blah again in the bitter elections of 1969. However, becoming unsure of his hold over an increasingly Christian constituency, he had previously persuaded Matalam to stand aside in his favor for the gubernatorial elections. His principal opponent in this election was the leader of the Ampatuan family, till then supporters of Matalam, but assuming increasing importance in two Upper Valley municipalities. Pendatun chose as his running mate a young attorney, Simeon Datumanong, whose mother was an Ampatuan and whose kin crossed party lines to vote for him. When, despite his fears, Pendatun won the congressional seat in 1969, Datumanong became governor, though he lost the position to a Christian in the elections of 1971.

The Sinsuat family, which had been influential in the Lower Valley since the 1880s, remained a force throughout the period of electoral democracy, notwithstanding repeated defeats, which were due largely to internal rivalries (see Sinsuat genealogy). Its base was the large rural municipality of Dinaig, which has always remained under family control. However, the Sinsuats also had sufficient representation in Cotabato City to secure the election of Mando, half-brother to Duma and Blah, as mayor. In 1949, with Blah in Congress, Duma in the provincial capital, Mando as mayor of Cotabato, and another brother, Udin, as mayor of Dinaig, the Sinsuats reached their zenith. By 1953, however, Mando was competing with Blah for the congressional seat with the support of Udin and 70 percent of the Dinaig vote.[26] Blah could count only on the voters living on and around his plantation on the coast and in sections of the city. Being a man of considerable means, however, he was able to assemble a sizable, if insufficient, vote from among Christians and nonrelatives.

Duma Sinsuat reunited the family for the gubernatorial elections of 1957, though without success. But after the second defeat the incoming administration appointed him to an important position in Manila, where he remained until his death in 1979. Blah Sinsuat again ran for Congress in 1961 but once more he failed to win the support of his powerful brothers. He did, however, secure the division of Dinaig municipality, and the mayorship of the new municipality, Upi, went to his son Puti. In 1965, a younger brother, Mama, ran against Mando for the Cotabato City mayorship but the resulting split vote allowed the position to pass to a Christian. Although Mama was subsequently appointed Commissioner for National Integration, the Sinsuats had reached their lowest point in Cotabato. Perhaps this is what persuaded them to unite behind Blah in a bid for Congress in 1969.

Despite their reconciliation, the Nacionalista Sinsuats lost the congressional election to the Liberal Pendatun, though the vote was so close, and the fraud so widespread, that the result was contested in the courts for months. Duma Sinsuat was among those elected to the Constitutional Convention but this contest had attracted mainly untried aspirants. In 1971, President Marcos backed the nomination of a Christian, Carlos Cajelo, as Nacionalista candidate in the gubernatorial race against the incumbent, Datumanong, who had the Liberal nomination. The Sinsuats confined their activities to defending their two municipalities and attempting to regain the mayorship of Cotabato (by now a city). Given the overwhelming predominance of Christians there, they found it politic to field Blah's Christian wife but they made it clear that she was the family candidate by appearing with her on the platform at a rally in the plaza.

By the time of the election, widespread fighting between Christian and Muslim irregulars, and the partial interventions of the Philippine armed forces, resulted in both the displacement of Maguindanaon voters and the immobilization of the armed men of Maguindanaon politicians. As a result, Cajelo won the governorship, displacing Datumanong, and Christians displaced many Muslim mayors. Reversing previous practice, people voted along communal lines, disregarding party slates. The Sinsuats also failed to regain the Cotabato mayorship, although they retained their two municipalities.

Sultan Kudarat Municipality

Sultan Kudarat is a large, relatively progressive municipality, situated across the river from Cotabato City, and extending down to the seashore. Traditionally the seat of the sultans of Maguindanao, it has always been dominated by descendants of the royal line, although the family did not enter the wider political arena until the 1970s (see Mastura genealogy).

The sultanate had ceased to be a political force by the middle of the nineteenth century, and Spain effectively determined who held the title. Although Sultan Mangigin moved elsewhere to avoid the wars at the turn of the century, upon his death the title returned to the traditional seat, and to the main descent line, in the person of Sultan Mastura. After Mastura's death in 1928, the succession

The Sinsuat Family: A Political Genealogy

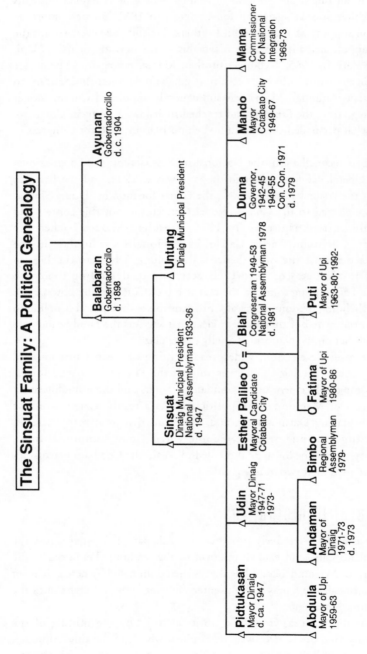

Ayunan
Gobernadorcillo
d. c. 1904

Balabaran
Gobernadorcillo
d. 1898

Untung
Dinaig Municipal President

Sinsuat
Dinaig Municipal President
National Assemblyman 1933-36
d. 1947

Mama
Commissioner
for National
Integration
1969-73

Mando
Mayor
Cotabato City
1949-67

Duma
Governor,
1942-45
1949-55
Con. Con. 1971
d. 1979

Blah
Congressman 1949-53
National Assemblyman 1978
d. 1981

Esther Palileo O
Mayoral Candidate
Cotabato City

Puti
Mayor of Upi
1963-80; 1992-

Fatima O
Mayor of Upi
1980-86

Pidtukasan
Mayor Dinaig
d. ca. 1947

Udin
Mayor Dinaig
1947-71
1973-

Bimbo
Regional
Assemblyman
1979-

Andaman
Mayor of
Dinaig
1971-73
d. 1973

Abdulla
Mayor of Upi
1959-63

Key: The chart shows only patrilineal ties. Marriages (numerous in the earlier generation) are not indicated except when politically significant. Male descendents are indicated by a triangle; females by a circle; marriage by an equal sign.

Descendants of Mastura, Sultan of Maguindanao

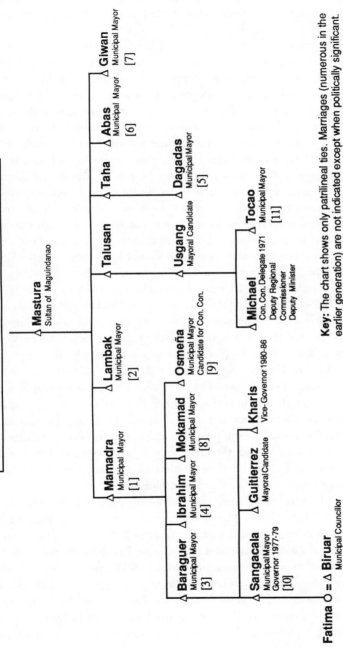

Key: The chart shows only patrilineal ties. Marriages (numerous in the earlier generation) are not indicated except when politically significant. Male descendants are indicated by a triangle; females by a circle; marriage by an equal sign.

Bracketed number indicates the order of succession to the mayorship of the municipality of Sultan Kudarat under U.S., Japanese, and Philippine administrations.

was disputed, and the descendant of Mangigin who claimed the title also chose to live elsewhere. Meanwhile, the descendants of Mastura remained dominant in what is now Sultan Kuderat municipality.

Sultan Mastura had numerous wives, and his descendants must now exceed three hundred, though not all of them remain within the bounds of the municipality. The American authorities appointed his eldest son, Mamadra, the first mayor. He was succeeded by a brother, and later by a son. As the Mastura genealogy shows, even after the office became elective it remained with the sultan's descendants. Prior to the war there seems to have been little in the way of competition for the position, perhaps because the rewards were few. In the 1950s, however, the incumbent was challenged both within the family and outside it. In 1951, Osmeña, son of Mastura's eldest son, Mamadra, succeeded despite a challenge from Osman, the head of a commoner family that was becoming wealthy in another part of the municipality. In 1955, he faced a double challenge from a first cousin, Talusan, and his elder brother's son, Sangacala. Although the family monopoly was not at risk because all three candidates were descendants of the sultan, Osmeña won not by reuniting the family but by making a deal with the outsider Osman. In 1959, Osmeña was defeated by his nephew, Sangacala, who held the position until President Marcos appointed him governor in 1977.

In the 1963 election, Sangacala's unsuccessful challenger was Osman's nephew but in 1967 he faced his own brother, Guitierrez, who with some of his other brothers decided that it was time for the spoils of office to be shared. Although Sangacala prevailed, Guitierrez resumed his challenge in 1971. As an attorney and a former district judge, he could claim professional status but he lacked financial resources of his own. The three brothers who supported him each had married into small communities, where their rank and their outside connections gave them ascendancy and some economic advantage. He also moved among his other kinsmen, making promises and exploiting dissatisfaction. His largest gain came from a deal with the Osman family whereby he took one of their number as his vice-mayoral candidate and undertook to support the establishment of their part of the municipality as a separate administrative unit.

Sangacala defeated his brother easily, drawing upon a wide repertoire of connections in which his family played but a minor part. Having acquired land during his years in office, he could mobilize laborers and tenants. The owners of businesses that had enjoyed his protection during his thirteen years in office delivered the votes of their workers and undertook to find positions, often nominal, for protégés who then busied themselves mustering the support of kith and kin. Two vice-mayoral candidates promised to deliver their personal followings in the hope of securing his support, as did several councilors, though Sangacala evaded a final commitment to either of them, and the results indicate that last-minute reneging occurred on both sides.

Among the family, Sangacala had the support of his father, Baraguer; his father's brother and former rival, Osmeña; several brothers; and another paternal uncle who controlled a small labor union. Tocao, a second cousin and great-grandson of Mastura, also campaigned on his behalf, for which he was later rewarded with the job of municipal secretary. Finally, through his wife and his wife's brother, who was a business associate, he gained access to another parcel of votes.

Political Families Under Martial Law

Fighting between Muslim and Christian irregulars began early in 1971. According to some Muslims, President Marcos backed the Christians as a means of repaying an old score against Congressman Pendatun. There was widespread complaint that the Philippine armed forces were shielding Christian elements and dispersing the Muslims. (The Nacionalista candidate for governor, Carlos Cajelo, was himself a member of the Philippine Constabulary and was associated with the Christian forces.) As early as 1968, former governor Ugtog Matalam had announced the formation of a Mindanao Independence Movement. About this time word spread that what later became known as the Moro National Liberation Front was training outside the country.[27]

By the time of the elections of November 1971, many voters had been displaced and the private armies of the Maguindanaon politicians had been neutralized. As a result, Christian candidates won the governorship and five mayorships from Muslim incumbents. As usual, the two parties had included both Muslims and Christians on their slates but, while the Sinsuats delivered Muslim votes to the Christian gubernatorial candidate, the majority voted along religious rather than party lines.

For some years Maguindanaon peasants had been fighting a rear-guard action against Christian encroachment. Maguindanaon politicians had largely ignored the fact, being more concerned with maintaining good relations with Christian voters. The 1971 election made it clear that this game was over. The politician, too, would be fighting a rear-guard action; Pendatun, in particular, had no prospect of retaining his congressional seat.

In 1972, the Moro National Liberation Front declared a war of secession. Its Cotabato forces reached the outskirts of the city the following year, after which the army drove it back into the marshes and mountains of the interior. Since that time, Cotabato has had a large military presence, albeit one never fully in control of the hinterland.

With the support of the armed forces, President Marcos declared martial law in 1972, dissolving Congress and postponing indefinitely the congressional and presidential elections that would have been held in 1973. The offices of governor and mayor were retained but with reduced powers. Incumbents now held their positions at the president's pleasure, which essentially meant that his personal advisors, including the military, had considerable influence in the matter.

Several of the old Maguindanaon leaders threw in their lot with the rebels during the first months. The government made surrender easy, however, and as the army reasserted itself most accepted this option. Congressman Pendatun went to the United States, and then to Saudi Arabia, while former governor Matalam retired to his estates in the Upper Valley. The government then set about subdividing Cotabato into new provinces, arranging the boundaries in such a way that Muslims constituted a majority in only one of them. The mayor of Sultan Kudarat municipality, Sangacala Baraguer, served as governor of the new province, called Maguindanao, but for reasons that were never made public he was dismissed in 1978. He is believed to have fallen out with the local military authorities. The position then passed to Sandiale Sambolawan, who did not belong to an established political family but had been one of the most popular candidates in the elections for the Constitutional Convention in 1970.

Sangacala owed his initial advancement not just to his experience as mayor of a large municipality but to his descent from the old sultan. When the new province was announced, a party of Sultan Mastura's descendants waited upon President Marcos and presented him with a family heirloom; it was presumed that Sangacala's subsequent appointment was in recognition of the family's importance. However, this left the problem of who would succeed him in the mayor's position. Sangacala proposed his son-in-law who, having no base of his own, could be expected to remain under his influence. Other members of the family objected to the office going to an outsider, however, and it passed instead to Tocao Mastura, a great-grandson of the sultan who had briefly served as municipal secretary and recently had surrendered from the MNLF. Tocao's cause was no doubt furthered by his brother, Michael, an attorney who had begun his career with election to the Constitutional Convention in 1972, and was shortly to take up an important executive position in the newly constituted regional administration.

Ironically, Sangacala's brief advancement opened the door to this previously unimportant branch of Sultan Mastura's lineage, and when he fell from grace the balance shifted decisively. Sangacala fought back but, despite several ambushes, Tocao succeeded in holding the mayorship from which position he was able to undermine Sangacala's supporters.

In 1978, Marcos announced elections for the Interim Batasang Pambansa (IBP), or National Assembly. Although the process took the form of an election, the odds were usually in favor of the president's KBL Party, so that the real contest occurred over the nomination, which this time went to Blah Sinsuat. In 1979, Marcos announced additional elections, this time for a new Regional Assembly, a body purportedly established to meet rebel demands for regional autonomy. Although a number of outsiders put their names forward, there was a general expectation that the KBL would select the four candidates allocated to Maguindanao Province from among the leading families, leaving the families to decide which of their number it should be. Not all of them were able to agree.

Two names were mooted among the Ampatuans but most of them finally agreed to unite behind former governor Datumanong whom the president had already appointed as regional commissioner. The Sinsuats failed to meet, and sons of brothers Udin and Mando, together with a daughter of Blah, all announced their candidacies. It was left to the president, presumably on local advice, to appoint Udin's son, Bimbo Sinsuat. Since the latter was only twenty-two, and inexperienced, one can presume that this gesture was in recognition of his father's control of a large municipality on the edge of the rebel domain. At the same time, Marcos fulfilled his obligation to the family as a whole.

Descendants of the old sultan (formally headed by the only surviving son, Giwan, but mainly identified with Michael and Tocao) proposed Guitierrez, Sangacala's brother and former rival. Guitierrez withdrew when Sangacala announced his own candidacy but, since the latter was still out of favor, he failed to win the KBL nomination and his success running as an independent was predictably meager.

The third KBL nomination went to the son of an up-country mayor, who had scored well as an oppositionist in the 1978 contest and whose territory also abutted the rebel domain. The fourth position was supposed to have been reserved for a nominee of the MNLF but since they declined to cooperate it passed to a "rebel returnee," a son of the old governor, Ugtog Matalam. Since the voting was exquisitely organized,[28] all the KBL nominees secured election to a body whose principal function was to provide recognition for political reputations in the region.

Encouraged by the success of these "elections," the government announced provincial and municipal contests for 1980. This time so many old names reemerged that it must have seemed like the old days. Former governor Sangacala ran for the governorship with a son of Ugtog Matalam as his running mate. A resuscitated Nacionalista Party, chaired by Mama Sinsuat (half-brother to Udin, Blah, and Duma), nominated a dissident member of the Ampatuan family for governor and slated Mama's brother, Mando Sinsuat, to run for the mayorship of Cotabato City, a post he had held from 1949 to 1967. (Mama, it will be remembered, had earlier run against his brother for this position and had been responsible for his losing it.) The bid for the mayoralty failed, however, and the governorship went to the incumbent, Sambolawan, who had secured the KBL nomination.

Sambolawan's running mate for vice-governor was Kharis, a brother of Sangacala, who had aligned himself with the Giwan-Michael-Tocao branch of the family. While his nomination highlighted the increasing importance of this group in the official party, their strategy was to try to include the two principal branches of the family while isolating the still-hostile Sangacala. Michael's appointment as deputy minister of Islamic affairs in 1981 represented a further advance.

In 1984, President Marcos announced further congressional elections, giving the Maguindanao nominations to Regional Commissioner Simeon Datumanong and to the incumbent, Blah Sinsuat. Unexpectedly, Blah's old rival, Salipada Pendatun, made a bid for the KBL nomination, although he was not a member of the party. Blah's sudden death gave the president an opportunity to bring his old enemy, Pendatun, into the fold but Pendatun, too, died in a car accident a few months later. Since former governors Duma Sinsuat and Ugtog Matalam also had died a few years before, Pendatun's death marked the passing of the political generation that had emerged in the 1940s.

Although a formidable figure in his own right, Pendatun had left no political heir: his children had never lived in Cotabato and they did not attempt political careers. Among the Sinsuats, two or three of the next generation made bids for minor office but they had no success outside their two municipalities and the Regional Assembly. However, one of the winners in the congressional elections held under the Aquino presidency was Gimi Matalam, son of the old governor, Ugtog. The other successful candidate was Michael Mastura.

Conclusion

The foregoing account of Maguindanaon politics has assumed that family constitutes a significant structural and organizational factor in it. However, it must be noted that the Christian politicians in the region became increasingly powerful without the benefit of family.[29] But, while migration tended to fragment family groupings, ethno-linguistic affiliation and town of origin in the long term provided an alternative framework for mobilization.[30] Even among the Maguindanaon, family was only one element in a heterogeneous complex of political forms. Indeed, Blah Sinsuat's lone campaigns against fraternal opposition demonstrate that one could make a good showing without family support if one had money, Manila connections, and political skills.[31] Nonetheless, a survey of congressional election results from the 1940s on suggests that family was a factor of declining importance. In the early years, the vote was distributed fairly evenly among four or more candidates, so that the winner needed only a plurality—in several instances no more than one-third of the vote—a substantial part of which might be mobilized by his family if they were influential and strategically situated. Later, as the electorate increased in numbers and heterogeneity, the costs of campaigning rose, a tendency aggravated by the nationwide escalation of election spending.[32] This reduced the number of serious contenders, often to just two, one of whom must gain a majority. Congressional elections, since they coincided with presidential races, became increasingly linked to national politics. Here national connections were likely to be as important as local standing. In this respect Salipada Pendatun, with his twenty-five years in national politics, was at a considerable advantage. Emerging as much as a result of his own achievements as of his family connections, he must be regarded as one of Machado's professional politicians.

The fact remains that most Maguindanaon politicians were members of family coalitions, and that the public viewed them as such, even when they were divided. Kinship and lineage were central elements in the precolonial social structure, and they persisted both as cultural codes and in the persons of such long-established families as the Sinsuats and the Masturas. As I suggested at the outset, the explanation for this survival seems to be the lack of other bases for differentiation, factors such as ideology, class, or sectional interest. Although this pattern could be observed in much of the Philippines between 1946 and 1972, it particularly held true for the Maguindanaon, whose frontier situation gave rise to a generalized economic elite, active in diverse areas. And, with the opening of so many economic opportunities, politics assumed unusual importance. Finally, class conflict was muted, first by a strong tradition of hierarchy—whether traditional or parvenue—and later by the land-based conflict between indigenous and settler populations, which was defined in religious terms.

The frontier situation also favored the political family in the sense that it enabled the more ambitious members to disperse and establish independent bases. This both reduced the likelihood of competition over resources and created the possibility of broadly based, family alliances that would prove attractive to national parties and politicians. The Sinsuats, spread throughout their vast home municipality and with considerable influence in Cotabato City, constituted a formidable coalition in the postwar period. Their decline was due to an inability to contain internal rivalry. The Ampatuans likewise had dispersed over three Upper Valley municipalities, and, although rivalry over the control of one of them resulted in an intrafamily shoot-out, they managed to remain unified for several provincial-level contests. The sultan's descendants, by contrast, were almost all resident in one municipality, many in one *barrio*, and they agreed only on the necessity of keeping outsiders out of office. In fact, power became the monopoly of one branch, with the others eventually reduced to supporting roles.

With the declaration of martial law and the consequent centralization of power, the importance of the family as a political coalition declined further. However, it did remain a means of articulating national and local levels of political life. While nationally the Marcos regime produced major social as well as political and economic changes, these have been more apparent in Manila than in the provinces, and occurred more in industry than in primary production. Moreover, in war-torn Cotabato, economic change took second place to the issue of reaching a settlement with the Muslim insurgency. Many old families, deprived of their armed followers, and forced either by the army or the insurgents to abandon their bailiwicks, lost control of their people in the countryside. And yet they remained the only effective link with the people, including the insurgents, and so remained important to the government, which courted them accordingly. When Marcos resumed elections under international pressure, the need to secure high numbers of votes for himself and his nominees brought the family coalitions back into prominence. They were thus in a state of preparation when unorchestrated elections resumed under the Aquino presidency.

The Maguindanaon elite, having suffered considerable losses as a result of the fighting, were eager for government jobs and assistance. Unfortunately there was never enough to satisfy everyone. Here the administration followed the practice of other influential people, who, when constantly badgered for recommendations and patronage, deem a favor to an individual a favor to the whole family, thus protecting themselves against further claims from this quarter. This principle was clearly at work in the distribution of official nominations for the Regional Assembly in 1979. Other family members might have found little joy in this arrangement but there was nothing they could do about it short of joining the rebels. Defecting to another family was unlikely to make a difference, since that group would be suffering the same problems. Thus, even when the family was not functioning as a coalition it remained an aggregation in the distribution of rewards, a way of breaking a mass into more manageable parts. As such it continued to provide its members with better-than-average life chances, the prestige of connections, and a name that was known.

The definitions of the family are not fixed, as I indicated above, but respond to demographic change and the pressure of internal competition. The old hereditary titles fell into disuse with the sultanate before the Japanese occupation. Most members of title-owning families then resorted to the commoner practice of taking the father's given name after one's own, so that Ali, son of Karim, was known as Ali Karim, and his son would take Ali as his surname. Others followed the Christian practice of patronymics. In the absence of a norm, choice of surname may be an indicator of relations within the family. Thus, during their heyday, all of Sinsuat's sons' children carried his name and some of his daughters' children did also.[33] By contrast, the descendants of Sultan Mastura bore various surnames. The branch that was dominant during the first half of the century carries the name of his eldest son, Mamadra, with the exception of Sangacala and his brothers. These, when they began to monopolize power, assumed their father's name (Baraguer) as did their children. Michael and Tocao, as they began their political careers, resumed Mastura as their surname. This practice later provided them with a rhetorical basis for claiming leadership of the entire family. On the other hand, regardless of an individual's choice of surname, people tended to refer to him or her as a Mastura, a Sinsuat, or an Ampatuan if it was the wider aggregation they had in mind.

Like the old titles, famous patronymics commemorate a family's continuity in political life and so provide a kind of legitimation. But, while members, and perhaps their long-standing associates, may be inspired by the born-to-rule mystique, for society at large such status stands relative to parallel claims made by other families. The traditional system of nobility based on claims of descent from the Prophet Mohammed provided a means of differentiation among such families, and also helped legitimate the political structure. So far as we can tell from the indigenous and foreign records, power and nobility coincided quite closely until the late Spanish period. There are now only vestiges of the traditional order but politicians who can claim noble descent still do so, while those on the way up try to get access to the royal genealogies in the hope of finding a connection.[34] Others pay the high bride-price required to obtain a wife who can transmit nobility to their children. But, whether or not they are strictly entitled to do so, Maguindanaon politicians usually adopt and are accorded the honorific *datu*. This practice can be understood as an attempt to tap the old sources of traditional legitimation in a setting in which new forms have failed to develop. Today, however, tradition is no longer beyond criticism. Some Maguindanaon professionals of humbler origin have demanded a place in politics for the "middle class," while educated social critics have called for an end to what they call "*datuism*," referring as much to entrenched political families as to the true nobility. The insurgent forces have attempted to maintain Islamic law, in the areas under their control, in place of the *adat* (customary law) that protects datu privilege.[35]

The ideals of the Muslim insurgents could provide a basis for a new, more ideological kind of politics. Figures such as Blah Sinsuat, Ugtog Matalam, and Salipada Pendatun were more or less devout Muslims but, having to appeal to Christian voters, they could not make too much of the fact. The younger generation of politicians depends on an overwhelmingly Muslim constituency. Congressman Mastura has been actively engaged in the instituting of Shariah law and other issues connected with the negotiations for some kind of regional autonomy. There is also talk of establishing a religious party, which would reflect religious revival within the region and in the Islamic world at large. It remains to be seen whether Cotabato's political families, which have endured the changes of the last century, will survive this new challenge.

N OTES

The research upon which this paper is based was funded by the University of Sydney and the Myer Foundation. Local sponsorship was provided by the National Museum in 1971 and the Institute of Philippine Culture, Ateneo de Manila University, in 1973 and 1979. The writer is indebted to Brian Fegan, Edward Hansen, Alfred McCoy, Corocoy Moson and Michael Mastura for their comments on earlier drafts. They are, of course, in no way responsible for what appears here.

The writer spent some twelve months in Cotabato, mainly in the second half of 1971 and the first half of 1979, with short visits in 1973 and 1976. The first visit coincided with the last elections held before the declaration of martial law; the last coincided with the elections for the Regional Assembly. The material presented here is largely drawn from extended discussions with a small circle of friends, all of them with experience at some level of the political process, and shorter formal interviews with some other political figures. My thanks are particularly due to Datu (now congressman) Michael Mastura, former governor Sandiale Sambolawan, Judge Corocoy Moson, Datu (and former mayor) Giwan Mastura, Dr. (now ambassador) Alunan Glang, and the late Nasrullah Glang. Additional data have come from the archives of the Commission on Elections (Comelec) in Manila, and from the pages of the weekly *Mindanao Cross*, which has been published in Cotabato City for more than thirty years.

[1]Dennis Gilbert, "Cognatic Descent Groups in Upper-class Lima (Peru)," *American Ethnologist* 8 (1981): 737–57, 759. See also Linda Lewin, "Some Historical Implications of Kinship Organization for Family-based Politics in the Brazilian Northeast," *Comparative Studies in Society and History* 21 (1979): 262–92.

[2]Kit Machado, "Changing Patterns of Leadership Recruitment and the Emergence of the Professional Politician in Philippine Local Politics," in *Political Change in the Philippines: Studies of Local Politics Preceding Martial Law*, edited by Benedict Kerkvliet (Honolulu: University of Hawaii Press, 1974).

[3]The Maguindanaon are something of an artifact of colonialism, ethnography and the ethnic politics of the Philippine Republic. The group does share a language, albeit with dialect variations, but it takes its name from the sultans who controlled the mouth of the river. It is unlikely that people in the Upper Valley of the Pulang (Tao sa Raya) would have answered to the term before this century. Indeed, many of the people living near the mouth of the river identify themselves as Iranon.

[4]Carl H. Lande, *Leaders, Factions, and Parties: the Structure of Philippine Politics* (New Haven: Yale University, Southeast Asian Program, 1965).

[5]Lande, *Leaders*, 18–20, 25–40.

[6]George M. Foster, "The Dyadic Contract: A Model for the Social Structure of a Mexican Peasant Village," *American Anthropologist* 63 (1961): 1173–92.

[7]Cf. Eric Wolf, "Kinship, Friendship and the Patron-Client Relationship," in *The Social Anthropology of Complex Societies*, edited by M. Banton (London: Tavistock, 1966).

[8]Lande, *Leaders*, 9–11.

[9]Cf. Peter Schneider, Jane Schneider, and Edward Hansen, "Modernization and Development: The Role of Regional Elites and Non-corporate Groups in the European Mediterranean," *Comparative Studies in Society and History* 14 (1972): 328–50.

[10]The history of the sultanate and the Upper Valley rajahs of Buayan has been outlined in Reynaldo Ileto, *Magindanao, 1860–1888: The Career of Datu Uto of Buayan* (Ithaca: Department of Asian Studies, Cornell University, 1971); Cesar Majul, *Muslims in the Philippines* (Quezon City: University of the Philippines Press, 1973); and Ruurdje Laarhoven, *The Magindanao Sultanate in the 17th Century: Triumph of Moro Diplomacy* (Quezon City: New Day, 1989).

[11]For structural analyses of segmentary states in the region, see D. Brown, *The Structure and History of a Bornean Malay State* (Brunei: Brunei Museum Journal, 1970); J. M. Gullick, *Indigenous Systems of Western Malaya* (London: Athlone Press, 1973); and Thomas Kiefer, "The Tausug Polity and the Sultanate of Sulu: A Segmentary State in the Southern Philippines," *Sulu Studies* 1 (1972): 19–64.

[12]See Najeeb Saleeby, *Studies in Moro History, Law and Religion* (Manila: Bureau of Public Printing, 1905).

[13]These genealogies, known as *tarsila*, are written in Arabic script. Some of them have been translated (see Saleeby, *Studies in Moro History*). The genealogy of the sultans of Maguindanao dates from the mid-nineteenth century and is accessible only to the immediate descendants. Genealogies from the Upper Valley have been copied by various hands and are more readily accessible.

[14]See Ileto, *Magindanao*, 46–65.

[15]For an account of the colonial period, see Jeremy Beckett, "The Defiant and the Compliant: The Datus of Magindanao under Colonial Rule," in *Philippine Social History: Global Trade and Local Transformations*, edited by A. W. McCoy and E. C. de Jesus (Sydney and Quezon City: George Allen and Unwin and Ateneo de Manila University Press, 1982), 391–414.

[16]For an account of these figures, see Beckett, *The Defiant and the Compliant*, 401–5. Sinsuat's father and paternal uncle had been significant figures during the Spanish period.

[17]Beckett, *The Defiant and the Compliant*, 404.

[18]Ralph Thomas, "Asia for the Asiatics? Muslim Filipino Responses to Japanese Occupation and Propaganda during World War II," *Asian Forum* 12 (1971): 43–60.

[19]Chester Hunt, "Ethnic Stratification and Integration in Cotabato," *The Philippine Sociology Review* 5 (1957): 13–38.

[20] The rate of tenancy in Cotabato remained low by Philippine standards until 1971 but the estimates are not wholly reliable because many traditional occupants of land paid a share of their harvest to local datus. See Beckett, *The Defiant and the Compliant*, 402–3.

[21] See Hunt, "Ethnic Stratification," 200–201.

[22] For an account of the fighting between Muslim and Christian elements and the subsequent Muslim uprising, see T. J. S. George, *Revolt in Mindanao: The Rise of Islam in Philippine Politics* (Kuala Lumpur: Oxford University Press, 1980).

[23] He previously had been married to a Maguindanaon from the Upper Valley but there were no children.

[24] Before that time, Christians had been appointed to the office.

[25] Edward Haggerty, *Guerilla Padre in Mindanao* (Manila: Bookmark, 1964).

[26] It should be noted that the main rivals were half-brothers, and some Maguindanaon speculated that they were perpetuating the jealousy among co-wives in a large polygynous family.

[27] George, *Revolt in Mindanao*.

[28] Skillful manipulation of the voting process not only insured the "election" of the chosen candidates but also achieved their ranking in a predetermined order. Since Lanao was included in the vote, and there was considerable mistrust between Maranao and Maguindanaon, the achievement was truly remarkable.

[29] There appears to have been a similar lack of political families in occidental Mindoro, another frontier province settled by immigrants from other islands. See Remigio Agpalo, *The Political Elite and the People: A Study of Politics in Occidental Mindoro* (Quezon City: College of Public Administration, University of the Philippines, 1972).

[30] The "magnificent seven" who organized the Ilaga units around 1970 were all Ilongos, as was the Philippine Constabulary colonel, Carlos Cajelo, who won the governorship in 1971.

[31] Good public relations is sometimes mentioned as an essential asset of the gladhanding politician. However, Blah Sinsuat was notably reserved in manner. He was known as the "silent millionaire."

[32] This observation was made by David Wurfel in "The Philippines," *Journal of Politics* 25 (1963): 757–73.

[33] The Sinsuats are also remarkable for the frequency of cousin marriage.

[34] The typical procedure followed in the genealogies (called *tarsila*) is to list a number of sons (and sometimes daughters) of a particular sultan but only the descendants of the one who succeeded him. Descent from one of the others nevertheless entitles one to be called *datu*. Salipada Pendatun kept a genealogy under the glass of the desk in his congressional office.

[35] I refer here both to the Moro National Liberation Front and to the breakaway Moro Islamic Liberation front, the latter of which has commanded a greater following during the last decade.

The Dream Goes On and On:
Three Generations of the Osmeñas,
1906–1990

Resil B. Mojares

One of the most dominant political families in the Philippines is the Osmeñas of Cebu Province in the central Philippines. Except for brief interruptions (1942–44, 1947–51, 1972–86), and despite the challenge posed by rival Cebuano politicians and families (Sotto, Cuenco, Durano), the story of the Osmeñas is one of remarkable success in maintaining political power.

From 1906, when Sergio Osmeña, Sr., won the Cebu governorship, until the present, the Osmeñas have effectively translated local dominance into supralocal power and vice versa. Entrenched in metropolitan Cebu, the premier transport and communications hub of the southern Philippines, as well as the home ground of a large, ethnic Cebuano population (comprising 25 percent of the country's total), they have assumed the role of leading power brokers in the country. With this base, they have gained preeminent roles in the Philippine government. Sergio Osmeña, Sr., was the highest-ranking Filipino official of the land from 1907, when he was elected speaker of the Philippine Assembly, to 1922 when he was eclipsed by Manuel Quezon. Later he served as the country's vice-president from 1935 to 1944 and as president from 1944 to 1946. His son, Sergio, Jr., a senator, was a serious contender for the vice-presidency in 1961 and the presidency in 1969. Cut down by Ferdinand Marcos during the martial-law era (1972–86), the Osmeñas have since reinstalled themselves in power. An Osmeña (Minnie, daughter of Sergio, Jr.) would have been Salvador Laurel's vice-presidential running mate in 1986 had the Aquino-Laurel unification talks collapsed. In the elections that followed Marcos's downfall, another Osmeña (Tomas, brother of Minnie) was elected mayor of Cebu City. Brothers John and Emilio R. Osmeña (grandsons of Sergio, Sr.), a senator and Cebu governor, respectively, were touted as candidates for president or vice-president in 1991.[1]

How does one explain the dominance and durability of one family? The experience of martial rule, the so-called EDSA revolution, and the ascension of Corazon Aquino raised hopes for the prospect of a more democratic form of politics in the post-Marcos era. The fall of some traditionally dominant families, the never-again lessons of authoritarian rule, and the politicization of new sectors of Philippine society pointed towards a more open political system. A spirit of new politics, in the wake of the change of government, found expression in the multiparty and antidynasty provisions of the new Constitution, changes in electoral law, increased private-sector activism, and the widening of what Filipinos call the "democratic space."

The emerging reality, however, is different. The results of the 11 May 1987 elections show that out of 200 congressmen in the House of Representatives, 130 belong to so-called traditional political families while another 39 are relatives of these families. Only 31 have no electoral record prior to 1971 and are not directly related to these old dominant families. Of the 169 congressmen who are members of or are related to dominant families, 102 are identified with the pre-1986, anti-Marcos forces while 67 are from pro-Marcos parties or families.[2] Despite a few nontraditional figures among the 24 elected members of the Senate, the cast is largely made up of persons belonging to prominent, pre-1972, political families.

Asked recently about the dynasty issue, Senator John Osmeña remarked, somewhat disingenuously, "One member of the family who does not do good is one too many, but 10 members in the family doing good are not even enough." Seriously, he added, "The anti-dynastic move runs contrary to the social vein of our society."[3] Governor Emilio (Lito) Osmeña, Jr., has a dismissive response to the same question: "Dynasties are inherited, we are elected."[4]

Many Filipinos would offer a simple explanation for the continuing political dominance of a few old families: "society itself has not changed." In Cebu they would say *nakagamot na* (literally, 'they have taken root') meaning that certain persons or families are rooted, established, and thus have a built-in advantage over the rest. These explanations tend to be reductive, however, when there is a clearer need to inquire into the dynamics of power maintenance in the Philippines.

The Osmeñas are an interesting case study of power maintenance not only because their prominence spans a century but because they do not conform to certain stereotypes about political kingpins, or "warlords," in the Philippines. They do not exercise monopolistic economic control in their bailiwick; they do not maintain "private armies" or engage in a rule of systematic, direct repression; and they are not gladhanding, traditional patrons. Their main base of electoral support—Cebu Province, particularly metropolitan Cebu—is a highly urbanized area with a heterogeneous population, a complex occupational structure, a developed media infrastructure, high levels of literacy, and a large concentration of modern, voluntary organizations.[5]

The Osmeña case, therefore, should shed an interesting light on such concepts of elite dominance as neo-patrimonialism, clientilism, machine politics, and corporatism. These are concepts useful in the analysis of power building. There are pitfalls, however, one of which is the tendency to focus attention on rulers, leaders, and big men; another is a concern for models and typologies based on selected features and variables of a state or system. The first of these directs analysis to the strategies and tactics of big men in building followerships, welding alliances, and deploying rewards and sanctions. Such focus on the power game and power manipulators tends to privilege the role of those who actively participate and it slights the importance of those who are not playing the game, reducing them to the status of passive masses.[6] The second approach slights the scope and variability of social practice. In particular, it undervalues the creativity and effect of the various forms of misparticipation or nonparticipation in the system. Moreover, it does not adequately problematize indicators of political development such as literacy, education, and urbanization.

In the case of the Osmeñas, there is a built-in temptation to focus on the more instrumental, leader-oriented aspects of power building. The political career of the Osmeñas has one dominant theme: their considerable skill in electoral *realpolitik*. They have combined, in fulsome measure, the virtues of Machiavelli's prince and Schumpeter's entrepreneur. Their deeds provide the stuff for manuals on how to win elections and advance a career in Philippine politics. Their story is a story of elections fought and frequently won.

In reading their story one is tempted by an epistemic and political bias: the construction of politics as a narrative of electoral battles. Two recent autobiographies of Cebuano politicians—Congressman Ramon Durano and Mayor Vicente del Rosario—read too much like chronicles of elections, embroidered with testaments of good deeds and acts of "public service" and philanthropy, leading one to suspect that politics-as-electoral-battle is how Filipino politicians themselves construct political reality.[7] Political memoirs and commissioned biographies, persuasive in their claim to be presenting the "official" or "inside" view, generally select and structure events in a way that emphasizes the agency of the subject and centers the leader where events are generated and things "happen."

Questions may be raised at this point. By so attending to the game as played by rulers and politicians, are we not privileging a preconstructed field, thus neglecting and misjudging the degree to which boundaries have shifted or the degree to which the field itself, or its axis, has changed? This underscores the importance of perspective, of taking in the entire field of political practice rather than overemphasizing one aspect of that field (such as elections) or the elements of the field preselected by either a model of analysis or the politician's own construction of political action.

In this paper we shall refrain from detailing how the elections of 1922, or 1951, or 1987, were won—thus avoiding in certain ways a reexploration of the handy truth that former first lady Imelda Marcos herself had occasion to use:

"Some are just smarter than others." Instead we shall attend to the more general problem of ideological domination of which elections are not just field but instrument.

Capturing Politics

Elections were a key institution in the American project of building a democratic structure of government in the Philippines at the turn of the century. The country, however, was not a blank slate. Spain had left behind a system of municipal and village governments manned by Filipinos, and the Revolution had created a Filipino republican government with (in varying degrees of formation) a constitution, executive and legislative bodies, and a network of local governments. More important, a weak and decrepit Spanish colonial state had allowed the flourishing of a native elite that had capitalized on the nineteenth-century transformation of Philippine agriculture, and in the process had accumulated local power. This building of power from the ground up was, in fact, a primary condition of the Philippine Revolution.

When the Americans moved in with their project of political democracy, they faced a native elite wise in the processes of power accumulation. Touched by imperial naiveté, the Americans' realization of this fact was surprisingly slow. Responding to impulses within their own political tradition, the practical imperative of using local intermediaries to govern the colony, as well as pressures from Filipinos, the Americans widened the field of "politics" for the native elite. Having dismantled the leadership of the Malolos Republic, they reorganized municipal governments. From 1901 to 1906 they appointed and then arranged the election of Filipino provincial governors, a position previously reserved for Spaniards. Until 1907 these elections were an elite activity (only municipal councilors cast votes for governor)—a procedure not unfamiliar to members of the propertied elite who had exercised similar, albeit limited, rights under Spain. The difference was that these rights were now exercised for higher stakes as more and higher elective posts were made available to Filipinos. Equally important, particularly for the Osmeñas, with the evolution of countrywide "representative democracy" a premium was now placed on development of a strong local or regional electoral base.[8] This process culminated in 1907 in the creation of a national legislative assembly composed of elected representatives from across the country who gathered to share national policy-making with the American-dominated Philippine Commission. Thus, a new era of "national politics" was inaugurated, one in which local power structures—what Andrew Turton calls the "secondary complex of predatory interests" that constitute so much of the state in transitional societies—have played an important role.[9]

The family's founder, Sergio Osmeña (1878–1961), rose on the crest of these developments. An illegitimate child (see genealogy) of a secondary branch of the rich and prominent Osmeña family of Cebu City, a Chinese-*mestizo* clan with considerable interests in real property, agriculture, and shipping, Osmeña was set on the road to a career in the Spanish colonial service. He studied law at Manila's University of Santo Tomas, worked as a court recorder of the Cebu Audiencia and later as personal aide to the Spanish politico-military governor of Cebu, and wrote journalistic pieces in defense of Spain when the Revolution broke out in Luzon in 1896. By 1898 the winds shifted: the Revolution came to Cebu in April and Admiral Dewey defeated the Spanish fleet in Manila Bay in May. Osmeña waited out the April anti-Spanish hostilities in Cebu City by seeking refuge in a northern provincial town. In 1899 he reemerged as a sympathizer of the Aguinaldo government and an associate of Juan Climaco, the leading *ilustrado* among Cebu's republicans.

By 1900, however, it was clear to Filipino *ilustrados* that American rule had become a reality. Few leaders perceived the opportunities for political advancement in the new order more acutely than Sergio Osmeña, and in the space of a few years he crafted the beginnings of a highly successful political career.[10] Between 1900 and 1906, when he was elected governor, he created a political base in the province by consolidating his position within Cebu's economic elite (in part through his marriage to a daughter of a wealthy Chinese merchant, Nicasio Chiong-Veloso), by building a reputation as a "nationalist" publisher and lawyer, and by skillfully welding a network of alliances with American officials, political groups in Cebu, and Filipino leaders in Manila. With his election to the speakership of the Philippine Assembly in 1907, he became the premier Filipino politician. He was twenty-nine years old. When he retired from public office, in 1946, he had not only served in the country's highest offices but had earned a reputation (still widely held) as the foremost Filipino statesman of all time.

The break in Osmeña dominance of Cebu politics that commenced in 1946 lasted only a few years. In 1951 a new family member emerged upon the scene when Sergio Osmeña, Jr. (1916–1984) was elected governor of Cebu. The twelfth child of Sergio Osmeña and Estefania Chiong-Veloso, Sergio, Jr.—more popularly known as Serging—studied commerce at universities in Manila and New York. He was an established businessman, recently married to Lourdes de la Rama, daughter of a Philippine senator and shipping magnate, when the Japanese invaded the Philippines and forced the elder Osmeña, then vice-president, to evacuate the country with Douglas MacArthur. Left in Manila with other family members, Serging had to fend for himself. In occupied Manila he not only survived but prospered. After an attempt at cashing in on the wartime disruption of transport by organizing a company that used sailboats to ferry passengers from Luzon to the Visayas, he moved into the more lucrative buy-and-sell trade, cultivating contacts in the military administration and providing motor vehicles, machinery, construction materials, and scrap metal to the Japanese. When the Americans returned in 1945, Serging was imprisoned and convicted on charges of economic collaboration, although he was later acquitted on the basis of a technicality. At a time when the Philippine government was anxious to bury the politically sensitive issue of elite collaboration with the Japanese, something of this experience, as well as the defeat of his father in the 1946 presidential elections, must have impelled Serging into active politics. He made a move to run for Congress in 1947, and then withdrew, but in 1951 he launched a masterly campaign that won him the governorship, in the process wresting control of Cebu Province from the Osmeñas' arch-enemy, the Cuenco family. From this point on, he charted a career that had as its goal nothing less than the Philippine presidency.[11] He carefully protected his electoral base (winning five times the mayorship of Cebu City, the center of the vote-rich Second Congressional District) and skillfully combined elective posts (mayor, congressman, senator) for political advantage. He came close to his goal in 1961, when he almost won as an independent candidate for vice-president, and again in 1969 when he lost in a bid for the presidency to Ferdinand Marcos in a fraud-filled election.

The imposition of martial law in 1972 forced the family into political limbo. The Plaza Miranda bombing of 1971 had left Serging Osmeña badly injured.[12] He was out of the country undergoing medical treatment when martial law was declared, and he remained in exile in California until his death in 1984. Other Osmeñas were victimized. Sergio Osmeña III, then perceived as Serging's heir apparent, was arrested in 1972 for alleged complicity in a plot to overthrow the government. He stayed in prison until his dramatic escape to the United States in 1977.[13] John Osmeña, Serging's nephew (then, as now, a senator), also sojourned in the U.S. as an exile after a brief dalliance with the Marcos regime. Emilio Osmeña, Jr. (John's brother) was imprisoned for nine months and held under house arrest for two years. The other children of Serging, including Minnie and Tomas, also spent the martial-law years in the United States. The Osmeña wealth was also affected by martial law: the five-hundred-hectare Hacienda Osmeña in Carcar, Cebu, was appropriated by the government under a land-reform program in 1975, and the government's Public Estate Authority took the multi-million-dollar Cebu North Reclamation Project away from the family-directed Cebu Development Corporation. Only two years after Marcos fell, however, the Osmeñas regained their supremacy in Cebu, putting themselves once more in a position to exercise influence in national politics.

The saga of the Osmeñas shows us not a dynasty in the conventional sense but a family highly skilled in the craft of politics. Sergio Osmeña, Sr., was an outsider to the rich, turn-of-the-century Osmeñas, comprised of the descendants of the first marriage of Chinese-*mestizo* merchant and landowner Severino Osmeña, who died around 1860. He was forced to earn recognition for himself (while at the same time he maneuvered to take control of a large chunk of the Osmeña wealth). He did not encourage his sons to go into electoral politics, although besides Serging two of them dabbled in it. Nicasio sought the Nacionalista Party nomination for Manila mayor in 1951 and made an aborted run for a Cebu congressional seat in 1957; Edilberto ran for Congress and lost in 1953. Two more sons, wittingly or unwittingly drawn into the resistance-collaborationist politics of World War II, were executed by guerrillas for political collaboration with the Japanese (Jose and

Teodoro), and a third was executed by the Japanese for refusing the puppet governorship of Cebu Province (Emilio, Sr.).

Sergio Osmeña's relations with Serging were strained as a result of the collaboration case (the old man refused to use his influence in favor of his son), and because of a dispute between Serging and his stepmother (Esperanza Limjap, Sergio's second wife) over matters of inheritance. The father's attitude toward his son's political career was ambivalent: at times endorsing it, at others openly declaring himself against it. As a result, Serging had to build a career on his own as his father had done. And, though Serging "sponsored" younger members of the family in politics, the third-generation Osmeñas also had to prove both their skills and competence. Thus, the Osmeña family hardly constitutes a cohesive unit, as shown in the conflicts arising out of the second marriage of Sergio, Sr., and in current tensions over the political legacy of both he and Serging.

To speak of the conservation of dynastic wealth as a prime motive in Osmeña politics would be a crude oversimplification. In legal, economic, and even moral terms, the Osmeñas have not functioned as a dynasty. Legally and financially, they do not operate as a corporate unit. Severino Osmeña married twice, and after his death the contest over his estate left his heirs by his second wife (including Sergio Osmeña, Sr., the illegitimate child of Juana Suico Osmeña) with nothing but a small portion of it. The family of Sergio was dismembered as well when he married Esperanza Limjap in 1920, two years after his first wife died. Tensions between the politically active children and their father and stepmother became public during the acrimonious probate proceedings of the elder Sergio's last will and testament in 1953–54. Executed on 2 October 1952 and probated on 26 November 1954, the will left 75 percent of the estate (conservatively valued at P2 million) to Esperanza Limjap, leaving 25 percent to be divided among the ten surviving children of the two marriages.[14] The early demise of the first Mrs. Osmeña, the death of Sergio, Sr., in 1961, and the strained relations between the second Mrs. Osmeña and her stepchildren left the family with no living totems of collective solidarity.

Given these disruptions, long-term stewardship of dynastic wealth has not been a major theme in Osmeña family history. The Osmeñas have largely functioned as individual entrepreneurs or loosely coordinated nuclear units building on their portions of the inheritance through intraelite marriage, enterprise, and the use of public office. Sergio Osmeña, Sr., used his political influence in the early twentieth century to gain control of a major part of the estate of Severino Osmeña. Sergio, Jr.'s close links to President Elpidio Quirino gained him directorships in government corporations and preferential loans and guarantees for De la Rama Steamship Company, owned by his wife's family, of which he served as president from 1948 to 1952.

Realty, however, is the core of the Osmeña wealth and it is in this field that they have most characteristically combined public service and private gain. Three generations of Osmeñas have been accused of real-estate speculation, from the restoration of Cebu City's burned downtown district in 1905, to the selection of the Provincial Capitol site in 1936, the Cebu North Reclamation Project in 1962–67, and, today, in the building of the Cebu Trans-Central Highway and the establishment of Cebu Property Ventures and Development Corporation (CPVDC), a joint venture between the provincial government and Ayala Land, Inc. (ALI).[15] In all of these cases, however, the Osmeñas have been more than mere extractive rent seekers. Skillfully combining public benefit with private gain, they have maintained for themselves, in large measure, the image of disinterested "economic managers." They are not regarded as the wealthiest family in Cebu, they do not have a large corps of clients and employees on their payroll, and they do not wield monopolistic business powers. Partly for this reason, they have retained the support of the large Cebuano business community whose members see in them promoters of the city's entrepreneurial ethos.

It is clear that the Osmeñas have built their power not through bureaucratic, military, or even economic position but by electoral means. By winning "mandates" from the voters, they established themselves as "legitimate" spokesmen for critical blocs of the electorate: the Cebuanos themselves (comprising 25 percent of the Philippine population); by extension, the Philippine south (traditionally represented by the vice-president if the president is from the north, and vice versa); and, finally, "the Filipino people." Location has favored the Osmeñas' careers. Metropolitan Cebu, with a population of one million, is the country's second-largest urban complex and the center of Philippine shipping, with its own concentration of media facilities and educational institutions. It is also the sentimental capital of the Cebuanos, the second-largest Philippine language-group, the members of which are found throughout large sections of the Visayas and Mindanao. Thus, control of Cebu readily translates into national power. Location has also shaped the nature of Osmeña politics. Based in a highly urbanized, commercial area with fractionalized, loosely coordinated, economic interests (instead of monolithic economic blocs), the family has relied on its electoral machine and ideological appeals rather than on military or economic coercion.

The Osmeñas are distinctly twentieth-century politicians sired by a system in which power is won by the ballot. Understanding the dynamics of Philippine elections is crucial, therefore, if one is to gain an understanding of Osmeña dominance. Further, the problematization of elections is required in order to assess the legitimacy of this dominance.

Defining Elections

Elections are such a key arena of political action that many Filipinos equate "politics" with "electoral politics." An institution established at the municipal level in the eighteenth and nineteenth centuries under Spanish rule, and significantly enlarged and strengthened under American auspices, elections (Cebuano *piliay, piniliay*) have become so well established in Philippine political culture that they have become a metonym not only for politics but for democracy itself.

Elections are an exercise deeply inscribed in the Filipino political imagination. During this century, local and national elections have been held on average once every two to four years. They involve great numbers of Filipinos, with 26.4 million voters registered in 1988 (1.2 million of them in Cebu Province). With the coming of "universal suffrage," the number of registered voters has increased from slightly more than 1 percent of the population in 1907 to close to 50 percent today, a number that comprises virtually the entire adult population of the country. Elections are keenly contested and voter turnouts are generally high. Turnouts in presidential elections have ranged from 69 to 90 percent, much higher than comparable statistics in the United States. That "there is no rest from politics" is a common lament.

Even under martial law, Marcos was constrained to create legitimacy through a series of plebiscites, referendums, and elections. Since Corazon Aquino assumed power in 1986 the country has witnessed one plebiscite and two nationwide elections. In the 11 May 1987 elections there were 84 candidates for 24 senatorial seats and 1,899 candidates for 200 congressional posts. In the 18 January 1988 local elections, roughly 150,000 candidates contested 16,454 posts. This means that an average of 8.5 candidates ran for each local post, 9 candidates for each congressional seat, and more than 3 candidates for each senatorial seat. In addition, the immediate post-Marcos period witnessed a proliferation of parties, factions, and coalitions, both local and national, not to mention persons running as independent candidates. For example, in the 18 January 1988 elections in Cebu Province, there were 10 parties, factions, or coalitions. This period, which witnessed the sudden release of repressed energies, is hardly typical, yet it does communicate something of the considerable moral investment Filipinos have placed in the electoral process.

Theoretically an election provides the occasion for society to take cognizance of itself. This is the time when citizens are most self-conscious, a season of stock-taking, when voters reflect on their collective state and history and make choices about leaders, policies, and "futures." The "democratic space" is most visible in incumbents submitting themselves for popular judgment and candidates presenting ideas of government, in the public exchange of contrary views, and, finally, in the voter weighing his or her options and casting a ballot in the ritual's inner sanctum, the polling booth.

The reality, of course, is not so tidy. Intensive exploitation of mass media and propaganda techniques crowd public space during the electoral season. Beneath the surface layer of diversity and dynamism is found a rather restricted field of thought and action. There is already much in the literature on Philippine politics that points to its restrictive aspects: an undeveloped party system, elite dominance and the ideological sameness of candidates, exclusion of those who fail to muster the considerable resources needed to mount a campaign, the subordination of issues to particularistic concerns, elaborate forms of terrorism and fraud, and the cultural baggage of traditional values of power and dependence. Much less attention has been paid to the hegemonic functions of the electoral process itself and to the cultural meaning this process has for Filipinos.

An election is a rite of incorporation or reincorporation. It affirms the validity and viability of a political organization and its center, and renews the participant's sense of membership, or "citizenship," in that system. In this, it can be viewed as a rite of collective passage, with liminal phases, beginning with the preliminary period of "desubjectification" (the campaign period, during which space is created wherein persons can stand aside and reflect on their condition); the "limen" of Election Day; and the postelection period of "resubjectification" ("reaggregation," "requalification") during which results are validated, winners proclaimed, the state affirmed, and the people reconstituted as social subjects.

The efficacy of the ritual is not assured, for it may be problematized, its power weakened by defects in procedures, misexecution, or various forms of misparticipation or nonparticipation. Hence, while it may lead people to where everything is in its place, and power holders are at the source of everything, it also may unmask the flawed and vulnerable character of the underlying system. The efficacy of the ritual can be undermined from "above" by leaders (manipulating the rules, exercising the illegitimate means of intimidation or cheating) as well as from "below" by the people themselves (selling their votes, engaging in cynical commentary, refusing to participate).

It may be argued that the ritual and practice of elections provide a channel not only for simple renewal but for a meaningful reconstitution of the system. Elections, however, do not exist in isolation. They are interlocked with the functioning of other forces and institutions in society, of which the economic are the most decisive. They do not exist outside history. Elections, therefore, do not constitute a free field but are, in fact, an arena in which the existing limits on participation are further exercised and enforced.

In Philippine elections we have a case in which the elite or dominant class usually constructs political reality for citizens. This process may be seen in the centrality accorded to the election itself as field of action and a channel for effecting political change. Formal education in "civics," the force of custom and law, rhetoric that invests the event with the charter of the "traditional" and the "sacral," and other factors imbue elections with symbolic power. In elections obeisance is rendered to the "state" and the people are constituted or reconstituted as its "subjects." In effect, the periodic holding of elections nourishes and renews the system. In the process it also tends to reify the existing system and deemphasize other areas of political work such as mass organizing, interest-group lobbying, and "armed struggle."

Elections, by their very nature, provide us with a concentrated expression of the process of ideological domination. This is one area in which the Osmeña phenomenon is important since the Osmeñas have built their dominance less on sheer economic power (though the use of such power was basic to their rise) or physical repression (though they are not wholly innocent of its methods) than on their mastery of the instrumental aspects of electoral power building. From this they draw their distinctive character as Filipino kingpins. Skillful management of ideological practices takes precedence over reliance on superior economic leverage (as in the case of the Lopez family), a system of traditional patronage (as in the Durano family), a mix of religion and militarism (as in Ali Dimaporo), or systematic electoral fraud (as in Marcos).

The matter of ideology—both as the world of social meanings and as the politician's stance in this world—is germane to achieving an understanding of the Osmeñas. It also provides an instructive focus: to deal with it is to confront not only the problem of dominant leaders and families but the broader problem of political culture. It is to go beyond "big men" into the realm of followers and nonfollowers.

Specific questions are raised by this approach. Where is the power game played? Who defines the field and who are the participants? Who is excluded and how are such exclusions effected? What is the influence of the excluded? Broadly, this involves the problem of "hegemony," a concept that takes into account not just direct and overt forms of domination but the complex interlocking of political, social, and cultural forces that creates conditions of subjection.

Elections create space within which people can think about and act on their social and political condition. Electoral practice, however, shows how acts of restriction and exclusion delimit the space. Here we shall not attempt a full inventory of hegemonic institutions and practices but will limit ourselves to illustrations from the field of public discourse on politics.

The first act of exclusion is exercised through the monopoly on public space. Dominant groups occupy much of the public space available: air time and newspaper space are purchased by candidates and parties, public walls are papered with posters and handbills, streamers and other propaganda materials festoon electric posts and trees, and plazas are appropriated for political rallies and meetings. The mass media have played an important role in Cebu politics since the first decade of the century, when Cebuano journalism began to flourish, and particularly after the 1950s when the "transistor revolution" democratized ownership of radio sets. Radio, in particular, is a dominant medium. Cebu City, for example, has eighteen radio stations with a range extending to large sections of the Visayas and Mindanao. Radio sets may be found in about 75 percent of households in Cebu Province. At the height of the campaign season, as much as 50 percent of the combined daily air time of radio stations may be devoted to political propaganda (broadcasts of party meetings, commentaries or talk shows, and jingles). Because control of public space requires considerable resources, it favors dominant parties or groups. Millions of pesos are required to fund a campaign organization, produce literature and sample ballots, and buy radio time, television spots, and newspaper space.

Further exclusion is exercised in the style and content of political speech. Analysis of political speech reveals beneath the seeming multiplicity of voices not so much the expansion as the restriction of political consciousness through the selective deployment of themes and the use of rhetorical devices that keep the field of speech and thought bounded. Political speech constructs history and the collective situation selectively; it reveals as well as masks social ills and their remedies. It identifies participants (friends and enemies, leaders and followers) and the roles they play. In the process, it highlights certain themes above others, labels and excludes what is "unrealistic," and sets the boundaries of what is considered to be "relevant" or "legitimate" discourse.[16]

In electoral contests in Cebu, public discourse has been dominated by conservative politicians. Political speech gravitates around the two poles of personality and issues (the English words have been adopted in Cebuano: *pirsonal* and *isyu*). *Pirsonal* is the low mode of discourse and encompasses verbal abuse, muckraking, vulgar humor, and gossip. *Isyu* is the high mode, consisting of the presentation of government platforms or the qualifications and social ideas of candidates. *Isyu*, however, is not a systematic exposition of ideology but a minimalist statement of general and abstract principles ("democracy," "freedom," "progress") and a listing of specific projects (such as roads, artesian wells, and garbage collection schemes). The Osmeña discourse skillfully combines both approaches. The low mode is voiced by a battery of hired spokesmen, campaign speakers, and radio commentators, while the Osmeñas themselves hew to a high mode that blends a broken-down, "developmental" technocratese (which stresses the Osmeña values of efficiency and innovativeness in the design and administration of projects) with emotive invocations of "democracy" and "progress" and appeals to the primordial sentiments of family, locality, and ethnicity.[17]

The state of language in the country is itself a factor in restriction. The Cebuano voter inhabits at least three ill-joined linguistic universes, Cebuano, English, and Tagalog (the latter, as the "national language," is called Pilipino). While, beginning in the late 1960s, the pressures of ideological politics have expanded the vocabulary of politics, particularly in Tagalog, public discourse on politics still inhabits an intermediate area between the local language and English. In this space the politician acts as a broker regulating and restricting the exchanges between two or more linguistic fields.[18]

In short, public discourse on politics is neither wholly open nor free. Control of public channels of communication, elite construction of tradition, selective deployment of messages, and the limits of the Philippine language situation—in concert with material conditions that sustain attitudes of political subjection—foster ideological domination.

A Minimalist Ideology

It is in the context of factors such as those cited above that one sees the boundedness of the field of *pulitika*. The Osmeñas are masters in the management of this field and are, in fact, the ones who inaugurated in Cebu politics the systematic use of modern mass media for electoral purposes.[19] They are skillful in the selection of messages and the manipulation of symbols so effective in Philippine

The Osmeña Family: A Political Genealogy

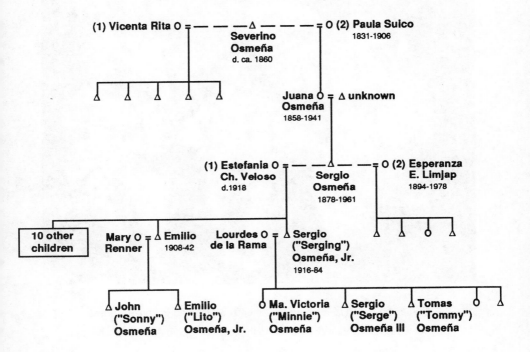

Sometime in 1907–8, Sergio Osmeña, Sr. (seated in center), poses
with the Cebu provincial delegation to the First Philippine Assembly where he
launched his national career by being elected speaker.
(*Credit:* University of Wisconsin-Madison, Memorial Library)

After his return from Washington, D.C., in early 1945, Commonwealth President
Sergio Osmeña, Sr. (upper right) speaks to thousands of supporters at a welcoming
rally on the Manila waterfront. In June 1960, Osmeña (lower right), then the country's
elder statesman, met U.S. President Dwight D. Eisenhower and Philippine President
Carlos Garcia at a Malacañang Palace reception.

After his return to the Philippines with General MacArthur in October 1944, Commonwealth President Sergio Osmeña, Sr., came home to Cebu for a family reunion. Shown in this family portrait are: (third row, left to right) Edilberto Osmeña, unidentified, Estefania Enriquez, Ramon Osmeña, unidentified; (second row, left to right) Mary Renner Osmeña, Milagros O. Gonzales, Esperanza Limjap Osmeña, Sergio Osmeña, Sr., unidentified, Vicenta Fortich, Guadalupe Veloso Osmeña; and (first row, sitting, second and third from left) the president's grandchildren, John and Emilio, Jr.

During the Liberation period, Mary Renner Osmeña, wife of Emilio, was photographed with her children: (left to right) Annabelle, Emilio, Jr. (seated), and John. Beside them is a photo of her father-in-law, Commonwealth President Sergio Osmeña, Sr.

A large, enthusiastic crowd waits on the Cebu City waterfront to greet Sergio ("Serging") Osmeña, Jr., arriving from Manila on an interisland ferry in August 1951. With ample funds from his successful marriage and business career, Serging was launching his career in Cebuano politics as a challenger to the established Cuenco family.

Already entrenched as the mayor of Cebu City, Serging Osmeña appears as a speaker on a panel at the Manila Overseas Press Club in March 1957.

'Wala Pa Gani, Naa Na'

Mga Marine Muabut Na Sa Sugbo

This political cartoon from the Cebu City newspaper *Kagawasan* portrays
Serging Osmeña as a knight errant who will sally forth from the world of business into
the field of politics to slay the monster Mariano J. Cuenco.

(*Kagawasan*, 7 November 1951)

In June 1969, launching his bid for the presidential nomination, Serging Osmeña
makes a dramatic entry at the Liberal Party convention in Manila. After the November
election, as early returns began to indicate defeat, candidate Osmeña (see facing
page) held a press conference at party headquarters in Manila to attack the media for
their unfavorable projections. At his right, party leader Senator Gerardo ("Gerry")
Roxas endorses Osmeña's criticisms.

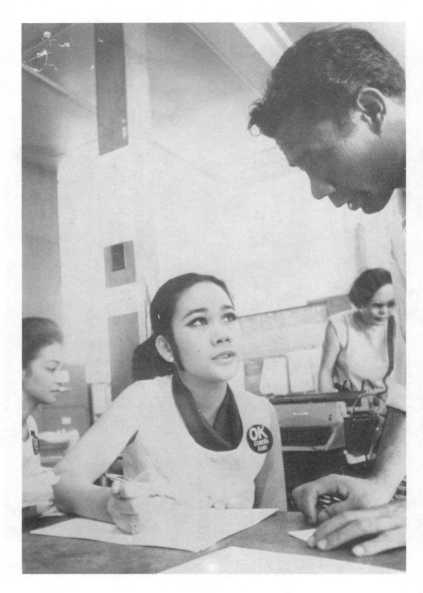

For the Osmeñas, the 1969 presidential election was a family affair. In September, Minnie Osmeña, daughter of presidential candidate Serging, fills out a voter registration form in Pasay City while wearing her father's OK ("Osmeña Kami") campaign button.

At an earlier Liberal Party caucus in Manila, Serging (above, left) shakes hands with politician Gerardo Roxas (wearing glasses) the son of former president Manuel Roxas. Accompanying Serging are (left to right) his daughter-in-law Marilita Barreto; her husband Sergio ("Serge") Osmeña III (smiling, at rear); and (partly concealed) Emilio ("Lito") Osmeña, Jr.

In May 1990, Cebu City mayor Tomas Osmeña and Cebu governor Lito Osmeña met to discuss development plans to sustain the pace of the local "economic miracle."

electoral politics, particularly in the context of the structurally undeveloped urbanism of Cebu, the Osmeña bailiwick. Theirs is an ideology of "developmentalism" and "modernity" with its promise of rational management, bureaucratic efficiency, and technocratic expertise in the design and execution of public projects. Theirs is the ethos of "good government" with its textbook values of honesty and efficiency in the conduct of public office and of efficacy and innovativeness in public service ("delivering the goods"). It is a minimalist ideology, however, in its loose aggregation of generalities and particulars and in its avoidance of a systematic critique of structures of social and economic domination.

The Osmeñas present themselves as effective and enterprising administrators, and by training and temperament they are well equipped for this role. University-educated and urban-based, they have entered politics through what remain largely nontraditional channels. Sergio Osmeña, Sr., who was educated in the Spanish period, studied law (the standard path into public life at that time, along with journalism, letters, and trade unionism). He seldom practiced law, however, as he was throughout most of his life a full-time politician and parliamentarian. Other Osmeñas have backgrounds in technology and entrepreneurship. Sergio, Jr., has a degree in commerce, John in mechanical engineering and public administration, Emilio in commerce, and Tomas in agricultural economics. Their principal economic interests are in real estate and commercial agriculture.

When Sergio Osmeña, Sr., launched himself into politics as councilor, provincial *fiscal*, and governor in the early years of the century, he built a reputation as an energetic and achievement-oriented public official. His impulses were shaped by the emerging American ethos of "public service" and he won the admiration and patronage of such high-ranking, colonial officials as William Cameron Forbes who saw in Osmeña's "reasonable, conservative, and pragmatic" style an approach congenial to their own notions of good government. For colonial administrators vexed by the "passivity" of the tradition-bound *tao*, the preoccupation with form of the Hispano-Filipino aristocrats, or the "irrationalism" of such volatile Filipino firebrands as Dominador Gomez and Vicente Sotto, Osmeña was *their* kind of politician. In the space of a few years he built a track record as a "modern," "rational" official replete with achievements in such areas as urban planning, fiscal management, public health, peace and order, and bureaucratic reform. He was probably the Philippines' first political technocrat.

Later Osmeñas were to exhibit the same efficacy and zeal. In 1951, when Serging Osmeña first became governor of Cebu, and throughout his ensuing political career, he promoted an image of himself as economist and technocrat. In 1988, when Emilio and Tomas launched their political careers by running for Cebu governor and Cebu City mayor, respectively, they also presented themselves as economists. It is not signally important that they have less-than-outstanding academic credentials. What is important is their ability to "deliver" with high-profile, large-impact projects. In the case of Serging, these included the Cebu North Reclamation Project, the Mactan International Airport, and the Mandaue-Mactan

Bridge. Today, capitalizing on a favorable political climate and the built-in assets of Cebu as a regional center, the Osmeñas, particularly Governor Emilio Osmeña, are aggressively moving to foster an "economic boom." This they aim to accomplish by attracting Filipino and foreign investors with an effective promotional campaign, through astute financial resource-building (including the sale of local government-owned properties), and with infrastructure initiatives (newly opened hinterlands, reclamation projects, and special economic zones).

They are not the only holders of special knowledge but they have the political skills to effectuate plans and "deliver the goods." They are connected to sources of power, and they know which levers to pull. They are linked to centers of influence to which common citizens have no access: the highest American officials, the Philippine president, big business in Manila, and foreign investors and financing institutions. Hence, Sergio Osmeña, Sr., enhanced his appeal through his friendship with Taft and Forbes; Sergio, Jr., was a poker buddy of business magnates and President Elpidio Quirino; Minnie (Ma. Victoria) is a successful stockbroker in the United States and former wife of the board chairman of Carnation International; and Emilio and Tomas are "successful real estate specialists" with projects in the Philippines and on the U.S. West Coast.

In addition, the Osmeñas have put their considerable entrepreneurial and organizational skills to good use in their electoral campaigns: in managing finances, contracting a quality staff for media packaging and opinion surveys, and running an efficient campaign organization. They have a fund of political experience, an organizational network built up through many elections, the support of big business, and the persuasive reputation of "winners."

By temperament, the Osmeñas are atypical political patrons: autocratic and brisk in their interpersonal dealings, averse to gladhanding, generally colorless and methodic in their political rhetoric, and more comfortable in the English language than in Cebuano. They have transformed their "take-charge, get-things-done" manner into a kind of charisma that has its basis in the evocation not of a traditional order but of a modern world in which technocrats and managers rather than feudal patrons and political *caciques* are the effective guides. The stigma of patronage they leave to their provincial political enemies, the Cuencos and the Duranos.

Yet Cebuano (and Philippine) society is imperfectly modern. The mechanics of public administration or fiscal planning do not make for stirring messages. In this wise, the Osmeñas have defined their electoral campaigns in terms of "crusades" that use primordial symbols of democracy, autonomy, and progress. Sergio Osmeña, Sr., was the "architect of Philippine Independence"; Sergio, Jr., was the "savior of democracy" standing against the "terroristic" Cuenco and Durano families. Similar themes have been raised by the third-generation Osmeñas, this time citing their somewhat dubious role as critics of the Marcos dictatorship.[20]

This rhetoric illustrates the use of a selective tradition for power building. In the cases of both Sergio, Sr., and Sergio, Jr., there is an oversimplification, if not a distortion, of history. The reputation of Sergio, Sr., as the "architect of Philippine independence" edits out of public memory his self-interested motives and the real character of the independence achieved, thereby reducing the complex of political and economic forces in the struggle for independence to comic-book proportions. The image of Sergio, Jr., as "savior of democracy" is also, in many ways, synthetic: it neglects to consider the political and economic roots of terrorism by reductively labeling it the work of a political enemy; it conveniently excludes the facts of the young Osmeña's own dalliance with the authors of large-scale terrorism (the Japanese military administration during the war years, for example, and President Quirino after the war). And today it is politically rewarding to be styled a critic of the dictatorship, blind to one's role in the shaping of the *pulitika* of which dictatorship was a consummation.

The use of a selective tradition is illustrated by the January 1988 local elections in Cebu City. Tomas Osmeña was running against Jose V. Cuenco, son of Manuel Cuenco, his father's opponent in the 1951 elections. In the initial stages of the campaign, Tomas was inhibited by the Osmeña-Cuenco Fusion (an alliance forged in 1959, the core of the dominant Partido Panaghiusa [Unity Party] in Cebu in 1986–88). A secret survey run among Panaghiusa followers had shown that the primary identification of the majority was Osmeñista rather than Cuenqista. Astutely, the Osmeña camp engineered an open break in the Fusion to force the polarization of Osmeña and Cuenco supporters, thus putting into high gear what the family's campaign strategists themselves called "the nostalgia trap."[21] This turned the contest into a battle over interpretations of the past: the Cuencos as perpetrators of terrorism in the 1940s versus the Osmeñas, the saviors of democracy in Cebu. On this ground, Tomas Osmeña emerged the winner.

More adept than their opponents in seizing the ideological high ground, the Osmeñas have defined political reality in advantageous terms. In the first decades of the century, when the imperative was the parliamentary formation of an independent, unified state, Sergio Osmeña, Sr., staked out the role of statesman and "apostle of national unity." In the postwar period, when the inefficacy of the central government, of "imperial Manila," became a popular lament, Sergio, Jr., and the third-generation Osmeñas appropriated local autonomy as their own cause. Today—with distrust of central government heightened by the experience of martial rule and the perceived weakness of the Aquino government—the Osmeñas have assumed the roles of vanguards of local autonomy, John with his registered political movement, Pilipinas 1992, batting for federalism, and Emilio with his Local Autonomy Movement of the Philippines (LAMP).

It is not difficult to see the roots of the Osmeñas' ideological appeal. For many Filipinos the story of government is a story of chronic frustration, from the immediate, day-to-day experience of inefficiency and corruption to awareness of the unchanging conditions of mass poverty. At the same time, the values of American-style democracy continue to dominate the popular imagination. Such are the ideological materials variously mined by Filipino politicians, from Ferdinand

Marcos, with his vision of a New Society rising out of the sins of the old, to perennial presidential candidate Pascual Racuyal, a Cebuano with a program of government involving plastic roads, a crime-free society, and a "World Peace Blood Compact" atop Mt. Arayat involving Reagan, Gorbachev, and Racuyal himself.[22]

The Osmeñas appeal to both the past and the future, on one hand by resurrecting selective images of the past, and on the other by evoking visions of a modern, progressive future. In his 1987–88 campaign, Tomas evoked the tradition of the Osmeñas with ads depicting the three generations: Sergio, Sr., Sergio, Jr., and Tomas. Under the portraits was the campaign slogan "The dream goes on." Indeed, the dream goes on and on and on.

Beyond Pulitika

The dream lives on, but only in a fashion. Political instability in the Philippines attests to the fact that hegemonic domination is far from total. Above it was remarked that elections create the space, or margin, in which people can stand aside from their social positions and formulate a potentially unlimited series of alternative social arrangements. Such space is often narrow and illusory. Yet popular practice and reinterpretation can also protect it, or they can create unintended spaces.

What is the popular conception of *politics* and *elections*? Cebuano does not have a clear equivalent for either term. Commonly used are the Spanish/English loanwords *pulitika* and *eleksiyon,* as well as two Cebuano terms, *piliay* (literally, the process of 'choosing') and *lugaynon* ('political' or 'what pertains to politics'). The latter is an early-twentieth-century coinage used in expressions like *bugnong lugaynon* ('electoral battle') and *kinabuhing lugaynon* ('political life'). One source credits the coinage to writer Uldarico Alviola (1883–1966) and claims that the word *lugaynon,* or *lugaynan,* is derived from the phrase *iniLUGAY sa katungdaNAN* ('competition for offices').[23] An alternative explanation holds that the now somewhat archaic word *lugay* refers to anything one roasts in a pan or oven (such as coffee beans) or dries on a mat under the sun (like copra). *Lugay,* therefore, is associated with that which is 'roasted' or 'exposed'. Frequently used in conjunction with *bugno* (which means 'battle' or 'contest' but has an older reference to chase-and-assault in hunting), it suggests the association of politics not only with electoral contests but with combat and sportive fighting.[24]

There is a gap between elite and popular constructions of *politics.* Spanish administrators spoke of *politica* in terms of governance, public order, and obedience of the law. Those who later wielded state power, the Americans and Filipinos, used *politics* to mean the craft of government and civic responsibility. Leaders like the Osmeñas represented politics in terms of "public service" and mystified elections as rituals of development and change. In Cebuano popular speech (including vernacular literature and journalism), however, *pulitika* is imaged in terms of elite factional competition (*inilugay sa katungdanan*), manipulation (*maneobra*), spectacle, and dissimulation. Hence, the frequent use of theatrical and sporting images in popular representations of *pulitika* (for example, politics as *moro-moro, linambay, sarsuela, gubat-patani,* and cockfight). *Pulitiko* ('politician') connotes one who is dissembling and skillful in interpersonal relations. In a study of early-twentieth-century political rhetoric in Tagalog, Reynaldo Ileto points to this cultural meaning:

> *Pulitika* is the perception of politics as a process of bargaining, with implicit self or factional interests involved. The interaction between the colonial power and its native wards was *pulitika.* At another level, it refers to the practices by which leaders cultivate ties of personal loyalty and indebtedness to them, or simply attract votes.[25]

The relationship between elite and popular conceptions of politics is not one of static opposition. While popular notions of *pulitika* distance and problematize allegiance to an order by disenchanting politics, stripping away the claims of disinterested service made by politicians, the sheer skill of those who are masters of the game can exercise its own kind of enchantment. Elite politicians can turn the fascination of the powerless for men of prowess to their advantage. Manipulating the discourse on politics, Cebuano warlord Ramon Durano can define politics, as he does, as "a game of devils" (*dula sa mga yawa*) and suggest how, given the rules of the game, people need their own devil to protect their interests and extract rewards from a morally indifferent state. In the same idiom, Sergio Osmeña, Jr., can foster a following built around the principle of *bisag unsaon* ("no-matter-what": an Osmeña campaign slogan), the blind faith in his infallibility as leader and guide. Finally, Governor Emilio Osmeña can turn arrogance into a virtue by fostering in his followers a sense of his command and control. Asked how he felt about charges that he uses his public office to advance family interests, he retorted, "If I don't move because it will benefit my family, then nothing moves in Cebu."[26]

Such acts of exclusion and appropriation classify and reclassify the boundaries of political action. In the Philippines, *pulitika* is not *politics* (whether construed broadly as the totality of public or civic life or narrowly as democratic bargaining or consensus building). Rather, it is that field of politics largely constructed and dominated by the elite. Attention, therefore, can be drawn fruitfully to dereifying this field by coming to understand how it is bounded and restricted, on one hand, or broken down and expanded, on the other. The former addresses the actions of dominant personalities and groups, their acts of restriction and exclusion. The latter deals with the actions of followers and nonfollowers, their acts of reinterpretation and negation. Such acts cannot be considered in isolation: they are tied not only to elections or overtly political institutions but to the functioning of other institutions in society (such as the economy or education) in which the process of hegemony is at work.

Yet even in the electoral field itself we can see the multifarious acts that extract from elections true political meanings (even if they be dismal and closed), deflect the claims of authority (even if temporarily, as do political jokes), or sabotage the practice of elections (even if individualistic or makeshift in character, as in vote selling or not voting). Such common acts are not without consequence. If they are widespread, they will problematize elections to the extent that the electoral institution (and, necessarily, its wider context) will have to be meaningfully reformed or more radical political options will have to be taken.

And what of politicians like the Osmeñas? Antonio Gramsci says that parties and politicians propagate conceptions of the world and organize the spontaneous consent of the ruled. The politician is engaged in the project of reconstructing past history as well as building present and future history. Yet, as Gramsci points out, "The active politician is a creator, an awakener, but he neither creates from nothing nor moves in the turbid void of his own desires and dreams."[27] To be understood, a politician must be seen in relation to ideological forces and social formations. The politician is successful to the extent that he bases himself on effective reality (the existing relationships of forces); he looks to the future to the extent that he bases himself on the progressive forces, giving them the means to triumph.

Underlying the Osmeña phenomenon is the practice of a conservative politics, one that restricts the distribution of power and constructs politics as *pulitika*. It is in this context that families with economic resources and political skills can perpetuate themselves in power. The specific character of the Osmeña dominance has been shaped by such factors as the American ethos of rational government, the personality and temper of the Osmeñas themselves, their belief in the electoral system, and the characteristics of the region in which they have founded their careers. To a significant extent, they are not only instrumentalists but true believers in the precepts of liberal democracy and free enterprise. Theirs, however, is a minimalist ideology subordinated to the exigencies and demands of action in the realm of *pulitika*. It is also an ideology that mobilizes people around their leadership but does not empower them nor seriously address the structural problems of Philippine society. The Osmeña dominance has been shaped as well by the practical, grosser realities of power maintenance in the Philippines, which require of leaders not only ideological competence but expedient skills in *realpolitik*, in the lower-order devices of lying, bribery, horse trading, and thuggery.

While the Osmeña dominance has its specific characteristics, it expresses a general phenomenon with deep historical foundations. The structure of precolonial politics in Southeast Asia has been described as a "contest-state" characterized by a weak center and a marked diffusion of power among diverse regions and rival principalities.[28] While Spanish colonialism helped to establish, both positively and negatively, the framework of a nation, it did not create a strong state. It intensified stratification through the co-optation of the elite, the award of contracts, licenses, and monopolies, and the introduction of new property rights and sources of power (such as race, education, and language). A ramshackle bureaucracy and military, however, allowed a native elite to accumulate local power within the colonial confines. In its turn, American colonialism, despite its avowals of democratization, strengthened tendencies towards the monopolization of power by local and regional elites. In this context, and in the relative absence of other principles around which power can be organized (class, ethnicity, or religion, for example, at least in large parts of the country), elite families became focal points for power accumulation. History thus underlies the continuing dominance of families like the Osmeñas.

It has been pointed out that lineage is relatively unimportant in Southeast Asian cultures; power is not inherited and the premium is on the virtue and achievements of the present generation.[29] Yet, in a system in which the circle of power is drawn around big men and men of prowess, those near or within the circle are in a position to inherit the resources or implements of power: contacts, networks, skills, money, or the name that affords the public visibility important in elections. In a society in which strong family ties are the result of economic and ideological factors, sons, brothers, and other relatives are strategically positioned to inherit power.

Moreover, we must attend to how political culture has constructed families like the Osmeñas, for a political family is the sum not just of what its members possess or do but of how it is regarded in the community. Invested with a mystique of expertise and efficacy, the reputation of the Osmeñas has not only underwritten their claims to power but has facilitated its intergenerational transfer.

Above I presented certain widely held assumptions: that martial rule was a radical break in the Philippine political experience, that the campaign against the Marcos dictatorship politicized large sectors of the population, and that these developments raised hopes for a "new politics" in the post-Marcos era. The persistence and reemergence of the old dominant political families in the elections of 1987 and 1988 force us to revise these assumptions. Not only did the reaction against martial rule fail to democratize power but it strengthened existing tendencies towards greater centralization. It did not break up the concentration of political and economic power; nor, despite its avowed aims of ideological reeducation, did it effect a progressive reform of political values. While it politicized a significant sector of the population in ways not wholly intended, to a great extent this sector has placed itself outside the arena of an electoral process still largely controlled by dominant groups. The experience of the left-wing Partido ng Bayan in 1987 and the dispersal of small ideological groups and parties in the current drift towards the old two-party system appear to portend a situation in which the significant tension will be between those who operate "inside" and those who work "outside" the electoral field, between the "included" and the "excluded."

There is a widespread sense that the Philippines has returned to the status quo ante martial rule. Indeed, for many the ravages of martial rule have rendered the past more politically congenial than it really was. And for many politicians the agenda now seems to consist simply of picking up where they left off, returning to where things were before they were rudely interrupted by martial law. Yet, 1988 is neither 1951 nor 1969. The field of elections itself has undoubtedly changed.

Two important factors will continue to affect the institution of elections: demobilization among voters and politicization outside the electoral field. The former refers to various forms of voter withdrawal, as a result of which elections do not exercise as much symbolic power as they once did. At various points, this symbolic power has been renewed, as in the election of Ramon Magsaysay in 1954 and the assumption of Corazon Aquino in 1986. Yet, so much symbolic capital has been dissipated and economic changes have fragmented old patterns of dependence to such an extent that it will become increasingly difficult to "bring the voters out." In many parts of the country, Carl Lande's image of the structure of Philippine politics as a multitiered system of patron-centered factions and followings has collapsed into complex, minuscule groups that are increasingly difficult to mobilize around old leaders, loyalties, and symbols.[30] The experience in Cebu (and, I suspect, in most of the country) over the past decades has been the advanced fragmentation of the electorate, so that candidates now must go further afield to reach the voters. The result is increasing investments in the use of mass media, the development of new and more elaborate techniques of intimidation or fraud, organization of a more complex and involuted campaign machinery, and adoption of more sophisticated polling and voter-behavior analysis. The "resistance" of voters undoubtedly will continue to influence both the style and content of elections.

The second factor, political mobilization outside the electoral field, has created new alignments that are not yet effectively organized as an electoral force, by choice or otherwise. These groups (radical trade unions, Basic Christian Communities, various "cause-oriented" groups, and the Communist Party of the Philippines), to the extent that they continue to build, will undoubtedly have an impact on the practice of elections.[31]

How have these factors affected the style and content of Osmeña electoral practices? An illustration is provided by Tomas Osmeña's 1987–88 mayoral campaign. In Cebu, the most popular issues with voters at this time were urban poverty and the breakdown of public order (both insurgency and common criminality). In the Osmeña campaign the politically sensitive issue of insurgency was skirted in favor of the more general theme of economic development. The campaign line was "Let us attend to economic projects and the insurgency issue will solve itself." On one hand, Tomas Osmeña projected his competence in economic matters (employing, among others, Asian Institute of Management dean Gaston Ortigas as campaign consultant). On the other hand, he cultivated the image of advocacy for urban-poor causes by means of such tactics as sleeping in the houses of campaign supporters in the city's depressed *barangays*, articulating "urban-poor" planks in his platform, and, after his election, staging his inauguration in the impoverished Pasil district of Cebu City. Using personal contacts and links to local development agencies, his staff devised the "People's Alternative" scenario, under which a group of private, voluntary organizations (PVOs) and nongovernmental organizations (NGOs) organized the Cebu Development Forum, which launched the People's Alternative project on 30 November 1987, just fifty days before the election. Ostensibly its purpose was to develop an urban-poor agenda for the city government, lobbying for the candidates' commitment to it, staging nonpartisan forums, and then openly endorsing the candidates "who can best serve the cause of the urban poor." It was an Osmeña scenario: top strategists in the Osmeña camp had direct links to the PVOs and NGOs involved, drew up the agenda, and directed the project. On 11 January 1988, at a convention attended by four hundred delegates, Tomas Osmeña was declared the "People's Choice."[32]

Among many Filipinos, there is the sense that times have not changed. But times *have* changed. Politicians like the Osmeñas are themselves adjusting to altered conditions: modifying their rhetoric by adding new messages, revising their campaign style, and addressing new issues. By doing so they can appropriate new symbols, co-opt new leaders, and reestablish the old borders that keep political action bounded. Yet pressures from below will make it increasingly difficult to give new life to old symbols or maintain the old boundaries. To the extent that these pressures are contained and the Philippine state continues to develop in a corporatist direction, the Osmeñas, with their political and technocratic skills, are superbly positioned to remain in power. To the extent that these pressures build and are not meaningfully confronted, the Osmeñas may find that *pulitika* no longer holds sway, that the terms of the struggle have shifted radically, and that the struggle for power is now taking place elsewhere.

NOTES

This is a revision of a paper presented at the Fortieth Annual Meeting of the Association for Asian Studies, held in San Francisco, California, 25–27 March 1988. I wish to thank Michael Cullinane for his help in the preparation of the manuscript, and Ben Anderson for his insightful comments at the San Francisco panel presentation.

[1]This paper was written in 1988 and slightly revised in 1990. I have chosen not to update the main text of the essay. In the complex, multicornered, 1991 presidential elections, Emilio Osmeña lost in a bid for the vice-presidency, running on the ticket of Fidel Ramos's LAKAS-NUCD Party. His brother John, who initially launched a vice-presidential campaign in Eduardo Cojuangco's Nationalist People's Coalition, changed course, ran for senator, and won. Tomas Osmeña won reelection as Cebu City mayor but his brother Sergio III lost a bid for a congressional seat in Cebu Province. Annette V. Osmeña (Emilio's wife), standing in for her husband, lost the race for Cebu governor. Marcelo Fernan, long-time Osmeña lawyer and *consiglieri*, ran and lost as the vice-presidential running mate of Ramon Mitra of the Laban ng Demokratikong Pilipino (LDP) Party. Esteban Osmeña, brother of Tomas, also lost in a maverick bid for the Senate in Miriam Santiago's People's Reform Party. Cousin Renato V. Osmeña was reelected to a seat on the Cebu City Council. The electoral reverses suffered by some of the Osmeñas were occasioned by intrafamilial feuding caused by a surplus of claimants to leadership in the family. These reverses have not significantly dented the power of the family itself.

[2]"Between Deadlines," *Philippine Daily Inquirer*, 24 January 1988, 4, citing a survey by the Institute of Popular Democracy, Manila.

[3]"Sonny Move vs. Barcenas Explained," *Sun Star Daily*, 29 October 1987, 1, 2.

[4]"The Kingpins of Cebu," *Metro* (July 1989): 23.

[5]Per the 1980 census, Cebu Province has five cities, forty-eight municipalities, and a population of 2,091,602. The urban core of the province (and the Osmeña stronghold) is Metropolitan Cebu, which consists of three cities and six municipalities and is home to

almost half the provincial population (928,000), with Cebu City itself accounting for 490,000. The provincial population is classified as 44.25 percent urban and 55.75 percent rural. It is ethnically homogeneous with 99.30 percent of the population speaking Cebuano. Literacy stands at 77.68 percent. Ownership of radio and television sets stands at 68.06 and 11.15 percent of total households, respectively, and at 74.24 and 22.88 percent in the urban areas. Of the major occupational groups resident in the province, 45.91 percent of the population are gainfully employed in agriculture, fishing, and forestry; 23.92 percent in industry and allied fields; and the rest in service, sales, professional, managerial, and clerical fields. Cebu City is a focal point for transport, trade, and service firms, with some 90 percent of the city's business establishments engaged in trade and commerce. See *1980 Census of Population and Housing: Cebu* (Manila: National Census and Statistics Office, 1983).

[6]See H. V. E. Thoden Van Velzen, "Robinson Crusoe and Friday: Strength and Weakness of the 'Big Man' Paradigm," *Man* 8, no. 4 (1973): 592–612.

[7][Ramon Durano], *Ramon Durano: An Autobiography* (Danao: Ramon Durano Foundation, 1987); Vicente S. del Rosario, *Fighting is My Love* (Cebu City: V. S. del Rosario, 1986).

[8]See Michael Cullinane, "Playing the Game: The Rise of Sergio Osmeña, 1898–1907," in *Philippine Colonial Democracy*, edited by Ruby R. Paredes (Quezon City: Ateneo de Manila University Press, 1988), 70–113.

[9]Andrew Turton and Shigeharu Tanabe, eds., *History and Peasant Consciousness in Southeast Asia* (Osaka: National Museum of Ethnology, 1984), 29–30.

[10]See Cullinane, "Playing the Game," for a detailed and incisive analysis of the early career of Sergio Osmeña, Sr. For an appreciative "official" biography, see Vicente Albano Pacis, *President Sergio Osmeña: A Fully Documented Biography*, 2 vols. (Quezon City: Phoenix Press, 1971).

[11]See Resil B. Mojares, *The Man Who Would Be President: Serging Osmeña and Philippine Politics* (Cebu City: Maria Cacao, 1986), for an account of the political life of Sergio Osmeña, Jr.

[12]The grenade bombing, perpetrated by unknown assailants, decimated the top leadership of the oppositionist Liberal Party gathered for a political rally on the eve of the 1971 senatorial elections. Among those severely injured, apart from Serging, were Liberal Party president Gerardo Roxas, Jovito Salonga, and the eight opposition senatorial candidates, including John Osmeña, Serging's nephew.

[13]See Steve Psinakis, *Two "Terrorists" Meet* (San Francisco: Alchemy Books, 1981).

[14]The last will of Sergio Osmeña, Sr., executed in 1952, reveals an estate, valued at P2 million, principally consisting of 1,743 hectares of urban and agricultural land in Cebu. In 1987, Emilio Osmeña, Jr., claimed assets of P49 million while his brother John declared P17 million when he assumed his Senate seat in 1987. On the controversy over the Osmeña will, see Cebu Court of First Instance (Fourteenth Judicial District, Branch III), Cebu Provincial Capitol, Cebu City, Case No. 1004–B, Probate of the will of Sergio Osmeña, "Memorandum for petitioners" (1 August 1954), "Amended record on appeal" (27 January 1955), "Inventory, estate of Don Sergio Osmeña, Sr." (24 February 1962), and "Summary showing allocation of estate principal and income as of December 31, 1963." Also see Mojares, *The Man*, 99–100.

[15]See Cullinane, "Playing the Game," 76–79, 106–8 (nn. 10, 11, 25); and Mojares, *The Man*, 36–38, 67–69, 110–12.

[16]For background on political rhetoric, see Maurice Bloch, "Symbols, Song, Dance and Features of Articulation," *European Journal of Sociology* 15, no. 1 (1974): 55–81; and Robert Paine, *Politically Speaking: Cross-Cultural Studies of Rhetoric* (Philadelphia: Institute for the Study of Human Issues, 1981).

[17]Verbal texts for the analysis of the "Osmeña discourse" include not only the speeches delivered by the Osmeñas themselves but by surrogates and subalterns (*liders*, "speakers bureaus," and hired radio commentators). Much of this material has not been

preserved. Only scattered texts of Osmeña speeches exist and there has been no systematic effort to record and archive rally speeches and radio programs. For a discussion of and extracts from some Osmeña speeches, see Mojares, *The Man*; and Resil B. Mojares, "Talking Politics: The *Komentaryo* on Philippine Radio" (paper presented at the Center for Southeast Asian Studies, University of Wisconsin, Madison, 28 April 1989).

[18]See Benedict Anderson, "The Languages of Indonesian Politics," *Indonesia* 1 (1966): 89–116.

[19]Mojares, *The Man*.

[20]The Osmeñas claim that they were blackmailed into silence in the early years of martial rule out of fear for the safety of the imprisoned Sergio III. Even after 1977, however, they played a less than prominent part in the anti-Marcos opposition, both in the Philippines and in the United States, reassuming an active public role only after the Aquino assassination in 1983. Senator John Osmeña publicly endorsed martial law in its early days. In a speech delivered in 1974, he lauded the achievements of the regime: "A peace-and-order condition has been attained to a degree never dreamed of. Economic prosperity has reached a new level." Stating that the price paid in terms of restrictions on civil liberties had been worthwhile, he concluded: "We must consider it an obligation to do everything in our power to make this new order a success." See John Osmeña, "Rights and Liberties During a Period of Reform," in *The Living Constitution*, edited by H. E. Gutierrez, Jr. (Quezon City: University of the Philippines Law Center, 1976), 128. John Osmeña later left for the United States, returning only after the Aquino assassination. In 1978, Emilio R. Osmeña was "pressured" to run as a Marcos candidate (under the banner of the Kilusang Bagong Lipunan Party) in the National Assembly elections. He later said that he agreed to run in order to gain "immunity and leverage to operate against Marcos." Despite the endorsement of Sergio, Jr., and brother John (in taped messages sent from the United States for public airing in Cebu), Emilio lost the election.

[21]The use of nostalgia in the Tomas Osmeña campaign included the recycling of old Osmeña campaign buttons and slogans, replays of the 1971 post–Plaza Miranda speech of Sergio Osmeña, Jr., and the projection of Tomas as his father's look-alike and political heir.

[22]Pascual Racuyal, whose quixotic career is a leitmotif in Philippine electoral politics, was born in Cebu in 1911. He now resides in Bulacan. He has run in every presidential election since 1937, except in 1981 when he "was not in the mood." His campaigns provide a farcical mirror-image of Philippine politics. Born "during strong thunder, lightning, and heavy rain," his qualifications include a "certificate of mental health," a record as a marathon public speaker, and "knowledge of military tactics from Hannibal to MacArthur." In the presidential campaign of 1985, he promised to be a "real model bribe-proof credible president," stating that "The best government in the world is 'make people happy.'" See Fe B. Zamora, "Stop the Elections, Stop His Candidacy, Stop the World but Racuyal Will Not Get Off," *Mr. and Ms.* (9 January 1986); and Efren L. Danao, "The Also-rans," *Veritas* (29 December 1985): 11–12.

[23]Francisco Labrador, "Lantugi mahitungud sa dilang Bisaya," *Bag-ong Kusog* (17 May 1929): 10, 22.

[24]Juan Felix de la Encarnacion, *Diccionario Bisaya-Espanol*, 3d ed. (Manila: Tipografia de Amigos del Pais, 1885); Vicente Gullas, *English-Visayan-Spanish Dictionary* (Cebu City: La Prensa, 1937).

[25]See Reynaldo C. Ileto, "Orators and the Crowd: Philippine Independence Politics, 1910–1914," in *Reappraising an Empire: New Perspectives on Philippine-American History*, edited by Peter W. Stanley (Cambridge: Harvard University Press, 1984), 10.

[26]"Ceboom!" *Metro* (July 1989): 19.

[27]Antonio Gramsci, *The Modern Prince and Other Writings* (New York: International Publishers, 1983), 163.

[28]Michael Adas, "'Moral Economy' or 'Contest State'? Elite Demands and the Origins of Peasant Protest in Southeast Asia," *Journal of Social History* 13, no. 4 (1980): 530–40.

[29]O. W. Wolters, *History, Culture, and Religion in Southeast Asian Perspectives* (Singapore: Institute of Southeast Asian Studies, 1982), 1–15.

[30]Carl H. Lande, *Leaders, Factions, and Parties: The Structure of Philippine Politics* (New Haven: Yale University, Southeast Asian Studies, 1965).

[31]The Communist Party of the Philippines/New People's Army (CPP/NPA) has remained largely outside the electoral field, opting for boycotts or "selective participation" depending on the party's analysis of conditions. In the 18 January 1988 local elections, it chose a policy of selective participation and revenue-raising, the latter accomplished through "taxes," the sale of safe-conduct passes to candidates wishing to campaign in NPA-influenced territory. Such taxes ranged from P25,000 to P100,000 per pass. In the Bicol region, it is claimed that the CPP/NPA raised no less than P3 million in cash and arms in such a manner ("Top Rebel Boasts of Gains in Elections," *Manila Chronicle* [18 January 1988]: 6). Current (1988) estimates of CPP/NPA strength range from twenty-three to thirty thousand part- or full-time armed guerrillas deployed in sixty provinces. The party is reported to be "in control" of eight thousand *barrios*, 20 percent of the country's total.

[32]A key figure on the 1987–88 Osmeña campaign staff was Francisco L. Fernandez, former classmate of Tomas and now commissioner of the Presidential Commission on the Urban Poor (PCUP). An organizer of the Federation of Free Farmers/Christian Social Movement in the years preceding martial rule, Fernandez has had extensive mass-organizing experience in Cebu, Negros, and Tondo (Manila). He brought into the Osmeña campaign staff Salvador Loyola, Jr., his associate in Pagtambayayong, Inc. (a social-housing NGO organized with the assistance of the Cebu-based Ramon Aboitiz Foundation, Inc., or RAFI). Fernandez and Loyola are also leaders and facilitators of Philippine Partnership for the Development of Human Resources in the Rural Areas (PHILDHRRA), the Visayas Institute for Cooperative Training Organization (VICTO), and other NGOs that joined to form the Cebu Development Forum. Linkage was provided by the RAFI, owned by the Aboitiz family, of which Annabelle Osmeña (sister of John and Emilio) is a member by virtue of her marriage to Luis Aboitiz. The NGOs/PVOs involved in the scenario had "direct influence" on 180,000 members or clients, although the Osmeña staff used these organizations more for effect than for mass mobilization (drawn from various interviews; also see the leaflet "The People's Alternative" [Cebu City, n.p., 1988]).

Ilustrado Legacy:
The Pardo de Taveras of Manila

Ruby R. Paredes

In August 1983, Dr. Mita Pardo de Tavera stood among the crowd of mourners at the funeral of Philippine senator Benigno ("Ninoy") Aquino. Several weeks before, Aquino had been killed by a shot to the back of the head as he stepped onto the tarmac of Manila's International Airport. Overflowing Santo Domingo Church, the mourners felt a sense of outrage overwhelming their grief.

The murdered man had been returning from a three-year exile in the United States to unify the opposition to Ferdinand Marcos's eleven-year dictatorship. Executed within earshot of his mother and his political supporters, the murder was an act of cruelty that sparked protests by millions of mourners who marched in the senator's cortege as it criss-crossed Central Luzon. The people saw Aquino's murder as the culmination of years of repression. The scenarios sketched by Marcos's spokesmen to exculpate him and his regime from any guilt in the murder infuriated the crowds.

Mita Pardo de Tavera's years as a medical doctor for the masses gave her an intuitive understanding of the people's mood. Rising to address the mourners, she knew what needed to be said. Gripping the podium as she eulogized the murdered man, she turned her oration into a challenge to the regime with the words "I call on Ferdinand Marcos to resign." In an atmosphere of repression, her boldness struck a responsive chord. Many began to echo her call for Marcos's resignation. But, whether from want of opportunity or courage of the moment, no one before Mita Pardo de Tavera had so effectively exposed the dictatorship's spurious claim to legitimacy. She believed Marcos to be guilty of subverting constitutional rule and fraudulently asserting the right to represent the Filipino people. Drawing upon the experience of years of contact with people of all classes, she concluded that Marcos had lost his mandate. After this latest crime, she felt it was time to bring down the dictator.

Although she seemed inspired by the passions of the moment, the wellsprings of Mita's words and her idealism lay deeper, in the principles of her grandfather, Trinidad Hermenegildo ("T. H.") Pardo de Tavera, and his generation of intellectuals, the *ilustrados* of 1896. As Mita saw it, her stand against Marcos was in the best traditions of her grandfather, who had challenged the Americans, and his uncle, who had challenged the Spanish.

Over the next decade, this inspiration would propel her from political ostracism as an opponent of the Marcoses' grand scheme for health to the core of state power. Between 1983 and 1992, Mita would move successively from the chair of the national women's coalition of GABRIELA to the cabinet of President Corazon Aquino where she served as secretary of social welfare and development from 1986 to 1992. As such, her authority over a broad policy area of critical importance to millions of Filipinos made her one of the most influential officials in government. Ultimately, she would become the longest-serving departmental secretary in the Aquino government, surviving fundamental, sometimes acrimonious, shifts in cabinet personnel.

In an interview she gave not long after her appointment, Mita attributed her rise to a family tradition of idealism and public service: "I would say you are what you are because of how you were prepared." Explaining the source of her inspiration, she said, "You learn from your family . . . 'serve your country,' 'be honest,' 'your country first'. . . . These are things I carried with me all the time, not just now but long before this job, these things have been with me." More specifically, she attributed her commitment to the influence of one person.

> My grandfather was a doctor of medicine, and since I was a little child I have always wanted to be like him . . . everything like him, even to be a doctor like him, and to serve the country like he did. Everything was after him. He was my idol, you know. . . . Although I'm the fourth generation since my great grandfather, I'm the third generation that participated in something of national importance.[1]

While Mita perceives her family as one that embodied service to the nation, most Filipino nationalists have held the diametric view that the Pardo de Taveras are the personification of elite betrayal. Focusing upon her grandfather's prominence in the transition to American colonial rule, nationalist historians have denounced his collaborationist role as traitorous. Thus, in 1981, only two years before Mita's moving tribute to Ninoy Aquino, the Philippine Educational Theater Association staged a play by nationalist Nicanor Tiongson entitled *Filipinas Circa 1907*. The antihero of this political drama was a strutting, manipulative *mestizo* named Tiyo Pardo, a transparent pseudonym for Mita's grandfather, T. H. Pardo de Tavera. Among the many crimes committed in four acts, Tiyo Pardo tried to sell the national patrimony to the colonial Americans, a dramatized treason that drew a chorus of boos and hisses from the enthusiastically nationalist audience.

This dissonance between the Pardo de Taveras' personal and public images lies at the heart of the problematic position occupied by the family and others of their class in Philippine politics. Like it or not, Filipinos must come to terms with the fact that the Pardo de Taveras, more clearly than any other politically prominent family, have played a central role in the formation of the Philippine nation-state for more than a century. The history of the Pardo de Taveras is in a sense the national history in microcosm.

Under Joaquin Pardo de Tavera's leadership in the late 1860s, his generation of Philippine-born Spanish and mixed-blood *mestizos* assumed a political identity as "Filipinos." Placed in opposition to the peninsular-born Spaniards by their support of colonial reforms, they gave the term Filipino its earliest connotation of inchoate and unformed nationalism. In the subsequent phase of national formation, T. H. Pardo de Tavera was a scholar whose work gained for Philippine studies the European recognition to which Filipino propagandists aspired. As the leading Manila *ilustrado*, he won the respect of the first American colonial administrators, and his expertise and political agenda shaped U.S. policy in the Philippines. In her generation, Mita led the women's movement to oppose Marcos in the early 1980s. An influential advocate for people's health care before and during the martial-law period, she won support for her nongovernmental organization AKAP from international agencies that had grown wary of Marcos's opportunism.

At each critical moment of national development a Pardo de Tavera has inspired the next generation to sacrifice for the nation. Yet in the public realm, even at their apex of power, the family has suffered from a mingled perception of admiration and animosity. The image of service and excellence is clouded by rumors of intrigue, murder, and infidelity that grow cumulatively with each corresponding generation of detractors.

Dispelling this double image of private and public perceptions requires careful analysis of both family and national histories. Significantly, it requires the ability to discern the extent to which the nationalist historiography limits perspective. With a clearer focus, the national record shows that, despite the prevailing nationalist view of T. H., he served the nation. As reflected and recorded in the family's memory, that tradition of service passed through two generations to his granddaughter Mita.

When asked to identify the support network that was responsible for propelling her to high office, Mita Pardo de Tavera unhesitatingly referred to the Concerned Women of the Philippines, a group of activists with whom she became identified during the last decade of the Marcos regime.[2] She won the support of this women's group, she believes, because she had maintained a principled opposition to the regime. Her life of service to the people as a medical doctor, and her advocacy on behalf of the need for basic medical care, marked her as one of the most powerful women in Philippine society. Simultaneously, however, she was aware that in Manila's gossipy milieu her connections to the Aquinos would be seen as central in her rise to power. Detractors would attribute her appointment to her niece's marriage to Cory Aquino's brother.[3] How much such connections contributed to the appointment may never be known. In Mita's own view her ability weighed more heavily than her connections.

In 1972, when Marcos declared martial law and established his dictatorship, Mita had just been appointed executive director of the tuberculosis research and treatment hospital known as the Quezon Institute. First hired as a medical fellow in 1946, she had risen through the ranks.[4] She saw her directorship, with its supervisory control over seventeen hospitals and twenty-one clinics, as a chance to implement some of the tuberculosis treatment policies she had developed over the years. She explained that as she came to weigh the operating costs of the hospital system and its provincial units she became convinced that "the institutional approach was too expensive." It cost ten times more to keep one patient in the hospital than to attend to many in their communities. More importantly, she knew from long experience at the Quezon Institute that hospitalization did not produce improved health for two-thirds of all patients confined for an average of thirty to sixty days. So she began to change direction, pressing her staff to take what she called a domiciliary approach, "one that would have us go towards the community."[5] She recalled that there was considerable resistance from the medical staff. In her words,

> This was understandable. Medical doctors are trained to stay in the hospital; they are not prepared to go to the community. My staff were not trained to become country physicians. So it was a question of attitudes. But I was able to institute this [change] in all our provincial units, and in the congressional districts around Manila. And things were moving very well until the issue of the property came up.[6]

Although what Mita was advocating came to be known as primary health care, her approach at that time "had no name."[7] Given the state's weak infrastructure, the family remained the main source of welfare for the majority of Filipinos. Mita argued that a sound national health policy should build upon the strengths of the local communities. Trained as a medical doctor, she was not opposed to the hospital system but she came to believe that the most efficient way of using scarce resources was to enable the family and local community to meet basic health needs. It was a perspective not often found among medical professionals but her years with tuberculosis patients allowed her to look "through the people's eyes."

In 1972, she had a chance to align national health policy with that perspective. But "my ideas were beginning to sound threatening to people in the medical group."[8] After the declaration of martial law, her views led her into a head-on clash with First Lady Imelda Marcos who was posing as a populist by building a series of lavish, organ-specific hospitals. With its aging wards the Quezon Institute lacked the grandeur that Imelda's ambition required. Sprawling over nineteen acres in suburban Manila, the outmoded colonial pavilions of the institute were unimpressive. Although the buildings housed hundreds of patients who could not afford other care, Mrs. Marcos wanted monuments to the regime's success. She shut down the Quezon Institute and built another organ hospital, the Philippine Lung Center. Mita's recollection of her sacking reveals the pain and humiliation she experienced.

> I was viewed as an obstructionist to Imelda's grandious plan, and the only way was to declare my position vacant. I'll never forget this. It was at a Board meeting on May 3, 1974. Right there and then, a motion was presented to declare the position of the Executive Secretary vacant. I objected vehemently. But the Board pointed out that although I had done wonders for the Institute, they still wanted a change at the top. It was within their legal prerogatives to relieve me, and they did. They did not say, "You can go back to your former position." Not at all. They just dropped me. I was the Executive Secretary, a position held at the pleasure of the Board. I was a career official. I thought that if the Board was not happy with me serving as Executive Secretary, I would go back to my former position. I had not realized that by assuming the post of Executive Secretary, I had given up my rights and I no longer had security of tenure. When I questioned how they could do that to me after nearly thirty years of service, their answer was, "Well, that's another matter. You will have to submit your resignation." I took it very badly. I decided that I would not go back like a beggar and say, "Well, I want to retire, please give me my retirement [pay]." What I did was to consult attorneys. I remember going to [Edgardo] Angara and Lorenzo Teves. They all talked about how difficult it would be to take on protagonists who were so important, and implied I was foolhardy to think of suing them. But I went on searching until I found one who was not intimidated by the establishment, Juan C. David. He said, "Yes, I'll take it over." So he filed my case. All I wanted was to file a protest against an act of injustice. This is when I really felt that truly we had a government that was unjust.[9]

Years later, when Mita regained power as chair of the Philippine Charity Sweepstakes, she would find out how much more directly the rise of the Lung Center caused the decline of the Quezon Institute.[10] Angry and frustrated after her dismissal by the Marcos regime, Mita found herself isolated. She had lost more than position and income. She had lost the object of sixteen years of hard work and with it the chance she had waited for to direct health care policy. In her words, "I believed, and still do, that the institute was meant to be a teaching hospital for tuberculosis and lung diseases. I hoped that what would continue was the learning and research into lung diseases among Filipinos."[11]

Despite political ostracism, Mita continued her private medical practice, and by 1975 she was working closely with Jose Diokno, a human-rights lawyer. Her dissociation from the Marcos dictatorship proved beneficial to her credibility. She recalls that:

> I found an opportunity to follow through my avant garde ideas about how TB should be handled. I met a British physician who had been in the Malaysian public health system and now headed a company based in Singapore. He liked my ideas and offered me a small grant, with a supply of TB medicines, to begin my community-based approach to TB treatment. I began right away. The program involved training volunteers, mostly women in the community, to act as health workers. Our first concern was to identify all contagious cases of TB. We taught our volunteers how to use microscopes for sputum examinations, how to give vaccinations. We trained them in starting treatment, and in follow-up treatment, doing repeat sputum examinations to find out how the patients were progressing, educating their families and neighbors. That was when I formed AKAP, Tagalog for 'to enfold' or 'to embrace'. What I envisioned was a health movement for the people.[12]

Strategies of Survival

In traditional historiography, there would be three main characters in the history of the Pardo de Taveras. Two are men: Don Joaquin (1829–84) and T. H. (1857–1925). The woman is Mita Pardo de Tavera (1919–). The attributes of achievement pertain to all three: formal education, high office, and elite social status. Such a story might be interesting but it would be limited in view and therefore familiar. It would trace only, in a very simple way, the family's rise.

When we broaden our view and, as Linda Gordon suggests, "rearrange relationships within old stories," we find ourselves rewarded with a fuller understanding of the family and its strategies of survival in the context of Philippine society.[13] The real story, then, is one of rise and decline, of endurance and reemergence. The prominence of the Pardo de Taveras continues because in each generation family members have grasped the source of the family's strength— their own—and built upon it.

The Pardo de Taveras are among a handful of Filipinos who can name their ancestors beyond the generation of their great-grandparents. This memory is the legacy of T. H. Pardo de Tavera. Drawing upon personal records and his research in European archives, he produced a history that traces the family's descent through both the Pardo de Tavera and Gorricho lineages.

The original name was Pardo. De Tavera was added in the 1640s when identifying an aristocrat by the family's place of origin became customary. It seems the Spanish nobility who were identified as "of Tavera" had Portuguese roots, and there is a town called Tavira, or Tabeira, close to the present Spanish border on the southeastern coast of Portugal. Those roots reach back into the sources of early peninsular history. When the Castilian Alfonso VIII waged war on the Almohad ruler in the thirteenth century, he led a coalition of forces from the kingdoms of Aragon, Navarra, and Portugal. One of those who fought heroically under his command was Don Gonzalo Paez de Tabeira.[14]

Recognition of the nobleman of Tabeira for distinguished service appears to have included titles and influence in the royal court. By the sixteenth century, the family "de Tavera" was counted among the powerful nobility of Toledo in the populous core of Spain, south of what became the metropole at Madrid. The cardinal of Toledo, Don Juan Pardo de Tavera, was inquisitor general and regent of Spain during the reign of Charles I. Descended from one of the cardinal's brothers and named for him, Don Juan Pardo de Tavera, Marques de Magahon by virtue of his marriage to one Doña Giomar, formed the branch from which the Philippine Pardo de Taveras' *arbol genealogico* (family tree) sprung.

T. H. Pardo de Tavera omits childhood and personal details but provides the name, year of birth, and name of spouse for each of his lineal ancestors.[15] To the main line of Pardo de Taveras he adds that of his mother's family, the Gorrichos. Combining cross-generational depth with the breadth of intrafamilial linkages, the genealogy is a remarkable expression of descent consciousness.

The founder of the family's Philippine branch was Don Julian Pardo de Tavera, born in Toledo in 1795. At the age of thirty, he married a Spanish woman, Doña Juana Gomez, daughter of Don Juan Gomez and Doña Catalina Duran. They married at Puerto Real in Spain on 1 December 1825 and shortly afterwards set sail for Manila. In two ways Don Julian broke the family mold. He left Spain for the Philippine colony, and, although his ancestors traditionally had held posts in the judiciary, he became a lieutenant in the Spanish Army.

Don Julian was the first member of this prominent Spanish family to relocate in the colony.[16] That he intended to settle in the Philippines is fairly clear. He did not come as an appointee, commissioned for a tour of duty in a far-flung post. He came with his new wife, and once in the colony he took up a profession quite different from those of his peninsular forebears. Why did he choose to emigrate, and why to the Philippines? Perhaps he saw opportunities there. Spain's attitude towards its colonies had begun to change in the eighteenth century. Spanish reformists were convinced that colonies were not mere pastoral burdens but potentially productive dominions. Arguing that colonies could and should benefit the mother country, they pressed for reforms that would stimulate colonial development. During the thirty-odd years that preceded the opening of Manila to foreign traders in 1809, a succession of Philippine governors had focused their attention on encouraging agriculture and industry. One of them, Rafael Maria de Aguilar y Ponce de Leon, touted the Philippines in 1806 as "the most valuable colony in the world." Perhaps Governor Aguilar's effusive praise of the Philippine dominions as "so extensive, so valuable and so productive that there are no limits to their possibilities" sounded a siren call to Spaniards of Don Julian's generation, if not of his social class.[17] Perhaps he was a younger son and stood to inherit less than an older, more favored brother. Those family details are not known. Julian Pardo de Tavera's reasons for breaking with the family's peninsular traditions and branching out on his own are difficult to discern in the faint light of surmise.

Don Julian and his wife went to live in the colonial society of the nineteenth-century Philippines. Within four years of their arrival, two sons were born, Felix and Joaquin, and the family became "Filipino." Used with discriminatory intent, the term referred to full-blooded Spaniards born in the islands in order to distinguish them from those who had been born in Spain. Yet, as the Pardo de Taveras settled in the colony, the pull of their peninsular traditions seemed to grow stronger. Reversing their father's lapse from the family's long devotion to judicial service, both Felix and Joaquin studied law. As bright, highly regarded young lawyers, the Filipino Pardo de Taveras moved into the select community of Spanish intellectuals whose career paths led directly into the law.

In the closed confines of the colony, fierce contests for prestige and rank often raged. In battles for social survival, genealogy proved a powerful weapon. With an indisputably distinguished lineage, the Pardo de Taveras were well armed. They could trace their descent from the family that had produced Spain's powerful sixteenth-century regent, Cardinal Don Juan Pardo de Tavera. Moreover, in the petty brawls for preferment, the burial place of one's honored dead was taken as a lasting indicator of rank. The family could silence the most vociferous opponent with the fact that the remains of "El Gran Cardenal" rested with those of Mother Spain's most venerated rulers in the Escorial, the palace-mausoleum of Philip II. The family's Spanish alliances through marriage with such noble families as the Medinaceli, Villar, Villanueva del Fresno, Alcala, Alameda, Palma, and Medellin y Montijo were impeccable. Beyond establishing the Spanish lineage then considered crucial for social acceptability, their genealogy commanded respect, even awe. Research attributed to the Spanish-Filipino biographer Manuel Artigas y Cuerva, a contemporary of T. H. Pardo de Tavera, corroborates the family's version of its history.[18]

The manuscript of the *Arbol Genealogico de los Pardo de Tavera* is written in the hand of Doña Paz Lopez Manzano, wife of T. H.'s second son, Alfredo, and mother of his granddaughter Mita. In the margin, Paz notes that the history was dictated by her father-in-law. That T. H. cherished recollections of family preeminence is obvious. That he regarded his knowledge of family history as a trust, a legacy to his descendants, is demonstrated in the care with which he drew the *arbol genealogico*. Was it his intent to raise the coming generations' sense of self-worth, to spur their ambitions with the family's lore? Perhaps. At the very least, his account of the lineage ensures that rising generations of Pardo de Taveras will know to whom they are related, and why. This trust has been vindicated already in his granddaughter Mita's sense of responsibility to uphold these family traditions. In providing her and her descendants with a historical sketch, T. H. created the framework upon which a fuller family history can be woven. Like the product of Penelope's endless loom, the Pardo de Tavera tapestry continues to unfold.

Joaquin: Liberal Reformist

Few details are known about the early years of Joaquin, son of Don Julian Pardo de Tavera. Aside from the mention of his birth at San Roque, Cavite, on 19 September 1829, all recorded information focuses on the brilliance of his career as a lawyer, professor of law, government dignitary, and leader of the liberal reformists in Manila.[19] Even T. H.'s published and personal histories omit the details of his uncle's childhood, portraying him at the peak of his public life as "Don Joaquin."

But the formal dates and milestones can be interpreted to bring life to the stiff portraiture. Thus, one finds that Joaquin was only twenty years of age when he began his studies of canonical law at Manila's Universidad de Santo Tomas, and only twenty-three when he received his first law degree. At twenty-four, he began another law course at the same university, finishing four years later, in 1857. By age twenty-eight, he was licensed to practice law in Manila and forthwith received an offer of appointment as law reporter in the colony's highest court, the Real Audiencia. But his health was poor and he declined the offer.

The young Joaquin was considered a rising star even in his university days. Working with such highly regarded lawyer-professors as Don Jose Jugo and Don Francisco de Marcaida, he quickly developed a reputation for brilliance. It seems that he combined a keen, incisive mind with a charisma that drew some of Manila's legal lions to him as mentors and advocates. Yet it would be a mistake to attribute those connections solely to the young man's rising reputation. His older brother Felix had preceded him at the university and in Manila's professional circles. By the time Joaquin completed his second law course, Don Felix was already a prominent lawyer with a reputation for excellence. Representing his in-laws, the Gorricho family, in a property dispute, the elder brother had appealed for and won a reversal of a colonial Audiencia decision from the Supreme Court in Madrid. Included among his associates was the famous Manila lawyer, Don Juan Francisco Lecaros, who became one of Joaquin's mentors. Indeed, it was in the distinguished practice of Lecaros that the younger brother cut his professional teeth. Don Felix's association with Don Juan Francisco was more than a professional one. At the baptism in 1857 of Don Felix's first-born son, Trinidad Hermenegildo ("Trini," later T. H.), Don Juan Francisco stood as godfather.

The year of his nephew's birth was also the year in which Don Joaquin was admitted to the bar. A second nephew, Felix, was born soon after, followed by a niece, Paz ("Chiching"). The young uncle Joaquin appears to have doted on his brother's children. It is not clear whether he was married by that time but perhaps the attentiveness with which he filled the avuncular role provides a clue. Felix's wife Juliana had a younger sister, Gertrudis ("Tula"), who at some point became Joaquin's wife. Both were daughters of Don Jose Damaso Gorricho, a wealthy landowner and industrialist of Manila and Cavite. If Joaquin was already married when Felix and Juliana began their family, his closeness to the young Pardo de

Taveras—Trini, Felix, Jr., and Chiching—would have been natural. They were not only his brother's but his wife's sister's children—a twofold filial tie.

When Don Joaquin was thirty-five years old, his brother Felix died. Without hesitation, he stepped in as the adoptive father to his three young kin, a role he filled with grace and affection. Joaquin's own children were not born until much later.[20] Perhaps, concerned with raising his brother's children, he and Tula postponed their own family. But seeing Don Joaquin's belated parenthood as proof of his devotion to filial duty is at best only conjecture. The finest testimony is in T. H.'s *Arbol Genealogico,* wherein he described the man he remembered as his father figure.

> Don Joaquin Pardo de Tavera was widely esteemed for his nobility of
> character. People who were drawn to him saw not only a man of intellect but
> a person whose elegant manner, kindness and tact won their loyalty and
> admiration.

Don Joaquin filled not only the paternal void left by his brother's early death but the gap it had opened in Manila's professional class. That segment of Philippine society was not extensive and the loss of a prominent member was apt to be sorely felt. As few young Spaniards sought access to professional education, replacing someone of Don Felix's stature must have been problematic. Among the colony's approximately 13,500 Spaniards, only a small percentage would have been considered suitable.[21]

It came as no surprise, then, when a Royal Order dated 6 December 1864 arrived in Manila appointing Don Joaquin as his brother's successor on the governor general's advisory council, the *Consejo de Administracion.* The post of *consejero* was largely honorary because the council could advise the governor only on matters he chose to bring before it.[22] Nonetheless, to sit in council meant prestige and influence. It brought the opportunity to mingle with the highest officials in the colony: the governor general, who presided; the archbishop of Manila; the admiral of the Navy; the Army's commander in chief; the president of the Royal Audiencia; the director general of the Civil Service; the head of the Exchequer; the fathers superior of the religious orders; the president of the Chamber of Commerce; the president of the colony's institute for development, the Sociedad Economica de Amigos del Pais; and six delegates representing the regions of Luzon and Visayas. The four at-large members were particularly notable, as they were appointed by the Spanish Crown. Like his brother Felix before him, Don Joaquin was one of these four. He received the royal appointment, the highest official recognition in Spain and all its dominions, when he was thirty-five years old.

There seemed no end to the honors, accolades, and favors showered upon Don Joaquin. Academic titles and appointments, the governor general's patronage, and memberships on directorial boards were all evidence of the high regard in which he was held.[23] At thirty-seven years of age, after passing a rigorous examination, he was named to the law professorship formerly held by his mentor,

Don Francisco de Marcaida. Don Joaquin thrived in the professoriate. He had won the admiration of his professors and mentors as a student. Now a professor himself, he found that his students were loyal. They gathered in throngs in his law class, in the hallways, at the gate of the university. Among his students were those of the next generation who would lead the struggle for Philippine independence— Antonio Maria Regidor, Mamerto Natividad, Florentino Torres, Hugo Ilagan, and Felipe Buencamino, Sr. Recalling his uncle through the eyes of the fifteen-year-old boy he was at that time, T. H. Pardo de Tavera captured the image that attracted and inspired so many university students.

> A man of principle, he defended issues of justice with tenacity, courage and a characteristically passionate commitment to democratic ideals. He gave himself to the study of matters Philippine, for which he professed a deep and abiding love. He was highly esteemed for his liberalism and gracious personality, and he was so popular that he was often found, following his lectures at the Universidad de Santo Tomas, surrounded by large groups of students at the university gates eager for his attention and inspiring ideas.

During these years of achievement and recognition, Don Joaquin also became the leading light in a movement attempting to bring liberal reform to the Philippine colony. Ardent and articulate, he was a passionate advocate of justice, bringing both his commitment to constitutionalism and his intellectual gifts to the study and teaching of Philippine matters.[24] In all questions that touched upon the interests of the colony, he invariably took a progressive stance. Also invariably, he took the side of the colony against Spain. In a conflict over control of Philippine parishes that broke out between the peninsular regular orders and Filipino secular priests, he took up the latter's cause, standing alongside Fathers Pelaez, Ponce, and Jose Burgos.[25] One of his students, Felipe Buencamino, Sr., asserts that it was from Don Joaquin and the men of the *comite de reformadores* that he first tasted the waters of liberal thought, inspiring him to lead the university students in an unprecedented strike, demanding for Filipinos the right to use Spanish rather than Latin in classes.[26]

Events in Spain during the late 1860s gave the impression that the liberal cause had won. The conservative Isabel II was overthrown, the liberal Constitution of 1868 was declared, and a liberal governor general was sent to the colony. The victory of the liberal faction in the metropole encouraged their colonial counterparts. Basking in the glow of success, Don Joaquin and a group of *reformadores* celebrated the arrival of the reputed liberal, Governor General Don Carlos Maria de la Torre. Although it was impromptu, the celebration was decorous and Don Joaquin and his fellow reformists were presented by Manila's governor himself. Remarkably, it was the first time the Manila liberals had identified themselves publicly to the colonial power as a group. How they had now positioned themselves in relation to that power would become apparent in subsequent incidents.

The Filipinos made another public display during a funeral procession convened to transfer the bones of former governor Simon de Anda from the Manila Cathedral to a niche in one of the churches within Intramuros, the walled city. The cathedral was in ruins, the result of a massive earthquake that had occurred on 3 July 1863, and a temporary transfer was required. Don Joaquin recalled the scene.

> On the day set for the transfer, the public, as if in response to some secret call, turned out *en masse*, all dressed in mourning, at the place for the ceremonies. The funeral cortege left the ruined cathedral and, after passing through the principal streets, amidst immense throngs of people, entered the Augustinian church where the Benediction was to be chanted before the actual transfer to the Franciscans' church. On the way, perfumes, flowers and wreaths were showered upon the bier. At the moment that the *Responso* was about to begin, a young Filipino priest separated himself from a group made up of his fellow clergy. He bore in one hand a beautiful wreath of laurel and forget-me-nots. Bowing as he passed in front of the astonished Captain-General, he ascended the steps of the catafalque and laid upon the casket a long ribbon which bore these words upon it: *"The Secular Clergy of the Philippines to Don Simon de Anda y Salazar."*[27]

The dignified demonstration seemed effective. Don Joaquin thought it would influence the governor general to do something on behalf of the colony, although in De la Torre's *junta*,

> there was not a mestizo, much less a Malay Filipino, summoned to represent his race, so numerous and important.[28]

Despite initial misgivings, the Filipino liberals took heart. Madrid's commission and Manila's *junta* rendered reports that concurred on points the Filipinos deemed crucial to the colony's good—reform of primary and secondary instruction, the establishment of a School of Civil Administration to end the sending out from Europe of new employees with each change of Cabinet, and the abolition of the tobacco monopoly.[29]

The liberals were elated. They carefully followed developments in Madrid and knew that the presence in the Spanish cabinet of the liberal Don Segismundo Moret y Prendergast would be instrumental in enacting the reforms. They must have felt certain that change was underway. On 12 July 1869, they gathered once again before the governor general's residence to acknowledge his efforts on behalf of their cause. The conservative *peninsulares* were outraged.[30] Here was a group of *creoles* and *mestizo* upstarts,[31] flaunting distinctiveness and nonpeninsular sympathies, clearly pro-Philippines in orientation. Because these Filipinos were among the more prominent of Manila's professionals, businessmen, and intellectuals, they were difficult to ignore. The highest officials in the colony certainly did not appear to disregard them. At a reception celebrating his promulgation of the Spanish Constitution hosted on 21 September 1869, the governor general favored the leading *reformadores* with prominent places.

Despite his liberal reputation and encouraging demeanor, Governor General de la Torre was still a minion of the colonial state. He drew the Filipino liberals to him, disarming them with apparent acceptance. Then, marking each one, he quietly ordered surveillance of their activities and correspondence. Although there were no specific criminal acts, nothing upon which to base a warrant of arrest, he found that there was cause for great caution. The Philippine-born Spaniard and liberal lawyer Don Antonio Maria Regidor had a brother, Manuel, who lived in Madrid, where he was busily involved in radical politics as a close associate of the radical Cuban-born deputy to the Spanish Cortes, Rafael M. Labra. In 1869, under the pseudonym Raimundo Geler, Don Manuel published a primer on reform for the Philippines entitled *Islas Filipinas: Resena de un organizacion social y administrativo y breves indicaciones de las principales reformas que reclaman*. He also was engaged in publishing, anonymously, many articles in Madrid's radical newspaper *La Discusion*.[32]

As men in positions of power are apt to do, De la Torre considered the demands for reform a threat. It was not that he and others like him misunderstood the intent of liberal reformists, for he grasped, even concurred in, what they wanted. But he held major reservations about the liberals.

> The country needs administrative and economic reforms . . . [G]iven the nature of this people, whose civilization is unfortunately quite rudimentary, their implementation demands great and special care. The state of the country also demands a good system of public education, inasmuch as that which it now has is reduced to a university in which they only form theologians and lawyers, two classes which are here the least necessary and which, moreover, are the nucleus of those who represent the anti-Spanish party.[33]

He could only perceive the change envisioned by reformists as leading to diminishing control. So he accused the Manila liberals of coveting independence. He knew there could be no response from the state other than to thwart the reformists, and a thwarted reformist was no less than a separatist, a lesson the Spanish were learning in the Americas. Thus, in December 1869, Governor General de la Torre reported as follows to his superior, the overseas minister.

> With very rare exceptions there is not a priest or a lawyer born in this country with some education and influence who, both now and always, has not employed them in creating around him aspirations for independence. At present, unfortunately, in spite of my efforts and the exquisite care I dedicate to this matter, as is my duty, I have not been able to find out anything concrete about their projects. Nonetheless the whole country points its finger

at certain individuals of the clergy and certain lawyers, all mestizos and
Philippine Spaniards. Without any doubt, these men, according to private
information and confidences I have received, and from the indications
emerging in the confidential dossiers drawn up for this purpose—everything,
I repeat, leads one to believe that these lawyers and priests are the only ones
here who dream of the independence of the country. . . . I am exercising
special vigilance, and I have adopted the means I believe necessary that public
order should be in no way disturbed. Moreover, I am determined to take
such dispositions as my fervent patriotism will suggest to me.[34]

Although De la Torre did not make obviously repressive moves, some of his policies
tipped his hand to the Filipino liberals.

[The] aggrieved [Filipino] clergymen [had] proposed to take advantage of the
new freedom of writing in the Peninsula, to defend themselves in the Spanish
press, but the Governor-General of the Philippines prohibited the entry into
the Islands of the Spanish newspaper *El Correo de Ultramar* [the Over-Seas
Post], notwithstanding that it was not devoted to any particular policy.[35]

Yet the villain in the eyes of the liberals was not Carlos Maria de la Torre. In
1871, their real enemy arrived in the person of Governor General Rafael Izquierdo y
Gutierrez who "ended immediately all the hoped-for reforms." Casting aside De la
Torre's precedents Izquierdo made no pretense of affability. Don Joaquin recalled that

On the very day of taking office, Don Rafael Izquierdo let it be plainly
known what were his intentions and the instructions he had received in
Madrid. "I shall govern," he told the civil and ecclesiastical officials who
surrounded him, "with a cross in one hand and a sword in the other." Then,
pointing to the portraits of Magellan and Legaspi which adorned the hall, the
governor expressed his regret at not seeing beside them portraits of the grand
men that founded the friar orders whose sons were there present. It would
have been impossible to imitate more perfectly the speech of the captains who
conquered Mexico by steel and the Gospel.[36]

Don Joaquin believed that escalating conflict between the secular Filipino
clergy and the peninsular friars caused Izquierdo's "policy of persecution." The
liberal faction, feeling embattled, "abandoned its propaganda in the newspapers of
the Peninsula." They watched with dismay as a policy of persecution unfolded, "a
disastrous policy which could only end in an attempt at revolution and in its most
rigorous repression."[37] In the realm of public instruction, an area of great concern
to the reformists, "the Governor, with the avowed intention of stamping out the
germs of liberal education there, suspended the opening of Manila's new School of
Arts and Trades on the very eve of the day set."[38] A recent law "had authorized

friars to free themselves from their vows but those who made use of that right were expelled and deprived of their property." Governor General Izquierdo "dismissed from office a great number of mestizos and natives who were in important positions in the civil and military services. He also required the resignation of some Peninsulares in the city as too zealous for the reforms." Don Joaquin noted evidence of injustice that rankled.

> Always before, in order to avoid danger of rivalry between the two battalions of
> artillerymen stationed in Manila, one of Peninsulares and the other of Filipinos,
> there had been maintained the strictest separation of the two races. As no
> injustice had ever been known, the most perfect goodwill existed between these
> two battalions of different colors. But the zeal for reform of the Governor
> destroyed this brotherhood of arms—there arose dissensions upon his ordering
> their consolidation with the difference that the Peninsulars should form the
> ranking companies and the native artillery have a subordinate position.[39]

The mutiny of a group of soldiers in the Cavite garrison provided the governor general with the pretext to move against the liberals. Since Don Joaquin had taken the lead in demanding reforms, the state equated his assertiveness with rebelliousness and charged him as a traitor to Spain.

Thus, in the sixth year of his professorship, at the height of his intellectual vigor, Don Joaquin was arrested. Before a special court, he and several colleagues were charged "with complicity in the crime of proclaiming the establishment of the republic."[40] The accusation was preposterous. Even more ludicrous was the connection made by the state between Don Joaquin and his co-accused, and the mutineers from the Cavite garrison.

At eleven o'clock on the night of 15 February 1872, the verdict was announced. One of Don Joaquin's colleagues, a brilliant young Spanish-Filipino priest, Jose Burgos, was sentenced to execution by *garrote*, the particularly cruel Spanish form of strangulation. Don Joaquin was sentenced to serve four years' imprisonment. By April he was on board the *Flores de Maria* bound for exile in the Mariana Islands.

In hindsight, his downfall seems inevitable. He had challenged the colonial state. His convictions had put him on a collision course with the power of Spanish repression. But at the time of his heady rise nothing had hinted at defeat. In his circumstances, his professional conduct, his business and personal associations, family, and character he was fortune's favorite. The facets of his life and career were brilliant. Even being Filipino in the racist atmosphere of Manila was acceptable. But he had projected his work and personality to reflect brilliance upon his identity as a Filipino. Seen through the paranoia of a repressive colonial state, that facet contained the flaw.

Don Joaquin was not a Filipino nationalist. The sentiments of people like him, who regarded the Philippines as their home, did not necessarily translate into aspirations for separation. They yearned for the dignity and political rights of full citizens so that they could correct the faults of the order under which they lived. Spain continued to loom large in their consciousness but the Philippines loomed larger. The islands became the focus of their energies and aspirations, the core of their passion. Their actions were driven by a fervent wish to raise up their homeland and improve its standing.

Were the feelings of Don Joaquin in sympathy with those of the Indios and others not Spanish in race? It is impossible to discover how his intellectual and political convictions were formed, or whether he was aware of the segment in colonial society that eventually would comprise the majority of the Filipino nation. No journal, letter, or other written record of his thoughts survives. The only direct source is an interview conducted with him and his close friend, fellow reformist, and comrade-in-exile Antonio Maria Regidor. The interviewer was the French writer Edmund Plauchut and the year was 1877, five years after the cataclysm that shook the foundations of their lives. By this time they were in Paris, out of reach of the power that had devastated them. Speaking freely and with emotion, they recalled the events of 1872.

> The French Revolution compelled Spain to concede political rights to the inhabitants of its over-seas possessions in Mexico and the Philippine Islands. As soon as it became known in Manila that the 'sons of the country' had the right to sit in the *Cortes,* currents of liberty electrified the Philippine people, who with enthusiasm acclaimed the constitutional regime in the Spanish peninsula proclaimed by the revolution. It was an era of short duration, for the reaction returned menacingly and the absolute despotism of the Spanish Kings hid the colonies in new clouds. Spain then lost a great part of her American possessions. Fears lest there should arise there a Bolivar or an Iturbide caused Spain to apply those means of oppression which constitute the most perilous of political systems. A hateful lack of confidence began to arise against the Filipinos, who from 1820 to 1823 were enthusiastically welcoming the spirit of equality and justice shown by the liberal regime. Spaniards born in the country, mestizos, natives, alike were deported without trial, without even the shadow of any judicial order. Moneyed men, priests, lawyers, natives, were torn from their peaceful homes. Some were thrown into prison and others were sent to convict camps in Europe for the 'crime' of having voiced their political opinions in favor of the just measures of the government.[41]

Indeed, divided by class and status, the non-*peninsulares* in the colony had not yet begun to see how their sentiments and aspirations should be linked by origins and experience. Don Joaquin would have felt akin only to those Malay Filipinos and "*mestizos*" with whom, using Spanish, he could discuss, argue, and agree about subjects they understood and the reforms they demanded. Now they were among his comrades in exile.

Exile in the Marianas

As the *Flores de Maria* put out to sea and the shoreline of Manila receded, what thoughts filled Don Joaquin's mind? As the ship sailed past the mouth of the harbor, did he shut out thought and reflection? Less than half a century earlier, his own father had set out from Spain for a remote colony, thousands of miles across the oceans. But that voyage was voluntary and Don Julian had been embarking for a new home. Don Joaquin's journey was made under duress. He was a prisoner of the Crown, disgraced and humbled. He had been torn from his home, from family, friends, and students, and from the life that he loved. Would he ever return? Would the torn fabric of his community be mended? What would his life be like in the Marianas? Where were these islands, out in the heaving ocean, unknown, obscure?

Without a doubt, it was some consolation that Don Joaquin was not alone but in the company of colleagues who, like himself, had been falsely indicted. There were twenty-two such *confinados*: Antonio Maria Regidor, Bartolome Serra, Jose Mauricio de Leon, Gervasio Sanchez, Pedro Carrillo, Balbino Mauricio, Maximo Paterno, Jose Basa Enriquez, Ramon Maurente, Jose Maria Basa, and the priests Jose Guevara, Agustin Mendoza, Feliciano Gomez, Pedro Dandan, Anastacio Desiderio, Miguel Laza, Toribio del Pilar, Justo Guason, Vicente del Rosario, and Mariano Sevilla. Among them was a woman, Doña Gertrudis Gorricho de Pardo de Tavera, Don Joaquin's wife.[42]

It was extraordinary that a wife should accompany her husband into exile. But Doña Tula was a remarkable woman. Although her family was rich, and she had a large inheritance, the Gorrichos were distinguished not simply by their wealth but by the vigor and creativity that had produced it. Her father and mother, with their backgrounds, marriage, and achievements, exemplify the emerging Filipino elite.

Like the Pardo de Tavera brothers, Doña Tula's father, Jose Damaso Gorricho, had been born in the Philippines. Although he was of Spanish blood, he was not considered a *creole* because he was also part Tagalog. Doña Tula's grandfather, Miguel Ignacio Gorricho, a Basque from the Unanoa Valley of Pamplona in Navarra, had been *alcalde mayor* of the Visayan province of Capiz.[43] His mother was Rafaela Doyle, the daughter of Jose Doyle (an Irishman who had come to Manila in 1750 in the entourage of Governor General Marques de Obando) and Maria Apostol (the daughter of a Greek father and a Tagalog mother). As Doña Rafaela was a quarter Tagalog, her son, Jose Damaso Gorricho, was one-eighth Tagalog.

Tula's mother was Ciriaca Santos of Cavite. To her the family attributes the vitality that spurred the Gorrichos' rise. She met Don Jose Damaso in her home town of Imus during one of his trips to the nearby provinces to procure supplies in his capacity as quartermaster for the Spanish army in Intramuros. The family story is that Don Jose Damaso was invited to Imus by the parish priest. During his visit, he saw a young woman fetching water from the well. He followed her, discovered her name, courted, and married her.[44]

As the wife of a quartermaster of the Spanish army, Doña Ciriaca began her own trade. She started by supplying *zacate* (hay) to the Spanish cavalry. As her business flourished, she purchased land across the river on which to grow her own *zacate*. Eventually she came to own large tracts of land further along the river in the rapidly growing section of Manila known as Binondo. Its location at the mouth of the Pasig River, across from Intramuros, favored Binondo's development as the city's commercial district. The center of the district and its most prestigious street was the Escolta. Doña Ciriaca and Don Jose Damaso owned most of the property on both sides of this street, from the bridge of San Gabriel to the street known as Soda. As a result of her business skills, and the properties inherited by her husband from his mother, Don Jose Damaso and Doña Ciriaca accumulated a large fortune. But their wealth derived not only from their large holdings on the Escolta. Don Jose Damaso also developed manufacturing and banking services, and is credited with initiating some of the Philippines' earliest industries. Even divided among their seven children, the properties remained considerable.

In deciding on the Marianas as Don Joaquin's place of exile, the Spanish colonial authorities added harshness to a punishment that was, for a man of his stature, virtually a sentence of death. The islands lay some fifteen hundred miles east of Manila. Although Ferdinand Magellan, when he reached them in 1521, gave the small group of islands a polite name,[45] they were known derogatorily as the Ladrones, meaning 'thieves', because the local people had taken things from the explorer's ships. They were considered obscure and isolated from the Philippine colony, which was itself one of the Spanish Crown's more distant dominions.[46]

The Marianas lay along the route between the Spanish Viceroyalty of Nueva España, the lofty administrative title for Mexico, and the Philippines. They became a way-station for galleons that carried the *real situado* (royal subsidy) from Acapulco to Manila, returning with Chinese silks and trade goods. The galleon trade ended when Spain's American colonies began waging their wars of independence, and the last galleon sailed in 1810. In 1817, the Marianas were transferred from the Mexican Viceroyalty to the Capitania General de Filipinas. One of the effects of the change was a decline in their importance and prosperity. That was especially clear in the reduction of the *situado*.[47] Though governor after governor in the nineteenth century tried to make the Marianas a port of call, their pleas fell on deaf ears in Manila.

The Spanish authorities had other uses for the Marianas. Over time they had learned that simply expelling undesirables from Spain to the Philippines did not diminish their activities. If they did not take care to isolate radical troublemakers, the exiles spread their treasonous ideas among the Filipinos. On the other hand, troublesome Filipinos deported to Spain came into their element, soaking up the politics of the metropole, associating with other agitators, and growing even more radical in their demands. To be effective, exile and banishment had to result in total alienation, the removal of the radical activist from any relevant context. The reformers were considered pestilential, and they had to be alienated from Spanish society on all levels. The remote Marianas provided punitive isolation.

On 22 April 1872, when the *Flores de Maria* reached the island of Guam, the *deportados* had their first glimpse of their place of exile. The shoreline was forbidding, indented with steep cliffs and mostly ringed with reefs against which the sea crashed.[48] The upper half of the east coast was steep and rugged, with no sheltering reefs, so the ship made its way to an anchorage on the western coast at San Luis de Apra. It was two miles from that anchorage to the *pantalan*, or pier, at Punta Piti. To disembark, the passengers had to take a lighter from the outer harbor through the channels formed by the reefs, to the pier. The channels could be navigated only at high tide.[49] From the ship, the island looked lush and green under clear skies. The northern half was a plateau rising sixty-six meters above the sea. The other half was mountainous and irregular, with steep slopes and deep gorges.

As the exiles landed, they would have noted that the *pantalan* looked recently built.[50] The *embarcadero* was floored with heavy timbers, which must have been cut from the forests in the northern part of the island, and was topped with a roof thatched with fronds of the *nipa* palm. The four sides were enclosed with walls of woven cane strips, and along them were fixed wooden benches. The doorways had carved balustrades.

Punta Piti was only the landing. The *deportados* had to travel a road that ran along the shore to reach the town of Agana. Perhaps, as became the mode fifteen years later, *calesas* (carriages) transported them the eight kilometers to the town center. It is more probable that they traveled in *carretas*, or carts, built with solid wooden wheels encased in iron tires made from old gun barrels.

Guam is the southernmost and the largest of the Marianas islands. But the *deportados* would not have thought it large. In size Guam is only a little more than 600 square kilometers, while their home island of Luzon is almost 106,000 square kilometers. It is not likely that they hoped for a comfortable exile. The humiliation of their arrest and trial, and the degradation and rejection that followed their fall from grace, had steeled them for the worst. Still, they must have been struck by the stark contrasts between Manila and Agana. Both were colonial capitals with buildings that housed officials and their functions but there the resemblance ended.

By the second half of the nineteenth century, Manila had become, in social and economic terms, two cities. There was the old city of Intramuros, and beyond it, centered in Binondo and sprawling into ricefields, was the new city. A fortress carefully planned to meet Spain's real and symbolic needs, Intramuros had massive gun emplacements guarding the entrance to the Pasig River.[51] As the center of colonial power, its purpose was to impress, inspire awe, and command obedience. It was filled with stately buildings of solid construction—the Ayuntamiento, the governor's palace, the cathedral, the churches, and the convents. There was no air of stylishness or frivolity about its structures. It was "an arena for religious pageantry, social interaction, political ceremonies and military parades."[52] It was a stage set for the reenactment of power rituals by both Church and state. In sharp contrast to Intramuros, the commercial center of Binondo lay open, its wharves,

Muelle de la Reina and Muelle de Silva, crowded with warehouses and businesses. Linking the old city with the heart of the new was a bridge, the Puente de España, which spanned the Pasig.

The opening of Manila to foreign commerce in 1809 so spurred its growth that by the 1880s it had seven suburbs, or *arrabales*, ranged in a loose radial pattern to the north, east, and southeast of Intramuros, encompassing close to 97,000 hectares. San Miguel, along the Pasig, became the *arrabal aristocrático*, with wide streets and imposing houses reminding one of stately Intramuros. Property values continued to rise, so that by the 1890s the price of good houses in San Miguel ranged from 30,000 to 83,000 pesos.[53]

In Agana the inhabitants lived "huddled beneath a protective cliff."[54] A nineteenth-century description reflects the discouraging picture that must have greeted the exiles.

> The city of Agana is located along the shore of the roadstead that bears the same name. The road is open to the north with a passage through the reef that allows small boats and large ones with light tonnage to pass through it. The town is situated on a strip of low sandy land about 600 meters wide. Behind it is a hill 30 to 40 meters high. A stream rises to the east and runs the length of the town through an artificial canal that lies between the houses and the beach. Most of the streets are wide, measuring between ten and twelve meters. The principal ones run from east to west and, although they are not straight, they run approximately parallel to one another. There are four streets and several alleys that run north and south. . . . All told there are 777 houses in the city and its barrios. Of these, forty-seven are built of masonry with tile roofs, two of masonry with wooden roofs, forty-six of masonry and *gigay* [woven coconut fronds], one of wood with zinc roof, 463 of wood and woven coconut fronds, and 218 of cane and woven coconut fronds."[55]

Don Joaquin, Doña Tula, and their fellow *deportados* would have been deposited at either the *casa gobierno* (government house) or the *mayoria de la plaza*, which was the office of the commander of the garrison (the Tribunal) and functioned as a combination town hall, municipal building, courthouse, and jail.

Don Joaquin and Doña Tula spent 997 days in exile on Guam, excluding the days of arrival (22 April 1872) and departure (16 January 1875). Where they lived, how they fared, and what they did to pass the hours is not known. As *deportados* it is unlikely that they were housed in the *presidio* like *confinados* (criminals) since official records show that the Marianas differentiated between their undesirables. T. H. Pardo de Tavera wrote that Doña Tula used her considerable wealth to ease the life of exile. Probably they lived in one of Agana's larger private houses. It also was common for occasional visitors to Guam, and *deportados* who could afford it, to lodge with local families.[56] As political prisoners, Don Joaquin and his fellows would not have been warmly received by the colonial officials, some of whom traveled to their Guam postings with them on the *Flores de Maria*.[57] But, because as a transport colony Guam got more than a fair share of "Spaniards who were nothing more than thieves,"[58] *deportados* of education and social status were probably well received by this element. The colonial officials acknowledged that "the deportation of small groups, especially of learned persons—and there have been some—has perhaps brought to these islands more advantages than disadvantage."[59]

The population of Guam was not large in 1872. Since there had been no major epidemics after smallpox reduced the number of inhabitants to 4,902 in 1863, it seems reasonable to estimate the population at the time of Don Joaquin's arrival at a figure between 6,000 and 6,400.[60] If, as was the case in 1886, more than 70 percent of the island's population lived in Agana, then the town had between 4,400 and 4,600 residents.[61] There was one native priest, Jose Bernardo Palomo y Torres. Born in Agana in 1836 and ordained in 1859, he was living and working on Guam when the *deportados* arrived. Whether they were friendly with him is not known.[62]

The difference between living in Manila and Agana can be seen as a matter of scale. In Agana, everything, including hope, must have been diminished. It is not that one stopped hoping but that one hoped for different things, smaller things.

On 5 May 1872, the *Flores de Maria* sailed out of San Luis de Apra, leaving the *deportados* in exile. After 701 days, on 25 March 1874, two of them escaped. These were not, as T. H. Pardo de Tavera states in his family history, Don Joaquin and Doña Tula escaping to Hongkong in the guise of friars. Rather they were Don Joaquin's close friend Antonio Maria Regidor and Manila businessman Balvino Mauricio, who arranged for the captain of a schooner to smuggle them to Hongkong.[63]

The eighty-ton schooner, commanded by a Captain Holcomb, had sailed from Hongkong under American colors with a cargo of "assorted merchandise." "Approximately two thousand pesos worth" was sold in Guam. Apparently Captain Holcomb intended to distract the Agana officials, inviting them to dine on board the day of the escape. The governor, the doctor, the administrator of the *presidio*, and the parish priest (Fr. Luis Ibañez) accepted. Father Ibañez recalled that "the captain appeared to be most attentive" but later he realized that Captain Holcomb "hid what he was scheming in his heart." Holcolmb informed the officials that he was sailing to the village of Umatac to take on water.[64] Genially, he insisted on taking along several members of the *principalia*.

Holcomb left for Umatac, using the presence of the *principales* as a distraction for his two escapees. At Umatac, he put his guests ashore and set sail for Hongkong with Don Antonio and Don Balvino on board. Although they could not return to Manila, their exile on Guam was over. They had no way of knowing it then but they had cut short their term on the island by less than a third.

In Agana the days dragged by. Storms blew in and out, tremors shook the island at regular intervals, officials came and served briefly, then were replaced by others. In early August of 1874, five months after the escape, the merchant steamer *Panay* arrived. More official replacements had come, including an *alcalde* (mayor) and two *escribanos* (scribes) who were to continue the *residencia* (review) of a former governor, familiar procedures from Don Joaquin's administrative past. There was also an armed escort composed of a captain of the guard, a lieutenant, and 40 soldiers accompanying a large group of Spanish "subversives." Plucked from their home cities of Cartagena, Jerez, Cadiz, Sevilla, and Madrid, 233 men and 4 women arrived to begin their exile. One wonders what the Filipinos thought at the sight of "those unfortunate *deportados* [who] arrived with no clothing, wretched and despondent after an extremely long journey made under the worst possible conditions."[65] Was it encouraging to discover that political activism persisted, or were they disheartened to see in yet another group of unfortunates evidence of continuing repression?

On 13 January 1875, nearly three years from the day of Don Joaquin's arrest, the Spanish merchant steamer *Legazpi* anchored at San Luis de Apra, bringing news of a pardon for the Filipino *deportados*. Immediately the Filipinos made plans to leave. Don Joaquin's fellow *reformador*, the wealthy Maximo Paterno, chartered the *Legazpi* for eight thousand pesos. The Filipinos were being allowed to leave the island for Europe, not for Manila, so their initial destination would be Hongkong.

The day of departure must have been a day of exhilaration. Perhaps they felt some twinges at leaving those of Agana who had been kind and generous. Fray Aniceto noted that the *Legazpi* sailed from San Luis de Apra at 4 o'clock in the afternoon. They must have waited for the tide before leaving the *embarcadero* at Punta Piti and sailing the two kilometers to the anchorage in the outer harbor. It might have been a happier day if they had been bound for Manila but perhaps not. Once branded as a *deportado*, could a person pick up the threads of a former life? Could Don Joaquin resume teaching, revive his law practice, return to the council? Clearly he and his wife must begin a new life. On board the ship were

> the priests Don Agustin Mendoza, Don Pedro Dandan, Don Anacleto Desiderio and Don Justo Guason. Also aboard were Don Maximo Paterno, Don Joaquin Pardo and his wife, Don Ramon [Maurente], Don Jose Baza, Don Pio Baza, Don Jose Baza [*sic*] and Don Pedro Carrillo. May God grant them a good voyage.[66]

The Pardo de Taveras in Paris

Don Joaquin and Doña Tula chose to reside in Paris. After the remoteness of Agana, the city must have seemed the center of life and movement. Their friend Antonio Maria Regidor had set himself up as an advocate in Spanish law in London, which was not far away. Madrid, with its community of Filipinos and *mestizos*, was accessible. Most importantly, the Parisian traditions of liberal thought and republicanism were vital. Don Joaquin would thrive.

As soon as they were settled, Don Joaquin and Doña Tula arranged to have brother Felix's eldest child join them in Paris. They regarded T. H. as a son, and no doubt wanted their closest kin near them in their new home. An increasing number of young Español/Filipinos and *mestizos* were traveling to Spain and other parts of Europe to study, so it would be entirely appropriate for the young man to earn his degree at the Sorbonne. Eventually T. H.'s mother, Doña Juliana, and the younger children, Felix and Paz, made the move to Paris as well.

The Paris migration of most of the Pardo de Tavera family was clearly an expression of Don Joaquin's concern for the well being of his dead brother's family. His concern was not for their financial well being, since Doña Juliana had a considerable share of the Gorricho wealth. Undoubtedly his real intent was to shield them from the slights and cruelties sure to be inflicted by vengeful *peninsulares* in the Philippines.

Although in his *genealogico* T. H. goes to some length to describe Don Joaquin's life and career, he says nothing about the family's experience of ostracism. Just as he gives not the slightest hint of remorse neither does he express even faint regret for the suffering that the family must have endured.

Although there is no written evidence that the Pardo de Taveras were mistreated in Manila after the banishment, it is impossible that the *peninsulares*, in self-righteous wrath over the *creoles* whom they maligned as anti-Spanish, would have spared victims' families. After the departure of Don Joaquin and Doña Tula the only Pardo de Taveras left in the Philippines were Doña Juliana and her children, perhaps their grandparents, and a few more distant kin.[67] Although Doña Juliana's family was closely knit, they were Gorricho. And it was painfully obvious that their wealth and social standing could not shield the Pardo de Tavera branch from the colonial state's displeasure.

It is possible to reconstruct the Pardo de Tavera family's fall from grace through the recollections of oppression of yet another prominent Filipino family, the Roxases. The discovery by the Spanish of the revolutionary group, the Katipunan, in 1896 brought a wave of terror in Manila reminiscent of the 1872 executions and arrests. One of the highest-ranking *creoles* to be executed on false evidence was Francisco L. Roxas. Like Don Joaquin a generation earlier, Don Francisco was a *consejero de administracion*. Again like Don Joaquin, his accumulated prestige, influence, and wealth could not deflect the power of the colonial state. Led out to Bagumbayan in Manila, tied at the elbows like his fellow prisoners, he was shot as a traitor to Spain. A cousin, Felix Roxas, recalled that after the execution "ordeals, humiliations, insults, restrictions, ingratitude and head-to-foot sneers [were] levelled at whoever was surnamed Roxas." When Felix tried to leave Manila for the relative safety of Europe, he first had to deal with disdainful Spanish officials. The Spaniard who grudgingly approved his travel papers refused to hand them over directly, tossing them on the floor at his feet.[68]

It would seem, from T. H.'s account of this period in his family's history, that to express anything other than stoic endurance would be, by implication, to cringe and acknowledge defeat. The refusal to do so is understandable. Even as he faced the full force of the colonial state, Don Joaquin always maintained that he was guiltless. Indeed, he claimed that he had fought against the injustice and oppression that threatened to destroy Spain.

His uncle's protestation is echoed in T. H.'s account and is given even greater force by the perspective from which the latter wrote in the 1920s. In light of Filipino nationalism and its hailing of the 1872 liberals as heroes, T. H.'s recollection is as much a celebration of Don Joaquin's principles as it is a memorial to his suffering. His admiration for his uncle's character and achievement is, in the obverse, an indication of how deeply the family must have suffered. In his straightforward narrative of events lies the inevitable yet unstated conclusion—that Don Joaquin's downfall was undeserved because the colonial state had erred.

Trinidad Hermenegildo Pardo de Tavera was eighteen years old when he left for Paris. He was in every sense young, with a baccalaureate from the San Juan de Letran, who had just begun medical studies at the Universidad de Santo Tomas. By the time he returned to Manila twelve years later it was 1887. He was thirty years old, more Frenchman than Spaniard, and more humanist than French. Whereas his grandfather had first arrived at Manila, also thirty years of age, armed only with an illustrious genealogy, T. H. returned impeccably educated. He held a Doctor of Medicine degree from the Sorbonne and a diploma in Malay languages from the École Nationale des Langues Orientales Vivantes. He was a published and translated author in the fields of medicine and linguistics, and had earned recognition for ground-breaking theoretical research.[69]

In 1884, his "Medicine a l'Ile de Luçon (Archipel des Philippines)," published in the Parisian *Journal de Medicine*, was translated into the Spanish and German. He was invited to membership in the learned Société Academique Indo-Chinoise in Paris. The same year, his *Contribucion para el Estudio de los Antiguos Alfabetos Filipinos* caused a stir among linguists and Filipino nationalists in Europe. His translator, the respected German linguist Ferdinand Blumentritt, recognizing its implications for theories on linguistic borrowing and for developing a new orthography, referred to T. H. as "the eminent Filipino linguist."[70]

T. H.'s immediate reasons for returning to Manila were twofold. By virtue of his medical research he was granted a royal commission in 1887 to study the medicinal properties of Philippine plants. Whether he sought the commission is not known but it certainly was timely. A year earlier, his mother had hosted a friend from Manila, Carmen Barredo. Doña Carmen was the widow of Ramon Gonzalez Calderon, one of the founders of Manila's largest commercial bank, the Banco Español Filipino. Traveling with Doña Carmen was her granddaughter and heir, Concepcion Cembrano y Gonzalez-Calderon. Concha, as her grandmother called her, was the daughter of Vicente Cembrano y Kerr and Carolina Gonzalez-Calderon.[71] Was it serendipitous that a perfect candidate for a suitable match came along just when T. H., on the threshold of an impressive career, was becoming optimally "marriageable"? It was not uncommon at the time for parents or grandparents to arrange a match. If Doña Juliana and Doña Carmen had intended a betrothal, they got their wish. But, since Concha was also the heir of her paternal grandmother, Concepcion Kerr, *viuda de* (widow of) Cembrano, who was in Manila, Doña Carmen thought it appropriate that the wedding should take place there.[72]

Was it foreordained that T. H. would return? Was he inextricably linked to the Philippines or was it a confluence of circumstances that brought him back? Certainly there were ties but were these strong enough to draw him and his family back?

Like Don Joaquin, T. H. was Philippine born, and so in the peculiar sense that the Spaniards used the term he was Filipino. But unlike Don Joaquin, who was full-blooded Spanish, T. H. was part Tagalog and part European. In fact, he was so distinctively European in his features that the Filipino painter Juan Luna chose him as the model for a painting of the Spanish explorer Miguel Lopez de Legaspi.[73] In the distinction that later Filipino nationalists would make, T. H. was a Filipino *de corazon* (of the heart) but he would never be a Filipino *de cara* (of the face).

There were, of course, property links. The wealth that maintained the family in Paris was largely derived from Manila-based real estate. But property is transferable and can be liquidated, for capital, as a timeless economic tenet testifies, has no nationality. Thus, the property of his family did not necessarily tie T. H. or his siblings to the Philippines.

After the Pardo de Taveras left Manila they did not break their ties to the Philippines. Indeed, as they came to thrive in the cosmopolitan world of Europe, they seemed to enhance their contacts with Filipinos and Philippine issues. T. H.'s earliest linguistic scholarship focused on the Philippines, and he was drawn to it as well in his studies of medical and humanist questions. Even if T. H. had not yet begun to identify himself as Filipino, his continuing links to the Philippines were seen as indicators of his roots. Like it or not, he was perceived as a Filipino.

The drawing room of Doña Juliana's home in Paris was a *salon*, a meeting place for young intellectuals, artists, and writers. The young Pardo de Taveras were "full of enthusiasm for new ideas," forming friendships with "South Americans and Filipinos, who were visionaries of patriotism and liberty."[74] In particular, Doña Juliana opened her home to the group of young, idealistic *ilustrados*, or intellectuals, from the Philippine colony who called themselves "Los Indios Bravos."

These young men were part of a larger group of Filipinos—*creoles*, Spanish, and Chinese *mestizos*—who in the latter part of the nineteenth century traveled to various European cities to study in the particularly European way expected of young men of substantial means.[75] With many of them, if not all, having achieved higher education before they arrived in these metropoles, they set themselves to earning additional university degrees in law or the sciences. Long subjected to the inequities and colonial inefficiencies that were aggravated by the *peninsulares'* discrimination, they were invariably liberal politically. Inevitably they gravitated toward the circles of liberal writers and intellectuals. Although most gathered in Madrid and Barcelona, they found themselves frequently in Paris, Rome, Heidelberg, and London. Among these *ilustrados* were Graciano Lopez Jaena, Julio Llorente, Salvador Vivencio del Rosario, Eduardo Lete, Jose Albert, Tomas del Rosario, Ramon Genato, Matias Gonzalez, Maximino Paterno, Pedro Paterno, Miguel Zaragoza, Felix Resurrección Hidalgo, Juan Luna, Baldomero Roxas, Mariano Ponce, Valentin Ventura, Jose Maria Panganiban, Antonio Luna, and Jose Rizal. Beginning with the last, these names comprise the litany that modern Filipinos invoke to commemorate the progenitors of the consciousness that begot the Filipino nation.

Yet, as in all things, these men hold varying ranks in the national memory. Some, whether or not they wrote tracts or promoted the reform movement, were clearly at the core of the group now known as the *propagandistas*. Some of these won higher recognition than the others, and their names inspire greater reverence.[76] Jose Rizal was a writer and artist of impressive breadth. Juan Luna and Felix Resurrección Hidalgo were gifted artists who won medals and citations, giving the community of Filipinos in Madrid, Rome, and Paris cause for public celebration and a high profile. Eduardo Lete was a newspaper editor and political writer, as were Mariano Ponce and Graciano Lopez Jaena.[77] But some of these men are enshrined in the national memory for more than their achievements in Europe as young men. After the outbreak of the Philippine Revolution, Rizal's execution as a traitor to Spain, in 1896, raised him to the status of a national martyr. Elevated to military leadership in the revolutionary government, Antonio Luna later took an uncompromising stance against U.S. colonial rule. His assassination in 1899, resulting from an unresolved conflict with the leader of the victorious Katipunan faction, Emilio Aguinaldo, has given him in the national memory the aura of unfulfilled promise.[78]

But in the 1880s these differentiations lay in the future. The gatherings at the Pardo de Tavera home on Avenue Wagram were warm and convivial, and the Filipino "Indios"—including Rizal and Luna—were frequent visitors. Rizal wrote to his parents about how much he enjoyed these gatherings.

> The Pardo [de Tavera] family who live here also invite me to eat at their home from time to time. Then Luna, Resurrección and I go there. On such days we do nothing else but talk about our country—its likes, food, customs, etc. The family is very amiable. The mother (widow) is a sister of Gorricho and remains very Filipino in everything. Her sons Trinidad and Felix Pardo are both physicians; her daughter Paz speaks French and English and she is very amiable and also very Filipino. She dresses with much elegance and in her movements and manner of looking she . . . is beautiful and svelte . . . .[79]

Juan Luna was, as T. H. put it, "the shining star" of the group. His painting, *Spoliarium*, had just won the gold medal at the Exposición Nacional de Bellas Artes in Spain, and he was the toast of the art world in Madrid, Rome, and Paris. Juan Luna courted Paz Pardo de Tavera who at twenty-four was tall, slim, and fair, with the refinement of a young woman of a cultured family.[80] No doubt Luna was encouraged by the warmth and cordiality with which the Filipino expatriates were received. On 7 December 1886, at the Civil Court in Paris, Paz and the twenty-nine-year-old Juan were married. As T. H. puts it, Luna had achieved much fame and glory but was impecunious.[81] Yet the couple seemed happy, supported by an indulgent Doña Juliana. Just as the Pardo de Tavera-Gorricho marriages had merged intellect and wealth, so had that of Luna and Pardo de Tavera.

T. H. and Concha Cembrano y Gonzalez-Calderon, heiress of her maternal and paternal grandparents, were more evenly matched. They were married in Manila in 1887, a year after the wedding of Paz and Juan Luna, and spent the next two years in the city. During these years T. H. did not teach nor did he have a public life. But his presence in the city did not go unnoticed. In 1889, the Chamber of Commerce named him as its delegate to represent the Philippines at the Universal Exposition in Paris. With his wide knowledge of Philippine culture, he was given the responsibility of organizing and cataloging the country's exhibits.[82] He and Concha sailed for Marseilles at about the end of March or the beginning of April 1889. With them was their first-born son, Carlos.

The reaction of one expatriate Filipino to the Philippine exhibit at the Paris Exposition is interesting. It is a mixture of sharp criticism for the colonialists, and gratified praise for a compatriot, T.H. Pardo de Tavera.

> In the wake of the miserable exhibit of our colonial products, we recall those sick and anemic wet-nurses who feed robust children, and we ask ourselves if there is no penalty in the Codes so that this class of criminals who poison the hopes of a people and mercilessly discredit an entire generation could be punished. . . . There was not sufficient time to prepare an exhibit worthy of the Philippines. It was impossible to find exhibitors who would send the industrial and natural products of the country within such a short time. An exposition no matter how common it might be needs years of preparation and such hasty improvisations of our officials, who are not used perhaps to this type of serious work, are inadequate. . . . We congratulate the delegate of the Manila Chamber of Commerce, the noted Doctor Pardo de Tavera, for his untiring efforts to have the Philippines participate with a modest presentation. The Chamber of Commerce in naming him their representative has recognized his fine zeal in overcoming the difficulties and problems which have arisen. Mr. Pardo has rendered an unselfish service to the Philippines, his native land.[83]

Although the exhibitors included Hidalgo and Felix Pardo de Tavera, Luna was not allowed to exhibit his painting *La Batalla de Lepanto*.

The family life of the Pardo de Taveras continued to change with the inexorable rhythms of death, marriage, and birth. In March 1884, Don Joaquin had died at the age of fifty-five. Now both Gorricho sisters were widows. Each had three children. Doña Tula's Eloisa, Beatrice, and Joaquin had been born in Paris and they were much younger than their cousins. T. H., at twenty-seven, had become the oldest male in the family. He began fulfilling the duties of *pater familias* at a much younger age than had Don Joaquin when Don Felix died in 1864.

A new generation of grandchildren came into the family. The first was a grandson, Andres, born 9 September 1887 to Paz and Juan Luna. The second grandson was Carlos, born in Manila to T. H. and Concha during their sojourn in 1888. Then on 24 June 1889 came a granddaughter, Paz and Juan Luna's second child, whose christening as Maria de la Paz on 9 September was celebrated by her parents with a large party of *los Indios Bravos*. A year later, in 1890, another grandson was added—Alfredo, second son of T. H. and Concha. That same year, Felix married Agustina Manigot, and set up his own household. With their growing family, Paz and Juan Luna moved to Villa Dupont, at 28 rue Pergolese. Doña Juliana, who maintained and supported the couple's household, came to live with them. The following year, 1891, Antonio Luna, Juan's younger brother and future general of the Philippine Revolution, then a student at the Pasteur Institute, also came to live at the house.

The cadences of the Pardo de Taveras' personal lives were changing. The circle of kin was widening. But the pace of their professional achievement did not diminish. When T. H. returned to Paris he resumed his research and writing. His brother Felix was proving himself a competent medical doctor and a talented sculptor, winning prizes, awards, and admiring reviews. In 1886 in Madrid, Felix won silver medals for his works *A Man, A Girl* and *Juan Salcedo*. A description of the artistic entries to the Paris Exposition in 1889 noted that "the young Filipino D. Felix Pardo de Tavera" had created a "handsome work of art . . . of an exquisite taste revealing in the author a sculptural talent bordering on genius."[84]

Then disaster struck. The terse words of a police investigator's report, dated 23 September 1892, flay emotion from the event.

> I have the honor of informing the Prefect of Police that yesterday at 10:30 a.m., Mr. Luna de San Pedro Juan fired four successive revolver shots in his home, Villa Dupont 28, on one of his brothers-in-law, Mr. Pardo de Tavera Felix, doctor of medicine, Pirachot Avenue 2 bis, on his mother-in-law, Mme Pardo de Tavera, and finally on his wife.

> Dr. Pardo de Tavera is wounded in the upper right chest; his condition gives no cause for alarm.

> The widow, Mme Pardo de Tavera, was killed instantly.

> As for Mme Luna de San Pedro, she is fatally injured. She received a bullet in the left [cranial] region

> Mr. Luna de San Pedro was arrested immediately after.

Another curt statement, dated 9 October, informed the procurator and prefect of police that "Mme Luna de San Pedro of Villa Dupont 28, wounded by her husband on 22 September, died yesterday evening at 6:15 p.m."[85] On 3 December, the judge of the Court of Justice of the Seine ordered transmittal of the evidence to the attorney general. On the sixteenth, the Paris Court of Appeals, "after having deliberated, considered that the evidence and the investigation resulted in sufficient charges against Luna de San Pedro, J[u]an."[86]

The police investigation described Juan Luna as being "of a calm nature, even indolent," although he "sometimes had outbursts of a certain intensity." His wife "was kind, and was not harsh with him." His mother-in-law "was full of reserve and delicacy in her relations with him, and he "had the most cordial relations" with his two brothers-in-law, Trinidad and Felix. "Luna de San Pedro seemed therefore to be in happy conditions regarding his life and the future. . . . But sorrow and bereavement were not long in troubling such serenity."[87]

In March 1892, the Lunas' three-year-old daughter, Maria de la Paz, had died. Several weeks later they received news from the Philippines that Juan Luna's father had died the previous September. In July, the couple's five-year-old first-born, Andres, became ill, and Madame Luna was suffering from asthma. Mother and son left Paris for Mont Dore to recuperate, returning on 12 August. On 4 September, Monsieur Dussaq, a fifty-five-year-old man with whom Paz had become acquainted at Mont Dore and "about whom she had spoken with praise in one of her letters to her husband," called upon the couple at their residence. Juan Luna's "temperament from then on pushed him to acts of violence without limit." Threatening his wife, "he rose against her in assault and battery." On 5 September, he beat her and destroyed her clothes. On 10 September, when she left their residence, Luna followed her to 25 Mont Thabor Street. He lost sight of her but met Monsieur Dussaq at the entrance to the building. Luna was convinced that this was "proof of his wife's relations with this individual." On 11 September, another "extremely heated" scene occurred. Luna threatened his wife with his revolver and beat her with his cane so that "her back was but a wound." His mother-in-law, Doña Juliana, urgently summoned her eldest son to intervene and protect his sister. Threatened by Luna with a revolver, T. H. became convinced that the family "needed judicial counsel to put an end to the Lunas' marriage, a situation which was already lost."

On the morning of 22 September, T. H. arrived at the Villa Dupont and went to see his sister in her room. Arriving shortly after, Felix Pardo de Tavera went directly to see his nephew, Andres, who was still sick in bed. Family friend Antonio Maria Regidor, newly arrived from London, also came that morning to Villa Dupont. With the two brothers upstairs, Don Antonio was left alone with Luna, who began to appear agitated. Then the brothers and Don Antonio left to discuss matters at a nearby cafe. Before long a maid arrived to call them back, saying "Come quickly, *monsieur* wants to kill *madame*."

When the three men reached the lane, Juan Luna, who was at a first-floor window, fired a shot at the brothers. Felix was wounded in the upper right breast. While T. H. and Don Antonio moved the wounded man out of the garden, Luna went upstairs and forced the door of the bathroom in which the women had sought refuge. Paz, holding her little son, was by the window crying for help. Doña Juliana was crouched near a decorative chimney by the bathtub. Luna fired point blank at his mother-in-law, killing her instantly. He fired another shot, which wounded no one, then aimed at his wife's head, and fired. The bullet split the left parietal bone and a fragment deeply penetrated the brain. Paz died sixteen days later without regaining consciousness.[88]

The detached bureaucratic tone of the police report and related documents seems to diminish the horror of the deaths of the two women. But the full impact of the family's devastation is recorded in the anguished voice of T. H., recorded in an article in the newspaper *Echo de Paris*. Two days after the murders, T. H. returned to the Villa Dupont to respond to a police reporter's questions. He explained,

> [Y]esterday, I was still experiencing the shock of the horrible tragedy that was played out before my eyes. . . . I was incapable of linking two ideas. . . . I am better today, calmer. . . . But let's leave this place. . . . Here I don't have my head about me; the cadaver of my mother is always before my eyes, I hear the death-rattle of my sister. . . . I don't know what makes me suffer more in this house, the sight of my dying sister or the memory of that ferocious scene of carnage.[89]

In his interview, T. H. recounted that the Pardo de Taveras had misgivings when Juan Luna sought Paz's hand in marriage. T. H. thought that his sister had been "carried away by the enthusiasm of youth, and also because her heart was full of love for the Philippines." Paz had married Luna

> without thinking on the conquences of the difference between them in social and economic standing, in education and physical type. She was tall, slim, fair, carefully groomed, and refined. He was short and very dark, like majority of the Ilocanos, with a thick moustache, short on manners. Truly opposites.[90]

Predictably, there came realization and disillusionment. At first, the Pardo de Taveras combined their efforts in an attempt to preserve the marriage. Despite her reserve, Doña Juliana was determined to support her daughter and son-in-law: "she saw to all their needs . . . even giving them a stipend of 500 francs a month."[91] Lacking a confession of infidelity from their sister or confirmation from any other source, Trinidad and Felix sought to appease Luna's jealousy.[92] Anxious to avert dissension, T. H. acknowledged that "I faulted my sister, I supported my brother-in-law from the beginning." Accepting Luna's demand that he be allowed to "cleanse his honor in blood," on 14 September the brothers had tried to arrange a duel with Monsieur Dussaq, Paz's alleged lover.

Dussaq was affronted. He "vehemently protested th[e] accusation," insisting that he had had "only fleeting and mundane relations" with Madame Luna.[93] He designated two friends, Monsieur Clogenson and Monsieur Fremy, to deal with Luna's seconds. On 15 September, the two sets of seconds formally exchanged accusations and denials. Dussaq's advocates stood firm. There "could be no question of indemnification . . . for the alleged relations with [Luna's] wife. . . . In the absence of all proof" that could discredit his denial, Dussaq refused to "comply with [Luna] on his conditions." T. H. and Felix were encouraged. Would Dussaq consider a formal deposition stating his denial of the "alleged facts"? His seconds "agreed immediately . . . and the declaration was given and accepted."[94]

The brothers were elated. A senseless bloodletting had been averted. More importantly, here was proof that Luna's suspicions of their sister were unfounded. Dussaq had sworn "on his honor that he has never corresponded with [by letter], nor had any rendezvous with Mme. Luna, to whom he had the honor of being presented at Mont Dore last July." But rushing to him with Dussaq's disclaimer, they found Luna obstinate, and "th[e] attestation . . . only exasperated him." Luna insisted that "only one thing was left for him to do since he could not cleanse his honor in blood: [he had to] leave his wife."[95]

Juan Luna was unaware that divorce was the solution his wife and in-laws were now determined to reach. So, if he had intended to use divorce as a threat to scandalize the staunchly proper Pardo de Taveras, he was disappointed. T. H. readily agreed to the idea, stating:

> Do what you want to do . . . whatever you do will be all right. My sister will come live at our house, we will look after her. . . . Time will make you forget things, perhaps you will reconcile . . . and you will only take her back with you when I give you my word of honor that she has been good.[96]

For Paz, her mother, and her brothers, the decision to seek a divorce had not been made easily. Divorce would confound the pattern of their lives. Doña Juliana and her sister, Doña Tula, were exemplars of wifely devotion. Testimony given during the murder trial verified that Paz had imbibed those family values and was herself a model wife and mother.[97] But Juan Luna's "obstreperous behavior towards her" gradually eroded her regard for him. He provoked ugly, terrifying scenes.[98] One such incident was witnessed by Concha, T. H.'s wife, who related that at the breakfast table one morning Luna had become infuriated when Paz intervened as he corrected their young son's manners. Luna threw everything on the table at Paz— cups, teapot, sugarbowl, dishes—and grabbed her by the wrists and shook her.[99] Imputing his latest rages to Paz's alleged adulterous liaisons, Luna became even more violent. Doña Juliana, living within earshot of Luna's tantrums and beatings, became convinced that the marriage was a disaster.

As Paz never told her brothers about the violence, they reached this conclusion much later.[100] When, from their mother, they finally learned the extent of Paz's alienation, they determined to extricate her from the marriage. The French courts would grant a divorce on grounds of domestic violence only on the testimony of witnesses.[101] While Paz remained in the marriage, however, attempts to provoke a confrontation with Luna would put her at risk. The Pardo de Taveras hesitated. So, when Luna himself decided that divorce was desirable, the family concurred with alacrity. But the family was destined for disappointment. Juan Luna changed his mind. He conceded, after all,

> I don't want a separation. . . . I am going to leave Paris with her and our son . . . we will go live at Vigo. . . . We'll live there alone, all alone; I will leave on Sunday.

This time T. H. was not so ready to acquiesce. It was a hasty, ill-conceived decision. T. H. knew that "[m]oney mattered little" to Luna, that "he didn't even sell his paintings." Still he tried to convince Luna to reconsider: "He only had eighty francs. I made him recognize that he couldn't go to Spain with such a small sum, that he needed to live, too, and I offered him some money." But Luna had his calculus. He brushed T. H.'s suggestion aside.

> No . . . I want nothing of my wife, nothing of you, either. I will live down there in poverty, and I don't want to receive anything from you. . . . No, no, nothing, nothing, I want nothing from you. I will live from the sale of the canvases I paint down there.

Later T. H. learned that on the same day Luna "threw all my sister's dresses into the fire, saying 'I want you to live simply, to behave simply. . . . It's not your dresses that I love, it's you . . . plus, you will not attract the looks of men.'"[102]

It was common knowledge in the Filipino community that Juan Luna had "no personal fortune," and that "it [wa]s in fact his wife who provide[d] for the needs of the family."[103] Forced at regular intervals to turn to the Pardo de Taveras for money, Juan Luna was unable to assume more than titular leadership of the household. Doña Juliana, though always circumspect in her dealings with him and increasingly fearful of his temper, was clearly the head of the house.[104] After his brother Antonio moved to Paris and joined the household as a student, Luna's dependence upon the Pardo de Taveras became even more urgent.[105] Leaving Paris for the remote town of Vigo could be seen as an attempt by Luna to regain control over his life. His refusal to concede the fact that his wife no longer wanted to be part of that life was symptomatic of his need to dominate. Luna told the family that Paz had agreed to go with him. But her mother was convinced Paz did so only after lengthy emotional scenes during which Luna harangued, threatened, and finally wore her down.

Vigo, on the northwestern coast of Galicia, north of Portugal, was remote but accessible by land over the difficult mountainous region of northwestern Spain. Yet it was not Vigo's remoteness that troubled Doña Juliana. She had, after all, seen her younger sister survive a life of exile on Guam. It was what she had seen and heard of Luna's abuse that made her adamant. Paz's departure for Vigo would remove her from the family's protection. Doña Juliana protested vehemently to T. H. that "It would be criminal on my part to allow Paz to leave." Convincing him to act on his sister's behalf, she admitted that Paz had confessed to her mother that she could "no longer tolerate my life with this man. I hate him with all my soul."[106] Before T. H. could do anything, however, his mother sent him a frantic message: "Come save your sister. Her husband wants to kill her."

T. H. rushed to the Villa Dupont where he, later claimed, "Luna received me very badly, [and] . . . threatened me with his revolver." He left the house "in a panic." His brother Felix was away on an extended holiday with his wife. Feeling "alone in Paris, without advice, without support," he "went to the police commissioner [from] whom [he] asked for counsel." The commissioner advised him to "take your sister away from there, it is prudent [to do so]." But, when T. H. asked the commissioner to accompany him, the official replied, "No, that's impossible . . . all I can do for you is give you a letter." T. H. protested, explaining, "I can't go there alone; my brother-in-law will kill me." But the police would not intervene in a domestic dispute. Left to his own resources, T. H. sent telegrams to Felix and to Don Antonio in London, urging them to come "as soon as possible." Felix returned that night, and the brothers went to Villa Dupont immediately, "fearing a catastrophe." T. H. later said that Luna "received us coldly, but he did not make a scene."[107]

The next day was Sunday, 22 September, the day Juan Luna and Paz, with their son Andres, were supposed to leave for Vigo. Early that morning T. H. and Felix made their way separately to Villa Dupont. While the brothers were upstairs talking with their mother and sister, Antonio Maria Regidor arrived. Luna was instantly suspicious. Don Antonio regularly provided legal counsel to the Filipino expatriates, and his sudden presence at Villa Dupont was surely part of a family plan. Luna asked why he had come to Paris.

According to Don Antonio, the Pardo de Taveras had not had a chance to brief him, so he did not know that the situation was explosive. He answered Luna's question directly, informing him that "Trinidad telegraphed me to come and set the conditions for the separation."[108] It was this information that triggered Luna's rage. When T. H. and Felix entered the room, he screamed:

> What does all of this mean? A reunion of the family council. . . . What do you have the presumption to do. . . . Ah! You know I will defend myself. . . .[109]

Soon after, in the impersonal format of a news article, T. H. recounted what he would later suppress in his family history.

> With that Luna went upstairs alone. We calmed him as best we could, and to let Regidor know all that had happened and why I had made him come, I

whispered in his ear: "Let's go outside, I have to talk to you." Then, I rushed to where my sister and mother were and said to them: "Close yourselves in your room; Luna is very upset . . . and don't open the door. If he knocks, call us, we are staying in the house."

I went downstairs again and, before leaving the house, I recommended that the maid come find me immediately if Luna provoked a scene.

Instead of staying in the villa, we went—my brother Felix, Regidor and I—to a cafe on Pergolesi Street. We were sitting there only a few seconds, we hadn't even been served yet, when we saw the maid enter: "Come quickly, she said, come, something terrible is going to happen." I ran. I had just approached the house when I heard the voices of my mother and my sister calling for help. My brother and Regidor had caught up with me; we hastened our step and reached the front of the home. Twenty or thirty people were already there, watching, having heard the screams. Not one of them tried to enter or call for help.

As we approached the iron gate, one of them called to me: "Watch out; he has a revolver." And in fact, at a first-floor window, my brother-in-law had a revolver, an enormous revolver, pointed at us. We hesitated a moment. But at a second-storey window, my mother and my sister with their little baby called to us: "Trinidad, Felix . . . help us."

The iron gate was closed, I opened it. I went to dart through the garden toward the house and I heard a shot. I stopped. I was not wounded. I took one step forward, but at that moment, someone stopped me. A hand held my shoulder: "Trinidad," Felix said, "I am wounded . . . ah! it is finished, I'm shot through the lung." I did not lose my composure but held up my brother who was going to faint. I opened his jacket and saw a small hole, in the upper right chest. I tore the buttons of his waistcoat and I saw his shirt already stained with blood. And when my brother murmured: "Ah! Trinidad, I'm lost; the lung is pierced, I assure you . . . trust me," I touched the wound a little, at some risk. To put him at ease I said: "No, the wound is not serious, it's nothing, it's nothing." But he fainted in my arms and I had to lie him down along the wall.

All of this happened in a matter of seconds. I got up and saw at the window that Luna was watching me, his revolver always in his hand as he leaned against the handrail.

And among the crowd that had gathered in front of the house, no one intervened. I shouted to those closest to me: "So enter, rescue my mother. In the name of God, I beg of you. Do you want money? . . . Here, here are ten francs, here are twenty, here are one hundred francs, but go in, I beseech you. . . . No one will hurt you, it is me he wants. . . ." No one moved. No one.

A Selected Genealogy of the Pardo de Tavera Family

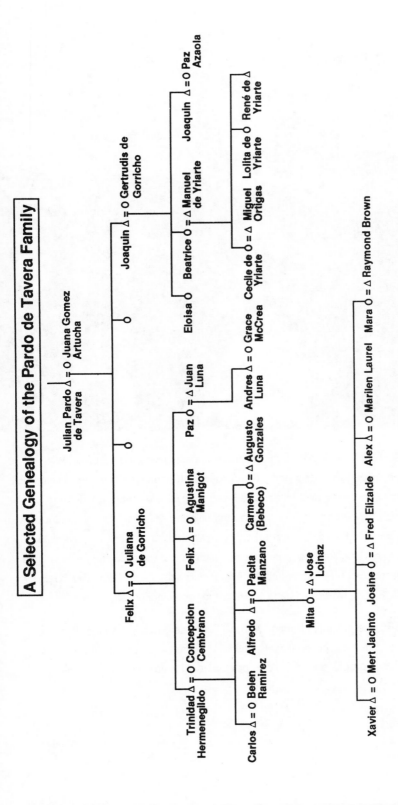

In 1890, at the Paris studio of Filipino painter Juan Luna (above), his fellow expatriates gather for a party. Surrounded by his canvases are (rear, left to right) unidentified, nationalist leader Jose Rizal, artist Felix Resurreccíon Hidalgo, unidentified, Paz Pardo de Tavera Luna, and unidentified. Seated in the front row is Juliana Gorricho Pardo de Tavera, holding her grandson Andres Luna, the child of Luna and her daughter Paz. In another photo taken that same day (upper right), the exiles dress up for a less formal portrait—(standing, left to right) Rizal, Paz Pardo de Tavera, unidentified, Hidalgo, and unidentified.

In 1886, the matriarch Juliana Gorricho Pardo de Tavera, mother of Paz and Trinidad, posed (lower right) for a portrait at a Paris studio. (Photographs and identifications courtesy of Mita Pardo de Tavera)

A formal portrait of Commissioner T. H. Pardo de Tavera taken at Manila's Sun Studio. In May 1920, he presented it to his son Alfredo and daughter-in-law Paz with a warm inscription, "A mis queridos hijos."
(Photograph and identification courtesy of Mita Pardo de Tavera)

The sons of T. H. Pardo de Tavera: Carlos (seated, left) and Alfredo (standing, right), students at the Taft School in Connecticut. (Photograph and identification courtesy of Mita Pardo de Tavera)

Mita Pardo de Tavera, aged four, photographed in 1924 at a Manila studio
with her mother Paz Lopez Manzano Pardo de Tavera.
(Photograph and identification courtesy of Mita Pardo de Tavera)

In 1927, a year before his death, Alfredo Pardo de Tavera sits for a studio portrait with his daughter Mita.
(Photograph and identification courtesy of Mita Pardo de Tavera)

In 1937, Mita Pardo de Tavera achieved considerable renown as a dancer at the international Eucharistic Congress held in Manila. Shown with classmate Martita Brown in Filipino dress, she was a student at the Assumption Convent, an exclusive Catholic girls' school in downtown Manila.
(Photograph and identification courtesy of Mita Pardo de Tavera)

In 1964, at the age of forty-four, Dr. Mita Pardo de Tavera served as chief of the Chest Pediatric Service of the Philippine tuberculosis center, the Quezon Institute. She is photographed (upper right) while treating a patient.
(Photograph and identification courtesy of Mita Pardo de Tavera)

A portrait of Mita (lower right), after the 1986 mass uprising, as one of the architects of Marcos's overthrow, by financier Jaime Zobel de Ayala.
(*Credit:* Jaime Zobel de Ayala)

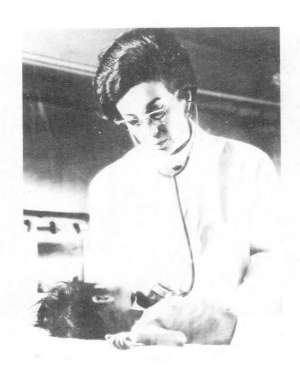

In July 1988, Mita, secretary of social welfare and development, speaks with President Corazon Aquino during a meeting of the Cabinet Officers Regional Development Committee at Malacañang Palace. In a tumultuous time with many cabinet changes, Mita was the president's longest-serving secretary.
(Credit: Philippine Daily Inquirer)

And then . . . I heard three deafening shots. . . . I looked at the windows of the house; no one. The miserable man has just killed my mother and my sister, I thought.

So, as if crazed, I made my way into the house with other people. I climbed the stairs and on the first floor I met Luna who had just handed over the revolver to the maid of the villa. He said to me: "Trinidad, you are the cause of all that happened here, you are the cause of everything."

"But I won't stop; I want to know what you did to my mother and my sister." And in the bathroom, I found the two unfortunates covered in blood with terrible head wounds, horrible, huge holes, huge . . . as if an egg could pass through. Ah! those poor women, those poor women. . . . I brought my mother and my sister over to their bed, tried to calm my sister and console my little nephew who was screaming and crying. . . .[110]

T. H. recalled that afterward Juan Luna suddenly "regained his calm, his composure," and said to Regidor, "Yes, you came to confirm that I had beaten my wife, that I hit Maria . . . you came to counsel them to take my wife away from me . . . . But I figured out your plan. . . . I am avenged now . . . you can do what you want with me." Later, at the police station, he said Luna again insisted that "these scoundrels wanted to take my wife from me, to separate me from her, to possibly give her to another."[111]

Initially, T. H. appeared to burden himself with guilt. Could he have averted the murders? He had done what he could, given what he knew of Luna's propensity for violence. Perhaps inadvertently, he began laying the basis for his brother-in-law's defense.

He was jealous, fiercely jealous, like a Malayan. Because he was born in the Philippines, he was born in the bad part of the island of Luzon, in the north, which is only inhabited by Malayans. Moreover the morals of the inhabitants of that part of the island are legendary, and jealousy made them commit horrible crimes there, veritable massacres.[112]

Juan Luna went to trial. On 8 February 1893, the president of the Assize Court of the Seine signed the following decree.

Considering the declaration of the Jury in favor of Luna de San Pedro, Jean, born 23 October 1857 at Badoc (the Philippines), painter, resident of Paris, Pergolese Street 48, Villa Dupont 28; accused of murder and attempted murder;

The said declaration bears that the accused is not guilty;

We declare the said Luna de San Pedro acquitted of the accusation brought against him and order that he be freed if not detained for another cause.[113]

Luna was ordered to pay a fine of one franc. In addition, the court ruled that it "Condemns Luna de San Pedro to pay Mr. Trinidad and Mr. Felix de Tavera the sum of . . . sixteen hundred fifty-one francs and eighty-three centimes, plus twenty-five francs for postage in addition to the interest on damages." It further attached a caveat that "any failure [by Luna] to pay . . . would be strongly to the advantage of Mr. Giot, lawyer of the plaintiffs, whose representation in this case is recognized as necessary."[114]

As if a fulfillment of a researcher's nightmare, the Assize Court records of cases heard between 1893 and 1930 were burned in a fire that destroyed the judiciary archives in Paris. Thus, no official record of the trial survives. On 18 February 1893, however, a hearing was held to consider an appeal by the plaintiffs to overturn Luna's acquittal. A copy of the impassioned address to the appellate court on behalf of the plaintiffs by Felix Decori does exist. It is possible to reconstruct the case for the defense from Decori's statements.

The defense in the trial had claimed that Luna was a devoted husband. Decori refuted this, citing the numerous instances of abuse. He denied another defense contention that the Pardo de Taveras had plotted to deprive Luna of his wife's love and companionship. More importantly, Decori focused his efforts upon refuting the contention that Paz was a frivolous woman, an uncaring mother, and an unfaithful wife. Exposing the manner in which Luna's defense impugned his victims, Decori protested that the acquittal had been won in part because the defense had presented the aggressor as the victim. Nonetheless, the acquittal was not overturned.

T. H. had concluded his interview by the French newspaper's police reporter with the following statement.

> I pardon [Luna] for whatever harm he did to me, he is irresponsible, and as I leave you, Monsieur, I repeat my recommendation of yesterday: since you have to reproduce this conversation, don't weigh down on him too much. Have pity on him.[115]

Indeed, the recollection of the murders continues to evoke pity. But there is also condemnation, and the purpose of the recollection—whether to pity or to condemn—depends upon whether the memory serves the murdered or the murderer.

In 1977, the National Historical Institute in Manila published a chronology of Juan Luna's life and work. Recalling the murders, author Carlos E. Da Silva paints a sympathetic image of Luna. In portraying Paz, however, Da Silva transforms her husband's suspicions of infidelity into fact. Subtly, but with ruinous effect, he depicts her with tints that deepen into the colors of an adulterous wife.[116]

Da Silva notes that after the death of their daughter, Paz was "so upset that her health was affected." While "Pacita, on advice of the family doctor, took a vacation at Mont Dore . . . together with their son, Andres," Luna stayed behind in Paris to work on "his greatest canvas, *Peuple et Rois*." With an implicit rebuke, Da Silva notes that Paz was away for "two months vacation."[117] He claims that

Luna heard rumors "about the behavior of Paz at Mont Dore . . . [which] strained the relations between husband and wife." Nowhere does Da Silva provide proof of Paz's infidelity, yet he asserts that she "refused to confess about her secret rendezvous and the intimate relations with a certain friend she had met at Mont Dore."[118]

In describing T. H.'s efforts to mend the failing marriage, Da Silva implies that Paz was unfaithful and that T. H. "failed to extract the truth from her." Again implying infidelity, he writes that Paz "promised to amend her ways." In contrast, Juan Luna is presented as the "aggrieved husband." Unable to ignore Luna's abusive treatment of Paz, Da Silva exculpates him by claiming that he "loved her deeply, forgave her and was willing to forget everything, suggesting they leave Paris immediately for Vigo, Spain." But in Da Silva's account ultimately Paz proves herself incorrigibly corrupted.

> During the week which followed, Luna observed that his wife was still going out, more frequently, and was discarding her mourning dress for colored dresses, bought colored eye-pencils and was using more facial make-up. This infuriated him when she refused to hand over the makeup pencils, whereat he tore her mourning dresses to pieces and beat her with a cane.[119]

Finally, it is claimed that Juan Luna fired through the door to open it, and broke through to find that he had killed his mother-in-law and mortally wounded his wife. Thus, Da Silva's account of Juan Luna's life exculpates him of any guilt in the murders.

On the other hand, E. Arsenio Manuel's extended biographical essay on Juan Luna has only this to say about the killings.

> The tragic family affair of Sept. 23, 1892, when he shot to death his wife and mother-in-law and wounded his brother-in-law, Felix Pardo de Tavera . . . arrested to a marked degree his artistic activities.[120]

More recently, Manila columnist Hilarion M. Henares, Jr., recounting what he calls a "tale" of the Pardo de Tavera family, drew this angle on his summary of the murder.

> Juan Luna was a respected painter in the Queen's Court at Madrid. He suspected that his wife Maria Paz Pardo de Tavera was having an affair with a Frenchman in Paris. He went there, confronted her and in a fit of jealousy shot her dead along with her mother. There was a celebrated court case that eventually exonerated him for defending his honor. . . . This of course earned him the enmity of Dr. Trinidad Pardo de Tavera whom he accused of plotting against his life. In a dramatic gesture Juan Luna uttered a curse against all the Taveras—a curse that has plagued them throughout the years.[121]

Henares uses his treatment of the murders as a prelude to political commentary on an issue involving another Pardo de Tavera in another time. Nonetheless, in examining the obvious distortion of fact and historical interpretation, one detects the source of the biases he reflects and the hidden agenda in his *ad hominem* attack on the family.

The murder of the Pardo de Tavera women presents a paradigm of the problematic perspective in Philippine nationalist historiography. Although Rupert Emerson's analysis of the nationalist viewpoint is itself problematic, it provides useful insight into the biases in the existing literature, in which compassion is reserved to the aggressor and condemnation is meted out to his victims.[122] Emerson defines "ex post facto reasoning," that is, "reasoning back from the fact of the nation to the things that must have caused it," as a paradox in Asian nationalism.[123] Indeed, in Philippine nationalist historiography there is a marked tendency to exclude people and events, or to denigrate them, if these cannot be shown to have furthered the rise of nationalism. My objection to this "nationalist" approach is not meant to suggest that historians should avoid making judgments but to point out that the historical perspective thus focused is bound to be narrow and confining. It produces a history with an *a priori* case to defend, a brief to hold, instead of a truth to analyze and understand. Furthermore, nationalist history, as in the writing of familial hagiography, succumbs to an irresistible temptation to ignore flaws that diminish the stature of one's forebears within the national family. If not ignored, these perceived faults are viewed in light refracted through the prism of nationalist fervor.

Thus, historical embarrassments are omitted, justified, remitted, rationalized, or excused. Philippine history practiced in such a politically charged environment does not readily confront the fact that Jose Rizal, Juan Luna, and Antonio Luna, like many of the *ilustrados* arrested in 1896, recanted their masonic beliefs; that Antonio Luna declared that he had denounced the Katipunan to his laboratory supervisor; or that the unresolved killings of Andres Bonifacio in 1898 and Antonio Luna in 1899 remain shrouded in omission and silence.

At the time, the Pardo de Tavera murders were seen as Juan Luna's "abyss," his "tragedy," his "misfortune."[124] But his status as the first Filipino artist to gain widespread European recognition has survived. In the intervening years of the revolution against Spain and the war against the United States, the activities of Juan Luna and his brother Antonio on behalf of the independent Philippine government heightened their nationalist aura. T. H. Pardo de Tavera, on the other hand, became the foremost advocate of Philippine statehood within the framework of the U.S. Constitution. Nationalist historians have rejected his rationale for this position as not germane to the case.

In the curious half-light that nationalist historiography casts upon the murders, the story is transformed into a morality play. Juan Luna is the Filipino patriot, a talented painter who brought glory to his native land, an Indio, and therefore a real Filipino. The Pardo de Taveras are the wealthy, Hispanicized elite, incapable of being, or becoming, Filipino. Paz Pardo de Tavera abjures the ideals of

Filipino womanhood, particularly those of fidelity and steadfastness. Her rejection of Juan Luna has become a metaphor for the family's rejection of the ideals of the Filipino. Her mother and her brothers do not chastise her but abet her corruption. The avenging Juan Luna destroys the faithless wife and with her the mother whose permissive negligence has allowed the daughter to slide into self-indulgence. The acquittal of Juan Luna by the Parisian court is seen by the nationalists as the ultimate vindication of the Filipino hero and the defeat of the unfaithful. Da Silva notes, with an unmistakable ring of satisfaction, that Luna was sentenced to pay a fine of only one franc.

The death of the two women was a blow from which the family struggled to recover, and the magnitude of its loss should be seen in perspective. Although the Pardo de Taveras are a very old Spanish family, their Philippine branch was at the time only in its third generation. Don Felix's early death and Don Joaquin's fall from favor ended the swift ascent of the second generation. But the family's moral and material resources helped offset the losses. The Gorricho women brought into the family a large measure of the strength of will, and the wealth, to survive those crises.

Doña Juliana was thirty-three years old when her husband Don Felix died in 1864. Their eldest son was seven years old, the young Felix five, and Maria de la Paz an infant of two. Endowed by her parents with a large inheritance, Doña Juliana combined it with her husband's estate. She managed her investments shrewdly and with considerable entrepreneurial skill enlarged the family's fortune. Although she was a young widow, she did not remarry, focusing her life on raising her children. In that task she had support of her brother-in-law, Don Joaquin, and his wife, Doña Tula, her own sister.

When Don Joaquin's crisis came eight years later, Doña Tula abandoned her comfortable life in Manila and accompanied her husband into exile. For more than two years she shared his banishment. When that proscription ended, and her husband was not allowed to return to Manila, she went with him to Paris. There their life was untroubled but it was nonetheless a life of exile. Again, through force of will and by means of their considerable resources, the Pardo de Taveras drew together. Doña Juliana and her children joined the rest of the family in Paris.

T. H. Pardo de Tavera identifies two integral aspects of his uncle's success in Paris—a distinguished lineage, and a proven commitment to the liberal cause.[125] He leaves implicit, however, the fact that the family's wealth greatly increased their chances of success. Wealth gave them the means to move beyond the reach of the Spanish colonial state, and it guaranteed the next generation's access to higher education and the refinements of a life of the intellect. It made possible alliances through marriage that ensured the continuity of family achievement.

Thus, the growing professional reputation of the third generation—Trinidad and Felix—marked the family's restoration. Paz's marriage to the "shining star" of the Filipino *propagandistas* continued the family's tradition of aligning itself with talent and wealth. T. H.'s return to Manila and the recognition of his expertise by the Manila Chamber of Commerce was the beginning of the family's vindication.

Throughout the Parisian years of recovery Doña Juliana was her children's strength and support. It is telling that even in their maturity, she maintained the family property undivided and in her name, retaining full control.

To a family in which moral strength and material sustenance were inherent to the roles of wife and mother, the loss of two generations of women, mother and daughter, was devastating. The family was close knit, the traditional bonds intensified by the shared experience of crises and exile. Thus, as the malaise in the marriage of Paz and Juan Luna deepened, mother, sons, and daughter instinctually drew together for support and safety. But, unable to deflect Luna's violence, the Pardo de Taveras suffered the destruction of the family's core. The murder was, and continues to be, a cause of deep pain to the family.[126]

During the awful days following the murders, the brothers had to confront the reality of their mother's will, her estate and its division. The family had lived in Paris for at least sixteen years, and, as Antonio Regidor put it, they had "exhausted a tidy fortune."[127] With Doña Juliana's death came the apportioning of her property. This meant a diminution, not a consolidation, of resources.

For the few days that Paz had survived her mother, the law provided that she had inherited a third of Doña Juliana's estate. With Paz's death, that inheritance passed to her five-year-old son, Andres. After Juan Luna's acquittal, he established guardianship over his son and Paz's inheritance.

Although Andres was the first in the family's rising generation, his connection to Luna meant alienation from the Pardo de Taveras. Sorrow and anger mingled in T. H.'s reaction to the Luna infamy. Juan had been a close friend. T. H. had supported his courtship of Paz, going so far as to allay his mother's doubts. He had tried to patch the crumbling relationship between his sister and her husband. He had helped in every way he could, with advice, patience, sympathy, and money. Afterward, he never spoke of Luna and would not allow the mention of his name. He destroyed the paintings that he and his mother had bought to support the artist and affirm their family bond.[128] But he could not deny his sister's son when Andres came to him after Luna's death in 1899, seeking to reestablish the ties of kinship. Until that time, however, the alienation between the Pardo de Taveras and Andres was complete.

Luna left Paris on 12 February 1893, less than a week after his acquittal, without waiting for the decision in the appeal against his release. Accompanied by his brother Antonio, and taking Andres along, he fled to Madrid. On 12 July, he moved to Portugalete in Bilbao. He left for Barcelona in April 1894 and from there set sail for Manila with Andres and Antonio. He reached Manila in May, the same month as T. H.

Return to Manila

With the division of property also came the physical breakup of the family. The Parisian sojourn ended. As much to escape the painful memories as to renew themselves, Doña Juliana's sons and their families left Paris.[129] Felix and his wife, Agustina Manigot, moved to her family's home in Buenos Aires. He never returned to Manila. T. H. and his wife returned to the Philippines with their sons, five-year-old Carlos and Alfredo, who was two. A daughter, Carmen, called Bebeco, was born in Manila.

Despite Antonio Regidor's comment in Paris that the Pardo de Taveras had "exhausted a tidy fortune," there remained considerable wealth. Available records of Manila's Fincas Urbanas in 1896 show that the property values listed in the names of T. H. and his mother reached an impressive total of 183,100 pesos.[130]

In an appointment reminiscent of his uncle Joaquin's earlier career, T. H. joined the Faculty of Medicine at the Universidad de Santo Tomas in May 1894. His European credentials so impressed the Spanish officials that he also was appointed to numerous advisory boards.

It was in the half decade between 1890 and 1895, when his domestic life was anything but tranquil, that T. H. produced some of his finest contributions to Philippine studies. His productivity leads one to suppose that he turned to work for its restorative effect. The anguished voice recorded in his interview by the Parisian newspaper is nowhere heard in his own writing, where he speaks in the authoritative tone of the scholar. Among the work published during this period were projects he had begun after his brief return to Manila in 1887. There he had been exhilarated by the opportunity for primary research, and he mined the Manila libraries of the religious orders for sources to enhance his study of the Philippines' indigenous cultures. In so doing, he uncovered two treasures.

The first was Fr. Juan de Plasencia's unpublished study of Tagalog society at the time of Spanish contact, the second a map of the Philippines drawn by Fr. Pedro Murillo Velarde. Based on his knowledge of Philippine culture and history, T. H. edited, annotated and published these bibliographic gems in 1892 and 1894.[131] In addition, he extended his research into the Tagalog language, developing linguistic theories along the lines of the approach now known as gluttochronology.[132] In 1892, he also published his work on Philippine medicinal plants, and a year later his study of printing and printmaking in the Philippines.[133] In 1895, he published a booklet of instruction in basic health and popular medicine. In recognition of his scholarly research and publications, he was admitted to membership in Madrid's Royal Academy of Languages and Royal Academy of Science.[134]

In August 1896, a Spanish friar came upon the existence of the Katipunan,[135] a secret revolutionary society, and promptly reported it to the authorities. Immediately the state's machinery of repression shifted into high gear. Spanish officials proceeded to persecute anyone they regarded as suspicious. Under the circumstances, the *katipuneros* decided that this was the time to declare the Philippines independent of Spain. They launched a full-scale war and were fighting the first battles by the end of August. By mid September it was clear that the

Spanish, concerned with the gravity of the threat, were bent on a policy of terror. They cast their nets widely, arresting anyone who seemed remotely suspicious in attitude or association, and applied torture and other forms of intimidation. As had been the case in previous episodes of repression, Filipino intellectuals became prime suspects.

Although many of the *ilustrados* held strong negative opinions about the Spanish colonial system, they were not anti-Spanish as such. Many were anticlerical, however, expressing their sentiments through membership in secret masonic lodges, which proliferated in late nineteenth-century Manila.[136] To the conservative Spanish, freemasons were the personification of evil, and they reserved special vitriol for the masonic *filibusteros*. These were arrested in large numbers, imprisoned or tortured, and urged to expose more of their hated membership.[137]

Joaquin Pardo de Tavera had been persecuted in similar circumstances in 1872. But in 1896 T. H. was spared. Although he had imbibed his uncle's liberal ideals, there the similarity ended.[138] While Don Joaquin's liberal politics permeated his work and associations, his nephew maintained a scholarly demeanor. T. H.'s Philippine contemporaries in Europe were well aware that he wanted nothing other than a tranquil life of the intellect, and it was generally understood that he intended only to "enjoy, study and write."[139] His appointment to the Faculty of Medicine at the Universidad de Santo Tomas had bolstered an unwavering commitment to the academic life. When fighting broke out, he was commissioned a captain in the Spanish army. But he was not attracted to the military mode and he resigned his commission in April 1897.[140] Thus, as Filipinos and Spanish moved towards greater conflict, T. H. stood at a distance.

Most of the beleaguered *ilustrados* did not play dynamic roles during the first phase of the Revolution. Moreover, as the Katipunan's separatism exceeded their immediate goals, they were for the most part excluded from the society's leadership. They were reformists, not revolutionaries, and what they had demanded was Filipino assimilation and equality within the Spanish polity. Yet, even after the *ilustrados* identified themselves more closely with the Revolution, the fighter's role remained one for which most of them were ill-fitted.

There were a few notable exceptions. During their sojourn in Europe in the 1880s, a small group of Filipinos became students of fencing. Two, Juan Luna and his brother Antonio, were especially devoted to the martial art and became skilled swordsmen. In addition, Juan was an *aficionado* of firearms. In Paris, during the months of the Exposition, the Lunas had formed the "Club Kidlat" (Tagalog for 'lightning') with Rizal and the Indios Bravos. Given this background, it is not surprising that in the Revolution's later phase Antonio Luna would take to the field as one of its foremost generals, and then assume the revolutionary government's position of minister for war. Juan would express a preference for fighting alongside him.[141]

Although the *ilustrados* were not at the forefront of revolutionary activity, many fell victim to Spain's policy of terror. A group of revolutionary *katipuneros* had implicated the *ilustrados* as a tactic designed to force their affiliation with the cause. Thus, many were arrested, imprisoned, or exiled, and they spent much of the Revolution's first phase preoccupied with freeing themselves.

Juan Luna's record during this period shows that, like many other *ilustrados*, he was simply struggling to survive. On 16 September 1896, he and his brothers Antonio and Jose were arrested. Antonio testified in November that he "knew nothing of the [Katipunan] conspiracy until July." He insisted, "I am not a rebel, nor a Mason, nor a filibuster. . . . I believe I have fulfilled my duties as a loyal son of Spain."[142] He claimed to have "denounced" both the Katipunan and another group, Jose Rizal's Liga Filipina, to the chief of his laboratory, Dr. Panzano, and to the governor general himself, testimony later confirmed by both officials.[143] Despite these efforts, Antonio failed to convince the Spanish of his loyalty and they continued to hold him in prison.

Juan Luna tried a similar tactic. On 17 January 1897, four months after his arrest, he retracted his masonic beliefs. That, too, proved ineffectual. Juan remained in prison until 27 May when he received a pardon from the Queen Regent of Spain. Through an intermediary she had been informed that one of her court artists had been unjustly imprisoned. Almost immediately after his release, Juan Luna left Manila for Madrid to work for Antonio's pardon. He left his son in the care of his brother Jose who had been released earlier. In Madrid, by August, Juan appealed directly to the Queen Regent and won Antonio's release. Freed from prison, Antonio left Manila for Ghent in Belgium.

Not all *ilustrado* imprisonments ended so fortuitously. At the end of December 1896, T. H. and his young sons had watched from a window in their house at Intramuros as Jose Rizal, his friend of Paris days, was escorted from Fort Santiago to his execution by firing squad just outside the walls at Bagumbayan.[144] For T. H. that moment must have seemed a point in cyclical time. A quarter century earlier, his uncle's friend, Fr. Jose Burgos, had been executed for espousing the cause of the Filipino seculars. Now he was witnessing the death of a man whose passion for Philippine studies he shared and whose political writings he admired.[145] To this point in his life, he had not translated his passion for Philippine studies into a political agenda. Yet, within three years of Rizal's execution, he would rise to become the most highly placed Filipino in government precisely because he was perceived as the foremost authority on the country's history and society. T. H.'s emergence during this period was part of the larger wave of political change that saw the *ilustrados'* knowledge and expertise become the major currency of political transactions.

Initially, the Philippine colonial equation was simple: the Spanish resisted Filipino demands first for reforms, then for separation. Filipino separatism ended the interminable, fruitless bargaining between Spain's conservative colonialists and the Filipino *propagandistas*. But even in the fighting that replaced the propagandists' verbal campaigns neither side could gain dominance. By the end of 1897 a stalemate had been reached, and both sides agreed to a truce. The revolutionary government under Emilio Aguinaldo went into voluntary exile in Hongkong.

When American interests intruded, the equation turned complex. In the ensuing three-sided contest, force of arms was no longer the most viable means of victory and negotiation became a major mode of discourse. As each side worked out its calculus, it found that the Filipino intellectuals were a factor worth considering.

Now facing not one but two adversaries, the Spanish were determined to prevent an alliance between the Filipinos and the Americans. Their first plan was to appeal to Filipino loyalty by finally conceding the long-demanded reforms. To make the offer credible, the Spanish sought the *ilustrados'* leadership and participation.

Dismissing the Spanish concessions as too little too late, the Filipinos under Aguinaldo declared the formation of the Philippine Republic on 12 June 1898. The circumstances of its creation required that the Republic demonstrate the capacity for self-rule and thereby gain international recognition and legitimacy. For this the revolutionaries needed the country's best-educated lawyers and professionals to lay the constitutional foundations and frame policy for a viable independent government.

The Americans were newcomers to the colonial sphere. Still grappling with their own frontier, they had no framework within which to organize and administer a territory so far removed from the United States. They, too, needed the knowledge and advice of the *ilustrados*.

On 21 April 1898, the U.S. Congress declared war on Spain, a decision that rested on an intricate meshing of U.S., Cuban, and Pacific interests. Tactical preparations had included the transfer of the Pacific Fleet's base of operations to Hongkong early in February. On 1 May, the American admiral George Dewey defeated the Spanish fleet under Admiral Montojo in Manila Bay.

Shocked by the turn of events and the enormity of the American threat, the Spanish government at Manila formed a consultative assembly only four days later. The most prominent Filipino intellectuals were appointed to the assembly, with the obvious aim of winning them as allies. T. H. Pardo de Tavera was among the appointees.[146]

Taking advantage of this turn of events, the revolutionary government renewed its struggle. Aguinaldo returned to Manila on board a U.S. transport on 19 May, and met with Dewey on his flagship, the *Olympia*. On 21 May, Aguinaldo resumed hostilities with Spain, and three days later formed a dictatorial government. On 27 May, the first consignment of American arms to the revolutionary forces were unloaded at Cavite. The Filipinos quickly established control over the area surrounding Manila Bay while the American navy controlled the harbor. The Spanish were confined to Intramuros. Confidently, the Filipinos declared their independence from Spain on 12 June 1898.

On 30 June, when the first American land forces arrived, the Filipinos conceded a part of the bay area for use as a troop landing. Then, to the Filipinos' dismay, the Spanish and Americans reached an agreement for the surrender of Manila to U.S. forces on 13 August. In response, on 10 September, the Philippine Republic proclaimed the town of Malolos, in Bulacan Province, its capital. It opened the Philippine Congress there five days later. The appointees to the

Congress were predominantly Manila *ilustrados*.[147] T. H. was designated the representative of the province of Cebu. In addition, he was appointed to the faculty of medicine and surgery of the newly created Universidad Literaria de Filipinas.

Even as the leaders of the Philippine Republic were appointing Manila *ilustrados* to high office, the Americans were confronting their own administrative difficulties. They were attempting to assume control over an area about which they knew next to nothing. In their need for expertise they, too, turned to the Manila *ilustrados*. On 28 September, Military Governor Elwell Otis invited T. H. Pardo de Tavera to join the Board of Health as an honorary member.

It was as if the arena in which Filipino and U.S. interests struggled was being widened just enough for the Americans to avail themselves of the knowledge and ability of the *ilustrados*. On 1 October 1898, T. H. was sworn in as Aguinaldo's director of diplomacy. That same month, Otis closed the College of San Jose, the university's medical college. In view of T. H.'s later involvement with issues in medical education,[148] it is safe to assume that Otis drew on his advice as the only Filipino member of the newly constituted Board of Health.

On 29 November, the Congress at Malolos approved the Constitution of the Philippine Republic. It was drafted by Felipe Calderon, a Manila *ilustrado* and maternal cousin of T. H. But barely two weeks later, on 10 December, the United States and Spain signed the Treaty of Paris transferring sovereignty over the Philippines to the United States. By that time Juan Luna was among the Philippine government's diplomatic agents in Europe and America, his appointment clearly in line with the Aguinaldo government's strategy of drawing upon *ilustrado* knowledge and experience.

From December 1897 until the American entry into the Philippines in May 1898 Luna had been in New York. In July he left for London. There he received word from the exile government in Hongkong that he was to serve with the Philippine delegation in Paris, headed by fellow *ilustrado* Felipe Agoncillo. Their mission was to prevent the signing of the Treaty of Paris.

With his experience in European capitals and at the Court in Madrid, Juan Luna undoubtedly was aware of the enormity of the task. The mission to seek recognition was itself daunting. The Philippine Republic was a new government, with no international stature and very few funds. Luna stated that he would prefer fighting on the battlefield alongside his brother. He also spoke in favor of a U.S. protectorate as a means of preventing bloodshed and misery among Filipinos.[149] Despite such views, and to his credit, he contributed his efforts to Agoncillo's diplomatic team. From September 1898 to March 1899, his work took him from London to Paris to confer with fellow *ilustrados* Ramon Abarca and Pedro P. Roxas on diplomatic strategies. By October he was in Hongkong, and by November in Manila. By way of Hongkong, Japan, the United States, and Canada, he was back in Paris by March of 1899. In June his brother Antonio, who had become minister for war under the Aguinaldo government, was assassinated, although Juan did not hear of his death until November. With the failure of the diplomatic mission now all too evident, Luna decided to return to the Philippines. His son, Andres, then twelve years old, was still in the custody of brother Jose. On 5 December 1899, at the age of forty-two, Juan Luna suffered a heart attack in Hongkong. A second attack killed him two days later.

It is not known when T. H. made the decision to fully dissociate himself from the Aguinaldo government and work only with the American colonialists. But no attempt has been made to link T. H.'s disaffection with the fact that Antonio Luna was directing Aguinaldo's negotiations with the Americans. Quick to anger and insult, Luna violently opposed those who sought a peaceful solution to the conflict with the United States.

In May 1899, T. H. Pardo de Tavera launched a daily newspaper, *La Democracia.* The paper's objectives were, simply put, T. H.'s political agenda: peace ("without which we can do nothing, expect nothing"), the separation of church and state, autonomy for the Philippines along with representation in the U.S. Congress, and the country's eventual admission as a state in the American union.[150]

On 5 May 1899, Aguinaldo's cabinet president, Apolinario Mabini, who like Luna was unalterably opposed to seeking peace, resigned. His replacement, Pedro Paterno, a Manila *ilustrado* and European contemporary of T. H. and Jose Rizal, immediately pursued negotiations for peace. Angered, Luna formed his own cabinet on 3 June with himself as president and war minister. On 5 June, Luna and an aide, Col. Francisco Roman, were assassinated in Aguinaldo's absence at the revolutionary headquarters in Cabanatuan, Nueva Ecija. Although T. H. makes no mention of it, the violence of Antonio's death must have been a reminder of the murders in Paris.

T. H. and the American Regime

The Manila *ilustrados'* authoritative role in shaping U.S. colonial policy in the Philippines has been described and analyzed elsewhere.[151] Here it should be noted that Jacob Gould Schurman said, in January 1899, at the time of his appointment as head of the First Philippine Commission, that "no definitive policy had been adopted or even thought out by the President." The commission was appointed to produce the recommendations that would serve as the foundation of a basic policy. According to Schurman, the commission's main sources of information were "the educated Filipinos" who form "possibly ten per cent at most—of the people." America's main concern "in devising a form of government for the Philppines [is] to frame one which, to the utmost extent possible, shall satisfy the views and aspirations of educated Filipinos."[152]

A month after Schurman and his commissioners arrived in Manila, in March 1899, he issued an invitation by proclamation to the Philippines' "leading and representative men . . . to meet for personal acquaintance and for the exchange of views and opinions."[153] Predictably, the men who responded to the call were the country's best educated and most articulate professionals.

The *ilustrados* who made the strongest impressions on the American colonialists were Filipino-Spanish lawyer Cayetano Arellano and T. H. Pardo de Tavera. The most favorable reactions came from their counterparts on the commission, the American academics. Commissioner Dean C. Worcester described Arellano in glowing terms as "universally admitted to be the ablest of living Filipinos and respected by natives, Spaniards, English and Americans alike." William Howard Taft, who later became the first civil governor, considered T. H. "the leading Filipino," being impressed by his command of western learning.[154]

It is not surprising that these Americans sought the counsel of the *ilustrados* whose learning they so admired. They sought Arellano's advice on everything juridical and organizational, and his assessment of the court system was incorporated in its entirety as part of the military governor's report to the president and Congress.[155] On virtually every other subject they consulted T. H. Pardo de Tavera. He was not only an authority on public health and medical questions. His grasp of the historical background of such controversial issues as the educational system, the agricultural "friar estates," and the political economy of the colony also made him an invaluable resource.

T. H. did not hesitate to speak his mind and publish his opinions. He was convinced that Aguinaldo's government was a "homegrown tyranny," and said so. He felt that the Americans should establish a protectorate in the Philippines and extend the full rights of the U.S. Constitution to the Filipino people. Kantian in his political philosophy, he was convinced that only through education and reason could Filipinos achieve their goals. He believed that the American system offered the best opportunity for the country's advancement.

The Americans viewed T. H.'s position as one that rendered them a "service." Borrowing T. H.'s own term, they described him as an "Americanista." They were impressed with his European background and quick to highlight his academic credentials. Commissioner Worcester described him as

> mostly Spaniard, with a bare trace of native blood. Born here, but has spent twenty-four years in Paris; he is one of the most pronounced Americanistas here and has been indefatigable and invaluable in his efforts to serve us.[156]

But who did T. H. and his *ilustrado* cohort serve? Obviously the American colonizers thought the Filipino intellectuals were in their service. American historians such as Glenn May have concurred, depicting the *ilustrados* as passive instruments of policy at best, and at worst as minions with no decisive role to play.[157] Philippine nationalist historians have excoriated them, and T. H. in particular, for collaborating with the Americans and allowing themselves to be co-opted for high office. T. H. saw himself as fulfilling the responsibility that his background and education had thrust upon him, that of serving the interests of the Filipino people whether they recognized it or not.

On 4 July 1901, William Howard Taft took office as the first U.S. civil governor of the Philippines. He immediately announced the appointment of T. H. and two other Filipinos—Benito Legarda and Jose Luzurriaga—as members of the Philippine Commission, the colony's governing body. Vested with legislative as well as executive authority, the Philippine Commission was dominated by Americans but the Filipino members were appointed to executive committees dealing with matters in which they had expertise. As such they participated in forming and implementing policy. When the Filipino appointments were announced, T. H. said, "We consider [this] a great day because three Filipinos have been appointed [to high office] regardless of who we be."[158]

The end of T. H.'s public life as a Philippine Commissioner came in 1909. Either he had not "played the game,"[159] or he had played it too well. He had been remarkably consistent in pursuit of what he considered to be in the best interest of the Filipinos. He had fought the highest colonial official, Governor General Luke E. Wright and succeeded in getting him recalled from the Philippines. In the process, he had made an enemy of the American commissioner William Cameron Forbes, whose devotion to Wright was virtual sycophancy. When Forbes proved himself capable of negotiating alliances with the younger, popular politicians of Osmeña and Quezon's generation, he won the approval of William Howard Taft. As the new colonial proconsul, Forbes succeeded in removing T. H. from the Philippine Commission in retaliation for Wright's dismissal.

The Americans could no longer allow T. H. to be perceived as influential. Colonial officials and their advisors now considered the generation of intellectuals he led to be troublesome and intractable. Taft's key advisor, James LeRoy, explained that it had been the intention of the commission to recognize "mainly the upper class at first" while "creating as far as possible conditions that will tend to social improvement and thus the lessening of their power." The long-range plan was to "win over the best element among the radicals" and

> get hold of the young men whose ideals are sufficiently defined to themselves
> so that they will never accept the guidance of the caciques, yet who have not
> the knowledge and experience to frame a program for themselves. . . . I would
> give a good deal for the chance to try reconciling this element of 'young
> Filipinos' who I believe represent the future of their country, to the new
> regime, weaning them from their false leaders, and making them a new
> political element of force in the country . . . one that would be the most
> important, because it would hold the possibility of growth along the right
> lines.[160]

In place of the *federalistas* and the Manila *ilustrados*, ambitious American colonialists such as William Cameron Forbes had begun cultivating a Filipino clientele. Led by Sergio Osmeña of Cebu and Manuel Quezon of Tayabas (now Quezon Province), the rising young politicians were, almost to a man, products of provincial political processes. Operating with the blessing of their colonial patrons, who saw them as effective levers of control over the Filipino masses, these politicians were a new breed to whom T. H.'s credo of service and reform seemed idealistic but detached from the realities of political power.

T. H.'s writing in his later years consisted of detailed descriptions of the paths he believed the Filipino people should take. No doubt he realized the futility of holding public office under the colonial system. With his analytical mind he must have understood the bankruptcy of representative leadership in the flawed system of colonial democracy that the United States was constructing in the Philippines.

The only chronological account of T. H. Pardo de Tavera's life is found in E. Arsenio Manuel's *Dictionary of Philippine Biography*, published in 1955. Reflecting what has become a traditional view of the "periodization" of T. H.'s life, Manuel identifies three phases. The first, 1884–98, "was devoted to investigational work of scientific nature which is of cultural value." It is of enormous interest in understanding Philippine historiography that the period from 1898 to 1909, when T. H. was at his most politically active, is described as "just an interlude in his life that ushered in the third period of intellectual introspection." While Manuel concedes that this period, although shorter, was "historically more meaningful," he claims that T. H.'s political activities only served to give "his ideas weight and audience." Echoing the nationalist view, he sums up T. H.'s political role in a dismissive way.

> The role he played in national politics may not be impressive—in fact he came to be regarded as a figure of anti-nationalistic views—but his actuations were those of a man of strong persuasions and could be justified by the peculiar conditions of the times, for as soon as the Federal Party had accomplished some of its aims in that period of transition between war and normalcy, he considered his task finished and thereafter [was] ready to dedicate himself to other labours.[161]

T. H.'s defeat by the American colonial state was not as dramatic as that of his uncle Don Joaquin in 1872 by the Spanish. But there are similarities. In both instances, the Pardo de Taveras held positions at the pleasure of a colonial master. Although they were appointed to those positions because they were qualified for them by virtue of their professionalism and personalities, the final arbiter of their influence was caprice—the whim of the colonialist.

T. H. always spoke his mind freely.[162] Too freely, the Americans felt. Freed from the constraints of officialdom, his writings in the years following his retirement from political life (Manuel's third "phase," 1909–25) constituted a virtual "crusade for intellectual liberation from the traditional ways, superstitions, feudalistic customs, class pressure and dominance, established modes of thinking, religious intolerance and the dogmatism of the preceding regime."[163] He had been a scientist in his younger, inquisitive days. He became a politician in his vigorous forties. In his retirement, he resumed his studies as a philosopher.

The range and pace of activity that T. H. maintained between 1898 and 1909 distinguished the public from the domestic phases of his life. In private he focused his efforts upon restoring the family patterns that had been profoundly shattered by Juan Luna. Although he would retain close fraternal ties to Felix, their moves to Manila and Buenos Aires left each with only a fraction of the family structure they once had. At its core, T. H.'s immediate family in Manila now comprised only himself, his wife Concha, their two sons, Carlos and Alfredo, and daughter Bebeco.

Nonetheless, his return home gave T. H. a fairly wide network of more distant kin. Doña Tula and the Pardo de Tavera cousins, Eloisa, Beatriz, and their father's posthumously born namesake, Joaquin, Jr., had returned to Manila after Don Joaquin's death in Paris in 1884. At least two decades younger than T. H., these cousins in effect comprised part of the rising generation. When T. H. was named to the Philippine Commission, the young Joaquin was just beginning legal studies at his father's alma mater, by that time referred to by its Americanized title as the University of Santo Tomas.

The maternal Gorricho relatives, who had married into various Manila and European families, provided an even wider circle of affinal relations. As T. H. broadened the range of his political activity, the public and domestic strands of his life became interwoven in his various networks. To take one example, his cousin Mauro Prieto was the son of his mother's sister, Josefa Gorricho, whose husband Antonio Prieto was descended from a Manila family with French origins. Though younger than T. H., Mauro was already a well-respected businessman in Manila, and when T. H. organized the Partido Federal in 1901 he became one of its founding members. In another instance, T. H.'s business associate and political ally on the Philippine Commission, Benito Legarda, was the father of Consuelo Legarda, Mauro Prieto's wife.

The flow of achievement from the brothers Don Felix and Don Joaquin to the brothers T. H. and Felix seemed to slow to a trickle in the following generation. Carlos, Alfredo, and Bebeco did not attain a university education. Neither they nor their spouses achieved any semblance of their father's public prominence. Paz's son, Andres Luna, did study architecture in Paris and in the 1930s was one of the Philippines' foremost architects. But clearly his achievement fell short of the high standards set by his forebears. Thus, the family's *ilustrado* achievements—high education and high office—eluded the generation of T. H.'s offspring. Yet in the succeeding generation Alfredo's daughter Mita became a medical doctor, a public figure, and a minister in the cabinet of the president of the Philippines.

There is evidence that T. H. devoted much thought and planning to the education of his sons. One of Governor Taft's letters to T. H., for example, refers to a previous discussion about the boys' education. In discussing a possible appointment to the post of resident commissioner in Washington, Taft suggested:

I should think . . . that place would be one quite suited to your tastes and certainly would be one suited to your talent and capacity. . . . I am sure you would find the life in Washington most delightful. You could then put your sons in school in America, where they could learn English and get familiar with the institutions of the country.[164]

Although T. H. did not accept the appointment, he took Taft's suggestion. Carlos, who was about fourteen, and Alfredo, who was twelve, became students at the Taft School in Connecticut, a preparatory institution owned by Taft's brother. As a reflection of the high regard in which their father was held, the boys were accorded many courtesies, including an invitation to the Roosevelt White House. But the boys showed little interest in the school and did not prosper in its environment. Their father, seeming to conclude that the frequent changes in their lives had to be mitigated, sent them to school in France. There they attended a Jesuit college in Paris before returning to Manila to finish their secondary education.[165]

Living in the aura of a father who was not only politically powerful but intellectually eminent should have provided Carlos and Alfredo with a compelling role model. There is no facile explanation for the fact that they did not follow in the paternal footsteps. There was a marked difference in temperament between T. H. and his wife but how much that proved to be a factor in the upbringing of Carlos and Alfredo is impossible to determine.

Publicly, T. H. and his wife were well matched. She was almost certainly of *creole* background, fair and attractive, her eyes pewter in color. Moreover, she was extremely wealthy. In addition to being the heiress of her grandparents—the paternal Cembrano y Kerr and the maternal Gonzalez-Calderon—her father's sister was Doña Kukang Cembrano de Ossorio, whose children owned the Victorias Sugar Mill. Another of her father's sisters married a Spaniard named Torrontegui, whose daughter Matilde married a brother of the Admiral Montojo of the Manila Bay disaster. A daughter of the Torrontegui-Montojo union married Enrique Zobel de Ayala after his wife Consuelo Roxas died in the cholera epidemic of 1900.[166] On Concha's maternal side, the family was *ilustrado*. Her cousin, Felipe Calderon, drafted the Constitution that was approved and adopted at Malolos in 1899 by the Revolutionary Congress.

As the wife of the highest-ranking Filipino in the American colonial government, Concha Pardo de Tavera was eminently respectable. Invariably she was escorted to dinner or led in the opening steps of the official *rigodon de honor* on the arm of the highest American official present.[167] By the dictates of protocol, she more often than not found herself on the arm of Governor Taft. In fact, the most visible sign of T. H.'s fall from power came on the evening of the Assembly's Inaugural Ball in 1907, when Secretary Taft relinquished Mrs. Pardo de Tavera to William Cameron Forbes and led Mrs. Sergio Osmeña into the *rigodon*.[168]

In their private lives, however, there was an underlying incompatibility. Concha was given to the gaming table while T. H. was extremely disciplined.[169] Whether focused on study, political activity, or family life, he devoted his considerable energies to excellence. Mita recalls that her grandfather meticulously observed a schedule of work, dining, correspondence, and a daily afternoon walk at the Luneta. He gathered his children's children around him as he grew older, teaching them good habits, rewarding them with highly polished centavo coins which he rubbed until they shined, writing them little notes with funny sketches, and telling them in ways they could understand something of the rationality with which he viewed the world.

There were few, if any, shared interests between husband and wife. Concha's preoccupation with gaming no doubt explains why T. H. banned playing cards and similar games in his household. As their children grew into adulthood, the need for shared responsibilities in parenting lessened. In the end they became estranged. After T. H. left the Philippine Commission, he moved to a house in the outlying suburb of Santa Mesa while Concha remained at the house on Legarda Street in Manila. Until his death in 1925 they maintained separate households.

The evidence of the family records and recollections indicate that T. H. was a loving parent. In his travels abroad, he was frequently accompanied by one, two, or all three of his children. During a trip to Paris with Bebeco in 1912, he learned that his younger son, Alfredo, had been assaulted by an American army officer. It had been three years since T. H. had left the Philippine Commission, and it was clear that with the rise of his colonial enemy, Forbes, to the position of governor general, his influence was on the wane. The incident is interesting for the light it sheds upon T. H.'s own view of his role as a parent and for the insight it provides into his growing sense of powerlessness within the American colonial system juxtaposed with his continuing influence with Manuel Quezon, the rising leader in Philippine politics.

In the incident in question, Alfredo, then twenty-two, had been in the company of an American friend named John Stevenot at a dance in the Manila Auditorium during Carnival. The two friends were at the bar when a group of drunken American cavalry officers walked in. One of them, a Lieutenant Hicks, accosted Alfredo. When he remonstrated, Hicks grabbed his whip. Cursing and staggering, he beat Alfredo about the head. Alfredo left the hall bleeding, and reported the incident to a police officer. The matter was brought to the attention of Alfredo's uncle Joaquin who in his capacity as the city *fiscal* questioned the American. Hicks admitted the assault and defiantly threatened to beat other Filipinos as well.

Despite the circumstances, which clearly defined the incident as a civil matter, the case was brought before a court martial. A letter from T. H. to Quezon, who was then in Washington serving as resident commissioner, describes his worry that political enemies would vent their anger toward him by making Alfredo suffer. He asked Quezon to use his good standing with the American administrators to prevent any injustice.

The letter also explains why the issue went beyond the Pardo de Tavera family. In the previous year Forbes had issued an executive order proclaiming that cases involving imprisonment for one year or less would not be brought before civil authorities but before the military. T. H. did not believe that Forbes would carry his tendencies towards authoritarianism this far. He asked Quezon to bring the matter before the U.S. Congress as evidence of what abuses the colonial government could perpetrate in its name. He decried the situation as another consequence of the status of the Philippines: a country to which the United States could do whatever it chose.[170]

In 1913, when T. H.'s term on the Board of Regents of the University of the Philippines expired, he was conferred the degree of Doctor of Laws, *honoris causa*. He left soon after for an extended visit with his brother Felix in Buenos Aires. The following year, he was in Lausanne, Switzerland, when Germany attacked Belgium and started the First World War. He spent the war years in Barcelona where he developed an interest in agriculture, particularly in wheat and fruit growing.[171] He lived off the proceeds of his properties just as his family once had done in Paris. There were some anxious moments over the reliability of money transfers from Manila to Barcelona but despite delays the service was not disrupted.[172] He returned to Manila in 1918.

The Next Generation

Although T. H.'s children achieved neither academic honors nor public prestige, they enjoyed high social status. Alfredo, for example, was regularly seen at the Baguio Country Club, which was reserved to the elite Americans and Filipinos. Thus, the younger generation succeeded in forming marriage alliances with families of similar position. Carlos, at twenty-four, married Belen Ramirez, the daughter of a tobacco industrialist who was among the exhibitors at the Paris Exposition under T. H.'s directorship in 1889. The elder Ramirez managed the Pardo de Taveras' financial affairs, and the families had a long-standing, close relationship. Bebeco married Pepito Ventura, son of a well-to-do family from Pampanga, but after she had borne two sons the marriage ended. According to family lore, the relationship failed for two reasons. Pepito, with T. H. as his guarantor, started a tobacco business with a loan of approximately one million pesos. When the business failed because of mismanagement, Pepito's insolvency engulfed his father-in-law in serious indebtedness. In addition, Pepito reportedly was "playing around with women." Despite the scandal in Manila society that invariably attached to divorce or separation, T. H. supported his daughter in her decision to end the marriage. Perhaps recalling a similar circumstance when divorce might have spared the family great pain, he arranged for Bebeco to obtain a divorce in the United States. He used his connections with American officials and former colonial administrators to smooth the process, so that Henry Stimson is said to have met Bebeco when her ship docked in San Francisco.[173] Eventually, she met and married Augusto Gonzales, whose family was prominent in Pangasinan.[174] But Bebeco's divorce and remarriage brought family tensions to the surface. Her mother objected strongly to her daughter's decisions, and mother and daughter became estranged.

In the traditional writing of family history, each generation is examined for the attributes of familial success. If no such marks of achievement are found, the family in that period is characterized as being "in decline" and its members are dismissed as lackluster. With achievement by a following generation of the familiar attributes of success, the family is said to have experienced a revival. In the family's taxonomy, a hiatus in the flow of achievement becomes an "aberrant" phase, interesting because it enhances the image of resurgent vitality in the achieving generation but uninspiring in the assumed torpidity of its members.

To take such a view of the generation that followed T. H. and preceded Mita would be unfortunate for familial historiography. It would overlook the crucial fact that the Pardo de Taveras of that period devised the strategies of survival that ultimately allowed the revitalization of the family. This view in no way diminishes the powerful way in which Mita reasserted Pardo de Tavera influence in Philippine society. But it does recognize the family's indebtedness to the generation that achieved survival.

Mita claims that the memory of her grandfather was the impelling force behind her success. Although she was only six when T. H. died in 1925, and twenty-four when she fulfilled her ambition to become a doctor, her grandfather's influence was so vital that he still looms large in her sense of self. Unless one believes that this influence could have survived purely by the force of a six-year-old girl's recollections, one must look elsewhere for the determination that embodied the family tradition in T. H. and kept his memory alive.

In 1918, Alfredo married Paz Lopez Manzano. She was Filipino-Spanish, her father (Narciso Lopez Manzano) a native of Asturias, and her mother (Josefa Samson) a Filipina of Chinese background from Santa Maria, Bulacan. Her father had come to the colony to make his fortune, and apparently did so in the copra trade. Ranked among the most wealthy Spanish-*mestizo* families, he sent his children to Spain for their education. He chose the Instituto Poligliota as the best school in Barcelona for his sons and entrusted his daughters to the Spanish nuns for their training in deportment.

One of these daughters, Paz, had recently returned to the Philippines when she met and married Alfredo. It was not a long courtship, nor was it an enduring marriage, for Alfredo died only ten years later, in 1928. But it was a remarkably fortunate alliance for the family. Alfredo was exceptionally devoted to his father. Although he did not emulate T. H.'s academic interests, he helped collect and maintain a library of valuable Philippine books and antiques.[175] But perhaps his most significant contribution to the family was that he drew his wife and daughter into his filial bond with his father.

Following their marriage, Alfredo and Paz set up their household in Cebu where he worked for Standard Vacuum Oil. A year or so after Mita's birth in 1919, they were relocated by the company to Zamboanga. But when T. H.'s health began to fail in 1923, Alfredo brought his wife and daughter back to Manila to live in his father's house. Although no doubt reduced in stature by returning to a household of which he was not the head, Alfredo encouraged the bond between grandfather and grandchild that proved critical to the survival of the family tradition. Mita came to love her grandfather with the pure innocence of which only children seem capable. Yet her affection might not have matured into devotion had it not been nurtured by her mother.

During the seven years that had elapsed since she married Alfredo, the rapport between Paz and her father-in-law had deepened into a relationship of shared values and mutual respect. T. H. seemed to recognize in Paz the strengths that had seen the Pardo de Taveras through their earlier crises. He loved her as a daughter, seeing in her the strength that had been lost to the family with the deaths of his mother and sister.[176] In the tradition of the Gorricho women, Paz imbibed the family's ideals and contributed her energies to ensuring their preservation. By the time her father-in-law died, Paz had become his trustee of family tradition.

Living in her father-in-law's household during the last two years of his life, Paz had an intuitive grasp of T. H.'s need to endow his descendants with the family history. She wrote down as much as she remembered of his stories and recollections, and recorded the history he dictated.[177] If recalling the painful events of the past proved cathartic for T. H., imparting his story to someone who listened with love and sympathy gave him affirmation. As a genealogy, T. H.'s *Arbol Genealogico* strengthened the family's sense of pride. As a memoir, it enhanced its understanding of its past.

Many signs pointed to T. H.'s declining political influence. But at the same time numerous accolades and honorary appointments indicated that he retained the people's respect. Although he refused to negotiate political arrangements with officials—American or Filipino—Manuel Quezon, the rising master of political maneuvering, called upon him regularly and sought his opinions.

Early in 1920, the Spanish consul in Manila requested an interview with T. H. Consul Palmaroli wished to discuss the reported intention of the Philippine government to appoint T. H. as president of the Commission of the Fourth Centennial of the Discovery of the Philippines, which would occur in 1921. The Spanish goverment was unhappy with the appointment because T. H. had made critical statements about Spain during the revolutionary period.[178]

T. H. was incensed. Apparently the Spanish government had forgiven those who deserted her cause, burned her property, and killed her citizens during the Revolution but would not overlook his valid criticisms of her policies. More to the point, this was a blatant attempt by another power to influence the Philippine government. T. H. noted caustically that it seemed the Philippine government was "not at liberty to give me an appointment without the O.K. of the Manila

Spaniards and their consul." Although he was appointed president of the
commission, the incident contributed to his belief that there was a need to keep a
clear record of his past actions and motives.

In January 1923, T. H. was appointed director of the Philippine Library and
Museum. In October, he formed the Philippine Library Association and became its
first president. In June, the Board of Regents of the University of the Philippines,
of which he was a former member, appointed him head of the newly created
Department of Philippine Languages. He held the position until 31 October 1924
when he resigned because of poor health. There was a final appointment to the
Board of Educational Survey of the Philippines but he did not live to hold that
office.

On 25 March 1925, Alfredo waited for his father to awaken from his
afternoon nap. Paz and his sister Bebeco had taken their children to Baguio City for
a holiday, and the house was quiet. Although it was half an hour past the time
when T. H. normally rose, Alfredo thought he should not disturb his father. When
an hour passed, he became anxious and entered his father's bedroom. He found
that his father had died quietly in his sleep.

The two decades between T. H.'s death in 1925 and Mita's emergence as a
medical doctor mark a long and difficult period for the family. Themes of crisis and
survival occur throughout, and an account of the family's endurance must
acknowledge all the sources of its strength. In a summary of those strengths the
tenacity with which the survivors upheld the family's values and traditions should
be recognized.

On 21 August 1928, after a prolonged depression, Alfredo took his life,
hanging himself in the garage of his residence above the old Cabaret de San Juan.
He left a note to reassure those "[t]o whom it may concern," stating that he had
decided to "kill myself of my own free will." The morning before his death he had
written a check in the amount of thirty pesos to a young woman, Julia Soriano, a
cabaret dancer.[179] He left nothing else.

Mita, who was nine at the time, remembers nothing about the death. She
remembers her father as kind and loving, an image consistent with that of Alfredo
the devoted son. She recalls that shortly after her grandfather's death Alfredo
seemed depressed and that he began to travel frequently to Japan for treatment.
Eventually her parents became estranged.

The fragmentation of the family at this time must have had a telling effect on
Alfredo's sense of bereavement. The bond between his father and his uncle Felix
had not been duplicated in Alfredo's relationship with his brother. Carlos spent
most of his time in Paris where he had developed a problem with alcohol and his
marriage was on the verge of collapse.

Nearer to home, the breach between Bebeco and their mother had been
healed. But the separation of T. H. and Concha had made Alfredo's attachment to
his father an alignment that distanced him from his mother. In the end, the
desperation that led Alfredo to the noose is comprehensible only in light of the

traumas of his life, of finding a beloved parent dead, of a sense of dysfunction in a society in which he was expected to replicate his father's achievements.

With the death of Alfredo, Mita's mother became her strongest link to the Pardo de Tavera family.[180] Struggling to maintain that linkage, Paz resolved to fight for her daughter's birthright. Mita's recollections of her mother juxtapose images of a gracious, handsome woman and a dauntless, protective parent whose adversaries at times included the Pardo de Taveras themselves.

When Mita was seventeen, Paz joined her brother-in-law Carlos in opposing the claim of his sister Bebeco to certain family properties. Mita's grandmother, Concha Cembrano, had died that year, and at the probate of her will Paz was stunned to learn that the extensive Cembrano properties were no longer part of the estate. In 1912, Concha had given some property to her children—Carlos, Alfredo and Bebeco. Paz, and apparently Carlos as well, had been told that the bulk of the estate would remain undivided. Sometime after Alfredo's death in 1928, however, Concha transferred most of her remaining assets to Bebeco. Carlos and Paz opposed the probate, arguing that Concha's properties should remain undivided for at least five years under the management of T. H.'s old friend and administrator, J. V. Ramirez, but they won only a temporary court order. Following an appeal filed by Concha's sisters in 1936, the court confirmed Bebeco's claim to the Cembrano estate.[181] Mita retained only what her father had received in 1912, the house and lot in Intramuros.

Perhaps Paz would have pursued Mita's claims with less temerity had the family not suffered a serious reversal five years before. During the famous Crystal Arcade case of 1931, the Supreme Court of the Philippines had ruled the Pardo de Tavera holdings on Manila's premier commercial street, the Escolta, forfeit to a creditor, El Hogar Filipino. The properties had been used as collateral in a large development project undertaken by the family firm, Tavera-Luna, Inc.

Ironically, the incorporation of Tavera-Luna had marked a resurgence of family unity. The son of the murdered Paz, Andres Luna, had at last joined his mother's family—a reconciliation he had begun with his uncle T. H. years before. Educated in Paris, Andres had eventually returned to Manila, a talented architect who seemed destined to equal his father's artistic achievements. In the 1920s, he became obsessed with the design and construction of a glass palace, to be called the Crystal Arcade, which he envisioned as a grand commercial center. He was certain the building would enhance the Escolta's commercial primacy and increase the value of the family's holdings. He urged the family firm to make the investment. Paz was fiscally conservative in administering her daughter's inheritance. Worried that the project was too ambitious, she cast a dissenting vote. But, as his mother's sole heir, Andres held the majority of shares and prevailed. Paz's misgivings proved well founded. Building on the quay side of the Escolta, contractors encountered a high water table. The building's foundation became a complicated and costly construction, a veritable sinkhole into which the corporation's resources drained. As the grandiose scale of both building and budget became obvious, people began to refer to it as the Pardo de Taveras' mausoleum.

The Crystal Arcade was magnificent,[182] a study in light and space, with a central staircase that seemed to float upward into a vast foyer. Indeed, it decorated the Escolta and drew many admiring visitors. But the very qualities that made it an attraction weakened its value as commercial property. There was insufficient room for office and retail activities. Saddled with an enormous debt, the corporation soon found, to the consternation of its shareholders, that the building did not generate enough income. Despite frantic efforts, the Pardo de Taveras were unable to forestall financial ruin. In a sequence of events that left Paz filled with unresolved resentment, the lending company El Hogar Filipino foreclosed.[183]

Dismayed, the Pardo de Taveras witnessed the dissolution of their corporation. Since wealth was only part of the meaning they attached to their Escolta properties, the loss meant more than the end of their fortune. The legacy of their ancestor, the *zacatera* from Cavite, was gone. With it went the family's visible connections to the city's commercial and social core. Their preeminence on the Escolta had been evidence of how closely their rise had been linked to the growth of the city. The family had lived in various homes on the Escolta, and in one of them T. H. had been born.[184] His grandmother, Doña Ciriaca, had held court in a home with large windows across the street from the house in which T. H. had lived as a boy. Mita recalled stories of his grandmother hanging bunches of ripe mangoes at her window to signal her grandchildren that she had returned from one of her many trips to the Cavite farm. That emotional investment in the family's Escolta legacy was gone. The ordeal was painful and marked not just the end of a tradition but the end of an identity.

Mita recalls that quite suddenly her mother began to say things like "We cannot afford this, we cannot afford that." Though not given to an ostentatious lifestyle, the Pardo de Taveras had maintained a level of comfort and refinement that now had to be scaled back. It marked a sharper decline than T. H. had experienced during the 1892 dispersal of wealth that had followed the deaths of Doña Juliana and his sister Paz. Honest and decidedly not entrepreneurial, T. H. accumulated little wealth despite his influential position on the Philippine Commission. Only through careful management did he preserve his patrimony and keep the "jewel" of the family's real estate largely intact.[185]

The rancor over who was to blame festered and finally came to a head during the probate of Concha's will. Coping with greatly reduced finances, Carlos returned from Paris with his son to find that his mother had effectively disinherited him in favor of his sister Bebeco. Paz resented her sister-in-law for her seemingly unmitigated selfishness. Yet the final break did not come until 1941 when Paz, by court order, forced Bebeco to comply with T. H.'s will and relinquish what was left of his library to Mita.[186] Considering T. H.'s books and papers to be the symbolic core of his legacy, Paz fought for possession because she was convinced that Mita was T. H.'s true heir. Preparing Mita to assume that role, Paz carefully chose the directions in which she steered her daughter.

Mita and the Legacy

At age six, Mita began her education at the Assumption school, where the nuns imposed high standards of deportment upon the young women.[187] Satisfied that the school reinforced her own values of honor and self-respect, Paz kept Mita at the Assumption through high school. Since she was determined that Mita should have more than the traditional transition from girl to wife and mother, she encouraged her daughter to aspire to a profession. Watching her schoolmates begin to opt for marriage, Mita set her sights on enrolling at the University of the Philippines for a degree in medicine. That her grandfather had been instrumental in establishing the university and its medical program in 1908, and subsequently served as a regent on its governing board, gave a certain poignancy to her determination to succeed there.[188] The choice, she said, was really between ballet, which she loved, and medicine, to which she felt a deep personal commitment. She decided that "With ballet, my energy would decrease as I grew older. With medicine, the older I got, the better I would be."[189]

Her medical studies would require a heavy commitment of resources—money, time, and energy—and Paz was prepared to sell a large portion of Mita's inheritance to finance them.[190] But, if a career in medicine would provide opportunities for achievement and self-realization, it would close others. While Mita was a student at the Assumption, she had met Serging Osmeña, whose father, Sergio, Sr., was the man who had displaced Mita's grandfather as the "first Filipino" in 1907.[191] Before long, Mita and Serging reached a tacit understanding that they would become formally betrothed when both were ready for marriage. But two obstacles were insurmountable. Paz opposed the match, arguing that Serging did not want Mita to pursue a career in medicine. With budding political ambitions, Serging required a wife who would assume all the domestic responsibilities, releasing him to the demands of his constituents. A Pardo de Tavera–Osmeña marriage would have been a brilliant alliance—the granddaughter of the quintessential *ilustrado*-statesman would have enhanced the political chances of the ambitious young politician. But family ties and tradition proved decisive. Acceding to her mother's counsel, Mita entered the University of the Philippines premedical program in 1939. Soon after, Serging married a woman whose family's widespread shipping interests provided him with valuable support.[192]

In December 1941, the Japanese invaded the Philippines, causing massive disruption in the lives of all Filipinos. Mita, then twenty-two, was required by her medical-school dean to live with her classmates in a downtown dormitory. With thousands of Manila residents, she endured a regime of cruelty that threatened them daily with death and destruction. But her mother had foresight, and Mita to some extent was better off than other Manileños. Paz had followed the unfolding of world events in the Manila media. By 1936, a combination of circumstances allowed her to make decisions that ensured her family's survival. Soon after the battle over Concha's will, she sold the lot in Intramuros but retained the house, which she ordered dismantled. Built of huge wooden beams and flooring salvaged from discarded Manila galleons, the house was a relic that Paz was determined Mita should keep. Paz had the materials carted to the outskirts of Manila, to a property that Mita's father had bought years before. There, in 1937, she built a house and began keeping a garden as well as chickens, pigs, goats, and cows.[193] When the Japanese invasion of December 1941 threw Manila into a panic, looters broke into the Port Area and began to empty the warehouses. Paz drove to the waterfront and bought cases of canned goods for a fraction of their cost. Thus, when food shortages later began plaguing Manila's residents, Mita had a modest but steady supply of chicken, often stewed *adobo* style, tinned sardines, and beef.

Mita's stories of the war years convey the image of a young medical student indistinguishable from her peers. She recalls waking at dawn to catch a tram and walking for miles to meet the *calesa* (a horse-drawn rig) that took her home to the farmhouse. There she would pack a small sack of rice and some fresh greens to augment the "awful" dormitory food before rushing back to the city and the safety of her room before curfew. In an environment drastically different from that of the Assumption, Mita learned the leveling lessons of the merit system. She began her studies with a chemistry course for which she was sure she was insufficiently prepared. She recalled the others "talking about 'valenses', about this and that, and I didn't know what they were talking about."[194]

In medicine proper, she developed a camaraderie with her classmates. They supported each other when studying for an anatomy test in which pieces of rubberlike tubing were the nerves to which one had to give specific names. They overcame their misgivings at being presented with their first cadaver for dissection on a laboratory slab. Together they endured unending anxiety over the "torture" exams, the grades, and the possibility of "flunking out." As Mita recalled,

> I worked so hard. . . . I told myself, "You've got to make it yourself, be respected for what you can do, not because you are the granddaughter of so-and-so. . . ." It was the most rigorous education. I don't know how I made it. At night I would stay very late with my books, studying, studying. There was no fun life, like going to parties, everything stopped.[195]

In 1942, Mita consented to marry Jose Loinaz. The decision marked a coming of age because it arose out of her need to care for her mother. She had passed the difficult premedical and core science courses and was dealing well enough with the stresses of living in an enemy-held city. But, as she traveled between her dormitory and the farmhouse, she became increasingly anxious about leaving her mother and her aunt Matilda with only a few servants in the isolated outskirts of the city. Paz had a stubborn streak, and once, when she would not bow as a Japanese sentry ordered, he had slapped her and threatened her with a bayonet. The thought of her mother under threat convinced Mita that it was now her responsibility to look to her mother's well-being. With her marriage, she acknowledged that the responsibility of the parent had passed to the next generation. If the details of her future life were unknown, its patterns were clear. As she said, "I was always sure about what I wanted to be."[196]

Thus, during the war years, a time of flux and uncertainty for most Manileños, the trajectory of Mita's life was set. Through her marriage and education, she had prepared herself for succession to leadership within the family. Her marriage would bring her four children, and she would, as her mother had done before her, provide them with the resources and education with which to make sound career and marriage choices. Similarly, her career at the Quezon Institute and her inheritance made her an established member of Manila's upper class. And, like her grandfather, her mix of ideology, intellect, and integrity would ultimately thrust her into political prominence.

Yet there is more to Mita's story than a tale of triumph over adversity. In a society in which class and family are closely intertwined, individuals and families can rise and fall with surprising speed. Since the rise of the export economy more than 150 years ago, there has always been a Filipino upper class whose position is based on combined economic and political power. But the composition of this class, the actual families that comprise it, is constantly changing.

The Pardo de Taveras are unique in that they are one of the few early prominent families to have survived. The story of their rise, descent, and resurgence could just as easily have been a tale of their rise, decline, and extinction. Their survival allows us to track a single family through a century and a half of change, and to see a whole class through the lives of its members. We could just as well have strung together studies of three or four families and achieved the same effect. But focusing on the Pardo de Taveras highlights the process of Philippine social change. Most importantly, this approach allows us to see clearly the legacy of the *ilustrados*. Just as T. H. Pardo de Tavera has served as Mita's personal mentor in the context of one family, so the *ilustrados* as a class left behind a tradition of erudition, ideology, and integrity that serves as a standard of national service. Despite their concentration of power, presidents Quezon and Marcos both were judged in a certain sense by these same standards, and both knew that they would have to answer to a historical tradition that begins with the *ilustrados*.

Notes

The author gratefully acknowledges the support so generously given her during the research and writing of this history from: Mita Pardo de Tavera; Mara Pardo de Tavera; Liana, Tara, Miel and Robert-Alfredo Paredes; Jan Opdyke; Sean Kirkpatrick; Franca Barricelli; Rory Paredes; Michael Cullinane; and Al McCoy.

[1] Mita Pardo de Tavera, interview, Manila, September 1986.

[2] Mita Pardo de Tavera, interview, Manila, 12–18 July 1992.

[3] Mita's mother, Paz Lopez Manzano, had a brother, Angel, whose daughter Lita married a de los Reyes. Lita's daughter, Margarita ("Tingting") de los Reyes, married Jose Cojuangco, the brother of Corazon Aquino, whose influence over his sister's political decisions was well known. Moreover, Mita's son Alex is married to a niece of Cory Aquino's vice-president, Doy Laurel.

[4] Mita had moved through all the career stages of junior resident, senior resident, and section chief at the institute. At a time when there were no medicines for tuberculosis, she was a young physician in the female ward. She said rest and three meals a day had an almost instantaneous, positive effect on her patients. "That's what they needed. . . . They were hungry, poor . . . so, you gave them three meals a day and they blossomed . . . they gained weight, they would stop coughing, they would really improve" (ibid.).

[5] Mita Pardo de Tavera, interview, Manila, June 1991.

[6] Mita Pardo de Tavera, interview, 12–18 July 1992.

[7] Ibid.

[8] Ibid.

[9] Mita Pardo de Tavera, interview with the author, Manila, June 1992.

[10] In Mita's words: "I was told that the property [of the institute] was used to borrow money to build the Lung Center. Yet the Center does not belong to the Department of Health. That's the same thing with the Heart Center, the Kidney Center and the various centers that Imelda built. They were built with government money but they do not belong to the Department of Health. The Lung Center was built with money borrowed by the Philippine Tuberculosis Society using Quezon Institute real estate as collateral. If that loan were repaid by the Society, it would gain ownership of the Lung Center" (Mita Pardo de Tavera, interview, 12–18 July 1992).

[11] Mita Pardo de Tavera, interview, June 1992.

[12] Ibid.

[13] Writing in the context of women's history, Linda Gordon makes the observation that "most historiographical progress—perhaps most intellectual progress—proceeds by rearranging relationships within old stories, not by writing new stories." Indeed, I found that regarding family history with the "new eyes" that women's studies has opened for me reveals a rich source to mine for the crucial, yet often informal, roles that women and other nonstellar persons have played in movements of social change. See Linda Gordon, "What's New in Women's History," in Teresa de Lauretis, ed., *Feminist Studies/Critical Studies* (Bloomington: Indiana University Press, 1986), 20-21.

[14] Such service was crucial to the rulers of Christian Spain. Their forces were at bay for much of the twelfth century when Islamic power over the peninsula had swept as far north as Huesca, in Zaragoza. Only the northern kingdoms of Galicia, Leon, Castilla, Navarra, Aragon, and Catalonia were under Christian rule. Thus, Alfonso VIII's victory at Las Navas de Tolosa in 1212 was a turning point. Halting the spread of Islamic power in the peninsula, it began the Reconquista that reached its height in the reign of the Catholic monarchs Ferdinand of Aragon and Isabela of Castilla with the beginning of a unified Spanish kingdom.

[15] Enrique, born in 1603, married Maria Montes; Juan, born in 1638, married Catalina de Arevalo; Diego, born in 1678, married Juana Padilla de Cordoba; Alfonso, born

in 1715, married Antonia de Cardenas; Joaquin, born in 1749, married Maria Alvarez; and Julian, born in 1795, married Juana Gomez (T. H. Pardo de Tavera, *Arbol Genealogico de los Pardo de Tavera, por T. H. Pardo de Tavera,* manuscript in the private collection of Mita Pardo de Tavera, Manila).

[16]Noted in E. Arsenio Manuel, *Dictionary of Philippine Biography* (Quezon City: Filipiniana Publications, 1955), 1:313.

[17]Rafael Maria de Aguilar y Ponce de Leon, who was governor general from 1793 to 1806, opened Manila to foreign trade. Quotations are from Nicholas Cushner, *Spain in the Philippines* (Rutland, Vt.: Charles E. Tuttle, 1971), 188.

[18]See Manuel Artigas y Cuerva, *Galeria de Filipinos Ilustres* (Manila: Imp. Casa Editoria "Renacimiento," 1917).

[19]See biographical entry in Manuel, *Dictionary of Philippine Biography,* 1:313–17, which summarizes the available biodata.

[20]His youngest daughter, Beatrice, was born in Paris in 1882 when Don Joaquin was fifty-three years old (ibid., 1:317n).

[21]Government statistics for the year 1870, six years after Don Felix's death, show that there were 3,823 *peninsulares* (residents born in Spain). Of that number, 516 were women. Among the remaining 3,300-odd, about 1,000 belonged to various religious orders, another 1,000 or so were soldiers, and the rest, roughly 1,300, were civil officials. The balance of what comprised the Spanish community numbered some 9,700. These were the Filipinos, or Español-Filipinos, who included both full-blooded, Philippine-born Spaniards and *mestizos.* The latter group were the offspring of Spanish and Indio (indigenous Malay) unions or those of Chinese parentage. Cited in James Leroy's "Bibliographical Notes" (in Emma Blair and James A. Robertson, *The Philippine Islands* [Cleveland: Arthur H. Clark 1907], 52:115, 6n), these figures were derived from Agustin de la Cavada's *Historia geografica, geologica y estadistica de Filipinas* (Manila: Impr. de Ramirez y Giraudier, 1876).

[22]Rafael Palma, *Historia de Filipinas* (Quezon City: University of the Philippines Press, 1968), 1:235–36.

[23]In 1865, Don Joaquin received the title Doctor of Jurisprudence and was named professor of law at the Universidad de Santo Tomas. He sat on the board of directors for the Obras Pias, a charitable fund that also functioned as a lending institution; the College of Santa Ysabel; the Royal Hospital of San Jose; and the Sociedad Economica de Amigos del Pais (Pardo de Tavera, *Arbol Genealogico*).

[24]T. H. uses the phrase "con verdadero carino" (ibid.).

[25]T. H. Pardo de Tavera writes, "Cuando se pusieron ante el tapete las problemas de mayor importancia para el pais, Don Joaquin siempre se mantuvo en las avanzadas desarrollando sus actividades y energias en pro de la causa de la cuestion de la libertad y asi se le ve figurar en la cuestion del clero, al lado de los Pelaez, Ponce y Burgos" (ibid.).

[26]Manuel Artigas y Cuerva, *Reseña Historica de la Real y Pontifica Universidad de Santo Tomas de Manila (En Celebracion del Tercer Centenario de su Establecimiento)* (Manila, 1911), 246-47.

[27]Joaquin Pardo de Tavera and Antonio Maria Regidor, interview with Edmund Plauchut, Paris, 1877, quoted in Austin Craig, *The Filipinos' Fight for Freedom,* rpt. of 1933 ed. (New York: AMS, 1973), 388–89.

[28]Ibid., 389–90.

[29]Ibid., 391. The other reforms included: "Tariff modification and reform in the manner of collecting duties at the custom house; No more discrimination between ship carriers; Reduction of export duties on native products; Permission for foreigners established in the country to acquire real estate, to worship freely according to their own religions, and to own trading ships under the Spanish flag; Creation of a council to report to the Over-Seas Ministry in Madrid upon the needs of the country." Don Joaquin noted in 1877 that the customs reform had been effective: "The custom house receipts under the revised tariff in 1874 showed a gain of sixty million pesetas over those of 1867, or a sixty per cent increase."

[30]John N. Schumacher claims that the *peninsulares* regarded the demonstration as a "scandal." See his *Revolutionary Clergy: The Filipino Clergy and the Nationalist Movement, 1850–1903* (Quezon City: Ateneo de Manila University Press, 1981), 16.

[31]Like the term *Filipino*, the word *creole* was used to describe Philippine-born Spaniards.

[32]Ibid., 19.

[33]Ibid.; John N. Schumacher, *Father Jose Burgos, Priest and Nationalist* (Quezon City: Ateneo de Manila University Press, 1972), 120–23.

[34]See ibid.

[35]Joaquin Pardo de Tavera and Antonio Maria Regidor, interview with Edmund Plauchut, 388.

[36]Ibid., 390–91.

[37]Ibid., 391.

[38]Ibid.

[39]Ibid., 391–92.

[40]Ibid., 395.

[41]Ibid., 383.

[42]The names of the exiles are provided in Fr. Aniceto Ibanez del Carmen, et al., *Chronicle of the Mariana Islands*, trans. Marjorie G. Driver (Agana: University of Guam, Micronesia Area Research Center, 1973), 26. About Doña Tula, T. H. Pardo de Tavera wrote, "A este destierro le acompano heroicamente su esposa, llamada Tula, que pertenecia a la prominente y acaudalada familia Gorricho, que con sus amplios recursos le hizo la vida de desterrado mas llevadera" (*Arbol Genealogico*).

[43]The date of Don Miguel's arrival in Manila is unknown but by 1779 he was commissioned by Governor General Basco as a lieutenant in the artillery. The next year he was appointed mayor of Capiz. In 1785, he was named chief auditor of the tobacco revenue, and two years later his responsibilities were enlarged to include the alcohol revenue (*Procedencia de la familia de Gorricho en Manila, copia de un escrito por T. H. Pardo de Tavera*, manuscript in the collection of Mita Pardo de Tavera, Manila).

[44]Ibid.

[45]The given name was *Velas Latinas*, descriptive of the shape of the sails on the canoes of the indigenes. See Francisco Olive y Garcia, *The Mariana Islands, 1884–1887: Random Notes of Governor Francisco Olive y Garcia*, trans. and annotated by Marjorie G. Driver (Guam: University of Guam, Micronesia Area Research Center, 1984), 3 (originally published in Manila by M. Perez e Hijos, 1887).

[46]The Philippines are located at 14.25° North latitude and 125° East longitude; the Marianas are at 17.20° North and 145° East.

[47]In 1788, the *situado* was 20,137 pesos, of which 3,000 were paid to the governor of the Marianas. By 1828, the *situado* had been reduced to 8,016 pesos (Olive y Garcia, *Mariana Islands*, 4).

[48]This description of Guam is taken from an account written some twelve years after Don Joaquin's exile (see Olive y Garcia, *Mariana Islands*, 15–19).

[49]Olive y Garcia, *Mariana Islands*, 53. The date and time of Don Joaquin's arrival is noted in Carmen et al., *Chronicle of the Mariana Islands*, 26.

[50]The *pantalan* was built in 1872. Since construction projects in the tropics are likely to be undertaken in the dry season, and because the Manila exiles arrived close to the end of the dry period, it seems safe to assume that the pier was completed, or close to it. See Olive y Garcia, *Mariana Islands*, 134–35.

[51]Juan Gutierrez-Gay, *Manila en el Bolsillo; Indicador para el forastero* (Manila: Imp. de Amigos del Pais, 1881), 5ff. Some 3,500 meters of thick masonry surrounded a rectilinear grid of twenty-nine streets. These streets were lined by massive stone houses, sometimes only three or four per block, each with walls six meters high. Every night the heavy timber gates of Intramuros were barred and armed garrisons patrolled the battlements.

[52]Robert R. Reed, *Colonial Manila: The Context of Hispanic Urbanism and Process of Morphogenesis* (Berkeley: University of California Press, 1978), 68.

[53]*Fincas Urbanas*, Manila, 1890–1896, Philippine National Archives.

[54]Olive y Garcia, *Mariana Islands*, 5.

[55]Ibid., 27.

[56]See Carmen et al., *Chronicle of the Mariana Islands*.

[57]Arriving with the *deportados* were the chief of the *presidio*, Don Antonio Valero y Tenorio; the *mayor* of the *presidio*, Don Juan Cumplido, with his wife and two daughters; and the *medico mayor primer ayudante de sanidad militar*, Senor Armendariz (ibid., 26).

[58]Olive y Garcia, *Mariana Islands*, 129.

[59]Ibid., 45.

[60]The population in 1881, eighteen years after the epidemic, was 7,890 (ibid.).

[61]The 1886 assessment is given in ibid., 26.

[62]See Carmen et al., *Chronicle of the Mariana Islands*.

[63]Ibid., 34.

[64]Umatac is on the Orote Peninsula, south of the harbor at San Luis de Apra. With good anchorage and plentiful water, it was a regular stopping place for the Manila galleons (Olive y Garcia, *Mariana Islands*, 28).

[65]Ibid., 45.

[66]Carmen et al., *Chronicle of the Mariana Islands*, 38.

[67]As the dates of death of Don Joaquin's parents are unknown, they may still have been living in 1872. Don Julian would have been seventy-seven years old. Possibly Doña Juana was ten years younger. Before his marriage to Doña Tula, Don Joaquin had had two daughters by a *mestiza* in Albay. One of them married a Madrigal and bore a son, Vicente (Pardo de Tavera, *Arbol Genealogico*).

[68]Felix M. Roxas, *The World of Felix Roxas; Anecdotes and Reminiscences of a Manila Newspaper Columnist, 1926–36*, trans. Angel Estrada and Vicente del Carmen (Manila: Filipiniana Book Guild, 1970), 131.

[69]A complete list of T. H. Pardo de Tavera's publications is provided in Manuel, *Dictionary of Philippine Biography*, 1:342–47.

[70]Guadalupe Forès-Ganzon, trans., *La Solidaridad*, rpt. (Quezon City: University of the Philippines Press, 1967), 695.

[71]Doña Concha's mother was a cousin of the Filipino lawyer Felipe Gonzalez Calderon who drafted the Constitution of the first Philippine Republic (Pardo de Tavera, *Arbol Genealogico*).

[72]T. H. Pardo de Tavera describes the background of the visit in the *Arbol Genealogico*.

[73]The painting, entitled *La Pacto de Sangre*, depicts the Rajah Sikatuna of Bohol and Legaspi in the traditional ceremony of the blood compact. Filipino nationalist Jose Rizal sat for the figure of Sikatuna. See Carlos E. Da Silva, *Juan Luna y Novicio* (Manila: National Historical Institute, 1977), 52.

[74]Pardo de Tavera, *Arbol Genealogico*.

[75]John N. Schumacher, in his *Propaganda Movement, 1880–1895* (Manila: Solidaridad, 1973), describes the young Filipinos as highly educated, noting that since "the cost of travel and expenses of studying abroad were considerable these early students came generally from well-to-do families and were . . . mostly creoles and mestizos" (pp. 17–18).

[76]Schumacher's *Propaganda Movement* is an excellent study of the politics of and interactions among the Filipinos in Europe.

[77]For the writings of the Filipinos who came to be known as the *propagandistas*, see Forès-Ganzon, *La Solidaridad*.

[78]See Teodoro Agoncillo, *Malolos: The Crisis of the Republic* (Quezon City: University of the Philippines, 1960).

[79]Jose Rizal to his parents, from Paris, 1 January 1886, in *Letters Between Rizal and Family Members*, vol. 2(Manila: National Heroes Commission, 1964), 204.

[80]The description is from ibid.

[81]Ibid.

[82]T. H. published the *Catalogo Memoria de la Exposicion de Productos de las Islas Filipinas* (Manila: T. H. Pardo de Tavera) in 1889.

[83]Forès-Ganzon, *La Solidaridad*, 483, 485.

[84]The passage continues, "the young Filipino D. Felix Pardo de Tavera presents a sculpture, a life-sized figure representing a Parisienne in Japanese dress. To all of us who have had the pleasure of admiring such a handsome work of art, the statue has seemed without an imperfection, of admirable reality, of an exquisite taste revealing in the author a sculptural talent bordering on genius." See "Letter from Paris, 28 March 1889," in ibid., 127–28.

[85]Telegram, Police Commissioner Muette to Procurator and Prefect of Police, 9 October 1892, Police Archives, Paris.

[86]Paris Court of Appeals, Case Number 1750, 16 December 1892, "Arrest: Luna de San Pedro, Assize Court de la Seine," Police Archives, Paris. The full indictment includes the following counts.

I. of having, on 22 September 1892 in Paris, tried to commit voluntary homicide on the person of Felix Pardo de Tavera, an attempt [which was not carried out due to] circumstances independent of the intention of the accused. With these circumstances the said attempt was committed: 1. with premeditation; 2. that it was followed by the crime of murder, committed on the woman Juliana Gorricho, widow Pardo de Tavera, as specified below.

II. committed voluntary homicide on the person of Juliana Gorricho, widow Pardo de Tavera, with these circumstances: 1. that the said voluntary homicide was committed with premeditation; 2. that it preceded, accompanied and followed the crime of murder, committed on the person of Maria de la Paz Pardo de Tavera, wife of Luna de San Pedro as identified above; 3. that it followed the attempt to commit the crime of murder on the person of Felix Pardo de Tavera.

III. of having committed voluntary homicide on the person of Maria de la Paz Pardo de Tavera, wife of Luna de San Pedro. With these circumstances: 1. with premeditation; 2. that it followed the crime of attempted murder as aforementioned, committed on the person of Felix Pardo de Tavera; 3. that it followed the crime of murder as aforementioned, committed on the person of Juliana Gorricho, widow Pardo de Tavera.

[87]Ibid.

[88]Quotations are from ibid.

[89]"The Affair of Villa Dupont, Mr. Trinidad Pardo, His Account of the Murder," *Echo de Paris*, 26 September 1892, copy in clipping file, Police Archives, Paris.

[90]Pardo de Tavera, *Arbol Genealogico*.

[91]"Affair of Villa Dupont."

[92]In Antonio Maria Regidor's testimony, he claims that at no time did Paz Luna "ever admit to her brothers that she became the mistress of M. Dussaq" ("Testimony of Antonio Regidor," in *The Drama of Pergolese Street, the Victims, the Account of a Witness [Don Antonio Maria Regidor y Jurado]*, transcript in clipping file, Police Archives, Paris).

[93]"Affair of Villa Dupont."

[94]Ibid.

[95]Ibid.

[96]Ibid.

[97]See *Proceso seguido contra el parricida Juan Luna San Pedro y Novicio, Discurso por Maitre Felix Decori, Abogado de la Corte de Apelacion de Paris* (Paris: Imp. Polyglotte Hugonis, 1893), especially pages 6–8.

[98]"Testimony of Antonio Regidor." Although Don Antonio was an old friend and counselor to the Pardo de Taveras, he also was well acquainted with Juan Luna. As a Filipino-Spanish lawyer practicing in London, his clientele were for the most part Filipino expatriates whose interests required an expert in Spanish law. Through these activities, as well as his connections to the exile community in Europe, he came to know all the *propagandistas* well. See also *Proceso seguido contra el parricida Juan Luna*, 15.

[99]Recounted by Doña Concha in ibid.

[100]"Testimony of Antonio Regidor."

[101]Pardo de Tavera, *Arbol Genealogico.*

[102]All quotations are from "Affair of Villa Dupont."

[103]"Testimony of Antonio Regidor."

[104]See, for example, excerpts from Luna's letters to his wife, reproduced in *Proceso seguido contra el parricida Juan Luna*, 18. Written the day before her death, on 21 September 1892, Doña Juliana's last letter to T. H. describes her fear of Luna and her worries over her daughter's safety (ibid., 23–25).

[105]Doña Juliana refers to this in ibid.

[106]Ibid.

[107]"Affair of Villa Dupont."

[108]"Testimony of Antonio Regidor."

[109]"Affair of Villa Dupont."

[110]Ibid.

[111]Ibid.

[112]Ibid.

[113]Case Number 1750, 8 February 1893, "Ordinance Which Acquits Luna de San Pedro," Assize Court de la Seine, copy filed in Police Archives, Paris.

[114]Ibid.

[115]"Affair of Villa Dupont."

[116]Da Silva, *Juan Luna,* 16–21.

[117]Ibid., 16.

[118]Ibid., 18.

[119]All quotations are from ibid.

[120]E. Arsenio Manuel, "Luna y Novicio, Juan," *Dictionary of Philippine Biography* (Quezon City: Filipiniana Publications, 1970), 2:240–66.

[121]Hilarion M. Henares, Jr., "Make My Day!" *Philippine Daily Inquirer,* 1 July 1989. A copy the clipping was provided by Cecilia Hofmann, a niece of Paz Lopez Manzano Pardo de Tavera. The latter was the mother of Mita Pardo de Tavera.

[122]Rupert Emerson, "Paradoxes of Asian Nationalism," in *Man, State and Society in Contemporary Southeast Asia,* edited by Robert O. Tilman (New York: Praeger, 1969).

[123]Ibid., 248.

[124]The titles of a collection of articles on the Luna murders published in *La Ilustracción Filipino* (7 November 1892) were "Luna al borde de la gloria y del abismo," "La tragedia de Luna," and "La desgracía del pintor Luna."

[125]T. H. writes, "Su procedencia de sangre de la nobleza española le habrio las puertas de la mas alta sociedad de Paris" (*Arbol Genealogico*).

[126]"Affair of Villa Dupont."

[127]See "Testimony of Antonio Regidor."

[128]Manuel's biography of Juan Luna includes a list of the missing paintings. See E. Arsenio Manuel, *Dictionary of Philippine Biography* (Quezon City: Filipiniana Publications, 1970), 2:63–4.

[129]Mita Pardo de Tavera, interview, Manila, June 1991.

[130]*Fincas Urbanas,* 1896, Philippine National Archives, Manila. The following houses were owned by the Pardo de Tavera-Gorricho family.

Address	Value (in pesos)	Owner
Pasaje de la Paz		
No. 11	38,200	Juliana
17	22,500	Juliana

Address	Value (in pesos)	Owner
Pasaje de la Paz		
No. 23	18,000	Juliana
25	30,000	Gertrudes
unknown	55,700	Juliana
unknown	13,200	Juliana
Calle Victoria, Intramuros:		
No. 4	6,000	Juliana

[131] *Las Costumbres de los Tagalogs, Segun el Padre Plasencia* (Manila: T. H. Pardo de Tavera, 1892) was meant to be a sequel to the annotated edition, by Jose Rizal, of Fray Antonio de Morga's *Sucesos de las Islas Filipinas* (Manila: National Historical Institute, 1890 [1991]). T. H.'s second work was entitled *El Mapa de Filipinas del P. Murillo Velarde* (Manila: T. H. Pardo de Tavera, 1894). A catalog of T. H.'s published work is provided in Manuel, *Dictionary of Philippine Biography*, 1:342-47.

[132] His study of Malay philology became the basis for the nationalist reform in Tagalog, in particular the change in the use of *c* with *k*. In 1887, he published *Sanscrito en la Lengua Tagalog* (Paris: Imp. de la Faculte de Medicine, A. Davy), followed by *Consideraciones Sobre el Origen del Nombre de los Números en Tagalog* (Manila: Tip. de Chofré y C.ª, 1889), which traced the origins of Tagalog numerical terms to three sources: Polynesian, or oceanic; indigenous, or native; and Arabic, or Hebrew and Sanskrit.

[133] *Noticias Sobre la Imprenta y el Grabado en Filipinas* (Madrid: Tip. de los Hijos de M. G. Hernandez, 1893).

[134] The health manual, *Arte de Cuidar Enfermos* (Manila: Tipo.-lithografia de Chofré y Comp., 1895), was translated into Tagalog by Inigo Regalado y Corcuera and published as *Paraan sa Pag-aalaga sa Maysaquit* (Manila: Imprenta de J. Atayde y Comp., 1895). It was intended to provide Filipinos with basic knowledge about primary health care (Manuel, *Dictionary of Philippine Biography*, 1:323).

[135] The organization's full name was Ang Kataastaasan, Kagalanggalang na Katipunan ng mga Anak ng Bayan, meaning "The Highest and Most Venerable Society of the Sons of the People."

[136] Masonry was not revolutionary, although it was clandestine. The *ilustrados* were attracted to membership because of the Masonic ideals of solidarity, education, and organization. John Schumacher analyzes the Filipino intellectuals' involvement in Masonry in his *Propaganda Movement*, 155–59.

[137] Instances of torture are described by Teodoro Kalaw in *Philippine Masonry*, trans. Frederic H. Stevens and Antonio Amechazurra (Manila: McCullough, 1956), 129.

[138] T. H.'s political writings show a strong affinity with Kantian political and moral philosophy (Lauran Schultz, University of Wisconsin–Madison, personal communication, 1992).

[139] Evaristo Aguirre to Jose Rizal, 10 March 1887, reproduced in Jose Rizal, *Rizal's Correspondence with Fellow Reformists* (Manila: National Heroes Commission, 1963), 88.

[140] *El Diario de Manila*, 22 April 1897 (clipping supplied by Mita Pardo de Tavera).

[141] In 1898, when Juan Luna was named to the commission seeking recognition for the revolutionary government, he supposedly said that he preferred to fight alongside his brother who by that time was a general under the command of Emilio Aguinaldo (see Da Silva, *Juan Luna*). On the "Club Kidlat," see Guadalupe Forès-Ganzon, *La Solidaridad* (Quezon City: University of the Philippines Press, 1967).

[142] John Taylor, *The Philippine Insurrection Against the United States: A Compilation of Documents with Notes and Introduction* (Pasay City: Eugenio Lopez Foundation, 1971), exhibit 12, 1:237.

143Ibid., 1:238.

144Mita Pardo de Tavera, interview, June 1991.

145Rizal gave T. H. a copy of his annotation of Morga's *Sucesos de las Islas Filipinas* with the following inscription: "A mi querido amigo y paisano, el filipinista Dr. T. H. Pardo de Tavera" [To my dear friend and countryman, the Philippinist Dr. T. H. Pardo de Tavera]. This book is in the private collection of Mita Pardo de Tavera, Manila. During his early, two-year visit to Manila, T. H. had attempted to defend Rizal's first novel, *Noli me tangere*, to the Jesuits by suggesting that Rizal tried to strike the friars with his stone but had hit religion instead. When Rizal's second novel, *El Filibusterismo*, appeared, T. H. wrote to his friend:

> Yesterday I received your book, today I have just devoured it. . . . I am already asking you when the third part is coming out. Please accept my congratulations, my sincere and moving felicitations, and as God has given you talent and energy for it, continue on the path that he has traced for you.

See Schumacher, *Propaganda Movement*, 152n. The quote is from T. H. Pardo de Tavera to Jose Rizal, 23 September 1891, reproduced in Rizal, *Rizal's Correspondence*, 601.

146T. H. referred to it as the "stillborn assembly" in a letter to Fr. Evaristo Arias dated 5 September 1898 (private collection of Mita Pardo de Tavera, Manila).

147The list of their names is found in Teodore M. Kalaw, *The Philippine Revolution*, rpt of 1924 ed. (Kawilihan: Jorge Vargas Filipiniana Foundation, 1969).

148In June 1899, T. H. formed the Society of Physicians and Pharmacists. In July, when the rector of the Universidad de Santo Tomas appealed for the reopening of San Jose, Otis issued an order "at the instance of the president and directors of the Philippine Medical Association" that forbade it. The president of the association was T. H. Pardo de Tavera. See *Lands Held for Ecclesiastical or Religious Uses in the Philippine Islands, etc.: Message from the President of the United States*, U.S. Congress, Senate, 56th Cong., 2d Sess., Sen. Doc. 190 (Washington, D.C.: Government Printing Office, 1901), 27.

149A chronology of Juan Luna's travels is given in Da Silva, *Juan Luna*, 21–33. The passage describing Luna's opinion on a U.S. protectorate occurs on page 25.

150Manuel, *Dictionary of Philippine Biography*, 1:326.

151See the chapter "Creation of a Colonial Policy," in Ruby R. Paredes, "The Partido Federal, 1900–1907: Political Collaboration in Colonial Manila" (Ph.D. diss., University of Michigan, 1989), 168–201.

152Jacob Gould Schurman, *Philippine Affairs: A Retrospect and Outlook* (New York: Charles Scribner's Sons, 1902), 49.

153U.S. Congress, *Report of the Philippine Commission to the President* (Washington, D.C.: Government Printing Office, 1900), 1:5.

154Jacob Gould Schurman was formerly the president of Cornell University; commission member Dean C. Worcester was a professor at the University of Michigan.

155See U.S. Congress, House, *Report of the Military Governor of the Philippine Islands on Civil Affairs*, 56th Cong., 2d Sess., House Doc. 2 (Washington, D.C.: Government Printing Office, 1900), 154–61.

156Dean C. Worcester, Letter, 23 April 1899, in Documents and Papers, Vol. 16, Worcester Papers, University of Michigan Libraries.

157See Glenn May, *Social Engineering in the Philippines: The Aims, Execution, and Impact of American Colonial Policy, 1900–1913* (Westport, Conn.:Greenwood Press, 1980).

158Quoted in Kalaw, *The Philippine Revolution,*, 294. T. H. was appointed to the committees for public instruction, health, municipal and provincial governments, non-Christian Filipinos, and appropriations.

159Michael Cullinane's article presents a paradigm of patronage and clientelism in colonialist politics. See "Playing the Game: The Rise of Sergio Osmeña, 1898–1907," in

Philippine Colonial Democracy, edited by Ruby R. Paredes (Quezon City: Ateneo de Manila University Press, 1989), 70–113.

[160]James LeRoy to William Howard Taft, 6 February 1906, William Howard Taft Papers, Library of Congress, Washington, D.C.

[161]All quotations are from Manuel, *Dictionary of Philippine Biography*, 1:341–42.

[162]Katherine Mayo, an American writer who studied the Philippines in the 1920s, characterized T. H. as "a man who is not afraid to be quoted." See Katherine Mayo, *Isles of Fear: The Truth About the Philippines* (New York: Harcourt, Brace, 1925).

[163]Manuel, *Dictionary of Philippine Biography*, 1:342.

[164]William Howard Taft to T. H. Pardo de Tavera, 24 March 1902, William Howard Taft Papers, Library of Congress, Washington, D.C.

[165]Mita Pardo de Tavera, interview, June 1991.

[166]Pardo de Tavera, *Arbol Genealogico*.

[167]The *rigodon de honor*, adapted from the Spanish-French *rigadoon*, is a stately dance-procession in which participants display great dignity of carriage and motion. It is usually performed at Philippine formal gatherings not as entertainment but as a presentation of dignitaries.

[168]Peter Stanley, *A Nation in the Making: The Philippines and the United States, 1899–1921* (Cambridge: Harvard University Press, 1974), 133.

[169]Mita's recollections, no doubt reinforced by those of her mother, are of a strict regimen of study and an orderly life (Mita Pardo de Tavera, interview, June 1991).

[170]T. H. Pardo de Tavera to M. L. Quezon, 26 March 1914, Series VI, Box 27, File: Pardo de Tavera, T. H., 1914–1920, Manuel L. Quezon Papers, Philippine National Library.

[171]T. H. Pardo de Tavera to Manuel L. Quezon, 21 September 1914, Series VI, Box 27, File: Pardo de Tavera, T. H., 1914–1920, Manuel L. Quezon Papers, Philippine National Library.

[172]Ibid.

[173]Mita Pardo de Tavera, interview, June 1991.

[174]The family is related to the husband of Vicky Quirino, whose father, Elpidio Quirino, was the second president of the Republic of the Philippines.

[175]Mita Pardo de Tavera, interview, June 1991.

[176]According to Mita, "My grandfather loved my mother very much. That's why many of these things that I know, I know because my mother would take the pains to write them down. My grandfather would tell her things and she would write them down, as much as she remembered. So these recollections were handed down through a daughter-in-law" (ibid.).

[177]Ibid.

[178]The incident is described in T. H. Pardo de Tavera to Manuel Quezon, 14 February 1920, Series VI, Box 27, File: Pardo de Tavera, T. H., 1914–1920, Manuel L. Quezon Papers, Philippine National Library.

[179]Quoted in Finis C. Opus, "Notables Casos de Suicidio en Manila," *National Review* (Manila), 21 February 1936, 41.

[180]Sometime after T. H.'s death, and during her estrangement from Alfredo, Paz and Mita went to live in Paz's mother's household. After Alfredo's death this living arrangement continued, and Mita's formative years were spent in her grandmother Manzano's house. Paz took charge of rearing her daughter, although some of the responsibilities of care and chaperoning were shared with Paz's unmarried sister Matilda as Mita grew older .

[181]See No. 45218, May 25, 1939, "In the matter of the will of the deceased Concepcion Cembrano Viuda de Pardo de Tavera," *Report of Cases Determined in the Supreme Court of the Philippines from May 5, 1939 to October 18, 1939* (Rochester, N.Y.: Lawyers Co-operative Publishing), 68: 175–78.

[182]Mita Pardo de Tavera, interview, June 1991.

[183]Mita recalls that her mother suspected bribery and denounced the court's haste in finding for El Hogar Filipino. Moreover, Paz felt that the rest of the family should have been more actively opposed to Andres's risky venture.

[184]In 1982, the Philippine National Bank commemorated the site with a plaque and a ceremony identifying the location of their Escolta offices as the property on which T. H. had been born.

[185]As commissioner, T. H.'s mandatory statement of property acquisitions since the American takeover showed a hacienda in Floridablanca, Pampanga Province. He had developed an interest in agriculture, particularly wheat and fruit production, and wanted a farm on which he could experiment with modern techniques and new seed varieties. But as commissioner charged with provincial and educational matters, his time was heavily committed to his official duties and he was unable to pursue the project. Stranded in Spain during World War I, he revived his interest. In some of his correspondence with Manuel Quezon during this period, he requested up-to-date information on wheat and fruit cultivation.

[186]T. H. acknowledged Alfredo's help in expanding the library and collection of antiques, and he bequeathed half of it to him. After Alfredo's death, Bebeco refused to transfer his half to Mita as her father's heir (ibid.).

[187]Among Mita's schoolmates were the daughters of old, wealthy, or powerful families, including those of President Quezon, Senator Magalona, and Secretary of Health Fabella (ibid.).

[188]Mita promised herself that she would not transfer to another university if she failed to make the grade in the selective medical program at the University of the Philippines (ibid.).

[189]Ibid.

[190]Mita had inherited properties in Raon, in Quiapo, and in the Ermita district of Manila. Holdings on M. H. del Pilar, Padre Faura, and in Paco (Pennsylvania Street) were sold to finance her education (ibid.).

[191]The term was used in various accounts of the 1907 Nacionalista Party victory in the elections for the first Philippine Assembly in 1907. See Stanley, *A Nation in the Making*, 126–34.

[192]Campaigning for the presidency years later, Serging telephoned Mita from Balayan, Batangas, a place they had visited during their brief engagement, to tell her that he recalled that visit with nostalgia (Mita Pardo de Tavera, interview, June 1991).

[193]The lot was in Quezon City, in the area now bounded by Ateneo University de Manila's Loyola Heights campus and the Philippine Army's Camp Aguinaldo. Mita thinks the property had been a farm. During a trip with her father to inspect it, she recalled that the caretaker had pointed out a well into which a carabao had fallen (ibid.). Mita has preserved the house. In 1977, she dismantled it one more time and moved it to Dasmarinas Village. There the materials were used in the construction of her current residence on Paraiso Street. The original house in Intramuros was located just outside the Manila Cathedral. Mita said that her father recalled T. H.'s description of the incident in 1896 when T. H. and Alfredo stood at one of the windows as Jose Rizal was escorted past on the way to his execution. In a gesture of farewell, Rizal paused and waved to T. H. (ibid.).

[194]Ibid.

[195]Nonetheless, she was among the top ten students in her class when she graduated from the University of the Philippines' College of Medicine (ibid.).

[196]Ibid.

Rent-Seeking Families and the Philippine State: A History of the Lopez Family

Alfred W. McCoy

In June 1972, Eugenio Lopez, Sr., stood at the summit of Philippine public life. Starting as a provincial bus operator, he had risen in only sixteen years to become chairman of the country's largest media conglomerate and president of its leading utility, the Manila Electric Company.[1] His brother was finishing a third term as vice-president of the Philippines. His closest friends dominated the sugar industry, the country's leading export. His fortieth wedding anniversary had been a brilliant spectacle "where champagne flowed as freely as a fountain" and "he had royalty and crème de la crème of Asia, Europe and America flown in."[2] Using his formidable media assets, he had recently defeated the country's president, Ferdinand Marcos, in a bitter battle over the spoils of power. Appearing at the Harvard Business School that June to receive its Distinguished Service Award, Lopez heard one speaker hail him as a man whose "story brings a unique message of inspiration."[3]

Only three months later, President Marcos declared martial law and destroyed Eugenio Lopez. After imprisoning his eldest son on capital charges, Marcos forced Lopez to sign over his shares in the Manila Electric Company and to watch silently while a presidential crony plundered his media conglomerate. Forced into exile, stripped of his wealth, and tortured by the threat of his son's execution, Lopez died of cancer in 1975 in a San Francisco hospital—a death ignored by Filipinos who had once sipped his champagne and celebrated his achievements.[4]

More vividly than any other, the story of Eugenio Lopez illustrates the close connection between state power and private wealth in the Philippines. For over thirty years, Lopez had used presidential patronage to secure subsidized government financing and dominate state-regulated industries, thereby amassing the largest private fortune in the Philippines. After declaring martial law in 1972, Marcos used the same state power to demolish the Lopez conglomerates and transfer their assets to a new economic elite composed of his kin and courtiers. Despite their deep personal enmity, Lopez and Marcos were in some respects more similar than either might have imagined. Putting aside their rhetoric, both acted in the apparent belief that the state should reward a self-selecting, economic elite instead of using its resources to strengthen the public sector or uplift the country's poor. Both used their political influence to benefit private corporations controlled by their families. During the period of the Philippine Republic (1946–72), the two became master manipulators of the state, operators without peer within their respective realms. Although Marcos was a career politician and Lopez an entrepreneur, their common commingling of business and politics drew them into the political arena where they met face-to-face, first as allies and later as enemies.

The Philippine state's pairing of substantial resources with a politicized system for their allocation has encouraged careers like those of Lopez and Marcos. Under the doctrine of national development, the Philippine state has accumulated substantial financial resources and broad regulatory authority. But, instead of using these economic powers to promote development, as in South Korea or Singapore, the Philippine executive branch has expended these resources as "rents" to reward retainers. Although no single factor can account for such a cluster of problems, the role of rents explains a good deal about the weakness of the Philippine state and the corresponding strength of Filipino political families.

The theory of "rents" can help us explain some significant aspects of this complex relationship between Filipino elites and the Philippine state. As defined by James Buchanan, rents appear when the state uses regulation to restrict "freedom of entry" into the market. If these restrictions create a monopoly, the economic consequences are decidedly negative—slowing growth and enriching a few favored entrepreneurs. Competition for such monopolies, a political process called "rent seeking," can produce intense conflict. To illustrate this point, Buchanan offers a parable that seems surprisingly germane to both electoral politics under the Philippine Republic and to "crony capitalism" under President Marcos.[5]

> Suppose that a courtier persuades the queen to grant him a royal monopoly to sell playing cards throughout the kingdom. The courtier so favored will capture sizable monopoly profits or economic rents, and this will be observed by other persons who might like to enter the industry. But their entry is effectively prevented by enforcement of the royal monopoly privilege. What the queen gives, however, the queen may take away, and the potential entrants are not likely to sit quietly by and allow the favored one . . . to enjoy his differentially advantageous position. Instead of passive observation, potential entrants will engage actively in "rent seeking." They will invest effort, time, and other productive resources . . . to shift the queen's favor

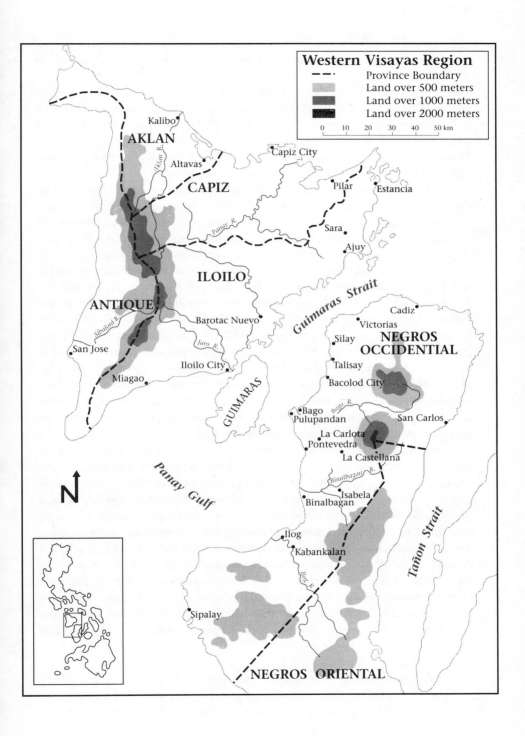

Western Visayas Region

- – · – Province Boundary
- Land over 500 meters
- Land over 1000 meters
- Land over 2000 meters

0 10 20 30 40 50 km

Kalibo

AKLAN

Capiz City

Altavas

CAPIZ

Pilar

Estancia

Aklan R.

Panay R.

Sara

Ajuy

ILOILO

Guimaras Strait

Cadiz

ANTIQUE

Barotac Nuevo

Victorias

Silay

NEGROS OCCIDENTAL

Sibalom R.

Jaro R.

Talisay

San Jose

Iloilo City

Bacolod City

Miagao

GUIMARAS

Bago

Pulupandan

Bago R.

San Carlos

La Carlota

Pontevedra

La Castellana

N

Binalbagan R.

Panay Gulf

Isabela

Binalbagan

Ilog

Kabankalan

Ilog R.

Tañon Strait

Sipalay

NEGROS ORIENTAL

toward their own cause. Promotion, advertisement, flattery, persuasion, cajolery—these and other attributes will characterize rent-seeking behavior.

In many Third World countries, as Anne Krueger has argued, rents are "pervasive facts of life." In India such restricted economic activity accounted for 7.3 percent of national income in 1964, while in Turkey rents from import licenses alone represented about 15 percent of the gross national product (GNP) in 1968. Given the importance of rents in both countries, the struggle for these restrictive licenses through rent-seeking activity is "highly competitive."[6]

Arguing, at least by implication, that these parasitic rents expand as the state increases its intervention in the economy, First World proponents of the concept have become acolytes for a neo-conservative idealization of the free market. "Scholars of development often vent their frustrations by identifying the culprits that keep their theories from working," notes Peter Evans in his critique of the literature on rents. "Recently . . . the state bureaucrat, strangling the golden goose of entrepreneurship and lining his pockets with unproductive rents, has again become the central villain."[7] Rejecting the idea that states are "standardized commodities," Evans posits a wide spectrum of public-sector performance ranging from a "predatory" state such as Zaire to "developmental states" such as Japan. Both have wielded a heavy interventionist hand in their economies but there have been some obvious and dramatic differences in the outcomes—misery in Zaire and prosperity in Japan. Seeking the reasons for these differences, Evans argues that a developmental state depends upon a meritocratic bureaucracy with both autonomy of action and a strong corporate identity. Above all, Evans argues that we must examine specific cases before we generalize about the relationship between the state and rents.[8]

Recent Philippine writing can serve as a useful corrective to these apparent biases. Surveying the economic wreckage of the Marcos era, Filipino political economists have applied this theory to explain how the Palace's rent-seeking courtiers used state power to plunder the country. Although sharply critical of a particularly venal regime, these economists still manage to avoid wholesale condemnation of the state, thereby jettisoning the antiregulatory, antistate biases that inform much of the original theory. Despite this creative adaptation of the concept, most of the Filipino work lacks detailed empirical evidence and thus suffers from an apparent superficiality. For example, in his seminal study of the role of businessmen in state economic planning, Manuel Montes, an economist at the University of the Philippines, argues that "the economic structure of the country . . . stimulates, encourages, and provides the greatest rewards to 'rent-seeking' activities."[9]

> In a "profit-seeking" economic structure, assets and income are won and lost on the basis of the ability of the business owner to develop the property. . . .
> In a "rent-seeking" society, ownership of property alone guarantees the access to wealth. . . .

In the case of the Philippines, we can generalize "property" to include protection from competition through quotas, tariffs, and measured capacities, subsidized credit, access to foreign reparations, loans, and grants.

In a profit-seeking society, the existence of a state that protects property is a necessary but not sufficient condition for maintaining such property. In contrast, in a rent-seeking society, the operations of the state determine the assignment of and the continued enjoyment of economic advantages. . . .

With this distinction in mind, there is a need to reinterpret accounting profits of Philippine enterprises and distinguish between that portion that arises out of the internal efficiencies and investments of the firm ("profits") and that portion that is due to its success in obtaining and retaining some economic advantage by the state. . . .

The rent-seeking economic structure is consistent either with an authoritarian political system or a democratic one, as long as a system of patronage determines political and economic relationships.

As evidence for this provocative reconceptualization of rent seeking, Montes offers his readers a superficial catalogue of businessmen who have served regimes from Quezon through Marcos. "In the presidency of Manuel Roxas," says Montes in a typical passage, "Soriano, Eugenio Lopez . . . and Jose Yulo were influential businessmen."[10] Foreign academics reading these long lists of names, broken by brief, inconclusive biographies, probably would regard such a chronicle as insufficient evidence for his broad, bold theory. For an informed Filipino audience, however, each family name—Soriano, Yulo, Lopez—is encoded with layers of meaning, and their mere recitation evokes a convincing resonance of shared knowledge. This style of argumentation testifies to the power of the family paradigm within the Philippines but it also presents problems for those of us who would like to translate indigenous knowledge into academic analysis.

In the Philippine setting, the study of a single rent-seeking family may be the most appropriate way of bridging this gap between western economic theory and the Filipino familial paradigm. Indeed, by adding elements of depth and detail missing from the current literature, such a study can contribute to the validation of both perspectives.

Among the leading Filipino families, the Lopezes are, by virtue of their history, well suited for such a case study. Seeking knowledge of the family's origins and early character, this essay begins in the late nineteenth century when the Lopezes enter the historical record as substantial sugar planters on the plantation frontier of Negros Island. While the second generation consolidated property and position within a regional planter elite, their children made a successful transition to sugar milling during the 1920s, thereby creating the capital that Eugenio Lopez would later employ in his climb to the apex of national power. The essay then becomes a biography of the family's greatest individual success, the financier Eugenio Lopez, Sr. Spanning a half century, Eugenio's career as a rent-seeking entrepreneur began in the 1920s when the infant Philippine state was still taking form and ended in 1972 when Marcos destroyed the Republic with his declaration of martial law. Following the patterns of Eugenio's progress, the essay surveys his relations with a succession of Philippine presidents—from his patron Quezon to his nemesis Marcos. Finally, in a coda on the restoration of the family's fortunes under President Aquino, it is argued that Eugenio succeeded in handing down enough of his capital and skills to perpetuate his family's position within the national economic elite.

The Philippine State

The strength of leading Filipino political families, as noted in the introduction to this volume, springs from the emergence of the Philippine Republic as a weak postcolonial state.[11] During its forty years of rule, the American colonial regime practiced a contradictory policy of developing a centralized administration of civil servants in Manila and promoting the autonomy of elected politicians in the provinces. To maintain the fiscal integrity of the bureaucracy, the colonial executive created the post of insular auditor, using it to punish corruption and thereby restrain what we now call "rent seeking" by rising elites. Although these controls weakened after 1935 with the establishment of an autonomous Commonwealth, the residual American role in approving legislation and supervising the budget still served as a brake on wholesale corruption.

After independence in 1946, the Philippines finally faced the problem of indigenizing a modern bureaucratic apparatus and integrating it with electoral politics based upon familial factions. In Weberian terms, the "rational bureaucratic," colonial state had given way to its opposite, the Philippine Republic's "neo-patrimonialism" with all the particularism, privilege, and corruption the term implies.[12] During the Republic's first decade, there were two main forms of interaction between state and political elites: while Manila's rival families maneuvered to manipulate the state's licensing powers to their advantage, provincial warlords challenged the Philippine Constabulary for control of the countryside.

Under the Republic, successive presidents used the state's licensing powers to win votes from Manila politicians and provincial warlords, thereby creating benefices that favored the dominant political families. Elite politics did not involve issues of production per se but revolved around a struggle among wealthy families over rents created by the manipulation of economic regulations. As Manuel Montes noted in his discussion of the postwar economy: "What has turned out to be important in accumulating wealth is not talent for efficient operation . . . but one's closeness to political rulers."[13] Whether they dealt in air travel, bus transport, radio, television, mining, logging, exporting, or importing, the profit structure of most major Philippine corporations depended upon the state for "protection from competition."[14]

In focusing upon the role of the state in economic development, it is important to distinguish between the Philippines and the dynamic economies of eastern Asia. Not every alliance between the state and entrepreneurial elites fosters rents that retard real economic growth. In South Korea or Singapore, where the state remains strong, bureaucracy can operate autonomously to direct, regulate, and finance growth without necessarily restricting access to the market. Moreover, in such societies state and private interests share a commitment to the promotion of national development that allows both to play by the unwritten rules of the game.

In the Philippines the alliance between the state and elite political families seems to lack such balance. Although the Philippine state has extensive financial resources and strong regulatory powers, the bureaucracy has rarely been able to exercise its authority in an impartial way. Over the past half century, a succession of Philippine presidents has played partisan politics with the state's economic powers, awarding loans and creating rents to reward the political brokers who assured their election. Since government expenditures accounted for 15 percent of the GNP in the 1970s and 1980s, the executive clearly had access to substantial resources.[15] Underlying the executive's partisan use of state power are political elites who fuse public office with private business. Campaigns for provincial or national office require heavy investments, which have, of course, a guaranteed failure rate of 50 percent. For the elites to justify the high risk of such investments, public office must promise extraordinary rewards. More than any other entrepreneur of the Republican era, Eugenio Lopez, Sr., mastered the logic of political investment, risking great capital in presidential elections and reaping even greater rewards.

The spectacular postwar climb of the Lopez brothers was based in large part, then, on their masterful manipulation of the state's regulatory and financial powers. Among the Republic's national entrepreneurs, they were the most successful rent seekers, prospering largely because they were skilled in extracting special privileges from a "state apparatus . . . choked continually by an anarchy of particularistic demands."[16] Indeed, at every step, from the founding of their provincial bus company during the 1930s to the formation of corporate conglomerates in the 1960s, the rise of Eugenio and Fernando Lopez relied in some way upon state licenses that restricted access to the market. Since all of their major corporations were in some sense rents, their commercial success involved a commingling of business and politics.

Unlike most postwar Filipino politicians, the Lopezes made little use of violence. Although the brothers maintained a strong political base in their home province, they did not form a private army nor did they forge close alliances with local warlords—making them in effect a purely rent-seeking family whose power rested largely upon their relations with the state and its executive. When they launched their careers as provincial politicians during the late 1920s, they, like others of this stratum, did use violence to advance their interests. But, like most oligarchic families, once they moved to Manila after World War II they traded in influence and avoided violence. No longer rooted in the land or dependent upon the social power of the provinces, the Lopezes came to depend upon the state, through the medium of the presidency, for the financial and regulatory concessions that would assure the prosperity of their corporations.

After declaring martial law in 1972, President Marcos used the same licensing powers that had built the Lopez wealth to destroy the family's fortune and foster a new oligarchy composed of his own kin and courtiers. Rather than breaking this system of rent seeking, Marcos's martial-law regime represented its apogee. His major achievement, and ultimate failure, lay in his attempt to restructure the national elite, replacing established families with a coterie of his own. In Weberian terms, he transformed the state from one of neo- or decentralized patrimonialism, that is, one with elites strong enough to reduce the ruler's authority, to one with power so centralized that it could be said to approach "sultanism." Although two protracted insurgencies and the existence of rival factions within and without the regime provided some restraint, at his peak in the late 1970s Marcos enjoyed exceptional authority for a ruler of a complex, modern society.

While foreign observers analyzed Marcos's regime in terms of issues and institutions (land reform or insurgency, for example), ordinary Filipinos more often focused on the familial resonance underlying a protracted power struggle among elite factions. In declaring martial law, Marcos posed as an institutional reformer battling the vested interests of the old oligarchy. But his attack on privilege, as many Filipinos observed, sprang from a bitter personal and political dispute with his former patron, Eugenio Lopez. Similarly, Marcos portrayed his dictatorship as a "revolution from above" but his regime soon lost its populist thrust and became a coalition of rising families expropriating the wealth of established elites. In the words of political scientist Paul Hutchcroft: "Marcos was merely expanding on earlier patterns of patrimonial plunder."[17] Using the state and its army, he became the first president since Manuel Quezon in the 1930s to reduce the autonomy of provincial elites. With considerable dexterity, he then employed economic regulations, backed by the threat of armed force, to pursue the main aim of his rule: changing the composition of the country's economic elite.

Marcos's demolition of the old oligarchs was a skillful exercise in the use of state power. After disarming the provincial warlords and stripping opposing oligarchs of their wealth, he transferred their assets to his relations and retainers. Since the old oligarchs had won much of their wealth through successful rent seeking under the Republic, their corporate holdings were vulnerable to an unfavorable regulatory climate and quickly collapsed. Faced with such fragile opposition in the corporate board rooms, Marcos was able to manipulate the national economy with relative ease. Before martial law, the authority of the central state had been limited by the autonomy of regional warlords and the influence of Manila's political families. Under the Marcos dictatorship, the balance of power shifted sharply towards the center as the Palace manipulated financial regulations to reallocate the rents accruing from major industries—a process epitomized in his destruction of the Lopez family and his expropriation of their assets. Marcos apparently intended this transfer of wealth to facilitate a restructuring of provincial politics. Enriched by monopolies in such key sectors of the economy as coconuts and sugar, his cronies assumed political control over their home regions when elections resumed in 1978. Backed by presidential authority, they became provincial plenipotentiaries who dictated the legislative, provincial, judicial, and military appointments in their respective regions.

Thus, by the late 1970s, a new system of national power was emerging in the Philippines. Instead of breaking the entrenched provincial elites and ruling through the central bureaucracy, Marcos tried to control them by creating a new stratum of supralocal leaders whom he financed with rents. In Negros Occidental, for example, the three politically dominant families of the north, center, and south survived the declaration of martial law. But now they reported to the ruling party's regional chief for the Western Visayas, Marcos's de facto sugar czar Roberto S. Benedicto.

Indicative of the impact of Marcos's reforms, a 1980 study of 453 corporations by Fr. J. F. Doherty found that his regime had encouraged an enormous concentration of wealth. Since more than 98 percent of all sectors had "four or fewer companies controlling 35 percent of sales," profits were excessive. For example, under two leading cronies, Juan Ponce Enrile and Eduardo Cojuangco, the coconut industry was maintaining a remarkable profit ratio of 111 percent. Significantly, the eighty-one individuals who owned the corporations studied by Doherty came from only three groups: once-obscure businessmen close to the first family who "had expanded their corporate empires at a fantastic rate"; a pre–martial law elite closely allied to the regime; and another pre–martial law elite that survived but had to "endure periodic harassments."[18]

As the Marcos dictatorship demonstrated with such destructive force, much of modern Philippine politics involves competition for rents among kin-based coalitions. A prime example of the rent-seeking family, the Lopezes relied on kinship to organize their internal finances and then used this support to compete in the political arena for economic advantage.[19] If Eugenio Lopez, the most successful entrepreneur of the Republican era, had any spark of genius, it lay in his capacity to divine the character of the Philippine state and to exploit its weaknesses. It is, then, Eugenio's mastery of the craft of rent seeking that distinguishes him from hundreds of other Lopezes and makes him a significant subject of study.

The Lopez Family Character

Unique among the Philippine political elite, the Lopez family has compiled an elaborate history and genealogy, now in four volumes, with sufficient documentation to allow close study of its history. Unlike their Central Luzon counterparts, who left few paper footprints during their shift from province to nearby metropolis, the Lopezes trace their origins to the more distant Western Visayas and they have thus made a more distinct and better documented move to Manila.

Emerging as sugar planters on the Negros frontier in the 1870s, the Lopezes were leaders of a regional industry that quickly became integrated into the national economy. Thus, the growth of their political and commercial influence paralleled the emergence of a national political elite. Indeed, their family history converges at almost every significant point with the major political changes of the past century. As with other Negros families, there were several distinctive phases in their rise to prominence. They first appeared as local merchants and *barangay* leaders in Iloilo Province during the 1850s, and then became pioneer planters in Negros from the 1870s to the 1890s. They diversified into sugar milling and commerce during the 1920s and 1930s, and shifted their capital, contacts, and residence to Manila after independence in 1946. As the state's role in the economy, particularly the sugar industry, expanded after the 1920s, rent seeking became an increasingly important source of family wealth.

Over the past century the Lopez family has exhibited distinctive characteristics in its business and political dealings, something akin to a recurring family "world view."[20] In five generations it has produced a number of dynamic entrepreneurs, men and women capable of expanding their family's capital through new investments. Two of these must rank among the most successful entrepreneurs the Philippines has produced—the colonial sugar baron Eugenio Jalandoni Lopez (1839–1906) and his grandson, Republican financier Eugenio Hofileña Lopez, Sr. (1901–75). Over time the Lopezes have demonstrated an almost intuitive understanding of capital and a seemingly innate capacity to make it grow. While the Cojuangcos have a history of skillful female entrepreneurs, and the Laurels of successful male politicians, the Lopezes have both. The Lopezes did not waste their women. Indeed, several Lopez women have proved formidable in business, and, despite marriage, they have retained exclusive control over their assets. A number of Lopez men have been successful politicians. In a society with bilateral inheritance, the family has preserved its position by profiting from the endeavors of both male and female entrepreneurs.

Although there have been intrafamily battles over business, the Lopezes generally have managed to maintain solidarity. Indeed, many ventures have been financed with capital borrowed from first-degree relatives. Preferring closed, joint-stock ventures, they have avoided publicly listed corporations. At several critical points in their history, the Lopezes also have formed important, kin-based, political alliances. For nearly forty years after they launched their careers in the 1920s, for example, Eugenio and Fernando Lopez cooperated closely in business and politics with two of their distant relatives, Oscar Ledesma and Alfredo Montelibano, Sr.

The leading Lopezes have shown skill in their dealings with both foreign financiers and the emerging nation-state. Although they have borrowed capital, technology, and personnel from abroad, they have never engaged in the joint ventures or excessive indebtedness that would threaten their control. Well aware of the strength of the state, both colonial and national, the Lopezes, like the Navarros of Mexico, have proved pragmatic in their cultivation of the powerful.[21] Although nationalistic in the late nineteenth century, they never openly challenged Spanish rule. After the United States occupied the islands in 1898, they worked effectively within the colonial system and then cooperated with the Japanese during World War II. After the war, the most dynamic Lopez line reacted to the rise of the independent nation-state by combining business and politics to build one of the Philippines' largest private fortunes.

Among the family's five generations and more than twenty-six hundred descendants, it was the brothers, Eugenio and Fernando, who initially rose beyond the family's position within an entrenched regional elite to the first rank of national prominence. When they began their political careers in Iloilo City, they were neophyte politicians who used a mix of local violence and national patronage to advance their business interests. During this period, however, through their political alliance with Commonwealth president Manuel Quezon, they discovered the state's power to bestow preferential access to restricted markets upon its followers. When they moved to Manila after the war, the brothers joined the upper echelon of the country's economic elite—in effect, entering a world of business and political contacts and leaving behind the violence of provincial warlords such as Ramon Durano or Justiniano Montano. By abandoning the territorial base that only violence could secure, the Lopezes became a strictly rent-seeking elite. Their dramatic rise to the apex of economic power in just sixteen years, and the destruction of their corporate empire in only two, provides clear evidence of the rent-seeking character of Philippine politics.

In surveying the fifty-year career of the Lopez brothers, it is important to give equal weight to their prewar provincial origins and their postwar role as national leaders. If we were to focus exclusively on their postwar careers in Manila, we would ignore the lessons that they offer us about the dynamics of political violence in the provinces. The spatial dimension of provincial politics appears to encourage the use of force. In the monocrop sugar economy of Negros, transport presented the sole opportunity for entrepreneurs of the Lopezes' middling scale, and the struggle for territorial control—over bus routes, waterfronts and waiting areas—made violence a useful, even necessary, instrument of commercial competition. Once in Manila, however, they operated in an open universe of political connections and financial paper, an arena lacking the spatial constraints that made violence rational in the provinces. Like the rest of Manila's cultured and cosmopolitan elites, the Lopezes came to disdain rural gun play as something of a social atavism.

Within the familial politics that underlay the martial-law era, it was Marcos's continuing use of violence, more than any other factor, that distinguished him from Eugenio Lopez. Both began their careers as provincial politicians who engaged in violence but Marcos introduced it, albeit refined and strengthened by state power, into national politics. Through violence, legal and extralegal, Marcos gained a significant advantage over the Lopezes, one that allowed him to declare martial law and destroy their wealth. Over the long term, however, reliance on violence discredited the regime, forcing Marcos into exile and facilitating the revival of the Lopez fortunes.

The Negros Plantation Frontier

The history of the modern Lopez family begins with the marriage of Basilio Lopez and Sabina Jalandoni in the Jaro district of Iloilo City sometime in the early 1830s. Between 1834 and 1859, Sabina gave birth to sixteen children of whom ten survived to maturity. Although these progenitors left few documents, family historian Oscar Lopez found that Basilio was a prosperous, Chinese-*mestizo*, timber merchant sufficiently prominent to serve as one of Jaro's *cabeza de barangay* (ward leaders) from 1842 to 1862 and as its *gobernadorcillo* (mayor) for one term in 1849. Aside from birthing a child every nineteen months for a quarter century, Sabina was known for her love of ostentation and was prosperous enough on her own account to bequeath a 148-hectare hacienda in Sarabia, Negros Occidental, to her heirs in the late 1870s.[22] Despite Sabina's legacy, neither spouse participated in the opening of the Negros plantation frontier, leaving that venture to their sons.

Among the ten surviving children, seven were active as entrepreneurs. While five sons crossed the Guimaras Straits to become major Negros sugar planters, two of the five daughters stayed home in Iloilo where they prospered as merchants and speculators. Indeed, the entrepreneurial character of the Lopez women is marked even in this second generation (see genealogy, page 477). The eldest child, Clara (1836–87), was an active merchant and moneylender, often serving as banker to her brothers' plantation ventures.[23] An inventory of her estate prepared in 1887 shows assets totaling P126,175.50. Only P55,000 was invested in agricultural lands and P42,053.50, a full third, was on loan to twenty-nine creditors.[24] Indicative of her exceptional wealth, housing assessments for 1891 show that her former home (a timber-framed, iron-roofed dwelling on Palacio Street in Iloilo City) was worth P12,000—comparable to the P15,000 home of Lucio Lacson, the second-largest sugar planter in Negros.[25]

The second child, Eulogia (1838–97), was also a banker to her generation. In 1879, she loaned P40,000 to her planter brother Eugenio at 12 percent interest and in 1889 extended P90,000 at 15 percent to her brother Claudio, also a planter. Both loans were comparable in size to those that British merchant houses were making to major Negros planters.[26] Incidental to her moneylending operations, she acquired two haciendas in Victorias, Negros, one with 125 hectares.[27] She was also active in commodity trading, and the 1891 tax register lists her as owning a substantial masonry warehouse on the Iloilo waterfront. The building was valued at P2,500, somewhat smaller than the P9,000 warehouse owned by the largest Negros planter, Teodoro Yulo.[28]

In the words of the family's genealogy, the third son, Eugenio (1839–1906), was "the central figure among the second generation Lopezes."[29] In his teens he acquired 1,500 hectares of sugar land in Balasan, Iloilo, before crossing the straits to Negros in the early 1860s where he spent the next fifteen years developing sugar plantations. According to a notarial document Eugenio signed in 1887, acknowledging a P40,000 loan from his sister Eulogia, he then owned a total of 2,592 hectares divided among eleven haciendas in Negros and Iloilo.[30] The Lopez genealogy states that between the 1850s and 1890s he purchased 4,000 hectares and sold 1,000, leaving him with 3,000 hectares at the time of his death—holdings that ranked among the region's largest.[31]

Returning home to Jaro in 1876, after the death of his father, Eugenio became the town's *gobernadorcillo* and a prominent member of the community. A leading philanthropist, he established schools for the city's workers and provided extensive relief during the disastrous famine of 1878. Although he was a nationalist, and his brother Claudio was patron to the firebrand *propagandista* Graciano Lopez-Jaena, Eugenio never used his position to challenge Spanish authority. He was a moving force behind the colonial government's investiture of an elected municipal council, the Ayuntamiento de Jaro, in 1891, and served as its *regidor,* or councilor.[32] When news of the Revolution reached Jaro in 1896, Eugenio joined the council in passing a ringing endorsement of Spain's civilizing influence in the islands. In March 1897, he was one of the main contributors to the five-hundred-man Ilongo Volunteer Battalion sent to fight General Emilio Aguinaldo's revolutionary army on Luzon.[33] Upon his death in 1906, Eugenio left a substantial estate and twelve surviving children, the first of 605 direct descendants among whom are found the family's most dynamic leaders. [34]

While Eugenio was one of the largest Negros planters, he also had six siblings with substantial haciendas. Although the largest Lopez farm was only 550 hectares, the four Lopez brothers that were listed in the Spanish census of 1896 had combined holdings of 1,440 hectares, comprising one of the five largest blocs of sugar land on the Negros frontier. Significantly, the Spanish census identified only six Negros planters with holdings over 1,000 hectares.[35] Thus, by every possible index—urban property, sugar lands, and liquid capital—the Lopezes had by the 1890s emerged as one of the region's wealthiest families. No longer mere local merchants and parochial politicians, they had spread far beyond Jaro to achieve wealth and influence throughout the Western Visayas region.

From Plantations to Sugar Mills

While the Lopezes' second generation made their fortunes during the sugar boom of the late nineteenth century, the third had to survive adverse conditions that ruined lesser families. Like all Negros planters, the third-generation Lopezes had to overcome three threats: a protracted sugar crisis from 1896 to 1913, the upheaval of the Philippine Revolution (1896–1902), and, gravest of all, the Philippine laws of inheritance. Most importantly, the third generation negotiated the transition to the new technology of mechanized milling, becoming one of the few planter families to acquire a major sugar factory.

When the long boom that built planter fortunes ended in the 1880s, the Philippine sugar industry went into a protracted crisis, which continued until the colony won free-trade access to the United States in 1913. Compounding these difficulties, the Philippine Revolution was particularly hard fought in Negros where insurgent workers burned plantations and murdered planters. As indicated by notarial documents preserved in the Philippine Archives, the combination of economic crisis and class war drove many planter families to bankruptcy.

During the first decades of American colonial rule, the Lopezes survived by mastering the new electoral politics and learning to deal with the nascent Philippine state. Just as Eugenio exemplified the family's success as plantation pioneers, so his son Benito (1877–1908) discovered the power of the uncensored press. Founded soon after the Revolution, *El Tiempo* became Iloilo City's best daily newspaper, and it served as an effective vehicle for launching its publisher's political career.

For those who survived these larger crises, the laws of inheritance, which mandated bilateral division among siblings, were the ruin of many families. Standards of living acquired from childhoods spent on vast plantations could not be sustained on farms a tenth that size. Moreover, fragmentation denied second-generation planters the economies of scale in management, finance, milling, and transport that could save large haciendas from bankruptcy in times of low prices or lost crops. Seven of Basilio's ten children, including Eugenio, built large holdings during the thirty-year sugar boom. By contrast, Eugenio's twelve surviving children, born between 1866 and 1885, reached maturity during the long sugar crisis that followed. When Eugenio died, he owned some dozen haciendas totaling 2,500 to 3,000 hectares, leaving each heir just 200 to 250 hectares.[36] His ninth child, Benito, inherited only a half-share of the 535-hectare Hacienda Casalagan, located in Pontevedra, Negros Occidental.

Benito Lopez (1877–1908), like his father, remained aloof from the Revolution. In 1900 or 1901, he joined the conservative Federalista Party after a branch was established at Iloilo City. As publisher of *El Tiempo*, Benito became an influential political figure and won the first elections for Iloilo's provincial governorship in 1903. A dynamic and hard-working governor, he toured remote municipalities to support the educational reforms and infrastructure development sponsored by the American colonial regime. In October 1907, he ran for reelection on the conservative Progresista ticket against Nacionalista Party candidate Francisco Jalandoni, another wealthy Jaro planter. As the former chief of staff of the local revolutionary army, Jalandoni enjoyed strong support from Iloilo's veterans, led by the militant Colonel Quintin Salas. In an extremely bitter campaign, the Nacionalistas attacked Governor Lopez as a pro-American collaborator, charges that would later trouble his children as well. On 27 December 1907, two months after Lopez's reelection, one of Jalandoni's closest followers, a former revolutionary officer named Joaquin Gil, walked into the governor's office and shot him four times. Several weeks later he died in a local hospital, leaving a modest legacy. His widow, Presentacion Hofilena, and their two children, Eugenio and Fernando, inherited Benito's share of Hacienda Casalagan, a printing press, and miscellaneous properties. While Joaquin Gil was executed and his patrons were exiled for their role in the affair,[37] the Lopezes had lost their generation's most promising leader.

Benito's surviving siblings, who proved to be formidable entrepreneurs, were among the few planters who made the transition to mechanized sugar milling after World War I. Built in the years of peak wartime prices, Negros Occidental's seventeen modern mills restructured the economics of the region's sugar industry. Prior to construction of the centrifugal mills, each plantation, like Governor Lopez's Hacienda Casalagan, had its own steam-driven mill, usually six to twelve horsepower. Linked to the individual haciendas by a network of railroads and iron-clad milling contracts, each centrifugal factory replaced dozens of steam mills and split the once homogeneous planter elite into contending sectors.

Instead of organizing the mills as local planter cooperatives or as integrated farm-factory plantations, the president of the Philippine National Bank, Venancio Concepcion, offered capital for factory construction to the most powerful family in each Negros sugar district. In effect, through his selective distribution of capital, Concepcion, a former Iloilo sugar broker, nominated a few of the larger families to become a new class of millers—the Yulos in Binalbagan, Montillas in Isabela, Aranetas in Bago, and Lizareses in Talisay. To pay for the milling of their cane, Negros planters signed thirty-year contracts conceding the new factories 45 percent of their sugar. Riding the global sugar boom of World War I, most mills recovered their construction costs quickly and went on to make astronomical profits.[38] When sugar prices dropped during the Depression, Negros planters mobilized politically against the factory owners and spent the next twenty years battling to increase their share of the milled sugar from 55 to 70 percent.

As long as they remained planters, with their capital committed to agriculture, the region's elite could not accelerate the process of accumulation beyond the slow, natural rhythms of the crop cycle. Moreover, periodic disasters—rats, fungal plagues, drought, and political upheaval—could destroy one crop in every four or five, slashing profits and pushing planters towards bankruptcy. With their farms mortgaged to finance cultivation of a fragile crop, sugar planters lived at the brink of ruin, dependent upon the vagaries of the weather.

The millers, by contrast, accumulated capital with each turn of their grinders and crushers. Freed from the tyranny of a capricious nature, the mills made high, reliable profits virtually without risk. Fuel was a sugar by-product, labor costs were flexible, factory maintenance was minimal, and the essential technology did not change for decades. Although the world price could and did crash eventually, the Philippines enjoyed unrestricted access to the protected U.S. market from 1913 to 1934.

A 1939 survey of profit sharing in the sugar industry highlighted this contrast between the fortunes of planters and millers. In his final report, Justice Manuel Moran found that planters bore all the risks and enjoyed few of the profits under the industry's 55:45 sharing ratio. At Central Lopez, for example, planters made an average of 3.51 percent return on investment and the mill 61.74 percent.[39] Moreover, the mills were backed by capital resources that far exceeded those of the haciendas.[40] Thus, the introduction of factory milling not only modernized the

Philippine sugar industry, it initiated a few of the leading planter families into an intensified capitalism.

Of equal significance, with the advent of the mills rent-seeking politics began to dominate the sugar industry. Through the discretionary award of a scarce commodity, capital, the emerging Philippine state had effectively restricted entry into the milling industry while assuring selected investors extraordinary profits. Indeed, the state formalized this de facto arrangement in 1934–35 when it established the Sugar Quota Administration to regulate production by awarding each mill and planter a fixed percentage of the country's total export quota for the United States.

In May 1927, during a second wave of mill construction, seven of Eugenio Lopez's ten surviving children combined their capital to establish the Central Lopez factory at Cadiz, Negros Occidental. As was usual with the Lopezes, gender was no bar to power, and the eldest sibling, Doña Maria Lopez, chaired the board. Of the eight board members, four were women. Although they were not active in management, Eugenio and Fernando, orphans of Maria's murdered brother Benito, were among its founders and investors. While only twelfth in production capacity among Negros's seventeen mills, Central Lopez was one of the more efficient and soon added an alcohol refinery to maximize downstream returns. With total profits of P3.5 million over ten years, on an initial investment of only P700,000, Central Lopez enjoyed a 500 percent return—placing it seventh among the country's forty-five mills.[41] A significant factor in the mill's profitability was its location in the region's only drought-free area. In contrast to the two to five months of drought visited upon the southern La Carlota district from 1920 to 1927, the Lopezes' district on the island's north coast enjoyed continuous rainfall.[42] An annual dry season restricted Central La Carlota to a maximum of six months' grinding every year but mills in the north could operate for ten months.[43] Consciously or not, the Lopezes had sited their mill in the optimum zone for a higher rate of return.

Continuing the family tradition of women entrepreneurs, in May 1934 Doña Rosario Lopez Santos (1872–1965), one of the founders of Central Lopez, used her own resources to establish Central Santos-Lopez in the prime Panay sugar district of Barotac Nuevo. In 1937 her mill earned P432,680, less than the earnings of Central Lopez but still impressive since Doña Rosario did not share the return with partners nor did she pay dividends.[44] Although her husband, former ship's engineer Francisco Santos, worked at the mill, she dominated the factory's management. After her husband's death by suicide in 1938, she ran the factory on her own for another quarter century.

Thus the Lopezes became one of eight Negros families whose capital accumulation was released from the risks of tropical agriculture to accelerate with the constancy of their mills' machinery. Surviving the long sugar crisis and avoiding the dissipation of ostentation, those of the third Lopez generation who had invested in sugar milling created the capital resources that their orphaned nephews, Eugenio and Fernando, would later use to reach national prominence. By contrast, the

Lopez lineages that remained simply planters would suffer a slow decline of fragmentation through inheritance, and would remain lodged within the regional elite.

Rise of the Lopez Brothers

Although the Lopez family has produced many wealthy and accomplished members, none of their achievements equal the remarkable career of Eugenio Hofileña Lopez (1901–75). Born in Jaro, Iloilo, the eldest son of Benito, Eugenio was orphaned at age seven, with his only sibling, Fernando, when Governor Lopez was assassinated.

As a law student in Manila and at Harvard in the 1920s, Eugenio developed the national and international contacts that distinguished him from his more parochial kin. By completing his undergraduate education at Ateneo de Manila University, an elite Jesuit college, and his law degree at the University of the Philippines, the alma mater of the country's most active political lawyers, he acquired access to powerful social networks. In contrast to his often dour uncles, Eugenio became the darling of the Manila elite. He engineered the election of the city's 1923 Carnival Queen, and as her consort danced for a season at the center of Manila society.[45] After studying for a year at Harvard Law School, he broke the family custom of local unions to marry Pacita Moreno, a member of a prominent Manila family. Although we can only speculate, it is possible that Eugenio's marriage to a well-connected Manileña, exceptional for Lopezes of his generation, may have facilitated his ultimate move to Manila and his entry into the national business elite. Reinforcing these ties to the capital, Eugenio left management of his Negros hacienda to his uncle and began his career as a lawyer in the offices of Vicente Francisco, one of Manila's most influential attorneys and his future advocate. By contrast, Fernando finished his law degree at University of Santo Tomas in 1924, and married a close relative, Mariquit Javellana of Jaro, earning him abiding ties in his home region.[46] In effect, Eugenio's education and marriage gave him an entree to national circles, while Fernando's marriage to a relative facilitated a strong regional base.

The careers of the brothers form one of the most spectacular success stories of the postwar Republic. Beginning with a single hacienda and the small printing press inherited from their father in 1928, they had amassed assets worth U.S. $300 million by 1973. With capital borrowed from their wealthy aunts and uncles, they began their careers by organizing a series of medium-scale, joint stock-ventures in Iloilo City during the 1930s—a bus company, an airline, and an interisland shipping firm. When the war destroyed most of these assets, the Lopezes filed for compensation with the U.S. War Damage Commission. A generous American payment allowed them to liquidate their investments and Eugenio moved to Manila shortly after liberation to launch himself as a national entrepreneur. Following a series of successful acquisitions of ever-larger corporations, he became the country's leading capitalist when he purchased Manila Electric Company (Meralco) in 1961.

Although biographers now portray Eugenio H. Lopez as an entrepreneur of sterling individual qualities,[47] his rise was also a product of his family and class. His emergence as a national figure in the 1960s was, in effect, the culmination of commercial success by four generations of a massive family. Significantly, within the larger family he belongs to the single line that has demonstrated a consistent capacity to perceive and profit from socio-economic change. The leaders of each generation within this line have shared some discernible personal and professional traits, making their success seem in part a product of what David Musto has called "familial world views."[48]

To these traits, Eugenio H. Lopez added personal boldness, ruthlessness, and a broad vision that made him the first Lopez to achieve national success. A man of personal discipline and determination, he rose daily at 4:00 a.m. because, as he told his wife, "my enemies whoever they are, they are still asleep and I'm already planning how to attack them." Soon after his marriage he informed his wife that he intended to become a millionaire by the time he was thirty.[49]

Surveying Eugenio's half-century rise to national prominence, we can isolate several interrelated factors in his success. Instead of building single corporations slowly, he was a financier who mobilized capital to build a succession of interlocking conglomerates, acquiring rather than building to accelerate growth. Investing just enough capital to gain corporate control, he would then drain the company's assets through a percentage-basis management contract or lavish executive benefits, practices that often aroused charges of profiteering from minority stockholders.[50] With his financing for future acquisitions thus secured, he would then buy a controlling interest in a larger corporation. By means of this pyramid-building technique, and unrestrained by the feeble regulatory efforts of a weak state, Eugenio steadily increased the size of the consortia he controlled—from P250,000 in 1937 to more than P1 billion in 1973.[51]

Judging from his investment decisions, Eugenio Lopez had a clear understanding of the relationship between technology and capital accumulation. While sugar milling created great profits for the third Lopez generation during the twenty boom years following World War I, the business was still tied to nature's slow, seasonal rhythms. In partnership with his brother Fernando, Eugenio invested in regional transport—on air, land and sea. Unlike sugar mills, the transport industry operated dawn to dusk, seven days a week, twelve months a year. While sugar profits ultimately were determined by global prices, transport profits depended on traffic volume from diverse sources. With machines driving their capital accumulation year-round, the Lopez brothers soon emerged as the most successful entrepreneurs in their home province.

In addition to acquiring their own sugar mills after World War II, Eugenio and Fernando moved into information technology—newspapers, radio, and television. With the acquisition of the Manila Electric Company in 1961–62, Eugenio achieved a major breakthrough. For, no longer dependent upon machinery to produce a single good or service vulnerable to sudden downturns, he could now sell energy to a diverse range of industries. Moreover, Meralco's generating dynamos spun ceaselessly, accumulating capital twenty-four hours a day, 365 days a year. As Eugenio moved from passive natural energy, to mechanical power, to electrical and microwave energy, he simultaneously accelerated his capital accumulation, increased his profitability, and reduced risk.

Aside from his financial skills, Eugenio maintained excellent relations with his close kin and allies, avoiding the bitter internal battles that have damaged families such as the Cojuangcos. Perhaps because their father had died young, Eugenio and Fernando maintained an intimate working relationship throughout their lives. Lacking his brother's entrepreneurial flair, Fernando, an open, likable man, embarked upon a successful political career, building a formidable political apparatus on both the national and provincial levels after World War II. Elected mayor of Iloilo in 1945, he became a senator in 1947, and vice-president of the Philippines in 1949. Later returning to the Senate, he sought the Nacionalista Party presidential nomination in 1965 but withdrew to become Marcos's running mate and eventual vice-president. Fernando's political success afforded Eugenio access to government contacts for his business concerns. Indeed, this symbiosis of political influence and corporate growth was a key factor in Eugenio's spectacular rise from provincial bus operator to the Philippines' most powerful entrepreneur in only a quarter century.

Central to their success was the Lopezes' long-term relationship with several planters who comprised the core of their political faction. Through this network, they gained a powerful lobby in the legislature, liberal access to the state financial institutions that serviced the sugar industry, confidantes in the corridors of Church power, and a regional vote bank negotiable in national politics. The brothers' closest political allies were Oscar Ledesma, an influential Iloilo City political leader and Negros planter related by marriage; and Alfredo Montelibano, Sr., a wealthy Bacolod sugar industrialist who became the industry's leading advocate.[52] Although their blood relationships were distant, the group used marriage and fictive kinship to formalize their ties. When Fernando's daughter Mita married Alfredo Montelibano, Jr., in March 1953, the bride's mother, the bridegroom's mother, and Oscar Ledesma served as principal sponsors—binding Lopez, Ledesma, and Montelibano as *compadre*.[53] During the Republican era, they became known in the national media as the "sugar bloc." Indeed, the Lopez-Ledesma-Montelibano alliance lasted for half a century, giving them a remarkable collective influence over government, Church, and business. Ledesma gave the Lopezes access to the sugar planters and the Church. Industrialist Montelibano later chaired such key Lopez enterprises as the Philippine Commercial & Industrial Bank and Meralco Securities. Unlike most elite Filipino alliances, which usually last less than a decade, these friendships survived war, dictatorship, and even divorce.

From the time the first Filipino Bishop of Jaro was appointed in 1943, the Lopez brothers, through ally Oscar Ledesma, cultivated a close alliance with their home diocese. A devoted Christian and anticommunist, Oscar Ledesma became, after World War II, one of the most influential Catholic laymen in the Philippines. A native of Cebu, where his brothers were leading politicians, Monsignor Jose Ma. Cuenco came to Jaro as temporary bishop in 1943 and remained there until his death in 1972. Ledesma was one of his closest advisors. He dined frequently at the bishop's palace, contributed generously, headed many diocesan committees, and won high Papal honors as a knight of St. Sylvester.[54] Cuenco's brother, Senate president Mariano J. Cuenco, was instrumental in securing the Liberal Party vice-presidential nomination for Fernando Lopez in 1949, and the bishop campaigned personally for him.[55] The alliance was cemented when Bishop Cuenco arranged a marriage between a Ledesma woman and a Cuenco son. After Bishop Cuenco died in 1972, leading Jaro laymen, Ledesma included, supported the selection of Monsignor Jaime Sin as his successor, a debt the future cardinal would repay when the state attacked the Lopez family during Marcos's martial-law regime.[56]

More than any other factor, Eugenio Lopez's financial success seems to have sprung from his manipulation of the Philippine state to achieve extraordinary profits from the business activities that we now call rent seeking. Throughout his lifetime, he used his capital to secure political protection, investing in elections and taking his profits in the form of political favors. As he put it: "To succeed in business, one must engage in politics."[57] In both the provincial and national phases of his career, he built powerful media organizations, which he used, with unblushing control over editorial policy, to reward allies and embarrass enemies. Most importantly, he always recognized the unique power of the presidency and worked to cultivate close personal relations with the executive. His enterprises prospered when an ally occupied Malacañang Palace, and they suffered, often badly, under the administration of an enemy. If it was Eugenio's genius to perceive the profit potential of state-created rents, it is a tribute to his courage and cunning that he pursued them with unequaled skill and persistence.

Eugenio's Study of the State

In retrospect, Eugenio Lopez's manipulation of the Philippine state seems studied and self-conscious. During his year at Harvard Law School in 1923–24, he wrote a fifty-one-page essay on "The Council of State of the Philippine Islands." In its five-year bureaucratic life, from 1918 to 1923, the Council of State operated as the colony's supreme governmental organ, developing many of the country's basic laws and institutions. Since the council had collapsed only months before Lopez began work on his Harvard essay, he was, in effect, studying two key phenomena: the Philippines' first sustained experience of an indigenous executive, and the country's character as an emerging nation-state. Eugenio's essay reveals both insight into the elements of political theory and a surprisingly cynical view of their application in the Philippines. At twenty-two he demonstrates a good grasp of some elusive concepts, among them the constitutional basis for political authority, the significance of the separation of powers within a tripartite system, and the political realities that allow senior officials to govern in defiance of the law.

As Lopez explained in the first section of his paper, Governor General Francis Burton Harrison had established the Council of State to solve a knotty political problem that had arisen two years before. In 1916 the U.S. Congress had passed the Jones Law establishing the Philippine Senate. Since the opening of the First Philippine Assembly in 1907, Sergio Osmeña had fused the post of speaker with leadership of the dominant Nacionalista Party to become the country's most powerful leader. By dividing the legislature into two houses, the Jones Law diluted Osmeña's authority and threatened his position as the "the recognized leader of the people in the government."[58] Capitalizing on his close personal relationship with Governor Harrison, Osmeña engineered the establishment of the Council of State as a joint legislative-executive body under his de-facto control as its vice-president. The council's creation "solved all the difficulties" since "Osmeña once more became the recognized leader in the government."[59]

Although the council resolved a major political problem, it did so, Lopez argued, by violating the spirit and letter of the colony's fundamental law. By assuming legislative and executive powers without sufficient legal foundation, the council violated the Jones Law, the colony's de facto constitution, and defied the basic legal doctrine of separation of powers. Moreover, the council arrogated unto itself extraordinary, almost dictatorial, powers, interpolating itself into every aspect of government and acquiring considerable power over the economy.

Eugenio Lopez's study of the legislation and judgments relating to the council's legality is an insightful, impassioned critique. After reviewing the organic basis of the Philippine government, "the writer can not find a part in the Jones Law which would mean a reference to the Council of State. Not even a phrase or word by which an analytical mind may be led to argue that the law impliedly or indirectly refers to the Council of State."[60] Since the Jones Law "created the three departments of government . . . granting to each well-defined powers and rights," the council is "entirely foreign to the machinery of government" and is "completely subversive to well-known principles of government."[61] In acceding to Osmeña's request, Harrison had, in Lopez's judgment, defied the law. [62]

> The writer admits the right of the Governor-General to ask the advice and consent of those persons he wants to consult. . . . No law forbids him from doing that. But when the Governor-General creates an advisory body there is put forth a new question. . . . The Governor-General has the right to be advised but he has no right whatsoever to form a body of advisors like the Council of State.

Despite its patent illegality, Lopez continues, the council "has not limited itself in advising the executive . . . it has exercised legislative powers, encroached on executive functions . . . has controlled the policy of the government, nay it has assumed almost dictatorial powers."[63] Lopez also found that by 1920 the council had assumed a remarkable range of powers—distribution of P30 million to promote universal elementary education, dispersal of P300,000 for rinderpest serum, reviews of government salaries, approval of bonds floated by local governments, control over irrigation projects, and even the drafting of the 1920 budget.[64] "It stands to reason," he argues, "that the Council of State is performing [sic] not only questions of importance, but also the most trifle [sic] things in government. The powers of the Council of State have become unlimited. The accumulation of these powers in the Council of State is a danger and menace to our free institutions."[65]

Citing Montesquieu on the significance of this precept, Lopez further charges that the council "has violated the principle of separation of powers which is considered the basis of every democratic government."[66] He argues that the governor general's arbitrary control over the council's membership had profound implications for the country's republican form of government.[67]

> If in the past the Governor General have [sic] appointed persons having the confidence of the people, he has done it, not because he was debarred by law or by the order creating the Council of doing otherwise, but simply as a matter of favor or what we may call an executive concession. If the Council of State knowing as we do its tremendous influence as well as its powers and privileges, were composed of persons not bearing the popular confidence, how then can we assent that it is a representative body? . . . If it ceases to be a representative body, it is repugnant to the republican form of government which has been established in the Philippine Islands. . . . Its existence is subversive to the foundations of free government.

In Lopez's argument, the key test of the council's legality came during the rice crisis of 1919 when the governor general issued a proclamation fixing the retail price of rice. A week later, the government charged a Chinese merchant named An Tang Ho with selling rice at an excessive price and he appealed his conviction. In a unanimous decision, the Philippine Supreme Court found that the governor's proclamation represented an improper delegation of legislative powers to the executive and was therefore unconstitutional. After pointing out that the governor general was acting at the direction of the council, Lopez concluded that "it was not the Governor-General who exercised the delegated powers, it was the Council of State to which he belonged." By failing to confront the Council of State on this issue, the Supreme Court, in Lopez's words, "showed cowardice" and "abdicated the right of fearless judgment."[68]

The council was disbanded only when Leonard Wood succeeded Harrison as governor general. In October 1923, Wood criticized the council as a "violation of principles of constitutional government," and Senate president Manuel Quezon introduced legislation to strip it of its power to authorize local bond issues.[69] It collapsed soon after.

The implications of Lopez's critique of the Council of State are profound. Most importantly, he seems to discern that this powerful organ was able to defy the most fundamental laws and legal principles of the country as long as the executive willed it so. Moreover, it could continue to do so for an indefinite period of time. Osmeña and Quezon had trampled the country's constitutional precepts for the sake of political expediency, and then attacked their creation as unconstitutional when it no longer suited their interests. Simply put, there were no apparent restraints to the arbitrary exercise of executive power in the Philippines. Observing his country's first experience of executive authority from the vantage point of Harvard Yard, Eugenio Lopez had divined some of the essential attributes of his emerging nation—the arbitrariness of executive power, the weakness of law, and the consequent capacity of the state to advantage its allies in defiance of law or principle. In sum, he may well have concluded that the Philippines was a nation of powerful men not of laws.

Examining Lopez's later career in light of this study is instructive. He seems to have concluded that the state was beyond repair. Rather than committing himself to a correction of its failings, he used his formidable skills to manipulate its weaknesses—in effect, extracting its resources to construct an alternative social order of family-based corporations within the private sector. Over the next half century, then, his masterful manipulation of the Philippines' laws, legislature, and executive went far beyond simple intuition or improvisation.

Provincial Political Debut

After completing their educations and entering Manila society, the Lopez brothers returned to Iloilo City in 1928 to begin their careers. To claim their position in the planter elite, they took control of their two Negros haciendas from their guardian and uncle, Vicente Villanueva Lopez. As their father's younger brother and the husband of their mother's younger sister, Vicente was, in effect, a double uncle, a relationship that should have ensured his integrity as their guardian.[70] Notwithstanding this close kinship, he refused to relinquish their share of the 685-hectare Hacienda Casalagan in Pontevedra. With an assertiveness that seems to have won the respect of the family's older generation, the brothers filed a civil case and by 1931 had forced uncle Vicente to divide the disputed hacienda, winning thereby 390 hectares of prime sugar land.[71]

Most importantly, Eugenio revived their father's newspaper *El Tiempo* and used it to launch himself as a power broker in Iloilo City.[72] Creating a niche for a new Spanish newspaper in the city's glutted media market was a formidable task. Despite a population less than one hundred thousand, Iloilo already had a Hiligaynon newspaper, two English-language weeklies, and five Spanish-language dailies—including such influential political papers as *La Tribuna,* the organ of Senator Jose Ma. Arroyo's branch of the Nacionalista Party; and *El Centinela,* the voice of Ruperto Montinola's opposition Democrata Party.

Working through attorney Vicente Arenas, an in-law and a former reporter at Manila's *El Mercantil,* Eugenio launched the new *El Tiempo* in June 1929 as a Spanish-language daily with an English section for the younger generation. Three years later, Eugenio founded *The Times,* the city's only English-language daily, under the editorship of Ezequiel Villalobos, a former reporter at the *Manila Daily Bulletin* who soon became Iloilo's preeminent journalist. Selecting his staff carefully for their editorial and reportorial skills, Eugenio gave his *Tiempo-Times* publications a modern, metropolitan look that set them apart from the quaint, literary serendipity of the city's established Spanish press.[73] With these newspapers, and later a Hiligaynon edition, *Ang Panahon,* Eugenio Lopez maneuvered to establish himself as the city's most powerful and professional media voice.

In a brilliant exercise of media power, Eugenio Lopez launched *El Tiempo* with a crusade against urban vice, personified by the city's leading Chinese gambler, Luis "Sualoy" Sane, branding him Iloilo's "Emperor of *jueteng.*" *El Tiempo's* first issue appeared on 1 June 1929.[74] By September the paper was publishing the winning number in this illegal lottery every day in a bold-face box on page one—a tactic that soon sparked intense controversy.[75] In the 2 October edition, the paper's first extant issue, the box read "Jueteng—City of Iloilo. Yesterday morning No. 34 was the winner; and in the afternoon it was No. 10. The gold of the gambler is more powerful than public opinion."[76] Not content with exposing the Chinese "banker" behind this lottery, *El Tiempo* began hinting, with increasing bluntness, that Iloilo's governor Mariano Arroyo, brother and political heir of the deceased senator Jose Arroyo, together with city police chief Marcelo Buenaflor, brother of Congressman Tomas Buenaflor, had been influenced by "corruption and bribes" to protect illegal gambling.[77]

In effect, the Lopezes were launching a frontal assault on the entrenched local leadership of the Nacionalista Party. More broadly, their campaign exposed a system of corruption that was already enmeshed in provincial politics by the 1920s. Backed by his father, who was considered "one of the richest men in the province,"[78] Jose Ma. Arroyo had begun his political career in 1916 with an impressive win in the elections for the House of Representatives and then consolidated his control over Iloilo with three successful Senate races.[79] When a leadership struggle between Quezon and Osmeña split the Nacionalista Party in 1922, Arroyo sided with Senate president Quezon and became the first vice-president of his Partido Nacionalista-Colectivista.[80] Over the next three years, Arroyo served as Quezon's trusted leader in Iloilo with the authority to award patronage in an arbitrary, even quasi-legal, manner.[81]

After Senator Arroyo's sudden death, Dr. Mariano Arroyo, then director of St. Paul's Hospital in Iloilo, inherited his brother's clientelist ties to Quezon and was elected provincial governor in October 1928.[82] Although he employed the language of loyalty with Quezon, Governor Arroyo's relations with the powerful Senate president remained coolly proper, lacking the intimacy his brother had won during years of common service in the Senate.[83] Lacking support from Manila, Governor Arroyo forged close relations with Congressman Tomas Buenaflor and Democrata Party boss Ruperto Montinola. Using these local alliances to build an autonomous political base, Arroyo began to attack the machinery of established Nacionalista leaders, most notably that of Jose Zulueta in Iloilo's First District—a bid for independence that concerned Quezon.[84]

To finance this reach for autonomy, Arroyo secured a rich source of political funding by accepting secret payments from the *jueteng* lottery controlled by Sualoy. In taking these bribes the governor was exposing himself to the kind of political attack that, ironically, had been suggested by his own brother just three years before. In January 1925, Senator Jose Arroyo had written Quezon that the "famous smuggler" Luis Sualoy had recently arrived in Iloilo as the "impresario of a game called *jueteng* which is the ruin of many poor Filipino families."[85]

> This Sualoy is allied with local authorities and many have informed me in a reliable way that he is secretly paying a thousand pesos a month to the current Municipal Mayor of Iloilo, who is a Democrata . . . and thus has the advantage of this monthly support from Sualoy along with other means that are not licit. We can catch him at this in a flagrant way if the Constabulary in Manila will send secret agents in disguise who are not known in Iloilo, since no other means will work. By doing this, we can save the poor from this terrible game of *jueteng*, which has made a millionaire out of its organizer through these illicit gains, and we can block the advantage of a Democrata mayor, a candidate for reelection who has a gold mine while our own candidates have empty pockets.

As criticism of Governor Mariano Arroyo's independence from local Nacionalista leaders mounted, he wrote Quezon in January 1929 protesting his loyalty to the party. To rebut the specific charges against him, the governor denied that he had awarded the foremanship of road gangs to people nominated by the opposition Democratas. Further, he cited his assistance to Congressman Zulueta's brother, who had recently been arrested and charged with financing another *jueteng* game.[86] As *El Tiempo's* attacks on *jueteng* intensified, the governor's dalliance with the Democratas and his independence from the Nacionalista machine would prove critical failings.

Although *El Tiempo* printed the winning lottery numbers and published charges that an illegal casino was operating in the Mahinay Building on Ortiz Street,[87] Iloilo's local police, compromised by what one journalist later called "the grease money they got from the operators," refused to act.[88] As public anger rose, the city council considered a resolution calling for action by the Philippine Constabulary. Simultaneously, the provincial board debated a motion to ask Governor General Dwight Davis for an independent investigation.[89]

In October 1929, responding to this pressure, the local Constabulary command raided a gaming and opium den on Iznart Street and arrested fifteen Chinese smokers and two lottery runners. With a brazenness that hinted at protection, Luis Sualoy bailed out the runners and sent them home in his personal auto.[90] When the local press headlined these arrests, Governor Arroyo issued a statement denying the lottery's existence, thereby implicating himself in the scandal: "I am in complete agreement with the desire of everyone for a strong campaign against the supposed jueteng gaming in Iloilo, if it really exists; and for that reason I have always insisted that the city police cooperate with the Constabulary in continuing this campaign."[91]

In its English-language section, "Plain Talk," *El Tiempo* responded to the governor with broad hints of corruption: "What mysterious hold has the 'Jueteng Boss' over some of our officials that he seems immune?"[92] The paper's campaign gained further credibility several days later when a municipal court sentenced one of the Chinese arrested on Iznart Street, Oyo Guim, to a month in prison for the crime of working as a *wakha*, or runner, in the *jueteng* racket. In its coverage, *El Tiempo* implicated Sualoy by reporting that he had appeared at the municipal jail to console the runner Oyo Guim after sentencing.[93] The next day, 10 October, *El Tiempo's* editor Jose Magalona was beaten by a local thug, Luis "Toldo" Elipio, as he was entering the Wing Kee Restaurant on Plazoleta Gay.[94] Insinuation gave way to direct accusation as *El Tiempo* declared open war on Governor Arroyo. [95]

> Jueteng alone is responsible for this brutal aggression. The men behind the jueteng here and all those who are benefited financially by this vice have something to do with this act of a crude low-brow. . . . Several persons, one of them Governor Arroyo himself, directly or by indirections had made the members of the editorial staff of this paper understand that there were people who were determined to club some of the *El Tiempo* personnel if the paper did not stop bothering the jueteng "interests."

As the Constabulary escalated its campaign against the lottery, producing numerous arrests of runners and minor bankers,[96] the activities of Iloilo's police chief Marcelo Buenaflor seemed confined to harassing *El Tiempo's* key source.[97] In their columns and stories, Lopez reporters began naming local officials and charging them with corruption.

Although many of Eugenio Lopez's moves in this protracted battle seem spontaneous, his choice of issues in itself exhibited a certain political genius. By focusing on a nonpartisan issue of social morality and official probity, he drew support from two inherently contradictory elements of colonial society—the American executive, with its almost priggish aversion to corruption, and the urban working class, which yearned for a moral cum national regeneration. By raising the issue of official corruption, Eugenio gained what became the decisive factor in his victory—intervention by the colonial governor who otherwise would have remained aloof. When the American governor generalship gave way to a Philippine presidency after 1935, Eugenio would use the Filipino tactics of *compadrazgo* and factional alliance to gain a similar access to executive power.

Whether or not Eugenio Lopez understood its full implications, the conflation of gambling, Chinese influence, and official corruption aroused a strong emotional response among the city's colonized proletariat. As knowledge of the issue spread through rumor and reports in the vernacular press, workers responded with outrage, giving Eugenio a sudden, and probably unexpected, mass constituency for his campaign. In an era when the city's dock workers often exhausted their income in drinking and cockfighting, union and community leaders equated personal immorality with colonial subjugation. The day after editor Magalona was assaulted, the newspaper *Makinaugalingon* offered a free copy of Jose Rizal's nationalist novel *Noli Me Tangere* as a prize to the reader who provided the best answer to the question "What must we do to rid ourselves of the deathly specter of jueteng?" Dozens of workers responded with demands for draconian penalties and radical changes. "Send all the Chinese bankers to Iwahig, Palawan [a penal colony]," wrote an anonymous entrant of No. 99, Quezon Street, Interior. "Arrest the organizers of the jueteng, fine them P10,000, send them to jail for ten years' hard labor," urged Pablo Cusio of San Carlos, Negros Occidental. "Imprison the operators for at least one month, but on each Sunday afternoon march them around every turn in the road so we can scream at them," raged Ramon Quimsing, "a poor man from Molo."[98]

With its aversion to official corruption and freedom from factional ties to the provinces, the American colonial executive and its Constabulary were, like Iloilo's working class, natural allies in the Lopez antivice campaign. Over the next ten months *El Tiempo* kept the issue alive, prodding the local Constabulary to continue its investigations and arrests.[99] After months of careful preparation, the Constabulary finally raided Sualoy's bank in March 1930, arresting the "emperor" and fourteen of his runners. Three months later, Iloilo's Court of First Instance sentenced him to five months in prison and a fine of P500.[100]

The local controversy exploded into national notoriety in August when *El Tiempo* published a confidential report containing police chief Marcelo Buenaflor's admission to the Constabulary investigator, Captain Gaviola, that he, Governor Arroyo, and Congressman Tomas Buenaflor had run an illegal *monte* card game in the Mahinay Building to raise funds for the 1931 elections.[101] Within days, Arroyo retaliated by filing a criminal libel case against *El Tiempo's* entire staff, including publisher Eugenio Lopez.[102] Moving with exceptional speed, the Department of Justice dispatched Judge Manuel V. Moran from Manila to hear the case. After taking evidence from all the principals, Judge Moran found on 3 September that in an effort to amass P100,000 in anticipated election expenses, "Governor Arroyo and Representative Buenaflor operated a gambling den at the Mahinay Building from March 3rd to April 13th, 1929, and that Governor Arroyo received P1,000 per month as his share of the gambling proceeds." Under such circumstances,

Moran concluded that "a newspaper has reason to publish this excess so that the society can correct itself." He exonerated *El Tiempo's* staff from all libel charges.[103]

Governor Arroyo fared even worse at the administrative hearings into his conduct. After he had filed his libel suit against *El Tiempo*, the Lopezes responded with a formal administrative complaint against him. On 9 August, Governor General Dwight Davis appointed Judge Marceliano R. Montemayor "as my special investigator to hear the administrative charges made against Hon. Mariano B. Arroyo." In the ensuing hearings, the Lopezes, represented by leading Manila attorney Vicente Francisco, won admission of the evidence against Arroyo presented before Judge Moran in the antecedent libel case.[104] Some of the most damning testimony came from attorney Pio Sian Melliza, who described himself as a boyhood friend, a *compadre*, a patient, and an active supporter of the governor:[105]

> I was in the office of Governor Arroyo in February 1930 and spoke at length, saying to him if possible he should arrest the jueteng men, and he answered that I should trust him to make those arrests. For this reason I kept going back to see him four or five times in February with the aim of reminding him why he still had not arrested the jueteng runners, not even a surprise police raid. . . . In March I went again . . . and he said to me the following:
> *"Compadre* . . . why are you so determined to get rid of jueteng gambling? Isn't it clear to you that most of the jueteng runners and sellers are our own political *liders?* The elections are close and I am running for reelection. Not including the money they are giving us for election expenses, they can hurt us in this election because there are many of these jueteng runners in this province."

In his report to the governor general, Judge Montemayor found "that from the latter part of 1929 to the first months of 1930, jueteng . . . had been played rather scandalously in the city of Iloilo" and that the respondent "knowingly tolerated it so as not to incur the displeasure and animosity of friends and political leaders." Citing Judge Moran's hearings, Montemayor further concluded that the governor had "maintained a gambling house in the Mahinay Building . . . until April 13, 1929" and had received P1,000 per month from that house. On 7 October, Governor General Davis ordered that Arroyo be removed from office "for the good of the service,"[106] and later appointed Dr. Timoteo Consing, a "close friend of the Lopezes," as his replacement.[107] Pending outcome of Constabulary investigations into their culpability, Iloilo mayor Eulogio Garganera and police chief Marcelo Buenaflor were suspended from office.[108]

Throughout this painful process, Arroyo appealed to Senate president Quezon for help but without result. When the scandal first broke in May 1929, Ignacio Arroyo, the governor's father, wrote Quezon that the officer in charge of the investigation, Captain Gaviola, was "in continuous conference with Mr. Pepe Javellana who wants to control gambling in Iloilo."[109] After more telegrams from the Arroyos, Quezon finally wrote the governor on 13 June agreeing that the allegations of "tolerance for gambling . . . are undoubtedly the work of your enemies" but advising sternly that such "rumors . . . can only be defeated by irreproachable conduct in public affairs."[110] A few days later, Governor Arroyo himself wrote Quezon assuring him that the "perjured allegations of my supposed tolerance of illegal gambling . . . are pure calumny and the work of my enemies who are gamblers."[111] As the evidence against Arroyo accumulated, Quezon fell silent—in marked contrast to his intervention when the brother of Congressman Zulueta, a loyal party man, had been jailed on a similar charge.[112] In July 1930, Arroyo again wrote to Quezon pleading with him to stop Interior Secretary Ventura from sending special investigators to Iloilo.[113] There was no reply. In September, after Judge Montemayor recommended the governor's removal, Arroyo wired Quezon: "Our enemies moved heaven [and] earth to destroy Collectivism Iloilo. We ask justice. Please wire Governor General recommending acquittal. Reply prepaid."[114] Despite Arroyo's exceptional gesture in paying P11.60 for a response, none was forthcoming.

Landing at Iloilo from Manila a week after his dismissal, former governor Arroyo was met at the waterfront by a demonstration of supporters protesting his dismissal. According to *El Tiempo's* front-page report, a parade of ten automobiles, thirty-four horse-drawn carriages, and a battalion of school cadets escorted him home along J. M. Basa Street with supporters waving placards lettered with "Viva Arroyo," "We Are Still With You," and "We Demand Elections So The People Can Judge."[115] Comparison of this article with a surviving photo of the demonstration suggests that *El Tiempo* had dropped its anti-Arroyo slant, as, for the first time in over a year, the paper seemed almost objective in its coverage. Not only are the details accurate but the reporter conveys the sense of a major political event, an outpouring of anger over the sacking of a popular leader. The photograph, shot by the Agar Studio from the upper floor of a building at the corner of Plazoleta Gay, captures the length of J. M. Basa Street, the grand concourse of the business district. In the vanguard of the demonstration are some 250 marchers and horsemen followed by six men carrying placards. Behind them is arrayed a string of fourteen automobiles that stretches impressively along the two-story shop fronts, halting traffic and attracting the attention of pedestrians.

A careful reading of this photograph also highlights an important point easily lost in the density and detail of paper documents: the controversy had remained, despite an outpouring of working-class concern, a political struggle within a narrow elite, the educated few who could still read a Spanish-language newspaper. A major demonstration for the former provincial governor in a city populated by nearly 100,000 people had attracted only 250 participants. Taken during prime working hours at midday, the photograph shows the marchers, all men, attired in suits, hats, and shoes—clothing that most laborers did not possess. While teachers and clerks might have suits, only the affluent, planters or merchants, could afford automobiles.

Despite this outpouring of support, and later announcements of an Arroyo candidacy for high office,[116] the former governor's political career was ruined. Indicative of his disgrace, two years later he sent a gift to Quezon at Baguio with his brother's widow, Jesusa Lacson vda. de Arroyo. "I was doubtful whether I should accept it or not," Quezon later wrote to Arroyo, "but in the end I decided to knowing that you think of us as family in light of the fraternal love that I feel for your deceased son, my unforgettable Pepe."[117] Quezon's hesitation probably was less wounding than his uncharacteristic gaffe—the deceased Jose, or "Pepe," was not Mariano's "son" but his brother. This defeat, indeed destruction, of the province's leading politician was a stunning political victory for Eugenio Lopez who, at twenty-nine, was still a neophyte publisher.

The Courtship of Quezon

Aside from establishing Eugenio Lopez's reputation, this media campaign broke the Arroyos' control over Iloilo's branch of the Nacionalista Party, creating an opening for new leadership. The appearance of the Lopezes as a political force coincided with a bitter struggle for the leadership of the ruling party. During the critical battles over independence, Quezon was desperate for support in his struggle for control of Iloilo, a populous and prosperous province. In 1932 the U.S. Congress had passed legislation, the Hare-Hawes-Cutting Act, creating an autonomous Philippine Commonwealth with an elected president as a transitional stage leading to full independence. After passing the Act, the Congress forwarded the legislation to Manila for ratification, sparking an intense debate within the islands over the terms of independence. Realizing that the glory of having negotiated independence in Washington would prove a major advantage in the subsequent campaign for the Commonwealth presidency, the country's leading politicians—Senate president Quezon, Senator Osmeña, House Speaker Manuel Roxas, and Senate minority leader Ruperto Montinola—split over the specifics. Quezon, determined to reject the bill, which had been negotiated by his rivals, forced his opponents out of their legislative positions in mid-1933.[118] While he now dominated the legislature and ruled the Nacionalista Party's majority faction, his enemies still controlled Panay Island, the home of both Montinola and Roxas. Seeking to counter the strength of his rivals in this region, Quezon tried unsuccessfully to weaken Roxas's influence by engineering the election of Jose Zulueta, representative from Iloilo's First District, as House speaker pro tempore.[119]

During this battle, Eugenio Lopez became an important source of campaign financing for Quezon and made his newspapers "the organ of the Nacionalista Party in the Western Visayas." According to former *Times* reporter Godofredo Grageda, "the two papers brought [Senate] President Quezon and the Lopez brothers close to each other, particularly Don Eugenio, whom the President invariably addressed by his nickname, 'Ening.'"[120] Quezon read the papers regularly and "would call up Don Eugenio and suggest things for publication, or sometimes he would give his comments." During the battle over ratification of the Hare-Hawes-Cutting Bill, Eugenio sided with Quezon, becoming his "most trusted leader in Iloilo."[121]

Throughout this controversy, Eugenio Lopez again demonstrated his ability to use media for political advantage. When *Times* editor Exequiel Villalobos exercised editorial independence by opposing Quezon's position on the Hare-Hawes-Cutting Act, Lopez, without advising Villalobos, hired a new editor—Eliseo Quirino, brother of Quezon's close follower Elpidio Quirino. Upon his arrival at the *Times*, the new editor's first task was to hand a letter of dismissal to his predecessor—still working at his desk ignorant of his fate. This calculated humiliation made Villalobos a lifelong enemy of the Lopez brothers.

In the June 1934 elections, the final battle in this protracted warfare, Quezon relied upon Congressman Zulueta as political leader and Eugenio Lopez as financier for his faction's campaign in this key region.[122] Reflecting the extraordinary strength of the opposition, the election results from Panay were a disaster for Quezon. Although his candidates won sixty-seven of the eighty-nine House seats nationally,[123] they lost four out of five in Iloilo, making the province a citadel of opposition. While Zulueta was reelected by a narrow margin, Quezon's candidates in the other four districts, all prominent politicians, suffered humiliating defeats. [124]

Three days after this debacle, Quezon's local leaders—Zulueta, the provincial governor, and the four defeated congressional candidates—met to conduct a searching review. They attributed their defeat to "the appeal to the electorate with respect to regionalism, in the sense that the Visayan provinces do not have to follow the leadership of Quezon who is Tagalog, despotic and tyrannical." To revive their fortunes, they recommended suspension of all general funds to the province and a purge of government employees who had aided the opposition.[125] In his own detailed post mortem, Dr. Fermin Caram, Quezon's defeated candidate in Iloilo's Second District, identified the opposition's use of Panay Autobus to move its voters to the polls as the key factor. While Quezon's candidates had relied upon "small automobiles which cannot carry many voters," the bus company had committed its entire fleet to the opposition on election day and had assigned several vehicles per town, "carrying up to 50 voters on each trip." Significantly, added Caram: "I understand that Panay Autobus offered its coaches without charge."[126] Under these circumstances, Quezon was more than willing to support the Lopez brothers in their later takeover of the company.

But Panay Island was an exception to broad national trends. After chastening his rivals by winning a wide majority in the Assembly, Quezon negotiated the reunification of the Nacionalista Party and led a coalition ticket, with Osmeña as his running mate, into the 1935 presidential elections. Despite the nominal fusion, however, the campaign provided ample evidence of his rivals' continuing strength in the Visayas. In August, when Roxas campaigned in Iloilo on behalf of the coalition ticket, the local Constabulary commander reported to Quezon that he had attracted more than ten thousand listeners, "the largest crowd ever assembled in Iloilo to hear a political meeting."[127] In the election that followed, Osmeña won over thirty-eight thousand votes as vice-president while Quezon himself gained only thirty-two thousand as president.[128] Despite his easy election to the presidency and the apparent party unity, Quezon continued to maneuver to reinforce the strength of his own faction, trying thereby to lessen the chance of any future challenge to his authority. In this effort, the Lopez brothers would prove to be valuable allies.

Within the rituals of *compadrazgo*, the brothers formalized their relationship with Quezon through baptisms that celebrated their proximity to power. Some months after the birth of his third child, Presentacion, in October 1935, Eugenio brought the president to Iloilo as baptismal sponsor and guest of honor at the "brilliant reception and ball" that dedicated his new mansion. There one hundred Manila socialites and the cream of local society danced to one of the country's leading bands, imported from the capital for the occasion.[129] Two years later, Fernando celebrated the baptism of his daughter Milagros (also born in 1935) with a still more lavish display. After disembarking at the Iloilo waterfront before a crowd of ten thousand, Quezon drove directly to Jaro Cathedral in a cavalcade of thirty autos to stand at the baptism. He later attended a dinner dance at Fernando's mansion with seven hundred guests, including Vice-President Osmeña, Assembly Speaker Gil Montilla, Justice Secretary Jose Yulo, and four other prominent legislators.[130]

Until the outbreak of war, Eugenio used "the singular advantage of being close to President Quezon" to become the province's most influential political broker. Local politicians and aspirants frequented his office at the *Tiempo-Times* building seeking "a word from Don Eugenio to higher headquarters." According to reporter Grageda's recollections: "Recalcitrant officials either had to toe the line or find themselves packing up for another destination. . . . Officials who wanted other assignments, or professionals who aspired for government positions . . . could find no better route than . . . Don Eugenio's getting in contact with the President."[131] Although there were repeated reports that Quezon planned to appoint Eugenio to the Iloilo City mayoralty or as resident commissioner in Washington, Lopez apparently preferred to avoid office and use his political influence to advance his interests.[132] Local press reports of these refusals spoke of "those intimate friends President Quezon and Eugenio Lopez" or the president's "compadre Ening," reminding readers of Lopez's access to Malacañang Palace.[133]

As their investments moved beyond publishing into the state-regulated transportation business, the Lopez brothers found that good relations with President Quezon were essential. Their return to Iloilo in 1928 had coincided with the city's long slide from national sugar entrepot to provincial backwater. By 1932, the port had lost 76 percent of Negros sugar exports, a blow that created unfavorable conditions for these ambitious young entrepreneurs.[134] Willing to try anything that would turn a profit, the Lopezes launched a series of small enterprises—a dance band, an ice-cream parlor, and rental properties—until

Eugenio realized that transportation was the city's only profitable business. By 1933, he had built a comprehensive transport network: the Iloilo Shipping Co. (interisland ferries to Negros), the Iloilo Transportation Co. (urban buses), and the Iloilo-Negros Air Express Co. or INAEC (regional air transport to Manila).[135]

During the Depression years of the early 1930s, the region's transport interests competed intensely. When the Lopezes put their ferry on the Negros-Iloilo run, shipping tycoon Esteban de la Rama, one of the region's wealthiest men, retaliated with a fare war that slashed prices far below profitability. Retreating from open competition in the sea lanes to the regulated airways, the Lopez brothers negotiated a generous government subsidy of P75,000 and monopoly rights on key routes to launch INAEC in 1933.[136] Under the terms of the franchise granted by the National Assembly, INAEC received a twenty-year permit to open routes anywhere in the islands, subject to approval by the Public Service Commission, in exchange for 1 percent of gross revenues—a classic rent-taking arrangement.[137] By selling shares to family and planter friends, the Lopezes assembled a million pesos in capital, taking care to retain control through a family-dominated board. Significantly, a majority of INAEC's directors served simultaneously on the board of the Lopez Sugar Central mill, another family-owned enterprise.[138] Launching its Manila-Iloilo route in February 1933, INAEC started with the ten-passenger capacity of a single Stinson tri-motor. By 1936, however, the company had sufficient revenues to purchase an eighteen-passenger Sikorsky S-43 worth P260,000.[139] The airline expanded rapidly to four aircraft flying routes reaching from Manila to Mindanao.[140] After six years of operation, INAEC had carried 94,211 passengers over a million miles with only one accident.[141] As one of only three Philippine airlines, INAEC enjoyed a monopoly on several major routes and its return on investment was impressive. But volume was relatively low, gross profits were limited, and the small clientele for high-cost air travel restricted the possibilities for future growth.

The Struggle for Panay Autobus

Land transport had a far greater profit potential than even the most efficient airline but the Lopezes were blocked from expanding their urban bus routes into Iloilo's hinterland by the state's licensing system. Seeking to extend their urban monopoly into the countryside, Eugenio decided to attempt a takeover of the island's largest bus firm, Panay Autobus. In 1937, he began a protracted battle that eventually came to dominate provincial politics. Considering the success of their rent-seeking activities under the postwar Republic, the struggle for Panay Autobus is a revealing example of the ways in which the Lopez brothers later would use politics to secure rents.

The rural population of Iloilo had depended on small, local bus firms until August of 1930 when an American entrepreneur, W. C. Ogan, launched Panay

Autobus with capital of P300,000 and a license from the Public Utilities Commission to operate fifty vehicles throughout Panay Island.[142] By November the company's island-wide network had attracted such a large share of the local traffic that thirty-one local bus-operators, who together owned more than one hundred trucks, appealed, without success, to the Public Service Commission to reconsider its license for Panay Autobus.[143] Two years later, Miguel Borja, a thirty-year-old Tagalog who had learned the business at Pantranco under its American founder, Frank Klar, launched his Capiz Motor Bus Company. Starting with just three second-hand units, Borja quickly expanded his fleet to sixty-five buses and bought out most of the local operators on Panay's northern littoral.[144] After suffering bitter strikes throughout 1934, culminating in an assault on his chief of operations, Panay Autobus owner Ogan agreed to merge with Capiz Motor Bus on terms that made Borja the manager and main shareholder. The merger created a regional transport giant with over three hundred units and capital of P365,000.[145] In the same year competition in and around Iloilo City increased when Dr. Manuel V. Hechanova, a prominent local planter, organized the Jaro Express.[146]

In their campaign to dominate bus transport in Iloilo, the Lopez brothers first concentrated on eliminating competition within Iloilo City. The Lopezes' company introduced a fleet of new double-decker buses, which drew traffic away from Jaro Express. Owner Manuel Hechanova, realizing that he was handicapped by a poor route structure, applied to the Public Utilities Commission for an improved schedule. Apparently lacking sufficient influence in Manila, his application was rejected.[147] After two years of relentless competition, losses at Jaro Express amounted to P75,000. In July 1936, Hechanova agreed to sell his company to the Lopezes for P80,000, subject to approval by the Public Service Commission.[148] Ten years later, commenting on his defeat in an interview with *El Tiempo*, Hechanova offered an exoneration of the Lopezes, which, in light of the later violence at Panay Autobus, seems a subtle condemnation: "Let me take this opportunity to state publicly that in this struggle Don Eugenio and Don Fernando carried themselves like gentlemen. They never offered any illegal competition, nor did they use illicit or violent means to force me from the field."[149]

With their control over urban routes now consolidated, the Lopezes purchased a small, island-wide concern, the B. Hernandez Company, and declared open war on Panay Autobus.[150] The garage and main terminus for Panay Autobus were located in Iloilo City where the Lopez-owned Iloilo Transportation Company had its network of urban routes. Reflecting the increased competition for passengers, bitter territorial conflicts arose, exacerbated by the Panay Autobus practice of encouraging its provincial buses to carry local passengers within the city limits, a technical violation of its license that the Lopezes denounced as poaching. When Panay Autobus persisted in this illegal practice, the brothers had a pretext for their takeover bid.[151]

During its eleven-month duration in 1937–38, the struggle for Panay Autobus was a complex conflict that ranged from gang violence on the waterfront to factional competition in city-council elections. By mobilizing a coalition that spanned the political spectrum from waterside gangsters to President Quezon, the Lopez brothers won the battle for Panay Autobus. Since the company had contributed to his recent electoral defeats in Iloilo, President Quezon naturally sided with the Lopezes, his *compadres* and close allies. Although escalating violence accompanied the conflict, the Constabulary refrained from restoring order—a neutrality that favored the Lopezes. Moreover, a range of local leaders, many of them inveterate enemies, united in support of the brothers. The city's rival labor unions, for example, backed them against a populist coalition of city-council candidates who were campaigning on a platform that opposed the Lopez interests. Most importantly, the brothers allied themselves with Iloilo's toughest waterfront gangsters who ultimately out-fought the opposition.

Since the Lopez family later "denied the use of force or threats of violence or murder" in the acquisition of Panay Autobus,[152] their alliance with the Iloilo underworld merits close examination on both factual and theoretical grounds. After the war, when they joined the national economic elite, the Lopez brothers moved into a world of corporate connections remote from the provincial violence that marred postwar democracy. But before the war they had engaged in provincial struggles, with clear territorial manifestations, over bus routes, waterfronts, precincts, and congressional districts. The territorial specificity of local politics created a zero-sum game, a win-or-lose situation, that made violence a necessary instrument for every player. To understand why the Lopezes, future statesmen and philanthropists, used violence during the provincial phases of their careers, it is necessary to grasp the territorial dimension of the struggle for Panay Autobus and the logic of the brothers' alliance with organized crime.

Before the war, the main roads and rail line on Panay Island funneled peasant passengers along the coastal plains, south towards Iloilo City's waterfront, where interisland ships took on travelers bound for Negros, Manila, and the rest of the archipelago (see map). Many of the passengers on the profitable long-distance bus routes from Aklan and Antique provinces were *sacadas,* cane cutters who gathered in work gangs in Iloilo City at the start of every milling season to ride the ferries across the Guimaras Strait. In the competition for this trade, the city's bus and shipping managers paid the local waterfront gangsters, known as *comisionistas,* a 10 percent commission to deliver these valuable passengers. During the off-season, the *comisionistas* traveled the interior towns of western Panay, seeking agreements with the labor contractors (*contractistas*) who recruited the cane-cutting crews. During milling season, the *comisionistas* fended off the competition on the waterfront with bluff and blows, by means of boxing, *baston* stick-fencing, or *bolo* fighting. In effect, these *comisionistas* were Iloilo's organized criminal element—entrepreneurs in violence who sold their services during elections and controlled their waterfront territory through physical prowess.

Among the city's many *comisionistas,* the Lopezes allied themselves with the most violent—the gang led by boxer Manuel Lamadrid and his underlings, which included the famed *bolo* fighter Simeon Valiente and the notorious thug Jesus Astrologo.[153] Indicative of their outlaw status, reporters for *Makinaugalingon,* the city's nonpartisan, Hiligaynon-language newspaper, identified Simeon Valiente as a "well known bad character with a long police record" (*ang kinilala nga isa sang mga hurung sa sini nga siudad, nga may madamu na gid nga "record" sa departamento sang polisiya*).[154] The paper's headline for an article on the death of Manuel Lamadrid identified him as "one of the city's evil characters" (*ang isa ka sutil diri*).[155] Both phrases are Hiligaynon's circumlocutory way of saying *gangster* or *professional criminal.* More particularly, the words *hurung* ('bad character') and *sutil* ('evil character'), connote, within the context of Iloilo City, an abrogation of the search for good and an embrace of vice—terms that described social outlaws, if not outcasts.

This language was an apt approximation of social reality. A brief biography of Jesus Astrologo, the most murderous of Iloilo's *comisionistas,* indicates that the city's waterfront fostered a milieu of violent professional criminals. Starting with an assault on a woman in 1928 at age fifteen, Astrologo's career in violence culminated in the leadership of Japanese patrols that slaughtered some 250 civilians in 1943. A survey of his court appearances over a twelve-year period before the war demonstrates a transformation from petty assault to professional criminality with a psychopathic edge. After convictions for individual assaults in 1928 and 1932, Astrologo joined Lamadrid's waterfront gang in the mid-1930s and began committing more vocational crimes, including a gang assault against a street rival in 1935 and the murder of a bus driver in 1940.[156] When the Japanese occupied Iloilo in 1942, he served them as a spy, guiding their troops into the mountains of Panay to search for resistance leaders and later torturing suspected guerrillas at Bacolod. During the Japanese Army's bloody punitive sweeps through Panay villages in 1943, he led mixed patrols of Japanese soldiers and Filipino thugs that engaged in torture, rape, and mass murder—specifically, the torture and execution of "several civilians" at Leon in July 1943; the beheading of thirty-seven villagers and massacre of "around one hundred Filipino civilians" at Tigbauan in August 1943; the execution of twenty-five civilians selected after the mass torture of eighty at Leon in August 1943; and the murder of three villagers and massacre of eighty more at Altavas in October 1943.[157] In one of its harshest judgments of wartime collaborators, the postwar People's Court ordered Astrologo executed for crimes of "treason with murder," a sentence later commuted to imprisonment.[158] Significantly, his August 1945 confession to the U.S. Counter Intelligence Corps (CIC) begins as follows: "I, Jesus Astrologo, age 33, interned at the 503rd RCT Stockade, having been duly advised of my rights . . . do proceed to state as follows: Prior to the Japanese occupation, I lived in Iloilo with my wife and children working as an inspector for the Lopez Transportation."[159]

Miguel Borja's sole *comisionista* was Primo Doctora, a retired boxer who had fought professionally in Iloilo as "Kid Fuenteville" and in Manila as "Kid Reyes" for six years. "In 1932, I quit the ring," he recalled, "and became a hired goon in the city of Iloilo. Almost every month I wound up in prison . . . I would be released from prison, get drunk and fight, and be sent back to prison by Judge Mapa." After three years on this long slide, Doctora was approached by Miguel Borja and offered a monthly salary of P45 to recruit passengers for Panay Autobus.[160]

During the eleven months of its duration, the Panay Autobus conflict was exceptionally violent, with periodic public battles between rival *comisionistas*. When ships loaded with *sacadas* docked at the Iloilo waterfront, rival *comisionistas* rushed forward to shuttle them towards their vehicles, transforming the pavement between the bus door and the ferry gangplank into a battleground.[161] "As the sacadas came down the ramps," recalled Primo Doctora, "it was our work as *comisionistas* to get them to ride our bosses' buses. Against me were Lamadrid's whole gang—Jesus Astrologo, Simeon Valiente, Teodoro Caporzo, [Proilan] 'Poring' Jison, [Francisco] Pilapil, and Lamadrid. I was alone against them with only one companion, my uncle Pablo Dais. I used to take them on with fists and fighting bolo." When the daily shoving erupted into sporadic violence, fighting often continued for ten or fifteen minutes before city police could assemble a platoon to wade into the melee of fists, clubs, and blades.[162] "Almost at any time of day or night," recalled Lopez executive Jose Jimagaon, "the police would call me at home or in the office to say that they had Astrologo, Valiente, or their boys in prison, and I would go down and bail them out."[163]

These duels on the Iloilo waterfront became routine, punctuated by incidents of extraordinary violence that marked the turning points in the struggle. In March 1937, for example, *comisionista* Fausto Nuevo had just arrived from Libacao, Capiz, on Panay Autobus with a crew of cane cutters bound for Negros. He was dining at the Plaza Lunch on Ledesma Street when the Lopez *comisionista* Manuel Lamadrid entered with his gang, demanded twenty pesos, and struck Nuevo when he refused. According to the police report, Nuevo fired three shots from an automatic pistol, killing Lamadrid and scattering his gang.[164] Two weeks later, in a battle over passengers disembarking from the ferry *MV Kanlaon II*, Primo Doctora and his partner wounded Lamadrid's successor, Jesus Astrologo, sending him to St. Paul's Hospital for a prolonged recuperation.[165] In August, police broke up a battle at Compania Maritima's waterfront office between rival gangs armed with "knives, canes, swords and bolos," arresting their leaders, Borja partisan Doctora and Lopez ally Astrologo.[166]

At the midpoint of this struggle, the December 1937 local elections intervened, forcing both sides to divert their energies from the waterfront to the political arena. While the Lopez brothers were among the leaders of a Nacionalista coalition that scored a crushing victory for Tomas Confesor in the race for provincial governor,[167] Iloilo's municipal elections presented a direct challenge to their interests. Under a new city charter adopted in November 1936, Iloilo City had a mayor appointed by the Commonwealth president and a council of seven elected members.[168] In the weeks before the formal inauguration of the new city mayor in July 1937, Quezon solicited nominations from both Zulueta and the Lopez brothers, and then appointed Dr. Ramon F. Campos, a close Lopez ally.[169]

Within weeks, the Lopez influence at city hall was felt on the streets where the struggle for Panay Autobus was intensifying. Only a week after breaking up the brawl among *comisionistas* at Compania Maritima in August 1937, Iloilo police chief Jose Tando had signaled his partisanship by suddenly imposing a ban on parking by Panay Autobus along Guanco, Iznart, and Rizal Streets, thereby impeding the company's ability to pick up passengers in the city center.[170] Opening a new arena of conflict, the seven city councilors were to be chosen in the local elections in December. Led by three former municipal mayors whose careers were now eclipsed, the city's veteran politicians formed a council slate known as the "Banwa Boys" ('local lads') who used the Lopez brothers as their main campaign issue.[171] Indicative of the depth of the split within the local Nacionalista coalition, the Banwa Boys quit the party and ran as the official candidates of the weak opposition group, the Frente Popular.[172]

On 4 November, the Banwa Boys launched their campaign in a public meeting the tenor of which was captured in *El Tiempo's* headline the next day: "Vigorous Attacks Launched by the Discontented 'Pros' Against the Lopez Family at Last Night's Rally." Speaking before a crowd of two thousand people at the corner of Ledesma and Quezon streets, outgoing mayor Eulogio Garganera attacked the Lopez land transport monopoly, and former mayor Serapion Torre criticized INAEC's government subsidy.[173] Three days later, the Nacionalista Party hosted a rally at the same corner where its provincial board candidate, attorney Ceferino de los Santos, spoke at length in defense of the Lopez operations. With a transparent bias, the family-owned *El Tiempo* reported that the speaker had "refuted the accusations . . . against the Lopezes and their interests in this province in sober language and with clear, convincing reason." Speaking in a similar vein, Iloilo's deputy mayor Ramon Jimenea asked rhetorically, "Now that the governor, the mayor and a majority of the city council belong to the Lopez faction, can we cite a single resolution or ordinance that favors the interests of this family?"[174] A week later, the Banwa Boys were back on the stump with what *El Tiempo's* headline called their "rude attacks," charging that the Nacionalista candidates were nothing more than "Lopez Boys," hirelings who would do the bidding of their powerful masters.[175] At a rival rally, Jimenea again defended the Lopezes, reminding his audience that Banwa candidate Garganera, the city's self-styled savior from special interests, had been suspended from the mayorship in 1931 for taking bribes.[176]

With sixty-two mass rallies held on city street corners during the last two weeks of the campaign, the pro- and anti-Lopez rhetoric grew more intense.[177] At a Banwa rally on 22 November, speakers accused the brothers of stealing from the uncles who had raised them. They further warned that the Lopez transportation monopoly was a threat to the province's future. On the other side, bitter over the failure of his union's strikes against Panay Autobus, labor leader Jose Nava attacked the Banwa Boys at a series of mass rallies. At one street-corner meeting Nava's aides held up a placard reading "Banwa Boys" and then, with a dramatic flourish, changed one word to make it read "Borja Boys." According to *El Tiempo's* partisan account, Nava's defense of the Lopezes drew an enthusiastic response from the crowd:[178]

> "This," shouted Nava in the midst of frenetic applause and numerous shouts, "is the real meaning of Banwa Boys. . . . They are candidates of Mr. Miguel Borja of Panay Autobus. This is the other side of the story that Garganera and his comrades do not want to reveal. Those so-called 'Banwa Boys' are candidates financed by Panay Autobus as a tool for vengeance against the Lopez family since they have competed with his transport business."

Drawing upon mass support built up during more than a decade of municipal leadership, the Banwa Boys captured five of the seven council seats in the 14 December elections.[179] While Banwa leader Eulogio Garganera placed first, with 5,813 votes, and his ally Serapion Torre was second with 5,348, Lopez defender Ramon Jimenea received only 3,089 votes and failed to win a seat.[180] In the words of some Banwa supporters, "the Lopezes, Zulueta and Confesor gave their all and every influence they had, going to the extent of kicking all the inspectors of the Pros, yet what happened? The best they all could do was a sole seat—one chair in the city council."[181]

Despite the opposition's dominance of the city council, the Lopezes' influence with both the mayor and governor limited its ability to assist Borja in the battle over his bus line. The council elections had embarrassed the Lopezes but they managed to controvert the opposition's allegations and control the damage. With the elections over and their influence intact, the Lopezes soon revived their campaign against Panay Autobus.

By simultaneously shifting both the police (appointed by the mayor) and the prosecutors (assigned by Manila) to their side, and then raising the level of extralegal violence, the Lopez brothers eventually forced Borja's capitulation. Soon after the elections, Panay Autobus lost its main defender when two Lopez fighters disabled Primo Doctora. "Even before I had a chance to draw my bolo or knew they were coming for me," Doctora recalled, "Valiente came at me from the side and slashed me across the forehead. At the same time Jison stabbed me in the side of the stomach. . . . It was rumored that [Lopez employee] Jose Jimagaon had ordered Valiente to eliminate me."[182]

With Doctora removed, the violence against Panay Autobus escalated. In late January 1938, for example, a criminal from Capiz named "Kiting" stabbed a Panay Autobus driver after refusing to pay his fare.[183] In Iloilo City, Miguel Borja's brother was beaten by one of the Lopez goons and suffered a serious head wound.[184] In these final weeks of conflict, Panay Autobus suffered slashed tires, broken windows, nail punctures, and assault or intimidation of Borja family members. Although Borja allies Doctora and Nuevo had been indicted for earlier assaults on Lopez *comisionistas*,[185] the Lopez-influenced police and prosecutors now failed to act. Miguel Borja, considering his life at risk, finally decided to sell. When his daughter, a company employee, protested, he asked her: "What do you want, my daughter, the Panay Autobus or the life of your father?"[186] Finally, in February 1938, Borja's group accepted an offer of P565,000 for their shares in Panay Autobus from investors led by Eugenio Lopez.[187]

Soon after taking control of Panay Autobus, Eugenio Lopez began transferring corporate profits and assets to his private accounts, developing the tactics he would employ later with such spectacular success in Manila. At a meeting of the board of directors in October 1938, W. C. Ogan, the company's founder and board member, moved that the account statements tendered by the Lopez group be rejected on grounds that they contained "illegal, immoral and corrupt" transactions. Specifically, he charged that the Lopezes had mortgaged Panay Autobus assets to obtain a corporate credit of P250,000 from the Philippine National Bank. Then, using company funds, they had loaned themselves P99,018; had purchased 17/25ths of the Iloilo Transportation Company, their own firm, at inflated prices; had acquired all of the Iloilo Transit Company, another of their own enterprises; and had paid themselves fees of P15,632.21 from Iloilo Transit Company funds after its acquisition. Finally, in their capacity as corporate directors, they had awarded themselves lavish annual salaries totaling P25,000.[188] Although Ogan filed civil cases that dragged on through the courts for months, the Lopez group did not attempt to rebut his allegations. Instead, they sued him for libel.[189] As owners of 70 percent of the company stock, the Lopez brothers maintained managerial control throughout the litigation, earning impressive profits and purchasing additional shares.[190]

Business and Provincial Politics

As a public utility with competition, costs, and charges set by the state, the Lopezes found that the profitability of Panay Autobus, once acquired, could only be assured through active participation in politics. Thus, between 1937 and 1941, company operations became one of the main issues in Iloilo provincial politics. Throughout, the Lopez brothers used their newspapers to good effect, foreshadowing the sophistication of their national media management after World War II.

In the provincial elections of 1940, the Lopez brothers were targeted by populist candidates, the first of many such attacks that would recur over the next half century. Governor Tomas Confesor, a formidable populist speaker, had won a landslide victory in 1937 with the support of a unified Nacionalista Party and the Lopez financial interests. In contrast, his 1940 reelection campaign was one of the most divisive in the province's history. After the Panay Autobus battle, Confesor and the Lopezes broke over a range of issues. The brothers, for example, held Confesor responsible for blocking Fernando's appointment as Iloilo City mayor.[191] Most importantly, perhaps, Confesor refused to grant Panay Autobus reductions in the bridge tolls that comprised almost half of the company's total direct tax burden.[192] Financially pressed by Confesor's intransigence on this issue, the

Lopezes began to support the rival Zulueta-faction candidate with both money and media.[193] When the brothers and other leaders expressed their displeasure with Confesor in meetings with Quezon, the president evidently pressured the governor to withdraw for the sake of party unity. In a characteristic act of defiance, Confesor refused and decided to run on his own.[194]

Denied support from the province's elite, Confesor adopted an anti-Lopez theme in a bid to attract lower- and middle-class voters. Although the Banwa Boys had inaugurated the anti-Lopez rhetoric, Confesor sharpened its ideological overtones, waxing eloquent over his mass, or *tigbatas,* doctrine. During his first term he had adopted a populist position by denying the Lopez requests for reduced bridge tolls, by supporting Panay Autobus conductors charged with theft, and by remaining neutral in a strike at Central Santos-Lopez in Barotac Nuevo. Citing this record on the stump, Confesor portrayed the election as a clash between rich and poor,[195] and derided the rival candidate, Mariano Consing, as a "political stooge" of the Lopez brothers.[196] Seeking to tarnish these populist claims, opposition speakers charged that Governor Confesor was a "Stevenot boy"—a reference to Colonel J. E. Stevenot, the American president of the Philippine Long Distance Telephone Company and a former resident of Iloilo City.[197] Admitting his friendship with the American, Confesor retorted that "Stevenot did not ask for lower bridge fares like the Lopez brothers did." As the campaign intensified, Confesor charged the Lopezes with malfeasance in their administration of Panay Autobus and demanded an accounting of P25,000 in conductors' bonds and P40,000 in unpaid dividends.[198]

Scoring a stunning upset that attracted national attention, Confesor won reelection by a wide margin.[199] The Manila *Tribune* gave the triumph page-one coverage, noting that Confesor had defeated the combined forces of the Lopezes and Jose Zulueta's formidable machine.[200]

After these reverses, the Lopez brothers consolidated their factional strength and began building a machine of their own, one that would remain a force in Iloilo politics for several decades. To cover the provincial towns beyond their economic reach, they allied themselves with Congressman Zulueta, who had strong support in rural areas. Drawing their own support largely from Iloilo's commercial sector, they integrated business with politics by building their faction around wealthy friends and family members, most notably Mayor Ramon Campos, Oscar Ledesma, and their cousin Francisco Lopez Jison. Reflecting his close ties to the Lopez group, President Quezon appointed Alfredo Montelibano as mayor of Bacolod City in 1938, and Oscar Ledesma as mayor of Iloilo City two years later.[201] Reinforcing this political power with economic influence, Ledesma served three terms as president of the Confederation of Sugarcane Planters' Associations before yielding the office to Montelibano in 1941.[202]

In the 1941 elections for the legislature and the presidency, the Lopez brothers repaired the damage they had suffered at Confesor's hands. Although he had resigned from the governorship in favor of his ally Dr. Fermin Caram to take a post in Manila, Confesor ran a slate of legislative candidates against the Zulueta-

Lopez alliance in all districts except the second. Through Quezon's intervention, both factions backed Oscar Ledesma for this seat and he resigned as mayor of Iloilo City to run. Throughout the campaign, Zulueta accused Caram of secretly supporting the opposition against Ledesma.[203] Although he denounced the reports as "unfounded and false," it required the personal intercession of Vice-President Osmeña before Caram committed himself fully to Ledesma's campaign, for the latter was a rival of long standing.[204] In the November elections, all the Zulueta-Lopez candidates won with solid majorities, including Ledesma who thus became the congressman from Iloilo City.

On the eve of war, the Lopez group had established itself as the dominant political faction in Iloilo City. The Lopez commercial interests were not only the largest but they were among the few showing any growth in the midst of the city's steady economic decline. Although President Quezon usually was careful to play provincial factions against each other, he was uncommonly generous in his support of the Lopez group. Combining local support with Quezon's patronage, the Lopezes controlled the city hall while their intimate friend Ledesma represented the city in the National Assembly. Simultaneously, Bacolod City mayor Alfredo Montelibano was emerging as the preeminent political leader in neighboring Negros Occidental. Within the sugar industry, Ledesma and Montelibano had established themselves as leaders of the powerful planters' association. Although Eugenio was forty and Fernando only thirty-six, the Lopez brothers already were approaching the limits of Iloilo's commercial and political possibilities.

Family Survival in World War II

Although Japanese aircraft bombed Iloilo City only days after the November 1941 elections, the advent of war did not slow the pace of provincial politics. While combat swept Luzon after the Japanese invasion in December, Iloilo remained comparatively peaceful—beyond the battle lines and under nominal U.S. military authority. Despite the imminent threat of Japanese invasion, Iloilo's factional intrigues continued unabated, driven by renewed Lopez maneuvers to reduce the bridge tolls for Panay Autobus. After the Japanese occupation of April 1942, the provincial elite faced several threats to their survival—destruction of property, death by bandits or soldiers, expropriation of assets, loss of political power, and disruption of their key export industry. Through dexterous political maneuvering, the Lopez faction survived them all.

While the U.S. Army held the ultimate political authority in Iloilo (from December 1941 to April 1942), local politicians translated their factional conflicts into the rhetoric of military preparedness. For reasons of personality and political perspective, Governor Caram failed to impress the American military. Soon after his arrival at Iloilo in November 1941, the commander of the Sixty-first Division of the U.S. Armed Forces in the Far East (USAFFE), General Bradford Chynoweth, had found an "indefensible" military situation and sought civilian support for his mobilization efforts. Chynoweth described Governor Caram as "not a strong man" and later would complain of his lack of cooperation.[205] In contrast to the army's sense of crisis, Caram tried to calm the public with cautionary advice.[206] When the army's local civil administrator, American attorney Thomas Powell, wrote Caram urging him to organize a civilian food-production campaign, the governor offered instead the rhetoric of loyalty: "I am conducting an intensive personal campaign in all municipalities. . . . One of the topics I invariably touched . . . is to stress the benefits that we have and are receiving from the United States and the loyalty and debt of gratitude that we owe the people and government of the United States."[207]

While Caram was earning General Chynoweth's displeasure, the Lopez faction was burrowing into the U.S. Military Administration and using their new leverage to discredit the governor's emergency program. On 9 January, Don Carlos Lopez, uncle of Eugenio and Fernando, was appointed assistant to USAFFE's civil administrator Thomas Powell. A month later, Oscar Ledesma was given a similar post.[208]

Although Governor Caram had been on friendly terms with the Lopezes before the war, the issue of bridge tolls again aroused their bitter opposition. Pleading wartime conditions, the Lopez brothers asked Caram to suspend the tolls for Panay Autobus. When he refused, they began campaigning for his dismissal. In a postwar report to the army's Counter Intelligence Corps, Caram explained that the criticisms of his administration had been "due to the persistent request of my political opponents made in January 1942 . . . to suspend the collection of Toll Bridges [sic] . . . by alleging that it was wartime. They were paying P1.20 for each truck . . . and there were then thirteen toll bridges under operation in Iloilo. They were hard put."[209]

Rebuffed by Caram, the Lopez faction criticized his administration in the pages of the *Times*. The first attack was published on 1 February 1942, urging "high public officials" to implement policy instead of "making unnecessary speeches and public demonstrations."[210] Over the coming weeks, the newspaper accused the governor of incompetence and dishonesty. When a shipment of soap, a commodity in short supply, arrived from Cebu and was cornered by Chinese merchants, a *Times* columnist charged Caram with collusion: "The fact he [Caram] allows the soap business to gravitate into the hands of local Chinese merchants is another gesture of his munificence."[211]

The army was unimpressed by the governor's diffident managerial style and reacted favorably to pressure for his removal. While the Lopez faction was negotiating with General Chynoweth for Oscar Ledesma's appointment as Caram's successor, President Quezon escaped from Corregidor and landed on Panay where he spent a month playing local politics. Since Eugenio Lopez was his *compadre* and Ledesma had enjoyed the president's personal support in the 1940 elections, Quezon's partisanship was soon felt. On 1 March, the president dismissed Caram and appointed Oscar Ledesma as both provincial governor and concurrent mayor of Iloilo City, an unprecedented concentration of local power.[212]

Two weeks later former governor Tomas Confesor landed on Panay after fleeing from Japanese-occupied Manila, and the president restored some balance to provincial politics by appointing him governor of Iloilo. After Quezon left for Mindanao and Australia, factional fortunes changed dramatically. Defense preparations accelerated under Governor Confesor, an advocate of total resistance to the Japanese. Simultaneously, the U.S. Army imposed a scorched-earth policy on Iloilo City, expropriating Panay Autobus vehicles to move troops and supplies to the mountains over strong Lopez objections.[213]

When the Japanese Army invaded Panay Island in April 1942, most of Iloilo City's population, including its elite, evacuated to rural refuges under the loose protection of USAFFE. After the U.S. Army surrendered to the Japanese in May, small bandit groups began to prey upon civilian evacuation sites. Like most of the provincial elite, the Lopezes found survival difficult in the countryside and soon sought Japanese protection in the city.

The most notorious of Iloilo's wartime bandits was Juanito Ceballos, a former Panay Autobus conductor. Accused of theft in the late 1930s by Fernando Lopez, he was sentenced to prison by Judge Vicente Mapa but was released on the eve of the war.[214] With the support of fifty demobilized soldiers, Ceballos located Judge Mapa in rural Zarraga and murdered him. After raiding the nearby plantation of Sabas Gustilo (a planter known for his cruelty) and slaughtering his family, the bandit crisscrossed the Iloilo Plain in search of the Lopez brothers. On the morning of 16 July 1942, he was surprised by a local guerrilla unit not far from the Lopez camp and executed.[215]

When these killings "started a general exodus of well-to-do families back to Iloilo City," the Japanese Army gained limited support from the province's political elite. Like Oscar Ledesma, most of the Lopez faction found guerrilla resistance to the Japanese "pointless."[216] In a private conversation the day after he was sworn in as Japanese-sponsored mayor of Iloilo City, Ledesma commented: "I don't quite understand the attitude of [resistance governor] Confesor. . . . After the surrender of USAFFE in Panay, I don't see the utility of any civilian resistance. Their act may be interpreted to indicate excessive fear of the Japanese or exaggerated desire to show off."[217] To break the resistance, the Japanese Military Administration (JMA), led by Lieutenant S. Mihara, a sophisticated English-speaking officer, formed local governments in mid-1942, which took both local factions into account. As Dr. Caram explained to the U.S. Army after the war:[218]

> Lt. Mihara manifested to me that his plan was to preserve both political factions and he had selected me for the governorship as he knew . . . that I belonged to Confesor's political faction. He also told me that he was appointing Oscar Ledesma as City Mayor because Ledesma belonged to the Zulueta and Lopez Brothers' political faction.

Seeking a balance between the province's dominant factions, the JMA appointed Caram as Iloilo's provincial governor, and Ledesma, his rival for the governorship only a few months earlier, to the post of city mayor. Ledesma staffed his wartime administration with cronies drawn from the city's elite. When Monsignor Jose Ma. Cuenco was named the first Filipino Bishop of Jaro, in January 1943, Mayor Ledesma escorted him on the ship from Manila to Iloilo, beginning a life-long political alliance between these powerful families.[219] After Ledesma resigned in March 1943 to become regional director of the pro-Japanese Kalibapi and the Philippine Sugar Association, former congressman Vicente Ybiernas, a Lopez-Ledesma ally, succeeded him as Iloilo City mayor.

In keeping with his role as the most influential but least public member of his family and faction, Eugenio Lopez waited out the war at his summer home in Baguio, then a colonial hill station in the mountains north of Manila. There he lived quietly, restricting his business activities to ownership of a local restaurant. The surrounding mountains were the refuge of Luzon's largest guerrilla groups, however, and the Japanese military was particularly vigilant in Baguio. As the war progressed, even the most retiring citizens, Lopez included, were drawn into relations with both the resistance and the Japanese. Working through close friends among the guerrillas, Lopez supplied them with "medicine, shoes, bond papers, laundry soaps, clocks and liquor." Simultaneously, however, he cultivated a warm social relationship with the local Japanese command, hosting frequent parties for the most senior officers. Even after the war, when he was under investigation for treason, Lopez willingly admitted that he often entertained General Nagasaki, the head of the Japanese Military Administration for Northern Luzon. Citing his success in securing the release of eight American nuns and many Filipino guerrillas, Lopez denied that these parties represented collaboration in any sense. In the words of a postwar interrogation report, "if he wanted to help a guerrilla or an American in distress, his only means was to give them [the Japanese] a party and ask what he wanted between drinks."[220]

Many members of the Filipino elite who attempted a similar balancing act found that the smallest slip brought torture and execution by the Japanese military police, the Kempeitai. As a skilled manager of power relations within his society, Lopez survived. His abilities were tested in December 1943 when the accomplished prewar swindler, Franco Vera Reyes, came to Baguio posing as an American intelligence officer, "Lieutenant Colonel Reyes," who claimed to have landed by submarine from Australia with orders from General MacArthur to coordinate all guerrilla activities. Using a similar story, Reyes was already penetrating Manila's leading underground network and extracting funds for fictional resistance work. He eventually delivered some the country's most prominent persons to the Kempeitai for torture and execution, among them Enrico Pirovano, the manager of De la Rama Shipping; Rafael R. Roces, Jr., a member of the distinguished publishing family; and Juan Miguel Elizalde, a wealthy industrialist.[221]

As Reyes spun a similar web to ensnare the Baguio resistance, Congressman Ramon Mitra, despite some reservations, allowed himself to be drawn in. Working with the regional guerrilla commander, Colonel Manuel Enriquez, he convened a meeting of the local underground. The group was seating itself at the Tropicana Restaurant on Session Road when Reyes spotted its owner, Eugenio Lopez. Suddenly Reyes excused himself and early the next morning left Baguio for Manila. Lopez had instantly recognized Reyes as the swindler he had accused before the war. Although Lopez's intervention aborted Reyes's scheme, its victims were fearful that they had been compromised. To avoid possible arrest, Colonel Enriquez accepted President Laurel's amnesty decree for guerrillas, while Mitra, under pressure from the local Kempeitai chief, had to accept his offer to serve as mayor of Baguio.[222]

Suspicious of those who served the local Japanese administration, Lopez was similarly circumspect when one Judy Geronimo, a "hula hula dancer" at the Pines Hotel, approached him in September 1944 with a letter she claimed was from the guerrillas. "I called on Mr. Eugenio Lopez in his home and attempted to deliver the letter addressed to him," Geronimo recalled in a sworn statement after the war. "He refused to accept it, saying that it would first have to be cleared by the Kempeitai."[223] In his postwar interrogation about this incident, Lopez explained that another prominent Baguio resident had been arrested by the Kempeitai after accepting a similar letter. Since Lopez knew that Judy Geronimo was one of the Pines Hotel hostesses who were "very close friends of the Japanese military police," he naturally "suspected he was being tested by the Japanese."[224] As it turned out, her letter was legitimate. Two weeks later, the Kempeitai arrested her. "I was asked many other questions about the guerrillas, and I was kept for two weeks, during which time I was tortured," Geronimo recalled. "I was taken to Bining, Mountain Province on 16 October [1944], by three Japanese soldiers, where I was shot and buried. The Japanese then left, and some Igorots took me to the hills and took care of me." In April 1945, she made a formal complaint to the U.S. Counter Intelligence Corps that Lopez had betrayed her to the Japanese.[225] In September, CIC agents investigated her charges but uncovered contradictory evidence insufficient for an indictment.[226]

Four months later, the Philippine Department of Justice sent two confidential agents to Baguio where they interrogated the principals in the case, notably Eugenio Lopez. "During the interview, Subject was calm, very cooperative and spoke spontaneously and freely," wrote Agents No. 43 and No. 50. "He acted sincerely and showed no fear. It is the opinion of the undersigned agents that Subject is 100% Filipino and pro-American, and therefore recommend that . . . the case be considered closed."[227] Within weeks, Special Prosecutor Emmanuel Pelaez concurred and asked that the case against Lopez be "definitely dropped," a recommendation approved by his superior, Lorenzo Tañada.[228] As he had done with the Japanese Kempeitai, Eugenio Lopez had divined the logic of power relations even in extraordinary political circumstances and survived by turning his would-be persecutors into protectors.

There was also a familial dimension to Eugenio Lopez's mastery of these strained wartime circumstances. By protecting his family from suffering during these difficult years, he inspired reverence among his children, fostering memories, later myths, that could be passed on to succeeding generations. In a special supplement published in the *Chronicle* a decade after Eugenio's death, Oscar Lopez was asked "when he began to be aware of his father's importance and power." His answer is revealing.

> It was during the war that he showed his capacity for leadership. It really dawned on me. We were all in Baguio during the latter part of the war and he dealt with the Japanese. . . . The Japanese military leaders always respected him. The time came when he got caught with other prominent citizens in Baguio listening to the short-wave radio which was not allowed. They were all brought to the police—the Kempeitai—and interrogated. Of course, he was asked why he was listening to the radio and his answer was: "Well, I want to find out how the war was going and you wouldn't allow us, yet I felt I had to know." You'd have expected that he would be imprisoned but the Japanese let him go, because he told the truth. He kept telling us later, "This is one thing the Japanese respects—you should always tell the truth. You try to hide something from them and they will not respect you."

While Eugenio spent most of the war at his summer home in Baguio, Fernando Lopez remained in Iloilo where he published the pro-Japanese daily *Panay Shu-Ho*. Like most of the provincial elite, who cultivated allies on both sides of the battle lines, the Lopez faction had maintained contact with pro-American guerrillas through USAFFE intelligence officers, among them Captain Patricio Miguel, a prewar Lopez supporter in the city police, and Captain Alfredo Gestoso, who helped Fernando escape from the city at the war's end and later protected him from collaboration charges.[229] Indeed, throughout the war Zulueta supporters, still allied with the Lopezes, staffed the guerrilla headquarters of Colonel Macario Peralta. As tension built in the ranks of the resistance between resistance-governor Confesor and Colonel Peralta, Zulueta supporters issued orders for the arrest of Confesor and his aides on wartime murder charges. Although Confesor escaped to U.S. Army headquarters on liberated Leyte in late 1944, Peralta's guerrillas arrested his aides, including Deputy-Governor Mariano Benedicto, and imprisoned them for the duration.

As Allied armies approached the Philippines, local factional tensions revived over the issue of Lopez's gambling casinos. By early 1944, Fernando controlled a network of casinos in Iloilo City operating under the protection of the Japanese Army.[230] In anticipation of possible famine, Governor Caram was urging intensified food production. He ordered the closing of all casinos six days a week, an obvious attack on Lopez.[231] In November, soldiers from the Bureau of Constabulary, a force still under Caram's control, raided a *monte* card game at Fernando's La Paz mansion and detained him for questioning by a Japanese officer.[232] However, these ongoing factional fights were already being overshadowed by the landing of Allied forces at Leyte in October. As the U.S. Army swept the archipelago, the impending invasion of Panay focused the local elite's attention on the criminal charges of collaboration that would surely follow.

Collaboration Charges

Throughout much of 1945, the U.S. Army's occupation of the Philippines posed a significant threat to the Lopez brothers' political future. With a global reputation as a resistance hero, Tomas Confesor now became interior secretary in the cabinet of President Sergio Osmeña. As a passionate critic of wartime collaborators, Confesor emerged briefly as the country's most powerful politician. Moreover, the Lopez brothers had been steadfast in their support of President Quezon, who had died of tuberculosis in 1944, and now enjoyed limited access to his rival and successor, Osmeña. With their old enemy at the side of a neutral president, the Lopezes had to maneuver to protect their political and economic assets.

When the Allies invaded Iloilo in March 1945, General Courtney Whitney, MacArthur's staff officer for guerrilla operations, appointed Confesor's aide, Mariano Benedicto, as mayor of Iloilo City and his brother, Patricio Confesor, as provincial governor. With American soldiers to protect them from reprisals by rival guerrilla factions, the Confesor group quickly regained lost power. As a prominent wartime collaborator Fernando Lopez, by contrast, was under threat of arrest.

Until the end of the army's occupation of Iloilo in August 1945, the CIC investigated local collaborators for possible prosecution on charges of treason. Seizing any weapon in their incessant struggle, Iloilo's factions exploited the CIC's reliance on anonymous informers to attack local rivals. Rather than unifying to defend the principle of collaboration, the two most prominent wartime officials, Fermin Caram and Fernando Lopez, accused each other of treason. In an interview with the CIC, Francisco ("Frank") Lopez Jison, Fernando's cousin and close ally, informed an investigator that Oscar Nava, a former lieutenant in the Japanese-sponsored Bureau of Constabulary and Caram's son-in-law, had stolen two machine lathes from a Lopez family sugar central in 1943 and later sold them to the Japanese. To back their allegations that Nava was a war profiteer, Jison's wife, the daughter of Vicente Lopez, Sr., added that Mrs. Nava had bought diamonds from many of the province's wealthiest women during the war.[233] Five days later, on 4 July 1945, the CIC imprisoned Nava. Despite Dr. Caram's complaints to Senator Manuel Roxas that the arrest was the result of Lopez intrigues, the evidence was strong enough to keep Oscar Nava under indictment for treason until his accidental death in 1946.[234]

Caram and his supporters retaliated with detailed allegations that Frank Lopez Jison had collaborated with the Japanese. In a series of statements to CIC agents and Filipino investigators made between 1945 and 1947, Caram charged that "he knew of dinners and banquets offered by Frank Jison to high-

The Lopez Family: A Patrilineal Genealogy

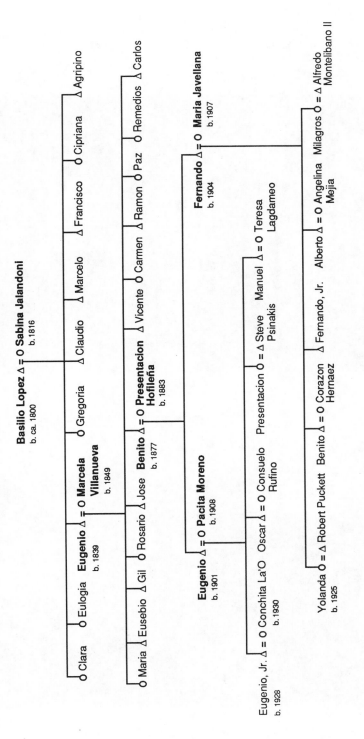

Sr. V. Lopez, Vicepresidente
Sr. R. MONTINOLA, FISCAL PROV.
(Sr. B. LOPEZ, Gob. Prov.) (Mr. J. F. SMIT, Gob. Gral.)

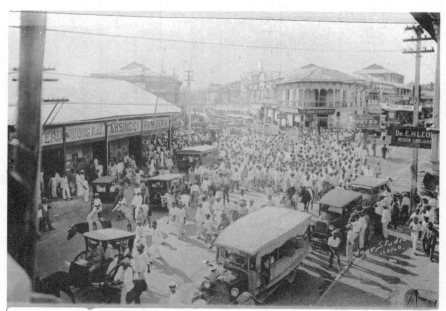

For three generations, Lopezes have courted the occupant of Malacañang Palace, whether colonial governor or Philippine president. In November 1906 (see upper left), Iloilo's provincial government held a reception for the U.S. governor general James F. Smith—including (left to right) Governor Benito Lopez, Smith, Municipal Vice-President Vicente Lopez, and Fiscal Ruperto Montinola.

In October 1930, after a press campaign mounted by Eugenio and Fernando Lopez, then neophyte newspaper publishers, Iloilo governor Mariano B. Arroyo was dismissed from office by the U.S. governor general. When Arroyo landed at the Iloilo waterfront from Manila (see lower left), supporters staged an automobile parade to protest his dismissal.

In March 1939, Commonwealth President Manuel Quezon (shown above) received the Lopez family at Manila's Malacañang Palace. Standing in the first row are the children of Eugenio and Fernando Lopez, including (left to right) Albertito, Fernando, Jr., Benito, Eugenio, Jr., and Presentacion, the president's godchild. Standing in the rear are Yolanda, Fernando, Sr., Mrs. Mariquit Lopez, Quezon, Mrs. Pacita Lopez, and Eugenio, Sr.

After independence in 1946, the Lopez brothers entered politics for better access to
executive power and courted President Elipidio Quirino. In the 1949 elections,
Fernando Lopez was Quirino's running mate on the winning Liberal Party ticket. After
a divisive campaign which split the party, rival leaders reconciled at Manila's Union
Club (see above). Emerging around midnight, they paused for a photograph,
including (front row, left to right) Vice-President-elect Lopez, President Quirino, Senator
Jose Avelino, and House Speaker Eugenio Perez.

At first, Lopez relations with Quirino were close, as could be seen (upper right)
when *Manila Chronicle* publisher Eugenio Lopez, Sr. (left) shared an intimate moment
with President Quirino beneath the pines of Baguio City, the Philippines' summer
capital.

Later relations became strained. During the 1953 presidential campaign
(see lower right), rumors circulated that Quirino was going to dump Lopez as his
running mate. The vice-president returned home to Iloilo City where he was met by a
torch-light parade of supporters rallying for their favorite son.

Denied renomination on the Liberal Party ticket, Vice-President Fernando Lopez joined Carlos Romulo's new Democratic Party as his running mate (see above). Shown at the party's formal launching in May 1953 are (left to right) Romulo, Lopez, and Mrs. Mariquit Lopez.

After the Democratic Party collapsed during the campaign, the Lopezes backed Nacionalista Party presidential candidate Ramon Magsaysay. Showing his influence with the new administration (see above right), in January 1954 *Manila Chronicle* publisher Eugenio Lopez, Sr. (far right) held a dinner party at his Manila home for (left to right) New York banker Dorsey Richard, former U.S. ambassador to the Philippines Myron Cowen, and President Magsaysay.

When Magsaysay died in an air wreck, the Lopezes allied themselves with his successor, President Carlos Garcia. In May 1961 (see above), Eugenio Lopez, Sr. (center) met with President Garcia (right) at Malacañang Palace and won approval for acquisition of the country's leading utility, the Manila Electric Company (Meralco).

Under President Ferdinand Marcos, the Lopez courtship of the Palace brought them triumph and disaster. At the climax of a deadlocked Nacionalista Party convention in November 1964 (see above), Fernando Lopez and Marcos, rivals for the presidential nomination, announced their alliance. On the stage at the Manila Hotel were (front row, left to right) Mrs. Imelda Marcos, Marcos (in dark suit), Lopez, and (partly concealed by an unidentified woman) disappointed candidate Emmanuel Pelaez.

Until their break in 1970, the Lopezes celebrated their proximity to President Marcos with public rituals. In a ceremony at Malacañang Palace sometime in 1969–70 (lower left), Marcos decorated financier Eugenio Lopez, his chief political patron, for services to the nation. In February 1969 (upper left), Marcos met with leaders of the National Federation of Sugarcane Planters at the Manila Hotel—including (left to right) Marcos, Philippine National Bank president Roberto S. Benedicto, industry leader Alfredo Montelibano, Sr., and Fernando Lopez.

In July 1969 (see upper left), Eugenio Lopez, Sr., celebrated his sixty-eighth birthday with a dinner party at the Manila Hilton. On the receiving line were (left to right) Mrs. Vicki Quirino Gonzalez, the daughter of President Quirino; Eugenio Lopez, Sr.; First Lady Imelda Marcos; Marcos; Mrs. Pacita Lopez, Eugenio's wife; Vice-President Fernando Lopez; and his wife Mrs. Mariquit Lopez.

The Lopezes were always careful to court the Church (see lower left). In November 1971, Vice-President Fernando Lopez (left) returned home to Iloilo City where he met with political ally Monsignor Jaime Sin (center), then auxiliary bishop of Jaro.

After declaring martial law in 1972, President Marcos confiscated many Lopez corporations. At a press conference in January 1985 (above), Oscar Lopez (far right), son of Eugenio Lopez, Sr., and president of the family holding corporation, presented the Lopez claims to ownership of the ABS-CBN media conglomerate seized by Marcos a decade earlier. Appearing with Lopez were Bienvenido Calleja (left) and Camilo Quiazon (center).

ranking Japanese Army and Navy officers." Through the sale of sugar, steel rails, and an electrical generator to the enemy, Jison and his cousin Fernando Lopez, in Caram's view, "made much money during the Japanese occupation." Most damningly, Caram claimed personal knowledge that Jison had warned the military of an impending guerrilla attack on Jaro in February 1945, leading to a successful Japanese counterattack in which "more than 500 Filipino guerrillas died." Freely admitting his antipathies towards the Lopez group, Caram told investigators that there was a "long-standing enmity (political in nature)" and alleged that "Fernando Lopez and Frank Jison have unjustly accused his son-in-law Oscar Nava . . . before the American CIC of treasonable collaboration."[235] In a supporting statement to the CIC, Caram's closest ally, union leader Jose Nava, gave evidence against both Frank Jison and Vicente V. Lopez, Fernando's uncle and former guardian. Jison's supposed crimes included the prewar rape and murder of a Manila waitress, brokering large quantities of sugar and machinery to the Japanese in 1943–44, and harboring a "notorious spy."[236]

For the American CIC agents, Dr. Caram's service as Iloilo governor under the Japanese may have lent some credibility to his version of events behind enemy lines. Perhaps unaware of the factional alliances across the battle lines, the American agents supplemented Caram's charges with a corroborating statement from Governor Confesor's aides in the resistance and recommended Jison's indictment.[237] In March 1946, the People's Court charged Jison with three counts of treason, all of them strikingly similar to Caram's original allegations.[238]

Although the case never came to trial, efforts directed at obtaining a dismissal embroiled Jison and the Lopezes in appeals and reinvestigations that dragged on for nearly two years. After a second investigation, Agent No. 160 of the Justice Department reported in August 1946 that the key witnesses in the case were allied with Caram and Confesor, "both bitter economic and political enemies of Mr. Fernando Lopez." Significantly, they supposedly had given their evidence "to put down the Lopez and Jison families." Moreover, Caram himself "suspected that it was Frank Jison who filed a treason charge against his son-in-law, the then Capt. Oscar Nava." Citing Jison's contributions to the guerrillas and his donations of food to the poor during the war, the agent described him as "a real, an unknown patriot." Consequently, Agent 160 recommended that "the complaint against Frank Jison be quashed."[239] In May 1947, nearly two years after the original investigation began, the People's Court prosecutor concurred with his agent's findings, writing that "the evidence was not sufficient" to sustain the allegations and urging a dismissal.[240]

In addition to the CIC investigations, the Confesor faction used the collaboration issue to harass the Lopezes during the U.S. Army's administration of the province. However, once the U.S. Civil Affairs Unit left Iloilo in August 1945, the Lopez faction rebounded with a strong political counterattack. The offensive opened with an editorial in the *Times* excoriating the inefficiency of the city police, most of whom had been guerrillas in wartime governor Tomas Confesor's provincial guard.[241] Through Congressman Jose Zulueta's intercession, President Osmeña appointed Fernando Lopez mayor of Iloilo City in September 1945, sparking a concerted anticollaborationist attack from Lopez's local rivals. Governor Patricio Confesor wired the U.S. interior secretary, Harold Ickes, the leading critic of Filipino collaborators, advising him that "pro-Japanese have been appointed to government positions."[242] When Malacañang refused to transmit Confesor's telegram to Washington, he wired the U.S. High Commission in Manila, complaining that "Fernando Lopez who has been refused CIC clearance . . . in view of serious charges against him has been appointed Mayor of Iloilo City."[243]

When the public outcry subsided after the mayor's inauguration, the editor of the pro-Confesor newspaper *Ang Tigbatas,* Ezequiel Villalobos, began a series of anti-Lopez editorials. Once the founding editor of the *Times,* the Lopez-owned daily, Villalobos had become an inveterate critic after his humiliating dismissal in the early 1930s.[244] He had survived the war years by serving as editor of Fernando's *Panay Shu-Ho,* but secretly he had documented his publisher's dealings with the Japanese in a detailed diary. "It seems that Fernando Lopez has perfected his self defense," he noted in an entry dated 2 August 1945. In reference to Fernando's reaction to collaboration charges, he wrote: "It is evident that he has bribed some guerrilla leaders."[245] In a 16 November *Tigbatas* editorial, he issued an ultimatum: Lopez must resign or he would publish a four-part series exposing Fernando for what he was—instrumental in the establishment of the *Panay Shu-Ho,* on intimate terms with the Japanese, a supplier of war materials to the enemy, and "general factotum" of the Japanese.[246] But, by the time the series was published in December, the collaboration issue was fading, and the exposé had almost no effect on Fernando's meteoric political rise.

Although Confesor's group had little political success in their fight against the Lopezes, they did succeed in destroying their land transport business. When the Lopezes tried to reopen Panay Autobus after the war, rumors of the company's collaboration became so strong that its assistant manager denounced them as "malicious reports . . . intended to destroy our enviable record of public service."[247] When the U.S. Civil Affairs unit ceased operations in August 1945, it sold thirteen of its thirty-five trucks to small operators and only sixteen to Panay Autobus—over the protests of the Lopezes who were desperate for units.[248] Unable to deny his competition access to vehicles, Fernando next tried to bankrupt them by reducing his fares from P0.03 per kilometer to P0.024.[249] Governor Patricio Confesor denounced the new fares as a Lopez attempt at "unrestrained monopoly," and produced an affidavit from Japan's Alien Property Custodian claiming that Lopez had sold Panay Autobus to a Japanese firm in 1943 for P260,000.[250] In retaliation, Mayor Lopez issued orders to city police for the arrest of any operator charging more than the P0.03 fare.[251]

In the end, it was the "jeepney" that destroyed the Lopez monopoly. In preparation for the invasion of Japan, General MacArthur's command had built sprawling supply depots around Manila and filled them with trucks, jeeps, airplanes, and landing craft. When Japan capitulated without invasion, the U.S. Army transferred the surplus to the Philippine government as war-damage payments, creating instant profit potential for postwar entrepreneurs. At the end of the war, the Philippine government sold surplus jeeps to Filipino buyers who began converting them into eight- and fourteen-passenger vehicles, dubbed "jeepneys," with a capital cost far less than the larger buses. The Lopezes fought a losing battle before the Public Service Commission seeking to block the licensing of the new operators. Felipe Ysmael, an intimate of Lopez rival Dr. Caram and a corporate lawyer who usually served only wealthy clients, personally represented ninety-six jeepney operators between 1946 and 1948. In almost every case he won their licenses over the objections of Lopez lawyers. Most of these clients claimed operating capital of P3,000 for their jeeps, a small investment compared to Panay Autobus's prewar capitalization of P500,000.[252] Unable to compete, the Lopezes sold Panay Autobus in the early 1950s. It was their last major investment in their home province. By 1955, only the Iloilo City Colleges, an unprofitable cement factory, and some real estate remained of the once substantial Lopez interests in Iloilo City.

The Move to Manila

Above all else, the rise of the Lopez brothers to wealth and power in the postwar decades sprang from their success at rent seeking under the new Republic. The family's formal move to Manila, and subsequent national prominence, followed similar shifts initiated in the 1930s by sugar families such as the Cojuangcos and Aranetas. But no other family experienced such an extraordinarily rapid rise into the first rank of the nation's economic elite. Viewed from within their faction and family councils, this success seems to stem from the symbiosis of Eugenio's skillful entrepreneurship and Fernando's political influence.

Backed by Eugenio's growing wealth, Fernando Lopez rose from mayor of Iloilo City to vice-president of the Republic in only four years. Following his appointment as mayor in September 1945, Fernando served for two years. He was then elected to the Senate in 1947. At the Liberal Party's 1949 presidential convention, he was chosen as President Elpidio Quirino's running mate over Jose Yulo, a bitter rival. Elected vice-president in 1949, Fernando provided important political support for Eugenio's corporate acquisitions, most notably the Biscom takeover of 1950.

Despite some factional tensions over Manuel Roxas's presidential campaign, Fernando Lopez and Jose Zulueta had remained allied against Tomas Confesor's faction throughout 1946 and into 1947. But Confesor disappeared as a political force after his followers suffered defeats in the postwar elections and he was indicted for wartime murders. With their mutual enemy eliminated, Lopez and Zulueta began a prolonged battle for control of Iloilo Province. Although Zulueta retained his base in the First District, south of the city, Fernando quickly secured overall leadership of the province, relegating Zulueta to the position of perennial challenger. Moreover, Rodolfo Ganzon, son of prewar Iloilo mayor Leopoldo Ganzon, used anti-Lopez rhetoric to win political control over Iloilo City in the 1950s. But Fernando remained the province's recognized leader until the declaration of martial law in 1972.

As the country moved from Commonwealth status to independence in 1946, relations with Malacañang Palace took on increased importance for the country's business leaders. Aware of the executive's power over the economy, the Lopez brothers prospered under the administrations of their allies, Sergio Osmeña (1945–46) and Elpidio Quirino (1948–53), but suffered somewhat from cooler relations with Manuel Roxas (1946–48).

The April 1946 presidential elections were the culmination of a bitter battle between Osmeña and Roxas for Quezon's mantle. The Lopez brothers reacted to this struggle by adopting an essentially pragmatic strategy. They began the long campaign cautiously inclined towards the incumbent, Osmeña, but in the final days, when they could no longer be punished for disloyalty, they jumped safely aboard the Roxas bandwagon. There were, of course, sound factional reasons for the Lopezes to prefer an alliance with Osmeña. Since mid-1945, their group had benefited from his appointment of their ally Alfredo Montelibano as secretary of national defense. Moreover, their enemies the sugar millers, led by Jose Yulo and Joaquin Elizalde, were Roxas's key supporters.

Not surprisingly, the Lopez group's outward support for Osmeña was evident from the beginning. In a letter dated December 1945, for example, Eulogio Garganera wrote his patron Roxas that the Lopez brothers and their newspapers "are more for the [Osmeña] administration than they are for you."[253] But from the outset the Lopezes were pursuing a more subtle strategy, with Fernando campaigning openly for Osmeña while Eugenio joined the wealthy Manila businessmen who financed Roxas. As early as June 1945, the American consul general at Manila had listed Eugenio Lopez as one of the "supporters of Roxas who have very large financial interests in the Philippines."[254]

In the campaign's last weeks, members of the Lopez group were arrayed between the rival candidates with a symmetry that seems calculated. As a cabinet member, Montelibano sided with Osmeña and campaigned actively for him to the end.[255] Fernando Lopez, having accepted Osmeña's appointment as mayor of Iloilo City in 1945, also remained loyal throughout.[256] Campaigning in his birthplace and bailiwick of Navalas on Guimaras Island, Mayor Lopez, in the words of a local rival, said that "if the people loves [sic] him. . . to give to Roxas a big zero in the poll, or the most that they give is ten (10) votes only"—a request fulfilled on election day when Roxas got 10 votes to Osmeña's 280.[257] Acting more cautiously in Iloilo City, Fernando tried to explain, if not excuse, his support for Osmeña as simple reciprocity, citing "my sense of honor," which "cannot permit that I go against a man who . . . cleared me from the charge of collaboration engineered by my political detractors."[258]

By contrast, Oscar Ledesma and Eugenio Lopez made an eleventh-hour leap to Roxas's side in the campaign's closing weeks. Cautiously allied with Roxas from the outset, Eugenio sent him a major contribution of P40,000 through a reliable intermediary in the campaign's critical final weeks.[259] Ledesma's switch was more dramatic. Only a month before the elections, a Roxas leader reported that "in Jaro . . . the Ledesmas are open for Osmeña."[260] Oscar himself, running for reelection to Congress in Iloilo's Second District, "revealed himself to be Osmeña's candidate" in a public meeting before the Cine Eagle.[261] In fact, Ledesma's position was more ambiguous. Praising Roxas as "a man of real worth whose ability and prestige are recognized not only in the Philippines but also in the United States," Ledesma told an Iloilo audience that he was supporting Osmeña because he felt "morally bound" by favors received from the president.[262] Then, only two days before voting commenced on 23 April, an ally wired Roxas with news of Ledesma's sudden reversal: "On Speaker Zulueta's pressure Ledesma changed attitude and now recommends your candidacy. In his meeting last night he praised you while not mentioning Osmeña."[263]

The strategy worked. In the months following the elections, the Lopez group formed an amicable alliance with the new president. Only a month after the voting, Fernando and the president became *compadre* when the first lady, Trinidad de Leon Roxas, stood as sponsor at the wedding of Lopez's daughter.[264] Roxas renewed Fernando's appointment as mayor of Iloilo City and sponsored his nomination for the Liberal Party senatorial slate in the 1947 elections.[265] During that campaign when Lopez complained that party leaders in Negros were "sabotaging my candidacy," Roxas wired the provincial governor explaining that Lopez is "loyally for our party in Negros as elsewhere" and ordering support for "our straight senatorial ticket."[266] With his election to the Senate, Fernando followed his brother to Manila. Although he would return to Iloilo periodically to maintain his provincial base, his home was now in the capital where he, like his brother, joined an emerging national elite.

After spending the war quietly in Baguio, Eugenio Lopez had moved to Manila following the city's liberation and soon emerged as a major entrepreneur. The war had, quite literally, liquidated most of his investments in Iloilo. Instead of rebuilding in the province, he transferred his capital to Manila. At war's end, he had filed a substantial claim with the U.S. War Damage Commission asking reimbursement for the army's expropriation of Panay Autobus vehicles. With the support of Colonel Francicso Offemaria, who had served as USAFFE transport officer (Sixty-first Division) in 1941–42, Eugenio claimed a huge daily rental from the time the units were commandeered in 1941 until liberation in 1945. In an interview given shortly before his death, Offemaria claimed that Eugenio recovered over a million dollars, an assertion that neither the Lopezes nor the documentary record has confirmed.[267]

Although his war-damage payments may have been significant during his first years in Manila, Eugenio's growing network of contacts gave him more than adequate access to private and public financing. Building upon the sugar industry's historic relations with state financial institutions, he secured credit for his corporations from the Philippine National Bank (PNB) and the Development Bank of the Philippines (DBP) that totaled P88 million by 1962. Among his thirteen major accounts, the DBP would provide P32 million for the Binalbagan-Isabela Sugar Mill and the PNB would lend P35 million for the Manila Electric Company.[268]

Apparently wary of depending upon the government for his corporate financing, Eugenio worked closely with allies during the 1950s to organize his own institution, the Philippine Commercial and Industrial Bank (PCIB). After long delays, the result of policy disputes between the sugar bloc and the Central Bank,[269] PCIB's incorporators finally won a license in 1958 and opened for business in February 1960. Although Eugenio and his wife Pacita were the bank's largest shareholders, with 12 percent of the stock, they apparently decided to distance themselves from its actual operations, and asked Alfredo Montelibano, the sugar bloc's preeminent leader, to serve as chairman.[270] Although Eugenio did not play a visible role, all the major shareholders were reliable associates. Montelibano held 2.4 percent of the stock and Roberto S. Benedicto, a Lopez corporate attorney, had 1.2 percent.[271] Starting from a position as the country's ninth-largest bank in 1960, PCIB grew quickly under Montelibano's chairmanship to become the third-largest within five years.[272] To fund this expansion, PCIB sold additional shares, 52.7 percent of the company, to investors outside the Lopez group. However, by expanding Eugenio's share to 19.3 percent and Montelibano's to 12.2, the group still retained corporate control.[273] Although it was launched with a broader ownership base than most of the Philippines' family-dominated private banks, PCIB soon came to serve the narrower interests of the Lopezes and the sugar bloc. "Eventually, they [PCIB] became over solicitous of one sector," recalled Jose ("Jobo") Fernandez, Central Bank governor and the founding president of the Far Eastern Bank and Trust Company. "They were a sugar bank, and they were fairly happy tagging themselves as a sugar bank."[274]

Drawing from these diverse sources of capital, Eugenio Lopez made a series of major acquisitions after the war. His first investment was in Far Eastern Air Transport, Inc. (FEATI), the successor to his prewar provincial airline, now reorganized as an international carrier and equipped with American war-surplus planes.[275] Reflecting the character of regulated airlines as rents, FEATI's fortunes would follow the ebb and flow of the Lopez group's relations with Malacañang Palace, expanding under Sergio Osmeña and collapsing when Manuel Roxas took office. Organized in 1945 under the Osmeña administration, FEATI soon grew into a major domestic and international carrier with routes reaching as far as Calcutta and Shanghai. Significantly, the cabinet officer responsible for aviation policy, Defense Secretary Alfredo Montelibano, was a Lopez ally who used his authority to grant FEATI a monopoly on international routes out of Manila and a disproportionate share of domestic routes. The rival Philippine Airlines (PAL) was controlled by a close Roxas associate, financier Colonel Andres Soriano, and consequently was handicapped in its dealings with Osmeña.

When Secretary Montelibano awarded FEATI a major expansion of its domestic routes on 20 October 1945, Soriano complained to President Osmeña that the apportionment of lines was "unfair, arbitrary and discriminatory to Philippine Air Lines." Soriano was particularly incensed that a Cebu-Mindanao route awarded to PAL in 1941 was now transferred to the rival FEATI.[276] A month later, Osmeña cabled Soriano at his hotel in New York City affirming the equity of the decision and asking that the issue "be held in abeyance until your return and the whole matter thoroughly examined."[277] By deferring the matter indefinitely, Osmeña, by default, confirmed Montelibano's allocation of the air routes to FEATI.

After his inauguration in 1946, President Roxas cancelled FEATI's monopoly by declaring an open-skies policy, in effect rewarding his ally Soriano and punishing the Lopez brothers who had qualified their support for him in the April elections.[278] Moreover, FEATI suffered a major crash in January 1947 that weakened its competitive position against PAL.[279] In May of that year Eugenio sold his family's 78 percent interest in FEATI to PAL for P2.8 million.[280]

With his profits from FEATI and other investments, Eugenio acquired the Manila Chronicle Publishing Company in September 1947 and then purchased a network of radio stations. As a well-edited paper staffed by the capital's best journalists, the *Manila Chronicle* quickly established itself as a leading national daily, providing the Lopez brothers with the same leverage in postwar Manila that *El Tiempo* had allowed them in prewar Iloilo. Throughout the next two decades of their controversy-laden climb to national power, the *Chronicle* served the Lopez interests as a flexible political instrument, hammering away at the venality of their enemies and trumpeting the virtues of their allies. The broadcasting operation grew more slowly from its beginnings as a small radio-manufacturing operation. Its evolution into a national radio and television network gave the brothers access to two very different audiences—peasant voters who listened to vernacular broadcasts on cheap, transistorized radios, and Manila's middle-class professionals who viewed television as a less-partisan medium than the daily press.

Recognizing the profit potential of U.S. Army surplus goods, Eugenio also established the Bolinao Electronics Corporation, in June 1946, to manufacture radio receivers from surplus parts. Three years later, when the exhaustion of these supplies and the imposition of import controls on new components hampered manufacturing, Bolinao switched to broadcasting and opened its first station, Radio DZBC, in the Manila suburb of San Juan. In 1953, Bolinao, now called ABS, opened Radio DZAQ, equipped with a fifty-kilowatt transmitter that could reach the whole country. That same year, ABS introduced television to the Philippines, operating at a loss for several years until there were enough consumer receivers to make the medium profitable. According to one account, President Magsaysay repaid a political debt to the Lopezes by foreclosing on government loans to radio stations owned by Antonio Quirino, younger brother of their enemy former president Quirino, thus facilitating expansion of the Lopez network.[281]

In 1956, the Lopezes established a separate network, the Chronicle Broadcasting Network (CBN), using it to operate a string of radio and television stations until they merged it with ABS to form ABS-CBN. Indicative of the corporation's success, Eugenio ("Geny") Lopez, Jr. (1928–), the first-born of Eugenio, Sr., opened the ABS-CBN "Broadcast Center" in December 1968, a facility described as the most modern studio in Asia with the exception of the NHK complex in Tokyo.[282] By 1972, ABS-CBN had become the largest media network in the Philippines with seven television and twenty-one radio stations nationwide. From the rented barn that had housed Radio DZBC in 1949, the network had grown into a conglomerate with twenty-three hundred employees and assets of P119 million.[283] Despite the capital requirements of such rapid expansion, the Lopez brothers financed the growth from internal sources and continued to control both ABS-CBN and the *Manila Chronicle* through the Benpres Corporation, an investment firm wholly owned by the brothers.[284]

Throughout this quarter century of steady growth, dozens of ABS-CBN broadcast licenses required initial government approval and periodic renewals, a process that would have been prohibitively expensive without political connections. If political impotence had doomed FEATI in 1947, when Fernando was just a freshman senator, then political influence assisted ABS-CBN's success after 1949 when Fernando became vice-president. As the Lopezes would discover when President Marcos declared martial law in 1972, broadcasting constituted an extreme form of rents, one that was exceptionally vulnerable to state regulation.

Battle Over Biscom

Perhaps the most profitable, and certainly the most politicized, of Eugenio Lopez's postwar acquisitions was the Binalbagan-Isabela Milling Company (Biscom). A consolidation of five damaged mills located in southern Negros Occidental, Biscom became, after its reconstruction in 1948, the largest sugar mill in Southeast Asia. Most Negros sugar centrals had become battlegrounds in postwar political struggles between planters and millers. Biscom was no exception. After decades of experience in the sugar industry, many of Negros's leading families had the capital and skill to expand their interests at a time when the new Republic lacked strong leadership. Moreover, the original thirty-year milling contracts were expiring almost simultaneously, opening a renewed debate over the division of milled sugar between mills and plantations. The result was a broad-front political battle, epitomized at Biscom, concerning both the sharing of processed sugar and ownership of the factories.

In its political essentials, the battle for Biscom seems a reprise of the prewar struggle over Panay Autobus. Most importantly, Eugenio's bid for the Philippines' largest sugar-milling factory was a revealing exercise in rent seeking. Through personal access to the executive, Lopez was able to secure state intervention to effect a major corporate takeover. Once he was in control of Biscom, he imposed a management contract that allowed him to siphon its assets into his other enterprises just as he had done at Panay Autobus.

Before the war, the future Biscom district had been divided among five mills—three small Spanish firms, the Filipino-owned Isabela Sugar Company, and the government's Binalbagan Estate, Inc. (see map). Owned and financed by the Philippine National Bank, Binalbagan Estate had operated as a model factory, showcasing improved labor relations, planter participation, and technological innovation. But, despite the government's good intentions, district planters demanded a larger share of the milled sugar and had lobbied Manila for the right to purchase the mill, a bid that President Quezon rejected in 1937.[285] Isabela Sugar, by contrast, was a private corporation controlled by the Montillas, a leading planter family. In 1924, Gil Montilla, then governor of Negros Occidental, had led the province's planters in lobbying the PNB to finance construction of modern mills. He had gained control of the Isabela Sugar Co., a medium-capacity factory erected in his home district.[286] With Gil's election as speaker of the National Assembly in 1935, the family-controlled board elected a younger relative, Enrique J. C. Montilla, to succeed him as Isabela's manager.[287]

After World War II, extensive damage complicated both reconstruction and planter-miller relations in southern Negros. During the war, Negros Occidental's sugar factories had suffered to such an extent that milling in many districts was suspended after liberation. Anti-Japanese guerrilla operations were particularly intense in southern Negros and all five sugar mills suffered heavy damage, particularly the Isabela factory. "We had decided to preserve several key centrals in Negros in order not to damage the economic development of the country," recalled Colonel Salvador Abcede, the island's wartime guerrilla commander. "In the Biscom area Binalbagan central was preserved and Isabela was destroyed. Isabela was producing alcohol in its distillery and it was close to guerrilla areas in the mountains. So on two counts it was necessary to destroy the Isabela central." Regarding the three Spanish-owned centrals in the Kabankalan area as "a remnant of Spanish colonialism," the commander "decided to eliminate them" as well.[288] Although Isabela's physical plant was largely ruined, the war allowed the Montillas to assume full ownership of the corporation. Runaway inflation had eroded the value of Japanese military currency, allowing Enrique Montilla to eliminate the family's indebtedness to the PNB by making a legally binding payment of "P1,200,000 in Mickey Mouse currency during the occupation." Thus, the Montillas emerged from the war in an improved financial position.[289]

Political conflicts between planters and millers resumed in 1946–47 when Jose Yulo and his brother-in-law, J. Amado Araneta, won an unprecedented concentration of milling capacity. In a proxy battle with the Gamboa-Lizares family, they captured a controlling interest in three of Negros Occidental's nine surviving mills. In other districts, the planters decided that the solution to the milling problem was planter acquisition of the sugar factories. Their takeovers intersected with the government's reconstruction activities and the ongoing planter-miller controversy to produce a complex politics that bore directly upon the sugar industry, providing the executive branch with extraordinary influence.

Through both his economic programs and political alliances, Manuel Roxas, the Republic's first president, played a central role in the rehabilitation of the sugar industry. At a conference with industry leaders held in November 1946, he announced that "he greatly favored consolidation of the milling districts wherever possible" and promised state financing through the new Rehabilitation Finance Corporation for "genuine rehabilitation projects."[290] The government's ownership of Binalbagan Estate and the extensive damage in southern Negros made this a prime area for consolidation. Indicative of the scale of financing required to resume milling in this district, an independent damage survey conducted in August 1946 by the Warner-Barnes Company, a leading sugar brokerage house, had calculated that the two mills, Binalbagan and Isabela, would require P6.5 million in reconstruction and development funds—P3.5 million to restore Binalbagan to its prewar capacity and the balance to finance an expansion that would serve an amalgamated district encompassing Isabela.[291]

Reflecting alliances forged for the April 1946 presidential elections, Roxas was sympathetic to the sugar millers. In the realignments within the Nacionalista Party that followed President Quezon's death in 1944, Joaquin ("Mike") Elizalde, owner of two mills, broke bitterly with Osmeña and led his closest ally among the millers, Jose Yulo, into an alliance with Roxas.[292] Similarly, the other leading miller faction, led by Amado Araneta and his ally Enrique Montilla, a prewar Yulo follower, financed the Negros branch of Roxas's Liberal Party.[293] Indeed, after the elections there were informed reports that "President Roxas leaned heavily on . . . Amado Araneta for advice in the sugar industry."[294] Since the Aranetas and Montillas had been allies within the industry since the 1920s, and both had supported Roxas's 1946 presidential bid, Enrique Montilla emerged as a powerful Liberal Party leader in southern Negros.[295] Moreover, within the overlapping alignments of factional politics in Negros, Montilla and the Lopez brothers were natural enemies. Not only were the Lopezes planters in Montilla's milling district but Montilla was married to Maria Arroyo, niece of the former Iloilo governor Mariano Arroyo whose career had been destroyed by *El Tiempo's* antigambling crusade of the early 1930s.[296]

In the ensuing negotiations over industry reconstruction, the Roxas administration offered Montilla a 46-percent share of the consolidated Binalbagan-Isabela Sugar Milling Company (known as Biscom), an offer that he accepted in early 1947.[297] As owner of the old Binalbagan Estate, the government retained control over the remaining 54 percent. In December, Biscom's ownership was restructured to finance a merger with the three small Spanish mills located near Kabankalan. Eighteen percent of Biscom's stock was awarded to the Spanish firms, reducing the government to the status of a minority shareholder with 44 percent, and increasing the potential power of Montilla's 38-percent share.[298] With Enrique Montilla serving as manager and vice-president, the newly organized Biscom applied to the Rehabilitation Finance Corporation (RFC) for P5 million in reconstruction funds and launched milling operations.[299]

After the first season proved the viability of the new mill, the political struggle for control over Biscom intensified. The sudden death of President Roxas in early 1948 and the accession of his vice-president, Elpidio Quirino, an Ilocano without direct ties to the sugar industry, introduced an unpredictable political element. Indicative of Quirino's flexibility, or malleability, on sugar issues, he campaigned for the presidency in 1949 with a leading planter, Fernando Lopez, as his running mate, and then ran for reelection in 1953 with a major miller, Jose Yulo. In March 1949, Enrique Montilla wrote to the Quirino administration asking that he be allowed to purchase its Biscom shares on the grounds that "the late President Manuel A. Roxas, advanced as an inducement . . . to join the merger, that in the event the government sold the shares . . . preference were to be given to Isabela Sugar Co."[300]

Fearful of Montilla's control, the planters served by Biscom countered with their own offer to purchase the government's shares. From the outset, planter-miller relations had been tense. When the new district's planters, led by Miguel Gatuslao, balked at signing new milling contracts with Montilla's management team, the RFC withheld approval of its financing for the mill.[301] As the 1948–49 season commenced, Gatuslao and Montilla exchanged hostile press releases over the mill's alleged failure to provide adequate rail transport to service the vast district.[302] "Enrique Montilla was very haughty and overbearing," recalled former congressman Carlos Hilado,[303]

> If you were a planter opposed to Montilla he would not give you the [rail]
> *vagones* due you so your canes would not be milled. And the planters thought
> Biscom was cheating them on the weighing and chemical analysis. Montilla,
> the planters said, was transferring tonnage to his friends. If you had seven tons
> of cane and were not close to Montilla, he would transfer two tons to a friend.

Initially, the government's sugar officials seemed inclined to extricate themselves from the controversy. In an internal memorandum to President Quirino, Binalbagan's administrators argued that "it has never been the policy of the Government, even from Quezon's era, to hold the control in the Sugar Centrals," and urged sale to the district planters. Failing that, they recommended that the government should act on Montilla's offer to purchase.[304] In December 1949, only weeks after his election to the presidency, Elpidio Quirino advised the parties concerned of his decision to sell all of the government's 177,941 Biscom shares at an auction restricted to Montilla and the district planters to be held in just two weeks.[305]

With President Roxas's death and Fernando Lopez's election as Quirino's vice-president, the Montillas had both lost their patron and seen their rival now ensconced at the right hand of the president. When Quirino announced that he would auction the government shares, the Lopez brothers, unbeknownst to Montilla, were already on the move.[306] Since they still owned their father's Hacienda Antolanga in Isabela, they identified themselves as district planters and led a challenge to the Montillas.

The bidding began on 3 January 1950. Enrique Montilla offered the government P1.95 million, equivalent to P11 per share, and forwarded a check for 10 percent of the purchase price to serve as deposit.[307] A week later, the district's planters, led by Miguel Gatuslao, informed Secretary of Justice Ricardo Nepomuceno of their intention to purchase the shares and requested a month's postponement of the bidding while they explored "ways and means" to organize "so considerable" an amount.[308] After the planters met on 7 February and unanimously endorsed the purchase, Gatuslao led a delegation that pressed Secretary Nepomuceno for another extension, explaining "how painful it is for us planters to find ourselves pitted against private capitalists when it comes to our desire to own the central in our district." He added that "unless we can own the Binalbagan Central ourselves, we prefer a thousand times to see the government . . . continue controlling it all the time."[309] Since the planters had failed to make a firm bid secured with a deposit, Nepomuceno wrote to President Quirino on 8 March recommending that the government extricate itself from "disputes of a private nature" by accepting Montilla's bid of P11 per share even though it was far below the stock's book value of P20.14.[310]

A month later, Miguel Gatuslao and Oscar Ledesma, the Lopez ally who was again serving as president of the National Federation of Sugarcane Planters, wrote to finance secretary Pio Pedrosa urging that the administration reject Montilla's bid to acquire the mill for "his family and relatives" because this purchase would cause "the great anxiety and prejudice of the large number of planters adhered to or milling at the central."[311] Further, since acquisition of all the government's shares would still not give the planters corporate control, the planters urged instead that the state cancel the sale and retain its interest to assure "the maintenance of the status quo in the present Central-Planter relations."[312] Accordingly, Secretary Pedrosa wrote to Quirino urging suspension of the Biscom sale "until such time as complete harmony obtains among the various components of the production in the industry."[313] Writing to the president directly on 11 May, Ledesma and Gatuslao amplified their case for government retention, arguing that Montilla's bid was far below the stock's book value.[314] Faced with such strong opposition to the sale from within his own administration, Quirino repeatedly postponed the bidding for nearly a year, allowing the planters time to locate financing.

From this point onward, the planters' campaign gained force, providing the Lopez group with an opening. Writing to President Quirino in May 1950, Ledesma and Gatuslao asked that the milling ratio at Biscom be set at "65% for the planter and 35% for the central," reminding him that resolution of this conflict was "entirely in your hands."[315] Working through sympathetic legislators, Ledesma introduced bills into the House and Senate with provisions that would raise the planters' share of milled sugar at all Philippine centrals to 70 percent.[316] Recognizing the threat this move held for his own company, Enrique Montilla advised Quirino that passage of the legislation "will mean bankruptcy of the Binalbagan-Isabela Sugar Co., Inc." and asked that he veto the legislation.[317] During this same period, the planters filed a case in the Supreme Court claiming exclusive ownership of the quota for sugar exports to the United States, an asset nearly equal in value to the mill's plant equipment.[318] Responding to the escalating pressure, and aware of a recent upward valuation of the mill's assets, Quirino's Council of State announced in June a new auction of the government's stock with two key provisions—the minimum price per share was set at P20 and the bidding would be closed to all but Montilla and the district planters.[319]

Following the announcement, Eugenio Lopez maneuvered skillfully, at both the local and national levels, to take control of the Binalbagan-Isabela Planters' Association, displacing the district's established leaders and reducing the pool of eligible planters, thereby positioning himself for a successful takeover. In elections for the presidency of the Binalbagan-Isabela Planters' Association, the Lopez group backed Emilio Camon, a local planter with strong ties to the district.[320] Camon was elected and soon joined another Lopez ally, Alfredo Montelibano, the new president of the National Federation of Sugarcane Planters, in successfully petitioning Quirino in October 1950 to restrict the bidding to those planters who had milled at the prewar Binalbagan Estate. The 195 planters to be eliminated claimed that a ruling in favor of this plan would constitute "a great injustice" and lobbied unsuccessfully against it. Significantly, these smaller planters later alleged that the Lopez group had accepted "substantial sums of money for the purchase . . . of the government's shares in Biscom" from investors with no ties to the district, in effect charging that the planters' reform movement had been subordinated to the interests of a single faction.[321]

After arranging a succession of calculated delays through President Quirino, the Lopez group finally secured the financing to bid for Biscom. Thus, in February 1951 the Philippine National Bank, proprietor of the government's shares, convened a formal ceremony for the opening of the sealed bids. With their assets pledged as collateral for individual bank loans, the planters allied with the Lopezes had quietly pooled their capital and submitted a sealed bid of P35 per share. Recalling this event a quarter century later, Congressman Carlos Hilado, who was present as an official observer, described Enrique Montilla as blinded by arrogance, which led him to make a series of blunders: "Montilla thought the planters had no money so he made his sealed bid for P21 . . . Montilla could have outbid the planters but he was too greedy." In the end, however, it was the 18 percent of Spanish-owned stock that proved pivotal. Knowing that the government's 44 percent share would not give them full control of the company, the Lopez planters had approached the Spanish stockholders before the bidding and "made a deal with the Spaniards that they would pay the same price as they paid for the PNB shares." According to Congressman Hilado, "Montilla could have purchased the Spanish shares before the auction. But Montilla was angry with the Spanish and wanted to get their shares for a song."[322] By the close of the bidding, the Lopez group had taken control of 62 percent of Biscom, a company with P22.4 million in assets, with a down payment of only P2.7 million.[323] Stunned by his defeat, Montilla flailed about, approaching the Spanish shareholders with a generous offer and pressing President Quirino to void the auction. Blocked at every turn, he found himself the focus of his family's anger and eventually committed suicide.[324]

Now in control of Biscom, the Lopez group convened a stockholders' meeting on 9 March, at which they increased the number of directors from seven to nine, elected Lopez allies to six of these seats, and appointed Eugenio Lopez as president and general manager.[325] Four months later, Eugenio led his board in approving a management contract with an outside firm, the Philippine Planters' Investment Company, for a fee set at 10 percent of "the gross income, sales, expenses, purchases and other receipts." Whether Biscom made a profit or not, it would now be making sizeable payments to Planters' Investment. Not surprisingly, the same Lopez group that controlled 62 percent of Biscom's stock also owned 81 percent of the shares in Philippine Planters' Investment.[326]

Several independent investigations concluded that this management contract was a legal mechanism that would allow Eugenio Lopez to plunder Biscom's resources, particularly the capital invested by the Montilla minority and the large loans from the state-owned RFC. Indeed, at the Biscom board meeting of July 1951, at which the contract with Planters' Investment was approved, minority director Marcial P. Lichauco objected that "such fee [sic] would deprive the minority stockholders, particularly the Isabela Sugar Co., Inc., of a substantial portion if not all of the profits to which they are entitled."[327] As aggrieved minority shareholders, the Montilla family sought redress in the courts. Responding to a motion by the Montillas enjoining the Lopez group from collecting its management fees, Judge Conrado Sanchez of Manila's Court of First Instance rendered a decision in October that was sharply critical of Lopez. After examining the membership of the boards of Biscom and Planters' Investment, Sanchez found that Eugenio Lopez was president of both companies and that his directors "perform the dual role of controlling majority directors in both corporations." The judge dismissed the defendants' "reverential reference" to Carlos Rivilla, the RFC's representative on the Biscom board, "as a protector of the RFC interests in the Biscom," by noting that he also was a founder of Planters' Investment and held stock in that company worth P50,000.[328] Although initially they invested only P2.7 million in Planters' Investment Company, the Lopez group was found to have collected "immense, staggering" management fees totaling P1.5 million pesos from Biscom in just six months, while the minority shareholder, the Montillas' Isabela Sugar Company, had earned nothing from an investment of P3.4 million.

Moreover, the Lopez group had paid itself these lavish fees, without precedent "in the records of sugar centrals in the Philippines," at a time when heavy losses threatened the company's profitability.[329] "Piercing the shard of corporate fiction," Judge Sanchez concluded that the Lopez directors "indirectly voted excessive compensation to themselves at a time when they performed the double role of giver and beneficiary." In granting the Montillas an injunction, he noted that "At the speed money finds its way out of the coffers of the Biscom, in the form of management fees, the cash position of said corporation, it is feared, may funnel down to the vanishing point."[330]

Two months later, the chief legal counsel for the RFC corroborated Judge Sanchez's findings. In an internal review, the RFC counsel concluded that the management contract "is illegal from the start because such an arrangement is an indirect way of paying dividends in violation of the provisions of the mortgage contract with the R.F.C." The counsel went on to state that Biscom would be paying the five directors in the Lopez group a remarkable fee of over P2 million per annum. Although such payments were clearly "excessive compensation," the contract was unassailable: "Whether they manage the Biscom efficiently or not, they will be entitled to exact payment of their fees, and yet, if the Biscom would want to do away with Philippine Planters' Investment Co., Inc., as manager, it will have to pay heavy damages."[331]

Despite such findings of illegality, Eugenio Lopez retained full control of Biscom. In September 1952, nearly a year after the Manila Court's injunction, Jacinto Montilla, a minority director, filed a complaint with the government's Integrity Board charging that the management contract with Planters' Investment was a mechanism for reducing the government's capital investment in Biscom, in effect allowing the Lopez group to purchase the government's shares "without paying a cent of their own money." Unable to explain why, under the circumstances, the government had not rescinded its sale of the Biscom shares to the Lopez group, Montilla pointed to the "hovering, long shadow of power which [Fernando Lopez] the Vice-President of the Philippines, brother and business partner of Eugenio Lopez, wields on Philippine officialdom, including those in the PNB and RFC."[332] This insight proved prescient, for in April 1954 another Manila court found in favor of the Lopez group, approving its management contract and dismissing the Montillas' complaint.[333]

Family Fortunes in the 1950s

After surviving these attacks and preserving their control over Biscom, the Lopez group used their expanded assets to contend for leadership of the ruling Liberal Party. Aggravated by the planter-miller conflict, which had peaked simultaneously, the Lopez-Yulo rivalry split the party in 1953. As owners of four sugar centrals, the Yulo-Araneta family represented the millers who were determined to block legislation adjusting the sharing ratio to 70:30 in favor of the planters. Thanks to their ally Alfredo Montelibano, the Lopezes were still identified with the planter faction and naturally supported the reform legislation. The battle began in August of 1952 when House speaker Eugenio Perez, an associate of J. Amado Araneta, charged that Lopez "vested interests" were trying to oust him from the speakership and alleged that they had been granted improper loans from the PNB. Then Jose Yulo himself went public, claiming that the Lopezes had cheated him in a 1946 sugar-trading deal. He demanded that the PNB collect an overdue loan from the Lopezes that had financed the transaction.[334]

When President Quirino bypassed Vice-President Fernando Lopez and gave the nomination to sugar miller Jose Yulo at the May 1953 Liberal convention, Lopez became the running mate of Carlos Romulo in the newly organized Democratic Party. Three months into the campaign, however, realizing that Romulo was weakening, the Lopezes engineered a merger of their new party with the Nacionalista Party, reportedly offering P2 million in campaign contributions if Ramon Magsaysay would make Fernando his running mate. Although the Nacionalista leadership refused these terms, they ultimately agreed to a coalition and awarded Fernando a position on a merged senatorial ticket. Lopez was elected to the Senate in November 1953 with the largest majority of any candidate, a reflection of his popularity and strong financial backing. Although Fernando, in effect, had been demoted from the vice-presidency to a Senate seat, the Lopez brothers managed to salvage some gains from the 1953 elections. The Quirino-Yulo ticket lost badly, weakening the worst of their enemies, while the Lopez group's support for Magsaysay gave it access to the Palace.[335] In January 1954, president-elect Magsaysay appointed Oscar Ledesma to his cabinet as secretary of commerce and industry, a post he would hold until he resigned to run for the Senate in 1957.[336] Moreover, Congress finally passed the new sugar legislation, Republic Act 809, strengthening the Lopez-Montelibano following among the planters.

Illustrating the continuing importance of proximity to the presidency, the Lopez fortunes waxed under the administration of Carlos Garcia and then waned when Diosdado Macapagal succeeded him. Fernando's Senate post was a more marginal position than the vice-presidency, denying the brothers the direct access to executive power they had enjoyed under Quirino.[337] After Magsaysay died in an airplane crash in March 1957, however, the Lopez brothers moved close to his successor, Carlos Garcia, becoming the "chief contributors" to his successful 1957 presidential campaign and the prime beneficiaries of his "Filipino first" program of economic nationalism.[338] Elected Senate president pro tempore in January 1958, Fernando increased his influence by means of a vigorous legislative record. His influence in the chamber also was amplified by Oscar Ledesma's election to the Senate in November 1957.[339]

In the final months of the Garcia administration, Eugenio Lopez finally achieved national economic preeminence by leading some of the country's foremost businessmen in the takeover of the Manila Electric Company (Meralco). Founded in 1903 by Detroit traction king Charles Swift, Meralco's profits as a tram operator and electrical corporation had long been determined by a favorable rate structure regulated by the colonial government. During the 1920s, its tram fares were among the highest in Asia, effectively denying many Manila workers access to public transport. With its profits dependent upon a sympathetic relationship with the state, Meralco's continued foreign ownership after independence was, as Eugenio understood well, an anomaly. Nonetheless, Meralco's enormous value, estimated at P244 million in early 1961, represented an almost insurmountable financial barrier to any potential Filipino buyer.[340] Incorporated in June 1961 by Eugenio and his closest associates, among them Alfredo Montelibano, the Meralco Securities Corporation (MSC) soon attracted six hundred stockholders prepared to support a takeover bid. In the largest transaction in Philippine business history, MSC purchased Meralco from its American owners on 5 January 1962. An all-Filipino board was elected, which included Eugenio, his son Geny, Salvador Araneta, and Mrs. Luz Magsaysay.[341] In contrast to their sole ownership of the Lopez media operations, the family held only 28 percent of MSC.[342] The control of Meralco, formalized only days after President Garcia left office on 30 December, had required six months of sustained government support, including permission for transfer of the franchise and state financing for the acquisition.[343] However, the Lopezes' generous financial support for Garcia's presidential campaign proved a liability when opposition candidate Diosdado Macapagal scored a surprising upset over the incumbent.

At War with Macapagal

As the leader of the opposition Liberal Party, president-elect Diosdado Macapagal had good reason to dislike the Lopez brothers. Not only had they financed his rival's campaign but they were maneuvering for control of Congress to position Fernando for a presidential bid in 1965. In the words of Dapen Liang: "President Macapagal's greatest concern in politics then was to prevent Senator Lopez from being elected president of the Senate."[344] Apparently realizing the economic basis of his country's rent-seeking politics, Macapagal tried to weaken Fernando's political position by attacking Eugenio's corporations. Within weeks of his inauguration, he denounced Fernando as the leader of the "sugar bloc," launching a campaign against the Lopez interests that would continue throughout his term. In a Senate speech, Fernando dismissed these charges as "unjust, unkind and unfounded philippics," and offered an impassioned defense of his career and family. In response to the president's allegations that his family represented "vested interests," Fernando replied that "we have share of stock only in two mills, the Binalbagan-Isabela Sugar Company . . . and the Pampanga sugar mills." Rebutting the charge that the *Manila Chronicle* is "our instrument of propaganda," he invoked the legitimacy of familial continuity.[345]

An insinuation has been made that we use the ABS-CBN radio and TV networks to promote the political interests of the "sugar bloc." The CBN network was organized as a complementary activity of the *Manila Chronicle*. As everybody knows, our family has been in the newspaper business since more than a generation ago when our parents started in Iloilo with *Tiempo-Times*.

The battle began in earnest six months later when Macapagal employed the full powers of the state to constrict the Lopezes' rent-based empire. Invoking the name of Harry Stonehill, an American expatriate notorious for his corruption, the president announced in a radio address that he would pursue "Filipino Stonehills who build and maintain business empires through political power, including the corruption of politicians and other public officials."[346] Within weeks, the administration was pressing criminal charges against Biscom's management for export violations,[347] the justice secretary had filed a criminal complaint against the Lopez brothers for corruption in a Manila land purchase,[348] and the Bureau of Internal Revenue was demanding P1.2 million in back taxes from the Lopez-owned Philippine Planters' Investment Company.[349] Believing that their ownership of the sugar mills made them politically vulnerable, Eugenio sold Planters' Investment and his shares in four affiliated companies to business associate Roberto Villanueva. To assure collection of the unpaid taxes, the revenue commissioner empowered a representative to manage the five remaining Lopez corporations and moved to seize the assets of Planters' Investment.[350] Deploying the skilled lawyers that would ultimately allow them to survive the Macapagal years, the Lopezes won a ruling from the Court of Tax Appeals blocking the government's confiscation of their company.[351]

Nonplused by this setback, the Palace intensified its pressure on the Lopezes in January 1963 by demanding that Meralco's directors remove Eugenio from the board for franchise violations. In making this demand, Executive Secretary Salvador L. Marino accused the brothers of being "engaged in a political power struggle in the country to the extent that Senator Lopez, apart from seeking the leadership of the Senate . . . also seeks political control of the country." Citing Meralco's status as a public utility and Meralco Securities' debt of $11.9 million to the PNB, Marino insisted the government had the right to regulate the utility's management.[352] After Fernando proclaimed that his battle with Macapagal would be a "fight to the finish,"[353] the president's press secretary cited government loans to thirteen Lopez-owned corporations totaling a remarkable P88 million in value, commenting that: "The adroit handling and application of political power and connections allowed the Lopezes to acquire these loans and a string of business enterprises like the Biscom . . . and a vast radio-television network." Expanding upon this critique, Senator Estanislao Fernandez, an administration ally, denounced Fernando's exploitation of his position as Senate president pro tempore: "It was during the term of Senator Lopez that the Lopez Sugar Bloc became so potent that President Garcia had to accede to its demands. It was during the term of Senator Lopez that his brother was able to buy the Meralco through a loan from the PNB." [354]

When the Meralco board defied the president's demand that they remove Eugenio Lopez "within a reasonable time," the Palace threatened to cancel Meralco's license to distribute electricity.[355] Four days later, public works secretary Brigido R. Valencia announced the immediate closure of nineteen Lopez-owned radio and four television stations. Citing the Lopezes' tardiness in applying for renewal of licenses that had now lapsed, the secretary announced his determination to end "the rotten set-up in the past when they could fix their way out of every violation."[356] Represented by former senator Vicente Francisco, the Lopezes soon won an injunction from the Supreme Court blocking the government's planned seizure of TV Channel 9 and later extended it to include nineteen radio and television stations owned by their Chronicle Broadcasting Network.[357] Simultaneously, Lopez lawyers convinced the Supreme Court to restrain the Manila *fiscal's* office from proceeding with another P10 million tax case against the brothers, one of several concurrent state pressures.[358] As these legal battles dragged on into the early stages of the 1965 presidential campaign,[359] Senator Lopez announced his "irrevocable decision" to seek the Nacionalista Party's presidential nomination.[360]

At the start of the election campaign, President Macapagal, using the state's regulatory powers, intensified his pressure on the Lopezes, focusing on the populist issue of Meralco's request for an increase in electrical rates. In October 1964, Meralco had petitioned the Public Service Commission (PSC) for a hefty 30-percent rate increase. After much partisan debate, the PSC finally granted Meralco a 23-percent rise in March 1965, a decision that aroused protest among administration allies.[361] Although the Supreme Court affirmed the PSC's decision, the commissioners rescinded their approval in July, prompting another Lopez suit before the Supreme Court, which eventually affirmed the original increase.[362] Throughout the campaign, the topic remained highly partisan with Macapagal supporters attacking the Nacionalista ticket, Ferdinand Marcos and Fernando Lopez, for betraying consumers with their silence on the issue.[363] Predictably, once the Marcos-Lopez ticket won the election, the issue died and Meralco proceeded with its rate increase.[364]

Alliance with Marcos

In 1965, the Nacionalista presidential candidate was, of course, Ferdinand Marcos. Fernando Lopez, despite his presidential aspirations, became his vice-presidential running mate, creating a ticket that married private wealth to populist appeal. The Lopez alliance with Marcos was a strategic blunder born of tactical necessity. To insure the defeat of incumbent President Macapagal, the Lopezes had felt compelled to ally themselves with Marcos. Eugenio Lopez used his money, media, and machine to make Marcos president in 1965 and to reelect him in 1969. By the time their inevitable break came in 1971, Eugenio had waited too long. In the final battle between Marcos's authoritarian state and the Lopez conglomerate, the family would suffer a devastating defeat.

The Lopezes' relationship with Ferdinand Marcos began in 1964–65 when the brothers were seeking a candidate to run against Macapagal.[365] Desperate for a sympathetic executive, Eugenio pursued two alternatives—supporting Fernando's now-official campaign for the presidency or forming an alliance with a sure winner. According to Primitivo Mijares, a former Lopez employee, Eugenio had long considered an alliance with Marcos against Macapagal. In a meeting with his legal advisers Roberto S. Benedicto and Claudio Teehankee early in the campaign, Eugenio had canvassed them on the subject. They advised him against supporting Marcos in light of the senator's prewar conviction for the murder of a political rival, an opinion supported by both Fernando Lopez and Alfredo Montelibano. Despite these warnings, Eugenio reportedly asked Mijares to liaise confidentially with Marcos as an overture to alliance.[366]

Meeting at the Manila Hotel in November 1964, the Nacionalista Party convention deadlocked on the first ballot. With 541 votes for Marcos, 382 for Emmanuel Pelaez, and 178 for Lopez, all candidates were short of the 771 votes needed for nomination.[367] After Pelaez refused Marcos's offer of the vice-presidency, and the other candidates released their delegates, Marcos won the nomination on the second ballot. With Pelaez eliminated, Marcos courted Lopez for the second slot as emissaries shuttled down the hotel corridors for twelve hours without success.[368] In a famous incident, Imelda Marcos broke the deadlock by approaching Fernando in tears, begging him to support her husband. Charmed by her beauty and apparent innocence, Fernando agreed, and the deal was done. The Lopez brothers committed their resources to the campaign in exchange for the vice-presidential nomination.[369] According to the recollections of family members, they threw their full support behind the ticket, using their media resources to the fullest, and spending P14 million to assure a victory.[370]

Marcos defeated Macapagal in the November 1965 elections. Not long after, Eugenio Lopez launched a major expansion and diversification program at Meralco. After purchasing adjacent electrical firms to give Meralco the widest possible distribution area, company management then created subsidiaries for the manufacture of transformers, the construction of power stations, and, in 1969, the refining of lubricating oil.[371] In the decade preceding martial law, the revenues of MSC, Meralco's public holding company, increased from P5 million (in 1962) to P69 million, a remarkable growth rate for a utility. During the same period, MSC assets grew seven-fold, from P155 million to P1,037 million.[372]

For six years, the Lopez-Marcos alliance remained amicable. With Lopez support, Marcos was reelected in 1969. An affable, self-deprecating man, Vice-President Fernando Lopez did not lay claim to his full rewards, seemingly content with the secondary post of secretary of agriculture. In January 1971, however, a break occurred, which erupted into what may be the most public and vitriolic split in Philippine political history. According to Marcos, the Lopezes were demanding concessions to advance their interests. According to the Lopezes, Marcos was demanding shares in their family corporations. "No, we should not yield any more to that s.o.b.," Geny Lopez reportedly told family members.[373] Using the *Manila Chronicle*, the Lopezes began an attack, publishing exposés of graft within the administration. For two months, in the words of Eugenio's second son, Oscar, "this public criticism reached its heights in a series of editorials, columns and editorial cartoons . . . which exposed the issue of the hidden wealth of the Marcoses."[374] Privately, the president reacted to the Lopez attacks with a mix of fear and rage. In a handwritten diary entry of March 1971, Marcos admitted that he was hurting: "The ABS-CBN TV and radio networks are blanketing the whole country with vicious lies and distorted propaganda. But Imelda feels that it is becoming effective in turning some of the people against us." In December a report of Don Eugenio's casual luncheon remark that Marcos "should not be allowed to go scot-free, but should be prosecuted" so upset the president that he agonized, in his diary, about suffering "imprisonment or worse" at the hands of his enemies. Publicly, using the Palace press corps, Marcos counterattacked, denouncing the Lopezes as "oppressive oligarchs" whose wealth and media power threatened the integrity of Philippine democracy. When a delegation of Tondo workers called upon the president at the battle's peak, Marcos vowed: "We will crush the Lopez oligarchy to pieces."[375] Indeed, with his love of grandeur and ostentation, Eugenio seemed typecast for the role of oligarch that Marcos would have him play. His fortieth wedding-anniversary celebration in 1968 had been the "party of the century," with champagne fountains, European royalty, an American society orchestra, and more than a thousand guests.[376]

In the end it was Marcos who blinked this time. After suffering five months of media criticism, he finally sued for peace by paying a call on Eugenio at his Paranaque residence and helicoptering to the Chronicle Building for a reconciliation with Fernando.[377]

Decline and Demise

When President Marcos declared martial law sixteen months later, the Lopez family became the main target of his "revolution from above." Just before midnight on 22 September 1972, Metrocom troops under Captain Rolando Abadilla, Marcos's trusted special agent, occupied the ABS-CBN Broadcast Center in Quezon City while other troops seized Lopez properties across the archipelago.[378] In exchange for "the unsealing of the Chronicle Building by the military" several days later, the Lopezes allowed Imelda's brother, Benjamin ("Kokoy") Romualdez, to take over the *Chronicle's* presses for the publication of his own newspaper, the *Times-Journal*. Under martial law, only Marcos relatives or close allies were allowed newspaper licenses. Kokoy paid only half the promised rent for the facility, and eventually purchased the Lopez presses, worth P50 million, for just P500,000.[379]

Marcos moved more slowly against the ABS-CBN network. With the declaration of martial law, all broadcasting companies automatically lost their licenses, rendering the Lopez network's P119 million worth of equipment useless to anyone other than a Palace favorite with access to a license. Negotiations dragged on for months through Kokoy Romualdez, apparently Marcos's chosen agent for the demolition of the Lopez empire. Then, on 6 June 1973, a fire destroyed the KBS television studios. Their owner, Roberto S. Benedicto, Marcos's fraternity brother and intimate, asked ABS-CBN chairman Alfredo Montelibano for temporary use of the Broadcast Center. Since Benedicto was a fellow Negros planter and old associate from the days when both had worked with Lopez, Montelibano supported the offer of short-term occupancy with rent. Arguing that "Malacañang could just issue a sequestration order," he persuaded the ABS-CBN board to accept.

On 9 June, "known to us at ABS as Looters Day," Benedicto's KBS employees moved in and "fought each other for choice office spaces and furniture." By August 1973, Benedicto's KBS was broadcasting on all the ABS-CBN channels with no lease agreement from the Lopez management. Three months later, Oscar Lopez, acting for his father Eugenio, met with Benedicto and offered to sell a network with a net worth of P50 million for a cash price of P36 million. Three days later, Benedicto rang back to "say that negotiations would have to be suspended temporarily because the government was contemplating seizure proceedings against ABS based on charges of unpaid taxes." Indeed, several weeks later, the ABS-CBN management was summoned to Camp Crame where the Bureau of Customs summarily announced cancellation of an exemption for equipment imported by the Broadcast Center eight years earlier. While the customs case dragged on for the next six years, Benedicto's KBS grossed over P1 billion in broadcast revenues without paying "a single centavo as rent or compensation." In October 1979, Philippine Customs finally ordered ABS-CBN to pay fines and back duties totaling P34 million, more than the network's sale price. Two months later, KBS transferred control of the Lopez facilities to the National Media Production Center, Marcos's state propaganda agency.[380]

While expropriation of the *Manila Chronicle* and the ABS-CBN network were crudely done, Marcos's campaign against Meralco was far more subtle. Since the media companies were private corporations, and had been tainted with factional partisanship by the fight with the president before martial law, Marcos could be confident that their expropriation would not disturb the business community. In the words of Oscar Lopez, the president "calibrated his attacks against the Lopez businesses. . . . Thus, in the case of MSC, Marcos knew that it would be scandalous to use the same crude methods he employed with the *Chronicle* or ABS-CBN . . . because MSC was a public corporation with 12,000 stockholders, including many foreign creditors." Instead of brute military force, Marcos used "conspiracy and [a] systematic campaign . . . to wrest control . . . from the Lopez family."[381]

In November 1972, Marcos employed a master stroke in the expropriation of Meralco when he used his martial-law powers to imprison Geny Lopez, Don Eugenio's eldest son. In the words of Oscar Lopez: "Geny's freedom was constantly dangled by Kokoy Romualdez before my father as the ultimate prize for accomplishing everything the Marcoses wanted from him." Although Eugenio had bested Marcos in their earlier battle, he was now forced to submit to the president's every demand. With Geny in custody to force compliance, Marcos used the full resources of the state to break the Lopez hold over Meralco, step by step. Through a series of legalistic maneuvers, Marcos gained control over a Lopez company with US $5.7 million in assets for a cash outlay of only $1,500:[382]

(1) In early 1973, the Board of Power slashed a scheduled Meralco rate increase from 36 to 21 percent, creating a serious revenue shortfall for the company.
(2) In March 1973, an Inter-Agency Team headed by Marcos's executive secretary Alejandro Melchor forced eight top Meralco executives to resign from the company's subsidiaries.
(3) In August-September 1973, Central Bank governor Gregorio Licaros refused all loans to Meralco until it had been sold and had paid its back taxes.
(4) In October 1973, Kokoy Romualdez forced an humiliating resignation of "30 trusted officers" from MSC at the annual stockholders meeting.
(5) Between February and November of 1973, Eugenio sent five letters to Marcos, most drafted by Kokoy's agent in Meralco, endorsing "your program to democratize wealth and property for the greater good of our people."
(6) Finally, in November 1973, Eugenio agreed to sell the Lopez family's 27 percent of MSC stock to the Marcos-controlled Meralco Foundation for only P150 million, which would be paid over a ten-year period.[383]

Despite broad hints that Geny Lopez would be freed once the Meralco matter was settled, Marcos did not release him even after Eugenio had signed over the company. When doctors diagnosed his cancer as terminal in early 1974, Eugenio, by this time exiled in San Francisco, California, contacted Marcos through intermediaries to request a final visit with his son. Capricious and cruel towards his former rival, Marcos summoned the dying man to Manila and then refused him a visit with his son.[384] Already emaciated, and extremely pale, Eugenio met with relatives in Manila and made a few public appearances in Iloilo, where he dedicated a hospital to his father's memory, before returning to San Francisco. Apparently "losing hope that he would be freed," Geny launched a ten-day hunger strike in November.[385]

With the opposition to Marcos still weak, Manila's Archbishop Jaime Sin, recently appointed to this post from the Lopez's home diocese of Jaro, was the only national figure who supported Geny. "We cannot jail a man indefinitely and still call ourselves Christian," said Sin in an impassioned defense of his parishioner.[386]

Despite Archbishop Sin's support and international press coverage, Marcos responded to Geny Lopez's hunger strike with characteristic cunning. Disturbed by the critical international coverage, Marcos delegated Defense Secretary Juan Ponce Enrile to negotiate with the Lopezes. After the secretary dangled the promise of a quick release once the hunger strike ended, Geny broke his fast on 28 November. A week later, however, Marcos announced that the Lopez heir would be tried in civil court for a capital crime—plotting to assassinate the president with an international team of hired killers.[387] Realizing that "the promise of Geny's release from prison was a hoax," Eugenio then broke his silence with two newspaper interviews given in the United States. On 2 January 1975, Eugenio responded to an interviewer's question about his agreement to sell Meralco to the Marcos-controlled Meralco Foundation: "I had agreed with Governor [Kokoy] Romualdez that he could take over all of the assets of Benpres [holding company] at no cost in exchange for the freedom of my son and the safety of the rest of my family."[388] Three weeks later, he stated that "the so-called [Meralco] 'Foundation' is just a front of the Marcos-Romualdez business interest."[389]

Eugenio's attacks apparently stirred Marcos, for on 24 January he summoned Fernando and Oscar Lopez to the Palace. In the course of two long meetings, he offered to place Geny under house arrest if Fernando and Geny would sign a letter accepting confiscation of their properties, endorse martial law, and admit their involvement in the alleged assassination plot. Geny refused to endorse martial law and the negotiations collapsed.[390] Bitter and close to death in San Francisco, Eugenio finally gave an impassioned interview to *Parade Magazine*, a glossy insert for Sunday newspapers across America, exposing Marcos's use of his son as a hostage.[391]

> I have already given up to the Marcos Foundation my holdings in Manila Electric which are worth at least $20 million. The Marcos Foundation had made to me the ridiculous down payment of $1,500 and claims they will pay some more if the company ever makes money. Meanwhile they control the company which is worth some $400 million.
>
> I signed over my holdings in the hope that President Marcos would release my son and let him join me here in San Francisco. But to date, Marcos has refused. He still holds my son captive and claims he will try him in a civil court.
>
> I accuse President Marcos of holding my son hostage so that he can blackmail me and my family into silence and have his front men take over all our business enterprises in the Philippines. Only recently the Marcos front men took over our family's six TV and 21 radio stations. They paid nothing for them. . . .
>
> I am an old man of 74. I am ill with cancer. I would like to have my son beside me, to see once more before I pass on. The report that Geny was involved in an attempt to assassinate Marcos is ridiculous. After all, Marcos was an old friend of ours. We supported him and Imelda until we realized his true aims.

My family has agreed to all of the Marcos demands to secure the release of our son. I have signed away the Manila Electric Company, the largest corporation in the Philippines. I have signed away the largest TV-radio chain in the islands, the ABS/CBN broadcasting networks. . . . But no sooner do I comply with one of their demands then they come up with another.

First, they demanded that my family keep quiet about everything and never criticize Marcos or his martial law. Then they asked me to visit the Philippines to prove that I was no political opponent in exile, threatening Marcos' position. I did that, too, in April 1974. I have been blackmailed into silence, into giving up millions of dollars in my company assets. Enough is enough. I refuse to be blackmailed further. The Marcos and Romualdez families have bled me dry. . . .

I, Eugenio Lopez, Sr., an old man, now appeal to public opinion. I have no other source to help me regain my son.

Four months later, on 6 July 1975, Eugenio Lopez died of cancer in San Francisco while Geny remained in prison on capital charges. From his deathbed, Eugenio pleaded with Marcos to send his son "under guard" for a last visit. Marcos refused. In a final act of cruelty, the dictator also denied the two Lopez sons not imprisoned permission to leave the country for a last visit with their father.[392] Two years later, Geny escaped from the Philippines in a chartered aircraft and won political asylum in the United States where he became a leader in the anti-Marcos movement.

Although Eugenio's death and Geny's dramatic escape eliminated the Lopezes from active participation in Philippine politics, Marcos still did not absorb Meralco. In 1978, his allies transferred the assets of MSC, the former Lopez holding company, to a new corporation, First Philippine Holdings, headed by Cesar Z. Zalamea, a long-time Kokoy Romualdez associate.[393] Although First Holdings' management claimed that the company was created to "pave the way for mutualization of Meralco's ownership to its customers," Marcos never seriously moved to implement his anti-oligarchic rhetoric of economic democracy. According to Oscar Lopez's analysis, the controlling interest in First Holdings remains the original 45 percent of the stock held by the Meralco Foundation, which "in turn is directly traceable to the interests of the Lopez family." Together, the top twenty stockholders of First Holdings, excluding the Foundation, hold only 9.2 percent of the stock. After breaking the Lopezes, even the Marcos regime seems to have had neither the capital nor the ability to absorb such a vast, complex corporation.[394]

Elite Restoration Under Aquino

Marcos's fall from power in 1986 heralded the restoration of the Lopez fortunes. After Geny Lopez's escape denied the president his hostage, the family's exiled members—Geny, his sister Presentacion, and her husband Steve Psinakis—stepped up their opposition in the United States. Reflecting President Reagan's close personal relationship with the Philippine dictator, the FBI hounded Psinakis after Marcos produced witnesses who claimed that he was the leader behind Manila's "Light-a-Fire" bombings in 1980. Despite this partisan harassment, the Lopezes became a major force in the American anti-Marcos movement.[395] In the Philippines, the family was as active as their weakened circumstances allowed. During the parliamentary elections of May 1984, Fernando Lopez allied his residual Iloilo machine with Fermin Caram, Jr., son of his prewar rival, to battle the government's regional KBL party candidates led by sugar czar Roberto S. Benedicto.[396] As the president's regional plenipotentiary for the Western Visayas, Benedicto used the resources of the state sugar monopoly and his vast cache of purloined wealth to finance KBL candidates in Panay and Negros Occidental.

Despite his great wealth and power, Benedicto suffered a humiliating defeat in the May 1984 elections. All his candidates on Panay lost and only a few survived in Negros Occidental. In a remarkable show of resilience, the Lopezes and others of the elite who had preserved their independent local machines defeated Benedicto's bid for regional leadership.[397] Six months later, Oscar Lopez, Eugenio's son and president of what was left of ABS-CBN, wrote Benedicto to "demand that you vacate our Broadcast Center on Bohol Avenue, Quezon City, and all our 22 provincial radio and television stations by January 19, 1985."[398] Although the manifesto was a bluff, it signaled the Lopezes' determination to recover their lost position.

When Corazon Aquino ran as an anti-Marcos presidential candidate in December 1985, Fernando Lopez emerged from retirement to raise her arm in proclamation rallies all around Manila.[399] Although hardly a major factor in Marcos's fall, the strategy gave the family access to Aquino when she became president. After seizing power in the EDSA uprising, President Aquino, in keeping with her policy of restoring the status quo ante Marcos, installed the Lopezes as acting managers of their old corporations during her first weeks in office. On 28 February 1986, only forty-eight hours after Marcos fled to Hawaii, Aquino appointed Manuel M. Lopez, Eugenio's fourth child and Geny's brother, as officer in charge of Meralco, a designation confirmed by the new board of directors in mid-April.[400] With the euphoria of the "People Power" revolution still strong, hundreds of Meralco employees met Manuel in the street on his first day back with placards emblazoned "Mabuhay Manolo Lopez" ('Long Live Manolo Lopez') and "Meralco Balik Lopez" ('The Lopezes Are Back at Meralco'), and carried him triumphantly into the building.[401] In April, President Aquino appointed Oscar Lopez president of First Philippine Holdings, the current holding company for Meralco.[402] Landing in Manila from San Francisco only four days after Marcos's flight to Hawaii, Geny Lopez began rebuilding the ruined media conglomerate he had headed before martial law.[403] Aquino appointed him board chairman of the Philippine Commercial & Industrial Bank (or PCI Bank), a former Lopez corporation expropriated by Kokoy Romualdez under martial law.[404]

At first, the Lopez restoration was little more than a fragile illusion. As Fernando and his nephew Geny noted in a letter to the newspaper *Malaya*, the three Lopez sons served "ultimately at the discretion of President Aquino and not because of equity ownership by the family in these corporations."[405] Seeking to strengthen the family position, and backed by eighteen friends who invested P1 million each, Geny revived the *Manila Chronicle*, which soon regained its reputation as the capital's journal of record. But, instead of the outright ownership his father had enjoyed, Geny controlled only 10 percent of the stock since he could not afford to invest more than P2 million on his own.[406] The family's return to broadcasting was similarly circumspect. In an open letter published on 12 June 1986, Philippine Independence Day, Fernando and Geny promised that "we do not seek to regain full control of our seized assets," adding that "we will seek the return of only one of our two previous television stations."[407] A month later, the Aquino administration leased Channel 2 to ABS-CBN and the Lopez company began broadcasting with a media splash on 17 August.[408]

At the outset, the restored network operated on the edge of extinction. With a single station, borrowed equipment, and heavy bank loans, the network could have gone bankrupt. But, through a mix of political manipulation and skillful management, Geny soon made Channel 2 Manila's premier television station and the most lucrative of the current Lopez investments. Using his "close ties with officials in the Aquino administration," he leased equipment from Roberto Benedicto's networks, now under government sequestration. Although the terms of the lease were generous, Lopez reduced the cost further by avoiding any payment during the six years of Aquino's rule.[409] By launching innovative programs and pirating top-rated shows from rival channels, Channel 2 placed first in the ratings in 1988. Two years later, the station captured an unprecedented 41 percent of Manila's television audience and earned P191 million, making it the most profitable station as well.[410]

Only nine months after his June 1986 denial of any such ambition, Geny petitioned the government for return of the entire ABS-CBN network of six television and twenty-one radio stations, including the government's Channel 4.[411] When the administration's arbitration committee began meeting to resolve the matter in May 1987, the Coalition Against Media Monopoly, led by former Constitutional commissioner Chito Gascon, fielded some one hundred demonstrators protesting the return of the stations to the Lopezes. Significantly, the anti-oligarchy ideology that had dogged the Lopezes for half a century had survived the collapse of the Marcos regime. In his arguments on behalf of the government, Assistant Solicitor General Eliseo Alampay claimed that "returning PTV-4 to the Lopezes would revive oligarchy which is inimical to public interest."[412]

Chastened by this outburst of populist hostility, Geny Lopez retreated to a less-aggressive stance until the outcry subsided. After building stronger support in the Palace and in Congress, he resumed his pursuit of media dominion. Like his father before him, Geny had found that success in the heavily regulated broadcast industry was basically political. Although the Lopez family came to realize that populist sentiment would bar them from ever regaining a second television channel, Geny mounted a vigorous legal campaign to recover the Broadcast Center, now occupied by the government's Channel 4. After a long process of negotiation and arbitration presided over by presidential counsel Adolf Azcuna, the Aquino administration agreed to return the Broadcast Center but asked for time to relocate Channel 4.[413] Although the negotiations dragged on until the end of Aquino's term, the Lopez family remains confident of ultimate success.[414]

But Geny Lopez had plans beyond the simple restoration of his family's position. In 1989, working through allies in the new Congress, he lobbied aggressively for approval of a "super-franchise"—a fifty-year license to operate a satellite-powered television channel that would integrate local broadcasting with global telecommunications.[415] Although Congress was supportive, the bill failed when President Aquino backed her transport and communications secretary in opposing Geny's radical redefinition of the broadcasting industry.[416] During the long, bitter controversy over this bill, Geny used Channel 2 as a partisan forum for his application, hammering at his enemies over the airwaves as his father had once done in the columns of the old *Manila Chronicle*.[417]

Banking is another area in which Geny Lopez has achieved success. In November 1987, the Lopezes achieved a major breakthrough when Geny allied the family with rising Chinese-Filipino financiers John Gokongwei and Antonio Chan to take control of PCIBank, one of the nation's largest. In the first independent test of his entrepreneurial ability, Geny organized a consortium, with a capital investment of P1.34 billion, to support a successful takeover bid against strong local and international competition. After skillful maneuvering, Lopez emerged with 14 percent of the stock, a significantly larger portion than the two 10-percent shares held by Gokongwei and his Robina Corporation.[418] An alliance with John Gokongwei, one of the country's most dynamic and domineering entrepreneurs, is not for the meek, and Filipino financial analysts waited for the inevitable rupture. But it did not come. Instead, the two entrepreneurs crafted a corporate structure— with Lopez as board chair and Gokongwei as head of an executive committee—that allowed an equitable division of authority.[419] To consolidate their control, the new owners replaced the bank's president, Ramon Ozaeta, a holdover from the Marcos era, with their own appointee, Rafael Buenaventura, then the highest-ranking Filipino executive at Citibank.[420] Under this triumvirate, PCIB posted an impressive 38.2 percent increase in gross earnings during 1989, and a 26.5 percent increase in 1990, while expanding its network to 226 branches, the largest among private banks in the Philippines.[421]

On the political side, Geny Lopez also negotiated a skillful shift of presidential patrons during the 1992 elections—a critical operation for any rent-seeking entrepreneur and one that had often confounded his father. In the tumult of the campaign Lopez seems to have invested in both the stability of the electoral process and an alliance with a single patron, Fidel Ramos, President Aquino's anointed successor. Apparently wary of the volatility of a presidential race with seven candidates, Lopez seems to have muted the partisanship of his media group and concentrated his resources on promoting honest balloting. Using the Electoral Code's provision for a private, media-based count to supplement the cumbersome tallying by the Commission on Elections, Lopez became chair and chief organizer of the Media Citizen's Quick Count (MCQC), leading other executives in a comprehensive effort to report the ballot results quickly and thereby frustrate systematic fraud by professional politicians.[422] Exercising great discretion, Lopez signaled his tacit personal support for Ramos by assigning a key ABS-CBN executive, vice-president Rod Reyes, to write the candidate's campaign speeches.[423] When an early surge of votes from Manila and the Western Visayas gave Miriam Defensor Santiago an early lead in the May 1992 tally, Lopez reportedly interceded to accelerate the reporting of votes by MCQC chapters in pro-Ramos regions such as Central Luzon and Bicol, providing an important boost to his would-be patron's flagging chances.[424] After Ramos finally took the lead in the MCQC tally on the fourth day of counting, Lopez rebuffed Santiago's charges of pro-Ramos bias and resisted her call for the dissolution of his organization. "We don't see any way of dissolving ourselves, much less stopping our count," he replied. "The law has mandated a media-based parallel count and we intend to fulfill our legal mandate."[425]

When the count was completed, after weeks of tension, and Fidel Ramos had been proclaimed president-elect, Lopez had a new patron in the Palace, a former employee as presidential press secretary, and prestige as the leader of a nonpartisan movement for good government. Perhaps most importantly, he had played a central role in defense of a pluralist system suited to his style of rent-seeking politics. After a lifetime in his father's shadow and fourteen years in prison or exile, Geny Lopez, the leader of the family's fifth generation, had demonstrated the entrepreneurial abilities that had sustained his family for so long. Like his father before him, he had proven himself skilled in securing the presidential patronage so central to the success of family-based enterprise in the Philippines.

Conclusion

Under three empires and five republics, succeeding generations of Lopezes have adapted and prospered—an exceptional performance in the history of any elite, Filipino or foreign. Over a span of five generations, the dominant line of the Lopez family has had the vision to perceive change and the dynamism to seize new opportunities. Since the century's turn, each generation has produced at least one entrepreneur who has grasped the import of both technological and political change. Most importantly, the last three generations of this line have seen the significance of the emerging Philippine state and entered politics to exploit its resources.

The family's adoption of new technology also has been central to its survival. Unlike most of the Negros planter class who continued to rely upon their haciendas, the third- and fourth-generation Lopezes moved beyond low-yield agriculture and sugar refining to seek new technology, simultaneously increasing capital and reducing risk.

Instead of mills and plantations, Eugenio Lopez, Sr., the most ambitious member of the fourth generation, moved the family into transport—air, land, and sea. His engines ran all day, twelve months a year, allowing a more rapid return on investment and freeing his capital from dependence on a crop that could be devastated by changes in weather or world markets. After the war, Eugenio shifted his resources into communications and energy technology, serving up information, generating power ceaselessly, and servicing a diverse market that could weather any economic downturn. Today, with his father's flair for innovation, Eugenio, Jr., the most skillful entrepreneur of the fifth generation, is attempting to recast the country's broadcast industry to exploit innovations in satellite technology, linking his regional television network to global telecommunications.

Above all, the history of the Lopez family illustrates the symbiosis between the weak Philippine state and the strength of the country's dominant political families. A contradictory pairing of the state's broad economic powers with the executive's role as a political patron has made rent seeking an imperative for major Filipino families. Through their reliance upon rents, these families can exploit the state's financial resources and regulatory powers to create optimum conditions for the growth of their corporations. Even if they are not so inclined, elite families are forced to cultivate alliances with the state, particularly its executive branch, if only to defend their established interests from unfair competition by ambitious courtiers. On the other side of this symbiosis, successive Philippine presidents have used their discretionary authority over the state resources to punish enemies and reward allies. By denying established elites access to rents, an administration can quickly reduce the wealth of a family. Similarly, a president can create vast wealth for a favored few by granting a de facto monopoly or approving low-interest loans.

The Philippine presidency has considerable short-term power to punish and reward but elite families have the strength of continuity. While administrations come and go, families remain to transmit their skills, contacts, and capital across the generations. Taking the struggle between Eugenio Lopez, Sr., and Ferdinand Marcos as an example, there seem to be limits on the executive's ability to either destroy an established family or elevate others to the first rank of the economic elite. The Philippines' capitalist economy imposes a certain rationality upon even this extreme system of political patronage, thereby limiting the long-term power of the executive to influence the composition of the country's elites. With the unprecedented power of his martial-law regime, Marcos could lavish vast resources upon his retainers and punish his enemies without legal restraint. But he could not command his coterie of economic incompetents to preserve their capital in the marketplace. Among the dozens of cronies favored with his largesse, only one, a member of an established family, managed to survive his fall with wealth intact. Similarly, through summary arrest, blatant manipulation of corporate regulations, and outright expropriation, Marcos stripped Eugenio Lopez, Sr., of his wealth and position. But he did not destroy the Lopez family's accumulated legitimacy, contacts, and skills. During his twenty years in power, Marcos tinkered with the composition of the elites without modifying the underlying political and social system that placed them at its apex. By harassing some older Filipino families and favoring selected Chinese entrepreneurs, Marcos did alter the membership of the country's economic elite. Simultaneously, however, his regime maintained the nexus of formal regulation and informal privilege that had long allowed family-owned corporations to control so much of the country's wealth. In the end, it was Marcos who fled into exile and Geny Lopez who returned to reclaim his family's wealth and position.

By skewing investments and regulations to favor its allies, the Philippine executive has, as an institution, compromised the integrity of the bureaucracy and allowed the privatization of public resources. Over the long term, then, we can conclude that such policies weaken the state and empower elite families, ultimately limiting the capacity of the bureaucracy to direct entrepreneurs and lead the country's development. Through this particular interaction between strong families and a weak state, the Philippine economy has declined markedly compared to its neighbors in eastern Asia. In South Korea, Singapore, and Thailand the state has played an active but less biased role in national development, avoiding the arbitrary and ultimately destructive partisanship rampant in the Philippines.

Such a system leaves an ambiguous legacy. By fusing politics and business, elite Filipino families have proved adept and aggressive at rent seeking, subverting public institutions to promote private accumulation. After a century, these political families have accumulated sufficient power, prestige, skill, and wealth to perpetuate a system that serves their interests. Indeed, any attempt to use the state to restrain these elites may, as it did in the Marcos era, merely mask a partisan attack by new, even more avaricious families. This subversion of the public weal in the service of private, familial wealth may be a corruption under law but it is also the dominant feature of politics as it is practiced in the Philippines.

NOTES

This essay has benefited from comments by Brian Fegan of Macquarie University, Vic Lieberman at the University of Michigan, and Oscar Lopez of the Lopez Foundation in Manila. At the University of Wisconsin-Madison, Michael Cullinane, Dan Doeppers, Paul Hutchcroft, and Don Emmerson gave the essay a close reading and offered useful comments. I thank them all for their generous assistance and assume full responsibility for the ways in which I have used, or misused, their ideas.

[1]Meralco Securities Corporation, *Annual Report, 1973* (Manila, Meralco Securities, 1973), 3, 14.

[2]*Manila Chronicle*, supplement, 14 March 1987.

[3]Ibid.

[4]Steve Psinakis, *Two "Terrorists" Meet* (San Francisco: Alchemy Books, 1981), 136–50; *Manila Chronicle*, supplement, 14 March 1987.

[5]James M. Buchanan, "Rent Seeking and Profit Seeking," in *Toward a Theory of the Rent-Seeking Society*, edited by James M. Buchanan, Robert D. Tollison, and Gordon Tullock (College Station: Texas A&M Press, 1980), 7–8.

[6]Anne O. Krueger, "The Political Economy of the Rent-Seeking Society," in Buchanan et al., *Theory of the Rent-Seeking Society*, 52–57.

[7]Peter B. Evans, "Predatory, Developmental, and Other Apparatuses: A Comparative Political Economy Perspective on the Third World State," *Sociological Forum* 4, no. 4 (1989): 561–62.

[8]Ibid., 570–74. Applying this critique to the Philippines, political scientist Paul Hutchcroft argues that there are two major types of rent-seeking regimes: "bureaucratic capitalism" wherein "a bureaucratic elite extracts privilege from a weak business class," and "booty capitalism" wherein "a powerful business class extracts privilege from a largely incoherent bureaucracy." With some qualifications, Hutchcroft feels that the Philippines falls within the latter category. See Paul D. Hutchcroft, "The Political Foundations of Booty Capitalism in the Philippines" (unpublished paper presented at the annual meeting of the American Political Science Association, 1992), 2.

[9]Manuel Montes, "The Business Sector and Development Policy" in *National Development Policies and the Business Sector in the Philippines*, edited by Aiichiro Ishii et al. (Tokyo: Institute of Developing Economies, 1988), 64–67.

[10]Ibid., 49. For other such studies of rents and recent Philippine economic history, see Raul V. Fabella, "Trade and Industry Reforms in the Philippines: Process and Performance," in *Philippine Macroeconomic Perspective: Developments and Policies*, edited by Manuel F. Montes et al. (Tokyo: Institute of Developing Economies, 1989), 183–214; and Manuel F. Montes, "Financing Development: The 'Democratic' versus the 'Corporatist' Approach in the Philippines," in *The Political Economy of Fiscal Policy*, edited by Miguel Urrutia (Tokyo: United Nations University, 1989), 84–148.

[11]For some theoretical literature on the state in the Philippines and the Third World, see Fermin D. Adriano, "A Critique of the 'Bureaucratic Authoritarian State' Thesis: The Case of the Philippines," *Journal of Contemporary Asia* 14, no. 4 (1984); Robert Stauffer, "The Philippine Political Economy: (Dependent) State Capitalism in the Corporatist Mode," in *Southeast Asia: Essays in the Political Economy of Structural Change*, edited by R. Higgot and R. Robison (London: Routledge and Kegan Paul, 1985); and Hamza Alavi, "The State in Post Colonial Societies," *New Left Review* (July/August 1972): 59–81. For sources that deal more directly with the idea of a "weak" Philippine state, see Temario C. Rivera, "Class, The State and Foreign Capital: The Politics of Philippine Industrialization, 1950–1986" (Ph.D. diss., University of Wisconsin, Madison, 1991), 184–214; and David Wurfel, *Filipino Politics: Development and Decay* (Quezon City: Ateneo de Manila University Press, 1988), 56, 340.

[12]Paul Hutchcroft has found Max Weber's concept of "patrimonialism" the most appropriate paradigm to explain the continuity of elite-state relations during the Marcos and post-Marcos eras in the Philippines. See Paul Hutchcroft, "Oligarchs and Cronies in the Philippine State: The Politics of Patrimonial Plunder," *World Politics* 43, no. 3 (April 1991): 414–50. According to Hutchcroft, the "heightened . . . role of the state in private accumulation" started with the end of the bureaucratic U.S. colonial regime in 1946, grew under the Republic, and achieved florescence under the Marcos regime (p. 423). Indeed, through the Republican era, Marcos's dictatorship, and the post-Marcos period, "there has been . . . little change in the way in which dominant economic interests interact with the Philippine state" (p. 415). Since Weber considered patrimonialism to be a form of "traditional authority," I, too, have used the term *neo-patrimonialism* to imply the revival of a traditional form of authority in a later era. According to Weber, patriarchalism gives way to patrimonialism "with the development of a purely personal administrative staff, especially a military force under the control of a chief. . . ." As the chief assembles his military force, he "tends to broaden the range of his arbitrary power . . . and to put himself in a position to grant grace and favors at the expense of the traditional limitations typical of patriarchal . . . structures." When the chief exercises "absolute authority," patrimonialism may be called "sultanism," and when an individual or a group exercises economic or political power patrimonialism may be described as "decentralized." See Max Weber, *The Theory of Social and Economic Organization* (New York: Free Press, 1964), 346–54.

[13]Manuel F. Montes, "11 Questions Regarding Nationalist Industrialization," in *Three Essays on Nationalist Industrialization*, edited by Emmanuel S. de Dios et al. (Quezon City: Philippine Center for Policy Studies, 1991), 38.

[14]Montes, "The Business Sector and Development Policy," 65.

[15]Ibid., 33.

[16]Hutchcroft, "Oligarchs and Cronies," 416.

[17]Ibid.

[18]J. F. Doherty, S.J., "Who Controls the Philippine Economy: Some Not Need Try as Hard as Others," in *Cronies and Enemies: The Current Philippine Scene*, edited by Belinda A. Aquino, Philippine Studies Series, no. 5 (Honolulu: Philippine Studies Program, University of Hawaii, 1982), 12–33.

[19]Under the Aquino administration, commentators from the center and left developed a cogent critique of these elite political families, which they called *clans* or *trapos*. See Eric U. Gutierrez, "Political Clans in Philippine Politics," *Conjuncture* 5, no. 3 (March 1992): 3, 15; Eric U. Gutierrez et al., *All in the Family: A Study of Elites and Power Relations in the Philippines* (Quezon City: Institute for Popular Democracy, 1992), 3–15; and Men Sta. Ana, "Trapos Still Rule," *Conjuncture* 5, no. 5 (May 1992): 1, 6.

[20]Similarly, in his study of the famous Adams family of Massachusetts, David Musto found a "familial cohesiveness, emotional and attitudinal" so marked that it became a familial world outlook with a "well organized view of our past, present, and future." See David F. Musto, "The Adams Family," *Proceedings of the Massachusetts Historical Society* 93 (1981): 41–42.

[21]Charles H. Harris, *A Mexican Family Empire: The Latifundio of the Sanchez Navarros, 1765–1867* (Austin: University of Texas Press, 1975), 314.

[22]Oscar M. Lopez, ed., *The Lopez Family: Its Origins and Genealogy* (Manila: Lopez Foundation, 1982), xxv–xxxix.

[23]Ibid., xli–xlii.

[24]Protocolos 1600, Negros Occidental, appendix, p. 47, Philippine National Archives.

[25]Fincas Urbanas, Iloilo, 1891, Philippine National Archives.

[26]Lopez, *The Lopez Family*, 1:xlii–xliv; Eugenio Lopez y Jalandoni, Reconocimiento de Obligacion, Protocolos, 1603, 30 August 1887, Philippine National Archives.

[27]Lopez, *The Lopez Family*, 1:xlii–xliv.

[28]Fincas Urbanas, Iloilo, 1891, Philippine National Archives.

[29]Lopez, *The Lopez Family*, 1:xliv.

[30]Eugenio Lopez y Jalandoni, Reconocimiento de Obligacion, Protocolos, 1603, 30 August 1887, Philippine National Archives.

[31]Lopez, *The Lopez Family*, 1:xliv–xlvi.

[32]Ibid., 1:xlvii–li; Pedro A. Paterno, *El Regimen Municipal en las Islas Filipinas* (Madrid: Sucesores de Cuesta, 1893).

[33]*El Eco de Panay* (Iloilo City), 16 March 1897.

[34]Lopez, *The Lopez Family*, 1:li–lii.

[35]Estadisticas, Negros Occidental, Philippine National Archives.

[36]Lopez, *The Lopez Family*, 1:xliv–xlvi, 167–68.

[37]Gov. Ruperto Montinola, "Report of the Governor of the Province of Iloilo," 30 June 1908, Bureau of Insular Affairs, U.S. National Archives; Chief, Law Division, "Give Result of Investigation of Joaquin Gil, Benito Lopez. . . ," 26 November 1907, Worcester Philippine Collection, Harlan Hatcher Library, University of Michigan.

[38]National Sugar Board, "Report of the National Sugar Board to His Excellency the President of the Philippines (mimeographed, 2 August 1939), 16–25, Elizalde Papers, Elizalde y Cia Offices, Iloilo City.

[39]Justice Manuel Moran, "Justice Moran's Report on the Sugar Industry" (mimeographed, 30 April 1939), 17, Elizalde Papers, Elizalde y Cia Offices, Iloilo City.

[40]Justice Moran found that the average capital investment for the country's 24,020 planters was P13,530, while the average for the country's forty-five mills was P3.96 million (see ibid., 10–11).

[41]Ramon M. Lacsamana, ed., *Negros Occidental 1938–1939 Yearbook* (Bacolod: Ramon M. Lacsamana, 1939), F3–4, F18–19.

[42]Yves Henry, *Conditions, Techniques et Financieres de la Production du Sucre aux Philippines* (Hanoi: Gouvernment Général de l'Indochine, Inspection Générale de l'Agriculture, de l'Élevage et des Forêts, 1928), 41–53.

[43]Asociacion de Agricultores de La Carlota y Pontevedra, Inc., *Memoria Anual de la Junta Directive y Comite. Ejercicio 1930–31* (Iloilo: La Editorial, 1931), 26–30; Don Carlos Locsin (president, Victorias Milling Co.), interview with the author, Hacienda Tagbanon, Manapla, Negros Occidental, 28 October 1975.

[44]National Sugar Board, "Report of the National Sugar Board to His Excellency The President of the Philippines," Manila, 2 August 1939, 20–21, Elizalde Papers, Elizalde y Cia Offices, Iloilo City. While her district planters made an average of 10.51 percent profit on their investments, Doña Rosario enjoyed an annual return of 42.73 percent ("Moran's Report on the Sugar Industry," 19).

[45]Doris G. Nuyda, *The Beauty Book* (Manila: Mr. and Ms. Publishing, 1980),1923.

[46]*Honorable Fernando Lopez, Silver Jubilee in Public Service, 1945–1970* (Iloilo: n.p., 1970), 5–6.

[47]Debbie Lozare, "Remembering Don Eugenio Lopez, Sr," *Manila Chronicle*, 14 March 1987, 33.

[48]Musto, "Adams Family," 42.

[49]Pacita Moreno Lopez, interview with M. N. Roces, quoted in Maria Natividad Roces, "Kinship Politics in the Post-War Philippines: The Lopez Family, 1945–1989" (Ph.D. diss., University of Michigan, 1990), 99.

[50]*The Times* (Iloilo City), 12 January 1939, 19 January 1939; Jacinto Montilla, "Memorandum to Integrity Board," 12 September 1952, Elpidio Quirino Papers, Ayala Museum, Manila; *Isabela Sugar Co., Inc., vs. Eugenio Lopez et al.*, Court of First Instance, Manila, Civil Case 14831 (1951), Enrique J. C. Montilla, complainant, filed in Elpidio Quirino Papers, ibid.

[51]A summary of his major transactions shows the effectiveness of this pyramiding tactic: the Iloilo Transportation Co. was valued at P250,000 in 1937; Panay Autobus was purchased in 1938 for P565,000; Far Eastern Air Transport, Inc., was sold in 1947 for P2.8

million; Binalbagan-Isabela Sugar Mill (Biscom) was acquired in 1951 for P2.7 million; the Manila Electric Company (Meralco) was purchased in 1962 for P54.4 million; and Meralco Securities Corporation's total investments were assessed at an aggregate book value of P1.02 billion in June 1973. See *The Times*, 12 January 1939; *Makinaugalingon* (Iloilo City), 2 March 1938; Andres Soriano, Memorandum Agreement, n.d., Elpidio Quirino Papers, Ayala Museum, Manila; *Sugar News* (Manila), January 1952, 31; Order, *Isabela Sugar vs. Eugenio Lopez*, and Meralco Securities Corporation, *Annual Report, 1973*, 28–35.

[52] *Philippines Free Press* (Manila), 28 March 1953, 34.

[53] *Manila Times*, 15 January 1953, 5 March 1953.

[54] *Veritas* (Iloilo City), 22 May 1949, 19 June 1949, 11 September 1949, 1 October 1950, 6 May 1951.

[55] Ibid., 22 May 1949, 3 July 1949, 10 July 1949.

[56] *Washington Post*, 23 November 1974.

[57] Ibid., 84.

[58] Eugenio Lopez, "The Council of State in the Philippine Islands" (unpublished paper, March 1924, Harvard Law School), 1. A copy of this work was consulted at the Harvard University Law Library.

[59] Ibid., 2.

[60] Ibid., 4.

[61] Ibid., 5–6.

[62] Ibid., 7–8.

[63] Ibid., 9.

[64] Ibid., 44–50.

[65] Ibid., 27.

[66] Ibid., 12, 20.

[67] Ibid., 34.

[68] Ibid., 36–38.

[69] Ibid., 43.

[70] Eugenio and Fernando's father, Benito Villanueva Lopez, had married Presentacion Javelona Hofileña, their mother. Their uncle and guardian, Vicente Villanueva Lopez, had married their mother's younger sister, Elena Javelona Hofileña. See Lopez, *The Lopez Family*, 1:168.

[71] Since none of the Lopez biographies or family histories mention this court case, the details remain obscure. For references to the dispute, see *El Tiempo*, 24 November 1937. The annual report of the La Carlota Planters Association for 1924–25 lists a single Hacienda Casalagan in Pontevedra with 685 hectares (Asociacion de Agricultores de La Carlota y Pontevedra, Inc., *Memoria Anual de la Junta Directive y Comite. Ejercicio 1924–1925* [Iloilo: La Editorial, 1925], 12). However, the association's report for 1931–32 shows Don Vicente Lopez as proprietor of "Hacienda Casalagan Viejo," with 295 hectares, and Eugenio and Fernando Lopez as owners of "Hacienda Casalagan Nuevo" with 390 hectares (Asociacion de Agricultores, *Memoria Anual, 1931–32*, 17). Since the area of the two haciendas totals 685 hectares, it seems safe to assume that this was the disputed property.

[72] *Manila Chronicle*, 14 March 1987 (Supplement: "Meralco's 84th Year").

[73] Godofredo Grageda, "The *El Tiempo* and *Iloilo Times*" (unpublished memoir, 15 November 1976), 1–5. According to his "Foreword," Grageda, "one of the original staff members of the *Tiempo-Times* publications," wrote this memoir for Oscar Lopez, Eugenio's second son, to satisfy his "curiosity" about "the power that both publications generated in bolstering the prestige and influence of his father in the affairs of Iloilo." Oscar Lopez shared it with me during an October 1988 interview, and I thank him for this kindness.

[74] *Makinaugalingon*, 4 June 1929.

[75] Ibid., 10 September 1929.

[76] *El Tiempo*, 2 October 1929. In 1974, while taking a break from reading the postwar issues of *The Times* at the Tiempo-Times Building in Iloilo City, I stepped into the work area behind the building. There I found, quite by accident, the extant prewar issues of *El*

Tiempo, discarded beneath a pile of garbage and soaked with rainwater. With the permission of Lopez executive Jose Jimagoan, I took this mass of wet newsprint home in a jeepney to nearby Jaro and turned a page or two every night as they dried. In this nightly journey through pages of the prewar *El Tiempo*, I was able to follow the progress of the *jueteng* scandal, albeit through a process that I found frustratingly slow. The first few pages of every volume had jagged tears, further complicating the continuity of the narrative. Informally, former *Times* employees told me that the paper's printers had torn pages from these prewar volumes to use to clean the presses. After rebinding and copying articles from the surviving volumes, I returned them to Mr. Jimagaon who forwarded them to the Lopez Museum in Manila where they are today. (The museum's director, Oscar Lopez, kindly reimbursed me for the cost of the binding.) This narrative therefore suffers a sometimes erratic and episodic quality arising from the random gaps in *El Tiempo*'s coverage and relies on the Hiligaynon newspaper *Makinaugalingon* for its chronological continuity.

[77] *El Tiempo*, 2 October 1929.

[78] Newspaper clipping entitled "Ignacio Arroyo Dies of Heart Failure in Residence in Iloilo," enclosed in a letter from Dr. Mariano Arroyo to Manuel Quezon, 19 January 1935, Box 65, File: Arroyo, Ignacio, Manuel Quezon Papers, Philippine National Library.

[79] Fernando Ma. Guerrero, *Directorio Oficial del Senado de Filipinas* (Manila: Bureau of Printing, 1921), 34–35; Fernando Ma. Guerrero, *Directorio Oficial del Senado y de la Camara de Representatives* (Manila: Bureau of Printing, 1917), 157–58.

[80] Dapen Liang, *Philippine Parties and Politics* (San Francisco: Gladstone, 1970), 129; letter from Jose Ma. Arroyo to Manuel Quezon, 15 April 1922, Box 182, File: Iloilo 1921–23, Manuel Quezon Papers, Philippine National Library.

[81] Letter from Jose Ma. Arroyo to Manuel Quezon, 27 December 1924, Box 182, File: Iloilo 1921–23, Manuel Quezon Papers, Philippine National Library.

[82] Letter from Dr. Mariano Arroyo to Senate President Manuel A. Quezon, 15 August 1927, and letter from Manuel A. Quezon to Dr. Mariano Arroyo, 23 August 1927, Box 182, File: Iloilo 1926–29, Manuel Quezon Papers, Philippine National Library.

[83] Resolution No. 1848, Provincial Government of Iloilo, 16 August 1929, Box 182, File: Iloilo 1926–29, Manuel Quezon Papers, Philippine National Library.

[84] Letter from Jose B. Ledesma to Manuel A. Quezon, 23 February 1929, and letter from Manuel Quezon to Senator Jose B. Ledesma, 29 May 1929, Box 182, File: Iloilo 1929, Manuel Quezon Papers, Philippine National Library; letter from Dr. Mariano Arroyo to Manuel Quezon, 5 January 1929, and letter from Manuel Quezon to Dr. Mariano Arroyo, 10 January 1929, Box 182, File: Iloilo 1929, Manuel Quezon Papers, Philippine National Library.

[85] Letter from Jose Ma. Arroyo to Manuel Quezon, 24 January 1925, Box 182, File: Iloilo 1921–23, Manuel Quezon Papers, Philippine National Library.

[86] Letter from Mariano Arroyo to Manuel Quezon, 31 January 1929, Box 182, File: Iloilo 1929, Manuel Quezon Papers, Philippine National Library.

[87] *El Tiempo*, 2 October 1929.

[88] Grageda, "*El Tiempo* and *Iloilo Times*," 8–10.

[89] *El Tiempo*, 2 October 1929.

[90] Ibid., 5 October 1929.

[91] Ibid.

[92] Ibid., 7 October 1929.

[93] Ibid., 9 October 1929.

[94] *Makinaugalingon*, 11 October 1929.

[95] *El Tiempo*, 11 October 1929.

[96] Ibid., 19 October 1929, 25 November 1929.

[97] Ibid., 29 October 1929, 13 November 1929.

[98] *Makinaugalingon*, 11 October 1929, 22 October 1929, 29 October 1929, 1 November 1929.

[99] *El Tiempo*, 3 January 1930, 14 January 1930.

[100] *Makinaugalingon*, 20 June 1930. Although he advertised in *El Tiempo* as an import-export dealer who "buys and sells all classes of local products" (*El Tiempo*, 3 October 1929), Sualoy could not withstand this pressure on his illegal operations. In October 1930, he sailed for China (ibid., 14 November 1930). After his return to Iloilo, the Constabulary raided his house on Iznart Street, in March 1933, seizing a notebook showing income from *jueteng* in January amounting to P2,175.60 and listing seven payments to police ranging from 5 to 30 pesos each (*Makinaugalingon*, 21 April 1933). In October 1937, a Manila court convicted Sualoy for possession of false bank notes and ordered him deported (*El Tiempo*, 31 March 1937). According to an obituary, he appealed the decision to the Philippine Supreme Court and finally fled to China where he died at Kinchang, Chingkang, of heart disease on 3 August 1940 (*Makinaugalingon*, 24 August 1940).

[101] Ibid., 6 August 1930.

[102] Ibid., 11 August 1930.

[103] Ibid., 22 September 1930.

[104] *Manila Times*, 27 September 1930.

[105] *Makinaugalingon*, 24 September 1930. The original Hiligaynon text of Arroyo's alleged statement reads: "Kumpare, ang siling niya, ngaa buut ka gid nga madula ang sugal nga hueteng? Wala ka makasayud nga ang kalabanan sang mga wakha kag mga magulibud sa pagpapatad mga lider natun? Malapit na lamang ang piniliay kag magapasulpu aku kag ina sila makagdaut sa atun gani madamu sila sa sini nga probinsia, wala'y labut nga ginahatagan kita nila sing pilak nga galastohon sa piniliay."

[106] *El Tiempo*, 24 October 1930.

[107] Grageda, "*El Tiempo* and *Iloilo Times*," 8–10.

[108] *El Tiempo*, 15 November 1930; *Makinaugalingon*, 3 October 1930.

[109] Letter from Ignacio Arroyo to Manuel Quezon, 11 May 1929, Box 65, File: Arroyo, Ignacio, Manuel Quezon Papers, Philippine National Library.

[110] Letter from Manuel Quezon to Mariano Arroyo, 13 June 1929, Box 65, File: Arroyo, Ignacio, Manuel Quezon Papers, Philippine National Library.

[111] Letter from Mariano Arroyo to Manuel Quezon, 22 June 1929, Box 182, File: Iloilo 1929, Manuel Quezon Papers, Philippine National Library.

[112] Letter from Jose Zulueta to Manuel Quezon, 2 April 1929, Box 70, File: Zulueta, Francisco, Manuel Quezon Papers, Philippine National Library.

[113] Letter from Mariano Arroyo to Manuel Quezon, 26 July 1930, Box 65, File: Arroyo, Ignacio, Manuel Quezon Papers, Philippine National Library.

[114] Telegram from Buenaflor/Arroyo to Manuel Quezon, 26 September 1930, Box 65, File: Arroyo, Ignacio, Manuel Quezon Papers, Philippine National Library.

[115] *El Tiempo*, 13 October 1930.

[116] Ibid., 14 October 1930.

[117] Letter from Manuel Quezon to Mariano Arroyo, 31 May 1932, Box 65, File: Arroyo, Ignacio, Manuel Quezon Papers, Philippine National Library.

[118] Vicente Albano Pacis, *President Sergio Osmeña: A Fully-Documented Biography* (Quezon City: Philippine Constitution Association, 1971), 49–51.

[119] Letter from Manuel Quezon to Jose Zulueta, 30 May 1934, Box 182, File: Iloilo 1934–35, Manuel Quezon Papers, Philippine National Library.

[120] Grageda, "*El Tiempo* and *Iloilo Times*," 10–13. In June 1933, the *Tiempo-Times* editors telegraphed Quezon citing a statement by his rivals Osmeña and Roxas (OSROX): "*Tiempo Times* request your comment immediately for public caution before OSROX arrival." That same day, Quezon responded with a long statement attacking the OSROX mission (telegram from *Tiempo-Times* to Manuel Quezon, 29 June 1933; and telegram from Manuel Quezon to *Tiempo-Times*, 29 June 1933, Box 51, File: 1933 General Correspondence—May-June, Manuel Quezon Papers, Philippine National Library).

[121] Quotation and the information in the following paragraph are from Grageda, "*El Tiempo* and *Iloilo Times*," 10–13.

[122]Letter from Jose Zulueta to Manuel Quezon, 10 May 1934, Box 182, File: Iloilo 1934–35, Manuel Quezon Papers, Philippine National Library.

[123]Dapen Liang, *Philippine Parties and Politics*, 182.

[124]For example, in Iloilo's Fourth District, two-term congressman Tomas Buenaflor lost badly (5,778 to 3,871) to an obscure opposition candidate. See Eulogio Benitez, *Directorio Oficial de la Camara de Representantes* (Manila: Bureau of Printing, 1938), 92–99.

[125]Confidential letter from Governor Jose Yulo et al. to Manuel Quezon, 8 June 1934, Box 182, File: Iloilo 1934–35, Manuel Quezon Papers, Philippine National Library.

[126]Letter from Dr. Fermin Caram to Manuel Quezon, 11 June 1934, Box 182, File: Iloilo 1934–35, Manuel Quezon Papers, Philippine National Library.

[127]Letter from Silvino Gallardo to Manuel Quezon, 19 August 1935, Box 118, File: 19 August 1935 Elections, Manuel Quezon Papers, Philippine National Library.

[128]Iloilo, Box 127, File: 1935 Election Returns Iloilo, Manuel Quezon Papers, Philippine National Library.

[129]*Makinaugalingon*, 19 August 1936, 29 August 1936.

[130]Ibid., 24 September 1938, 1 October 1938. Fernando's 1929 baptismal celebration for his firstborn, Benito, was a much more modest affair, with a guest list comprised entirely of Lopez relations and regional elite. These included the godmother Nelly Lopez, Oscar Ledesma, local attorney Thomas Powell, and Iloilo merchant Herbert Hoskyn. See *El Tiempo*, 21 December 1929.

[131]Grageda, "*El Tiempo* and *Iloilo Times*," 12–13.

[132]*Makinaugalingon*, 21 October 1936, 27 July 1940, 3 August 1940.

[133]Ibid., 21 October 1936.

[134]Bureau of Customs, Department of Finance, Philippine Islands, *Annual Report of the Insular Collector of Customs* (Manila: Bureau of Printing, 1925, 1932, 1934), 37, 31, 33, respectively.

[135]Jose Jimagaon (prewar manager of Lopez enterprises), interview with the author, Iloilo City, 19 April 1974.

[136]*El Tiempo*, 5 November 1937, 8 November 1937.

[137]Ibid., 17 February 1937.

[138]*Sugar Central and Planters News* 14, no. 1 (January 1933): 40; ibid., 14, no. 3 (March 1933): 152.

[139]Manuel H. David, ed., *Panay Directory and Souvenir Book* (Iloilo City: Ramon F. Campos, 1937), 49.

[140]*El Tiempo*, 3 December 1937; *The Times*, 1 March 1939.

[141]Ibid., 17 February 1939.

[142]*Makinaugalingon*, 30 May 1930, 9 June 1930. The 30 May issue gives a figure of fifty buses, while an article in *El Tiempo* published on 13 November 1930 refers to a license for thirty units. I have not found an alternative source to resolve this discrepancy.

[143]*El Tiempo*, 13 November 1930.

[144]Pacita Borja de Lezama (daughter of Miguel Borja), interview with the author, Iloilo City, 30 August 1974. The role of colonial Americans in the early development of bus transportation in the Philippines, as well as Klar's career, are treated in Lewis E. Gleeck, Jr., *Americans on Philippine Frontiers* (Manila: Carmelo and Bauermann, 1974), 133–36.

[145]On the labor troubles at Panay Autobus, see *Makinaugalingon*, 9 January 1934, 12 January 1934, and 10 April 1934. The conflict between Panay Autobus and its union, Federacion Obrera de Filipinas, resulted in an assault by Leon Nava, son of the union president, on the company manager, an American named John Barker. See ibid., 24 April 1934. For the details of the merger, I have relied upon David, *Panay Directory*, 50; and the interview with Pacita Borja de Lezama. Interestingly, I met Mrs. Lezama at a dinner party hosted by former vice-president Fernando Lopez at his home in La Paz, Iloilo City. She invited me to interview her on the subject of our host's takeover of her family's company nearly thirty years earlier. At the close of our interview, which took place in the office of the

Aboitez Shipping Company on Iloilo's Muelle Loney, I asked her why she socialized with the Lopezes given the bitterness of their former battle. With a certain irony, she attributed the frequent Lopez invitations to "guilt" and explained her acceptances as a business necessity (Pacita Borja de Lezama, interview, 30 August 1974).

[146] *El Tiempo*, 2 September 1946.

[147] Ibid.

[148] *Makinaugalingon*, 22 February 1936, 4 July 1936; *El Tiempo*, 8 November 1937.

[149] Ibid., 2 September 1946.

[150] Serafin Deza (station manager for Eagle Express bus company prior to its purchase by the Lopez brothers), interview with the author, Dumangas, Iloilo, 3 October 1975.

[151] Pacita Borja de Lezama, interview, 30 August 1974.

[152] In her elaborate denial of a Lopez alliance with the Iloilo underworld, Maria N. Roces reflected the concern of her main source, Oscar Lopez, the son of Eugenio Lopez, Sr., and the family historian, whom she interviewed in May 1988, two years after the ouster of Marcos. The political need to rebut Marcos's allegations about their violence underlying the vehement Lopez denial of any use of force, past or present, and the consequent contradictions in Roces's argument, are illustrated in this passage from the Roces dissertation.

> When questioned regarding these accusations of intimidation, Lopez family members and employees all agreed that the Lopezes quarreled with the Borjas but denied the use of force or threats of violence or murder. The Lopezes would probably not hesitate to use goons, the family's lieutenants may have resorted to violence, but it was another thing to imply that they would resort to murder without sufficient evidence to support the allegation. The post-war family history revealed no concrete evidence of their having ever planned an assassination despite all that President Marcos has done to them (although one in-law, Steve Psinakis, was associated with terrorists). In fact, as will be shown in this narrative, although the family members were fighters, once threatened, their reaction was not to risk everything to win, but to consolidate forces and move their business interests elsewhere. Although McCoy's arguments are persuasive, the blatant use of violence was not characteristic of the Lopez business or political panache (Roces, "Kinship Politics," 92).

During the postwar decades, the Lopezes, like most Manila-based political families, did not use violence in either politics or business. In the prewar period, however, the Lopez brothers were provincial politicians and like most of that elite stratum engaged in violence as both an offensive and a defensive tactic. Since President Marcos had jailed Eugenio Lopez, Jr., on charges of plotting his assassination, and then had used him as a hostage in order to extort much of the Lopez wealth, the family's determination to disassociate itself from violence is understandable.

[153] Lopez employee Jose Jimagaon confirmed his company's alliance with Jesus Astrologo and Simeon Valiente in an interview with the author conducted at Iloilo City, 28 September 1974. This assessment of Astrologo's reputation is based on a reading of reports of his activities in *Makinaugalingon*. At the time that Astrologo was active on the Iloilo waterfront in the Panay Autobus battle, the paper reported that he used a club to beat attorney Emilio R. Severino, a local labor leader, in Bacolod, "wounding his face and injuring other parts of his body" (*Si Gg. Severino napilas sa nawung kag may samad sa mga bahin sang lawas*). The paper charged that Astrologo had "been paid by the enemies of Mr. Severino because nothing had passed between them, not even an argument, before this happened" (*Ginahunahunaan nga si Astrologo ginbayaran sang mga kaaway ni Gg. Severino, kay wala mag-agi sa ila bisan nag-bangig sang wala pa mahanabu*). In closing, the article noted, "Excepting this incident, there are other criminal cases against Astrologo in this city and in Bacolod" (*Wala labut sini may mga panumbung pa nga kriminal batuk kay Astrologo sa sini nga siudad kag sa Bakolod*). See *Makinaugalingon*, 25 September 1937.

[154] Ibid., 30 December 1939.

155Ibid., 17 March 1937.

156Sentencia, 15 January 1928, *Pueblo vs. Astrologo,* Criminal Case No. 7982, Court of First Instance, Iloilo; Decision, 13 February 1932, *People vs. Jesus Astrologo,* Criminal Case No. 15317, Justice of the Peace, Iloilo; Sentencia, 4 February 1935, *People vs. Jesus Astrologo,* Criminal Case No. 11076, Court of First Instance, Iloilo; Sentencia, 12 December 1940, *People vs. Jesus Astrologo,* Criminal Case No. 12018, Court of First Instance, Negros Occidental, in *People vs. Jesus Astrologo,* Case No. 701, Fifth Division, People's Court, University of the Philippines Archives, Library, Diliman Campus.

157Amended Information, 2 August 1947, *People vs. Jesus Astrologo,* ibid.

158Judge Florentino Saguin, Decision, 11 December 1947, ibid.

159Jesus Astrologo, Confession, 16 August 1945, ibid.

160Primo Doctora (Panay Autobus *comisionista*), interview with the author, Iloilo City, 23 January 1975.

161Ibid.; Josue Javellana (a Lopez *comisionista*), interview with the author, Iloilo City, 15 July 1975.

162Primo Doctora, interview, 23 January 1975.

163Jose Jimagaon, interview, 15 July 1975.

164*Makinaugalingon,* 17 March 1937; Francisco Delgado (*comisionista* allied with Miguel Borja), interview with the author, Iloilo City, 30 August 1974.

165*El Tiempo,* 30 March 1937.

166*Makinaugalingon,* 18 August 1937.

167*El Tiempo,* 1 November 1937.

168David, *Panay Directory,* 120–53.

169Telegram from Vargas to Manuel Quezon, 18 June 1937, and telegram from Governor Timoteo Consing to Manuel Quezon, 26 June 1937, Box 182, File: Iloilo 1935–42, Manuel Quezon Papers, Philippine National Library.

170*Makinaugalingon,* 25 August 1937.

171Among the leaders of the Banwa Boys were Serapion Torre (mayor, 1923–28), Eulogio Garganera (mayor, 1929–31, 1934–37) and Leopoldo Ganzon (mayor, 1932–34).

172*Makinaugalingon,* 11 December 1937.

173*El Tiempo,* 5 November 1937.

174Ibid., 8 November 1937.

175Ibid., 15 November 1937.

176Ibid., 30 November 1937.

177Ibid., 2 December 1937.

178Ibid., 11 December 1937.

179Ibid., 22 December 1937, 24 December 1937.

180*Makinaugalingon,* 22 December 1937.

181Letter from Juan Tendencia et al. to Manuel Roxas, 8 March 1940, File: Correspondence—Volume 5, Manuel Roxas Papers, Philippine National Library.

182Primo Doctora, interview, 23 January 1975. *Makinaugalingon* published a slightly different account, reporting that in the midst of the usual morning struggle for passengers Valiente struck Doctora, after which his companion Hugo Onating stabbed the boxer, sending him to hospital with a serious wound (*Makinaugalingon,* 19 January 1938).

183Ibid., 29 January 1938.

184Pacita Borja de Lezama, interview, 30 August 1974.

185*El Tiempo,* 30 March 1937; *Makinaugalingon,* 17 March 1937.

186Pacita Borja de Lezama, interview, 30 August 1974. After the Panay Autobus struggle, which temporarily had elevated the status of their profession, the local *comisionistas* did not fare well. In January 1939, Valiente was sentenced to four months' imprisonment for slashing a patron at Iloilo's Follies Bergere. His companions, Jesus Astrologo and Hugo Onating, received lesser sentences for their role in the assault (*Makinaugalingon,* 14 January 1939). In December, the proprietor of Oxford Tailoring on Ledesma Street fatally shot

Simeon Valiente when this "well known bad character" entered the shop with an armed gang. After this incident, Iloilo police arrested three of Valiente's companions, including Hugo Onating (ibid., 30 December 1939). In December 1940, Jesus Astrologo was sentenced to fourteen years' imprisonment for the murder of a bus driver in an altercation over passengers on the Pulupandan pier (Sentencia, 12 December 1940, *People vs. Jesus Astrologo*, Criminal Case No. 12018, Court of First Instance, Negros Occidental, in *People vs. Jesus Astrologo*, Case No. 701, Fifth Division, People's Court, University of the Philippines Archives). During World War II, he was a notorious collaborator, for which he later served a prison sentence. After his release, he found a refuge working as a gardener at Fernando Lopez's home in Manila. During the course of my doctoral research in Iloilo City in 1974–76, I repeatedly requested an interview through Oscar Lopez but was informed that Astrologo refused to discuss these matters.

[187] *Makinaugalingon*, 2 March 1938.

[188] In addition to these transactions, Ogan criticized the Lopez group for purchasing 180 shares of Panay Autobus stock from various individuals, using company funds, at prices ranging from P110 to P210, then reselling the shares to themselves at a discounted price of P100. See *The Times* (Iloilo), 12 January 1939, 19 January 1939.

[189] Ibid., 12 January 1939, 10 February 1939, 18 February 1939, 22 February 1939, 9 March 1939, 22 March 1939.

[190] Ibid., 9 February 1939; *Makinaugalingon*, 17 July 1940.

[191] *The Tribune* (Manila), 7 November 1940.

[192] *The Times*, 23 February 1939.

[193] Juan Borra (Zulueta-faction candidate for the Iloilo Provincial Board in 1940), interview with the author, Manila, 6 November 1973.

[194] Cesario C. Golez (provincial secretary during Confesor's first term, 1937–40), interview with the author, Iloilo City, 30 October 1973; *The Tribune*, 6 November 1940, 7 November 1940.

[195] Mariano V. Benedicto (Iloilo City campaign manager for Confesor in the 1940 elections), interview with the author, Manila, 9 November 1973.

[196] *The Tribune*, 9 November 1940.

[197] Ibid., 14 November 1940.

[198] Ibid., 23 November 1940.

[199] "Result of the Special Election . . . December 10, 1940," Manuscript Tally Sheets, Electoral Commission, Fermin Caram, Sr., Papers, home of Fermin Caram, Jr., Iloilo City.

[200] *The Tribune,* 13 December 1940.

[201] *Sugar Central and Planters News* 22, no. 4 (April 1941): frontispiece; ibid., 21, no. 11 (November 1940): 453; *Makinaugalingon*, 24 September 1938. Alfredo was the son of Alejandro Montelibano who had been a prominent leader in a faction of Iloilo's Nacionalista Party allied with Senator Jose Ma. Arroyo and thus with Quezon himself. See letter from Alejandro Montelibano to Manuel Quezon, 10 December 1923, Box 128, File: Election Special—1923, Manuel Quezon Papers, Philippine National Library.

[202] *El Tiempo*, 16 January 1937; *Sugar Central and Planters News* 22, no. 4 (April 1941): frontispiece; ibid., 21, no. 2 (February 1940): 51.

[203] *The Herald* (Manila), 13 October 1941; *El Centinela* (Iloilo), issues of 11, 18, 24, and 28 October 1941.

[204] Ibid., 11 October 1941; *Hiligaynon* (Manila), 14 October 1941; Telegrams from Tomas Confesor to Manuel Quezon, 5 November 1941 and 6 November 1941, Box 128, File: Elections—November 1–6, 1941, Manuel Quezon Papers, Philippine National Library.

[205] Brigadier General B. G. Chynoweth, Report of Operations, "Historical Report, Visayan-Mindanao Force," RG-2, Box 4, MacArthur Memorial Archives, Norfolk, Virginia.

[206] On 14 January 1942, for example, Caram made his first independent policy statement on military preparedness by issuing orders to town mayors that "the people should

not be enjoined to commence any hostile act to invaders in order not to provoke reprisal" (*The Times*, 14 January 1942).

[207] Ibid., 6 February 1942.

[208] Ibid., 11 January 1942, 19 January 1942, 8 February 1942.

[209] Fermin G. Caram, Sr., "Memorandum for Col. Francis X. Cronan, C.I.C., U.S. Army," 20 April 1945, Fermin Caram, Sr., Papers, home of Fermin Caram, Jr., Iloilo City.

[210] *The Times*, 3 February 1942.

[211] Ibid., 22 February 1942, 1 March 1942.

[212] Letter from Manuel Quezon to General Douglas MacArthur, 25 February 1942, Box 55, Quezon Papers, Philippine National Library.

[213] Juan V. Borra, "The Guerrilla in Panay," *Southeast Asia Quarterly* (Iloilo City) 3, no. 2 (October 1968): 41–43; *The Times*, 14 April 1942.

[214] Jose M. Jimagaon, interview, 15 July 1975; Borra, "The Guerrilla in Panay," 40–42.

[215] Cesario C. Golez, *Calvary of the Resistance: The Price of Liberty* (Iloilo City: Cesario C. Golez, 1973), 30–32; untitled report from Deputy Governor Cesario C. Golez to Governor Tomas Confesor, 20 October 1944, Volume 36, World War II Papers, Central Philippine University.

[216] *Panay Times* (Iloilo City), 15 January 1944.

[217] Exequiel Villalobos (editor of *Panay Shu-Ho*), Diary, 30 June 1942, papers in the possession of the Villalobos family, Iloilo City.

[218] Caram, "Memorandum for Col. Cronan."

[219] Monsignor Jose Ma. Cuenco, *Memorias de un Refuiado* (Jaro: Catholic Publishing House, 1947), 105; *Panay Shu-Ho*, 20 February 1943, 6 March 1943, 15 March 1943, 10 April 1943.

[220] Agent No. 43 and Agent No. 50, Memorandum For: The Chief, Division of Investigation, Subject: Lopez, Eugenio (Treason), Department of Justice, Commonwealth of the Philippines, 18 January 1946, Counter Intelligence Corps, Case Report: Lopez, Eugenio, People's Court, University of the Philippines Archives, Library, Diliman Campus.

[221] Edmundo G. Navarro, *Beds of Nails* (Manila: Edmundo G. Navarro, 1988), 82–89; Theodore Friend, *Between Two Empires* (New Haven: Yale University Press, 1965), 250.

[222] Ramon P. Mitra, Letter to the Solicitor General, 30 January 1948, in *People vs. Ramon P. Mitra*, People's Court, Case No. 3468, pp. 11–14, University of the Philippines Archives, Library, Diliman Campus.

[223] Judy Geronimo, Confidential Affidavit, 14 April 1945, Counter Intelligence Corps, Case Report: Lopez, Eugenio, People's Court, University of the Philippines Archives, Library, Diliman Campus.

[224] Agent No. 43 and Agent No. 50, Memorandum.

[225] Judy Geronimo, Confidential Affidavit.

[226] Special Agent CIC 2216, Memorandum for the Officer in Charge, 11 September 1945, Subject: Lopez, Eugenio, Area No. 12, Counter Intelligence Corps, Case Report: Lopez, Eugenio, People's Court, University of the Philippines Archives, Library, Diliman Campus.

[227] Agent No. 43 and Agent No. 50, Memorandum.

[228] Emmanuel Pelaez, Memorandum for the Solicitor General, Subject: Lopez, Eugenio, 31 January 1946, Counter Intelligence Corps, Case Report: Lopez, Eugenio, People's Court, University of the Philippines Archives, Library, Diliman Campus.

[229] Letter from Relunia to Mac, 25 February 1944, vol. 5, World War II Papers, Central Philippine University; Colonel Pedro Serran (ret.), interview with the author, G-2 Sixth Military District, Manila, 21 January 1974.

[230] Villalobos, Diary, 30 March 1944.

[231] *Panay Times*, 19 April 1944.

[232] *The Times*, 8 November 1945.

[233] Special Agent 2763, Subject: Nava, Oscar, To: HQ-CIC, 1 September 1945, Fermin Caram, Sr., Papers, home of Fermin Caram, Jr., Iloilo City.

[234]Letter from Fermin Caram, Sr., to Helen Caram Nava, 31 July 1945, and letter from Fermin Caram, Sr., to Manuel A. Roxas, 29 July 1945, Fermin Caram, Sr., Papers, home of Fermin Caram, Jr., Iloilo City.

[235]Ignacio Debuque, Re. Reinvestigation, 9 January 1947, *People vs. Frank Jison*, Criminal Case No. 5400, People's Court, University of the Philippines Archives, Library, Diliman Campus.

[236]Jose Ma. Nava, To: CIC, Subject: Frank Jison, Vicente Lopez, Sr., Vicente Lopez, Jr., n.d., papers in possession of the Nava family, Iloilo City.

[237]Agent No. 160, Subject: Jison, Frank, 15 August 1946, Division of Investigation, *People vs. Frank Jison*, Criminal Case No. 5400, People's Court, University of the Philippines Archives, Library, Diliman Campus.

[238]Information, 18 March 1946, in ibid.

[239]Agent No. 160, Subject: Jison, Frank, 15 August 1946, Division of Investigation, in ibid.

[240]Special Prosecutor Ignacio Debuque, Motion for Dismissal, 5 May 1947, in ibid.

[241] *The Times*, 30 August 1945.

[242] *Ang Tigbatas* (Iloilo City), 28 September 1945.

[243]Ibid., 3 October 1945.

[244]Luther Garcia (staff writer at *The Times*), interview with the author, Iloilo City, 17 November 1974.

[245]Villalobos, Diary, 2 August 1945.

[246] *Ang Tigbatas*, 16 November 1945.

[247] *The Times*, 5 June 1945.

[248]Ibid., 15 September 1945.

[249]Ibid.

[250]Ibid., 27 September 1945; Reichi Ishii, Affidavit, 14 October 1945, Vol. 202, World War II Papers, Central Philippine University.

[251] *The Times*, 6 October 1945.

[252]See, for example, *Damaso Soriano in the PSC*, Case 27600 (1947), papers in the possession of the family of Felipe Ysmael, Iloilo City.

[253]Letter from Eulogio Garganera to Senate President Manuel A. Roxas, 31 December 1945, Box 51, File: Iloilo Politics, Manuel A. Roxas Papers, Philippine National Library.

[254]Ronald K. Edgerton, "The Politics of Reconstruction in the Philippines, 1945–1948" (Ph.D. diss., University of Michigan, 1975), 251, 40n.

[255]Letter from Jorge Villanueva to Manuel A. Roxas, 12 April 1946, Box 15, File: Elections Presidential 1946 April, Manuel A. Roxas Papers, Philippine National Library. Villanueva identified himself to Roxas as "one of your sympathizers."

[256] *The Times*, 29 September 1945.

[257]Letter from F. G. Caram to Manuel A. Roxas, 6 August 1946, File: Iloilo—1946, Manuel A. Roxas Papers, Philippine National Library.

[258] *The Times*, 16 April 1946.

[259]Ronald Edgerton confirmed this action in interviews with Primitivo Lovina, the man who carried Lopez's funds to Osmeña, and with Juan Borra, a veteran Iloilo politician and Roxas loyalist. See Edgerton, "Politics of Reconstruction," 219, 251, 40n.

[260]Letter from Eulogio Garganera, 20 March 1946, Box 14, File: Elections Presidential 1946 March, Manuel A. Roxas Papers, Philippine National Library.

[261]Letter from Eulogio Garganera to Manuel A. Roxas, 25 March 1946, Box 14, File: Elections Presidential 1946 March, Manuel A. Roxas Papers, Philippine National Library.

[262] *The Times*, 26 March 1946.

[263]Telegram from Buenaflor to Gen. Manuel Roxas, 21 April 1946, Box 15, File: Elections 1946 April, Manuel A. Roxas Papers, Philippine National Library.

[264] *The Times*, 25 May 1946.

[265] *Fernando Lopez, Silver Jubilee*, 5.

[266]Telegram from President Manuel A. Roxas to Mayor Lopez, 9 November 1947, File: Iloilo 1947–48, Manuel A. Roxas Papers, Philippine National Library.

[267]Colonel Francisco Offemaria (transport officer, USAFFE, Sixty-first Division, in 1941–42), interviews with the author, Manila, 5 November 1973 and 28 January 1974. In a 1988 interview, Fernando Lopez recalled receiving war-damage payments for Panay Autobus but gave no indication of the size of the reimbursement. See Roces, "Kinship Politics," 102, 43n.

[268]*Manila Times*, 24 February 1962.

[269]Frank H. Golay, "The Philippine Monetary Policy Debate," *Pacific Affairs* 29, no. 3 (1956): 253–64.

[270]Virginia Benitez Licuanan, *Money in the Bank: The Story of Money and Banking in the Philippines and the PCIBank Story* (Manila: PCIBank Human Resources Development Foundation, 1985), 131. Eugenio Lopez's invitation to Montelibano was described in interviews conducted by Paul Hutchcroft with Ramon S. Orosa, a former president of PCIB and the son of Sixto Orosa, Jr., its first president. The interviews took place in Manila on 30 April 1991 and 4 May 1991. For many of these details and much documentation on the postwar history of Philippine banking, I am indebted to Paul Hutchcroft who has completed a doctoral dissertation at Yale University entitled "Predatory Oligarchy, Patrimonial State: The Politics of Private Commercial Banking in the Philippines" (Ph.D. diss., Yale University, 1993).

[271]Licuanan, *Money in the Bank*, 131.

[272]Sycip Gorres and Velayo, "A Study of Commercial Banks in the Philippines" (annual reports for the 1960s), Sycip Gorres and Velayo Library, Makati, Metro-Manila.

[273]*SEC-Business Day 1000 Top Corporations, 1981* (Manila: Business Day, 1981), 219–20. The Lopezes expanded their shares through an increased investment in the company.

[274]Jose B. Fernandez (governor of the Central Bank of the Philippines, ret.), interview with Paul Hutchcroft, Makati, Metro-Manila, 6 April 1990.

[275]*The Times*, 25 October 1945, 17 November 1945.

[276]Letter from Andres Soriano to President Sergio Osmeña, 20 October 1945, Box 2, Sergio Osmeña Papers, Philippine National Library.

[277]Telegram from Sergio Osmeña to Colonel Andres Soriano, 22 November 1945, Box 2, Sergio Osmeña Papers, Philippine National Library.

[278]There are many indications of Andres Soriano's closeness to Manuel Roxas. In October 1945, for example, political leader Ildefonso Coscolluela of Negros Occidental wrote a letter to Roxas, addressing him as "my dear Manoling," and asking, "Please don't forget to take up with Don Andres Soriano the matter of the agency of the San Miguel products in this province, if and when they start the business again" (aside from his interests in PAL, Soriano was president of the San Miguel Corporation). See letter from Ildefonso Coscolluela to Manuel Roxas, 26 October 1945, Box 51, File: Iloilo Politics, Manuel A. Roxas Papers, Philippine National Library.

[279]*Manila Times*, 14 January 1947, 21 January 1947.

[280]Letter from Pio Pedrosa to President Manuel Roxas, 3 May 1947, File: Memorandum, Misc., Manuel A. Roxas Papers, Philippine National Library; Andres Soriano, Eugenio Lopez, Memorandum Agreement, n.d., Elpidio Quirino Papers, Ayala Museum, Manila. In his letter, Pio Pedrosa commented that "experience . . . has definitely proven that there is not enough inter island traffic to maintain two large organizations like PAL and FEATI," adding that "in the international traffic it would be suicidal for both FEATI and PAL to compete with foreign airlines." Indicative of the degree of state intervention in the airline industry, Pedrosa urged that the government buy enough PAL shares to maintain a holding of 34 percent of the company's stock. He also asked that the government support the airline as its chosen instrument for the president's policy of "having a Philippine company carry the Philippine flag into other countries."

[281]Rosalinda Pineda-Ofreneo, *The Manipulated Press: A History of Philippine Journalism Since 1945* (Manila: Cacho Hermanos, 1984), 124–25.

[282]*Manila Chronicle*, 14 September 1986.

[283]Augusto Almeda-Lopez, "Memorandum on the ABS-CBN Case," 14 December 1984 (copy provided by Oscar Lopez).

[284]Oscar Lopez, Affidavit, July 1987 (copy provided by Oscar Lopez).

[285]*Sugar Central and Planters News* 18, no. 3 (March 1937): 101.

[286]Narciso Pimentel, *Directorio Oficial de la Asemblea Nacional* (Manila: Bureau of Printing, 1938), 161–63.

[287]*Sugar Central and Planters News* 17, no. 1 (January 1936): 31. Sources are not explicit about Enrique's relationship to Gil Montilla. While Enrique's biography in *Sugar Central and Planters News* (18, no. 2 [January 1937]: 40) is uncharacteristically vague about his parentage, Jacinto Montilla's biography in the same journal states that "he had his early training under his father, Speaker Gil Montilla" (18, no. 4 [April 1937]: 141).

[288]Colonel Salvador Abcede, interviews with the author, Bacolod City, 26 October 1974 and 27 October 1974.

[289]Letter from G. M. Bridgeford, Warner-Barnes Manila, to Colonel F. Hodsoll, D.S.O., 1 March 1947, Warner-Barnes, Inc., Iloilo City.

[290]Letter from G. M. Bridgeford, Warner-Barnes Manila, to Colonel F. Hodsoll, D.S.O., 27 November 1946, Warner-Barnes, Inc., Iloilo City.

[291]"Binalbagan Sugar Project: Strictly Confidential," memorandum enclosed in letter from Colonel F. Hodsoll, D.S.O., to G. M. Bridgeford, Warner-Barnes Manila, 29 January 1947, Warner-Barnes, Inc., Iloilo City.

[292]In a letter to Commander Charles Parsons, Joaquin ("Mike") Elizalde, Philippine resident commissioner in Washington, D.C., complained that President Osmeña had written a "blunt and ungracious letter accepting my resignation" and that his press secretary had issued a statement about the resignation that was "almost insulting to me." Letter from Joaquin Elizalde to Commander Charles Parsons, 30 December 1944, Box 5, File: Elizalde, Joaquin, Manuel A. Roxas Papers, Philippine National Library. Six months later, Elizalde wrote to Roxas: "I am sincere in thinking that you are the one and only man who can save the country," 25 June 1945, Box 5, File: Elizalde, Joaquin, Manuel A. Roxas Papers, Philippine National Library.

[293]In the month before the elections, Enrique Magalona wrote Manuel Roxas that Araneta was contributing P15,000 and three jeeps to the party, while Montilla offered only P5,000 (letter from Enrique Magalona to Manuel A. Roxas, 3 March 1946, Box 14, File: Elections Presidential 1946 March, Manuel A. Roxas Papers, Philippine National Library). Indicative of their close prewar alliance, Montilla wrote Jose Yulo in November 1941 that he would give up P20,000 per annum for the next nine years. "I do this willingly to sustain our faction and your leadership in this district" (letter from Enrique J. C. Montilla to Jose Yulo, 8 November 1941, Box 128, File: Elections 1941—November 7–12, Manuel Quezon Papers, Philippine National Library).

[294]Letter from G. M. Bridgeford, Warner-Barnes Manila, to Colonel F. Hodsoll, D.S.O., 16 December 1946, Warner-Barnes, Inc., Iloilo City.

[295]Anexo "C," Convention of the Delegates of the Liberal Party of the Municipalities Comprising the Third Representative District of the Province of Negros Occidental . . . on September 10, 1947, Box 34, File: Negros Occidental, Manuel A. Roxas Papers, Philippine National Library.

[296]*Sugar Central and Planters News* 18, no. 2 (February 1937): 40.

[297]Ibid., 26, no. 5 (May 1950): 237.

[298]Memorandum on Voting Trust, Binalbagan Sugar Company, n.d., Elpidio Quirino Papers, Ayala Museum, Manila.

[299]Letter from G. M. Bridgeford, Warner-Barnes Manila, to Colonel F. Hodsoll, D.S.O., 8 March 1947, Warner-Barnes, Inc., Iloilo City.

[300]Letter from E. J. C. Montilla to Binalbagan Estate, Inc., 18 March 1949, Elpidio Quirino Papers, Ayala Museum, Manila.

[301]Letters from G. M. Bridgeford, Warner-Barnes Manila, to Colonel F. Hodsoll, D.S.O., 8 March 1947 and 13 March 1947; and letter from Colonel F. Hodsoll, D.S.O., to G. M. Bridgeford, Warner-Barnes Manila, 11 March 1947, Warner-Barnes, Inc., Iloilo City.

[302]*Sugar Central and Planters News* 25, no. 1 (January 1949): 30, 33.

[303]Carlos Hilado (congressman from Negros Occidental during this period), interview with the author, Bacolod City, 9 September 1975.

[304]Memorandum on Voting Trust, Binalbagan Sugar Company, n.d., Elpidio Quirino Papers, Ayala Museum, Manila.

[305]Letter from R. Nepomuceno, secretary of justice, to Binalbagan-Isabela Planters Association, Inc., 28 December 1949, Elpidio Quirino Papers, Ayala Museum, Manila.

[306]Letter from Oscar Ledesma, president of the National Federation of Sugarcane Planters, and Miguel Gatuslao, president of the Binalbagan-Isabela Sugar Planters Association, to Secretary Pio Pedrosa, 20 April 1950, Elpidio Quirino Papers, Ayala Museum, Manila.

[307]Letter from E. J .C. Montilla to R. Nepomuceno, secretary of justice, 14 February 1950, Elpidio Quirino Papers, Ayala Museum, Manila.

[308]Letter from Emilio Camon, vice-president, Binalbagan-Isabela Planters Association, to Ricardo Nepomuceno, 10 January 1950, Elpidio Quirino Papers, Ayala Museum, Manila.

[309]Letters from Miguel Gatuslao to Ricardo Nepomuceno, secretary of justice, 14 February 1950 and 15 February 1950, Elpidio Quirino Papers, Ayala Museum, Manila.

[310]Letter from Ricardo Nepomuceno, secretary of justice, to President Elpidio Quirino, 8 March 1950, Elpidio Quirino Papers, Ayala Museum, Manila.

[311]Letter from Oscar Ledesma, president of the National Federation of Sugarcane Planters, and Miguel Gatuslao, president of the Binalbagan-Isabela Sugar Planters Association, to Secretary Pio Pedrosa, 20 April 1950, Elpidio Quirino Papers, Ayala Museum, Manila.

[312]Letter from Pio Pedrosa, secretary of finance, to President Elpidio Quirino, 21 April 1950, Elpidio Quirino Papers, Ayala Museum, Manila.

[313]Letter from Pio Pedrosa, secretary of finance, to President Elpidio Quirino, 20 April 1950, Elpidio Quirino Papers, Ayala Museum, Manila.

[314]Letter from Oscar Ledesma, president of the National Federation of Sugarcane Planters, and Miguel Gatuslao, president of the Binalbagan-Isabela Sugar Planters Association, to President Elpidio Quirino, 11 May 1950, Elpidio Quirino Papers, Ayala Museum, Manila.

[315]Letter from Oscar Ledesma, president of the National Federation of Sugarcane Planters, and Miguel Gatuslao, president of the Binalbagan-Isabela Sugar Planters Association, to President Elpidio Quirino, 21 May 1950, Elpidio Quirino Papers, Ayala Museum, Manila.

[316]Carlos Hilado, interview, 9 September 1975.

[317]Letter from Enrique J. C. Montilla, general manager, Binalbagan-Isabela Sugar Co., 17 May 1950, to President Elpidio Quirino, Elpidio Quirino Papers, Ayala Museum, Manila.

[318]Memorandum from Enrique J. C. Montilla, general manager, Binalbagan-Isabela Sugar Co., 14 November 1950, Elpidio Quirino Papers, Ayala Museum, Manila. In February 1950, a presidential committee valued Biscom's shares at P20.14 including the value of sugar-export quotas and P11.76 excluding sugar-export quotas. See V. Carmona et al., letter to President Elpidio Quirino, 17 February 1950, Elpidio Quirino Papers, Ayala Museum, Manila.

[319]Letters from Enrique J. C. Montilla, general manager, Binalbagan-Isabela Sugar Co., 4 January 1951, 7 March 1951, and 17 May 1950, to President Elpidio Quirino, Elpidio Quirino Papers, Ayala Museum, Manila.

[320]Carlos Hilado, interview, 9 September 1975.

[321]Letters from Marino Rubin, acting president of Biscom Planters Association, to Binalbagan Estate, Inc., 21 February 1951, Elpidio Quirino Papers, Ayala Museum, Manila.

[322]Carlos Hilado, interview, 9 September 1975; *Manila Chronicle*, 22 February 1951.

[323]Binalbagan-Isabela Sugar Co., Inc., Statement of Account for Period Ending October 31, 1949, "Schedule C," in V. Carmona et al., letter to President Elpidio Quirino, 17 February 1950, Elpidio Quirino Papers, Ayala Museum, Manila; Judge Conrado V. Sanchez, "Order," 26

October 1951, in Enrique J. C. Montilla, Complainant, *Isabela Sugar Co., Inc., vs. Eugenio Lopez et al.*, Court of First Instance, Manila, Civil Case 14831 (1951), 3–4.

[324]Carlos Hilado, interview, 9 September 1975; *Manila Chronicle*, 22 February 1951.

[325]*Sugar Central and Planters News* 27, no. 3 (March 1951): 119; Judge Conrado V. Sanchez, "Order," 26 October 1951, in Enrique J. C. Montilla, Complainant, *Isabela Sugar Co., Inc., vs. Eugenio Lopez et al.*, Court of First Instance, Manila, Civil Case 14831 (1951), 3–5.

[326]Jacinto Montilla, *Squandering of the People's Money by Influential Politicians and Business Denounced to the Integrity Board* (Bacolod City, n.p., 1952), 3–9, Elpidio Quirino Papers, Ayala Museum, Manila.

[327]Judge Conrado V. Sanchez, "Order," 26 October 1951, in Enrique J. C. Montilla, Complainant, *Isabela Sugar Co., Inc., vs. Eugenio Lopez et al.*, Court of First Instance, Manila, Civil Case 14831 (1951), 10.

[328]Ibid., 14–15.

[329]Ibid., 18–19, 21.

[330]Ibid., 27–28. Not long after this decision, the Manila accounting firm J. S. Zulueta conducted an audit of Biscom's books, finding that the company had overstated its net profit by P946,881 (the correct figure should have been only P171,333). Aside from the "unusual management fees of 10%," the Biscom board had paid P79,500 in legal fees to Manila's most powerful political lawyers, "Attorneys Vicente Francisco (P25,000), [Lorenzo] Tañada, [Emmanuel] Pelaez & [Claudio] Teehankee (P25,000), Claro Recto (P25,000), Roberto Benedicto (P4,000), and Leon Ma. Guerrero (P500)" at a time when Biscom was not involved directly in a litigation" (Montilla, *Squandering the People's Money*, 14–15). While the accountants did not speculate on the reasons for these fees, Eugenio Lopez was probably retaining these influential advocates to defend his management contract with Planters' Investment.

[331]Letter from Sixto de la Costa, chief legal counsel, Rehabilitation Finance Corporation, to the chairman, 11 December 1951, Elpidio Quirino Papers, Ayala Museum, Manila.

[332]Montilla, *Squandering the People's Money*, 16–19.

[333]*Manila Chronicle*, 4 April 1954.

[334]Jorge R. Coquia, *The Philippine Presidential Election of 1953* (Manila: University Publishing, 1955), 80–81, 84–85, 92, 195–201.

[335]Ibid., 265–69; *Manila Times*, 23 February 1962.

[336]Republic of the Philippines, Senate, 4th Cong., *Official Directory, 1960–1961* (Manila: Bureau of Printing, 1960), 44.

[337]Coquia, *Presidential Election of 1953*, 261–77.

[338]Quentin Reynolds and Geoffrey Bocca, *Macapagal the Incorruptible* (New York: David Mackay, 1965), 183.

[339]Liang, *Philippine Parties and Politics*, 375; *Daily Mirror*, 24 February 1956; Philippine Senate, *Official Directory, 1960–1961*, 13–14, 44; Republic of the Philippines, Commission on Elections, *Report of the Commission on Elections to the President of the Philippines and the Congress on the Manner the Elections Were Held on November 12, 1957* (Manila: Bureau of Printing, 1958), 216–17.

[340]Manila Electric Company, *Manila Electric Company: A Brief History* (Manila: Manila Electric Company, 1976), 57.

[341]*Manila Chronicle*, 14 March 1987.

[342]*Malaya*, 12 June 1986.

[343]Manila Electric Company, *Manila Electric Company*, 59.

[344]Liang, *Philippine Parties and Politics*, 381.

[345]*Manila Times*, 23 February 1962, 24 February 1962.

[346]Ibid., 19 August 1962.

[347]Ibid.

[348]Ibid., 20 August 1962.

[349]Ibid., 28 August 1962.

[350]*Daily Mirror*, 31 August 1962.

[351] *Manila Times*, 1 September 1962; Eugenio ("Geny") Lopez, Jr., interview with M. N. Roces, 21 May 1988, cited in Roces, "Kinship Politics," 141, 177n.

[352] *Manila Times*, 4 January 1963.

[353] Ibid., 9 January 1963.

[354] Ibid., 14 January 1963.

[355] Ibid., 15 January 1963, 18 January 1963.

[356] Ibid., 17 January 1963.

[357] Ibid., 22 January 1963, 10 February 1963, 10 May 1963.

[358] Ibid., 18 January 1963, 22 January 1963.

[359] Ibid., 9 August 1964.

[360] Ibid., 14 April 1964.

[361] Ibid., 17 March 1965.

[362] Ibid., 31 July 1965, 7 September 1965.

[363] Ibid., 15 August 1965.

[364] Ibid., 14 January 1966.

[365] Lewis E. Gleeck, Jr., *President Marcos and the Philippine Political Culture* (Manila: Lewis E. Gleeck, Jr., 1987), 53–54, 129–30.

[366] Primitivo Mijares, *The Conjugal Dictatorship of Ferdinand and Imelda Marcos I* (San Francisco: Union Square Publications, 1976), 242–43.

[367] *Manila Times*, 22 November 1964.

[368] Ibid., 23 November 1964.

[369] Raymond Bonner, *Waltzing with a Dictator: The Marcoses and the Making of American Policy* (New York: Times Books, 1987), 24; Kerima Polotan, *Imelda Romualdez Marcos: A Biography of the First Lady of the Philippines* (Cleveland: World Publishing, 1969), 42–43.

[370] Pacita Moreno Lopez (widow of Eugenio Lopez), interview with M. N. Roces, 17 May 1988; Presentacion Lopez Psinakis, interview with M. N. Roces, 26 May 1988; and Vicente Lopez, Jr. (Lopez campaign manager), interview with M. N. Roces, 18 May 1988; all cited in Roces, "Kinship Politics," 143, 185n, 187n, respectively.

[371] Oscar Lopez, Affidavit, July 1987.

[372] Meralco Securities Corporation, *Annual Report, 1973*, 26–27.

[373] Mijares, *Conjugal Dictatorship*, 174.

[374] Oscar Lopez, Affidavit, July 1987.

[375] William C. Rempel, *Delusions of a Dictator: The Mind of Marcos as Revealed in His Secret Diaries* (Boston: Little Brown, 1993), 128, 130; Mijares, *Conjugal Dictatorship*, 177.

[376] *Manila Times*, 21 January 1968; *Daily Mirror*, 12 January 1968.

[377] Mijares, *Conjugal Dictatorship*, 180–81.

[378] Almeda-Lopez, "Memorandum on the ABS-CBN Case," 2–3.

[379] Oscar Lopez, Affidavit, July 1987, 2–3.

[380] Almeda-Lopez, "Memorandum on the ABS-CBN Case," 3–27.

[381] Oscar Lopez, Affidavit, July 1987, 1–5.

[382] Mijares, *Conjugal Dictatorship*, 200–201.

[383] Ibid., 3–9.

[384] Psinakis, *Two "Terrorists" Meet*, 138.

[385] Oscar Lopez, Affidavit, July 1987, 9.

[386] Mijares, *Conjugal Dictatorship*, 310–11. In the early 1970s, as the incumbent bishop of Jaro, Jose Ma. Cuenco, edged towards retirement, the Lopez group had cultivated his likely successor, the then auxiliary bishop of Jaro, Jaime Sin. When Fernando Lopez celebrated his "silver jubilee in public service" in 1970, it was Auxiliary Bishop Sin who had delivered the invocation (*Fernando Lopez, Silver Jubilee*, 12–13). As active Catholic laymen, the Lopez faction had supported Sin's promotion to bishop of Jaro in 1972 and his elevation to the Archdiocese of Manila a year later. In the midst of this crisis during the early years of martial law, the Lopezes' reliance on the Diocese of Jaro for political support was simply one more indication of their isolation.

[387] Mijares, *Conjugal Dictatorship*, 305–12.

[388] Ibid., 200–201.

[389] Ibid., 202.

[390] Ibid., 314–15.

[391] Psinakis, *Two "Terrorists" Meet*, 140–42.

[392] Ibid., 148–49.

[393] Ruben R. Canoy, *The Counterfeit Revolution: Martial Law in the Philippines* (Manila: Philippine Editions, 1980), 117; Business Day, *1000 Top Corporations in the Philippines* (Manila: Business Day, 1983), 272–73.

[394] Oscar Lopez, Affidavit, July 1987, 10–12.

[395] Psinakis, *Two "Terrorists" Meet*, 280–88, 310–24.

[396] *Malaya*, 8 June 1984. A Marcos crony, Benedicto had a vast private fortune that included a controlling interest in two major banks, Traders Royal and Republic Planters. Significantly, by 1980 the latter had assets of P4,800 million, four times those of Meralco Securities (*Sugar News*, January-February 1981, 5). Combined with his centralized control over the sugar industry, Benedicto controlled economic resources in the Western Visayas that dwarfed those of the Lopezes at their peak.

[397] *Malaya*, 8 June 1984.

[398] Letter from Oscar M. Lopez to Roberto S. Benedicto, 19 December 1985 (copy kindly provided by Oscar Lopez).

[399] *Mr. and Ms.*, 20–26 December 1985, 13.

[400] *Manila Chronicle*, 14 March 1987.

[401] Ibid.

[402] Oscar Lopez, Affidavit, July 1987, 1–2.

[403] *Malaya*, 2 March 1986.

[404] Business Day, *Corporate Profiles* (Manila: Business Day, 1983), 328; *Malaya*, 12 June 1986.

[405] Ibid., 12 June 1986.

[406] *Philippine Daily Inquirer* (Hilarion Henares, Jr., column), 5 January 1987.

[407] *Malaya*, 12 June 1986.

[408] *Manila Times*, 12 July 1986.

[409] *Manila Standard*, 14 April 1992, 13 April 1992.

[410] *Manila Standard*, 13 April 1992.

[411] *Business Day*, 20 March 1987.

[412] *Manila Chronicle*, 5 May 1987.

[413] *Tonight*, 13 February 1989.

[414] Oscar Lopez, interview with the author, Quezon City, 3 July 1992.

[415] *Philippine Daily Inquirer*, 2 April 1989.

[416] *Manila Standard*, 6 April 1989.

[417] *Philippine Daily Inquirer*, 2 April 1989; Henry Canoy, chairman of Radio Mindanao, letter to the *Philippine Daily Inquirer*, 12 April 1989.

[418] *Manila Chronicle*, 2 December 1987; *Manila Bulletin*, 2 December 1987.

[419] *Philippine Daily Inquirer*, 18 February 1988.

[420] Ibid., 13 May 1989.

[421] Ibid., 13 May 1990, 4 May 1991.

[422] *Philippine Daily Globe*, 22 April 1992.

[423] Anonymous journalist, Philippine Center for Investigative Journalism, interview with the author, Makati, 7 July 1992.

[424] Anonymous Manila newspaper publisher, interview with the author, Makati, 12 July 1992.

[425] *Philippine Daily Inquirer*, 18 May 1992.

INDEX